WASENSTEINER | FAASS

LONDON 1938

EXHIBITION OF

TWENTIETH CENTURY GERMAN ART

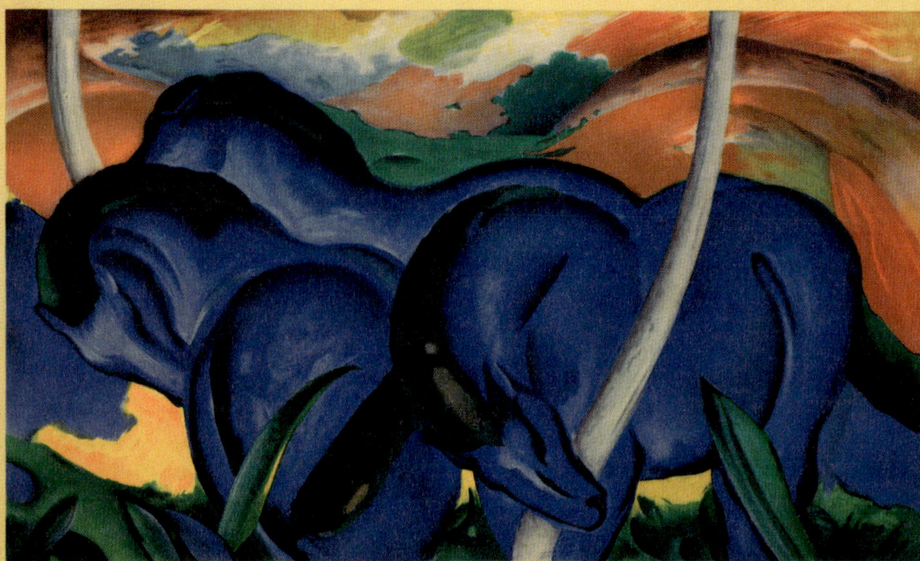

NEW BURLINGTON GALLERIES W.1.

JULY 8th - 30th

PATRONS INCLUDE:— Augustus John *(President)*, The Rt. Rev. the Lord Bishop of Birmingham, Sir Kenneth Clark, Lord Ivor Churchill, Pablo Picasso, Herbert Read, Esq., Sir Michael Sadler, C.B., K.C.S.I.

ADMISSION 1/6

Lucy Wasensteiner Martin Faass

Defending 'degenerate' art

London 1938

Mit Kandinsky, Liebermann und Nolde gegen Hitler

LIEBERMANN VILLA AM WANNSEE

The Wiener Library

GRUSSWORT

PROF. MONIKA GRÜTTERS MdB,
STAATSMINISTERIN FÜR KULTUR UND MEDIEN

Es war ein Licht der Hoffnung in der dunkelsten Zeit der deutschen Geschichte, ein ermutigendes Bekenntnis zur Freiheit der Kunst und ein Akt der Solidarität über Ländergrenzen hinaus: Im Sommer 1938 setzte die Londoner Ausstellung *Twentieth Century German Art* der unsäglichen Propagandaschau des NS-Regimes unter der verächtlichen Bezeichnung «Entartete Kunst» eine Würdigung der deutschen Moderne entgegen – ein demonstrativer Schulterschluss mit den im nationalsozialistischen Deutschland verfemten und verfolgten Künstlerinnen und Künstlern.

Ich freue mich sehr, dass die in deutsch-britischer Zusammenarbeit entstandene und maßgeblich von der Kulturstiftung des Bundes geförderte Rekonstruktion der Ausstellung nun 80 Jahre später in der Berliner Liebermann-Villa am Wannsee wie auch in der Wiener Library in London zu sehen sein wird. Sie erinnert an die verbindende Kraft der Kultur in Europa, aber auch an die Verdienste Großbritanniens um die Verteidigung demokratischer Werte – bis hin zur Unterstützung des Wiederaufbaus der Demokratie in Deutschland nach dem Zweiten Weltkrieg, für die wir Deutschen Großbritannien in Dankbarkeit verbunden bleiben.

Nicht zuletzt steht die Ausstellung exemplarisch für die zahlreichen exzellenten Kulturkooperationen, die Großbritannien und Deutschland – zum Glück! – auch in diesen nicht einfachen Zeiten des Umbruchs in der Europäischen Union verbinden. Möge sie all ihren Besucherinnen und Besuchern bewusst machen, wie kostbar Partnerschaft und Zusammenhalt in Europa sind!

It was a ray of hope during the darkest period in German history, an encouraging affirmation of the freedom of art and an act of solidarity across national borders: In the summer of 1938, the London exhibition *Twentieth Century German Art* countered the Nazi regime's unspeakable propaganda display of what it disparaged as 'degenerate art' with an homage to modern German art and a strong show of support for the artists who were being ostracized and persecuted in Nazi Germany.

I am very pleased that a reconstruction of this exhibition, the fruit of German and British cooperation, will be on view at the Liebermann-Villa in Berlin and the Wiener Library in London, 80 years after the original exhibition and with significant funding from Germany's Federal Cultural Foundation. This new exhibition reminds us of the unifying power of culture in Europe and of the United Kingdom's valuable services in the defence of democratic values, including its help in restoring democracy in Germany after World War II, for which we Germans remain truly grateful to our British friends. The new exhibition is also but one example of the many excellent cultural collaborations between Germany and the United Kingdom which – fortunately! – continue to bring us together, even in these times of uncertainty and upheaval in the European Union. I hope this exhibition will remind all its viewers how precious partnership and solidarity are in Europe!

PROF. MONIKA GRÜTTERS, MEMBER OF THE GERMAN BUNDESTAG
MINISTER OF STATE FOR CULTURE AND THE MEDIA

GREETING

SIR SEBASTIAN WOOD
BRITISH AMBASSADOR IN GERMANY

This book, and the exhibitions which it accompanies, commemorate a remarkable act of European cooperation that took place on the eve of the Second World War. In 1938, a group of artists, collectors, art historians and dealers – British, Swiss, and Germans in exile – joined forces to stage *Twentieth Century German Art*, a protest exhibition to the National Socialist campaign against so-called 'degenerate art'. This group of individuals recognised that an exhibition in London's fashionable New Burlington Galleries could be of vital practical assistance to those involved: creating new audiences for the artists for example, or providing émigré collectors with a chance to sell their works. But the organisers also believed that an art exhibition could effect real political change. Their exhibition stood as a remarkable public defence not only of German modernist art, but also of artistic freedom, internationalism, pluralism and the importance of cultural exchange.

The Europe of today is – thankfully – a very different place. Yet we still face many of the same challenges: mass migration, rapid economic and social change, and deep political divisions both nationally and internationally. As in 1938, collaboration, communication and exchange remain key to tackling these challenges.

At its heart, *London 1938* is a collaborative project between Berlin and London, and this book, with its contributions from Britain, Germany and further afield, is an important reminder of all that has been achieved in the post-War period. I am honoured to lend my support to this endeavour.

Dieses Buch und die Ausstellungen, die es begleitet, erinnern an ein bemerkenswertes Beispiel europäischer Zusammenarbeit am Vorabend des 2. Weltkriegs. Im Jahr 1938 schloss sich eine Gruppe von Künstlern, Sammlern, Kunsthistorikern und Händlern – Briten, Schweizer und im Exil lebende Deutsche – zusammen und organisierte die Ausstellung *Twentieth Century German Art* als Protest gegen die nationalsozialistische Kampagne gegen sogenannte «entartete Kunst». Die Gruppe war sich bewusst, dass eine Ausstellung in den angesagten New Burlington Galleries in London nicht nur den Künstlern ein neues Publikum verschaffen und den emigrierten Sammlern Gelegenheit geben würde, Kunst zu verkaufen. Die Ausstellung sollte auch politisch etwas bewirken, als öffentliches Plädoyer für die deutsche Moderne, aber auch für künstlerische Freiheit, Internationalismus, Pluralismus und kulturellen Austausch.

Das Europa von heute ist anders. Doch viele der Herausforderungen sind geblieben: Migration, rascher wirtschaftlicher und sozialer Wandel, tiefe politische Gräben sowohl national wie auch international. Wie schon 1938 sind Kooperation, Kommunikation und Austausch wichtige Voraussetzungen dafür, dass wir diese Herausforderungen meistern.

Im Kern ist *London 1938* eine Kooperation zwischen Berlin und London. Mit Beiträgen aus Großbritannien, Deutschland und anderen Ländern erinnert das Buch daran, wie viel in den Jahren seit dem Krieg erreicht wurde. Es ist mir eine Ehre, dieses Vorhaben zu unterstützen.

SIR SEBASTIAN WOOD
BRITISCHER BOTSCHAFTER IN DEUTSCHLAND

VORWORT

DR. HANS-GERHARD HANNESEN
VORSTAND DER MAX-LIEBERMANN-GESELLSCHAFT BERLIN

DR. MARTIN FAASS
DIREKTOR DER LIEBERMANN-VILLA AM WANNSEE

Die Liebermann-Villa am Wannsee ist ein Museum, das der Kunst Max Liebermanns, dem Vermächtnis seines Gartens und der wechselvollen Geschichte der Familie Liebermann gewidmet ist. Die Entrechtung und Verfolgung der Familie in der Zeit des Nationalsozialismus, der Zwangsverkauf der Villa und der verfolgungsbedingte Entzug der Kunstsammlung Max Liebermanns gehören damit ebenso zum Teil unseres Vermittlungsauftrages wie die kulturpolitische Situation dieser Jahre.

Eines der bemerkenswerten kulturpolitischen Ereignisse war die Ausstellung *Twentieth Century German Art*, die 1938 als Antwort auf die *Entartete Kunst*-Aktion in London stattfand. In dieser Ausstellung war Max Liebermann mit 22 ausgestellten Werken prominent vertreten. Und nicht nur das: Martha Liebermann, die Witwe des Künstlers, unterstützte die Ausstellung persönlich mit einer Leihgabe. Sie schickte ein Albert Einstein-Porträt ihres Mannes nach London.

Diese wertvollen Erkenntnisse verdanken wir Dr. Lucy Wasensteiner, die seit Ende 2015 Mitarbeiterin der Liebermann-Villa ist und mit ihrer fabelhaften wissenschaftlichen Arbeit über die Londoner Ausstellung alles ins Rollen gebracht hat. Hierfür gilt ihr unser allerherzlichster Dank. Denn das Thema stellte sich für unser Haus geradezu als Glücksfall heraus, da uns mit ihm gelang, namhafte Projekt- und Förderpartner zu gewinnen.

Für ihre großzügige Unterstützung danken wir allen voran der Kulturstiftung des Bundes, ohne die das Projekt nicht zustande gekommen wäre. Unser herzlichster Dank gilt darüber hinaus der International Music and Art Foundation, der Ernst von Siemens Kunststiftung, dem British Council und Sotheby's.

Zu großem Dank verpflichtet fühlen wir uns auch dem Britischen Botschafter in Deutschland Sir Sebastian Wood, durch dessen Schirmherrschaft sich manche Türen geöffnet haben.

Last but not least danken wir unserem Projektpartner, der Wiener Library in London, einem der weltweit bedeutsamsten Archive zum Holocaust und der Nazi-Zeit, für die hervorragende Zusammenarbeit.

FOREWORD

DR HANS-GERHARD HANNESEN
COMMITTEE OF THE MAX LIEBERMANN SOCIETY, BERLIN

DR MARTIN FAASS
DIRECTOR OF THE LIEBERMANN-VILLA AM WANNSEE

The Liebermann-Villa am Wannsee is a museum dedicated to the art of Max Liebermann, to the upkeep of his summer house and garden, and to the chequered history of the Liebermann family. Communicating the story of the family's persecution by the Nazi regime, their disenfranchisement, the confiscation of their property and the wider cultural-political context of the Nazi period is a central part of our mission.

One of the most remarkable cultural events of this time was the 1938 London exhibition *Twentieth Century German Art*, staged in response to the German campaign against so-called 'degenerate art'. Max Liebermann was not only represented by 22 works in this ground-breaking exhibition; his widow Martha also personally supported the exhibition with a loan. She sent one of her husband's portraits of Albert Einstein to the exhibition.

For this valuable knowledge we thank Dr Lucy Wasensteiner, who has worked at the Liebermann-Villa since 2015 and who has brought this project to fruition with her wonderful research on the topic of *Twentieth Century German Art*. For this we give her our heartfelt thanks.

This subject has proven particularly fortuitous for our museum, as it has allowed us work together with numerous renowned patrons and partners. We would like to thank the German Federal Cultural Foundation, without whose support the project could not have been realised. In addition we are extremely grateful to the International Music and Art Foundation, to the Ernst von Siemens Kunststiftung, to the British Council and to Sotheby's.

We would like to express our gratitude to the British Ambassador Sir Sebastian Wood, whose patronage has opened so many doors for the project.

Last but not least we thank for their outstanding cooperation our project partner, the Wiener Library in London, one of world's most significant archives relating to the history of the Holocaust and the Nazi period.

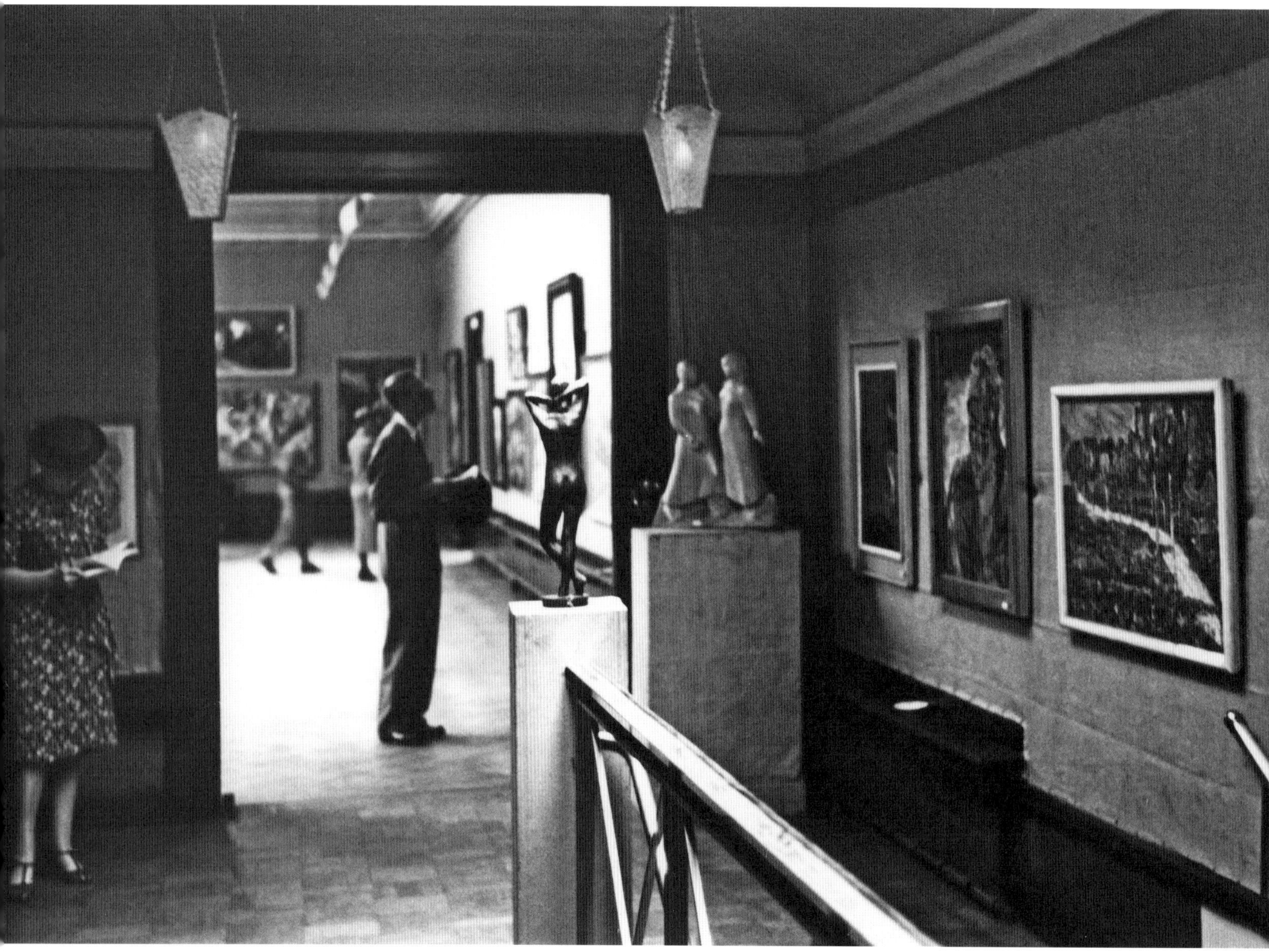

1 Austellung *Twentieth Century German Art*, New Burlington Galleries, London 1938, Innenansicht.

Die Ausstellung *Twentieth Century German Art*

LUCY WASENSTEINER

Am Donnerstag, den 7. Juli 1938, wurde die Ausstellung *Twentieth Century German Art* in den New Burlington Galleries im Londoner West End eröffnet. Sie zeigte mehr als 300 Meisterwerke der deutschen Moderne, von mehr als 64 herausragenden Künstlern (Abb. 1-4). Großformatige Ölgemälde von Max Beckmann, Otto Dix, Wassily Kandinsky, Paula Modersohn-Becker und Emil Nolde hingen neben grafischen Arbeiten von Paul Klee, Oskar Kokoschka und Käthe Kollwitz sowie Skulpturen von Wilhelm Lehmbruck und Collagen von Kurt Schwitters. Auch die Generation der Wegbereiter der Moderne war repräsentativ vertreten: 18 Werke von Lovis Corinth, acht Werke von Max Slevogt und wenigstens 22 Arbeiten von Max Liebermann, dem Vater der Berliner Secession.

Twentieth Century German Art war nicht nur die erste Retrospektive deutscher moderner Kunst in Großbritannien. Die Ausstellung fand genau ein Jahr nach der Eröffnung der von den NS-Machthabern in München organisierten Propaganda-Ausstellung *Entartete Kunst* statt. 62 der in London ausstellenden Künstler waren in München als ‹entartet› deklariert und von den Nazis ins Exil getrieben worden oder hatten der Entfernung ihrer Werke aus den deutschen Museen und deren Beschlagnahme machtlos zusehen müssen.

Indem sie jene modernen Künstler erneut in einem gebührenden Rahmen präsentierte, wurde *Twentieth Century German Art* schon längst als wichtigste internationale Antwort auf die Ausstellung *Entartete Kunst* gewürdigt.[1] Dennoch blieben viele Fragen jahrelang unbeantwortet: Woher kamen die Kunstwerke angesichts der schwachen Vertretung der deutschen Moderne in den damaligen britischen Sammlungen? Wer verfügte über die notwendigen Kontakte hinsichtlich der Organisation einer solchen Ausstellung, während Europa sich immer mehr in Richtung Krieg bewegte?

Diese Fragen konnten dank jüngster Erkenntnisse der Provenienzforschung beantwortet werden. Vor dem Hintergrund des gesteigerten öffentlichen Interesses für den von den Nazis verübten Kunstraub sowie für die Restitution der Werke wurden in den letzten zwei Jahrzehnten große Fortschritte hinsichtlich der Bestimmung der aufeinanderfolgenden Eigentümer der infrage kommenden Kunstwerke gemacht. Im Falle von *Twentieth Century German Art* konnten so anhand des Ausstellungskatalogs (eine unbebilderte Liste der Werke mit abgekürzten, ins Englische übersetzten Titeln, siehe S. 249-257) einerseits die gezeigten Kunstwerke eindeutig identifiziert, andererseits die Namen der Leihgeber festgestellt werden. Weiterhin konnte die Organisationsstruktur der Ausstellung erhellt werden: Die Schau entstand im Rahmen eines internationalen Projekts, an welchem deutsche Emigranten maßgeblich beteiligt waren.[2]

2018 jährt sich die Eröffnung dieser außergewöhnlichen Kunstveranstaltung zum 80. Mal. Deshalb widmen sich zwei Ausstellungen der Geschichte von *Twentieth Century German Art*: Die eine findet in der Londoner Wiener Library, die andere in der Liebermann-Villa in Berlin-Wannsee statt. Anhand einer Auswahl originaler Kunstwerke sowie Informationen zu den Leihgebern der damaligen Ausstellung sollen dieser wichtige Moment der deutsch-britischen Kulturbeziehungen sowie die Identität und Motivation der Organisatoren rekonstruiert werden.

Die vorliegende Publikation bezieht sich auf beide Ausstellungen. Der Hauptteil enthält eine Auswahl der 1938 ausgestellten Werke mit einer Kurzdarstellung des Lebenswegs der Leihgeber.[3] Darüber hinaus enthält das Buch drei Gruppen von Essays zum besseren Verständnis von *Twentieth Century German Art*. Die erste Gruppe spiegelt den historischen Kontext der Ausstellung: Entwicklung der Kulturpolitik der NS-Regierung; Großbritannien als Zufluchtsort deutscher Emigranten nach 1933; Rezeption der deutschen Kunst in London im Sommer 1938. Die zweite Gruppe von Essays widmet sich der Ausstellung: der Geschichte ihrer Organisation, dem ausstellungsbegleitenden Buch mit dem Titel *Modern German Art* und dem musikalischen Rahmenprogramm. Die dritte Gruppe schließlich behandelt die Nachwirkung von *Twentieth Century German Art*.

Ebenso wie die Ausstellung aus dem Jahr 1938 wurde das heutige Projekt in Teamarbeit verwirklicht. Erneut möchte ich mich bei den Leihgebern, den Katalogmitarbeitern sowie der Belegschaft der Wiener Library und der Liebermann-Villa herzlich bedanken. Mein Dank gilt auch dem Courtauld Institute und Dr. Shulamith Behr. Folgenden Institutionen sei zudem für ihre großzügige Unterstützung herzlich gedankt: der Kulturstiftung des Bundes, der International Music and Art Foundation, der Ernst von Siemens Kunststiftung, Sotheby's und dem British Council.

1 In den letzten achtzig Jahren beschäftigten sich zahlreiche deutsche, britische, schweizerische und amerikanische Autoren mit der Ausstellung. Besonders erwähnenswert sind folgende Bücher und Aufsätze: Paul Ortwin Rave: Kunstdiktatur im Dritten Reich, Hamburg 1949, S. 112-114; Cordula Frowein: The Exhibition of 20th Century German Art in London 1938. Eine Antwort auf die Ausstellung «Entartete Kunst» in München 1937, in: Thomas Koebner/Wulf Köpke/Joachim Radkau (Hg.): Exilforschung. Ein internationales Jahrbuch, München 1984, Bd. 2, S. 212-237; Stephan Lackner/Helen Adkins: Exhibition of 20th Century German Art, in: Eberhard Roters (Hg.): Stationen der Moderne. Die bedeutenden Kunstausstellungen des 20. Jahrhunderts in Deutschland, Berlin 1988, S. 315-337; Keith Holz: Modern German Art for Thirties Paris, Prague and London. Resistance and Acquiescence in a Democratic Public Sphere, Ann Arbour 2004, S. 195-240; Christian Weikop: The British Reception of Brücke and German Expressionism, in: Christian Weikop (Hg.): Bridging History. Perspectives on Brücke Expressionism, Farnham 2011, S. 234-276.

2 Vor dem Hintergrund der Diskussion bezüglich des bestzutreffenden Begriffs für die Bezeichnung der Menschen, die Deutschland nach 1933 verlassen mussten, haben die Autoren dieser Publikation sich für die Begriffe «Emigrant» und «Flüchtling» entschieden. Gleichwohl finden im Text die Begriffe «Exil» und «Emigration» Anwendung.

3 Ein in Vorbereitung befindliches Buch (Lucy Wasensteiner: *The Twentieth Century German Art Exhibition. Answering Degenerate Art in 1930s London*, New York) wird detailliert auf die ausgestellten Werke und deren Leihgeber eingehen.

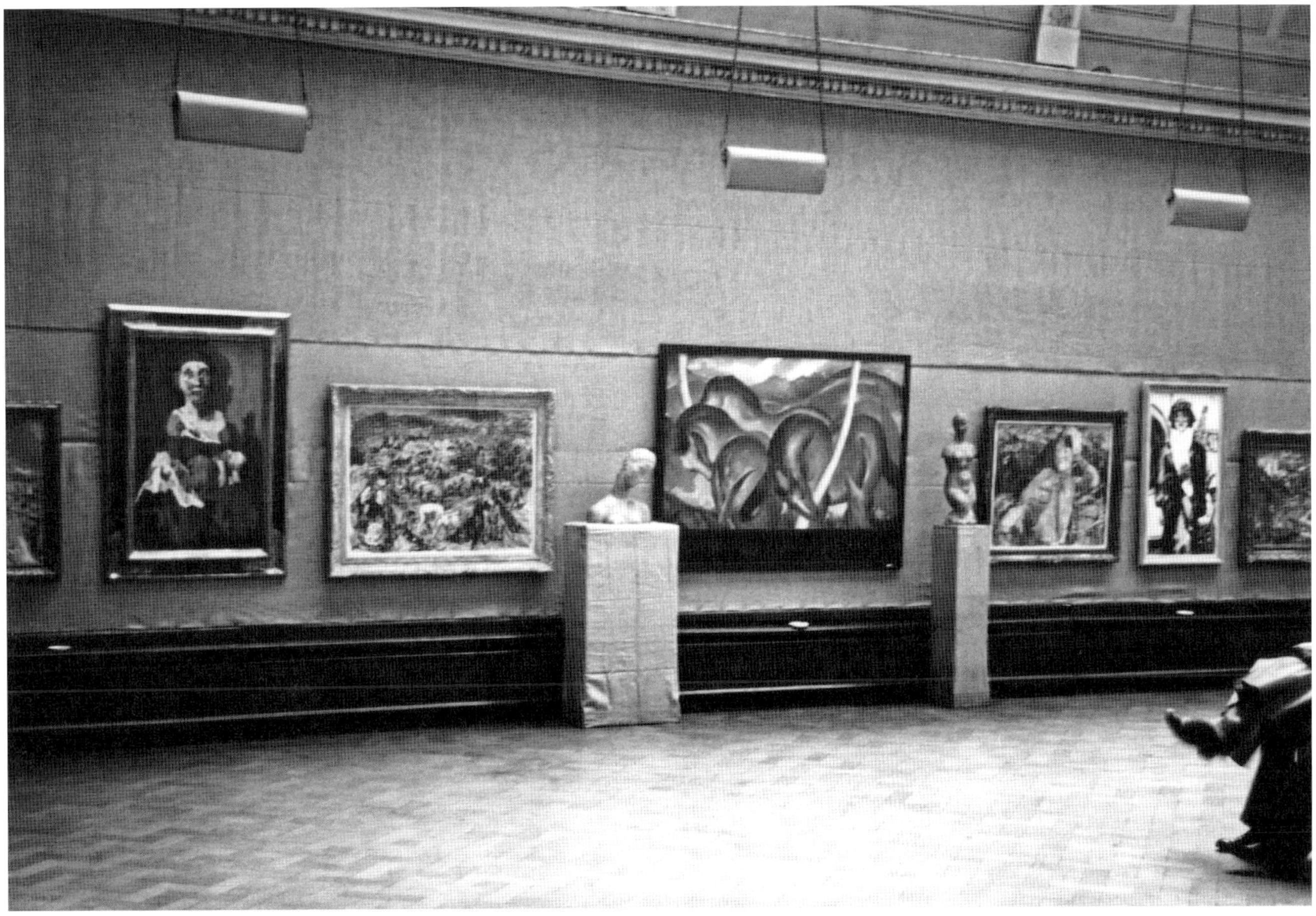

2 + 3 (folgende Doppelseite) Austellung *Twentieth Century German Art*, New Burlington Galleries, London 1938, Innenansicht

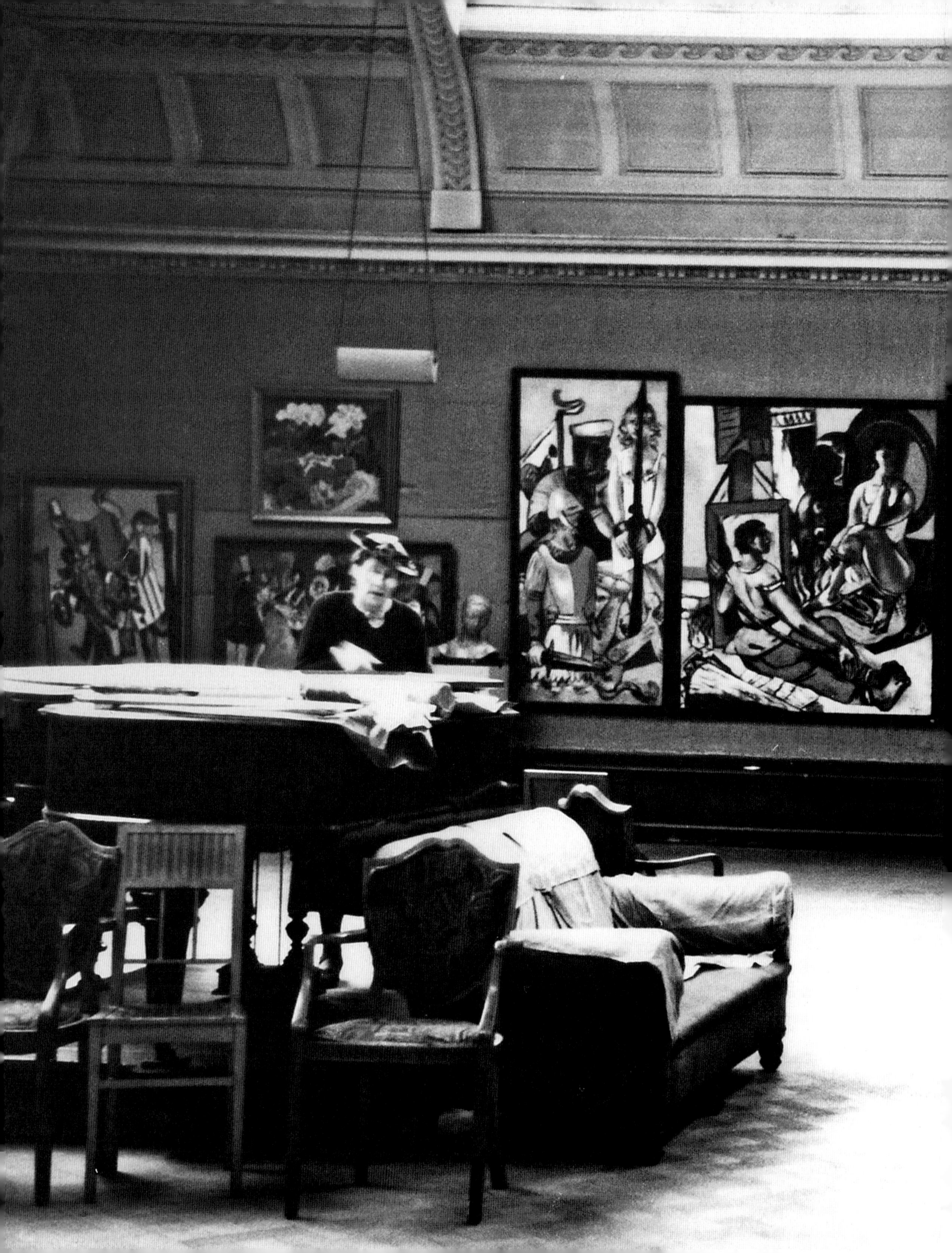

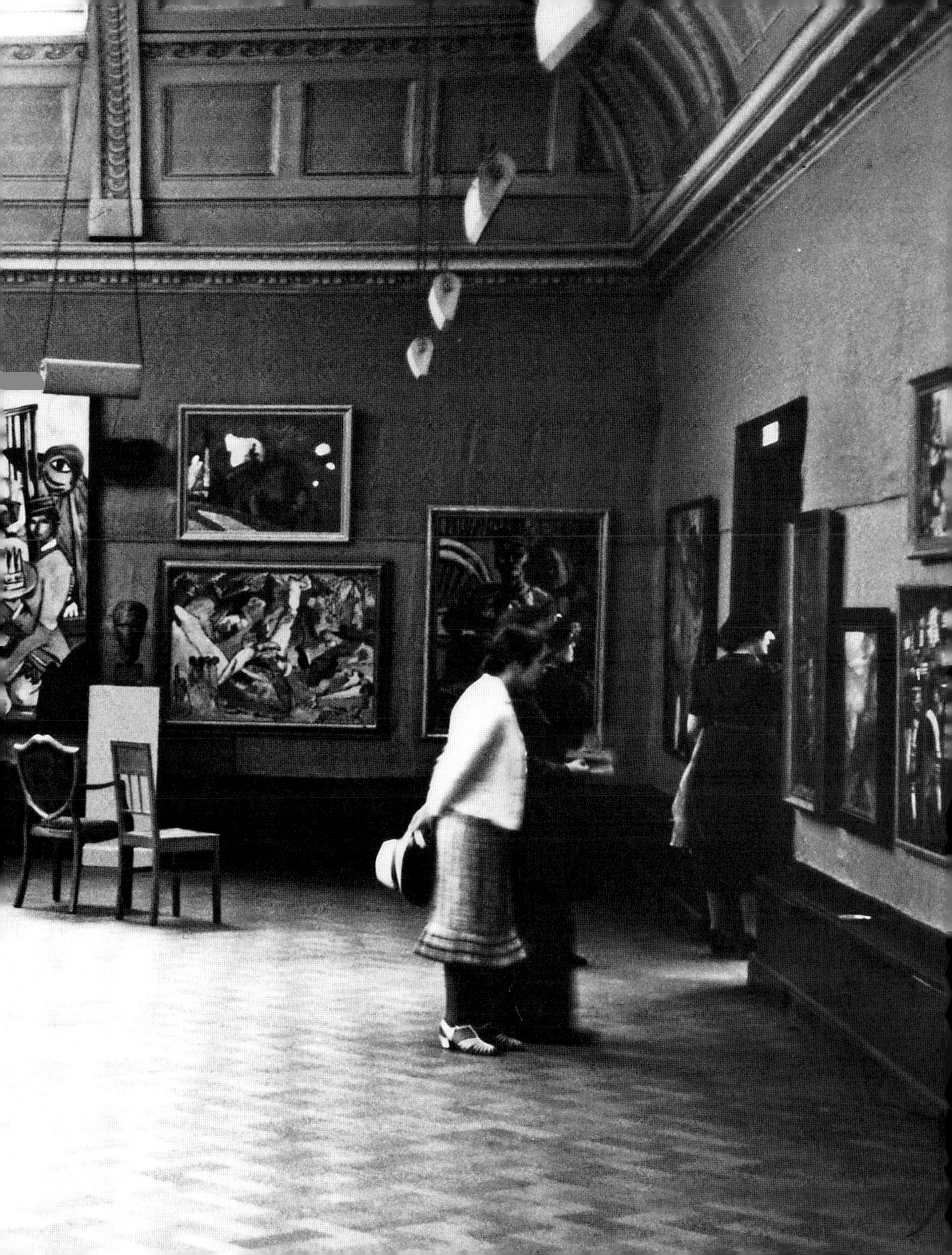

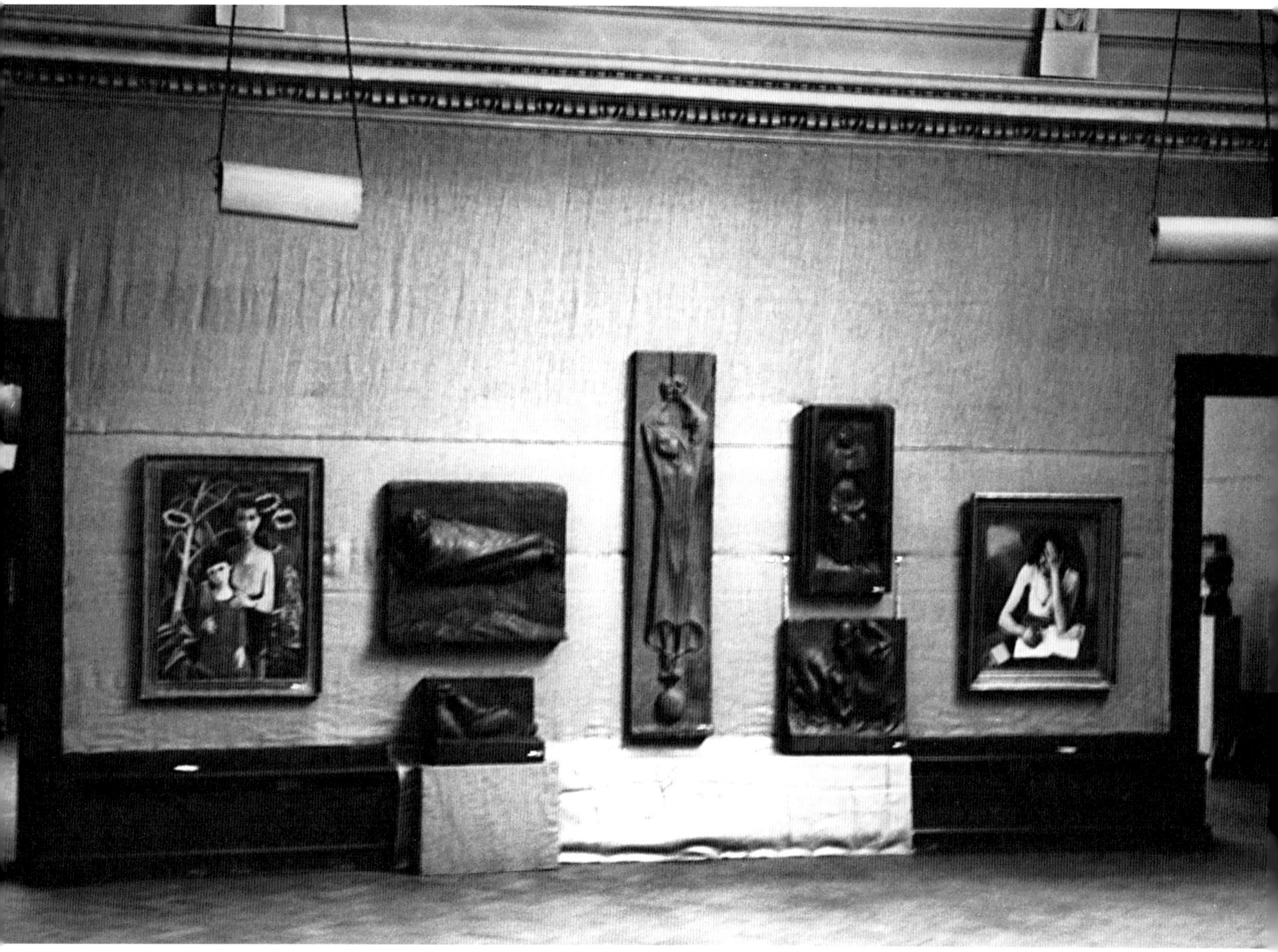

4 Exhibition *Twentieth Century German Art*, New Burlington Galleries, London 1938, Interior view

The exhibition *Twentieth Century German Art*

LUCY WASENSTEINER

On Thursday 7 July 1938 the exhibition *Twentieth Century German Art* opened its doors at the New Burlington Galleries, at the heart of London's West End. The show contained more than 300 masterpieces of German modernism, by at least 64 artists – among them, every key name from the last half century (fig. 1-4). Large-scale oils by Wassily Kandinsky, Max Beckmann, Emil Nolde, Otto Dix and Paula Modersohn-Becker hung alongside works on paper by Käthe Kollwitz, Oskar Kokoschka and Paul Klee, sculptures by Wilhelm Lehmbruck, and collages by Kurt Schwitters. The earliest generation of German modernists was also well-represented: 18 works by Lovis Corinth, eight by Max Slevogt, and at least 22 by the father of the Berlin Secession, the painter Max Liebermann.

This exhibition was not only the first British retrospective of these Germans, however. The show coincided exactly with the one-year anniversary of the National Socialist propaganda exhibition *Entartete Kunst* (*Degenerate Art)*, staged in Munich in 1937. Of the 64 artists listed in the London catalogue, 62 had been labelled 'degenerate' in Munich, had seen their works confiscated from German museums, or had been forced into exile by the Nazi regime.

By returning these modernists to a civilised gallery setting, *Twentieth Century German Art* was the most significant international response to *Entartete Kunst*, and indeed, has long been recognised as such.[1] Yet many aspects of the show have remained a mystery. Where did the exhibited artworks come from, given the dearth of German modernism in British collections? And who had the contacts to organise such a show, as Europe slid ever closer to war?

New developments in the field of provenance research have allowed us to answer these questions. With a growing public interest in Nazi art looting and restitution, the last two decades have brought many new resources for tracing the ownership histories of artworks. Applying these resources to the 1938 exhibition catalogue (pp. 249-257) – an unillustrated list of works, with their titles listed briefly and in English translation – it has become possible both to definitively identify the exhibited artworks, and to uncover who lent them to London. This has in turn unveiled the show's organisation: a fundamentally international project, in which German émigrés played a central role.[2]

The year 2018 marks the eightieth anniversary of this remarkable cultural event. To commemorate this milestone, the story of *Twentieth Century German Art* will be told via two exhibitions in Britain and Germany: at the Wiener Library in London, and at the Liebermann-Villa

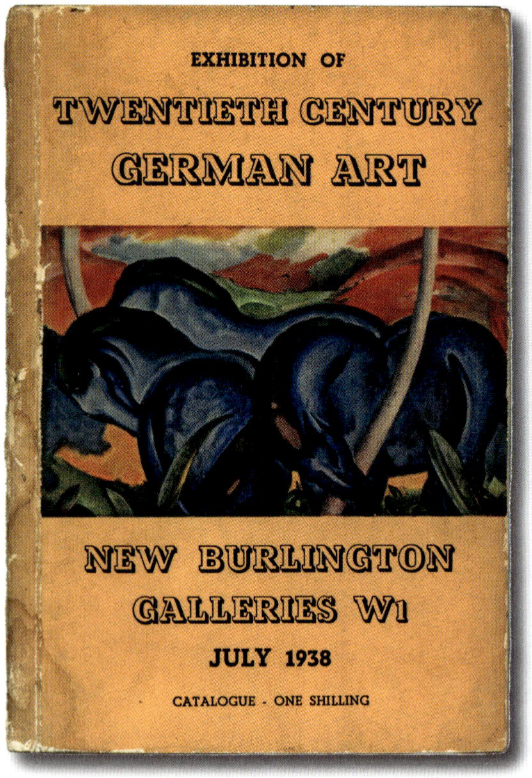

5 Front cover of the exhibition catalogue *Twentieth Century German Art*, New Burlington Galleries, 1938

am Wannsee in Berlin. Presenting a selection of the original exhibits together with details of their lenders in 1938, these shows aim to reconstruct this crucial moment in the history of UK-German relations, and to shed new light on the organisers and their motivations.

This book accompanies these two exhibitions. In its central section, it presents a selection of the original 1938 exhibits, together with the stories of their lenders.[3] The volume also contains three groups of essays, which provide space for a broader exploration of *Twentieth Century German Art*. The first group of essays is dedicated to context, with essays considering the development of National Socialist cultural policy, Britain as a German émigré destination after 1933, and the extent to which London audiences were aware of German art in the summer of 1938. In the second group of essays, attention turns to the exhibition itself, with texts considering the exhibition's organisation, the accompanying 'Festival of German Music' staged at the galleries during the show's run, and the book published for distribution at the exhibition under the title Modern German Art. In the final section, the impact and afterlife of *Twentieth Century German Art* are considered.

Like its 1938 predecessor, this book and exhibition project has been a true team effort. I would like to extend my thanks once again to both the exhibition lenders, and the contributors to this volume, as well as to the staff of both the Wiener Library and the Liebermann-Villa. I would like to thank the Courtauld Institute, and the supervisor of my research there, Dr Shulamith Behr. Particular thanks are also due to the German Federal Cultural Foundation, the International Music and Art Foundation, the Ernst von Siemens Kunststiftung, Sotheby's and the British Council for their generous support.

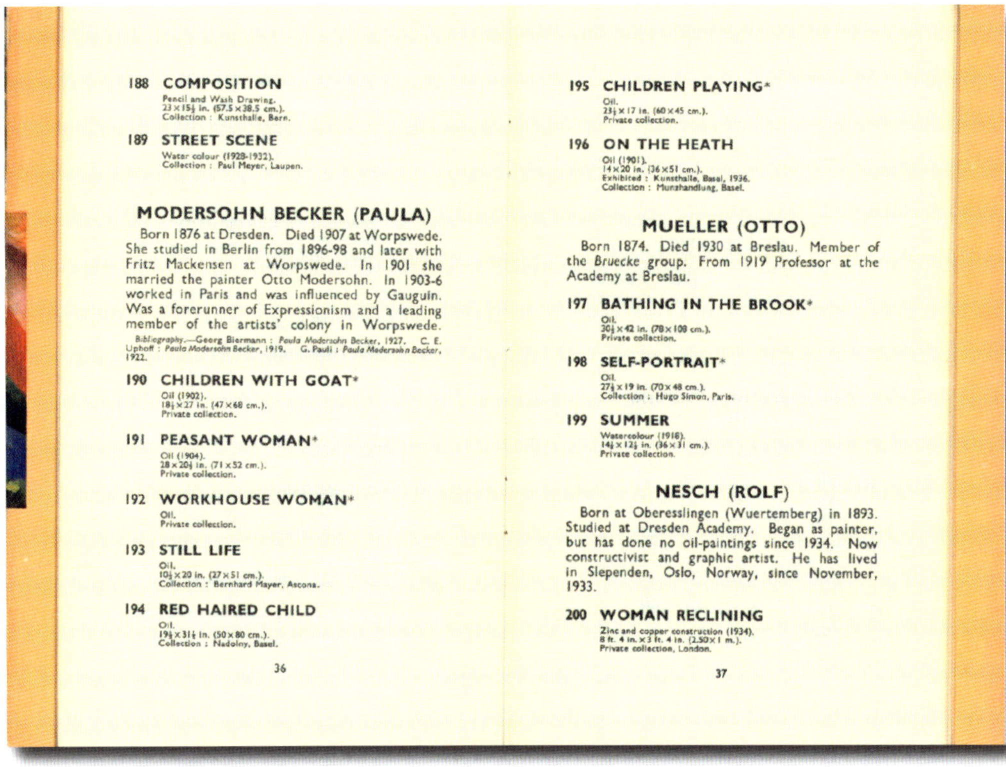

188 COMPOSITION
Pencil and Wash Drawing.
23 × 15½ in. (57.5 × 38.5 cm.).
Collection : Kunsthalle, Bern.

189 STREET SCENE
Water colour (1928-1932).
Collection : Paul Meyer, Laupen.

MODERSOHN BECKER (PAULA)

Born 1876 at Dresden. Died 1907 at Worpswede. She studied in Berlin from 1896-98 and later with Fritz Mackensen at Worpswede. In 1901 she married the painter Otto Modersohn. In 1903-6 worked in Paris and was influenced by Gauguin. Was a forerunner of Expressionism and a leading member of the artists' colony in Worpswede.

Bibliography.—Georg Biermann : *Paula Modersohn Becker*, 1927. C. E. Uphoff : *Paula Modersohn Becker*, 1919. G. Pauli : *Paula Modersohn Becker*, 1922.

190 CHILDREN WITH GOAT*
Oil (1902).
18½ × 27 in. (47 × 68 cm.).
Private collection.

191 PEASANT WOMAN*
Oil (1904).
28 × 20½ in. (71 × 52 cm.).
Private collection.

192 WORKHOUSE WOMAN*
Oil.
Private collection.

193 STILL LIFE
Oil.
10½ × 20 in. (27 × 51 cm.).
Collection : Bernhard Mayer, Ascona.

194 RED HAIRED CHILD
Oil.
19¾ × 31½ in. (50 × 80 cm.).
Collection : Nadolny, Basel.

36

195 CHILDREN PLAYING*
Oil.
23½ × 17 in. (60 × 45 cm.).
Private collection.

196 ON THE HEATH
Oil (1901).
14 × 20 in. (36 × 51 cm.).
Exhibited : Kunsthalle, Basel, 1936.
Collection : Munzhandlung, Basel.

MUELLER (OTTO)

Born 1874. Died 1930 at Breslau. Member of the *Bruecke* group. From 1919 Professor at the Academy at Breslau.

197 BATHING IN THE BROOK*
Oil.
30¾ × 42 in. (78 × 108 cm.).
Private collection.

198 SELF-PORTRAIT*
Oil.
27½ × 19 in. (70 × 48 cm.).
Collection : Hugo Simon, Paris.

199 SUMMER
Watercolour (1918).
14¼ × 12¼ in. (36 × 31 cm.).
Private collection.

NESCH (ROLF)

Born at Oberesslingen (Wuertemberg) in 1893. Studied at Dresden Academy. Began as painter, but has done no oil-paintings since 1934. Now constructivist and graphic artist. He has lived in Slependen, Oslo, Norway, since November, 1933.

200 WOMAN RECLINING
Zinc and copper construction (1934).
8 ft. 4 in. × 3 ft. 4 in. (2.50 × 1 m.).
Private collection, London.

37

6 Extract from the exhibition catalogue *Twentieth Century German Art*, New Burlington Galleries, 1938, p. 36-37

1 Over the last 80 years the exhibition has been frequently referenced in broader studies by British, German, Swiss and US authors. Key texts include: Paul Ortwin Rave: Kunstdiktatur im Dritten Reich. Hamburg 1949, p. 112-4; Cordula Frowein: The Exhibition of 20th Century German Art in London 1938. Eine Antwort auf die Ausstellung Entartete Kunst in München 1937; in: Thomas Koebner, Wulf Köpke, Joachim Radkau (eds.): Exilforschung. Ein internationales Jahrbuch. Munich 1984, vol. 2, pp. 212-37; Stephan Lackner and Helen Adkins: Exhibition of 20th Century German Art; in: Eberhard Roters (ed.): Stationen der Moderne. Die bedeutenden Kunstausstellungen des 20. Jahrhunderts in Deutschland,. Berlin 1988, pp. 315-37; Keith Holz: Modern German Art for Thirties Paris, Prague and London. Resistance and Acquiescence in a Democratic Public Sphere. Ann Arbour 2004, pp. 195-240; and Christian Weikop. The British Reception of Brücke and German Expressionism; in: Christian Weikop (ed.): Bridging History. Perspectives on Brücke Expressionism, Farnham 2011, pp. 234-76

2 The authors of this volume acknowledge the debate surrounding the most appropriate term for those who left German-occupied Europe in the years after 1933. In this catalogue, the terms 'emigre' and 'refugee' will be used interchangeably to refer to these individuals; the term 'exile' will similarly be used interchangeably with 'emigration'

3 A forthcoming book by the present author will provide a complete overview of the exhibition's contents and lenders. Lucy Wasensteiner: The Twentieth Century German Art Exhibition. Answering Degenerate Art in 1930s London. New York (forthcoming)

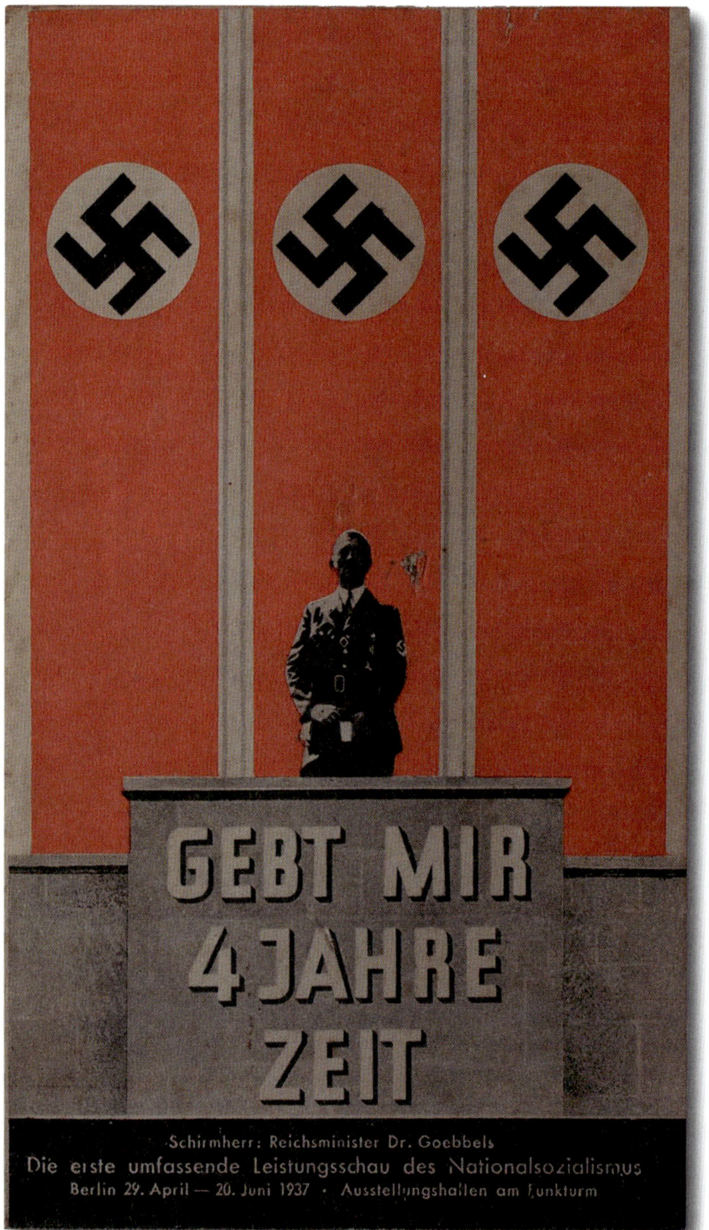

7 Broschüre zur Wanderausstellung *Gebt mir vier Jahre Zeit*, 1937

«Deutsches Volk, gib uns die Zeit von 4 Jahren». Die nationalsozialistische Kunstpolitik in ihrer Konsolidierungsphase von 1933 bis 1937

MEIKE HOFFMANN

Am 1. Februar 1933 – einen Tag nach der Machtübertragung an die Nationalsozialisten – richtete Adolf Hitler als neuer Reichskanzler erstmals einen *Aufruf an das deutsche Volk.* Darin prangerte er die Weimarer Republik als eine Zeit des wirtschaftlichen und politischen Verfalls an, in der angeblich Kommunismus und Anarchie das Wesen der Deutschen zersetzt hätten. Er dagegen versprach die Rettung des Vaterlandes, die Einheit der Nation, die Beseitigung der Arbeitslosigkeit und eine prosperierende Wirtschaft. Das einzige, was er dafür vom deutschen Volk verlangte, waren vier Jahre Zeit. «Die Parteien des Marxismus und seiner Mitläufer haben vierzehn Jahre lang Zeit gehabt, ihr Können zu beweisen. Das Ergebnis ist ein Trümmerfeld. Nun, deutsches Volk, gib uns die Zeit von 4 Jahren, und dann urteile und richte uns!»[1]

In den nächsten Monaten wiederholte Hitler seinen beschwörenden Appell bei jeder wichtigen Rede. Per Rundfunkausstrahlung und Parteizeitungen sowie Plakaten und Flugblättern taktete er ein Millionenpublikum auf die geforderte Karenzzeit von vier Jahren ein.[2] In seinen Heilsversprechen spielte die Wiederbelebung der deutschen Kunst und Kultur eine Schlüsselrolle. Laut Hitler sei sie die «stolzeste Verteidigung des deutschen Volkes».[3] Schon durch die Formulierung klingt eine Instrumentalisierung für die Kriegspropaganda an. Allerdings blieb er eine Erklärung schuldig, was genau er unter einer neuen Kunst im Sinne der NS-Ideologie verstand und wie er seine hochgesteckten Ziele erreichen wollte. Was also geschah in diesen vier Jahren der Konsolidierungsphase?

Goebbels – Rosenberg – Rust

Die Hauptprotagonisten der ‹Gleichschaltung› im Kulturbereich waren Joseph Goebbels (Abb. 13), Alfred Rosenberg (Abb. 8) und Bernhard Rust (Abb. 9). Hitler führte sie bewusst gegeneinander ins Feld, um den Konkurrenzkampf unter ihnen zu schärfen und Höchstleistungen erwarten zu können.

Rust, der als Gymnasiallehrer bereits 1922 in die NSDAP eingetreten war, übernahm im April 1933 die kommissarische Leitung des Preußischen Kultusministeriums und rückte so an die Seite von Hermann Göring, Ministerpräsident von Preußen. In seiner neuen Funktion sorgte Rust auf Grundlage des *Gesetzes zur Wiederherstellung des Berufsbeamtentums* vom 7. April 1933 für die Entlassung zahlreicher jüdischer und politisch missliebiger Museumsmitarbeiter, Akademie- und Hochschullehrer, um sie durch ‹arische› bzw. ideologiekonforme Kollegen zu ersetzen.[4] Nach Auflösung der Kulturhoheit der Länder wurde Rust 1934 zum

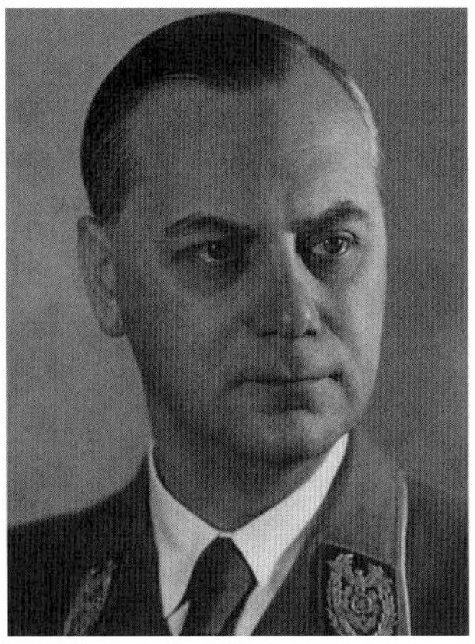

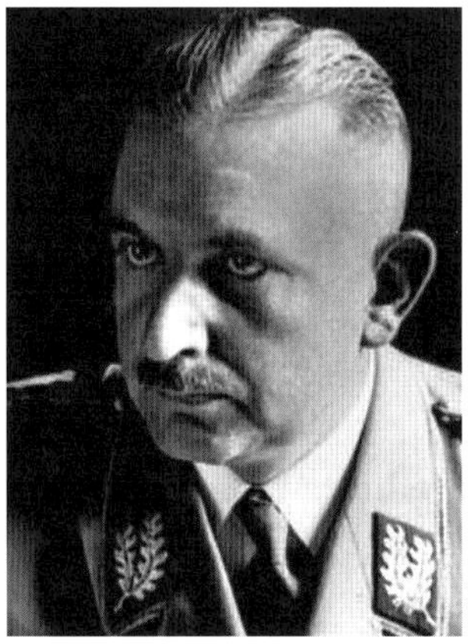

8 Alfred Rosenberg

9 Bernhard Rust

Reichsminister für Wissenschaft, Erziehung und Volksbildung ernannt, wodurch sein Verfügungsbereich auf die Museen und Ausbildungsinstitutionen in ganz Deutschland ausgedehnt wurde. Nach seinem tatkräftigen Debüt verlor er im Kompetenzgerangel mit Rosenberg und Goebbels jedoch zunehmend an Entscheidungswillen und Durchsetzungskraft.

Alfred Rosenberg, seit 1920 Mitglied der NSDAP, gründete 1929 den Kampfbund für deutsche Kultur, der zunächst überparteilich auf Vereinsebene eine völkisch gesinnte, antisemitisch und reaktionär ausgerichtete Kulturpolitik propagierte. In seinem 1930 publizierten Buch *Der Mythus des 20. Jahrhunderts* machte Rosenberg eine angeblich existierende jüdisch-bolschewistische Weltverschwörung für den Verfall der deutschen Kultur verantwortlich, was den Kerngedanken von Hitlers Rassenideologie prägte. 1934 wurde Rosenberg zum Beauftragten des Führers für die Überwachung der gesamten geistigen und weltanschaulichen Schulung und Erziehung der NSDAP ernannt. Jedoch war auch Rosenberg dem Machtstrategen Goebbels nicht gewachsen. Erst später erlangte er außerhalb Deutschlands als Leiter des Einsatzstabs Reichsleiter Rosenberg in den besetzten Westgebieten und als Reichsminister für die besetzten Ostgebiete die ersehnte politische Bedeutung.

Joseph Goebbels war von Anfang an ehrgeizig bestrebt, die Kontrolle über alle Kulturbereiche an sich zu reißen. Im März 1933 gründete er das Reichsministerium für Volksaufklärung und Propaganda (RMVP), das fortan für die inhaltliche Lenkung der Presse, Literatur, bildenden Kunst, Musik sowie des Films, Theaters und Rundfunks zuständig war. Goebbels erklärte dazu: «Das Ministerium hat die Aufgabe, in Deutschland eine geistige Mobilmachung zu vollziehen. Es ist also auf dem Gebiet des Geistes dasselbe, was das Wehrministerium auf dem Gebiet der Wache ist. [...] Die geistige Mobilmachung [ist] ebenso nötig, vielleicht noch nötiger als die materielle Wehrhaftmachung des Volkes.»[5] Mittels der Kultur sollte die deutsche Bevölkerung psychologisch auf den schon früh geplanten Krieg vorbereitet werden. Kurz darauf – im September 1933 – gründete Goebbels die Reichskulturkammer (RKK) mit Unterkammern zur Abdeckung aller Kulturbereiche. Hier musste jeder gemeldet sein, ob Künstler oder Kunstvermittelnder bis hin zum Postkartenverkäufer, um seinen Beruf weiterhin ausüben zu dürfen.

Mit dem RMVP und der RKK hatte Goebbels die wichtigsten Gleichschaltungsinstanzen der Kulturszene geschaffen. Damit griff er drastisch in die Kompetenzbereiche von Rust und Rosenberg ein. Aus den noch Jahre andauernden Rivalitäten ging Goebbels stets als Sieger hervor. Allerdings war er selbst in einem Zwiespalt gefangen. Sein Kunstverständnis deckte sich nicht mit dem von Adolf Hitler. So schätzte Goebbels durchaus einzelne Vertreter der modernen Kunst wie Edvard Munch, Emil Nolde oder Ernst Barlach, von letzterem besaß er zwei Plastiken.[6] Vielen Künstlern und Parteifunktionären galt Goebbels deshalb als Hoffnungsträger für die Etablierung des Expressionismus als Vorbild für die offizielle NS-Kunst. Bis 1936 fand die pro-moderne Bewegung ihre Foren. Immer wieder versuchte Rosenberg Goebbels aufgrund seiner Kunstanschauung bei Hitler anzuschwärzen. Dieser verhielt sich in der Frage jedoch zunächst indifferent. In seiner zweiten Rede auf der Kulturtagung des Parteitags der NSDAP in Nürnberg am 5. September 1934 verdammte er sowohl die «Kunstverderber», die «Neues um jeden Preis» anstreben, als auch die ewigen «Rückwärtse», die die «Neuzeit zugunsten des Mittelalters vergewaltigen» würden.[7] Was also waren die Parameter für eine neue Staatskunst?

Völkische Kunst

In wissenschaftlichen Abhandlungen zur Kunst im ‹Dritten Reich› ist das Fehlen eines konkreten Stilkanons – sowohl für die erwünschte als auch für die unerwünschte Kunst – häufig als Unvermögen oder Inkonsequenz der NS-Ideologen ausgelegt worden. Die Kunstanschauung der Nationalsozialisten war jedoch nicht auf ästhetische Theorien ausgerichtet, sondern auf eine völkische Ideologie. Stilistische Fragestellungen gehen daher unweigerlich am Kern der Absichten von damals vorbei. Die Debatte zur nationalsozialistischen Kunst wurde bewusst aus den intellektuellen Verhandlungsräumen herausgelöst und einem ganz neuen Referenzrahmen verpflichtet. Die verbindlichen Richtgrößen sollten gleichsam aus der neuen Weltanschauung erwachsen. Mit der Einführung von Kriterien wie ‹arteigen› oder ‹entartet› wurde der Bewertungsmaßstab an Kategorien der Rassenlehre gebunden und die Kunst eindeutig als eine Angelegenheit des Volkes deklariert. Jedermann war mit der Reduzierung auf zwei Kategorien nun in der Lage, über Kunst zu urteilen.

Im Sinne des Systems kann also nicht von Inkonsequenzen die Rede sein. Vielmehr wurden Reibungskoeffizienten geschaffen, um die Kunst einem Radikalisierungsprozess der Gesellschaft auszusetzen. Dass hierbei vor allem progressive Tendenzen auf der Strecke bleiben würden, war absehbar. Seit ihrer Entstehung war die Moderne starken Anfeindungen aus der Bevölkerung ausgesetzt gewesen. Zwar fiel nach Abdankung des Kaisers Ende 1918 die offizielle Hürde für ihre Verbreitung, und die moderne Kunst hielt während der Weimarer Republik landesweit Einzug in öffentliche Sammlungen, jedoch konnten die Vorbehalte auch im Zuge der Museumsreform samt volksnahem Bildungsprogramm nicht ausgeräumt werden. Nach 1933 fühlten sich die ungehörten Gegner aufgerufen, ihren Kampf endgültig auszufechten. Es dauerte nur wenige Monate bis die ersten Femeausstellungen auf lokaler Ebene organisiert wurden: Dessau, Mannheim, München, Erlangen, Karlsruhe, Nürnberg, Chemnitz, Stuttgart, Bielefeld, Ulm und Dresden öffneten ihre sogenannten ‹Schreckenskammern› mit moderner Kunst gleich 1933. Zahlreiche weitere Städte folgten in den nächsten Jahren.

1936 wanderte die drei Jahre zuvor in Dresden unter dem Titel *Entartete Kunst* gezeigte Ausstellung nach München (Abb. 10, 14 und 15). Erstmals trat hier das RMVP als mitverantwortliche Instanz auf.[8] Für Goebbels war es an der Zeit, Bilanz zu ziehen und eine klare Position einzunehmen. Das Klima in der Kulturszene hatte sich zunehmend verschärft. Nach den XI. Olympischen Sommerspielen 1936, bei denen sich Deutschland der Welt gegenüber noch tolerant präsentieren wollte, fanden vermehrt Ausstellungsschließungen statt, allen

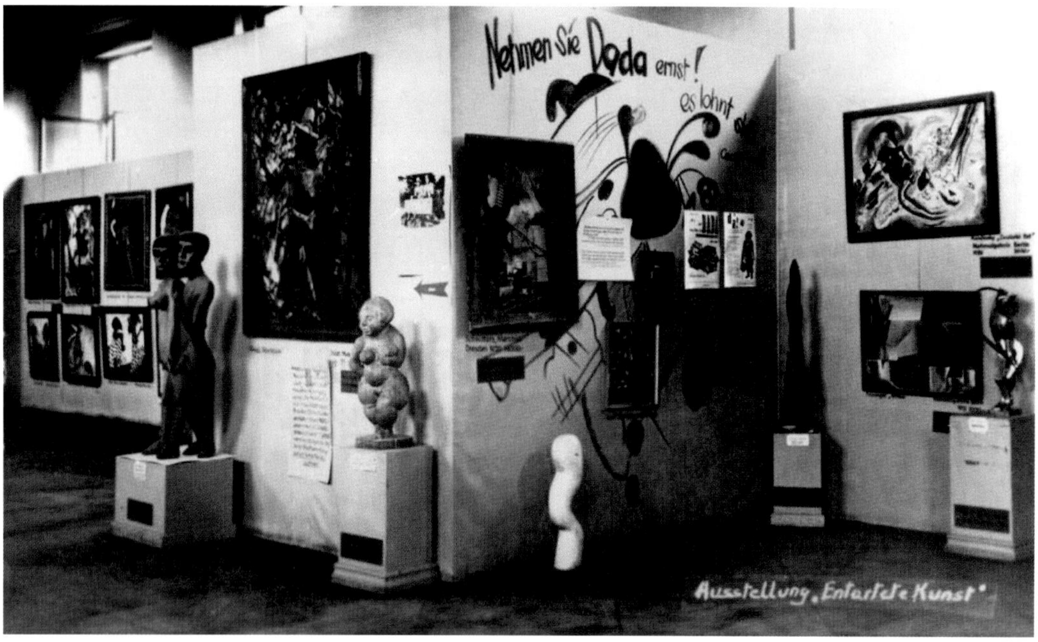

10 Ausstellung *Entartete Kunst*, München 1937, Innenansicht

voran die der Neuen Abteilung der Nationalgalerie im Kronprinzenpalais, in der bis dato noch Werke der Expressionisten gezeigt werden durften. Im Herbst des Jahres tagten in Berlin die Museumsleiter, denen Erziehungsminister Rust die «Säuberung der Museen» ankündigte.[9] Darauf folgten zunächst gezielte Umbesetzungen in der Reichskammer. Im Dezember übernahm Adolf Ziegler (Abb. 12), Maler und Kunstberichterstatter, mit ambitionierten Plänen das Amt des Präsidenten der Reichskammer der bildenden Künste. Zwei Monate später rief er die Landesleiter der Kammer zu einer Arbeitstagung ins Schloss Schönhausen in der Nähe von Berlin zusammen, auf der er ein energisches Durchgreifen und den Beginn einer «planvollen Kulturpflege auf lange Sicht» proklamierte.[10]

1937 hatte die ‹Gleichschaltung› weitestgehend ihren Abschluss gefunden, das Reich war ökonomisch saniert und innenpolitisch stabilisiert. Nachdem die Machthaber von April bis Juni des Jahres in Berlin mit einer gigantischen Reichsausstellung Rechenschaft über die wirtschaftlichen und militärischen Errungenschaften abgelegt hatten,[11] war der Kunst ein eigener Auftritt in München vorbehalten. Am 16. Juli begann in der sogenannten «Hauptstadt der Bewegung» ein pompöses Festprogramm mit Opern- und Theateraufführungen, Konzerten, Umzügen und volkstümlichen Veranstaltungen. Zwei Tage darauf öffnete das neu erbaute Haus der Deutschen Kunst an der Prinzregentenstraße mit der ersten *Großen Deutschen Kunstausstellung* seine Türen (Abb. 11 u. 16). Um die glanzvolle Darbietung noch zu erhöhen griff Goebbels erneut die Idee einer Femeausstellung unter dem Titel *Entartete Kunst* auf. Innerhalb kürzester Zeit ließ er dafür aus 32 Museen rund 700 Werke moderner Kunst sicherstellen. Als Ausstellungsort fungierte die Abgusssammlung des Archäologischen Instituts in den Hofgartenarkaden nahe dem Haus der Deutschen Kunst. Auf monumentale Weise visualisierte Goebbels so den Kontrast von ‹arteigen› und ‹entartet› in Anlehnung an den populären Vorher-Nachher-Vergleich, ohne dem Volk bei der starken Inszenierung beider Schauen wirklich eine freie Bewertung zu überlassen.

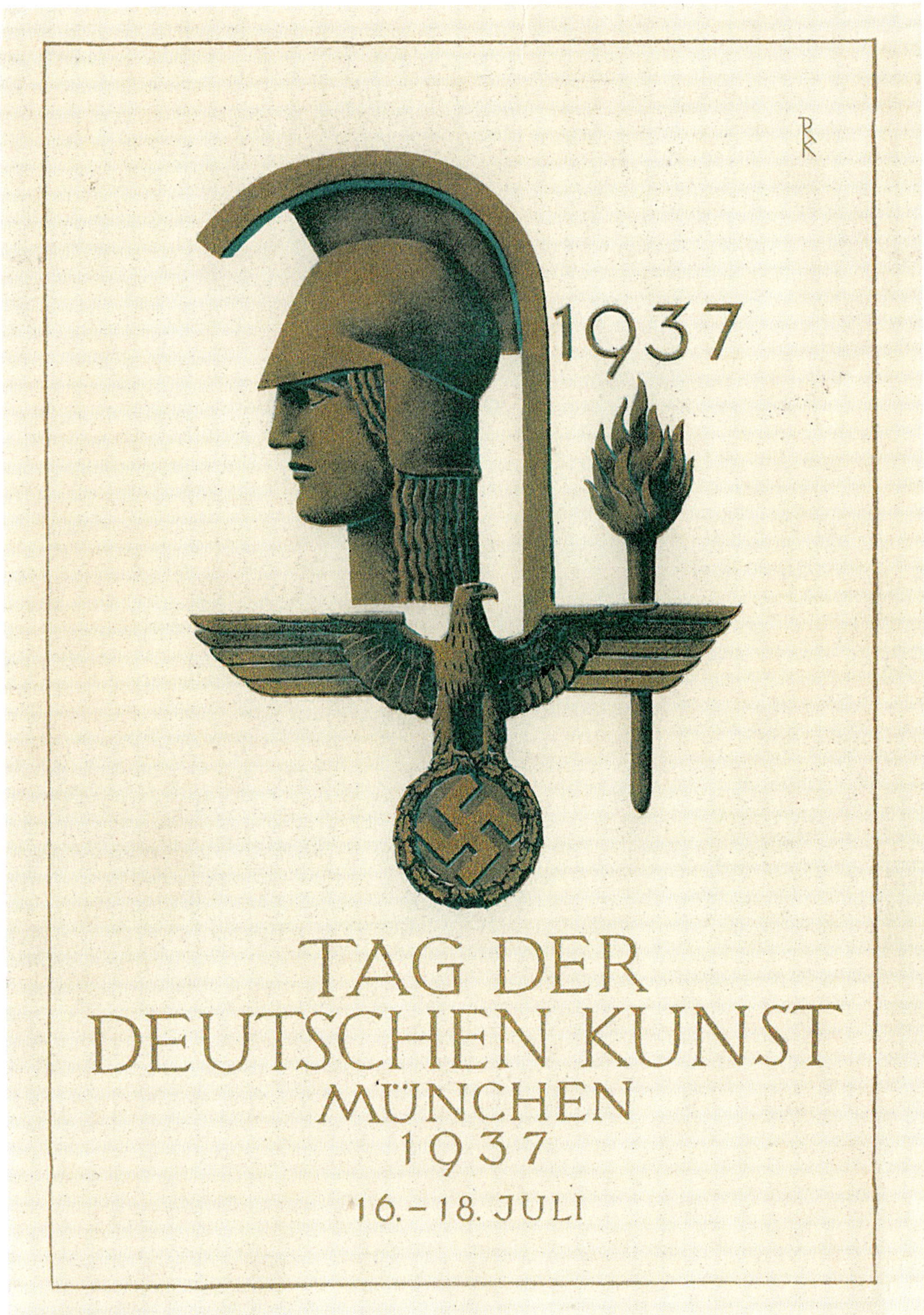

11 Plakat zum Tag der Deutschen Kunst, 16.-18. Juli 1937

Nach Ablauf der ausbedungenen Karenzzeit von vier Jahren war das Urteil gefällt. Hitler griff bei seiner Rede zur Eröffnung des Hauses der Deutschen Kunst den Vorschlag von Erziehungsminister Rust aus dem Vorjahr auf: «Wir werden von jetzt ab einen unerbittlichen Säuberungskrieg führen gegen die letzten Elemente unserer Kulturzersetzung.»[12] Ausführen durfte den Plan Goebbels, der nun endgültig in das Lager der leidenschaftlichen Gegner der Moderne übergewechselt war. Wie bei der Sicherstellung von Kunstwerken für die Ausstellung ordnete er auf Grundlage eines Führererlasses die Beschlagnahme aller restlichen Bestände moderner Kunstwerke in Museen und Institutionen an. Insgesamt waren mehr als 21.000 Kunstwerke betroffen. Bis zum Ende des Zweiten Weltkriegs waren sie dem Blick der Öffentlichkeit entzogen. Noch heute ist unsere Wahrnehmung der Klassischen Moderne von den damaligen Ereignissen geprägt.

1 Adolf Hitler: Aufruf an das deutsche Volk, Völkischer Beobachter, 2. Februar 1933.

2 Adolf Hitler: Kundgebung im Berliner Sportpalast, 10. Februar 1933, Stiftung Deutsches Rundfunkarchiv.

3 Adolf Hitler: «Die deutsche Kunst als stolzeste Verteidigung des deutschen Volkes», Rede auf der Kulturtagung des Parteitags der NSDAP, Nürnberg 3./4. September 1933, in: Robert Eikmeyer (Hg.): Adolf Hitler, Reden zur Kunst- und Kulturpolitik, 1933-1939, Frankfurt am Main 2004, S. 43 ff.

4 RGBl I, 7. April 1933, S. 175, vgl. insbesondere § 3 u. § 4.

5 Goebbels Erklärung RMVP, 25. März 1933.

6 Hubertus v. Tippelskirch: Amt oder Kunst. Die Kunstauffassung Joseph Goebbels. Kulturbiographie eines Wanderers, Sammlers und Berserkers, 1917-1939, unpubl. Magisterarbeit an der Freien Universität Berlin 2015.

7 Adolf Hitler: «Kunst verpflichtet zur Wahrhaftigkeit», Rede auf der Kulturtagung des Parteitags der NSDAP, Nürnberg 5. September 1934, in: Robert Eikmeyer (Hg.): Adolf Hitler, Reden zur Kunst- und Kulturpolitik, 1933-1939, Frankfurt am Main 2004, S. 63 ff.

8 Vgl. Christoph Zuschlag: «Entartete Kunst». Ausstellungsstrategien im Nazi-Deutschland, Worms 1995, S. 146 ff.

9 Wissenschaftlicher Pressedienst, Nr. 260, 6.11.1936, BArch NS 15/163.

10 Arbeitstagung der Reichskammer der bildenden Künste, in: Völkischer Beobachter, 14.2.1937.

11 Gebt mir vier Jahre Zeit, Ausstellungsgelände am Funkturm, Berlin April bis Juni 1937, vgl. Zuschlag 1995, S. 169 ff.

12 Adolf Hitler: Programmatische Kulturrede des Führers, Rede zur Eröffnung der Großen Deutschen Kunstausstellung in München, 18. Juli 1937, in: Robert Eikmeyer (Hg.): Adolf Hitler, Reden zur Kunst- und Kulturpolitik, 1933-1939, Frankfurt am Main 2004, S. 123 ff.

"People of Germany, give us four years". The Consolidation of Nazi Art Policy, 1933-1937

MEIKE HOFFMANN

On 1 February 1933 – the day after the Nazis seized power – Adolf Hitler issued a proclamation to the German people for first time as Chancellor. In his appeal, he decried the Weimar Republic as a period of economic and political decline, in which communism and anarchy had supposedly corroded the character of the Germans. He, by contrast, promised to save the Fatherland, unite the nation, end unemployment and revitalise the economy. The only thing he asked from the people of Germany was four years' time. "The Marxist parties and their followers had fourteen years to prove their worth. The result was ruin. Now, People of Germany, give us four years, and then pass judgement upon us."[1]

In the months that followed, Hitler reiterated his plea in every major speech, using radio broadcasts, Nazi party newspapers, posters and flyers to convince millions of Germans to give him a four-year grace period.[2] The revival of German art and culture featured strongly in his promise of salvation. According to Hitler, art was the "proudest way to defend the German people,"[3] wording which already suggested war propaganda. However, he was yet to explain exactly what he understood by new art in line with Nazi ideology and how he planned on achieving his ambitious goals. So how did things progress during this four-year consolidation phase?

Goebbels – Rosenberg – Rust

The main proponents of "Gleichschaltung" (Nazification of state and society) in the cultural sector were Joseph Goebbels (fig. 13), Alfred Rosenberg (fig. 8) and Bernhard Rust (fig. 9). Hitler deliberately pitted these men against each other to fuel their rivalry and encourage their performance.

Rust, a secondary school teacher who had joined the Nazi party in 1922, was appointed as deputy head of the Prussian Ministry of Cultural Affairs under the authority of Hermann Göring, Minister President of Prussia. In keeping with the Law for the Restoration of the Professional Civil Service passed on 7 April 1933, Rust arranged for the dismissal of numerous Jewish and politically undesirable museum employees, academy members and university teachers so they could be replaced with Aryan colleagues who conformed to the Nazi ideology.[4] After the cultural sovereignty of the federal German states was withdrawn, Rust was made Minister of Science, Education and Culture in 1934, which extended his sphere of influence to museums and educational institutions all over Germany. After his strong start, however, his decision-making and assertive powers soon faded in the turf war with Rosenberg and Goebbels.

A member of the Nazi party since 1920, Alfred Rosenberg founded the "Kampfbund", a Militant League for German Culture in 1929, an initially non-partisan association which advocated a nationalistic, reactionary and anti-Semitic cultural policy. In *Der Mythus des 20. Jahrhunderts* (*The Myth of the Twentieth Century)*, a book published in 1930 that helped shape Hitler's racial ideology, Rosenberg blamed an alleged Jewish-Bolshevist world conspiracy for the demise of German culture. Four years later, Rosenberg was appointed as Commissar for the Supervision of Intellectual and Ideological Education of the NSDAP. He was however no match for Goebbels's power games. It was only later that he eventually achieved the political importance he so coveted as Head of the Reichsleiter Rosenberg Taskforce for the Occupied Western Territories and Reich Minister for the Occupied Eastern Territories.

From the outset, Joseph Goebbels had set his sights on seizing control of all areas of culture. In March 1933 he founded the Reichsministerium für Volksaufklärung und Propaganda (RMVPM, Reich Ministry of Public Enlightenment and Propaganda), which from then on was responsible for controlling the German press, literature, visual arts, filmmaking, theatre and broadcasting. As Goebbels explained: "The Ministry is tasked with the intellectual mobilisation of Germany. Therefore, it is to the arts what the Ministry of War is to defence [...] because intellectual mobilisation is just as necessary, perhaps even more so, than the material militarisation of the country."[5] Through culture, the German population was to be prepared psychologically for the war, which was already being planned. Six months later Goebbels founded the Reichskulturkammer (RKK, Reich Chamber of Culture), thus establishing totalitarian control over all areas of culture: artists, art critics and even postcard vendors had to be registered in the Chamber and its various branches to be allowed to continue their work.

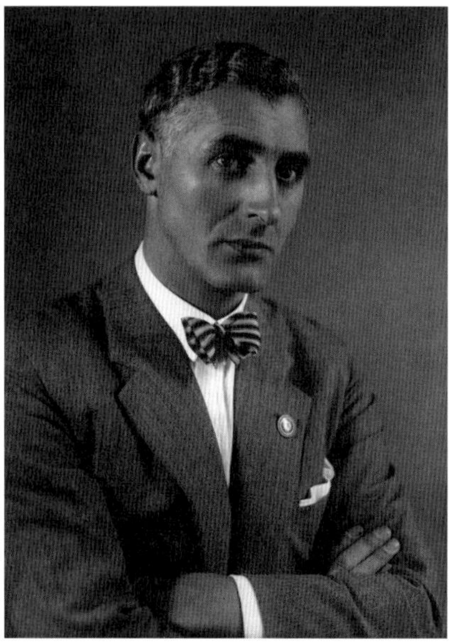

12 Adolf Ziegler, um 1937

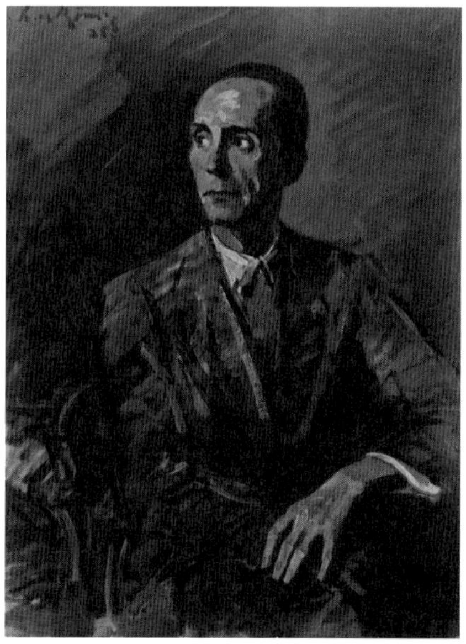

13 Leo v. König, *Porträt Joseph Goebbels*, 1935

With the two offices he had founded, RMVP and RKK, Goebbels had at his disposal very powerful tools for the Nazification of cultural life in Germany. He was able to impose himself within Rust's and Rosenberg's areas of responsibility, thus consistently emerging victorious over his rivals in the following years. He was however in something of a difficult situation, as his ideas about art did not entirely accord with those of Adolf Hitler. For instance, he rated such modern artists as Edvard Munch, Emil Nolde or Ernst Barlach highly and he even owned two sculptures by the latter.[6] Indeed, many artists and Nazi officials hoped Goebbels would be able to establish Expressionism as a model for national-socialist art. The pro-modern wing behind the minister was active until 1936, although Rosenberg repeatedly tried to bring Goebbels into disrepute for his views on art. Hitler however remained indifferent, stating in his second speech at the Congress of Culture held in Nuremberg on 5 September 1934 that he was condemning both the "spoilers of art, who aspire to create new things at all cost," and the "backward-lookers, who would rape the modern era in favour of the Middle Ages."[7] So what were the parameters for official Nazi art?

Art for the "Volk"

In academic literature considering art in the Third Reich, the lack of a firm stylistic canon – for both promoted and rejected works – has often been construed as an incapability or inconsistency on the part of the Nazi ideologists. Their approach to art, however, didn't originate from an aesthetic theory, but rather from their nationalist ideology. Stylistic issues therefore inevitably took a back seat in favour of political intentions. The debate on official Nazi art was deliberately left out of the intellectual sphere and bound by a completely new frame of reference, whereby the canons were supposed to spring directly from the new ideology. The introduction of criteria such as 'race-specific' or 'degenerate' not only bound the assessment standard for works of art to race theory; it also established a clear link between art and the German people, so that everyone was henceforth capable of passing judgement on works of art.

The Nazi approach to art was therefore not inconsistent. Rather it created friction coefficients, allowing the art scene to play a part in a radicalisation process that affected the whole of German society. The fact that progressive tendencies in particular would fall by the wayside was foreseeable under such conditions, all the more so since modern art had faced the hostility of the general public since its inception. Though official hurdles were repealed after the fall of the monarchy in late 1918, and works by modern artists found their way into public collections during the Weimar Republic, the German public remained hostile to modern art; even a popularisation programme accompanying museum reform during these years did little to alter the situation. After the Nazis seized power in late January 1933, opponents of modernism recognised the call to fight for their cause. Within months, so-called "chamber of horrors" exhibitions of modern art were organised in cities including Dessau, Mannheim, Munich, Erlangen, Karlsruhe, Nuremberg, Chemnitz, Stuttgart, Bielefeld, Ulm and Dresden.

In 1936 an exhibition of *Entartete Kunst* (*Degenerate Art*) shown in Dresden three years earlier moved to Munich (fig. 10, 14 and 15). The RMVP appeared as a co-organising body for the first time.[8] For Goebbels, it was time to take stock and adopt a clear stance as the climate on the cultural scene began to heat up. After the eleventh Olympic Games held in Berlin in 1936, during which the Nazi rulers had been looking to present a tolerant image

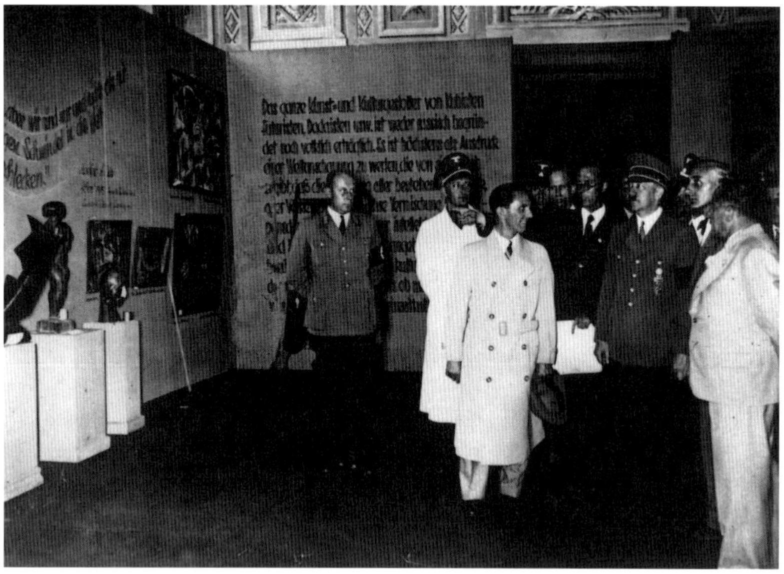

14 Goebbels, Hitler and Adolf Ziegler visiting the exhibition *Entartete Kunst*, Munich 1937

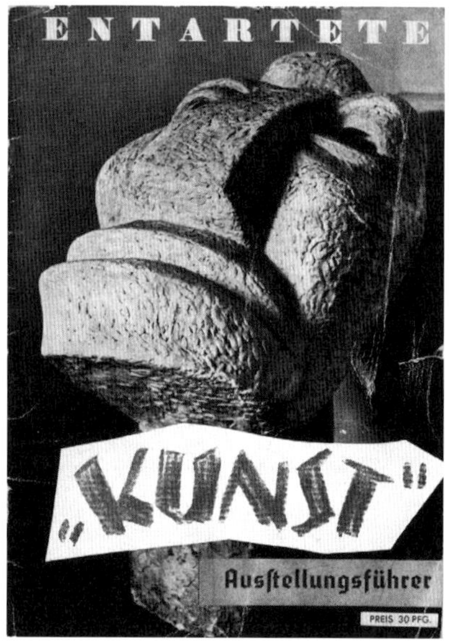

15 *Entartete 'Kunst'*, visitors guide, 1937

to the world, numerous exhibitions of modern art were closed down, among them a show of Expressionists in the Kronprinzenpalais, an annex of Berlin's National Gallery. In the autumn of that year, Education Minister Rust announced a "cleansing of the museums" to directors convening in the German capital.[10] This was followed by targeted reshuffles in the RKK: in December, Adolf Ziegler (fig. 12), a painter and ambitious art journalist, was appointed President of the Reich Chamber of the Fine Arts. Two months later, Ziegler summoned the heads of the regional branches of the RKK to a conference at Schönhausen Palace on the outskirts of Berlin, where he announced an emphatic clampdown and the launching of "long-term systematic cultural conservation measures."[10]

By 1937 *Gleichschaltung* was largely complete; the economy had been revived and the political power of the Nazis stabilised on the home front. After Hitler had flaunted his economic and military achievements with an enormous exhibition in Berlin from April to June,[11] art was given a stage of its own. On 16 July an ostentatious programme of events was launched in Munich – the "Capital of the Nazi Movement" – featuring opera and theatre performances, concerts and parades. Two days later, the newly constructed House of German Art on Prinzregentenstrasse opened its doors with the first *Große deutsche Kunstausstellung* (*Great German Art Exhibition*) (fig. 16). To round off proceedings, Goebbels turned again to the idea of a slander exhibition under the title *Entartete Kunst*. Containing over 700 works swiftly confiscated from 32 German museums, the exhibition was held in the Hofgarten Arcade, a building located near the House of German Art, which usually housed the collection of replicas of the Institute of Archaeology. Goebbels' concept was based on the popular before/after comparison to underscore the contrast between 'race-specific' and 'degenerate' art; the exhibition's startling design leaving visitors little choice but to share his conclusions.

At the end of the proclaimed four-year grace period, the verdict was clear. In his speech at the inauguration of the House of German Art, Hitler picked up Education Minister Rust's

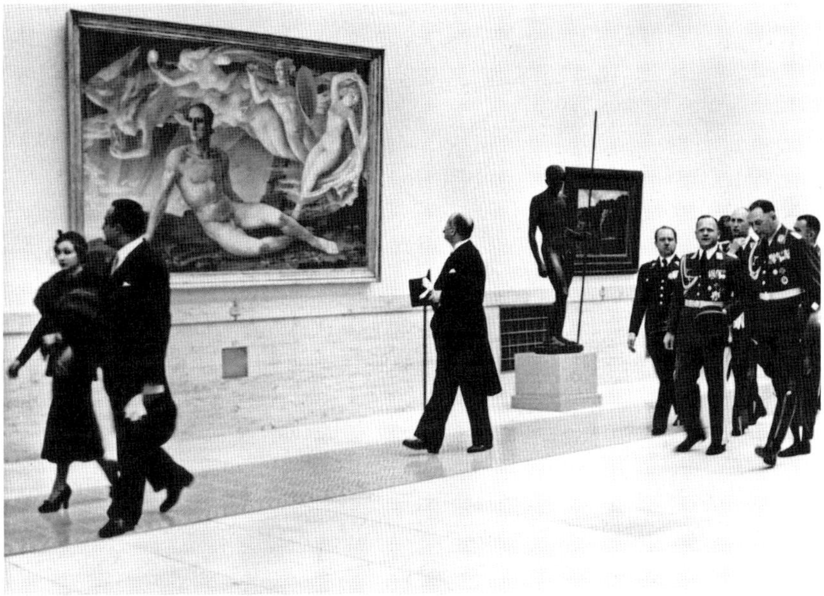

16 *Große Deutsche Kunstausstellung,* Munich 1937

proposal from the previous year, stating: "From now on, we will wage a bitter cleansing war on the last remnants of what caused our cultural decay."[12] Goebbels, who had meanwhile switched sides and become a staunch opponent of modern art, was to execute the plan. Continuing the project started for the Munich *Entartete Kunst* exhibition, and with the relevant decree from the Führer in hand, he ordered the confiscation of all works of modern art remaining in German museums and institutions. By the end of the Second World War, a total of over 21,000 artworks had been seized and removed from display. To this day, our perception of modern German art remains shaped by the events of that time.

1 Adolf Hitler: Aufruf an das deutsche Volk, in: Völkischer Beobachter, 2 February 1933.
2 Adolf Hitler, speech during the rally in the Berlin Sportpalast on 10 February 1933, German Broadcasting Archive Foundation.
3 Adolf Hitler: Die deutsche Kunst als stolzeste Verteidigung des deutschen Volkes (speech at the Congress of Culture at the Nazi party rally, Nuremberg 3-4 September 1933), in: Robert Eikmeyer (ed.): Adolf Hitler, Reden zur Kunst- und Kulturpolitik, 1933-1939, Frankfurt am Main 2004, p. 43 ff.
4 Reichsgesetzblatt I, 7 April 1933, p. 175, cf. particularly § 3 and § 4.
5 Joseph Goebbels, RMVP declaration, 25 March 1933.
6 Hubertus von Tippelskirch: Amt oder Kunst. Die Kunstauffassung Joseph Goebbels. Kulturbiographie eines Wanderers, Sammlers und Berserkers, 1917–1939, unpubl. MA thesis at Freie Universität Berlin, 2015.
7 Adolf Hitler: Kunst verpflichtet zur Wahrhaftigkeit (speech at the Congress of Culture at the Nazi party rally, Nuremberg, 5 September 1934), in: Robert Eikmeyer (ed.): Adolf Hitler: Reden zur Kunst- und Kulturpolitik, 1933–1939, Frankfurt am Main 2004, p. 63 ff.
8 cf. Christoph Zuschlag: "Entartete Kunst". Ausstellungsstrategien im Nazi-Deutschland, Worms 1995, p. 146 ff.
9 Wissenschaftlicher Pressedienst, Nr. 260, 6 November 1936, BArch NS 15/163
10 Arbeitstagung der Reichskammer der bildenden Künste, in: Völkischer Beobachter, 14 February 1937.
11 *Gebt mir vier Jahre Zeit* (exhibition at Berlin's trade fair ground, April–June 1937), cf. Zuschlag 1995, p. 169 ff.
12 Adolf Hitler: Programmatische Kulturrede des Führers (speech at the opening of the *Great German Art Exhibition* in Munich on 18 July 1937), in: Robert Eikmeyer (ed.): Adolf Hitler, Reden zur Kunst- und Kulturpolitik, 1933–1939, Frankfurt am Main 2004, p. 123 ff.

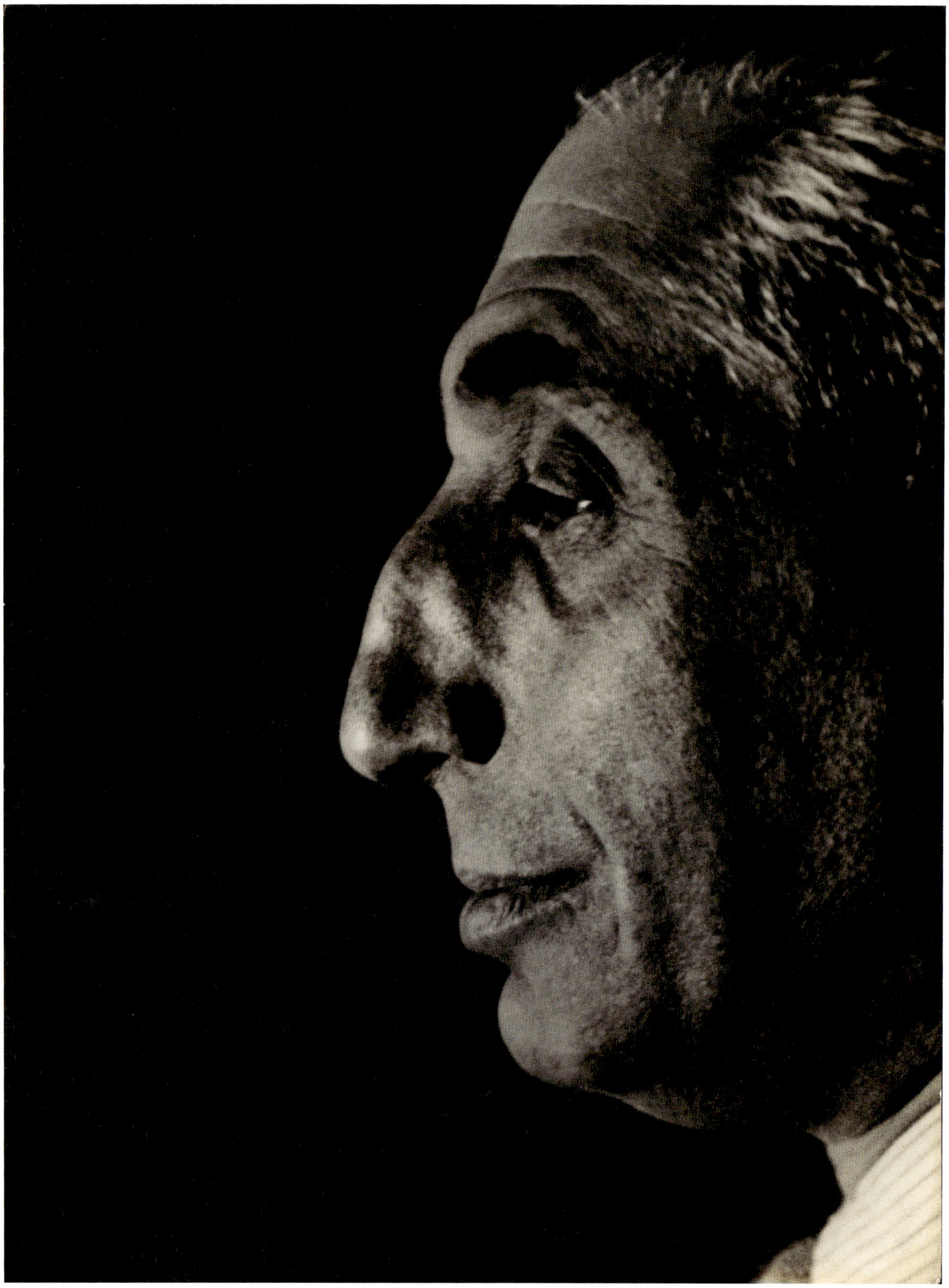

17 Gerty Simon, *Portrait of Alfred Flechtheim*, 1935, as featured in her Camera Club exhibition of 1935

Refugees and Émigrés from Nazi Germany to Britain 1933-1938

BARBARA WARNOCK

The London exhibition *Twentieth Century German Art* was in part a direct response to the 1937 Nazi campaign against so-called 'degenerate art'. It was also the product of the existence, since the Nazi accession to power in 1933, of a German Jewish émigré scene stretching across Europe.[1] As will be explored in this volume, the origins of the 1938 London exhibition were inextricably linked with the refugees and émigrés that Nazi oppression created, and it was in this context of persecution, flight and exile that *Twentieth Century German Art* was planned and staged. This essay traces some of this context in terms of the situation for those escaping Nazi Germany for Britain between 1933 and 1938.

From the moment the Nazis came to power in January 1933, people began to flee Germany, with many arriving in Britain. Events over subsequent months saw the numbers of new arrivals steadily increase.[2] Action against those the Nazis deemed their enemies increased after the Reichstag Fire on 27 February 1933, when political persecution against Communists and Socialists in Germany intensified. On 1 April 1933 there was a Nazi-organised boycott of Jewish businesses. The boycott was a particularly critical moment for many German Jews. It convinced the progressive educationalist Anna Essinger (fig. 20) for example that 'Germany was no longer a place in which to bring up children in honesty and freedom'; at this point she took steps to relocate her school near Ulm abroad.[3] Essinger settled upon Britain as her destination and, with Home Office permission, 75 mainly Jewish pupils and the staff of school re-settled in Kent.

The experience of Anna Essinger and her pupils points to the relative degree of flexibility that existed at that time in the British immigration system, at least for those with means. Regulations introduced in 1914 had removed the right of refuge in Britain, but visa-free travel was possible from many countries.[4] The main obstacle most faced, after the difficulties of exiting the Reich had been negotiated,[5] was inspection by immigration officers at points of entry. Those seeking to stay were required to demonstrate that they were able to support themselves, and conditions of entry were sometimes imposed.[6] The Home Office intended their system to allow room for discretion and flexibility, but equally, particularly at a time of mass unemployment, sought to avoid taking in those who might occupy a position that could otherwise go to a British citizen.[7] The British government did not use this flexibility to ease the passage of refugees in the context of Nazi persecution, however. Until the outbreak of war, the government offered no financial support to these new arrivals. Furthermore, many who came were only admitted into Britain as trans-migrants: that is, on the understanding that they would leave after a set period and migrate on elsewhere (although the eventual length of the war rendered this stipulation redundant for most who came in the 1930s).[8]

It was generally the voluntary sector rather than the government that provided assistance for refugees between 1933 and 1938. Following the April 1933 boycott in Germany, Jewish community organisations and Quaker groups in Britain mobilised to offer support and urge the government to do more for those seeking asylum from Germany.[9] One such group was the Jewish Refugee Committee (JRC), formed under the leadership of the German-born Otto Schiff, who had emigrated to Britain around the turn of the century. Schiff had worked since the First World War to assist Jewish refugees. On 6 April 1933 the JRC met with a committee of the British Cabinet, to advocate for assistance for those fleeing the Third Reich. Though the Committee refused to relax entry requirements, it did agree to the JRC's pledge that it would raise funds to cover the costs of the maintenance of those Jews who fled persecution in Germany.[10]

Another important voluntary sector group was the Central British Fund (CBF), founded in 1933 to aid Jews escaping Germany with paperwork, obtaining sponsorship to cover maintenance, housing, gaining employment and other advice. The left-wing Artists International Association, also founded in London in 1933, similarly formed a committee to aid refugees, and later helping a number of those connected with the *Twentieth Century German Art* exhibition.[11]

One area with which refugee organisations assisted was in helping refugees gain employment in Britain. For those who sought to work, a permit obtained in advance was required. The role of the voluntary sector here can be seen in the work of The Academic Assistance Council, established by William Beveridge to help some of the c. 1,200 German academics removed from their posts by the Hitler Regime. The Council managed to place 178 academics in British universities,[12] such as the Nobel-prize winning physicist Max Born, recruited from Göttingen for the University of Cambridge. The philosopher Prof. Ernst Cassirer was also invited to Britain thanks to the work of the council, travelling from Hamburg to Oxford in summer 1933; his cousin, the publisher Bruno Cassirer, followed in 1938. Other cultural figures and institutions arrived in Britain without this assistance. In late 1933, the Mayor Gallery in London offered Alfred Flechtheim the opportunity to work for them in the British capital (fig. 17), allowing him to relocate to London. His colleague Grete Ring of the Kunstsalon Cassirer – with whom Flechtheim had organised the three-part-exhibition *Lebendige Deutsche Kunst* (*Living German Art*) in Berlin early 1933 – was able to come to Britain in 1938, one year after Flechtheim's death in London. The critic and writer Alfred Kerr was another important cultural émigré to Britain, arriving in London from Paris in 1936.

Highly skilled professionals, well-connected businessmen and those with a degree of international renown found it easier to gain permits. However, even in these cases, the government sometimes consulted relevant professional groups, who frequently acted to block applications. By 1939 for example, only 25 permits for architects had been issued, as the Royal Institute of British Architects' numerous objections meant that only truly world-leading figures were able to enter Britain – such as Walter Gropius, who lived and worked in Britain between 1934 and 1937.[13]

Despite some of the obstacles, the arrival of even small numbers of creative figures in Britain served to stimulate British culture.[14] In 1935, the Jewish German architect, Erich Mendelsohn, who had fled from Berlin in 1933, won the competition to design the De la

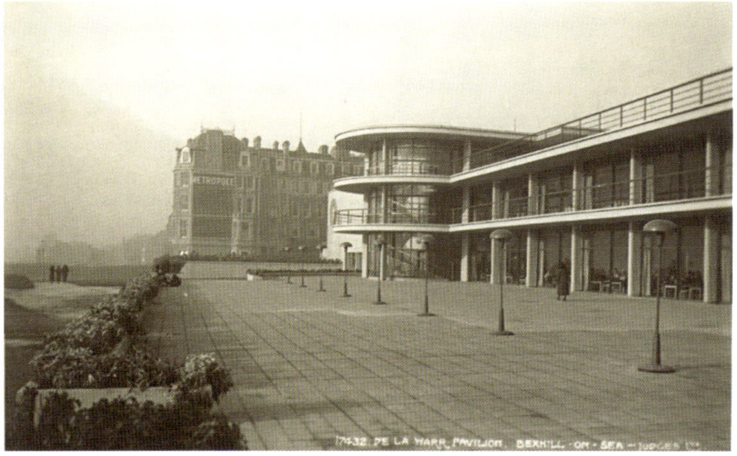

18 The De la Warre Pavillon in Bexhill, c. 1935

Warr Pavilion in Bexhill (fig. 18), a building today regarded as an outstanding example of modernism in Britain.[15] Refugees from Germany also helped to develop the Glyndebourne Festival from 1934 and the Edinburgh International Festival from 1944.[16]

One German photographer who was able to create a successful niche for herself in exile was Gerty Simon (fig. 22), whose son Bernd (later Bernard) was one of Anna Essinger's pupils (fig. 21). Simon had moved from Berlin to Britain with Essinger's school in 1933 and established a photographic studio in Chelsea. She was part of a well-connected artistic milieu in Berlin and once in London, she set about forging new connections with members of the cultural scene, establishing a kind of 'salon' at her London home. Her subjects in Berlin had included Lotte Lenya, Albert Einstein and Max Liebermann – in London, she photographed leading figures of the day ranging from Aneurin Bevan to Peggy Ashcroft and Sir Kenneth Clark, director of London's National Gallery from 1933 to 1945. Simon also staged a number of exhibitions in London, including one at the Camera Club in 1935 (see fig. 17).[17] Gerty Simon is an example of the way that it was possible for some creative figures to both connect with, and enhance, the cultural scene in Britain.

The British policy towards the refugees who fled Nazi Germany under 'threat of arrest and fear of penury' prior to 1938 is described by Deborah Dwork and Robert Jan van Pelt as, 'we'll take the best and let the French, Dutch and Czechs cope with the rest'.[18] There is indeed some truth in this characterisation. When one considers the social backgrounds of émigrés to Britain such as Gerty Simon, Walter Gropius, and indeed the lenders discussed in the catalogue section of this volume, it is tempting to conclude that Jewish refugees escaping Nazism tended to be highly educated and culturally engaged. But, as Tony Kushner argues, this view ignores another route by which some were able to escape, which was through obtaining a permit to work as a domestic servant (see fig. 23). From 1931, a work permit was required for those wanting to employ foreign servants, but a shortage of domestic staff in Britain meant that work in this area was relatively plentiful. Between January 1933 and late 1938, around 7,000 German Jewish refugees entered Britain this way, most of them women, and some among them from working-class backgrounds.[19] By the outbreak of war, the total was around 20,000.[20]

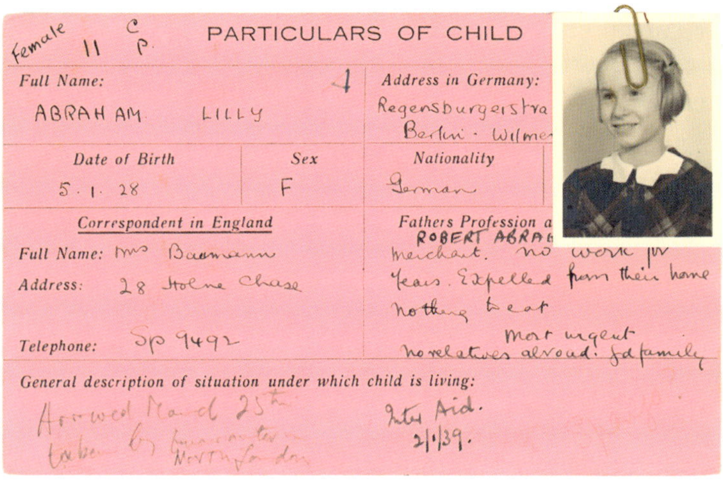

PARTICULARS OF CHILD

Full Name: ABRAHAM LILLY

Address in Germany: Regensburgerstra Berlin - Wilme

Date of Birth: 5.1.28

Sex: F

Nationality: German

Correspondent in England

Full Name: Mrs Baumann

Address: 28 Holne Chase

Telephone: SP 9492

Fathers Profession a: ROBERT ABRA merchant. no work for years. Expelled from their home nothing to eat. Most urgent. no relatives abroad

General description of situation under which child is living:

19 Index card for Lilly Abraham, who came to England under the *Kindertransport* movement

Those seeking to escape Germany for Britain between 1933 and 1938 had no right of refuge in the country and they were offered no British governmental assistance. Refugees were often selected according to their wealth and professional success, and generally offered only temporary admission. But at least no visa was required, meaning a significant reduction in onerous pre-departure preparations. In 1938 however – the year that Twentieth Century German Art was staged in London – this situation changed.

1938 was a particularly significant moment for Jews remaining in Germany and Austria. In March, the German Anschluss of Austria occasioned a dramatic upsurge in anti-Semitic violence and other forms of oppression in the country. Across the Reich, 1938 also saw the institution of the policy of Aryanisation – the seizure of Jewish property. These events, and the annexation of the Czech Sudentenland which followeg in autumn 1938, prompted a further significant wave of emigration towards Britain. Among those who arrived during this period, the painter Oskar Kokoschka; Walter Neurath and his wife, who would go on to found the art publishers Thames & Hudson; and the authors Elias Canetti and Erich Fried. In response to these new arrivals, in particular following the Anschluss of Austria, the emigration regime in Britain tightened up.[21] From May 1938 visas were required for those coming to Britain from Germany and Austria.

Yet despite these new regulations and the continued lack of official governmental financial assistance, more refugees from Nazism came to Britain between May 1938 and September 1939 than had in the whole of the period since 1933. Increasing persecution across the Third Reich and the occupation of Czechoslovakia only increased the need and the voluntary groups whose efforts had been so vital since 1933 stepped up their efforts. In some areas, for example in the issuing of domestic service work permits, the government relaxed restrictions.[22] The horrors of *Kristallnacht* (the November Pogrom) in November 1938 saw voluntary sector groups convince the government to allow a visa waiver scheme, known as the Kindertransport, to operate for children aged up to seventeen (fig. 19). Ultimately around 10,000 children, mainly from Germany and Austria, were able to escape to Britain this way. The entire effort and its costs (including the required £50 sponsorship for each child) was organised by voluntary sector organisations such as the CBF, with efforts coordinated by the Refugee Children's Movement.[23]

It was not only the Kinder who managed to escape between late 1938 and 1939, however. Between March 1938 and the outbreak of war in September 1939 – when leaving Nazi Germany or Nazi occupied Europe became extremely difficult – at least 50,000 Jewish refugees came to Britain.[24] In total between around 80,000 refugees from Nazism escaped to Britain between January 1933 and September 1939.[25]

The background to the *Twentieth Century German Art* exhibition was, then, not just the context of the vilification in Germany of modern art, but also the arrival in Britain of refugees from Nazism. Entry into Britain was not always easy. But once here, many managed to establish connections in Britain that would enhance and invigorate the country in ways that most would never have foreseen.

1 In this text, the terms 'émigré' and 'refugee' will be used interchangeably, given the difficulty of drawing meaningful distinction when considering those who left National Socialist Germany during this period
2 Deborah Dwork, Robert Jan van Pelt: Flight from the Reich: Refugee Jews 1933-1946. London 2009, p. 9
3 Ibid, p. 15.
4 Louise London: British Immigration Control Procedures and Jewish Refugees 1933-1942. London 1992, p. 490-1
5 In Germany, there was a flight tax and various bureaucratic measures to try to prevent foreign currency leaving the country and ensure that the government profited from any assets that those fleeing had: Zara Steiner: Refugees. The Timeless Problem; in: Jessica Reinisch and Matthew Frank (eds.): Refugees in Europe 1919-1959. A Forty Years' Crisis? London etc. 2017, pp. 21-32, p. 25
6 A considerably more open system operated in France than in Britain, but refugees arriving there often then faced destitution, see Dwork and van Pelt, p. 23-24
7 London, pp. 496-7
8 Tony Kushner: The Battle of Britishness. Migrant Journeys 1685 to the Present. Manchester 2012, p. 123
9 For information about these groups Werner E. Mosse (ed.): Second Chance. Two Centuries of German-Speaking Jews in the United Kingdom. Tübingen 1991
10 Dwork and van Pelt, p. 25
11 Peter Lasko. The Impact of German-Speaking Refugees in Britain on the Fine Arts; in: Mosse, pp. 255-274, p. 255.
12 Dwork and van Pelt, p. 22
13 Lasko, p.255
14 See Mosse.
15 Lasko, p. 256.
16 It should be noted that not all of the creatives who came found a conducive atmosphere for their work. Lasko points out the irony that Kurt Schwitters' work, damned in Germany as 'degenerate', 'met with an almost equally negative response in Britain', Ibid, p. 260
17 The Bernard Simon Collection, Wiener Library Archives
18 Dwork and van Pelt, pp. 18, 27
19 Although many of those that came by this route, particularly after the Anschluss, were in fact much more privileged women seeking escape by any means. See Tony Kushner: Alien Occupation. Jewish Refugees and Domestic Service in Britain 1933-1948; in: Mosse pp. 553-78.
20 Ibid.
21 In July 1938, as the Twentieth Century German Art exhibition was underway at the Burlington New Galleries, President Roosevelt's attempt to generate an international response, the Evian Conference, finished without any meaningful commitment to aid Jews in need of refuge, see Steiner, 'Refugees', 26. Some Jews managed to migrate to Palestine, although from 1939, that became more difficult: see Mark Levene: The Jewish Dimension; in Reinisch and Frank, pp. 85-100, pp. 91-92
22 See Kushner: Alien Occupation, p. 561.
23 The CBF is now called World Jewish Relief. For more on the Kindertransport see Vera K. Fast: Children's Exodus. A History of the Kindertransport. New York 2011; and Andrea Hammel and Bea Lewkowiczm (eds.): The Kindertransport to Britain 1938/39. New Perspectives. Amsterdam and New York, 2012. The Kindertransport was somewhat problematic in that parents and sometimes siblings were often not able to escape: Jennifer Craig Norton estimates that at least four in five of the Kinder lost one or both parents. Jennifer Craig-Norton, Contesting Memory: New Perspectives on the Kindertransport, University of Southampton, Doctoral Thesis, 2014
24 Grenville, p. 6
25 Kushner: The Battle of Britishness, p. 123

Emigranten und Flüchtlinge aus NS-Deutschland nach Großbritannien 1933-1938

BARBARA WARNOCK

Die Londoner Ausstellung *Twentieth Century German Art* war zum Teil eine direkte Antwort auf die Aktion *Entartete Kunst* der NS-Regierung von 1937. Gleichzeitig war sie das Produkt der deutsch-jüdischen Emigrantenszene, die nach der Machtergreifung der Nazis im Jahr 1933 in ganz Europa entstanden war.[1] Wie die Forschungsergebnisse des vorliegenden Bandes zeigen, entwickelte sich das Projekt der Londoner Ausstellung in einem durch Verfolgung, Flucht und Exil bestimmten Kontext, wobei die Emigranten aus Deutschland an der Vorbereitung und Durchführung der Veranstaltung maßgeblich beteiligt waren. Der vorliegende Essay versucht einige der Zusammenhänge nachzuzeichnen, welche die Situation zwischen Großbritannien und den aus Nazi-Deutschland Geflohenen zwischen 1933 und 1938 prägten.

Direkt nach der Machtergreifung der Nazis im Januar 1933 verließen zahllose Menschen Deutschland, wobei viele von ihnen nach Großbritannien gelangten. Die Ereignisse der folgenden Wochen und Monate ließ die Zahl der Neuankömmlinge weiter stetig ansteigen.[2] Nach dem Reichstagsbrand vom 27. Februar machte die NS-Regierung Jagd auf alle, die sie für Staatsfeinde hielt, vor allem auf Kommunisten und Sozialisten. Am 1. April organisierten die Nazis einen Boykott jüdischer Geschäfte, den viele deutsche Juden als eindeutiges Zeichen verstanden. So beispielsweise auch die fortschrittliche Pädagogin Anna Essinger (Abb. 20), die Deutschland fortan «nicht mehr als geeigneten Ort ansah, Kinder in Ehrlichkeit und Freiheit zu erziehen», so dass sie beschloss, das von ihr gegründete und geleitete Landschulheim Herrlingen (bei Ulm) ins Ausland zu verlegen.[3] Essinger entschied sich für England, und durfte mit Genehmigung des britischen Innenministeriums in der Grafschaft Kent eine neue Schule eröffnen, in der 75 meist jüdische Kinder von Lehrern aus Herrlingen unterrichtet wurden.

Das Schicksal Anna Essingers und ihrer Schüler beweist, dass das damalige britische Einwanderungsgesetz relativ flexibel war – zumindest für Einwanderer, die nicht mittellos waren. Auch wenn das Asylrecht 1914 abgeschafft worden war, konnte man aus vielen Ländern ohne Visum nach Großbritannien einreisen.[4] Für deutsche Emigranten bestand – nach der Überwindung der fortlaufend erhöhten Ausreisehindernisse[5] – die Hauptschwierigkeit in den Kontrollen, denen sie sich bei der Einreise durch britische Grenzbeamte unterziehen mussten. Dabei hatten sie vor allem nachzuweisen, dass sie für ihren Unterhalt selbst aufkommen konnten, wobei manchmal verschärfte Bedingungen angewandt wurden.[6] Das britische Innenministerium war einigermaßen flexibel, versuchte aufgrund der damals

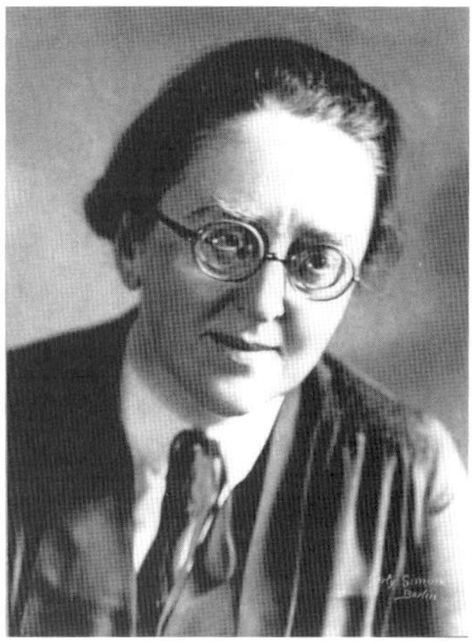

20 Gerty Simon: Porträt von Anna Essinger, um 1930

herrschenden Massenarbeitslosigkeit allerdings jene Emigranten abzuweisen, die den Arbeitsplatz eines Briten hätten einnehmen können.[7] Diese Flexibilität bedeutete jedoch keineswegs, dass die britische Regierung die Einreise von NS-Verfolgten begünstigte, zumal Neuankömmlinge bis zum Kriegsausbruch keinerlei staatliche Zuwendung erhielten. Darüber hinaus wurde vielen Flüchtlingen nur eine vorläufige Aufenthaltsgenehmigung erteilt mit der Auflage, nach einer gewissen Zeit in ein anderes Land weiterzureisen (was sich durch die ungewisse Dauer des Krieges dann erübrigte und für die in den 1930er Jahren Eingereisten noch nicht galt).[8]

Zwischen 1933 und 1938 wurden die Flüchtlinge in Großbritannien vorwiegend durch Privatinitiativen unterstützt. Nach dem von den Nazis im April 1933 organisierten Boykott jüdischer Geschäfte starteten britische Quäker-Gruppen und jüdische Gemeinden Unterstützungsaktionen und forderten die Regierung zu mehr Engagement für die Asylsuchenden aus Deutschland auf.[9] In diesem Zusammenhang sei das Jewish Refugee Committee (JRC) erwähnt, das von Otto Schiff gegründet wurde. Der in Deutschland geborene und um die Jahrhundertwende nach England ausgewanderte Schiff kümmerte sich seit dem 1. Weltkrieg um jüdische Flüchtlinge. Während eines Treffens mit Regierungsvertretern am 6. April 1933 forderte das JRC Hilfe für die aus NS-Deutschland Geflüchteten. Zwar lehnte die Regierung eine Lockerung der Einreisebedingungen ab, jedoch erklärte sie sich mit der Bereitstellung von Geldern für den Unterhalt jüdischer Flüchtlinge aus Deutschland einverstanden.[10] Ebenfalls erwähnenswert sind der Central British Fund (CBF), der ab 1933 jüdische Flüchtlinge beim Ausfüllen von Formularen sowie bei der Suche nach staatlicher Zuwendung, Unterkunft und Arbeit unterstützte, sowie die linksgerichtete, 1933 in London gegründete Artists International Association, welche Flüchtlingen half und Mitwirkende an der Ausstellung *Twentieth Century German Art* unterstützten sollte.[11]

Besonders wichtig war die Hilfe bei der Arbeitssuche und Erlangung der notwendigen Arbeitserlaubnis. Eine effiziente Hilfsorganisation in diesem Bereich war das Academic Assistance Council. Diese Einrichtung war von William Beveridge gegründet worden und versuchte den 1.200 von den Nazis entlassenen Akademikern zu helfen. Ihr gelang es, 178 deutschen Wissenschaftler eine Stelle an britischen Universitäten zu vermitteln[12] – darunter Max Born, Nobelpreisträger der Physik, der 1933 von Göttingen nach Cambridge wechselte. Auch der Philosoph Ernst Cassirer wurde eingeladen, nach Großbritannien zu kommen und reiste im Sommer 1933 von Hamburg nach Oxford. 1938 folgte ihm sein Vetter, der Verleger Bruno Cassirer. Auch ohne institutionelle Hilfe gelang es verschiedenen Persönlichkeiten des kulturellen Lebens nach Großbritannien zu gelangen. Im Herbst 1933 erhielt Alfred Flechtheim (Abb. 17) von der Mayor Gallery die Möglichkeit, kontinuierlich für sie tätig zu sein, so dass er seinen Lebensschwerpunkt an die Themse verlegte. Seine Kollegin Grete Ring vom Kunstsalon Paul Cassirer, mit der Flechtheim Anfang 1933 noch eine dreiteilige Ausstellung *Lebendige deutsche Kunst* in Berlin realisiert hatte, konnte sich erst 1938 in London etablieren, ein Jahr nachdem Flechtheim dort gestorben war. Auch der Kritiker und Schriftsteller Alfred Kerr siedelte, von Paris kommend, 1936 in die britische Hauptstadt über.

Für hochspezialisierte Fachleute, Geschäftsmänner mit guten Verbindungen und international anerkannte Akademiker war es zunächst relativ einfach, eine Arbeitserlaubnis zu erhalten. Allerdings holten die Behörden manchmal den Rat von Berufsgenossenschaften ein, wobei diese oft eine negative Stellungnahme abgaben. 1939 zum Beispiel erhielten nur 25 deutsche Architekten eine Arbeitserlaubnis, denn das Royal Institute of British Architects meinte, ausschließlich weltweit anerkannte Architekten sollten in Großbritannien tätig werden. Unter denen, die bereits früher eine Arbeitserlaubnis erhalten hatten, war Walter Gropius, der zwischen 1934 und 1937 im Vereinigten Königreich wirkte.[13]

Ungeachtet der Einreisehindernisse und der reativ kleinen Zahl von Vertretern kreativer Berufe, erfuhr die britische Kulturszene durch diese Ankömmlinge einige Anregung.[14] So beispielsweise durch den jüdischen Architekten Erich Mendelsohn, der 1933 Berlin verlassen hatte und zwei Jahre später den Wettbewerb zum Bau des De la Warr-Pavillons in Bexhill gewann (Abb. 18). Bis heute gilt dieses Gebäude als ein herausragendes Beispiel moderner Architektur in Großbritannien.[15] Darüber hinaus trugen Flüchtlinge aus Deutschland dazu bei, das Opera Festival at Glyndebourne (ab 1934) und das Edinburgh International Festival (ab 1944) zu bedeutenden Anlässen zu entwickeln.[16]

Auch die Fotografin Gerty Simon (Abb. 22), deren Sohn Bernd (später «Bernard») (Abb. 21) Schüler von Anna Essinger war, zählt zu den Künstlern, denen es gelang, sich im britischen Exil eine Nische zu schaffen. Nachdem sie 1933 Berlin verlassen hatte, eröffnete sie ein Fotostudio in Chelsea. Gerty Simon hatte Verbindungen zu vielen Berliner Künstlern besessen; auch in der Londoner Kulturszene konnte sie rasch Fuß fassen und etablierte bei sich zu Hause eine Art Künstlersalon. In Berlin hatte sie u.a. Persönlichkeiten wie Albert Einstein, Max Liebermann und Lotte Lenya portraitiert. In London fotografierte sie prominente Persönlichkeiten wie Aneurin Bevan und Peggy Ashcroft oder Sir Kenneth Clark, der zwischen 1933 und 1945 Direktor der National Gallery war. Darüber hinaus zeigte Gerty Simon ihre Werke im Rahmen vieler Ausstellungen, insbesondere bei einer Schau des *Camera Club* im Jahre 1935 (Abb. 17).[17] Ihre Geschichte zeigt, dass einige Künstler durchaus imstande waren, sich in der britischen Kulturszene zu integrieren und diese zu bereichern.

«Wir nehmen die Besten, während die Franzosen, Niederländer und Tschechen sich um den Rest kümmern.»[18] So beschreiben Deborah Dwork und Robert Jan van Pelt die Politik der Briten bei der Aufnahme von Menschen, die vor 1938 aus NS-Deutschland wegen «drohender Verhaftung und Verarmung» fliehen mussten. Angesichts der sozialen Stellung von Emigranten wie Walter Gropius, Gerty Simon oder den Leihgebern der Ausstellung *Twentieth Century German Art*, die im vorliegenden Band dokumentiert sind, könnte der Eindruck entstehen, die Mehrzahl der jüdischen Flüchtlinge seien Angehörige der Oberschicht

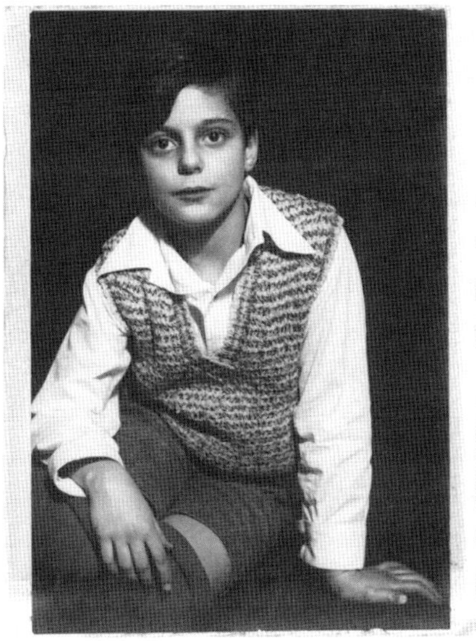

21 Gerty Simons Sohn Bernard als Junge, 1920er Jahre

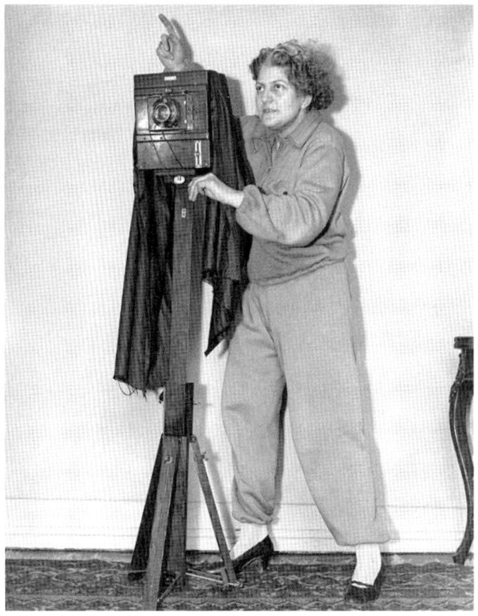

22 Gerty Simon 1934 in ihrem Londoner Fotostudio

gewesen. Tony Kushner relativiert diese Auffassung allerdings, indem er unterstreicht, dass viele deutsche Flüchtlinge in Großbritannien einreisen konnten, weil sie eine Arbeitserlaubnis als Hausangestellte vorweisen konnten (siehe Abb. 23). Seit 1931 konnte ausländisches Hauspersonal nur mit einer solchen Erlaubnis beschäftigt werden, doch waren viele solcher Stellen noch immer unbesetzt, so dass zwischen Januar 1933 und Ende 1938 circa 7.000 deutsche Juden (darunter viele Frauen aus der Arbeiterklasse) als Hausbedienstete in Großbritannien Zuflucht fanden.[19] Bei Kriegausbruch war diese Zahl sogar auf ca. 20.000 angestiegen.[20]

Zwischen 1933 und 1938 hatten deutsche Flüchtlinge kein Recht auf Asyl in Großbritannien und erhielten – wie erwähnt – keinerlei staatliche Unterstützung. Die Einreisewilligen wurden meist auf der Basis gesundheitlicher und beruflicher Kriterien ausgewählt und erhielten in der Regel nur eine vorläufige Aufenthaltsgenehmigung. Allerdings war kein Visum nötig, was die Kosten vor der Ausreise aus Deutschland maßgeblich verringerte. 1938 änderte sich die Situation jedoch schlagartig.

Das Jahr der Ausstellung *Twentieth Century German Art* war für die in Deutschland und Österreich verbliebenen Juden besonders schicksalhaft. Nach dem *Anschluss* Österreichs im März 1938 nahm die antisemitische Gewalt und andere Formen der Unterdrückung und Entrechtung dramatisch zu. In Deutschland wurde außerdem die Politik der Arisierung juristisch verankert, die Juden zum Verkauf ihrer Firmen zwang. Diese Entwicklungen und die Annektierung des Sudetenlandes im Herbst 1938 löste eine weitere Welle der Emigration nach Großbritannien aus. Unter den Flüchtenden, die zu dieser Zeit in England eintrafen, waren Oskar Kokoschka, das Ehepaar Walter und Eva Neurath (die später den Kunstverlag Thames & Hudson gründeten) sowie die Schriftsteller Elias Canetti und Erich Fried. Als Reaktion auf diese neue Einwanderungswelle, besonders aus Österreich, entschied sich die britische Regierung für eine Verschärfung der Einreisebedingungen.[21] Ab Mai 1938 galt für deutsche und österreichische Bürger die Visumspflicht.

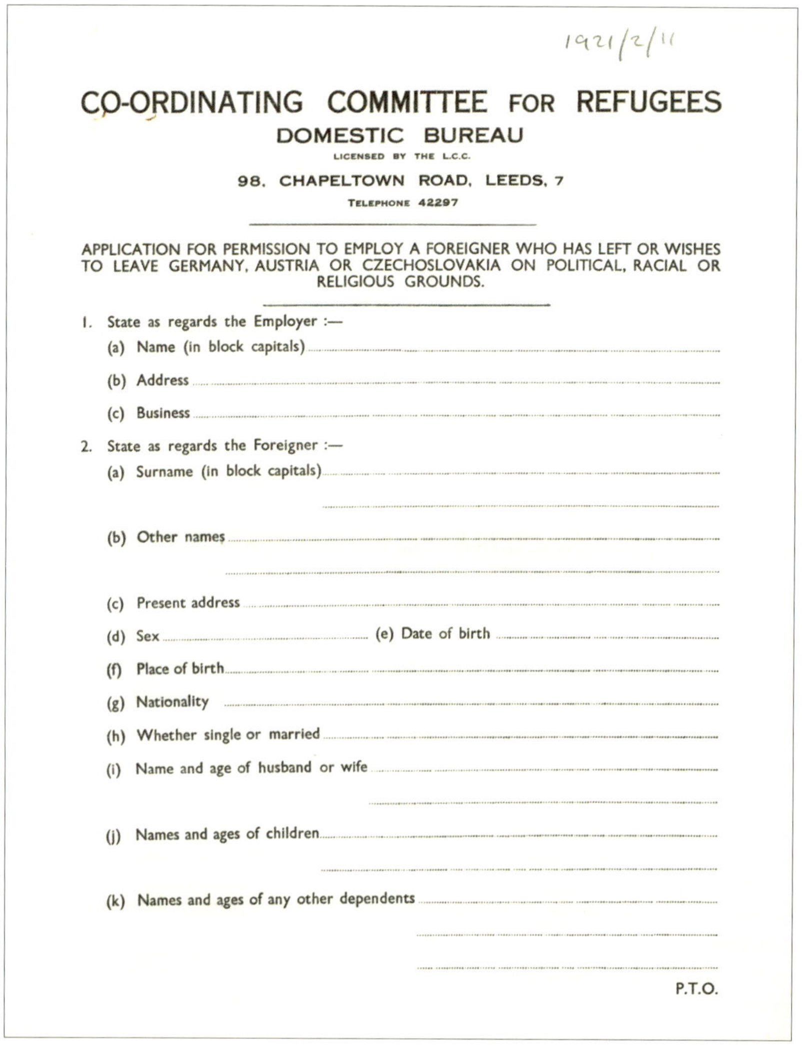

1921/2/11

CO-ORDINATING COMMITTEE FOR REFUGEES
DOMESTIC BUREAU
LICENSED BY THE L.C.C.
98, CHAPELTOWN ROAD, LEEDS, 7
TELEPHONE 42297

APPLICATION FOR PERMISSION TO EMPLOY A FOREIGNER WHO HAS LEFT OR WISHES TO LEAVE GERMANY, AUSTRIA OR CZECHOSLOVAKIA ON POLITICAL, RACIAL OR RELIGIOUS GROUNDS.

1. State as regards the Employer :—
   (a) Name (in block capitals) ....
   (b) Address ....
   (c) Business ....
2. State as regards the Foreigner :—
   (a) Surname (in block capitals) ....
   (b) Other names ....
   (c) Present address ....
   (d) Sex .... (e) Date of birth ....
   (f) Place of birth ....
   (g) Nationality ....
   (h) Whether single or married ....
   (i) Name and age of husband or wife ....
   (j) Names and ages of children ....
   (k) Names and ages of any other dependents ....

P.T.O.

23 Antragsformular des Co-ordinating Committee for Refugees in Leeds für die Erlaubnis zur Beschäftigung von Ausländern, die aus politischen, rassischen oder religiösen Gründen Deutschland, Österreich oder die Tschechoslowakei verlassen wollen; um 1938.

Trotz dieser Restriktionen und der Tatsache, dass Flüchtlinge weiterhin keine staatliche Zuwendung erhielten, kamen zwischen Mai 1938 und September 1939 mehr Menschen nach Großbritannien als in den vorherigen Jahren seit der Machtübernahme der Nazis. Angesichts der wachsenden Verfolgung im Deutschen Reich und der Zerschlagung der Tschechoslowakei verstärkten die britischen Hilfsorganisationen ihre Bemühungen. Gleichzeitig lockerte die Regierung verschiedene Vorschriften, unter anderem die Bestimmungen zur Vergabe von Arbeitserlaubnissen für Hausbedienstete.[22] Nach den November-Pogromen der ‹Reichskristallnacht› ließ sich die britische Regierung von den Hilfsorganisationen dazu bewegen, auf die Visumspflicht für Kinder bis 17 Jahre zu verzichten. Auf diese Weise konnten ca. 10.000 hauptsächlich deutsche und österreichische Kinder über sogenannten ‹Kindertransporte› Zuflucht in Großbritannien finden (Abb. 19). Die Organisation und die Kosten für die Aktion (inklusive der vorgeschriebenen 50 Pfund Unterstützungsgeld für jedes Kind) lagen in den Händen von Hilfsorganisationen wie dem CBF und dem Refugee Children's Movement.[23]

Außer den Kindern konnten zwischen März 1938 und dem Kriegsausbruch im September 1939 – d.h. einer Zeit, in der die Flucht aus Deutschland und den besetzen Gebieten äußerst schwierig geworden war – mindestens 50.000 jüdische Flüchtlinge nach Großbritannien gelangen.[24] Somit kann die Gesamtzahl derjenigen, die zwischen Januar 1933 und September 1939 in Großbritannien Zuflucht fanden, auf circa 80.000 geschätzt werden.[25]

Der Kontext der Londoner Ausstellung *Twentieth Century German Art* wurde demnach von zwei Faktoren maßgeblich bestimmt: Einerseits von der Hetze gegen die moderne Kunst in Deutschland, andererseits von der Ankunft der Menschen, die vor den Nazis geflüchtet waren. Auch wenn es keineswegs einfach war, in Großbritannien hereingelassen zu werden, so konnten doch viele hier Fuß fassen und ihr Zufluchtland stärken und beleben, obwohl dies kaum jemand für möglich gehalten hatte.

1 Im vorliegenden Aufsatz werden die Begriffe «Emigrant» und «Flüchtling» gleichbedeutend verwendet, da es kaum möglich ist, bei Menschen, die NS-Deutschland verließen, eine entsprechende Differenzierung zu treffen.

2 Deborah Dwork/Robert Jan van Pelt: Flight from the Reich: Refugee Jews 1933–1946, London 2009, S. 9.

3 Ibid., S. 15.

4 Louise London: British Immigration Control Procedures and Jewish Refugees 1933-1942, London 1992, S. 490-491.

5 Ausreisewillige mussten eine «Reichsfluchtsteuer» entrichten und Bank- und Wetpapierguthaben auf Sperrkonten einzahlen. Darüberhinaus verhinderten Devisenverkehrsbeschränkungen, die Mitnahme ausländischer Währungen; siehe Zara Steiner: Refugees. The Timeless Problem, in: Jessica Reinisch/Matthew Frank (Hg.): Refugees in Europe 1919–1959. A Forty Years' Crisis?, London u. a. 2017, S. 21-32.

6 Das Einreisen war in Frankreich einfacher und die dort ankommenden Flüchtlinge waren meist mittellos; siehe Dwork/van Pelt, S. 23/24.

7 London, S. 496/497.

8 Tony Kushner: The Battle of Britishness. Migrant Journeys 1685 to the Present, Manchester 2012, S. 123.

9 Siehe Werner E. Mosse (Hg.): Second Chance. Two Centuries of German-speaking Jews in the United Kingdom, Tübingen 1991.

10 Dwork/van Pelt, S. 25.

11 Peter Lasko: The Impact of German-speaking Refugees in Britain on the Fine Arts, in: Mosse, S. 255-274.

12 Dwork/van Pelt, S. 22.

13 Lasko, S. 255.

14 Siehe Mosse.

15 Lasko, S. 256.

16 Nicht alle heute bekannten Künstler fanden in Großbritannien Erfolg. Lasko erwähnt u.a. Kurt Schwitters, der in Deutschland als ‹entartet› galt und dessen Werk vom britischen Publikum ebenfalls abgelehnt wurde; siehe Lasko, S. 260.

17 The Bernard Simon Collection, Wiener Library Archives, London.

18 Dwork/van Pelt, S. 18/27.

19 Man beachte jedoch, dass – insbesondere nach dem Anschluss Österreichs – viele dieser Menschen bessergestellte Frauen waren, die unbedingt das Reich verlassen wollten. Siehe Tony Kushner: Alien Occupation. Jewish Refugees and Domestic Service in Britain 1933-1948, in: Mosse S. 553-578.

20 Ibid.

21 Die vom US-Präsidenten Roosevelt zur Lösung der Flüchtlingskrise organisierte Evian-Konferenz endete im Juli 1938 ohne konkrete Ergebnisse (siehe Steiner, Refugees, S. 26). Manche Juden konnten allerdings Zuflucht in Palästina finden, bevor dies ab 1939 schwieriger wurde (siehe Mark Levene: The Jewish Dimension, in Reinisch/Frank, S. 85-100 sowie S. 91/92).

22 Siehe Kushner: Alien Occupation, S. 561.

23 Das CBF wurde inzwischen umbenannt und heißt heutzutage World Jewish Relief. Für weitere Details zu den Kindertransporten siehe Vera K. Fast: Children's Exodus. A History of the Kindertransport, New York 2011, sowie Andrea Hammel/Bea Lewkowicz (Hg.): The Kindertransport to Britain 1938/39. New Perspectives, Amsterdam/New York, 2012. Das Problem bei den Kindertransporten war, dass die Eltern und manchmal sogar die Geschwister nicht mitflüchten konnten. Laut Jennifer Craig-Norton verloren mindestens vier von fünf geflüchteten Kindern ein Elternteil oder sogar beide Eltern. Siehe dazu Jennifer Craig-Norton: Contesting Memory: New Perspectives on the Kindertransport, University of Southampton (Dissertation, 2014).

24 Grenville, S. 6.

25 Kushner: The Battle of Britishness, S. 123.

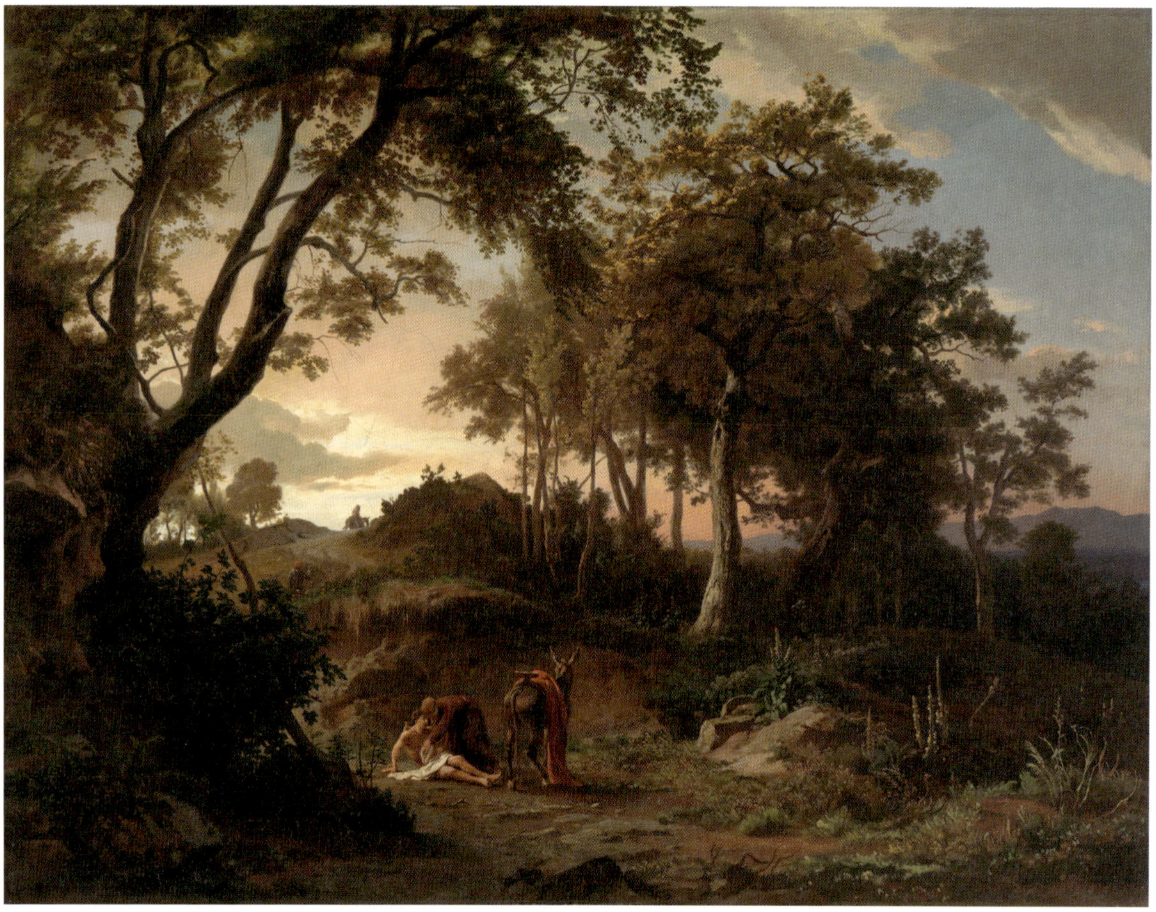

24 Johann Wilhelm Schirmer, *The Evening, The Good Samaritan helps the injured wanderer*, ca. 1850. Oil on canvas, 122 x 160 cm. Kunsthalle Karlsruhe

National intelligence, spiritual rapprochement, and mystic beefsteak: the reception of modern German art exhibitions in London, 1853-1934

MATTHEW C. POTTER

Following the Second World War, memories of previous cultural interactions between Germany and Britain became awkward and were deliberately forgotten. Evidence of past exhibitions of German art in London, and the responses of audiences in the British capital, provide an important corrective to this historical lacuna. This essay looks at three moments in this exhibition history to see how Anglo-German artistic relations developed in the years before 1938.

German Exhibitions in the Nineteenth Century

The second half of the Nineteenth Century saw numerous initiatives aimed at teaching the growing middle-class in London about German art. In 1853 for example, the Lawrence Gallery at 168 New Bond Street opened its first exhibition of contemporary German art with fifty pictures, including works by Karl Friedrich Lessing, Karl Ferdinand Sohn, Andreas Achenbach, and Johann Wilhelm Schirmer, among others.[1] Reviewers were not wholly positive – the critic in the London art journal *The Athenaeum* for example judged that the exhibition failed to adequately showcase the "national" character of the "Düsseldorf and Munich schools due to its overemphasis upon landscape paintings", lacking work by Wilhelm von Kaulbach, Johann Friedrich Overbeck, Eduard Bendemann, and Karl Hess. Despite the centrality of nature to German Romantic artists and the Düsseldorf Academy generation that followed them in the 1830s and 1840s, German art was preeminently associated in Britain with historical genre painting after 1850. *The Athenaeum* critic was however clear to point out that his own knowledge of German art had been gathered via visits to Germany, as self-consciously demonstrated by reference to Lessing's works in the Städel Museum in Frankfurt and the art gallery in Cologne. This justified the assertion that any negativity was not the result of "an insular spirit" or the "silly depreciation of the stranger, with the sillier view of feeding patriotic vanity" but was based on the solid criteria of judging how much the art represented "national intelligence".

Both the lack of German places as subjects for the landscapes on show, and the approach of their painters, were disappointing to *The Athenaeum*'s critic: Johann Wilhelm Schirmer's *The Good Samaritan* (ca. 1850, fig. 24), for example, though containing accurate forms, was considered "little more of a picture than a page of a *hortus siccus* [herbarium]." Yet despite the early rhetoric of this article, historical art was not wholly neglected in this 1853 show,

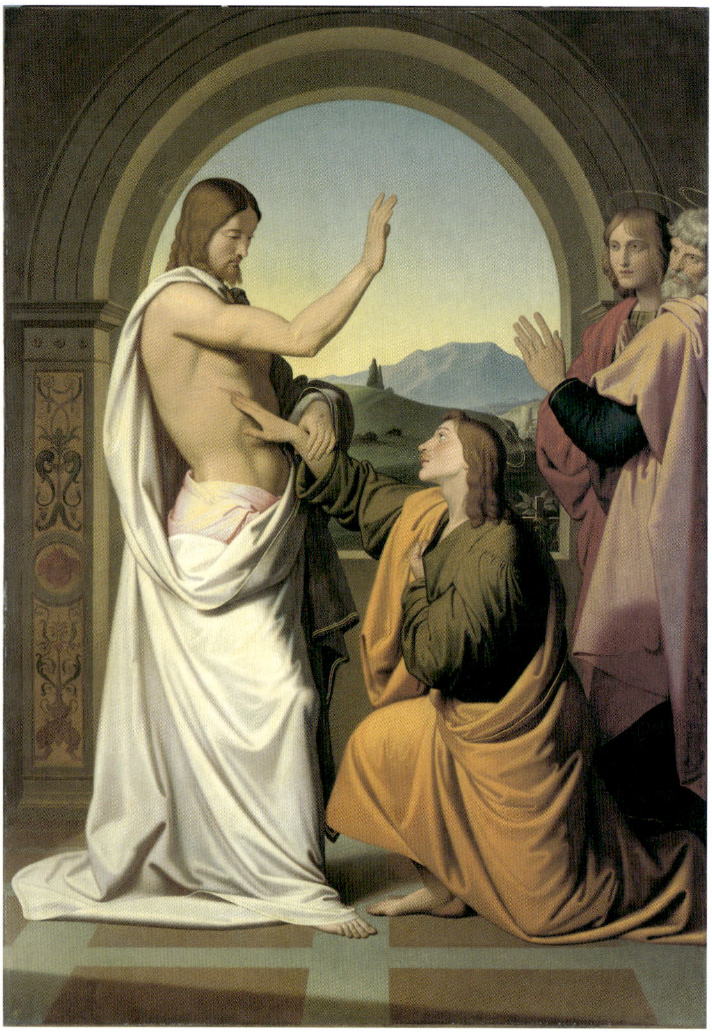

25 Johann Friedrich Overbeck, *Incredulity of St. Thomas*, 1851. Oil on canvas, 216.5 x 154 cm. Museum Georg Schäfer, Schweinfurt

and indeed was considered by the reviewer. Heinrich Carl Anton Mücke's *Ecce Homo* (1850 possessed the "propriety of great correctness and care" and while he had "not risen to his high argument, he has not treated it with flippant want of reverence. The figure is more academic than sentimental." Such German imagery had currency in Britain at this time.[2] Johann Friedrich Overbeck's *The Incredulity of St. Thomas* (1851, fig. 25) had for example been shown at the Royal Academy during 1853, and was also included in the groundbreaking exhibition *The Art Treasures of Great Britain*, staged in Manchester in 1857. In their review of the 1853 Lawrence Gallery show, the Art Journal noted with interest that Queen Victoria had purchased "the best landscapes" from the exhibition.[3] It was in fact Prince Albert who was responsible for these acquisitions: two landscapes by Oswald Achenbach, *Morning* (1850-4) and *Evening* (1850-4), and *The Jungfrau* (1853, fig. 31) by August Becker. The second of these artists was the brother of Ernst Becker, Librarian at Windsor and tutor to Victoria and Albert's two eldest sons.[4]

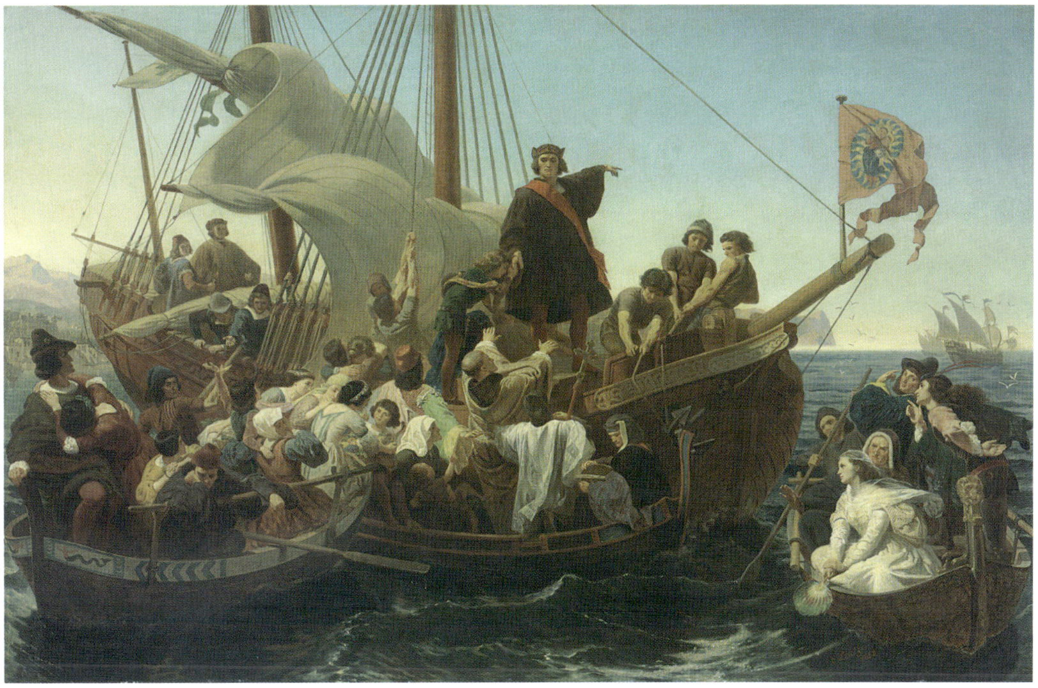

26 Emanuel Gottlieb Leutze, *Departure of Columbus from Spain*, 1855. Oil on canvas, 122 x 183.5 cm. Private Collection

In 1854 the Lawrence Gallery was renamed the 'German Gallery', with subsequent exhibitions – and their reviews – following similar lines. A show staged in 1854 offered, according to the review in *The Athenaeum*, "but a sorry specimen of the German school, both as to quality and quantity", with familiar criticism of poor colour, inferior landscapes (compared to the British school), and inadequate representations of the Nazarenes. Again, historical work however provided some redemption, for example, Adolf Seel's *Defense of a Castle during the Thirty Years' War*.[5] There was a similar response to an exhibition of one hundred artworks staged at the gallery in 1855. Here, it was Emanuel Leutze's *The Departure of Christopher Columbus from Spain* (1855, fig. 26) which was singled out for praise, characterised as "an historical work of great merit".[6]

The Athenaeum additionally welcomed these German exhibitions as a potential "trade speculation" allowing British artists to learn from their German colleagues. Such calls were echoed by critic Joseph Beavington Atkinson in his reviews of the Munich International Exhibitions of the 1860s.[7] The *German Academy of Art* exhibition at the Piccadilly Galleries (1861), and German and Austrian pictures at the International Exhibition at South Kensington in 1862 continued to spread the word. The Unification of Germany gave the British added impetus to learn about the country's art, though, ironically, the immediate result of the Franco-Prussian war (1870-1) was for the German Gallery to open its doors to French artist-refugees.[8] The next decade saw the publication of two important texts on the topic of German art, William Bell Scott's *Gems of Modern German Art* (1873) and Atkinson's *The Schools of Modern Art in Germany* (1880). Though exhibitions of German art were still rare, Adolph Menzel was honoured as a Foreign Academician by the Royal Academy in 1896, with his work "suitably introduced to the London public" at the French Gallery on Pall Mall in 1903.[9]

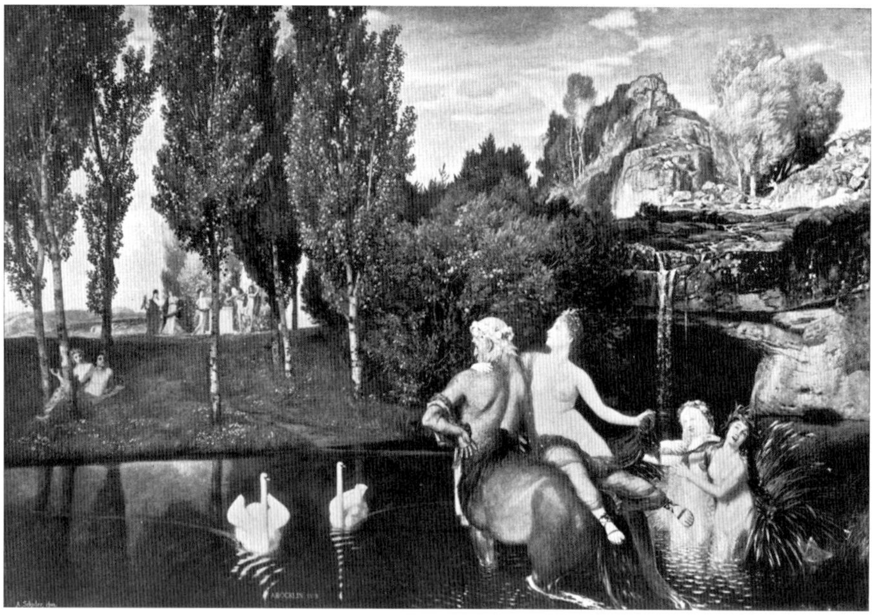

27 Arnold Böcklin, *Elysian Fields*, 1877/78. Oil on canvas, 170 x 250 cm. National Gallery Berlin (lost in the second world war)

The Importance of 1906

Exhibitions of German art gave opportunities for entente during the heightened Anglo-German diplomatic tensions at the turn of the twentieth century. The year 1906 saw two displays in London offering comprehensive accounts of contemporary German art. If the German Gallery exhibitions had provided only partial insights on contemporary practice, the same could not be said for the 1906 shows, with *The Times* declaring that "German art is making a serious invasion of London this season".[10] Between 2 May and 10 July, the Munich-based David Heinemann Gallery ran an exhibition at the Grafton Galleries in Mayfair, displaying "all the artists belonging to the different Munich schools" with 277 pictures by Franz von Lenbach, Wilhelm von Kaulbach, Fritz von Uhde, and Hans von Bartels among others.[11] The quality of the show was recognised even in Germany, with the London correspondent of the Munich-based *Die Kunst für Alle*, F. E. W. Freund, characterising it as a "truly representative exhibition".[12] In this article, Freund also noted the particular significance of the show as – with the exception of von Lenbach, Friedrich August von Kaulbach, Bartels and Franz von Stuck – the artists displayed were all but unknown, and furthermore the exhibition promised the "spiritual rapprochement of the two peoples."

The other German show of 1906 was Henry van der Velde's *Exhibition of the Works of German Artists*, staged at the Prince's Galleries in Knightsbridge between May and June – and including among others loans from the Berlin National Gallery. Again writing in *Die Kunst für Alle*, F. E. W. Freund noted the show's ground-breaking nature, "intended to present, for the first time to a foreign country, modern [German] art in the context of the English public; for even French art has not received such a thing here", providing "a good overview of German contemporary art".[13] In London, *The Times* agreed on the exhibition's inclusivity, even if it showed some reticence over Stuck's work.[14]

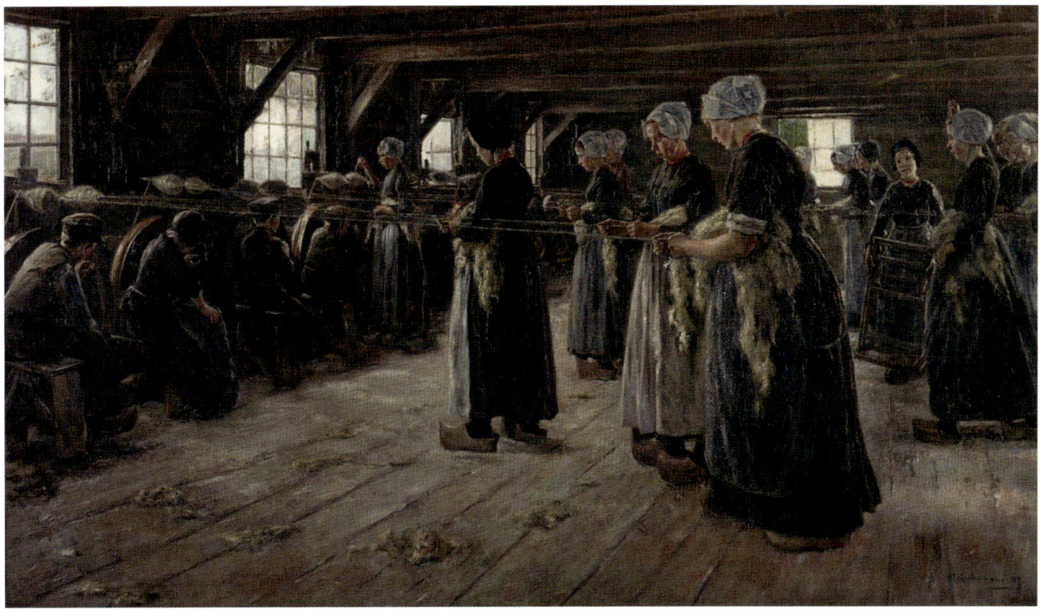

28 Max Liebermann, *Flax Spinners in Laren*, 1887. Oil on canvas, 134.5 x 231 cm. National Gallery Berlin

The diplomatic value of these exhibitions is evident from the attendance list of the Inaugural Dinner of the Prince's Galleries show. Sentiments expressed in a 1904 speech by German Ambassador to Britain Paul Wolff Graf Metternich – encouraging closer cultural connections between Britain and Germany – were supported at the dinner by Frank Lascelles (British Ambassador to Germany, 1895-1908) and Johann Heinrich von Bernstorff (Secretary to the Germany Embassy in London, 1902-8).[15] Speaking at the dinner, Richard Haldane, then British Secretary of State for War, also echoed Metternich's words, proclaiming that German art "had gone far beyond her own borders, and had penetrated profoundly the minds of us in England ... bringing the peoples together on a common basis, because, after all, it was the things of the spirit that formed the foundation of much that both Germans and English possessed", while the Anglo-German artist Hubert von Herkomer acknowledged the warm reception given to British artists in Germany.[16] Writing in the *Art Journal*, critic Frank Rinder congratulated British artists for returning the favour, concluding that Arnold Böcklin, Lenbach, Menzel, and Stuck all "emerge as men of power" from the Prince's Galleries exhibition.[17] While some paintings were criticised in Rinder's review – among them Böcklin's *Elysian Fields* (1877/78, fig. 27) and von Uhde's *The Entombment of Christ* – Max Liebermann's *Flax Spinners in Laren* (1887, fig. 28) was praised, as was Stuck's *Procession of Bacchantes* which Rinder described as the "most powerful work by a living artist". Perhaps due to the diplomatic tensions of the time both Rinder and *The Athenaeum* critic agreed, nevertheless, that British artists were not outdone by contemporary German art.[18]

The painter and illustrator Walter Crane also attended this dinner, and designed a poster for the Prince's Galleries show (fig. 33), presumably in thanks for his treatment by Germany: some of his works toured Germany in 1894, his work entered German before British public galleries, he designed a cover for *Jugend* (1898), and illustrated the 1882 English translation

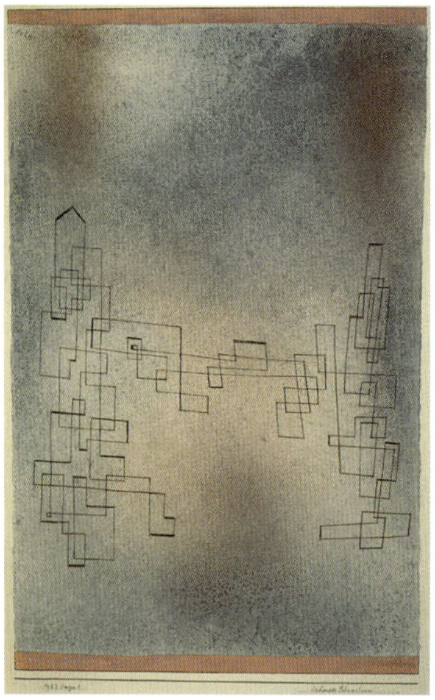

29 Paul Klee, *Approaching Snowstorm*, 1927, watercolor and ink on paper mounted on board, 49.9 x 31.6 cm. National Gallery of Scotland Edinburgh

of Grimms' *Kinder- und Hausmärchen* (1812-15).[19] His poster employed personifications of the two nations. The Union Jack which conventionally adorns Britannia's shield is replaced by the St. George of England on her robes. Her and Germania's shields are transformed into palettes with the latter decorated with the Imperial eagle, while the German imperial tricolour flag serves as a backdrop to the whole. Despite such nationalistic imagery, Crane showed the two figures shaking hands in accord.

German Modernist Exhibitions in Britain

With its contributions to Expressionism, Dadaism, Neue Sachlichkeit and the Bauhaus, German art between 1905 and 1933 was internationally recognised as a driving force of modernism. London audiences had various opportunities to see examples of this work during the 1910s and 20s, for example at the annual exhibitions of the Allied Artists' Association, and at the 1914 exhibition of *Modern German Art* staged at the Twenty-One Gallery in Westminster. This 1914 show included woodcuts by Wassily Kandinsky, Ernst Ludwig Kirchner, Franz Marc and Max Pechstein, greeted by British artist Wyndham Lewis as a "surgery of the senses."[20]

Following the National Socialist takeover in Germany, these German modernist exhibitions continued. Certain of the artists facing persecution in Germany had solo exhibitions in London during this period. Among them: Liebermann, Max Ernst, Oskar Schlemmer[21] and Paul Klee, who was – due to the efforts of the German art dealer Alfred Flechtheim's[22] – the subject of an exhibition at the Mayor Gallery on Cork Street in 1934.

The reactions of critics to this Klee exhibition were varied. Anthony Blunt was cooly dismissive in *The Spectator.*[23] Charles Marriott writing in *The Times* was more positive: although he felt Klee's work was at times silly, he nevertheless found him "an interesting artist, and one that was bound to happen. If you drive out Nature with a cube, she creeps in with a wriggle" for the neo-classicist Cubism of the Latins failed to "satisfy the Northern genius, once representation had been abandoned." Certain fantasy pictures on show demonstrated

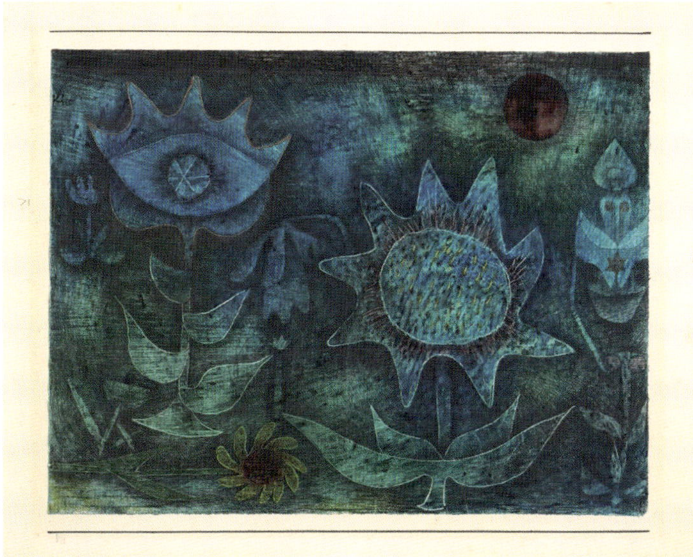

30 Paul Klee, *Blossoms in the Night*, 1930, watercolor and ink on paper mounted on board, 23.5 x 31.1 cm. San Francisco Museum of Modern Art

"the splendid phrase of the child", others, like *Approaching Snowstorm* (1927, fig. 29) Marriot compared to "air photographs of prehistoric cultivation – linear patterns imposed upon gradations of tone". *Blossoms in the Night* (1930, fig. 30) demonstrated Klee's skills as a "magical colourist", so, for his variety and ingenuity, the critic declared: "on the whole we are glad of Mr. Klee".[24]

The British art historian and critic Herbert Read provided a sturdy foundation for others with his deep reading of Klee in his books *The Meaning of Art* (1931) and *Art Now* (1933). The poet and critic Geoffrey Grigson for example, writing in *The Bookman* in October 1933, particularly praised Klee as one of the stand-out artists referred to in *Art Now.*[25] Writing in the same journal two months later, Grigson recognised Klee as "one of the most exquisite, one of the most peculiar and (excusing the word) one of the most important artists alive", regretting the long wait to see this work, infused as it was with the values of the "Northern pre-Renaissance" tradition.[26] Klee's works were "the mincemeat, the mystic German beefsteak, chopped from cubism and futurism", and, because of this, Grigson esteemed the artist's authenticity, and his witty and intellectual childlike vision.[27] The artist and critic Jan Gordon applied Read's definition in *Art Now* of modern art as "free fancy" to Klee. For Gordon, however, Klee's "mask of childishness" was superficial, for the surface textures and depths of meaning were comparable to the complex rhythms of nursery rhymes, as he concluded: "*Three Blind Mice* may outlast Milton's *Paradise Lost*, but Klee will hardly outlive Titian".[28]

From the 1850s to 1930s London audiences were exposed to infrequent but important exhibitions of contemporary German art. Critical responses were informed and aware both of the shortcomings of the early shows, and the accuracy of later displays, in capturing the spirits of their ages. As diplomatic climates changed, German art exhibition shifted from educational novelties, to become first a salve to the political tensions of the *Kaiserzeit*, and then evidence of the avant-gardism persecuted by the Nazis. Throughout the period, British viewers desired to learn as much as they could from the infrequent opportunities they had to look at German art in London exhibitions.

1 Lawrence Gallery: Catalogue of paintings, at the first annual exhibition of the works of modern German artists. London 1853; Anon.: Exhibition of the works of Modern German Artists, in: The Athenaeum, vol. 1333 (14 May 1853), p. 593

2 Matthew C. Potter: The Inspirational Genius of Germany. British Art and Germanism, 1850-1939. Manchester, 2012, p. 79

3 Anon.: Exhibition of the Works of Modern German Artists, in: Art journal (June 1853), p. 161

4 Jonathan Marsden (ed.): Victoria and Albert. Art and Love. London 2010, pp. 118-19

5 Anon.: Fine Arts. Exhibition of German Art, in: The Athenaeum, vol. 1381 (15 April 1854), pp. 467-8

6 Anon.: Fine Arts. Exhibition of German Art, in: The Athenaeum, vol. 1441 (9 June 1855), p. 678

7 Anon.: Exhibition of the Works of Modern German Artists, in: Art Journal (June 1853) p. 161; Potter, pp. 56-78, 80, 82, 109, 266

8 William Vaughan: German Romanticism and English Art. New Haven etc. 1979, p. 248; Anon.: German Gallery, 168 New Bond Street. Society of French Artists, in: Examiner, vol. 3281 (17 December 1870), p. 809

9 Potter, pp. 82,37,46,70,202-6; Anon.: Passing Events, in: Art Journal (June 1896), p. 190; Anon.: Menzel at the French Gallery, in: The Athenaeum, vol. 3946 (13 June 1903), p. 760; Anon.: Menzel, in: Art Journal (July 1906), p. 195; MaryAnne Stevens: The Royal Academy in the Age of Queen Victoria, in: Helen Valentine (ed.): Art in the Age of Queen Victoria. Treasures from the Royal Academy of Arts Permanent Collection. New Haven etc. 1999, pp. 26- 39, p. 36.

10 Anon.: Art Exhibitions, in: The Times (16 May 1906), p. 4. An exhibition of historic German art with Albrecht Dürer and the German Primitives was also mounted in London during 1906, at the Burlington Fine Art Club (see Anon.: Burlington Fine Arts Club, in: The Times (21 May 1906), p. 10)

11 See Anon.: German Art Exhibition in London, in: The Times (13 April 1906), p. 11, and Anon.: Art Exhibitions, in: The Times (16 May 1906), p. 4

12 F. E. W. Freund: Die Münchener Kunstausstellung in London, in: Die Kunst für Alle, vol. XXI, issue 18 (15 June 1906), pp. 423-4

13 F. E. W. Freund: Von Ausstellungen und Sammlungen, in: Die Kunst für Alle, vol. XXI, issue 19 (1 July 1906), pp. 451-2

14 Anon.: An Exhibition of German Art, in: The Times (5 April 1906), p. 10; Anon.: Art Exhibitions, in: The Times (16 May 1906), p. 4

15 Regarding the dinner, see: Anon.: Anglo-German Relations. Sir F. Lascelles at the Berlin Lyceum Club (From our own correspondent), Berlin, Jan.14, in: The Times (15 January 1906), p. 5; Anon.: German Artists' Exhibition. Inaugural Dinner, in: The Times (23 May 1906), p. 5; Anon.: International Society Of Sculptors, Painters, And Gravers, in: The Times (11 January 1906), p. 7; Johann von Bernstorff: My Three Years in America. New York 1936, pp. 16,28

16 Anon.: German Artists' Exhibition. Inaugural Dinner, in: The Times (23 May 1906), p. 5

17 Frank Rinder: London Exhibitions, in: Art Journal (July 1906), p. 220

18 Ibid.; Anon: Munich Exhibition at the Grafton Gallery, in: The Athenaeum, vol. 4099 (19 May 1906), p. 614; see also: Anon.: Contemporary German Artists at Knightsbridge, in: The Athenaeum, vol. 4102 (9 June 1906), p. 709

19 Potter, pp. 196-203, 208; Jeffrey L. Sammons: Kuno Francke's Edition of the German Classics (1913-15). A Historical and Critical Overview. New York 2009, p. 86: Crane's Der Mäher (The Mower) (1891) was gifted to the Karlsruhe Kunsthalle by Hans Thoma; Hans Ries: Deutsche Bilderbuchkritik zwischen Wolgast und dem Dritten Reich, in: Bernd Dolle-Weinkauff and Hans-Heino Ewers (eds.): Theorien der Jugendlektüre. Beiträge zur Kinder- und Jugendliteraturkritik seit Heinrich Wolgast. Weinheim etc. 1996, p. 93

20 Judith Collins: Omega and Hogarth Woodcuts, in: Jeremy Greenwood: Omega Cuts. Woodbridge 1998, pp. 9-18, p. 13

21 Regarding the earlier exhibitions of Max Liebermann, see the text by Martin Faass in this volume. Oskar Schlemmer enjoyed a solo exhibition at Noel Norton's London Gallery in 1937; Max Ernst at the Mayor Gallery in 1937

22 See Ottfried Dascher: "Es ist was Wahnsinniges mit der Kunst". Alfred Flechtheim – Sammler, Kunsthändler, Verleger. With a bibliography by Rudolf Schmitt-Föller and a familiy tree by Rico Quaschny. Wädenswil 2011, p. 350-1

23 cited in Hans Albert Peters: Alfred Flechtheim. Sammler. Kunsthändler. Verleger. Düsseldorf 1987, pp. 197-8, 200

24 Anon.: Art Exhibition. Mr. Paul Klee, in: The Times (17 January 1934), p. 17

25 Geoffrey Grigson: Unit One, Herbert Read, and The Mayor Gallery, in: The Bookman, 85, vol. 505 (October 1933), pp. 31-2

26 Geoffrey Grigson: Paul Klee, in: The Bookman, 85, vol. 507 (December 1933), p. 390

27 Ibid; Geoffrey Grigson, "Childishness" in Contemporary Art, in: The Bookman, 85, vol. 507 (December 1933), pp. 170-1

28 Jan Gordon: Art and Artists. Paul Klee's Work, in: The Observer (21 January 1934), p. 12

Nationalacharakter, geistige Annäherung und mystisches Beefsteak – Rezeption der Londoner Ausstellungen moderner deutscher Kunst 1853-1934

MATTHEW C. POTTER

Nach dem 2. Weltkrieg wurde es zu einer Peinlichkeit, über frühere deutsch-britische Kulturbeziehungen zu sprechen, so dass man diese lieber geflissentlich vergaß. Dieser historischen Gedächtnislücke kann nur durch eine Rückbesinnung auf die einstigen Ausstellungen deutscher Kunst in London sowie deren Rezeption durch das britische Publikum begegnet werden. Der vorliegende Essay konzentriert sich auf drei Aspekte der Ausstellungsgeschichte, an denen nachgezeichnet werden soll, wie sich die britisch-deutschen Kunstbeziehungen in der Zeit vor 1938 entwickelt hatten.

Ausstellungen deutscher Kunst im 19. Jahrhundert

In der zweiten Hälfte des 19. Jahrhunderts gab es verschiedene Initiativen, um die wachsende Mittelschicht Londons für die deutsche Kunst zu sensibilisieren. So zeigte die Lawrence Gallery an der New Bond Street im Jahr 1853 fünfzig Werke zeitgenössischer deutscher Künstler, unter ihnen Andreas Achenbach, Karl Friedrich Lessing, Johann Wilhelm Schirmer und Karl Ferdinand Sohn.[1] Allerdings waren die Reaktionen auf diese Ausstellung nicht ausschließlich positiv. Die Londoner Kunstzeitschrift *The Athenaeum* beispielsweise kritisierte die ungenügende Berücksichtigung des «nationalen Charakters aufgrund der übermäßigen Vertretung der Landschaftsbilder der Düsseldorfer und Münchner Schule». Auch vermisste man Werke von Malern wie Eduard Bendemann, Karl Hess, Wilhelm von Kaulbach und Johann Friedrich Overbeck. Obwohl in den 1830er und 1840er Jahren die Natur für die deutschen Romantiker und die Künstler der Düsseldorfer Akademie von zentraler Bedeutung war, assoziierte man in Großbritannien mit deutscher Kunst hauptsächlich das historische Genre. Der unbekannte Autor des *Athenaeum*-Aufsatzes betonte zudem, dass seine Einschätzung der deutschen Kunst auf mehreren Deutschlandreisen beruhe, bei denen er Gelegenheit gefunden hatte, Werke von Carl Friedrich Lessing im Frankfurter Städel sowie das Museum in Köln zu besichtigen. Damit bekräftigte er seine Versicherung, sein negatives Urteil entstamme keineswegs einer etwaigen «Inselmentalität» oder gar «einer dummen Abwertung des Fremden aufgrund noch dümmerer patriotischer Eitelkeit»; vielmehr ergebe sich sein Urteil aus klaren Kriterien, die ermitteln ließen, inwieweit Kunstwerke dem Nationalcharakter entsprächen.

Der *Athenaeum*-Aufsatz bemängelte an den ausgestellten Landschaften nicht nur das Fehlen typisch deutscher Schauplätze, sondern auch die Manier jener Werke. In der Kritik des

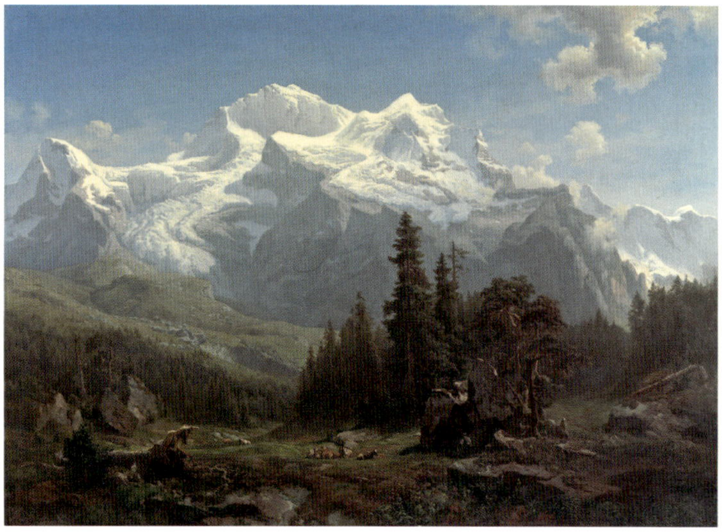

31 August Becker, *Die Jungfrau*, 1853. Öl auf Leinwand, 95.2 x 132.7 cm. Royal Collection Trust, London

Barmherzigen Samariters beispielsweise, einem Bild von Johann Wilhelm Schirmer (um 1850, Abb. 24), werden zwar die akkuraten Formen gelobt, doch sei das Gemälde als Ganzes «kaum mehr wert als eine Herbariumseite». Der Artikel behandelt im weiteren die Historienbilder, die auf der Ausstellung des Jahres 1853 gezeigt wurden. Die Ausführung eines Werkes von Heinrich Carl Anton Mücke – *Ecce Homo* (1850) –, wird als «höchst korrekt und sorgfältig» beschrieben, doch habe der Künstler die Szene «nicht mit der gebührenden Ehrfurcht» behandelt, so dass die Figur «mehr akademisch als vom Gefühl her» wirke. Deutsche Bilder dieses Genres standen damals in Großbritannien hoch im Kurs.[2] *Der ungläubige Thomas* von Johann Friedrich Overbeck beispielsweise (1851, Abb. 25) wurde 1853 in der Royal Academy gezeigt sowie ein weiteres Mal 1857 im Rahmen der wegweisenden Ausstellung *The Art Treasures of Great Britain* in Manchester. Zur Ausstellung der Lawrence Gallery von 1853 hob das *Art Journal* mit Interesse hervor, dass Königin Victoria «die besten Landschaftsbilder» gekauft habe. In Wahrheit war der Ankauf allerdings von Prinz Albert veranlasst worden.[3] Es handelte sich dabei um zwei Bilder von Oswald Achenbach (*Morgen* und *Abend*, beide 1850/54) sowie um ein Gemälde von August Becker (*Die Jungfrau*, 1853, Abb. 31). Letzterer war der Bruder von Ernst Becker, Bibliothekar im Schloss Windsor und Privatlehrer der ältesten Söhne von Königin Victoria und Prinz Albert.

1854 wurde die Lawrence Gallery in «German Gallery» umbenannt, und die anschließenden Ausstellungen – und Besprechungen – bewegten sich in ähnlichen Bahnen. Zu einer Schau vom gleichen Jahr war im *Athenaeum* zu lesen, sie gebe ein «bedauerliches Beispiel der deutschen Schule – sowohl in qualitativer wie quantitativer Beziehung». Die Kritik des Autors bezog sich auf die ärmliche Palette, die banale Landschaftsszenerien (im Vergleich zur britischen Schule) und die unzureichende Berücksichtigung der Nazarener. Erneut waren es die Historienbilder, die eine gewisse Entschädigung boten – beispielsweise die *Verteidigung einer Burg im Dreißigjährigen Krieg* von Adolf Seel.[5] Als die Galerie 1855 eine Ausstellung mit hundert Werken zeigte, war es einzig das Gemälde *Christopher Kolumbus verlässt Spanien* (1855, Abb. 26) von Emanuel Gottlieb Leutze, das Lob erntete und als «Historienbild von hohem Wert» bezeichnet wurde.[6]

Dennoch begrüßte das *Athenaeum* diese deutschen Ausstellungen als eine «Geschäftsmöglichkeit», von der die britischen Künstler nur lernen könnten – eine Einstellung, die auch vom Kritiker Joseph Beavington Atkinson geteilt wurde, der in den 1860er Jahren mehrere Internationale Kunstausstellungen in München besuchte.[7] Eine weitere Bestätigung fand diese Haltung 1861 durch die Ausstellung *German Academy of Art* in den Piccadilly Galleries sowie im darauf folgenden Jahr, als Werke deutscher und österreichischer Künstler an der internationalen Ausstellung von South Kensington gezeigt wurden. Die Reichsgründung von 1871 verstärkte das britische Interesse, mehr über die deutsche Kunst zu erfahren, obwohl das direkte Ergebnis des Franko-Preußischen Krieges ironischerweise darin bestand, dass die German Gallery sich für geflüchtete französische Künstler öffnete.[8]

In den 1870er Jahre erschienen in England zwei wichtige Publikationen zur deutschen Kunst: *Gems of Modern German Art* von William Bell Scott (1873) und *The Schools of Modern Art in Germany* von Joseph Beavington Atkinson (1880). Obwohl Ausstellungen deutscher Kunst weiterhin eher selten blieben, wurde Adolph Menzel 1896 als «ausländisches Mitglied» von der Royal Academy gewürdigt und sein Werk 1903 dem Londoner Publikum anlässlich einer Veranstaltung in der French Gallery am Pall Mall «angemessen vorgestellt».[9]

1906 – ein Schlüsseljahr

Als sich die politischen Konflikte zwischen Deutschland und England um die Jahrhundertwende verschärften, trugen die in Großbritannien organisierten Ausstellungen deutscher Kunst zur Entspannung bei. Besonders erwähnenswert sind zwei Londoner Ausstellungen von 1906. Hatte die German Gallery nur punktuell Einblick in das zeitgenössische deutsche Kunstschaffen geboten, so traf dies auf die Ausstellungen des Jahres 1906 nicht zu. Vielmehr schrieb die *Times*: «In dieser Saison erlebt London eine regelrechte Invasion der deutschen Kunst».[10] In Kooperation mit der Münchner Galerie David Heinemann zeigten die Grafton Galleries zwischen dem 2. Mai und dem 10. Juli in Mayfair Werke «aller Künstler der verschiedenen Münchner Schulen». Es handelte sich um 277 Bilder von Malern wie Hans von Bartels, Wilhelm von Kaulbach, Franz von Lenbach, Fritz von Uhde und anderen.[11] Die Bedeutung der Schau wurde auch in Deutschland selbst gewürdigt; so sprach F. E. W. Freund, der Londoner Korrespondent der *Kunst für Alle*, von einer «wirklich repräsentierenden Ausstellung».[12] Zugleich merkte er an, dass außer Bartels, Kaulbach, Lenbach und Stuck die meisten vertretenen Künstler in England so gut wie unbekannt seien und die Ausstellung «der geistigen Annäherung der beiden Völker nur förderlich sein» könne.

Die andere Ausstellung des Schlüsseljahres 1906 war die von Henry van der Velde organisierte *Exhibition of the Works of German Artists*, die im Mai und Juli in den Prince's Galleries in Knightsbridge gezeigt wurde – unter anderem mit Leihgaben aus der Berliner Nationalgalerie. Laut Freund bestand ihre Bedeutung darin, dass sie «zum ersten Mal eines fremden Landes moderne Kunst im Zusammenhang dem englischen Publikum [vorführe]; Denn selbst der französischen Kunst [sei] so etwas hier bisher nicht zuteil geworden», womit die Ausstellung «eine gute Übersicht des deutschen Kunstschaffens der Gegenwart» gebe.[13] Ein Artikel der *Times* lobte die Veranstaltung ebenfalls, obwohl darin zurückhaltend Kritik an den Werken von Stuck geübt wurde.[14]

Welche diplomatische Bedeutung die Ausstellung hatte, wird an der Teilnehmersliste zum Eröffnungsdinner der Prince's Galleries ersichtlich. Frank Lascelles, der britische Botschafter in Berlin, und Johann Heinrich Graf von Bernsdorff, der deutsche Botschaftsrat in London,

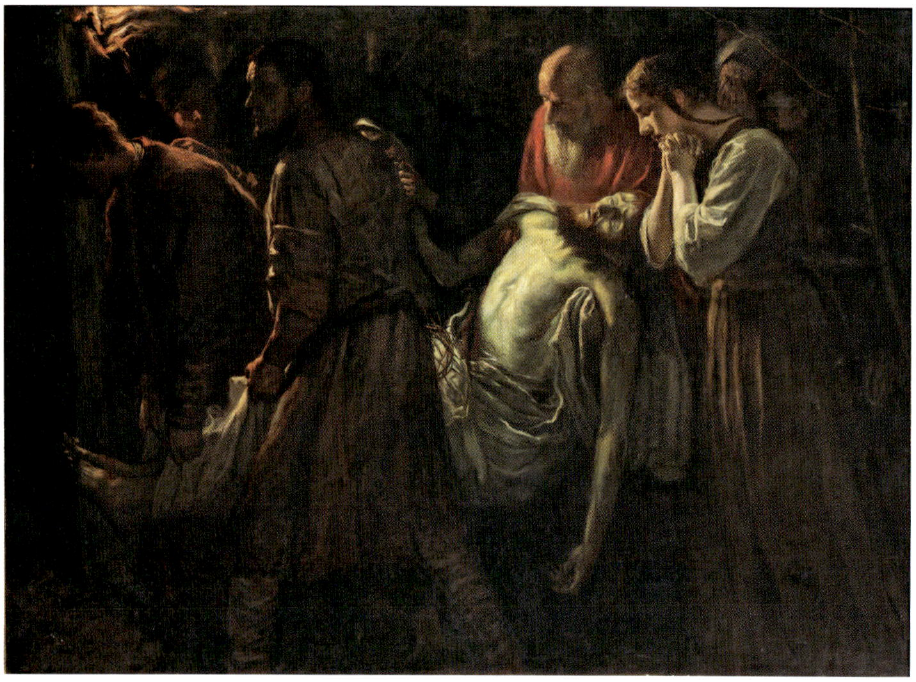

32 Fritz von Uhde, *Die Grablegung Christi*, 1894. Öl auf Leinwand,, 168 x 237 cm. Museum Bautzen

nahmen in ihren Ansprachen Bezug auf eine Rede von Paul Wolff Graf von Metternich, der 1904 als deutscher Botschafter in London beide Länder zu engeren kulturellen Beziehungen ermutigt hatte.[15] Auch Richard Haldane, der britische Kriegsminister, griff bei seiner Ansprache Metternichs Worte auf und sagte: «Die deutsche Kunst strahlt weit über die Grenzen Deutschlands aus und ist tief in unseren englischen Geist eingedrungen. [...] Indem sie Gemeinsamkeiten unterstreicht, trägt sie zu einer Annäherung unserer beider Völker bei, denn es ist letztlich der Geist, der den gemeinsamen Sockel der Deutschen und der Engländer bildet». Im Gegenzug anerkannte der deutsch-englische Künstler Hubert von Herkomer die positive Aufnahme britischer Kunst in Deutschland.[16]

In der Besprechung für das *Art Journal* gratulierte Frank Rinder den britischen Künstlern für ihre ebenfalls positive Haltung gegenüber der deutschen Kunst und schrieb, Böcklin, Lenbach, Menzel und Stuck hätten sich dank der Ausstellung in den Prince's Galleries als «Männer von wachsender künstlerischer Kraft» erwiesen.[17] Obwohl sich Rinder über manche Werke zurückhaltend äußerte – darunter die *Gefilde der Seligen* von Arnold Böcklin (1877, Abb. 27) und *Die Grablegung Christi* von Fritz von Uhde (1894, Abb. 32) –, fand er zugleich lobende Worte für die *Flachsscheuer in Laren* von Max Liebermann (1887, Abb. 28). Franz von Stucks *Prozession der Bacchanten* bezeichnete er gar als «ausdruckstärkstes Werk eines zeitgenössischen Künstlers». Dennoch stimmten Rinder und das *Athenaeum* darin überein, dass die englische Kunst von der deutschen keineswegs übertroffen werde, eine Ansicht, die vielleicht auch den politischen Spannungen der damaligen Zeit geschuldet war.[18]

Unter den Gästen des erwähnten Dinners befand sich auch der englische Maler und Graphiker Walter Crane, von dem der Entwurf zum Ausstellungsplakat stammte (Abb. 33). Diesen Auftrag hatte er vermutlich erhalten, da schon 1894 Werke von ihm in Deutschland

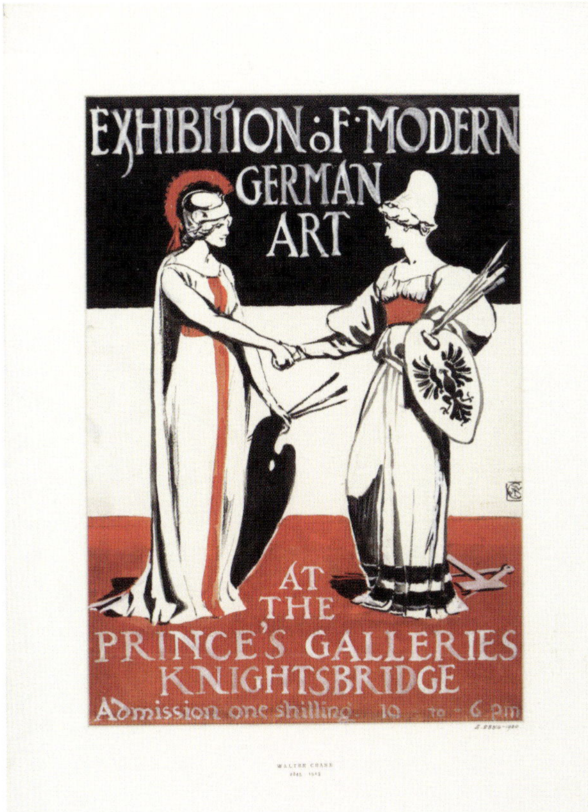

33 Walter Crane, *Exhibition of Modern German Art*, Plakatentwurf für die Ausstellung in den Prince's Galleries Knightsbridge, 1906. Victoria & Albert Museum, London

ausgestellt und in öffentliche Sammlungen aufgenommen worden waren. Darüber hinaus hatte er 1898 das Titelblatt einer Ausgabe der Zeitschrift *Jugend* sowie 1882 den Umschlag der englischen Ausgabe *Kinder- und Hausmärchen* der Gebrüder Grimm (1812/1815) gestaltet.[19] Auf Cranes Entwurf für das Plakat der Ausstellung sind Allegorien Deutschlands und Großbritanniens zu sehen. Das Kleid Britanniens ist nicht mit dem Union Jack, sondern nur mit dem Sankt-Georgs-Kreuz geziert. Anstelle von Schildern halten beide Gestalten Malerpaletten, wobei auf derjenigen Deutschlands ein Reichsadler zu sehen ist. Als Hintergrund dient die schwarz-weiß-rote Reichsfahne. Trotz dieses patriotischen Pathos reichen sich beide Figuren die Hand.

Ausstellungen moderner deutscher Kunst in Großbritannien

Dank ihres maßgeblichen Anteils an der Entstehung des Expressionismus, des Dadaismus, der Neuen Sachlichkeit und der Bauhaus-Bewegung war die deutsche Kunst der Jahre 1905 bis 1933 als treibende Kraft der Moderne international anerkannt. In den beiden ersten Jahrzehnten des 20. Jahrhunderts hatte das Londoner Publikum mehrmals die Möglichkeit, Werke dieser Kunstströmungen kennenzulernen, beispielsweise auf der jährlichen Präsentation der Allied Artists' Association oder auf der Ausstellung *Modern German Art* der Twenty-One Gallery von 1914. Hier waren unter anderem Holzschnitte von Ernst Ludwig Kirchner, Franz Marc, Max Pechstein und Wassily Kandinsky zu sehen, die vom britischen Künstler Wyndham Lewis als «Chirurgie der Sinne» gelobt wurden.[20]

Die Ausstellungen moderner deutscher Kunst in England gingen auch nach der Machtergreifung der Nazis weiter. Unter den verfolgten Künstlern, deren Werke in London im Rahmen von Einzelausstellungen gezeigt wurden, seien hier nur Liebermann, Max Ernst, Oskar Schlemmer and Paul Klee erwähnt,[21] der – dank der Bemühungen Alfred Flechtheims[22] – 1934 eine Ausstellung in der Mayor Gallerie an der Cork Street erhielt.

Das Kritiker-Echo auf diese Klee-Ausstellung fiel jedoch geteilt aus. Während Anthony Blunt in *The Spectator* ihr kühl ablehnend gegenüberstand,[23] schrieb Charles Marriott in der *Times* eine verhältnismäßig positive Kritik: Obwohl er manche Werke Klees als einfältig bezeichnete, beschrieb er den Maler als einen «interessanten Künstler, wie er einmal kommen musste». Weiterhin schrieb Marriott: «Wenn die Natur durch Kuben verdrängt wird, kehrt sie eben auf krummen Wegen zurück.» Dies sei unausweichlich, da der neoklassizistische Kubismus der Südeuropäer «dem nördlichen Genie nach der Abschaffung des Gegenständlichen nicht genügen könne». Manche fantastische Bilder Klees zeugten von der «wunderbaren Ausdrucksweise der Kinder», während andere wie *Drohender Schneesturm* (1927, Abb. 29) «durch ihre Linienraster auf einem farbig abgestuften Hintergrund an Luftaufnahmen vorgeschichtlicher Ansiedlungen» erinnerten. *Blüten in der Nacht* (1930, Abb. 30) schließlich offenbare die ganz Vielfalt und Erfindungsgabe des «magischen Farbenkünstlers», so dass der Kritiker zuletzt erklärte: «Alles in allem sind wir über Herrn Klee durchaus glücklich.»[24]

Mit zwei Büchern trug der Kunstkritiker und -historiker Herbert Read wesentlich zu einem tieferen Verständnis Klees in Großbritannien bei: *The Meaning of Art*, 1931, und *Art Now*, 1933. Der Poet und Kritiker Geoffrey Grigson teilte Reads Wertschätzung, indem er Klee in der Zeitschrift *The Bookman* gleich zweimal erwähnte: Im Oktober 1933 lobte er ihn als einen der herausragenden, in *Art Now* genannten Künstler;[25] zwei Monate später galt er ihm als «einer der außergewöhnlichsten, seltsamsten, ja sogar – verzeihen Sie das Wort – wichtigsten zeitgenössischen Künstler», und bedauerte, diesen «von der Tradition der nördlichen Frührenaissance» durchgedrungen Maler so lange verkannt zu haben.[26] Weiterhin meinte Grigson, Klee sei «deutsches Hackfleisch, ein aus Kubismus und Futurismus zusammengeschnittenes mystisches Beefsteak», jemand der aufgrund seiner Authentizität, seines Witzes und seiner kindlich-intellektuellen Vision Anerkennung verdiene.[27] Der Künstler und Kritiker Jan Gordon wiederum meinte, das Werk Klees entspräche vollkommen der von Read in *Art Now* formulierten Definition der modernen Kunst als «freie Fantasie». Dennoch meinte Gordon, Klees Maske der Kindlichkeit sei nur vordergründiger Art: Die Texturen und die Bedeutung seiner Werke seien so «komplex» wie Rhythmus und Reime von Kinderliedern. Daraus zog er den Schluss: «[Das Kinderlied] *Three Blind Mice* mag Miltons *Paradise Lost* überdauern, aber Klee wird kaum einen Tizian überleben.»[28]

Zwischen den 1850er und 1930er Jahren fanden in London zwar nur vereinzelte, jedoch wichtige Ausstellungen zeitgenössischer deutscher Kunst statt. Die Kritik reagierte jeweils informiert, bemängelte zunächst die Einseitigkeit der ersten Präsentationen, lobte dann aber die Genauigkeit der späteren Darbietungen bei der Erfassung des jeweiligen Zeitgeistes. Da das politische Klima zwischen den Ländern wechselte, wandelten sich auch die Ausstellungen deutscher Kunst. Galten sie anfangs einer Bildungsnovität, so dienten sie in der Kaiserzeit als Balsam für die politischen Spannungen, ehe sie die Verfolgung avantgardistischer Kunst durch die Nazis dokumentieren sollten. Während der gesamten Zeit blieb das britische Publikum lebhaft interessiert und versuchte, über die unregelmässig stattfindenden Ausstellungen so viel wie möglich über die deutsche Kunst zu erfahren.

1 Lawrence Gallery: Catalogue of paintings at the first annual exhibition of the works of modern German artists, London 1853; o. V.: Exhibition of the works of Modern German Artists, in: The Athenaeum, Bd. 1333, 14. Mai 1853, S. 593.

2 Matthew C. Potter: The Inspirational Genius of Germany. British Art and Germanism, 1850-1939, Manchester, 2012, S. 79.

3 o. V., Exhibition of the Works of Modern German Artists, in: Art Journal, Juni 1853, S. 161.

4 Jonathan Marsden (Hg.): Victoria and Albert. Art and Love, London 2010, S. 118-119.

5 o. V.: Fine Arts. Exhibition of German Art, in: The Athenaeum, Bd. 1381, 15. April 1854, S. 467-468.

6 o. V.: Fine Arts. Exhibition of German Art, in: The Athenaeum, Bd. 1441, 9. Juni 1855, S. 678.

7 o. V.: Exhibition of the Works of Modern German Artists, in: Art Journal, Juni 1853, S. 161; Potter, S. 56-78, 80, 82, 109, 266.

8 William Vaughan: German Romanticism and English Art, New Haven u. a. 1979, S. 248; o. V.: German Gallery, 168 New Bond Street. Society of French Artists, in: Examiner, Bd. 3281, 17. Dezember 1870, S. 809.

9 Potter, S. 37, 46, 70, 82, 202–206; o. V., Passing Events, in: Art Journal, Juni 1896, S. 190; o. V.: Menzel at the French Gallery, in: The Athenaeum, Bd. 3946, 13. Juni 1903, S. 760; o. V.: Menzel, in: Art Journal, Juli 1906, S. 195; MaryAnne Stevens: The Royal Academy in the Age of Queen Victoria, in: Helen Valentine (Hg.): Art in the Age of Queen Victoria. Treasures from the Royal Academy of Arts Permanent Collection, New Haven u. a. 1999, S. 26-39, S. 36.

10 o. V.: Art Exhibitions, in: The Times, 16. Mai 1906, S. 4. Eine Ausstellung deutscher Kunst der Vergangenheit mit Werken von Albrecht Dürer und anderen Altmeistern wurde auch im selben Jahr im Londoner Burlington Fine Art Club organisiert (siehe o. V.: Burlington Fine Arts Club, in: The Times, 21. Mai 1906, S. 10).

11 Siehe o. V.: German Art Exhibition in London, in: The Times, 13. April 1906, S. 11; o. V., Art Exhibitions, in: The Times, 16. Mai 1906, S. 4.

12 F. E. W. Freund: Die Münchener Kunstausstellung in London, in: Die Kunst für Alle, Bd. XXI, Heft 18, 15. Juni 1906, S. 423/424.

13 F. E. W. Freund: Von Ausstellungen und Sammlungen, in: Die Kunst für Alle, Bd. XXI, Heft 19, 1. Juli 1906. S. 451-452.

14 o. V.: An Exhibition of German Art, in: The Times, 5. April 1906, S. 10; o. V., Art Exhibitions, in: The Times, 16. Mai 1906, S. 4.

15 Siehe: o. V.: Anglo-German Relations. Sir F. Lascelles at the Berlin Lyceum Club (From our own correspondent), Berlin, Jan. 14, in: The Times, 15. Januar 1906, S. 5; o. V.: German Artists' Exhibition. Inaugural Dinner, in: The Times, 23. Mai 1906, S. 5; o. V.: International Society Of Sculptors, Painters, And Gravers, in: The Times, 11. Januar 1906, S. 7; Johann von Bernstorff: My Three Years in America, New York 1936, S. 16 u. 28.

16 o. V.: German Artists' Exhibition. Inaugural Dinner, in: The Times, 23. Mai 1906, S. 5.

17 Frank Rinder: London Exhibitions, in: Art Journal, Juli 1906, S. 220.

18 Ibid.; o. V.: Munich Exhibition at the Grafton Gallery, in: The Athenaeum, Bd. 4099, 19. Mai 1906, S. 614; siehe auch o. V.: Contemporary German Artists at Knightsbridge, in: The Athenaeum, Bd. 4102, 9. Juni 1906, S. 709.

19 Potter, S. 196-203, 208; Jeffrey L. Sammons: Kuno Francke's Edition of the German Classics (1913-15). A Historical and Critical Overview, New York 2009, S. 86. Das 1891 von Crane gemalte Bild *Der Mäher* ist ein Geschenk Hans Thomas an die Kunsthalle Karlsruhe; Hans Ries: Deutsche Bilderbuchkritik zwischen Wolgast und dem Dritten Reich, in: Bernd Dolle-Weinkauff/Hans-Heino Ewers (Hg.): Theorien der Jugendlektüre. Beiträge zur Kinder- und Jugendliteraturkritik seit Heinrich Wolgast. Weinheim u. a. 1996, S. 93.

20 Judith Collins: Omega and Hogarth Woodcuts, in: Jeremy Greenwood: Omega Cuts, Woodbridge 1998, S. 9-18.

21 Für die früheren Ausstellungen Max Liebermanns siehe in dieser Publikation den Aufsatz von Martin Faass. 1937 wurden in der Mayor Gallery Werke von Max Ernst gezeigt und in der London Gallery Noel Nortons eine Oskar Schlemmer-Ausstellung organisiert.

22 Siehe Ottfried Dascher: «Es ist was Wahnsinniges mit der Kunst». Alfred Flechtheim – Sammler, Kunsthändler, Verleger. Mit einer Bibliographie von Rudolf Schmitt-Föller und einer Stammtafel von Rico Quaschny. Wädenswil 2011, S. 350-351.

23 Zitiert in Hans Albert Peters: Alfred Flechtheim. Sammler. Kunsthändler. Verleger, Düsseldorf 1987, S. 197, 198, 200.

24 o. V.: Art Exhibition. Mr. Paul Klee, in: The Times, 17. Januar 1934, S. 17.

25 Geoffrey Grigson: Unit One, Herbert Read, and The Mayor Gallery, in: The Bookman, 85, Bd. 505, Oktober 1933, S. 31-32.

26 Geoffrey Grigson: Paul Klee, in: The Bookman, 85, Bd. 507, Dezember 1933, S. 390.

27 Geoffrey Grigson: «Childishness» in Contemporary Art, in: The Bookman, 85, Bd. 507, Dezember 1933, S. 170-171.

28 Jan Gordon: Art and Artists. Paul Klee's Work, in: The Observer, 21. Januar 1934, S. 12.

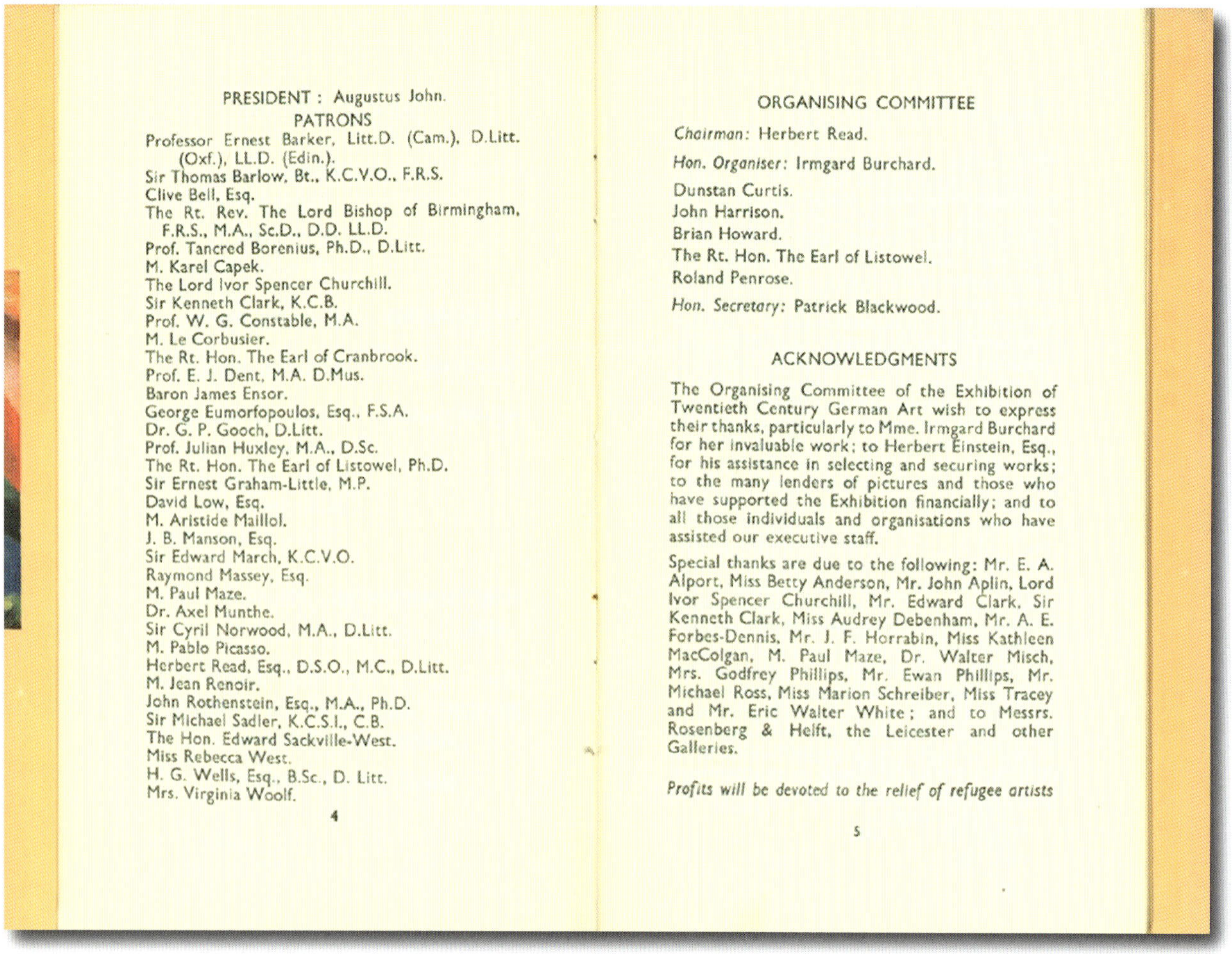

PRESIDENT : Augustus John.

PATRONS

Professor Ernest Barker, Litt.D. (Cam.), D.Litt. (Oxf.), LL.D. (Edin.).
Sir Thomas Barlow, Bt., K.C.V.O., F.R.S.
Clive Bell, Esq.
The Rt. Rev. The Lord Bishop of Birmingham, F.R.S., M.A., Sc.D., D.D. LL.D.
Prof. Tancred Borenius, Ph.D., D.Litt.
M. Karel Capek.
The Lord Ivor Spencer Churchill.
Sir Kenneth Clark, K.C.B.
Prof. W. G. Constable, M.A.
M. Le Corbusier.
The Rt. Hon. The Earl of Cranbrook.
Prof. E. J. Dent, M.A. D.Mus.
Baron James Ensor.
George Eumorfopoulos, Esq., F.S.A.
Dr. G. P. Gooch, D.Litt.
Prof. Julian Huxley, M.A., D.Sc.
The Rt. Hon. The Earl of Listowel, Ph.D.
Sir Ernest Graham-Little, M.P.
David Low, Esq.
M. Aristide Maillol.
J. B. Manson, Esq.
Sir Edward March, K.C.V.O.
Raymond Massey, Esq.
M. Paul Maze.
Dr. Axel Munthe.
Sir Cyril Norwood, M.A., D.Litt.
M. Pablo Picasso.
Herbert Read, Esq., D.S.O., M.C., D.Litt.
M. Jean Renoir.
John Rothenstein, Esq., M.A., Ph.D.
Sir Michael Sadler, K.C.S.I., C.B.
The Hon. Edward Sackville-West.
Miss Rebecca West.
H. G. Wells, Esq., B.Sc., D. Litt.
Mrs. Virginia Woolf.

4

ORGANISING COMMITTEE

Chairman: Herbert Read.

Hon. Organiser: Irmgard Burchard.

Dunstan Curtis.
John Harrison.
Brian Howard.
The Rt. Hon. The Earl of Listowel.
Roland Penrose.

Hon. Secretary: Patrick Blackwood.

ACKNOWLEDGMENTS

The Organising Committee of the Exhibition of Twentieth Century German Art wish to express their thanks, particularly to Mme. Irmgard Burchard for her invaluable work; to Herbert Einstein, Esq., for his assistance in selecting and securing works; to the many lenders of pictures and those who have supported the Exhibition financially; and to all those individuals and organisations who have assisted our executive staff.

Special thanks are due to the following: Mr. E. A. Alport, Miss Betty Anderson, Mr. John Aplin, Lord Ivor Spencer Churchill, Mr. Edward Clark, Sir Kenneth Clark, Miss Audrey Debenham, Mr. A. E. Forbes-Dennis, Mr. J. F. Horrabin, Miss Kathleen MacColgan, M. Paul Maze, Dr. Walter Misch, Mrs. Godfrey Phillips, Mr. Ewan Phillips, Mr. Michael Ross, Miss Marion Schreiber, Miss Tracey and Mr. Eric Walter White; and to Messrs. Rosenberg & Helft, the Leicester and other Galleries.

Profits will be devoted to the relief of refugee artists

5

34 *Twentieth Century German Art*, exhibition catalogue, list of patrons and thanks

A British Statement against Nazi Policy? The Organisation of *Twentieth Century German Art*

LUCY WASENSTEINER

Looking at the patrons listed on the *Twentieth Century German Art* exhibition poster (see p. 2), it is hard to imagine a set of names which better represented the British cultural establishment of the late 1930s. From the director of the National Gallery Sir Kenneth Clark, via a Bishop to a Churchill, the list also included names with a proven interest in German culture. The educationalist Sir Michael Sadler was one of the earliest collectors of German modernist art in Britain. Art historian Herbert Read meanwhile – then editor of the renowned *Burlington Magazine* – had written extensively on German art throughout the 1920s and 30s.[1]

It might therefore be safely assumed that *Twentieth Century German Art* was a squarely British project, a chance for German modernist sympathisers in Britain to oppose Nazi policy on a public stage. Yet this organising team, and their motivation for involvement, were in reality far more complex, as a look into the archives confirms.[2]

The Origins of the Organising Team

The earliest plans for what became *Twentieth Century German Art* were indeed articulated in London. Not by Read or Sadler however, but by the British dealer Noel 'Peter' Norton (fig. 35). Norton's 'London Gallery' on the city's Cork Street had come to specialise in central European modernism, perhaps spurred in part by her husband's career – Clifford Norton worked at the British Foreign Office during the mid-1930s, serving as private secretary to the notorious opponent of the Hitler regime, Sir Robert Vansittart. Following events as they developed in Germany, in September 1937 Norton began plans for an exhibition of *Banned Art* to be staged at her London Gallery: a commercial show, with a political message.[3]

Meanwhile in Zurich, another dealer was having similar ideas. Irmgard Burchard (fig. 36) had founded her dealership in 1934, as she witnessed increasing numbers of German modernists seeking new markets abroad. Assisted by the contacts of her husband, the artist and designer Richard Paul Lohse, by 1936 Burchard was dealing for numerous Swiss and German artists from her base in Zürich, among them Paul Klee and Willi Baumeister.[4] During 1937, her business brought her to London. Here she met Norton – by late September 1937 the two women had joined forces to realise the *Banned Art* project.[5]

A third name, which would prove central to the London exhibition, was the German Jewish art critic Paul Westheim (fig. 38). Westheim had made his name in Weimar-era Berlin as founder and editor of journal *Das Kunstblatt*.[6] Forced into exile in 1933, Westheim settled

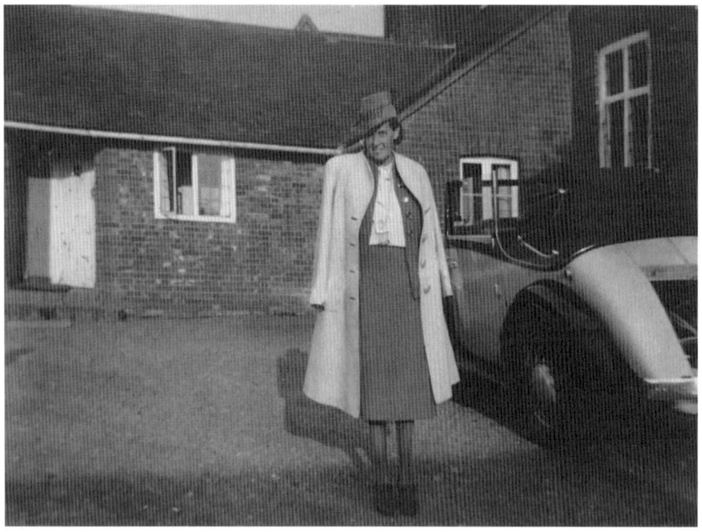

35 Noel 'Peter' Norton, c. 1930

in Paris, where he continued his pro-modernist advocacy. On 30 September 1937 he was among the founding members of the Paris-based Deutscher Künstlerbund (i.e. 'German Artists' Association'). Founded with the specific aim of counter Nazi cultural policy, their first project – as set out in their minutes – was an exhibition in Paris, "a fundamental demonstration against the Munich exhibition *Degenerate Art*".[7]

Some time during late September 1937, Burchard and Norton learned of the Künstlerbund's plans via mutual friends in Paris.[8] Burchard approached her Zürich contact, the émigré Yugoslavian writer Oto Bihalji-Merin, to reach out to Westheim, the two men being previously acquainted from Berlin.[9] The approach was a success. Though initially reluctant given the distinctly commercial nature of the London project, the DKb agreed to participate, hoping to 'interpret [the London exhibition] for our own propagandistic aims'.[10] By November Westheim had received a contract from Norton's gallery, undertaking to gather pictures for an exhibition in London in exchange for a fee of fifty pounds.[11]

The Work Starts

As November 1937 drew to a close, so Burchard, Westheim and Norton began work on the *Banned Art* project. Despite their disparate backgrounds, the three formed a highly effective team when it came to gathering exhibits.

Westheim for example was extremely well-connected within both the German modernist and émigré scenes thanks to his previous career at *Das Kunstblatt*. He provided instant access to prestigious Berlin collectors in exile in Paris – for example the banker and politician Hugo Simon, and the textile magnate Erich Göritz.[12] Where collectors were not known to him directly, he could also reach out to former colleagues for their recommendations. Particularly important among them was the art historian Charlotte Weidler (fig. 39). Weidler had worked with Westheim at *Das Kunstblatt* – she had remained in Berlin after 1933, where she was employed gathering works for the annual Carnegie International exhibitions in Pittsburgh.[13] In this position she could travel widely without arousing official suspicion, a freedom she was

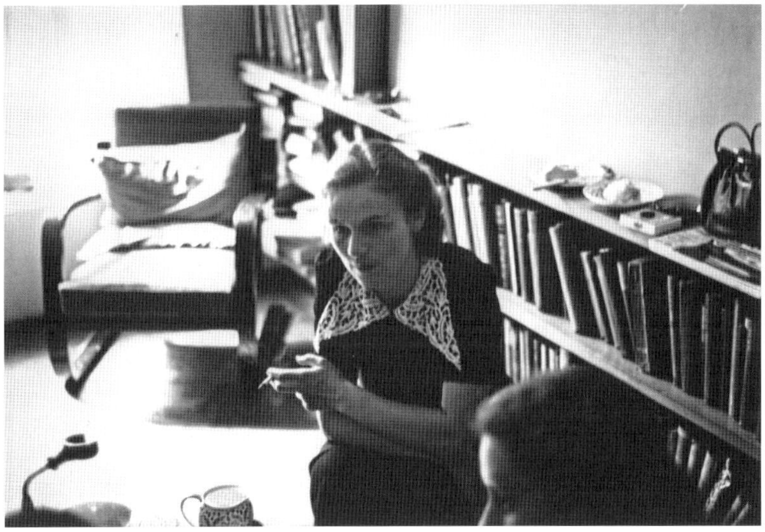

36 Irmgard Burchard photographed by Ewan Phillips at the New Burlington Galleries, July 1938

soon using for the benefit of the London exhibition. In November 1937 for example Weidler visited the artist Max Pechstein, still resident in Germany, gathering the names of his most important foreign collectors. These were in turn passed to Westheim (see cat. no. 16).

With Westheim and his network identifying potential lenders, the low public profile and Swiss passport of Irmgard Burchard meant she was ideally placed to gather up the identified works. During late 1937 she traversed Europe, collecting loans on Westheim's recommendations. She could also identify her own potential exhibits however – works from her dealership contacts and from private collections in Zurich and Basel (see cat. nos. 3 and 25). Burchard also initiated a letter-writing campaign to dozens of the so-called 'degenerate' artists, imploring them to send works to London. Many agreed, among them Kurt Schwitters, formerly of Hannover, who provided Burchard with at least five pieces from his exile in Western Norway.[14]

In London, the contacts of Noel Norton brought further key works within the reach of the exhibition team. Her neighbour on Cork Street for example was the American heiress Peggy Guggenheim, who through her 'Guggenheim Jeune' dealership lent works by Kandinsky and Kokoschka. Indeed it seems to have been Norton who first brought Herbert Read (fig. 40) to the London project. Read had prepared the foreword for an exhibition of Edvard Munch staged at Norton's London Gallery in 1936. By December 1937 he too was involved with the *Banned Art* project, agreeing to select the works gathered and arranged the exhibition's hang.[15]

A further asset to the team was the Vienna-born art historian Edith Hoffmann (fig. 37). Daughter of the Czech-Jewish diplomat and cultural journalist Camill Hofmann, after completing her studies in Munich she relocated to London in 1934. As a German-speaking art historian, with a diplomatic passport and the wealth of her father's connections, it did not take long for her to come to the attention of Norton and Burchard in London. By December 1937 she was also involved with the exhibition project, travelling between Britain and mainland Europe to assist with the gathering of works.[16]

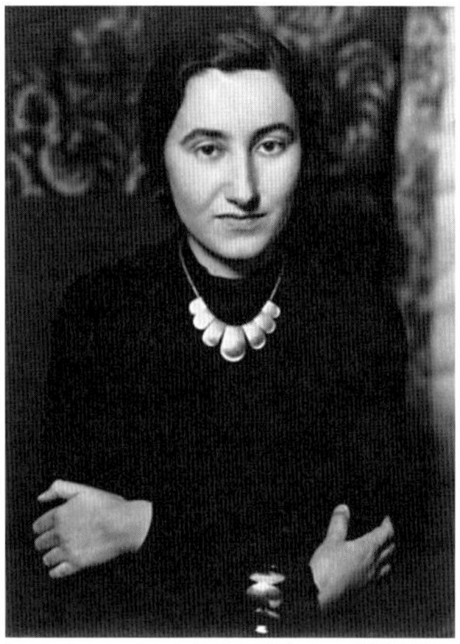

37 Edith Hoffmann, London 1937

Conflicting Motivations

In a little over eight months, the organising team were able to recruit over 90 individual lenders to the London exhibition. As indicated in the catalogue section of this volume, these were a highly varied group: Swiss, British and German émigré figures; museums, commercial dealers, private collectors and the 'degenerate' artists themselves.

Considering the development of the exhibition project during the winter of 1937-8, it is also clear that Westheim, Norton and Burchard in particular were far from united in their aims for the London show.

On 1 December 1937 for example, Norton wrote to her fellow organisers, informing them of a series of changes to the exhibition's title and its scope. Though eager to defend German modernism in London, Norton was also concerned that a show of *Banned Art* might have a negative impact on her husband's career. The title would therefore need to be changed, to the more politically neutral *Twentieth Century German Art.* Artists officially approved of by the German regime would also now need to be included.[17]

Neither Burchard nor Westheim were surprised by this change to the show's title: both had already received various negative reactions to the name, in particular from contacts in Switzerland.[18] They were however deeply unsatisfied with the proposed inclusion of 'official' German artists in the exhibition. Though both continued their work gathering exhibits for the show, both wrote to Norton to protest this change.[19] Westheim in particular was additionally irritated by the manner in which this decision had been made by Norton, namely without his involvement. As he wrote to her on 10 December, 'it would have been more pleasant, and more in line with my expectations, if I had been informed before the decision was taken'.[20] Ultimately only one work by an 'officially approved' German artist was included in the London show: a Georg Kolbe bronze of the dealer Paul Cassirer, loaned from the collection of Hugo Simon.

As December progressed, so Westheim grew yet more dissatisfied with Norton's working methods. Shortly before Christmas 1937 Clifford Norton was reposted to the British Embassy in Poland.[21] He and his wife immediately departed London for Warsaw, effectively ending Noel Norton's involvement in the exhibition project, and leaving the show without a venue.

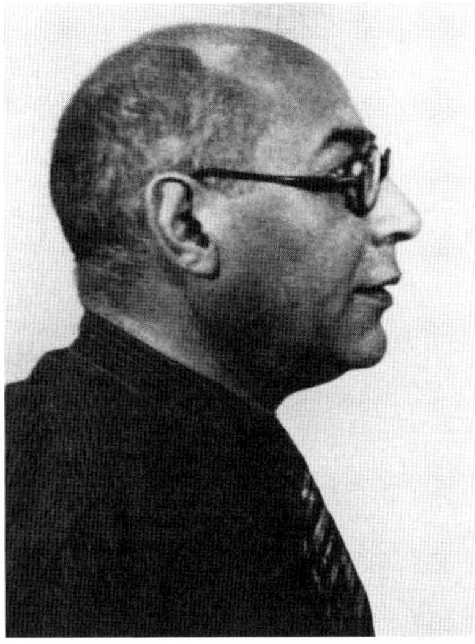

38 Paul Westheim, Paris 1937

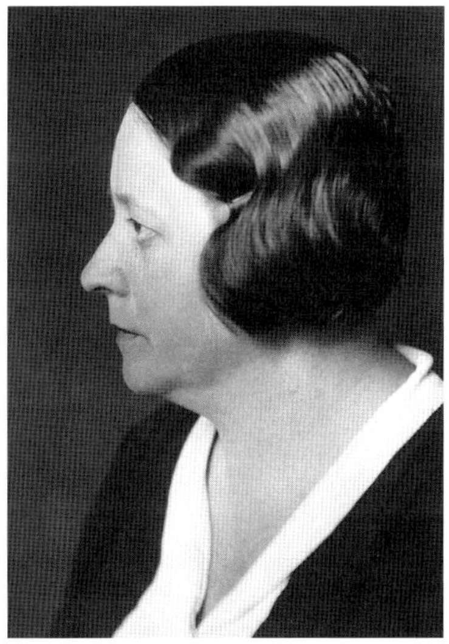

39 Charlotte Weidler, Berlin 1933

Learning of Norton's actions, Westheim was incensed. On 28 January he informed Burchard that he wanted 'nothing to do' with the London project, on grounds of 'the bluffs ... the misinformation ... the way I have been ripped off'.[22]

Irmgard Burchard meanwhile steadfastly continued to work. A generation younger than Westheim and Norton, and only three years into her career as a dealer, the planned exhibition had pushed her into a new professional league. The opportunity to work with some of Europe's leading artists, dealers and collectors was not to be abandoned lightly. During the early weeks of 1938 Burchard kept up her correspondence with lenders, working with Herbert Read to find a new venue for the show while continuing her travels across Europe to gather works. By February 1938 her hard work had paid off. With Read (fig. 40) newly instated as 'Chairman of the Organising Committee' the rooms of the New Burlington Galleries (fig. 41) were secured for the show – a fourth-floor space on Burlington Gardens. Under Read's leadership, these galleries had housed the first British retrospective of Surrealist art in 1936,[23] followed later that year by the similary impressive *Masters fo French 19th Century Painting.*[24] As Charlotte Weidler wrote to Westheim on 23 February, "Burlington is of course fabulous and very respectable ... it will surely make the Nazis blue and green with anger".[25]

Whether spurred by this promise of Nazi rage, or enticed by the respectability of the New Burlington Galleries, during March 1938 Westheim restarted work on *Twentieth Century German Art*, despite the continued neutrality of its title, and despite the presence of the officially-approved German sculptor Kolbe among the secured exhibits. Yet once again, it did not take long before his pride was again wounded by his fellow organisers. In March he became angered by Burchard's suggestion that time had been 'lost' by his absence from proceedings; less than two weeks later he heard rumours that plans were afoot to send the London show to Paris, without the involvement of his DKb group.[26] In a letter to Herbert Read of 6 April 1938, Westheim announced the end of his involvement with London. The reasons cited – Burchard's behaviour, and her failure to adequately apologise for it.[27]

Disappointment and Sabotage

The letter of 6 April from Westheim to Read, ending Westheim's involvement with *Twentieth Century German Art*, in fact crossed another of the same date from Read to Westheim. Unaware of Westheim's break with the project, in this letter Read informed Westheim of further changes he had planned to the show's public face. Namely, that Westheim would now not be named in the publicity materials, 'to avoid every suggestion that this exhibition is a project of Jews or émigrés'.[28]

Why did Read push for these changes, in the final weeks before the show's opening? The summer of 1938 certainly marked the highpoint of Britain's appeasement of Nazi Germany, with Chamberlain and Hitler signing the Munich Agreement on 30 September.[29] There is however little evidence that these policies could have impacted upon a private exhibition in this way. Perhaps more likely, is that Read's decision was prompted by a fear that 'Jews and émigrés' might compromise the popularity of the exhibition among London's gallery-going public. The spectre of the Jewish immigrant had haunted British imaginations since the first wave of Russian arrivals fifty years earlier. Though extreme anti-Semitism of the kinds seen in Nazi Germany remained rare, there was a strong expectation for the émigré in Britain to 'blend in', to avoid 'bringing discrimination among themselves'.[30] Read's personal engagement on behalf of the Hitler émigrés is well-documented.[31] His letter to Westheim does however indicate a concern that the wider London public may have been offended by the open participation of Jewish émigré figures in *Twentieth Century German Art*.

Receiving this letter from Herbert Read, Westheim not only continued to withhold his services from the exhibition. He actively set about attempting to sabotage the show, writing to artist contacts and imploring them to remove their works, while penning a series of articles criticising the exhibition's political neutrality for the pages of the Parisian émigré press.[32] Westheim and the DKb ultimately staged their own counter-exhibition to *Degenerate Art* in Paris in the November of 1938, under the title *Freie Deutsche Kunst* (i.e. *Free German Art*).[33]

Upon receiving Read's letter of 6 April, Westheim saw aspects of British society which he had perhaps, until that point, failed to consider. While he may have hoped to use the exhibition to restate his position as a leading historian and critic, for Read and his fellow Britons Westheim was clearly seen first and foremost among two categories of 'undesirables', namely 'Jews or émigrés'. The anger and disappointment which flowed from this realisation perhaps illustrates the optimism Westheim had initially held for *Twentieth Century German Art*, not only as a chance to answer Nazism, but also as a chance to continue his career in Britain.

The Show Opens

With Irmgard Burchard at the helm, during the early summer of 1938 over 300 artworks were brought to London – as many as 600, if correspondence between the organisers is to be believed.[34] Only 271 of these exhibits were included in the exhibition catalogue. This slim, unillustrated volume listed the exhibits alphabetically by artist – sometimes with dimensions and previous exhibitions, sometimes not, with all titles provided in English or French translation.

As promised by Read, Westheim was not named in the exhibition catalogue (fig. 34), nor in any of the exhibition's publicity materials . Irmgard Burchard was the only one of the original initiators to receive a mention – named in the catalogue as 'honorary organsier'. Herbert Read meanwhile used the catalogue's introductory pages to further emphasise the detachment between the exhibition, and the political situation in Germany (fig. 42), as he wrote, "the organsiers of the present exhibition are not concerned with the political".[35]

Despite its distinctly British presentation, *Twentieth Century German Art* was nonetheless a fundamentally international project: brought together by British, Swiss and German émigré figures, who between them gathered works from collections across Europe. It was also a show which served different purposes for each of the figures involved: certainly, a chance to make a statement against Nazism, but also a chance to sell works, to start one's career as a dealer, or to continue one's career as a writer and critic in exile. The eventual break between the organisers stands only as testament to the strength of the hopes held by each of them for the successful conclusion of the London show.

1 See for example Adrian Glew: "Blue Spiritual Sounds". Kandinsky and the Sadlers, 1911-1916, in: Burlington Magazine, vol. 139, no. 1134 (September, 1997), pp. 600-15; and Ben Read and David Thistlewood (eds.): Herbert Read. A British Vision of World Art. London 1993

2 A full reconstruction of Twentieth Century German Art, its organisation, lenders an impact will be provided in the forthcoming book by the present author: Lucy Wasensteiner. The Twentieth Century German Art Exhibition. Answering Degenerate Art in 1930s London. New York, forthcoming. The most important archival sources for the overview presented in the present text are: Russian State Military Archive, Moscow, 'Sonderarchiv', Fond 602, Paul Westheim collection (hereafter 'RSMA') and the Akademie der Künste Archive, Berlin, Eugen Spiro Collection (hereafter 'AdK')

3 As recounted in RSMA, letter from Patrick Blackwood to Paul Westheim, 14 February [1938]

4 Lucy Watling: The Irmgard Burchard Tableaux. An Anti-Nazi Dealership in 1930s Switzerland, in: Eva Blimlinger and Monika Mayer (eds.): Kunst Sammeln, Kunst Handeln. Vienna 2012, pp. 234-242

5 As recounted in RSMA, letter from Irmgard Burchard to Noel Norton, 5 December 1937

6 See Keith Holz: Scenes from Exile in Western Europe, in Stephane Barron and Sabine Eckmann (eds.): Exiles and Émigrés. The Flight of European Artists from Hitler. Los Angeles 1997, pp. 43-56, pp. 46-7

7 AdK, founding protocol and first minutes of the DKb, 30 September 1937

8 RSMA, letter from Charlotte Weidler to Paul Westheim, 1 June 1938, recalling the show's genesis

9 RSMA, letter from Oto Bihalji-Merin to Paul Westheim, 11 October 1937. Regarding Bihalji-Merin, see the text by David Elliott in this volume

10 AdK, minutes of the DKb, 17 November 1937

11 RSMA, letter from Patrick Blackwood to Paul Westheim, 18 November 1937

12 See cat. nos 12 and 8.

13 See Ines Rotermund-Reynard: Geheime Netzwerke . Charlotte Weidlers Briefe an den Kunstkritiker Paul Westheim (1933-1940), in: Burcu Dogramaci and Karin Wimmer, Netzwerke des Exils. Künstlerische Verflechtungen, Austausch und Patronage nach 1933. Berlin 2011, pp. 261-76

14 Sprengel Museum, Hanover, Kurt und Ernst Schwitters Stiftung, letter from Irmgard Burchard to Kurt Schwitters, 15 June 1938

15 RSMA, letter from the London Gallery to Paul Westheim, 1 December 1937

16 Biographical information with thanks to Yonna Yapou-Kromholz. Regarding Hoffmann's work gathering exhibits from Europe: RSMA, letter from Patrick Blackwood to Paul Westheim, 8 December 1937

17 RSMA, letter from the London Gallery to Paul Westheim, 1 December 1937; regarding Norton's concerns for her husband's career: RSMA, letter from Charlotte Weidler to Paul Westheim, 1 June 1938, recounting a conversation between Weidler and Norton

18 See for example RSMA, report of the organisers authored by Irmgard Burchard, dated 28 November 1937, in which she asked her fellow organisers to stop using the name banned art for fear of adverse reactions in Switzerland

19 RSMA, letter from Irmgard Burchard to Noel Norton, 5 December 1937; and letter from Paul Westheim to Noel Norton, 10 December 1937

20 RSMA, letter from Paul Westheim to Noel Norton, 10 December 1937

21 It seems this move coincided with Vansittart's transfer from the post of Permanent Undersecretary, also in December 1937, as the Chamberlain government sought to remove anti-appeasement voices from influential positions in London. See Frank McDonough: Neville Chamberlain. Appeasement and the British Road to War. Manchester etc, 1998, p. 52

22 RSMA, letter from Paul Westheim to Irmgard Burchard, 28 January 1938

23 'International Surrealist Exhibition', 1936

24 Alfred Flechtheim played a central role in this French exhibition; he also assisted with curating the Surrealist show. See Ottfried Dascher: “Es ist was Wahnsinniges mit der Kunst“. Alfred Flechtheim – Sammler, Kunsthändler, Verleger. With a bibliography by Rudolf Schmitt-Föller and a familiy tree by Rico Quaschny. Wädenswil 2011, p. 372-373.

25 RSMA, letter from Charlotte Weidler to Paul Westheim, 23 February 1938

26 See RSMA, letter from Paul Westheim to Irmgard Burchard, 24 March 1938; also RSMA letter from Paul Westheim to Herbert Read, 2 April 1938

27 RSMA, letter from Paul Westheim to Herbert Read, 6 April 1938

28 RSMA, letter from Herbert Read to Paul Westheim, 6 April 1938

29 See McDonough

30 See, for example, Jodi Burkett: Anti-Semitism and Racism in Britain. Assessing the Reaction to and the Legacy of Kristallnacht, in: Colin McCullough and Nathan Wilson (eds.): Violence, Memory and History. Western Perceptions of Kristallnacht. New York etc. 2015, pp. 16-33

31 See for example Read and Thistlewood, also James King: The Last Modern. A Life of Herbert Read. London 1990

32 See for example Westheim, P., ‘Die Vandalen: Der zerschnittene Kokoschka, wird er in London ausgestellt?’, Pariser Tageszeitung, 7 July 1938, p. 3; Westheim, P., ‘Kulturchronik: Ein Seltsamer Katalog’, Pariser Tageszeitung, 23 July 1938, p. 3; Westheim, P., ‘Ausstellung 20th Century German Art’, Freie Kunst und Literatur, September 1938. Correspondence in their respective archives suggests Westheim contacted Oskar Kokoschka and Otto Freundlich for example, emploring them to remove their works from the show. IMEC Abbaye d’Ardenne, Otto Freundich collection; and Zentralbibliothek Zürich, Oskar Kokoschka collection.

33 Regarding this Paris show, see for example Holz, pp. 195-240

34 RSMA, leter from Paul Westheim to Bruno Frei, 22 August 1938

35 Though anonymous, it is assumed that this introduction was penned by Read given the similarity between this and Read’s credited introduction to Peter Thoene: Modern German Art. London 1938

Die Organisation von *Twentieth Century German Art* – Ein britisches Statement gegen die Nazis?

LUCY WASENSTEINER

Ein Blick auf die Namen der Schirmherren, die auf dem Plakat der Ausstellung *Twentieth Century German Art* (vgl. S. 2) genannt sind, macht deutlich, dass sich das Patronat aus der Crème de la Crème der britischen Kunstwelt in den späten 1930er Jahre zusammensetzte. Von Sir Kenneth Clark, dem damaligen Direktor der National Gallery, über einen Bischof bis hin zu einem Churchill werden dort einige Prominente aufgeführt, die für ihr Interesse an deutscher Kultur bekannt waren. So beispielsweise der Erziehungswissenschaftler Sir Michael Sadler, der zu den ersten britischen Sammlern moderner deutscher Kunst zählte, oder der Kunsthistoriker Herbert Read, Herausgeber des renommierten *Burlington Magazine*, der seit den 1920er Jahren zahlreiche Artikel über deutsche Kunst geschrieben hatte.[1]

Es scheint deshalb die Annahme berechtigt, *Twentieth Century German Art* sei ein durch und durch britisches Projekt gewesen, über das englische Anhänger deutscher Kunst öffentlich gegen die Politik der Nazis Stellung nehmen wollten. Ein Blick in die Archive zeigt allerdings, dass die Motive der Ausstellungsorganisatoren in Wirklichkeit viel komplexer waren.[2]

Die Entstehung des Organisationsteams

Die ersten Pläne, aus denen die Ausstellung *Twentieth Century German Art* hervorgehen sollte, wurden in London entwickelt – allerdings weder von Read noch von Sadler, sondern von der britischen Kunsthändlerin Noel ‹Peter› Norton (Abb. 35). Sie betrieb in der Cork Street die London Gallery, die auf moderne mitteleuropäische Kunst spezialisiert war. Diese Ausrichtung dürfte teilweise mit dem Beruf ihres Mannes zu tun gehabt haben: Als britischer Diplomat war Clifford Norton Mitte der 1930er Jahre Privatsekretär von Sir Robert Vansittart, einem erklärten Hitler-Gegner. Aufgrund der politischen Entwicklung in Deutschland begann Noel Norton im September 1937 darüber nachzudenken, verbotene deutsche Künstler in ihrer Galerie zu zeigen – im Rahmen einer kommerziellen Ausstellung, aber mit einer politischen Botschaft.[3]

Zur gleichen Zeit beschäftigte sich eine Galeristin in Zürich mit einem ähnlichen Projekt: Irmgard Burchard (Abb. 36). Sie hatte 1934 ihre Kunsthandlung gegründet, da sie feststellte, dass die in Deutschland verfolgten Künstler neue Märkte im Ausland suchten. Dank der guten Verbindungen ihres Mannes, des Malers und Graphikers Richard Paul Lohse, verkaufte sie ab 1936 von Zürich aus Werke deutscher und schweizerischer Künstler, unter anderem von Paul Klee und Willi Baumeister.[4] 1937 führten sie ihre Geschäfte nach London. Hier traf sie Noel Norton, worauf die beiden Galeristinnen Ende September beschlossen, gemeinsam eine Ausstellung mit dem Titel *Banned Art* (*Verbotene Kunst*) zu realisieren.[5]

Der dritte Name, der für die Londoner Ausstellung zentrale Bedeutung gewinnen sollte, war derjenige des deutsch-jüdischen Kunstkritikers Paul Westheim (Abb. 38). Während der Weimarer Repuplik hatte er sich als Gründer und Herausgeber der Zeitschrift *Das Kunstblatt* einen Namen gemacht[6] – mit der Konsequenz, dass er sich 1933 gezwungen sah, nach Paris ins Exil zu gehen, wo er sich weiterhin für die moderne Kunst einsetzte. Am 30. September 1937 gehörte er zu den Gründern des neuen, in Paris beheimateten Deutschen Künstlerbunds, dessen Hauptziel es war, ein Gegengewicht zur NS-Kulturpolitik zu etablieren. Kaum gegründet, beschloss die Gruppe, eine Ausstellung zu veranstalten, die «eine grundsätzliche Demonstration gegen die Münchner Ausstellung *Entartete Kunst* werden» sollte.[7]

Irgendwann gegen Ende September 1937 erfuhren Burchard und Norton durch gemeinsame Pariser Bekannte von den Plänen des neuen Künstlerbundes.[8] Daraufhin wandte sich Burchard an den jugoslawischen Autor Oto Bihalji-Merin, der in Zürich als Emigrant lebte, und bat ihn, mit Westheim Verbindung aufzunehmen, den er noch von Berlin her kannte.[9] Der Kontakt kam zustande, und der Künstlerbund erklärte sich nach anfänglichem Zögern zur Zusammenarbeit bereit. Trotz des kommerziellen Charakters des Projekts hegte er die Hoffnung, die Veranstaltung auch «nach Möglichkeit für die eigenen Ziele propagandistisch auswerten» zu können.[10] Daraufhin erhielt Westheim von der Norton Gallery gegen ein Honorar von 50 Pfund Sterling den Auftrag, Leihgaben für die Londoner Ausstellung zu acquirieren.[11]

Die Arbeiten beginnen

Ab Ende November 1937 arbeiteten Burchard, Norton und Westheim gemeinsam an der Vorbereitung der Ausstellung *Banned Art.* Trotz ihrer verschiedenartigen Hintergründe bildeten sie ein höchst effizientes Team, als es darum ging, Kunstwerke für das Projekt zu gewinnen.

Aufgrund seiner früheren Tätigkeit als Herausgeber des *Kunstblatts* besaß Westheim ausgezeichnete Verbindungen zu den kulturell interessierten Kreisen der deutschen Emigration in Paris. So hatte er direkten Zugang zu bedeutenden Sammlern, die er noch aus Berlin kannte, unter ihnen der Bankier und Politiker Hugo Simon oder der Textilindustrielle Erich Göritz.[12] Wo noch kein persönlicher Kontakt bestand, halfen ihm Empfehlungen früherer Kollegen weiter. Eine besondere Rolle spielte dabei Charlotte Weidler (Abb. 39). Sie hatte für das *Kunstblatt* gearbeitet, war nach 1933 aber in Berlin geblieben und vermittelte von dort Kunstwerke für die jährlich stattfindende Ausstellung der Carnegie Foundation in Pittsburgh.[13] In dieser Funktion konnte sie Reisen ins In- und Ausland unternehmen, ohne den Verdacht der Nazis zu erregen – eine Freiheit, die sie umgehend zugunsten der Londoner Ausstellung nutzte. Im November 1937 besuchte sie beispielsweise Max Pechstein, der weiterhin in Deutschland lebte, und erhielt von ihm eine Liste seiner wichtigsten ausländischen Sammler. Die Namen teilte sie anschließend Westheim mit (siehe Kat.-Nr. 16).

Nachdem Westheim und seine Kontaktpersonen auf diese Weise potentielle Leihgeber ausfindig gemachte hatten, trat Irmgard Burchard in Aktion. Dank ihres Schweizer Passes und ihres politisch unbelasteten Namens war sie prädestiniert, die in Aussicht genommenen Werke zusammenzutragen. Gegen Ende des Jahres 1937 reiste sie kreuz und quer durch Europa, um – mit Westheims Empfehlungsschreiben versehen – die Leihgaben zu sammeln.

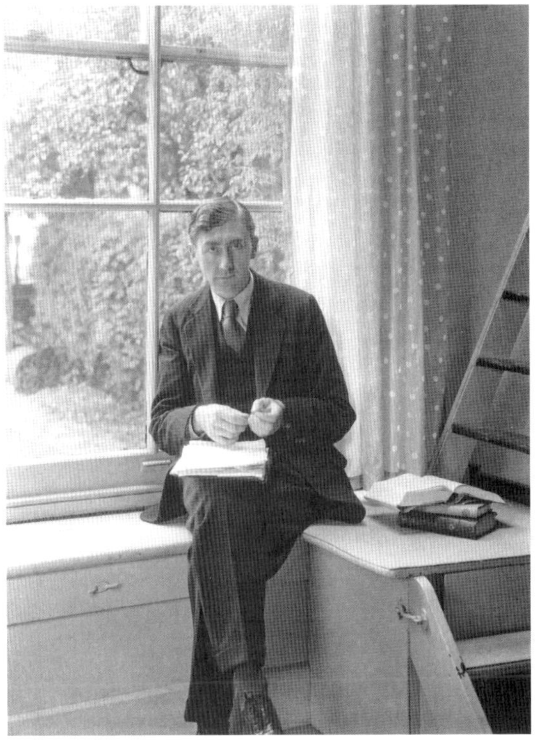

40 Herbert Read in London 1934

Gleichzeitig wählte sie selbst Exponate aus – zum einen Werke, die sie über ihre Galerie zum Verkauf angeboten hatte, zum anderen Bilder von bekannten Zürcher und Basler Sammlern (siehe Kat.-Nr. 3 und 25). Außerdem startete sie eine Rundbriefaktion und wandte sich an zahlreiche ‹entartete› Künstler mit der Bitte, Werke für die Londoner Ausstellung zur Verfügung zu stellen. Sie erhielt daraufhin viele Zusagen, unter anderem auch von Kurt Schwitters, der aus Hannover nach Norwegen geflüchtet war und von dort mindestens fünf Werke nach London schickte.[14]

Noel Norton brachte mit ihren Londoner Kontakten weitere herausragende Werke in Reichweite des Projekts. Zu ihren Nachbarn an der Cork Street zählte die amerikanische Erbin Peggy Guggenheim, die im Januar 1938 dort ihre Galerie Guggenheim Jeune eröffnete. Sie vermittelte der Ausstellung Werke von Kandinsky und Kokoschka. Noel Norton scheint es auch gewesen zu sein, die Herbert Read (Abb. 40) zur Mitwirkung an dem Projekt gewann. 1936 hatte Read bereits ein Vorwort zum Katalog einer Munch-Ausstellung der Norton Gallery verfasst. Ende Dezember 1937 sagte er zu, sich auch an der Auswahl und Hängung der Ausstellung *Banned Art* zu beteiligen.[15]

Weitere Unterstützung erhielt das Team von der aus Wien stammenden Kunsthistorikerin Edith Hoffmann (Abb. 37). Sie war die Tochter des tschechisch-jüdischen Diplomaten und Schriftstellers Camill Hoffmann, hatte in München studiert und lebte seit 1934 in London. Als deutschsprachige Kunsthistorikerin mit diplomatischem Pass und zahlreichen Kontakten aus der Welt ihres Vaters kam sie für Norton und Burchard wie gerufen. Im Dezember 1937 wurde sie ebenfalls in das Vorbereitungsteam aufgenommen, unternahm Reisen auf den Kontinent und half bei der Sammlung von Kunstwerken.[16]

Gegensätzliche Motivation

In weniger als einem Dreiviertel Jahr brachten es die Organisatoren fertig, mehr als 90 Leihgeber für die Londoner Ausstellung zu gewinnen. Wie dem Katalogteil des vorliegenden Bandes (siehe S. 94-150) entnommen werden kann, war die Leihgeberschaft äußerst heterogen. Sie bestand aus Schweizern, Briten, deutschen Emigranten, Museen, Kunsthändlern, Privatsammlern und den ‹entarteten› Künstlern selbst.

Berücksichtigt man die Entwicklung des Projekts im Winter 1937/38, so zeigt sich allerdings, dass Westheim, Norton und Burchard in ihren Zielen keineswegs übereinstimmten.

Beispielsweise schrieb Noel Norton am 1. Dezember einen Brief an ihre Partner und teilte mit, dass sie beabsichtige, beim Titel und Spektrum der Werke Änderungen vorzunehmen. Obwohl sie weiterhin für die Verteidigung der deutschen Moderne in London eintreten wollte, waren ihr beim Titel *Banned Art* Bedenken gekommen, da eine Ausstellung unter diesem Vorzeichen negative Auswirkungen auf die Karriere ihres Mannes haben konnte. Der Titel müsse deswegen durch einen politisch neutralen ersetzt werden: *Twentieth Century German Art*. Auch sollten Künstler berücksichtigt werden, die vom deutschen Regime ‹offiziell anerkannt› waren.[17]

Weder Burchard noch Westheim waren über die Änderung des Titels überrascht; beide hatten schon verschiedentlich negative Reaktionen darauf gehört, insbesondere aus der Schweiz.[18] Entschieden ablehnend zeigten sie sich jedoch gegenüber dem Vorschlag, auch ‹offiziell anerkannte› deutsche Künstler in die Ausstellung aufzunehmen. Sowohl Westheim wie Burchard reagierten darauf mit einem Protestbrief, setzten ihre Arbeit aber fort.[19] Westheim war vor allem über die Art irritiert, wie Norton die Entscheidung im Alleingang getroffen hatte. So schrieb er am 10. Dezember: «Unnötig zu sagen, dass es mir angenehm gewesen wäre und auch meinen Erwartungen entsprochen hätte, wenn man mich vor der Entscheidung unterrichtet hätte.»[20] Zuletzt wurde in der Ausstellung allerdings nur ein einziges Werk eines ‹offiziellen› Künstlers gezeigt: Georg Kolbes Bronzekopf des Kunsthändlers Paul Cassirer aus der Sammlung Hugo Simon.

Je länger der Dezember ging, desto mehr sah sich Westheim durch Noel Nortons Arbeitsweise vor den Kopf gestoßen. Kurz vor Weihnachten wurde ihr Ehemann Clifford an die britische Botschaft in Warschau versetzt,[21] worauf beide London binnen weniger Tage verließen und Noel Norton's Beteiligung an dem Ausstellungsprojekt ein Ende fand – was auch den Wegfall der Räumlichkeiten bedeutete. Westheim reagierte empört und informierte Burchard am 28. Januar, dass er «mit diesem Projekt nichts [mehr] zu tun habe. [...] Sie kennen auch die Gründe, den Bluff, die falschen Angaben, die Art, wie ich geneppt worden bin.»[22]

Irmgard Burchard ihrerseits blieb unerschütterlich und arbeitete weiter. Eine Generation jünger als Westheim und Norton, war sie erst vor drei Jahren in den Kunsthandel eingestiegen; die geplante Ausstellung hatte sie beruflich in eine neue Liga katapultiert, und die Chance, mit den führenden europäischen Künstlern, Galeristen und Sammlern zusammenzuarbeiten, konnte sie nicht leichtfertig aufgegeben. So versuchte sie in den ersten Wochen des Jahres 1938 die Korrespondenz mit den Leihgebern aufrecht zu erhalten und mit Hilfe Herbert Reads neue Ausstellungsräume zu finden, während sie zugleich fortfuhr, zur Beschaffung der Leihgaben durch Europa zu reisen. Schon im Februar zahlte sich ihr Engagement aus: Nachdem Read zugesagt hatte, als neuer «Vorsitzender des Organisationskomitees» zu fungieren, konnte sie die New Burlington Galleries (Abb. 41) als Ausstellungsort gewinnen. Die

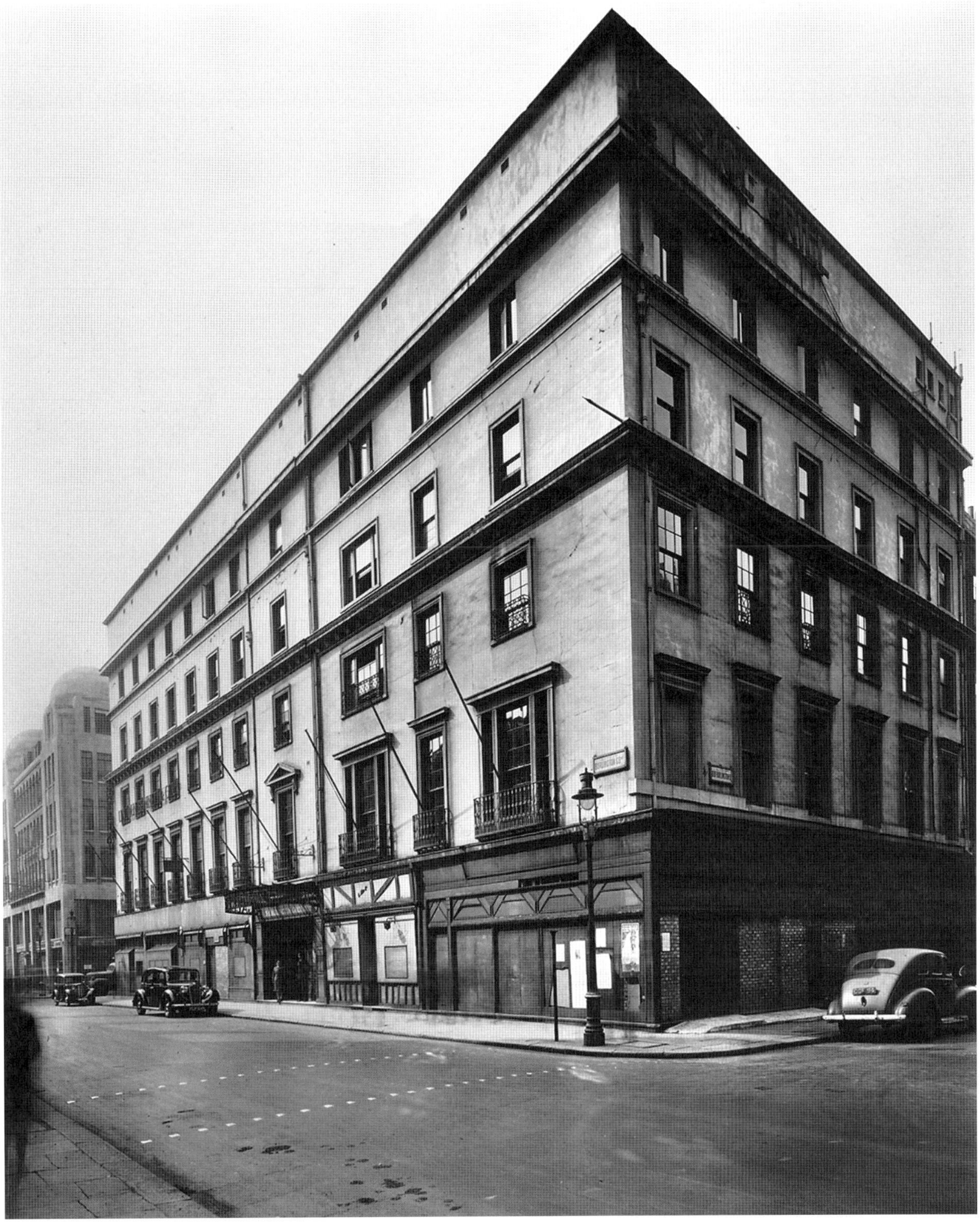

41 3-5 Burlington Gardens, Westminster, 1946. Die New Burlington Galleries hatten ihre Räume im vierten Stock des Gebäudes.

Räume befanden sich im vierten Stock eines Gebäudes in den Burlington Gardens und waren durch die erste Surrealisten-Ausstellung in England bekannt geworden, die 1936 unter der Leitung von Herbert Read dort stattgefunden hatte,[23] gefolgt von einer ebenfalls viel beachteten Retrospektive *Masters of French 19th Century Painting* im Oktober gleichen Jahres.[24] Oder, wie Charlotte Weidler am 23. Februar an Westheim schrieb: «Burlington ist natürlich fabelhaft und sehr seriös. Da werden ja die Nazis sicher grün und blau vor Ärger werden.»[25]

Einerlei, ob von der Aussicht angespornt, den Nazis ein Ärgernis bereiten zu können, oder verlockt vom außerordentlichen Renommee, das die New Burlington Galleries genossen – im März begann Westheim die Arbeit für *Twentieth Century German Art* wieder aufzunehmen, ohne sich an der Neutralität des Titels oder der Berücksichtigung eines ‹offiziell anerkannten› Plastikers wie Kolbe weiter zu stören.

Allerdings ging es nicht lange, und Westheim sah sich erneut von seinen Partnern brüskiert. Noch im März geriet er in Empörung, als Burchard ihm indirekt zu verstehen gab, durch seine vorübergehende Demission sei Zeit verloren gegangen. Kaum zwei Wochen später erfuhr er von Gerüchten, wonach beabsichtigt war, die Ausstellung von London nach Paris zu schicken, ohne den Deutschen Künstlerbund dabei zu involvieren.[26] Daraufhin schrieb Westheim am 6. April einen Brief an Herbert Read und erklärte das Ende seiner Mitwirkung am Londoner Projekt. Als Gründe gab er Burchards Verhalten und das Ausbleiben einer angemessenen Entschuldigung an.[27]

Enttäuschung und Sabotage

Westheims Brief an Read vom 6. April, mit dem er seine Mitarbeit an *Twentieth Century German Art* aufkündigte, kreuzte sich mit einem Schreiben gleichen Datums von Read an Westheim. Ohne von Westheims Bruch mit dem Projekt zu wissen, berichtete Read von weiteren Veränderungen, die er im Hinblick auf die öffentliche Wirkung der Ausstellung beabsichtigte. So sollte Westheim nach außen hin nicht mehr namentlich erwähnt werden: «Um jeden Anschein zu vermeiden, dass diese Ausstellung eine Unternehmung von Juden oder Emigranten sei, haben wir der Öffentlichkeit gegenüber sorgfältig alle Namen ausgeschlossen, die in diesem Sinne ausgelegt werden könnten.»[28]

Was trieb Read dazu, nur wenige Wochen vor Eröffnung der Ausstellung solche Änderungen vorzunehmen? Der Sommer 1938 bezeichnet bekanntlich den Höhepunkt der britischen Appeasement-Politik gegenüber Nazi-Deutschland – mit dem Ergebnis der Unterzeichnung des Münchner Abkommens durch Chamberlain und Hitler am 30. September.[29] Dennoch ist nicht erwiesen, dass diese politischen Entwicklungen eine private Kunstausstellung derart beeinflusst haben. Wahrscheinlicher ist, dass Read befürchtete, das Stichwort ‹Juden und Emigranten› könne die Attraktivität der Ausstellung beim Londoner Kunst-Publikum in Frage stellen. Seit der ersten Welle russischer Emigration fünfzig Jahre zuvor verfolgte das Gespenst des jüdischen Einwanderers die britische Phantasie. Extreme antisemitsche Aktionen wie in Deutschland waren zwar die Ausnahme geblieben, doch bestand ein hoher Erwartungsdruck zur Assimiliation, um nicht zur Zielscheibe von Diskriminierung zu werden.[30] Reads persönliches Engagement für die Flüchtlinge aus NS-Deutschland ist zwar gut dokumentiert.[31] Gleichwohl offenbart sein Brief an Westheim die Sorge, dass die erklärte Beteiligung jüdischer Emigranten an der Ausstellung *Twentieth Century German Art* bei einer breiteren Öffentlichkeit auf Vorbehalte stoßen könnte.

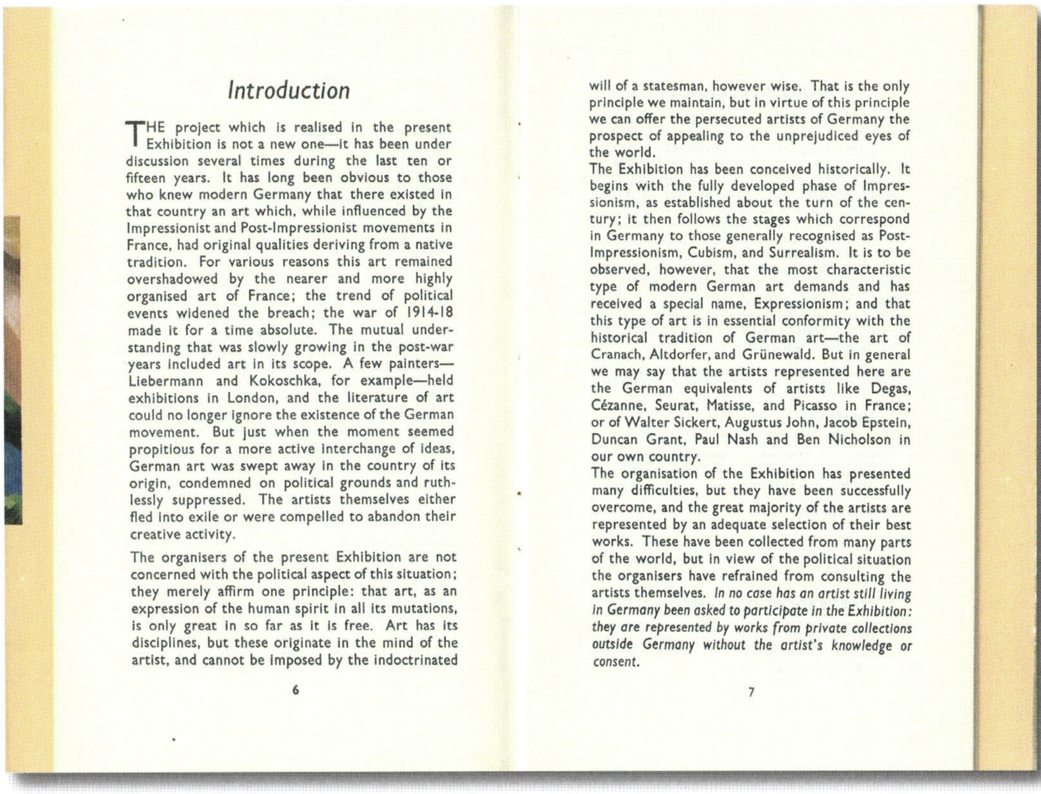

Introduction

THE project which is realised in the present Exhibition is not a new one—it has been under discussion several times during the last ten or fifteen years. It has long been obvious to those who knew modern Germany that there existed in that country an art which, while influenced by the Impressionist and Post-Impressionist movements in France, had original qualities deriving from a native tradition. For various reasons this art remained overshadowed by the nearer and more highly organised art of France; the trend of political events widened the breach; the war of 1914-18 made it for a time absolute. The mutual understanding that was slowly growing in the post-war years included art in its scope. A few painters—Liebermann and Kokoschka, for example—held exhibitions in London, and the literature of art could no longer ignore the existence of the German movement. But just when the moment seemed propitious for a more active interchange of ideas, German art was swept away in the country of its origin, condemned on political grounds and ruthlessly suppressed. The artists themselves either fled into exile or were compelled to abandon their creative activity.

The organisers of the present Exhibition are not concerned with the political aspect of this situation; they merely affirm one principle: that art, as an expression of the human spirit in all its mutations, is only great in so far as it is free. Art has its disciplines, but these originate in the mind of the artist, and cannot be imposed by the indoctrinated

6

will of a statesman, however wise. That is the only principle we maintain, but in virtue of this principle we can offer the persecuted artists of Germany the prospect of appealing to the unprejudiced eyes of the world.

The Exhibition has been conceived historically. It begins with the fully developed phase of Impressionism, as established about the turn of the century; it then follows the stages which correspond in Germany to those generally recognised as Post-Impressionism, Cubism, and Surrealism. It is to be observed, however, that the most characteristic type of modern German art demands and has received a special name, Expressionism; and that this type of art is in essential conformity with the historical tradition of German art—the art of Cranach, Altdorfer, and Grünewald. But in general we may say that the artists represented here are the German equivalents of artists like Degas, Cézanne, Seurat, Matisse, and Picasso in France; or of Walter Sickert, Augustus John, Jacob Epstein, Duncan Grant, Paul Nash and Ben Nicholson in our own country.

The organisation of the Exhibition has presented many difficulties, but they have been successfully overcome, and the great majority of the artists are represented by an adequate selection of their best works. These have been collected from many parts of the world, but in view of the political situation the organisers have refrained from consulting the artists themselves. *In no case has an artist still living in Germany been asked to participate in the Exhibition: they are represented by works from private collections outside Germany without the artist's knowledge or consent.*

7

42 Katalog der Ausstellung *Twentieth Century German Art*, Einleitung

Westheim wiederum sah sich durch Reads Brief nicht nur in seiner Entscheidung bestätigt, die Mitwirkung an der Ausstellung aufzugeben; das Schreiben veranlasste ihn sogar, das Projekt von nun an aktiv zu sabotieren. Er schrieb an Künstler und beschwor sie, ihre Beteiligung zu widerrufen. Außerdem startete er eine Serie von Artikeln in der Pariser Emigrantenpresse, in denen er die politische Neutralität der Ausstellung kritisierte.[32] Zuletzt organisierten er und der Deutsche Künstlerbund eine eigene Gegen-Ausstellung zur *Entarteten Kunst*, die im November 1938 unter dem Titel *Freie Deutsche Kunst* in Paris stattfand.[33]

Reads Brief vom 6. April enthüllte Westheim einen Aspekt der britischen Gesellschaft, der ihm bis dahin verborgen geblieben war. Während er womöglich gehofft hatte, über die Ausstellung seine Position als führender Kritiker und Kunsthistoriker wiederzuerlangen, musste er nun feststellen, dass er für Read und dessen britische Landsleute in erster Linie unter zwei Kategorien unerwünschter Menschen fiel: Juden und Emigranten. Die daraus resultierende Empörung und Enttäuschung mag andererseits zeigen, welch großen Optimismus Westheim mit der Ausstellung *Twentieth Century German Art* ursprünglich verband – nicht nur im Sinne einer Gelegenheit, den Nazis entgegenzutreten, sondern auch als Chance, in Großbritannien seine Karriere weiterzuführen.

Eröffnung der Ausstellung

Im Frühsommer 1938 wurden – unter Leitung von Irmgard Burchard – über 300 Kunstwerke nach London transportiert, wobei in der Korrespondenz des Organisationsteams sogar von 600 Werken die Rede ist.[34] Im unbebilderten Ausstellungskatalog sind allerdings nur 271 Exponate aufgelistet, alphabetisch nach Künstlern und mit Titeln auf Englisch oder Französisch, manchmal auch mit Maßangaben und Hinweisen auf frühere Ausstellungen.

Wie von Read angekündigt, taucht Westheims Name weder im Katalog (Abb. 34) noch in den Werbeprospekten der Ausstellung auf. Von den ursprünglichen Initianten ist Irmgard Buchard die einzige, die Erwähnung findet; im Katalog ist sie als «honorary organiser» genannt. Um die Distanz der Ausstellung zur politischen Situation in Deutschland zu unterstreichen , betonte Read in seiner Einleitung zum Katalog (Abb. 42): «Die Organisatoren der Ausstellung haben mit Politik nichts zu tun.»[35]

Ungeachtet des dezidiert britischen Auftretens der Ausstellung war *Twentieth Century German Art* ein durch und durch internationales Projekt. Zusammengebracht von Briten, Schweizern und deutschen Emigranten, versammelte es Werke aus Sammlungen in ganz Europa. Zugleich diente das Vorhaben jeder der beteiligten Personen zu unterschiedlichen Zwecken: Einerseits bot es die Möglichkeit, ein Statement gegen das NS-Regime zu artikulieren, andererseits verfolgte es das kommerzielle Interesse, Kunstwerke zu verkaufen, und schließlich bot es die Chance, Karriere als Kunsthändlerin zu machen oder sich im Exil weiter als Autor und Kritiker zu behaupten. Dass es dabei zu einem Bruch zwischen den Organisatoren kam, belegt nur, wie groß die Hoffnungen waren, die alle Beteiligten an den Erfolg der Londoner Ausstellung knüpften.

1 Siehe Adrian Glew: «Blue Spiritual Sounds». Kandinsky and the Sadlers, 1911-1916, in: Burlington Magazine, Bd. 139, Nr. 1134, September 1997, S. 600-615; sowie Ben Read/David Thistlewood (Hg.): Herbert Read. A British Vision of World Art, London 1993.

2 Eine detaillierte Beschreibung der Ausstellung *Twentieth Century German Art*, ihrer Organisation, Leihgeber und Auswirkungen wird im folgenden, bald erscheinenden Buch zu lesen sein: Lucy Wasensteiner, The Twentieth Century German Art Exhibition. Answering Degenerate Art in 1930s London, New York. Der vorliegende Essay wurde hauptsächlich auf der Grundlage von Dokumenten aus folgenden Archiven geschrieben: Rossiiskii Gosudarstvenni Voennyi Arkhiv, Moskau; Sonderarchiv, Fond 602, Paul Westheim (i. F. «RSMA»); Akademie der Künste Berlin, Sammlung Eugen Spiro (i. F. «AdK»).

3 RSMA, Brief von Patrick Blackwood an Paul Westheim, 14. Februar [1938].

4 Lucy Watling: The Irmgard Burchard Tableaux. An Anti-Nazi Dealership in 1930s Switzerland, in: Eva Blimlinger/Monika Mayer (Hg.): Kunst Sammeln, Kunst Handeln, Wien 2012, S. 234-242.

5 RSMA, Brief von Irmgard Burchard an Noel Norton, 5. Dezember 1937.

6 Siehe Keith Holz: Scenes from Exile in Western Europe, in: Stephane Barron/Sabine Eckmann (Hg.): Exiles and Émigrés. The Flight of European Artists from Hitler, Los Angeles 1997, S. 43-56.

7 AdK, Gründungsdokument und erstes Protokoll des Deutschen Künstlerbundes, 30. September 1937.

8 RSMA, Brief von Charlotte Weidler an Paul Westheim, 1. Juni 1938

9 RSMA, Brief von Oto Bihalji-Merin an Paul Westheim, 11. Oktober 1937. Für mehr Informationen über Bihalji-Merin siehe den Essay von David Elliott, S. 161-167.

10 AdK, Protokoll einer Sitzung des Deutschen Künstlerbundes, 17. November 1937.

11 RSMA, Brief von Patrick Blackwood an Paul Westheim, 18. November 1937.

12 Siehe Kat.-Nr. 12 und 8.

13 Siehe Ines Rotermund-Reynard: Geheime Netzwerke. Charlotte Weidlers Briefe an den Kunstkritiker Paul Westheim (1933-1940), in: Burcu Dogramaci/Karin Wimmer: Netzwerke des Exils. Künstlerische Verflechtungen, Austausch und Patronage nach 1933, Berlin 2011, S. 261-276.

14 Sprengel Museum Hannover/Kurt und Ernst Schwitters Stiftung, Brief von Irmgard Burchard an Kurt Schwitters, 15. Juni 1938.

15 RSMA, Brief der London Gallery an Paul Westheim, 1. Dezember 1937.

16 RSMA, Brief von Patrick Blackwood an Paul Westheim, 8. Dezember 1937. Für die biographischen Informationen über Edith Hoffmann danken wir Yonna Yapou-Kromholz.

17 RSMA, Brief der London Gallery an Paul Westheim, 1. Dezember 1937. Zu Noel Nortons Bedenken bezüg-

lich negativer Folgen auf die Karriere ihres Mannes siehe RSMA, Brief von Charlotte Weidler an Paul Westheim, 1. Juni 1938; Weidler berichtet darin über eine entsprechende Unterhaltung mit Noel Norton.

18 RSMA, Mitteilung von Irmgard Burchard an die anderen Veranstalter vom 28. November 1938, in welcher sie ihre Partner darum bat, den Titel «Verbannte Kunst» nicht weiter zu benutzen, weil sie diesbezüglich negative Äußerungen aus der Schweiz erhalten hatte.

19 RSMA, Brief von Irmgard Burchard an Noel Norton, 5. Dezember 1937, sowie Brief von Paul Westheim an Noel Norton, 10. Dezember 1937.

20 RSMA, Brief von Paul Westheim an Noel Norton, 10. Dezember 1937.

21 Die Versetzung fiel mit der Abschiebung von Unterstaatssekretär Vansittart auf einen unbedeutenden Posten zusammen. Im Dezember 1937 war Premierminister Chamberlain offensichtlich darum bemüht, die Gegner seiner Appeasement-Politik auszuschalten. Siehe dazu Frank McDonough: Neville Chamberlain. Appeasement and the British Road to War, Manchester u. a. 1998, S. 52.

22 RSMA, Brief von Paul Westheim an Irmgard Burchard, 28. Januar 1938.

23 International Surrealist Exhibition, 1936.

24 An dieser Ausstellung, die ebenfalls als Retrospektive über die Kunstepoche eines Landes gedacht war, hatte Alfred Flechtheim wesentlichen Anteil, der auch schon bei der Surrealisten-Ausstellung konzeptuell mitgewirkt hatte; vgl. Ottfried Dascher: «Es ist was Wahnsinniges mit der Kunst». Alfred Flechtheim – Sammler, Kunsthändler, Verleger. Mit einer Bibliographie von Rudolf Schmitt-Föller und einer Stammtafel von Rico Quaschny. Wädenswil 2011, S. 372-373.

25 RSMA, Brief von Charlotte Weidler an Paul Westheim, 23. Februar 1938.

26 RSMA, Brief von Paul Westheim an Irmgard Burchard, 24. März 1938, und Brief von Paul Westheim an Herbert Read, 2. April 1938.

27 RSMA, Brief von Paul Westheim an Herbert Read, 6. April 1938.

28 RSMA, Brief von Herbert Read an Paul Westheim, 6. April 1938.

29 Siehe McDonough.

30 Siehe u. a. Jodi Burkett: Anti-Semitism and Racism in Britain. Assessing the Reaction to and the Legacy of Kristallnacht, in: Colin McCullough/Nathan Wilson (Hg.): Violence, Memory and History. Western Perceptions of Kristallnacht, New York u. a. 2015, S. 16-33.

31 Siehe u. a. Read/Thistlewood und James King: The Last Modern. A Life of Herbert Read, London 1990.

32 Siehe u. a. Paul Westheim: Die Vandalen: Der zerschnittene Kokoschka, wird er in London ausgestellt?, in: Pariser Tageszeitung, 7. Juli 1938, S. 3, sowie: Kulturchronik: Ein Seltsamer Katalog, in: Pariser Tageszeitung, 23. Juli 1938, S. 3, und: Ausstellung 20th Century German Art, in: Freie Kunst und Literatur, September 1938, S. unbekannt. Darüber hinaus zeigen Briefe in verschiedenen Künstlerarchiven (IMEC Abbaye d'Ardenne, Collection Otto Freundlich, Zentralbibliothek Zürich, Oskar Kokoschka Collection), dass Westheim jene Künstler beschwor, ihre Beteiligung an der Ausstellung zu wiederrufen.

33 Bezüglich der Pariser Ausstellung siehe u. a. Holz, S. 195-240.

34 RSMA, Brief von Paul Westheim an Bruno Frei, 22. August 1938.

35 Obwohl die Einleitung des Katalogs nicht namentlich gezeichnet ist, deuten manche Ähnlichkeiten zwischen diesem Text und dem von Read verfassten Vorwort zu Peter Thoenes Buch *Modern German Art* von Peter (London 1938) darauf hin, dass der anonyme Text von Read stammt.

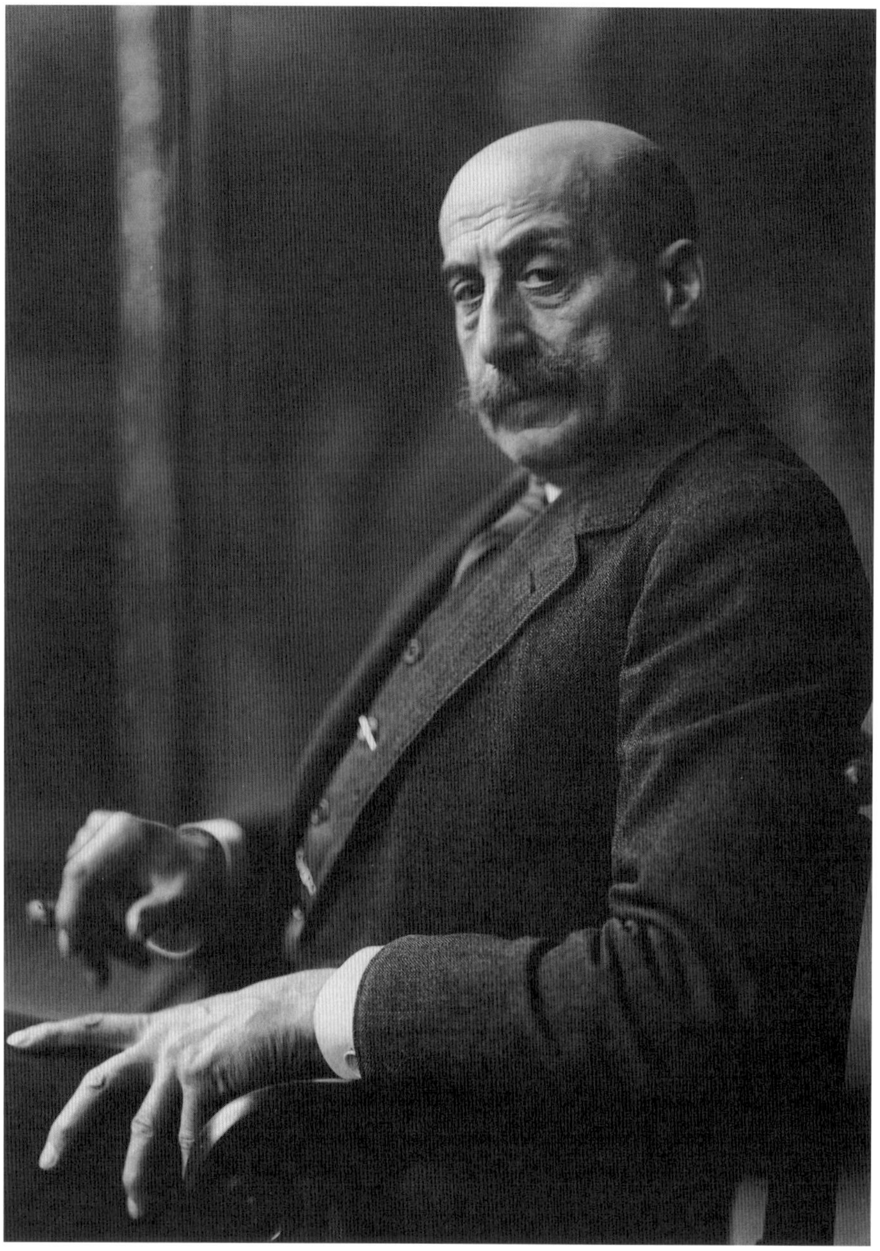

43 Max Liebermann, um 1930

Nur noch im Ausland als deutscher Künstler geehrt: Liebermann-Ausstellungen zwischen 1933 und 1938

MARTIN FAASS

«So peripher es in der Rückschau aussehen mag, der kulturelle Bereich war der erste, aus dem die Juden (und ‹Linke›) in großem Umfang vertrieben wurden»,[1] merkt Saul Friedländer an. Fast unmittelbar nach der Machtübernahme begann der Exodus jüdischer und linker Intellektueller aus Deutschland. Am 18. März verließ der Philosoph und Literaturkritiker Walter Benjamin Berlin, um nach Paris zu gehen. Die Dirigenten Otto Klemperer und Bruno Walter sahen sich zur Flucht gezwungen. Innerhalb weniger Wochen wurden die jüdischen Kulturschaffenden in Deutschland ihrer rechtlichen und sozialen Stellung beraubt und als Fremdkörper in der deutschen Gesellschaft stigmatisiert.

Als eine der bedeutendsten Kulturinstitutionen der Hauptstadt geriet auch die Preußische Akademie der Künste Berlin schnell in den Fokus der neuen Machthaber – und damit auch deren langjähriger Präsident Max Liebermann, der seit 1932 sogar Ehrenpräsident war (Abb. 43). Am 6. Februar 1933, wenige Tage nach dem politischen Umsturz, wurde der Nationalsozialist Bernhard Rust zum Minister für Kunst, Wissenschaft und Volksbildung in Preußen ernannt. Eine seiner ersten Maßnahmen war die ‹Säuberung› der Preußischen Akademie der Künste. Rust drohte offen damit, die Akademie zu schließen, falls ihr Präsident, Max von Schillings, nicht dafür sorgen würde, missliebige Künstler wie Käthe Kollwitz und Heinrich Mann zu entfernen. Das «Gesetz zur Wiederherstellung des Berufsbeamtentum» vom 7. April 1933 bot schließlich die Handhabe, alle jüdischen Mitglieder auszuschließen. Auf Anweisung des Ministers fanden diese Regelungen auch auf die Mitglieder der Akademie Anwendung, obwohl sie keinen Beamtenstatus hatten. Betroffen waren zunächst die Mitglieder der Abteilung Dichtung. Die ‹Säuberung› der Abteilung bildende Künste, der Max Liebermann seit über 35 Jahren angehörte, sollte am 15. Mai 1933 folgen. Dem ehrabschneidenden Ausschluss aus der Akademie kam Liebermann zuvor, indem er am 7. Mai presseöffentlich von allen seinen Ämtern zurücktrat.

Jetzt wurde es still um Max und Martha Liebermann. «Die Mitglieder der Berliner Gesellschaft, die jahrzehntelang um eine Einladung bei Liebermanns gebuhlt hatten, mieden nun das Haus am Pariser Platz. [...] Der greise Malerfürst, der nicht nur Jude war, sondern dem man darüber hinaus auch noch Sympathien für die bürgerliche Linke nachsagte, wurde zu einer Belastung.»[2]

Obwohl Liebermanns Werke in den Räumen der Nationalgalerie vom neuen Direktor Eberhard Hanfstaengl mit ministerieller Zustimmung zunächst unangetastet blieben, wurden sie aus den Sonderausstellungen anderer Museen, Galerien und Kunstvereine in Deutschland, die den berühmten Maler in den Jahren zuvor noch mit Bitten um Ausstellungsbeteiligungen bedrängten hatten, binnen kurzem entfernt. Einzig jüdische Kulturinstitutionen, wie die jüdischen Museen in Berlin und Frankfurt, boten für Ausstellungen mit Liebermann-Werken eine von den Nationalsozialisten gebilligte, vom Rest des deutschen Kulturlebens separierte Nische. Ähnlich wie der 1933 gegründete Kulturbund Deutscher Juden waren sie Teil eines behördlich überwachten parallelen Kulturbetriebes, zu dem ausschließlich Künstler und Werke zugelassen waren, die von der Zensur als jüdisch und/oder als nicht deutsch angesehen wurden. So fanden zwischen 1933 und 1945 die beiden einzigen Liebermann-Ausstellungen in Deutschland im Jüdischen Museum in Frankfurt und im Jüdischen Museum Berlin statt. Es handelte sich dabei um Gedenkausstellungen, die nach dem Tod des Künstlers im Jahr 1935 organisiert wurden.

Nur im Ausland war es für Liebermann noch möglich, in seinem alten Recht als herausragende Persönlichkeit der Deutschen Kunst wahrgenommen und ausgestellt zu werden. Deshalb kommen den Ausstellungen in der Schweiz, England und Österreich besondere Bedeutung zu. «Seitdem ich alle öffentlichen Ämter niedergelegt habe und als ‹privater› Maler lebe und arbeite», schrieb Liebermann am 9. November 1934 an Sir William Rothenstein, den Direktor des Royal College of Art in London, «hab ich im Ausland, in Zürich, Amsterdam mit Erfolg ausgestellt und namentlich Bilder, die ich in den letzten Jahren gemalt habe. Dazu haben mir ein paar befreundete Besitzer einige zur Verfügung gestellt, sodaß eine Übersicht über mein Schaffen seit nunmehr 65 Jahren – unglaublich aber wahr! – kenntlich wird.»[3]

Die erste in der Reihe der von Liebermann genannten Ausstellungen fand vom 8. April bis 2. Mai 1933 in der Zürcher Galerie Aktuaryus statt. Liebermann zeigte hier 55 Gemälde und 49 Druckgraphiken. Die Leihgaben für diese Ausstellung kamen zu einem großen Teil von Liebermann selbst und vermutlich Privatsammlern aus seinem Umfeld. Die Ausstellung war für Gotthard Jedlicka, der als Berater der Galerie und Redakteur der Hauszeitschrift *Galerie und Sammler* tätig war, Anlass, den deutschen Künstler in einem Essay als «Klassiker einer wirklichkeitsnahen Kunst»[4] zu feiern. In einem Sammelband, der 1933 unter dem Titel «Begegnungen» erschien, veröffentliche Jedlicka darüber hinaus einen ausführlichen Bericht über seinen Besuch bei Max Liebermann. Dankbar über so viel Aufmerksamkeit schrieb Liebermann im Dezember: «Sehr verehrter Herr Jedlicka, gestern erhielt ich vom Verleger Ihr Buch zugesandt: inzwischen habe ich es mit großem Vergnügen gelesen u ich sage Ihnen besten Dank, auch dafür dass Sie mich, der ich in Deutschland boykottiert bin, dem Auslande gegenüber in so liebenswürdige Erinnerung bringen.»[5]

Die erbarmungslose Ausgrenzung der Juden nahm im Frühjahr 1934 konkrete Formen an. Im Februar 1934 ordnete Reichswehrminister Werner von Blomberg an, dass der Arier-Paragraph auf das Militär anzuwenden sei. Weniger als einen Monat später verkündete Propagandaminister Goebbels, dass prinzipiell alle Juden aus der Reichskulturkammer ausgeschlossen bleiben und damit keine Möglichkeit mehr erhalten sollten, sich am kulturellen Leben in Deutschland zu beteiligen.

Daher war Max Liebermann umso mehr erfreut, als William Rothenstein im gleichen Jahr eine Liebermann-Ausstellung für die Leicester Galleries in London organisierte. «Ihr Brief hat mich ausserordentlich erfreut», schrieb der Künstler, «denn er bestätigte mir (was mir bereits Herr Flechtheim gesagt u geschrieben hatte), daß Sie mir in Ihren freundschaftlichen Gesinnungen treu, wie seit vielen Jahrzehnten, geblieben sind. Wie dankbar ich

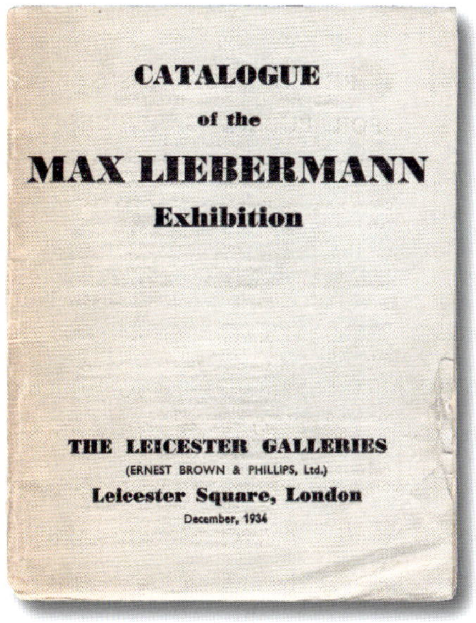

44 Katalog der Liebermann-Ausstellung in den Londoner Leicester Galleries, 1934

Ihnen für das opferwillige Interresse, mit dem Sie sich meiner Ausstellung in den Leicester Galleries angenommen haben, bin, kann ich Ihnen nicht sagen. Ohne Sie wäre die Sache einfach unmöglich gewesen, ja sogar bis Juli 1932 hätte auch der ‹phantasievollste Kunsthändler› kaum daran gedacht, einen Fünf und Achtzigjährigen in London in einer Ausstellung zu zeigen.»[6]

Rothenstein, selbst Künstler, bemühte sich, mit der Ausstellung eine repräsentative Übersicht zu Liebermanns Schaffen bieten zu können. Unterstützt wurde er dabei von einer Gruppe namhafter Londoner Persönlichkeiten, einem Committee of Honour, darunter Sir Thomans Barlow, Sir Kenneth Clark (Direktor der National Gallery), Prof. W. G. Constable (Direktor des Courtauld Institutes), James Manson (Direktor der Tate Gallery) und Sir Michael Sadler, die vier Jahre später auch zum Erfolg der Ausstellung *Twentieth Century German Art* beitragen sollten. Gezeigt wurden insgesamt 28 Zeichnungen, 5 Pastelle und 27 Gemälde, überwiegend Werke aus den zwanziger und dreißiger Jahren, aber auch zahlreiche aus früheren Schaffensphasen (Abb. 44). Die ausgestellten Arbeiten kamen bis auf drei von Liebermann selbst und von Sammlern aus Deutschland – unter anderem vom Chemnitzer Textilindustriellen Karl Göritz, der drei Jahre vor seiner Emigration nach Holland das Gemälde *Polospieler im Jenisch Park* (1912, Abb. 50) an die Leicester Galleries schickte. Liebermann schrieb an Rothenstein: «Zugleich mit diesen Zeilen gehn 25 Ölbilder etwa, ebensoviel Zeichnungen, Pastelle an die Leicester Galleries ab: was Sie davon ungeeignet halten, lassen Sie einfach zurück.»[7]

Wie wichtig für Liebermann die Ausstellung in der Leicester Galleries in den letzten Monaten seines Lebens war, geht aus einem Brief hervor, den er nur zwei Wochen vor seinem Tod, am 14. Januar 1935, seiner Frau Martha an Rothenstein diktierte: «Seit nunmehr zwei Monaten verhindert mich eine Grippe und deren Folgen Ihnen selbst meinen Dank für Ihre freundliche Hilfe und Sorge für meine Londoner Ausstellung zu sagen, an deren Erfolg Sie so großen Anteil haben. Ich wartete von Woche zu Woche auf Besserung, und muß nun doch, da die Zeit weiter fortschreitet, mich zu meinem Dank der Hand meiner Frau bedienen. Ohne die Freude und Genugtuung die mir Ihre Freundschaft und die Collegialität der englischen Künstler bereitet haben, hätte ich diese schreckliche Zeit der Krankheit wohl nicht überstanden.»[8]

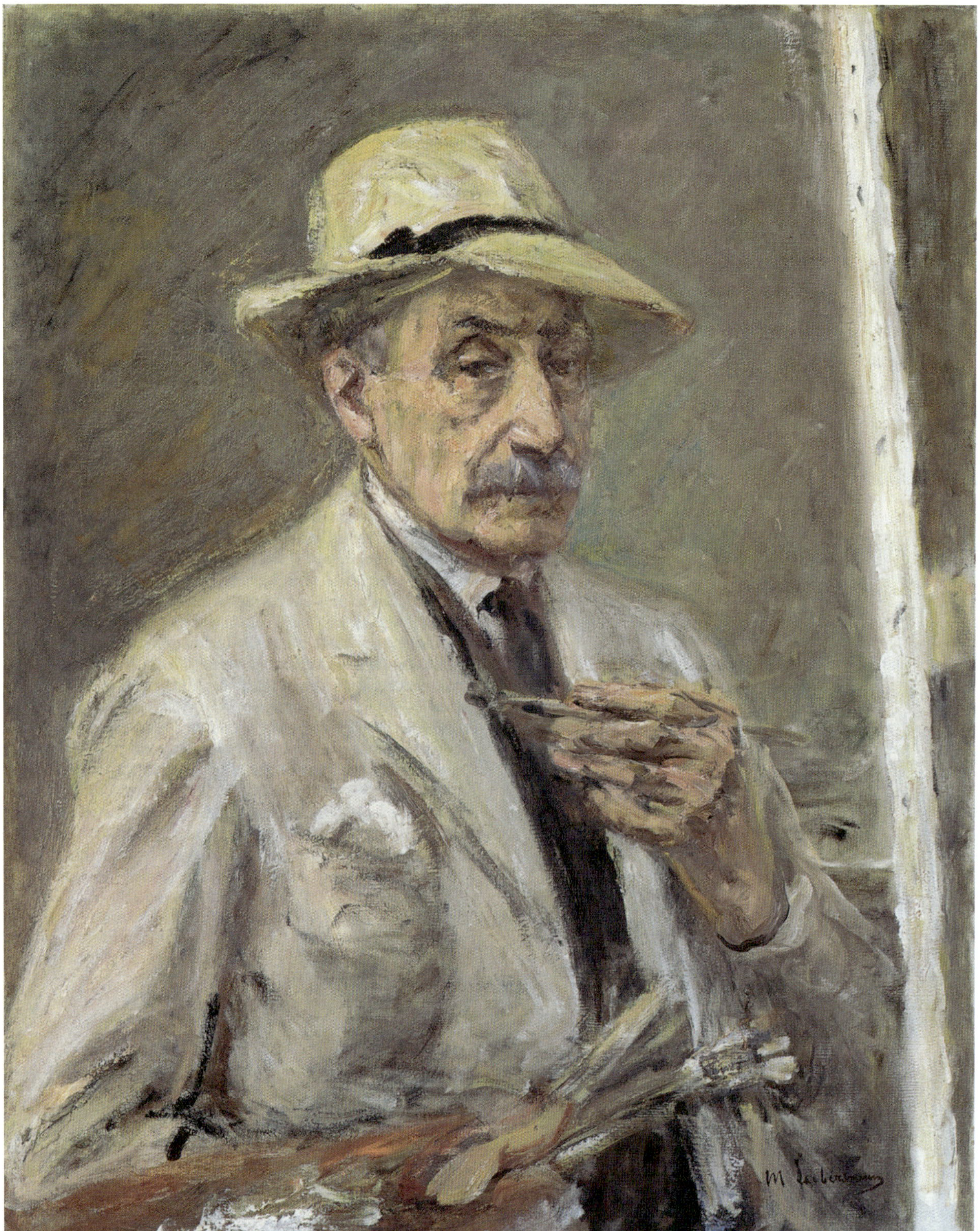

45 Max Liebermann, *Selbstbildnis*, 1934. Öl auf Leinwand, 92 x 73.5 cm. Tate Gallery London

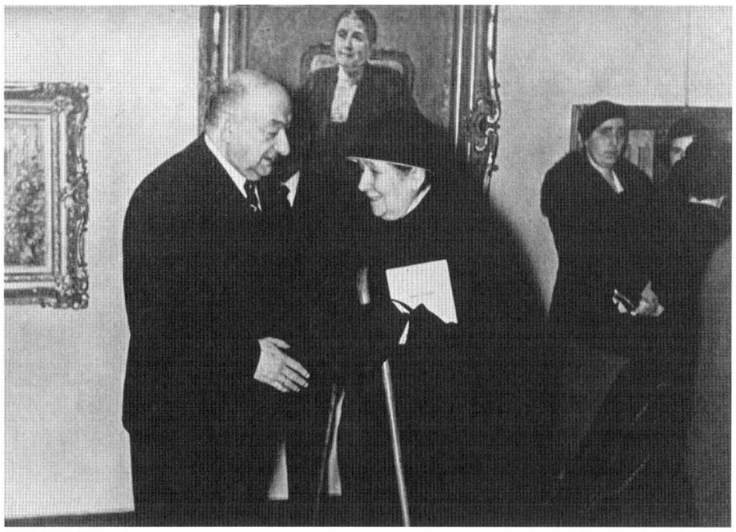

46 Heinrich Stahl und Martha Liebermann bei der Eröffnung der Gedächtnisausstellung für Max Liebermann im Jüdischen Museum Berlin, 1936

Der Ankauf des letzten Selbstporträts von 1934 (Abb. 45) durch Lord Marks und die Schenkung an die Tate Gallery ist die letzte offizielle Anerkennung, die dem greisen Künstler zuteil wurde. Gerührt bedankt sich der Maler am 28. Januar bei Direktor James Manson für die Aufnahme des Werkes in das berühmte Londoner Museum.[9]

In Deutschland dagegen herrschte bei den neuen Machthabern die Auffassung vor, «Juden seien für das deutsche Volk nicht repräsentativ und das Deutsche Reich werde daher von ihrem Wirken im Ausland keinen Nutzen haben.»[10] Dies hatte auch Auswirkungen auf die Leihpolitik der deutschen Museen, wie Lucas Lichtenhan, der Konservator der Kunsthalle Basel, feststellen musste, als er nach Liebermanns Tod eine Ausstellung von dessen Werk in Erwägung zog. Im September 1935 reiste er nach Berlin, um neben der Witwe des Künstlers (Abb. 46), die das Projekt ausdrücklich begrüßte, einige Sammler und Vertreter der Nationalgalerie zu treffen. Anschließend begab er sich nach Frankfurt, musste seinen Plan schließlich jedoch begraben, da es Ende 1935 bereits unmöglich geworden war, Liebermanns Werke aus öffentlichen deutschen Sammlungen auszuleihen.[11] Die Mechanismen des NS-Regimes zeigten Wirkung und verunmöglichten es, einem toten jüdischen Künstler noch Bedeutung beizumessen.

Etwas Ähnliches ereignete sich, als die Kunsthalle Bern auf Wunsch der Deutschen Botschaft 1936 die Ausstellung *Deutsche Malerei des 19. Jahrhunderts* veranstaltete. Präsentiert wurde 182 Gemälde von der Romantik bis zum Realismus, unter anderem 38 Werke aus der Sammlung der Nationalgalerie Berlin,[12] – allerdings kein einziges Bild von Max Liebermann. Die *Berner Tagwacht* kommentierte: «Im Rahmen der deutschen Kunst fanden die Schöpfungen eines Juden keinen Platz mehr [...], weil der Mann Max Liebermann von der ‹Nationalsozialistischen Kulturgemeinschaft› auf der Liste der deutschen Maler gestrichen worden war».[13]

Schließlich gelang es jdoch in Wien, eine Liebermann-Retrospektive zu veranstalten, die am 15. Januar 1937 eröffnet wurde. Es handelte sich um eine Verkaufs-Ausstellung, mit 58 Gemälden, 30 Arbeiten auf Papier und zahlreichen nicht im Katalog genannten Druckgraphiken, die der Galerist Otto Kallir-Nirenstein in seiner seit 1923 bestehende «Neue Galerie» zeigte. Wie Dokumente im Archiv des Belvedere in Wien belegen, stand er dazu in direktem Kontakt mit

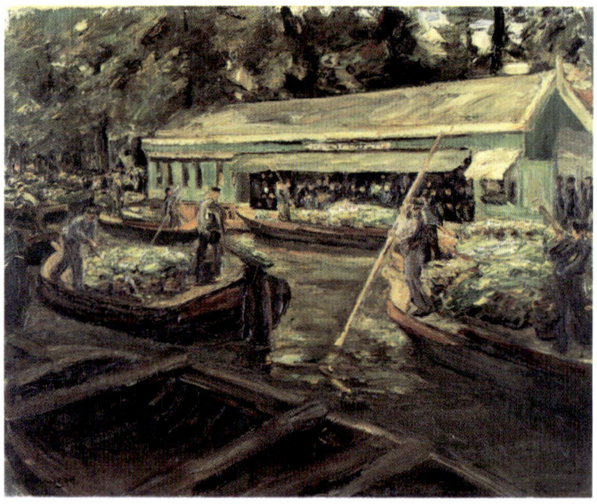

47 Max Liebermann, *Gemüsemarkt in Delft*, 1907. Öl auf Leinwand, 71 x 89 cm. Privatbesitz

dem Liebermann-Biographen Erich Hancke (Abb. 51) in Berlin, der Martha Liebermann, die Witwe des Künstlers, beim Ordnen und Verwalten des Nachlasses unterstützte.[14]

Hancke war eine zentrale Figur bei allen nach dem Tod des Meisters stattfindenden Ausstellungen. Er machte Vorschläge für die Auswahl, half als Kenner des Liebermannschen Werkes bei der korrekten Bezeichnung und Datierung der Werke und vermittelte Leihgaben aus Privatbesitz. Für Wien stellte er eine Gruppe von 36 Werken zusammen, die aus Berlin nach Österreich geschickt wurden. Etwa 20 davon stammten aus dem Nachlass des Künstlers, darunter 12 Arbeiten wie z.B. *Bildnis des Bruders Felix Liebermann* (1865), *Bildnis der Eltern des Künstlers* (1891) oder *Die Gattin des Künstlers* (1931), die aufgrund ihres überwiegend privaten Charakters nicht für den Verkauf bestimmt waren, sowie 8 Arbeiten wie *Fischstillleben* (1877) oder *Selbstbildnis im Anzug, sitzend* (1928), die Hanke gegenüber Nirenstein als verkäuflich deklarierte. Die übrigen 16 Gemälde der Berliner Sendung organisierte Hancke von befreundeten Sammlern aus Liebermanns Umkreis , u. a. von Heinrich Stahl, Geheimrat Nothmann, den Mitgliedern der Familie Cassirer, vom Auktionshaus Paul Graupe sowie aus der teils in Berlin gelagerten Sammlung Erich Göritz, einem der Brüder von Karl Göritz, der seit 1934 im Britischen Exil lebte. Ein Konvolut von 11 Gemälden wurde aus Paris nach Wien geliefert; 9 Zeichnungen und 148 Druckgraphiken steuerte der damals im Amsterdamer Exil lebende Kunsthändler Walter Feilchenfeldt bei. Sechs Gemälde brachte der 1936 von München nach St. Gallen emigrierte Kunsthändler Fritz Nathan auf den Weg nach Wien, darunter *Das Atelier des Künstlers* von 1902 (Abb. 48), das sich damals noch im Eigentum der Ludwigs Galerie München befand. Darüber hinaus bewegte Nathan den Sammler I. E. Sturzenegger aus St. Gallen dazu, das Bild *Gemüsemarkt in Delft* (1907, Abb. 47) zu leihen, und bemühte sich um 12 Zeichnungen aus der in Winterthur befindlichen Sammlung Julius Freund. Das Gemälde *Papst Leo XII erteilt den Pilgern in der Sixtinischen Kapelle den Segen* (1906, Abb. 52) wurde von der Galerie Thannhauser München zur Verfügung gestellt.

An der Leihgeberliste wird erkennbar, dass Liebermann-Ausstellungen nach 1933 im wesentlichen auf vier Quellen angewiesen waren: auf den Nachlass des Künstlers, auf Kunsthändler, die mit Liebermann verbunden gewesen, aber aus dem deutschen Kunstmarkt verdrängt worden waren, auf jüdische bzw. jüdischstämmige Sammler und auf Schweizer Privatsammlungen. Das gilt grundsätzlich auch für die folgenden Ausstellungen in Bern, Basel und London, wobei hier in Einzelfällen auch Schweizer Museen als Leihgeber fungierten.

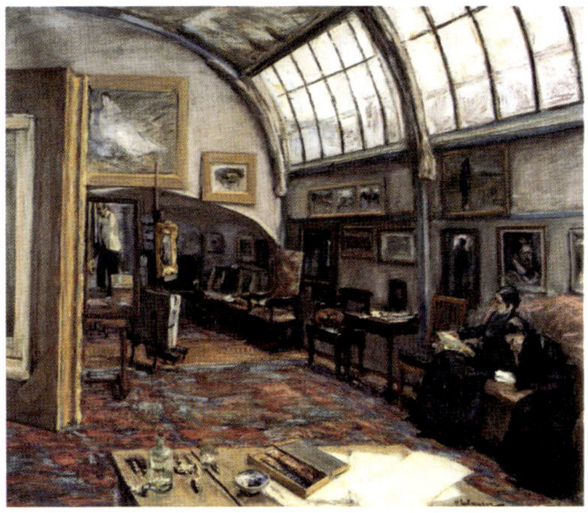

48 Max Liebermann, *Atelier des Künstlers*, 1902. Öl auf Leinwand, 68.5 x 82 cm. Kunstmuseum St. Gallen

Im übrigen war es zu diesem Zeitpunkt für Kunsthändler wie Kallir-Nirenstein, die ihren Sitz im Ausland hatten – noch gehörte Österreich nicht zum Reichsgebiet –, ohne weiteres möglich, Kunstwerke aus Deutschland zu verkaufen, da das Deutsche Reich ein großes Interesse an ausländischen Devisen hatte. «Werke der Moderne durften das Land ohne Probleme verlassen, weil sie in vielen Fällen ohnehin als minderwertig oder sogar als ‹entartet› eingestuft wurden.»[15] In dieselbe Kategorie fielen vornehmlich Werke jüdischer Künstler. Selbstverständlich mussten bei der Ausfuhr umfangreiche Zollformalitäten erledigt, Ausfuhr- und Einfuhrgenehmigungen eingeholt und die zuständige Devisenstelle mit einbezogen werden, die darüber wachte, dass keine Vermögenswerte unkontrolliert ins Ausland verbracht wurden.

Noch während der Vorbereitungen für die Wiener Schau kam Max Huggler, der Direktor der Kunsthalle Bern, der im Jahr zuvor die Ausstellung *Deutsche Malerei* ohne Liebermann gezeigt hatte, auf den Gedanken, die Wiener Verkaufsausstellung en bloc für Bern zu übernehmen. Erich Hancke teilte mit, dass ihm die Idee «spontan» gefalle.[16] Zwar war es schließlich nicht möglich, die gesamte Schau nach Bern zu bringen, doch kam durch Leihgaben von Privatsammlern wie Oskar Reinhart und dss Kunstmuseums Winterthur dennoch eine ähnlich umfangreiche Ausstellung zusammen, die vom 3. Jui bis 4. Juli 1937 in der Kunsthalle Bern zu sehen war. Im Katalog sind 63 Gemälde und 47 Zeichnungen verzeichnet. 22 der ausgestellten Werke gehörten zu dem von Hancke für Wien zusammengestellt Konvolut von ursprünglich 36 Gemälden. Von daher kann vermutet werden, dass in Wien einige davon wie z.B. das Gemälde *Düne und Meer – Auf der Düne* (1909) verkauft worden waren, sofern sie nicht aus anderen Gründen für eine weitere Station nicht zur Verfügung standen.

In abgewandelter Form und dank der tatkräftigen Mitwirkung Erich Hanckes konnte die Berner Ausstellung im August 1937 schließlich noch von Lucas Lichtenhahn für Kunsthalle Basel übernommen werden. Als man dort Eröffnung feierte, sah die Welt in Nazi-Deutschland düster aus: In München war kurz zuvor die Propagandaschau *Entartete Kunst* eröffnet worden, und in Berlin hatte man die Liebermann-Werke aus der ständigen Ausstellung der Nationalgalerie ins Depot verbannt. Damit wurde das Programm umgesetzt, das Hitler bei der Eröffnung der *Großen Deutschen Kunstausstellung* im Haus der Deutschen Kunst mit den Worten zusammengefasst hatte: «Wir werden von jetzt ab einen unerbittlichen Säuberungskrieg führen gegen die letzten Elemente unserer Kulturzersetzung.»[17] Da wirkt es wie aus der Welt gefallen, wenn es im Katalog der Basler Ausstellung heißt: «Hochgeschätzt und mit vielen Ehrungen ausgezeichnet, starb Liebermann als Nestor der deutschen Malerei 1935 in Berlin. Werke seiner Hand besitzen, außer fast sämtlichen deutschen Museen, öffentliche Sammlungen in Paris, Oslo, Stockholm, Zürich u.a.m.»[18]

Eine solche Würdigung der Kunst und Persönlichkeit Liebermanns war um diese Zeit nur noch im Ausland möglich. Daher werden sich Martha Liebermann und Erich Hancke im darauf folgenden Jahr gefreut haben, als die Organisatoren der großen Londoner Ausstellung *Twentieth Century German Art* an Liebermann dachten und ihm eine prominente Rolle in der Präsentation einräumten. Da sie viele der Beteiligten an den Liebermann-Ausstellungen in Zürich, Wien, Bern und Basel persönlich kannten, kam eine ansehnliche Gruppe von Werken zusammen. Max Huggler, Direktor der Kunsthalle Bern, spielte eine entscheidende Rolle bei der Aktivierung der Leihgeber in und um Bern und schickte auch Werke aus seinem eigenen Besitz an die New Burlington Galleries.[19] Fritz Nathan stellte das *Atelier des Künstlers* zur Verfügung, das 1937 bereits in Wien, Basel und Bern zu sehen gewesen war; vom Sammler Karl Göritz kam das *Polospiel in Jenisch Park* (Abb. 50), das er 1934 auch in die Liebermann-Ausstellung der Londoner Leicester Galleries gegeben hatte. Der Zürcher Sammler Sigmund Pollag beteiligte sich mit dem Werk *Konzert in der Oper* (Kat.-Nr. 3), das 1937 unter den Exponaten der Basler Ausstellung gewesen war. Zu den Leihgebern zählte außerdem der Sammler Weill aus Zürich, dessen Studie *Papageienmann* (Abb. 49) im vorherigen Jahr zur Berner Ausstellung gezählt hatte.

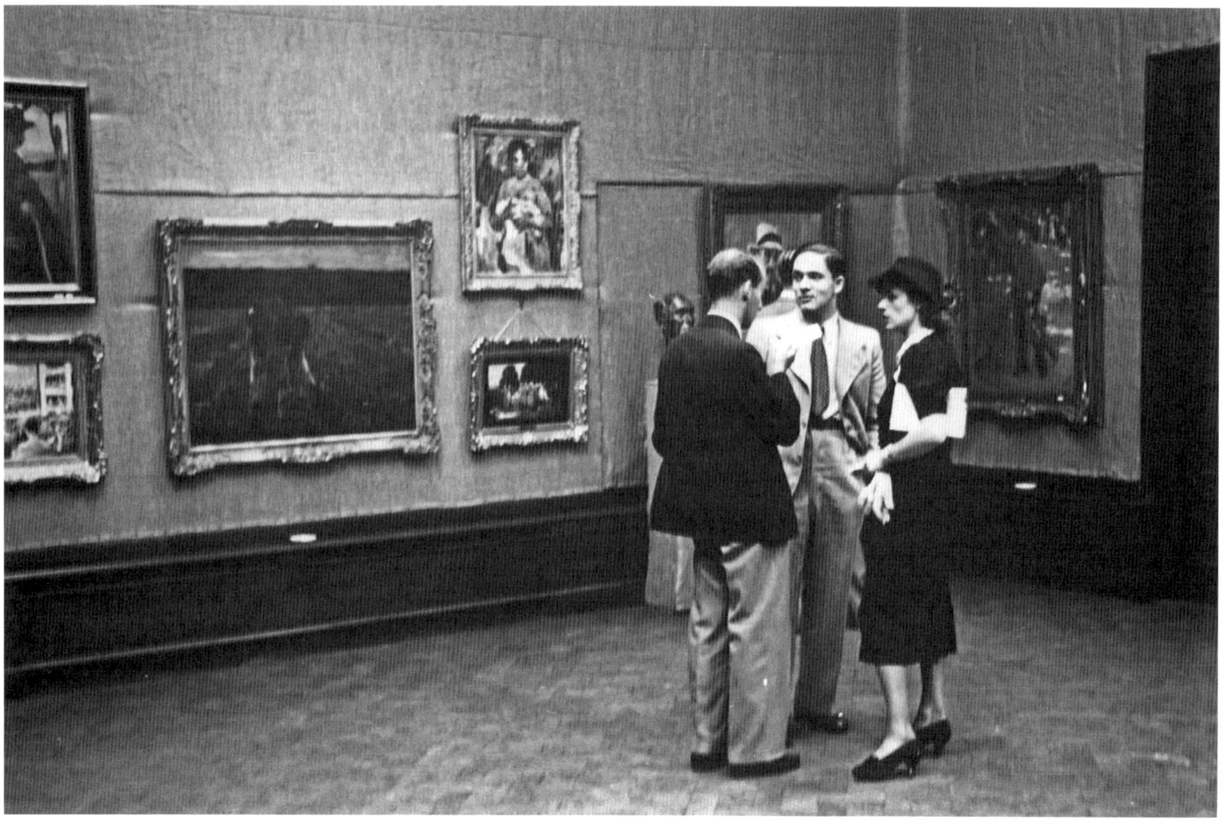

49 Ausstellung *Twentieth Century German Art* London 1938 mit Liebermanns Werken *Konzert in der Oper* (unten links), *Kartoffelpflücker* (Mitte), *Kirchgang in Laren* (rechts daneben), *Selbstbildnis*, 1928 (verdeckt) und *Papageienmann, Studie* (rechts).

Leider haben sich nach heutigem Stand der Forschung keine Belege für einen direkten Kontakt zwischen den Organisatoren von *Twentieth Century German Art* und Martha Liebermann erhalten. Fest steht jedoch, dass das *Porträt Albert Einstein* (1925, Kat.-Nr. 1), das einen Nachlass-Stempel trägt, zur Hinterlassenschaft des Künstlers gehörte und daher vermutlich von Martha Liebermann selbst für die Londoner Schau zur Verfügung gestellt worden ist. Um die Papiere und den Transport wird sich, wie in den vorangegangenen Jahren, Erich Hancke gekümmert haben.

In London waren schließlich 10 Gemälde und 8 Graphiken von der Hand des Meisters zu sehen. In den wohnlich ausgestatteten Räumlichkeiten der Burlington Galleries wurden die Liebermann-Werke wie in den besten Zeiten der Berliner Secession zusammen mit den Bildern von Lovis Corinth und Max Slevogt gezeigt. Dem ‹Dreigestirn des deutschen Impressionismus› stellten die Organisatoren noch die Werke Paula Modersohn-Beckers zur Seite, darunter *Stilleben mit Apfelsinen, Bananen, Zitronen und Tomate* (Kat.-Nr. 13). In dieser Kombination bildeten sie den Auftakt zu einer der beeindruckendsten Ausstellungen der Deutschen Kunst in der ersten Hälfte des 20. Jahrhunderts.

1 Saul Friedländer: Das Dritte Reich und die Juden. Die Jahre der Verfolgung 1933-1939, München 2000, S. 24.

2 Bernd Schmalhausen: «Ich bin doch nur ein Maler». Max und Martha Liebermann im Dritten Reich, Halaska: wissenschaftliche Abhandlungen. Hildesheim [u.a.] : Olms, 1994, S. 60f.

3 Max Liebermann an Wilhelm Rothenstein, Brief vom 9.11.1934, ML 3087, Houghton Library MS Eng 1148 (881), Max Liebermann Briefe Bd. VIII, zusammengetragen, kommentiert und herausgegeben von Ernst Braun, Schriftenreihe der Max-Liebermann-Gesellschaft Berlin; Baden-Baden (in Drucklegung). Mit herzlichem Dank an Herrn Braun, der die Briefe an Rothenstein aus seinem Manuskript vorab zur Verfügung gestellt hat.

4 Gotthard Jedlicka: Max Liebermann, in: Galerie und Sammler, Nr. 9/10, 1933, S. 160.

5 Max Liebermann an Gotthard Jedlicka am 15. Dezember 1933, zit. n. Kat. Max Liebermann und die Schweiz, S. 39.

6 Max Liebermann an Wilhelm Rothenstein, Brief vom 9.11. 1934, ML 3087, Houghton Library MS Eng 1148 (881), Max Liebermann Briefe Bd. VIII, zusammengetragen, kommentiert und herausgegeben von Ernst Braun, Schriftenreihe der Max-Liebermann-Gesellschaft Berlin; Baden-Baden (im Erscheinen).

7 Ebd.

8 Max Liebermann an Wilhelm Rothenstein, Brief vom 14.1.1935, ML 3088, Houghton Library MS Eng 1148 (881), Max Liebermann Briefe Bd. VIII (im Erscheinen).

9 Max Liebermann an James Manson, Brief vom 28.1. 1935, ML3042, Tate Archive TGA 7915, Max Liebermann Briefe Bd. VIII (in Drucklegung): «Dear Sir, It gave me great pleasure to receive your letter with the good news, that the Tate-Gallery has accepted the gift of my last self-portrait. I appreciate highly the honour you and your committee have conferred upon me, and I am proud and happy to know that a work of my hand is in your famous collection.»

10 Saul Friedländer, S. 134.

11 Max Liebermann und die Schweiz. Meisterwerke aus Schweizer hrsg. von Marc Fehlmann, Museum Oskar Reinhart, München 2014, S. 40.

12 Max Liebermann und die Schweiz, S. 41.

13 Zit. n. Max Liebermann und die Schweiz, S. 42.

14 Herzlichen Dank für den Zugang zum Material an Stefan Lehner und Dr. Rolf Johannsen Österreichische Galerie Belvedere.

15 Anja Tiedemann, Klees Tod war für mich der größte Schmerz, in: Markt und Macht im ‹Dritten Reich›, hrsg. v. Uwe Fleckner, Thomas W. Gaethgens, Christian Huemer, S. 191-215, S. 196.

16 Erich Hancke an Max Huggler, 19. Februar 1937, KHB Archiv, zit. n. Max Liebermann und die Schweiz, S.41.

17 Adolf Hitler, Rede zur Eröffnung der Großen Deutschen Kunstausstellung in München, 18. Juli 1937, zit. n. Marlies Schmidt, Die «Große Deutsche Kunstausstellung 1937 im Haus der Deutschen Kunst zu München»: Rekonstruktion und Analyse, Hochschulschrift Halle, Univ., Philosophische Fakultät I, Diss., 2010, S. 64.

18 Katalog Kunsthalle Basel: Max Liebermann 1947-1935. Graphisches Kabinett. 7. August bis 5. September 1937, Basel 1937, S. 11. Herzlichen Dank für die Zurverfügungstellung von Material an Andrea Lutz vom Museum Oskar Reinhard und Rainer Baum vom Kunstmuseum Basel.

19 Vgl. Lucy Wasensteiner: The Twentieth Century German Art Exhibition. Answering Degenerate Art in 1930s London. New York (im Erscheinen).

A German artist honoured only outside Germany: Liebermann exhibitions between 1933 and 1938

MARTIN FAASS

"Although it may seem peripheral in retrospect, the realm of culture was the first from which Jews (and 'leftists') were driven out in large numbers,"[1] notes the historian Saul Friedländer. The exodus of Jewish and left-wing intellectuals began almost immediately after the Nazis seized power: the philosopher and literary critic Walter Benjamin left Berlin for Paris on 18 March 1933; the conductors Otto Klemperer and Bruno Walter were forced into exile later that year. Within the first few weeks of National Socialist rule, Jewish Germans working in the cultural industries were robbed of their legal and social standing, and stigmatised as alien elements within German society.

As one of Berlin's most important cultural institutions, the Prussian Academy of Arts came quickly to the attention of the new regime. The painter Max Liebermann (fig. 43) had served as president of the Academy for over a decade, from 1932 in an honorary capacity. On 6 February 1933, just a few days after Hitler seized power, the National Socialist Bernhard Rust was appointed Minister for Art, Science and Education in Prussia. One of his earliest projects was the "cleansing" of the Academy, threatening its closure unless then-president Max von Schillings agreed to eject disfavoured artists such as Käthe Kollwitz and Heinrich Mann. The Law for the Restoration of the Professional Civil Service, passed on 7 April 1933, provided for Jews to be excluded from all civil service positions. The law was also applied to the Prussian Academy – though its members were not strictly speaking civil servants – beginning with the department of poetry. The "cleansing" of the department of fine arts was in turn scheduled for 15 May 1933. On 7 May, pre-empting this humiliation, Max Liebermann resigned from all his official positions.

Max and Martha Liebermann thus disappeared from public life. "The members of Berlin society, who had for decades vied for invitations to the Liebermanns', now avoided the house on Pariser Platz [...] The old 'prince of painters' – not only a Jew, but also an alleged sympathizer with the bourgeois left – had become a liability."[2]

In the Berlin National Gallery, the newly appointed director Eberhard Hanfstaengl was granted ministerial permission to leave Liebermann's paintings on display. Elsewhere in Germany however, his works gradually disappeared, removed from museums and galleries where they had previously hung with pride. Only venues approved by the National Socialist government could continue to show Liebermann's works – Jewish museums, or organisations such as the Kulturbund Deutscher Juden (Cultural Association of German Jews). These venues provided a state-controlled parallel cultural scene for Jewish or "non-German" artists. The only two Liebermann exhibitions staged in Germany between 1933 and 1945 took place in such institutions: memorial exhibitions, staged shortly after the artist's death in 1935, at the Jewish Museum in Frankfurt and the Jewish Museum in Berlin.

It was only outside Germany's borders that Liebermann could be exhibited and appreciated as a leading German artist. In this context, exhibitions of his works staged in Switzerland, England and Austria take on a particular significance.

On 9 November 1934, Liebermann wrote to Sir William Rothenstein, director of the Royal College of Art in London: "Since I resigned from all public offices and began living and working as a 'private' painter, I have successfully exhibited abroad, in Zurich, Amsterdam, particularly showing paintings created in recent years. Several friendly owners have loaned paintings, allowing an overview of my work from the past sixty-five years – unbelievable but true! – to be exhibited".[3]

The Zurich exhibition mentioned here by Liebermann took place at the city's Galerie Aktuaryus from 8 April to 2 May 1933, the show containing 55 paintings and 49 prints. Most of these loans came from Liebermann himself, or from private collectors in his circle. The exhibition prompted Gotthard Jedlicka, consultant to the Zurich gallery and editor of their in-house magazine *Galerie und Sammler*, to dedicate an essay to Liebermann, in which he described the artist as a "classic of realist art".[4] Jedlicka also included an account of a meeting with Liebermann in his 1933 volume Begegnungen, which was met with gratitude by the artist, as he wrote in December: "Dear Mr. Jedlicka, Yesterday I received your book from the publisher. I have read it with great pleasure and I want to thank you very much, boycotted as I am in Germany, for bringing me so kindly to the attention of those in other countries".[5]

As 1934 dawned, so the merciless exclusion of Jews from German life continued. In February 1934 the Reich Minister of War Werner von Blomberg ordered an "Aryan Paragraph" to be applied to the military. Less than one month later, Propaganda Minister Goebbels announced that all Jews were to be banned from the Reich Chamber of Culture, thus preventing their further participation in German cultural life. In this context, a Liebermann exhibition planned by William Rothenstein for London's Leicester Galleries was all the more welcomed by the artist, as he wrote to Rothenstein:

"I was extremely pleased by your letter, because it confirmed (as Mr. Flechtheim had already told me and written to me) that you have remained faithful in your friendly disposition toward me, as you have been for many decades. I cannot tell you how grateful I am for the selfless interest you have shown in organising my exhibition in the Leicester Galleries. Without you it would simply have been impossible, as up to July 1932 even the 'most imaginative' art dealer would hardly have thought of presenting works by an eighty-five-year-old painter in London."[6]

Rothenstein, himself an artist, set about organising a Liebermann retrospective for London. He was supported by a prestigious "Committee of Honour" including Sir Thomans Barlow, Sir Kenneth Clark (Director of the National Gallery), Professor W.G. Constable (Director of the Courtauld Institute), James Manson (Director of the Tate Gallery) and Sir Michael Sadler. Four years later, each of these names would go on to lend their support to the exhibition *Twentieth Century German Art*. The Leicester Galleries exhibition of 1934 (fig. 44) comprised total of 28 drawings, five pastels and 27 paintings, mainly works from the 1920s and

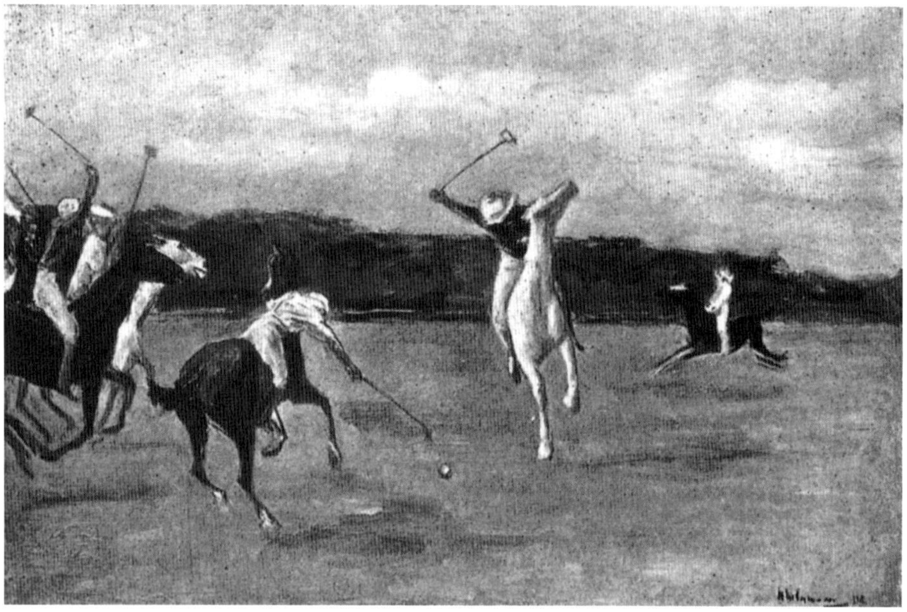

50 Max Liebermann, *Polo Game in Jenisch Park*, 1912. Oil on canvas, 55 x 82 cm. Lost in the second world war.

1930s, though some earlier works were also included. All but three of the exhibited works came either from Liebermann himself or from German collectors, among them the Chemnitz industrialist Karl Göritz, who provided *Polo Game in Jenisch Park* (1912, fig. 50) to the Leicester Galleries three years before his emigration to Holland. As Liebermann wrote to Rothenstein in November 1934: "Together with these lines, I send some twenty-five oil paintings and as many drawings and pastels to the Leicester Galleries. Simply leave out what you consider unsuitable."[7] The importance of this London retrospective for the artist in the last days of his life is illustrated by a further letter to Rothenstein, which Liebermann dictated to his wife Martha on 14 January 1935, just three weeks before his death: "For two months now, flu and its consequences have prevented me from thanking you myself for your kind help and concern for my London exhibition, to the success of which you have contributed so much. I waited from week to week for improvement, and now, as time marches on, I must rely on the help of my wife to express my gratitude. Without the joy and satisfaction that your friendship and the collegiality of the English artists have given me, I would probably not have survived this terrible time of illness."[8]

Following its exhibition at the Leicester Galleries, Liebermann's last self-portrait – dated 1934 (fig. 45) – was acquired by Lord Marks, who gifted it to London's Tate Gallery. The artist was deeply moved by this final act of official recognition, on 28 January 1935 writing to the Tate's director James Manson to thank him for accepting the work.[9]

Meanwhile in Germany, the government remained of the opinion that "Jews were not representative of the German people and the Reich would therefore not benefit from their activities abroad."[10] This view directly affected the lending policies of German museums, as discovered by Lucas Lichtenhan, director of the Kunsthalle Basel, when he sought to arrange a posthumous exhibition of Max Liebermann's work in Basel in 1935. In September 1935 Lichtenhan travelled to Berlin to meet with both the artist's widow (fig. 46) and a number of private collectors and representatives from the Berlin National Gallery. He then travelled

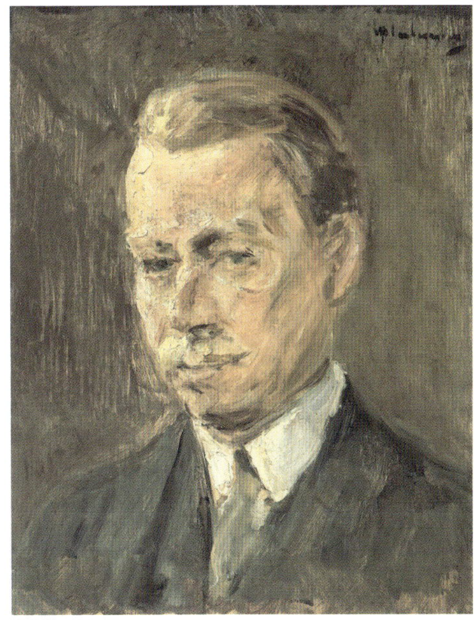

51 Max Liebermann, *Portrait of Erich Hancke – head study*, 1929. Oil on wood, 50 cm x 39.5 cm. Private collection.

on to Frankfurt, for similar discussions with collectors and museums. He was forced to conclude that – by late 1935 – it was already impossible to borrow Liebermann's works from public German collections.[11] The mechanisms of the Nazi state had successfully blocked any attempt to honour this dead Jewish artist. Liebermann was similarly excluded from an exhibition of nineteenth-century German painting staged at the Kunsthalle Bern in 1936, at the request of the German Embassy. The exhibition comprised 182 paintings from Romanticism to Realism, including 38 works from the Berlin National Gallery.[12] Among them, not a single painting by Liebermann. As the Bern newspaper *Tagwacht* commented: "Within German art there is no longer place for the works of a Jew. [...] because the 'National Socialist Cultural Community' has now crossed Max Liebermann off the list of German painters."[13]

Despite these difficulties however, it was possible for further Liebermann exhibitions to be staged abroad during the 1930s. From 15 January 1937 the Austrian gallerist Otto Kallir-Nirenstein opened a commercial exhibition of Liebermann's works at his 'Neue Galerie' in Vienna. The show contained 58 Liebermann paintings, 30 works on paper, and numerous prints not listed in the catalogue. As the gallery's archives at the Belvedere in Vienna make clear, the show was organised with the help of Liebermann's biographer Erich Hancke (fig. 51). Hancke was resident in Berlin in 1937, and was engaged in assisting Martha Liebermann with the administration of her husband's estate.[14]

Erich Hancke played a central role in each of the Liebermann exhibitions staged abroad after 1935. He made suggestions for the selection of works, gave expert advice on their correct designation and dating, and arranged loans from private collections. In the case of the above-mentioned Neue Galerie show, he arranged for the transport of 36 works from Berlin to Vienna. Twenty of these came from Liebermann's estate, of which eight were for sale, including *Fish Still Life* (1877) and *Self-Portrait in a Suit*, seated (1928). The remaining twelve works from the Liebermann estate were more private in nature, and were accordingly not for sale, among them the *Portrait of Felix Liebermann*, the artist's brother (1865), *Portrait*

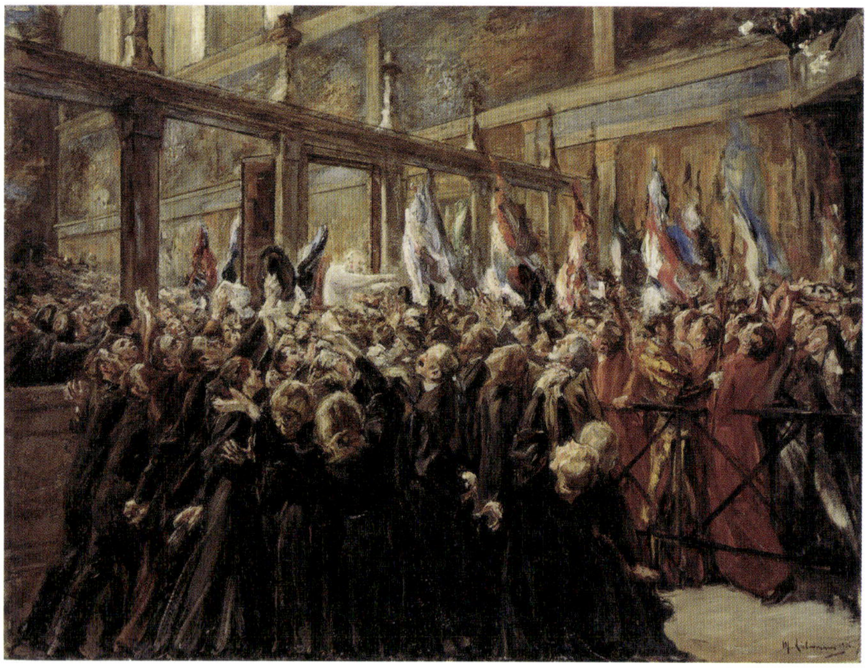

52 Max Liebermann, *Pope Leo XII Blesses the Pilgrims in the Sistine Chapel*, 1906. Oil on canvas, 112 x 154 cm. Westfälisches Landesmuseum Münster

of the Artist's Parents (1891) and *The Artist's Wife* (1931). Sixteen further works were sent to Vienna from collectors in Liebermann's Berlin circle, among them Heinrich Stahl, Privy Councillor Nothmann, members of the Cassirer family and the Paul Graupe auction house. Works also came from the portion of the Erich Göritz collection in storage in Berlin. Formerly resident of Berlin, Göritz was the brother of Karl Göritz, and had lived since 1934 in exile in Britain (see cat. no. 8, p. 110-111).

Another eleven paintings were sent to the Vienna exhibition from Paris; nine drawings and 148 prints from Walter Feilchenfeldt, then living in exile in Amsterdam. The art dealer Fritz Nathan, who had emigrated from Munich to the Swiss town of St. Gallen in 1936, sent six paintings to Vienna, among them *The Artist's Studio* (1902, fig. 48), which at that time was still owned by the Ludwigs Galerie in Munich. Nathan also persuaded the collector I. E. Sturzenegger in St. Gallen to lend the painting *Vegetable Market in Delft* (1907, fig. 47); he also attempted to secure twelve drawings from the Julius Freund collection in Winterthur. Finally, the Munich-based Galerie Thannhauser sent the painting *Pope Leo XII Blesses the Pilgrims in the Sistine Chapel* (1906, fig. 52). This list of lenders clearly illustrate that Liebermann exhibitions after 1933 were reliant on the artist's estate, on émigré art dealers formerly connected to the artist, on Jewish-owned collections and on private collections in Switzerland. This was the case for the successive exhibitions in Bern, Basel and London, through some individual works also came from Swiss museums.

For art dealers based outside Germany – such as Kallir-Nirenstein in Vienna, which in 1937 still remained outside the Third Reich – it was entirely possible to sell works from within Germany, particularly considering the German regime's interest in foreign currency. As noted by art historian Anja Tiedemann, "it was no problem for modern artworks to leave the country, since they were in any case largely categorised as inferior, or even 'degene-

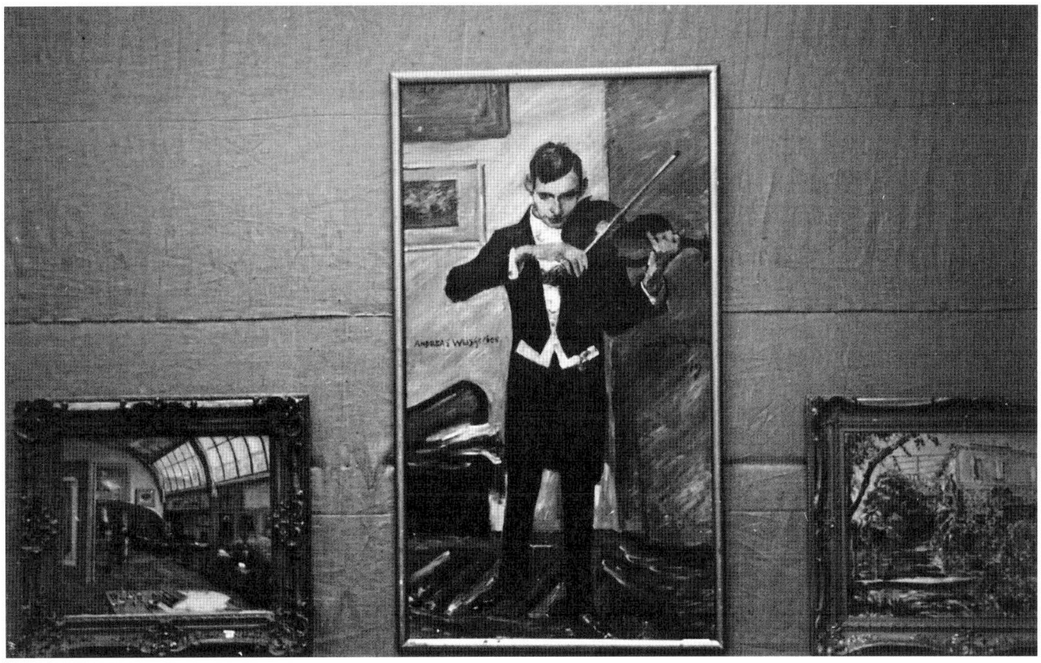

53 View of the exhibition *Twentieth Century German Art* with Liebermann's painting *The Artist's Studio* (left)

rate'."[15] This applied in particular to the works of Jewish artists. It was only necessary to ensure that customs regulations were fulfilled, that the relevant permissions for export and import were obtained, and that the foreign exchange office was informed of any potential cross-border asset transfers.

Witnessing the planning stages of the exhibition in Vienna, Max Huggler – director of the Kunsthalle Bern – was inspired to stage his own Liebermann exhibition. Just one year after his exhibition of nineteenth-century German painting from which Liebermann had been entirely excluded, Huggler suggested to Hancke that he take over the Vienna exhibition following its closure. Hancke's replied that he found the idea "pleasing";[16] Huggler's exhibition ran in Bern from 3 June to 4 July 1937, containing 63 paintings and 47 drawings. In the end it was not possible to transport the Vienna exhibition in its entirity to Bern. Huggler's exhibition contained 22 of the 36 paintings shown in Vienna, suggesting that some had already been sold – such as the painting *Dunes and the Sea – on the Dunes* (1909) – or were otherwise no longer available for the exhibition in Switzerland.

Thanks to the efforts of Erich Hancke, the Bern exhibition was in turn taken over in a slightly modified form by the Kunsthalle Basel in August 1937, the museum under the leadership of Lucas Lichtenhan. As this show opened in Basel however, the situation in Germany was worsening: while the propaganda exhibition *Entartete Kunst* opened its doors in Munich, Liebermann's works in the Berlin National Gallery were removed from view and sent into storage. As Hitler set out in his speech opening the first *Große Deutsche Kunstausstellung* at Munich's House of German Art on 18 July 1937: "From this point onward, we will wage a merciless cleansing war against the last remaining elements who intended to degrade our culture".[17] Against that backdrop, the words in the Basel exhibition catalogue seem taken from another world: "Liebermann, who died in Berlin in 1935, was the doyen of German

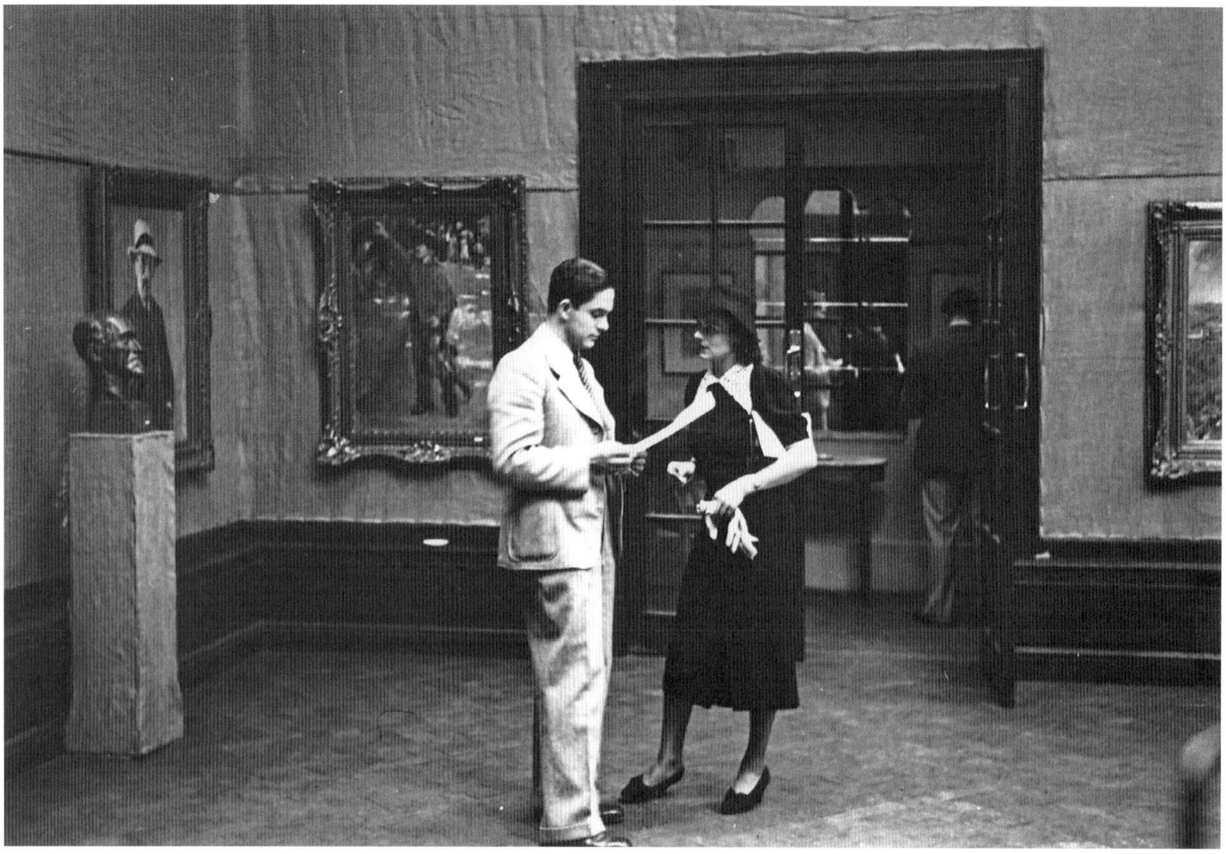

54 View of the exhibition *Twentieth Century German Art* with Max Liebermann's paintings *Self portrait 1928* (left wall), and *Parrot Man, Study* (facing wall, left)

painting, highly esteemed and distinguished with many honours. Owned by practically every German museum, his works are also found in public collections in Paris, Oslo, Stockholm, Zurich, among many other cities."[18]

Such praise and appreciation of Liebermann's life and work was now only possible outside Germany. Martha Liebermann and Erich Hancke must therefore have been all the more pleased to hear of the plans for *Twentieth Century German Art*, and the central role to be afforded to Liebermann. Many of those involved with the London show in 1938 had already contributed to the foreign exhibitions of the preceding years. Max Huggler, director of the Kunsthalle Bern, played a decisive role in identifying lenders for *Twentieth Century German Art*, also providing works from his private collection.[19] The émigré art dealer Fritz Nathan sent *The Artist's Studio* (1902) to the New Burlington Galleries, the work having already been shown in Vienna, Basel and Bern during 1937. The collector Karl Göritz provided his *Polo Game in Jenisch Park* (1912), as he had to the Leicester Galleries in 1934. The Zürich collector Sigmund Pollag provided the Liebermann oil *Concert in the Opera* (1922, cat. no. 3), which he had also lent to Basel in 1937. And the Liebermann painting *Parrot Man, Study* (1901, fig. 54), provided by an unknown lender to Bern in 1937, reappeared one year later at *Twentieth Century German Art*.

Unfortunately, the research to date shows no evidence of direct contact between Martha Liebermann and the organisers of *Twentieth Century German Art*. Nonetheless, the *Portrait of Albert Einstein* (1925, cat. no. 1) exhibited in London bears an estate stamp, meaning it was in Martha Liebermann's ownership in 1935, and thus strongly suggesting that it was she who provided it to *Twentieth Century German Art* three years later. Just as with her previous loans to foreign exhibitions, Erich Hancke would have organised the paperwork and shipping.

Twentieth Century German Art contained ten paintings and eight prints by Liebermann. Just as in the heyday of the Berlin Secession, his works hung at the New Burlington Galleries alongside his colleagues Lovis Corinth and Max Slevogt. The organisers in London added Paula Modersohn Becker to this triumvirate of German Impressionism, for example with works such as her *Still Life with Oranges, Bananas, Lemon and Tomato* (1906, cat. no. 13). These four artists provided the opening act for one of the most important exhibitions of German art in the first part of Twentieth Century.

1 Saul Friedländer: Das Dritte Reich und die Juden. Die Jahre der Verfolgung 1933–1939, Munich 2000, p. 24
2 Bernd Schmalhausen: "Ich bin doch nur ein Maler". Max und Martha Liebermann im Dritten Reich, in: Halaska, Wissenschaftliche Abhandlungen, Hildesheim etc., 1994, p. 60f.
3 Max Liebermann to Wilhelm Rothenstein on 9 November 1934, ML 3087, Houghton Library MS Eng 1148 (881), in: Max Liebermann – Briefe, Vol. VIII, collected, commented and published by Ernst Braun, Schriftenreihe der Max-Liebermann-Gesellschaft Berlin, Baden-Baden (forthcoming). With sincere thanks to Mr. Braun for permitting access to his manuscript with the letters to Rothenstein ahead of printing.
4 Gotthard Jedlicka: Max Liebermann, in: Galerie und Sammler, No. 9/10, 1933, p. 160.
5 Max Liebermann to Gotthard Jedlicka on 15 December 1933, in: Marc Fehlmann/Museum Oskar Reinhard (eds.): Max Liebermann und die Schweiz. Meisterwerke aus Schweizer Sammlungen, Munich 2014, p. 39.
6 Max Liebermann to Sir William Rothenstein on 9 November 1934, ML 3087, Houghton Library MS Eng 1148 (881), in: Max Liebermann – Briefe (forthcoming).
7 Ibid.
8 Max Liebermann to Wilhelm Rothenstein on 14 January 1935, ML 3088, Houghton Library MS Eng 1148 (881), in: Max Liebermann – Briefe (forthcoming).
9 Max Liebermann to James Manson on 28 January 1935, ML3042, Tate Archive TGA 7915, in: Max Liebermann – Briefe): "Dear Sir, It gave me great pleasure to receive your letter with the good news, that the Tate-Gallery has accepted the gift of my last self-portrait. I appreciate highly the honour you and your committee have conferred upon me, and I am proud and happy to know that a work of my hand is in your famous collection."
10 Saul Friedländer, p. 134.
11 Marc Fehlmann/Museum Oskar Reinhart, p. 40.
12 Ibid., p. 42.
13 quoted ibid, p. 43
14 Sincere thanks to Stefan Lehner and Dr. Rolf Johannsen, Österreichische Galerie Belvedere, for access to the material.
15 Anja Tiedemann: Klees Tod war für mich der größte Schmerz, in: Uwe Fleckner/Thomas W. Gaethgens/Christian Huemer (eds.): Markt und Macht: Der Kunsthandel im "Dritten Reich", Berlin 2017, pp. 191-215.
16 Erich Hancke to Max Huggler on 19 February 1937, KHB Archiv, quoted in Marc Fehlmann/Museum Oskar Reinhard, p. 41.
17 Adolf Hitler: Rede zur Eröffnung der Großen Deutschen Kunstausstellung in München, 18. Juli 1937, quoted in Marlies Schmidt: Die „Große Deutsche Kunstausstellung 1937 im Haus der Deutschen Kunst zu München": Rekonstruktion und Analyse, Hochschulschrift Halle, Univ., Philosophische Fakultät I, dissertation, 2010, p. 64.
18 Anon.: Max Liebermann 1847–1935. Graphisches Kabinett – 7. August bis 5. September 1937 (exhibition catalogue), Basel 1937, p. 11. Sincere thanks to Andrea Lutz from Museum Oskar Reinhart and Rainer Baum from Kunstmuseum Basel for access to the material.
19 cf. Lucy Wasensteiner: The Twentieth Century German Art Exhibition. Answering Degenerate Art in 1930s London, New York (forthcoming).

Katalog

LUCY WASENSTEINER

Bis heute zählt *Twentieth Century German Art* zu den größten Ausstellungen deutscher Kunst, die jemals in Großbritannien stattgefunden haben. Wie vorne bereits erwähnt, wurden damals mehr als 300 Werke der wichtigsten Vertreter der deutschen Moderne ausgestellt.

Auf den folgenden Seiten werden ausgewählte Werke der damaligen Schau vorgestellt. Es handelt sich dabei um die 29 Gemälde, welche die Liebermann-Villa am Wannsee in der Wintersaison 2018/2019 zeigt. Die Präsentation der Werke entspricht in etwa derjenigen in den New Burlington Galleries im Jahre 1938, die den Besucher auf eine mehr oder weniger chronologische Reise vom Impressionismus des späten 19. Jahrhunderts über den Expressionismus bis hin zur Abstraktion der folgenden Jahrzehnte führte.

Der vorliegende Katalog gibt einen Überblick über die damalige Ausstellung und versucht, auf der Grundlage von Ergebnissen der Provenienzforschung, folgende Fragen zu beantworten: Woher kamen die Kunstwerke? Was war die Motivation der Leihgeber? Und wie konnten diese für eine Teilnahme an der Ausstellung gewonnen werden?

Obwohl diese Fragen bei manchen Exponaten nicht vollständig beantwortet werden können, unterstreichen die vorgestellten Werke die Dimension und den Anspruch der damaligen Ausstellung sowie die Heterogenität der Beteiligten, seien es deutsche Emigranten und Nazi-Gegner, schweizerische Kunsthändler mit kommerziellem Interessen, britische Sammler und Unterstützer des Projekts oder auch ‹entartete› Künstler auf der Suche nach neuen Absatzmärkten.

Bis heute konnten mehr als 90 Leihgeber identifiziert werden. Da allerdings viele damals in London ausgestellte Kunstwerke im damaligen Katalog nicht aufgeführt wurden, geht die Suche nach diesen Werken und deren Leihgebern weiter.

Catalogue

LUCY WASENSTEINER

The London exhibition of *Twentieth Century German Art* stands to this day among the largest exhibitions of German art of any kind, ever to have been staged in Britain. As noted above, it contained over 300 artworks by every key name of the German modernist scene.

The following pages present a selection of these original 1938 exhibits – the 29 works exhibited during autumn and winter 2018-19 at the Liebermann-Villa am Wannsee. They are listed here broadly in accordance with how they were exhibited at the New Burlington Galleries in 1938, where the visitor was led in a loosely chronological progression from late nineteenth-century German impressionism to the expressionism and abstraction of the following decades.

While giving a sense of the visual impression of this remarkable 1938 exhibition, this catalogue also presents the results of provenance research into these London exhibits: exploring who provided these works to *Twentieth Century German Art*, their reasons for doing so, and how they were recruited for the project.

While in some cases, these details can be reconstructed with some certainty, in others we are left to speculate. What all of these works make clear however is both the scale and ambition of *Twentieth Century German Art*, and the mix of backgrounds of those involved: German émigrés seeking to answer Nazism, Swiss dealers seeking to sell their works, British collectors lending their support to the project, or the so-called 'degenerate' artists themselves, seeking new markets abroad.

To date, over 90 individual lenders to the London exhibition have been identified. With so many exhibits excluded from the catalogue however, exhibits and lenders continue to be identified.

Martha Liebermann

Im frühen 20. Jahrhundert wurde Max Liebermann für seine Portraits prominenter Persönlichkeiten berühmt. Einstein portraitierte er zwischen 1922 und 1925 z. B. drei Mal.

Das hier gezeigte Bild von 1925 trägt statt der Signatur des Künstlers einen Stempel, der darauf hindeutet, dass es zum Zeitpunkt von Liebermanns Tod 1935 noch Eigentum des Malers war und anschließend seiner Witwe Martha (1857-1943) gehörte. Es handelt sich um den sogenannten Nachlass-Stempel.

1938 wurde das Portrait im Katalog von *Twentieth Century German Art* als Leihgabe eines Londoner Privatsammlers aufgeführt. Solch vage Formulierungen wurden im Katalog oft benutzt, um die Identifizierung von Eigentümern zu verhindern, die damals noch in Deutschland lebten. Wahrscheinlich befand sich das Gemälde 1938 weiterhin im Besitz von Martha Liebermann und zählte zu den Werken, welche die Witwe des Malers ab Mitte der 1930er Jahre für verschiedene Ausstellungen zur Verfügung stellte (vgl. S. 81-83).

Während der Londoner Ausstellung versuchten die Organisatoren, das Portrait Einsteins zu verkaufen. Das Bild wurde zuletzt von der Londoner Royal Society erworben. Ob Frau Liebermann den Kaufpreis je erhielt, ist unbekannt. Fest steht nur, dass sie Deutschland nicht verlassen konnte und im März 1943 als 85jährige in Berlin Selbstmord beging.

In the early decades of the Twentieth Century the Berlin painter Max Liebermann became renowned for his society portraits. He painted Albert Einstein's portrait three times during the 1920s: once in 1922, and twice more during 1925.

This painting is one of the 1925 portraits. It was not signed by the artist, instead bearing the artist's estate stamp, meaning it was in the artist's possession upon his death in 1935, passing into the ownership of his widow, Martha (1857-1943). In 1938 the painting appeared in the *Twentieth Century German Art* catalogue, listed as a loan from a 'Private collection, London'. These kinds of general descriptions were often used by the exhibition organisers to conceal a painting's true owner – in particular, if that owner was still living in Germany. It seems likely that this painting remained in Martha Liebermann's owner-ship until 1938, and that it was one of the many works sent by her to exhibitions across Europe during the mid-1930s (see pp. 88-90). Once on show in London, the organisers set about finding a buyer for this Einstein portrait. Eventually a buyer was found for the painting – London's Royal Society. Whether these funds ever reached Germany is unknown. Ultimately unable to find safe passage out of Germany, Martha Liebermann committed suicide in Berlin in March 1943 at the age of 85.

Literatur

Matthias Eberle: Max Liebermann 1847–1935. Werkverzeichnis der Gemälde und Ölstudien, München 1995.
Bernd Schmalhausen: «Ich bin doch nur ein Maler». Max und Martha Liebermann im Dritten Reich, Olms 1994.
o. V.: London day by day. Rescuing Einstein's Picture, in: Daily Telegraph and Morning Post, 12. August 1938, S. 10.
Royal Society Archives (London), mit bestem Dank an Keith Moore.

Literature

Matthias Eberle: Max Liebermann 1847-1935. Werkverzeichnis der Gemälde und Ölstudien. Munich 1995
Bernd Schmalhausen: "Ich bin doch nur ein Maler". Max und Martha Liebermann im Dritten Reich. Olms 1994
Anon.: London day by day. Rescuing Einstein's Picture, in: Daily Telegraph and Morning Post (12 August 1938), p. 10 Royal Society Archives (London) – with thanks to Keith Moore

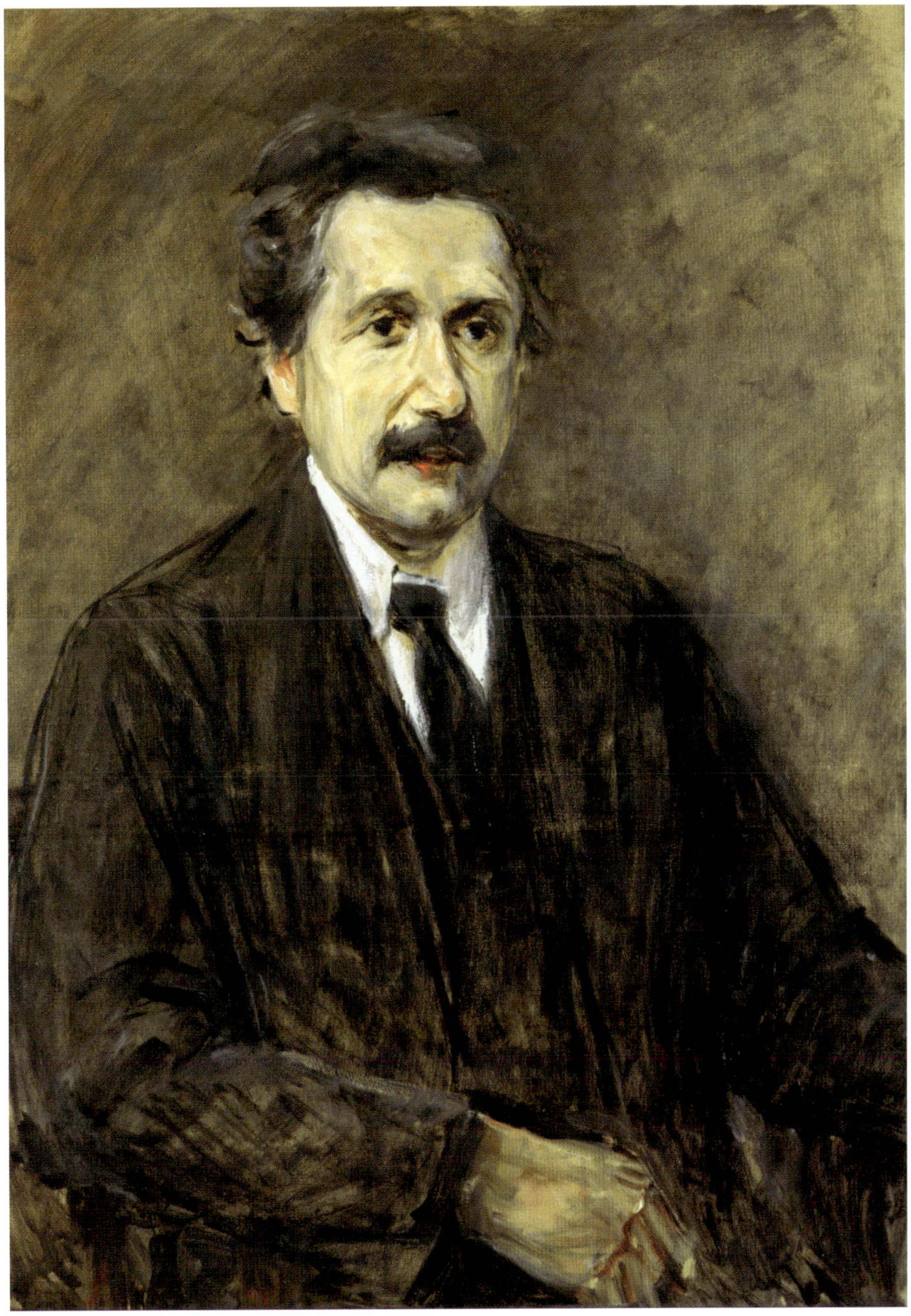

1 Max Liebermann
Professor Albert Einstein, 1925.
Öl auf Leinwand | oil on canvas, 99 x 74.9 cm
The Royal Society, London

Theodor + Ellen Plaut

Theodor Plaut (1888-1948) wurde in Leipzig als Sohn einer jüdischen Familie geboren. Nachdem er in Berlin, München und London Wirtschaft studiert hatte, wurde er 1924 zum Wirtschaftsprofessor an die Universität Hamburg berufen. 1920 heiratete er Ellen J. Warburg (1899-1940), die Tochter eines Hamburger Bankiers, die ihm zwei Kinder schenkte.

Während der 1920er Jahre reiste Plaut regelmäßig nach Großbritannien, um dort Vorlesungen zu halten und Forschungen zu betreiben. Nach der Machtergreifung der Nazis und seiner Entlassung aus der Universität Hamburg übernahm er im Oktober 1933 eine Gastprofessur an der Universität Hull in Nordengland.

Das hier gezeigte Pastell hatte der Vater von Ellen Plaut 1916 vom Berliner Kunsthändler Paul Cassirer erworben. Nachdem es 1938 in der Ausstellung *Twentieth Century German Art* gezeigt worden war, blieb es im Besitz der Familie Plaut bis zu seiner Veräußerung in London im Jahre 1995.

Theodor Plaut (1888-1948) was born to a Jewish family in Leipzig. He studied Economics in Berlin, Munich and London, before being appointed Professor of Economics in Hamburg in 1924. In 1920 he married Ellen J. Warburg (1899-1940) of the Hamburg banking family. Together the couple had two children.

Plaut had been a regular visitor to Britain during the 1920s, to conduct research and hold lectures. Following the National Socialist takeover in 1933, and his dismissal from the university in Hamburg, he was offered a Visiting Professorship at Hull University in northern England, which he took up in October 1933.

This pastel had been acquired by Ellen Plaut's father in 1916, from the Berlin dealership of Paul Cassirer. The family were able to bring it with them to Britain in 1933. Five years later, they loaned it to *Twentieth Century German Art*. The work remained in the Plaut family collection until its sale in London in 1995.

Literatur
Leo Baeck Institute (New York), Theodor Plaut collection.
Christie's (London): German and Austrian Art '95, Auktionskatalog, 11. Oktober 1995, Lot-Nr. 128.

Literature
Leo Baeck Institute, New York, Theodor Plaut collection
Christie's (London): German and Austrian Art '95. Auction catalogue (11 October 1995), lot 128

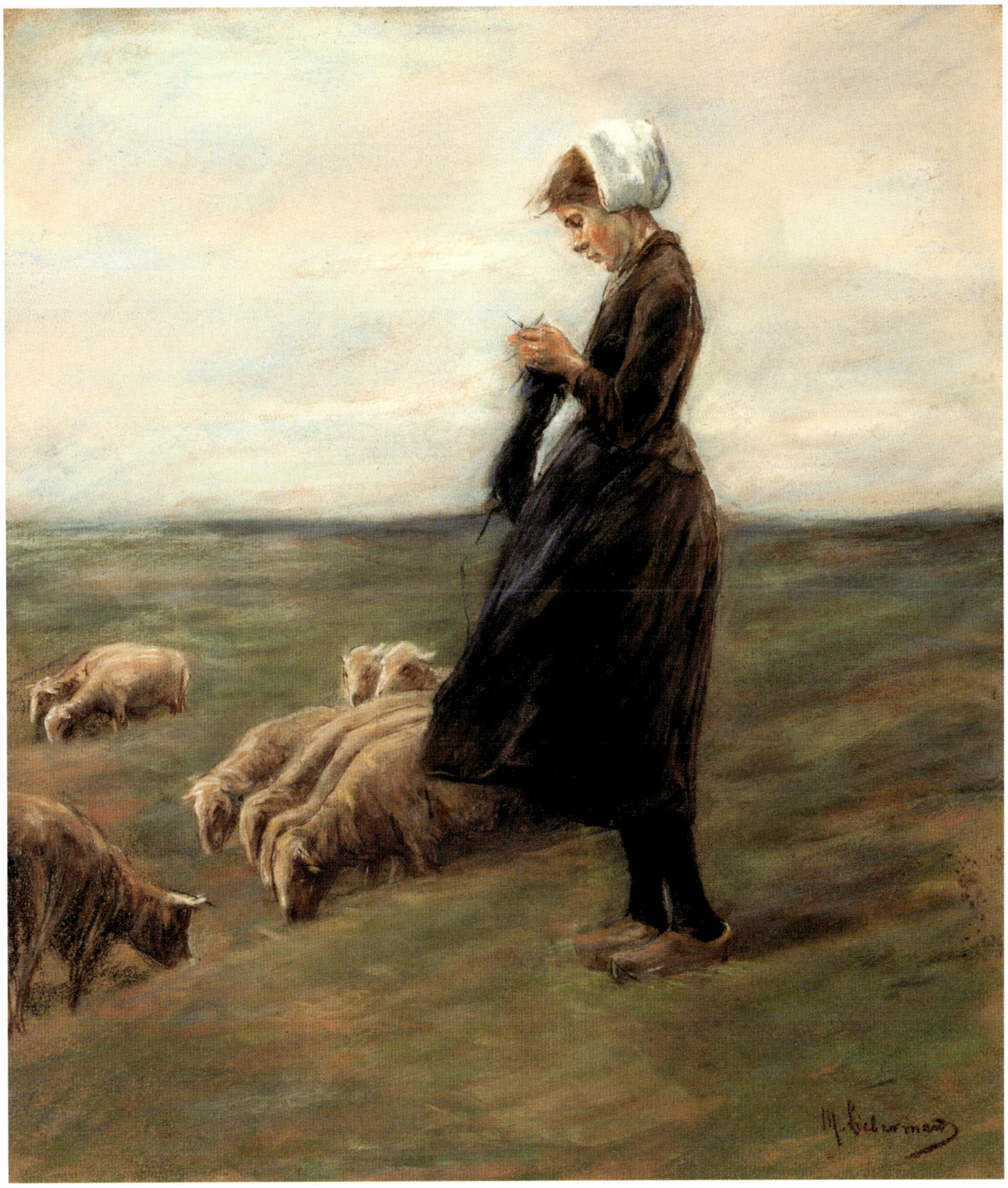

2 Max Liebermann
Schafhirtin | *Shepherdess*, 1887
Pastell auf Papier auf Pressspan | pastel on paper, on board, 74 x 66 cm
Privatsammlung | private collection

Sigmund Pollag

Leihgeber dieses 1938 ausgestellten Werks war Dr. Sigmund Pollag (1888-1977). Der gebürtige Basler hatte in Zürich und München Medizin studiert und wurde Assistent des deutschen Chirurgen Ferdinand Sauerbruch. Obwohl ihm in Deutschland eine Professur angeboten wurde, kehrte Pollag 1919 in die Schweiz zurück und eröffnete in Zürich eine Praxis, die er 57 Jahre lang betrieb.

Nicht nur als Mediziner, sondern auch als Mäzen und Sammler war Dr. Pollag in Zürich bekannt. 1925 legte er den Grundstock zu einer Sammlung, die hauptsächlich Werke französischer Künstler wie Pissarro, Renoir und Matisse sowie sämtliche graphischen Blätter von Maurice de Vlaminck umfasste.

Irmgard Burchard, die als Züricher Galeristin Kenntnis von dieser Sammlung gehabt haben dürfte, wird vermutlich den Kontakt zu Pollag hergestellt haben. Das hier gezeigte Ölgemälde war unter den zehn oder mehr Werken, mit denen sich Pollag an *Twentieth Century German Art* beteiligte. Weitere Leihgaben aus seiner Sammlung waren Arbeiten auf Papier von Max Liebermann und Max Slevogt.

The lender of this painting in 1938 was the Swiss doctor Sigmund Pollag (1888-1977). Born in Basel, he trained as a doctor in Zürich and Munich. He began his career in Germany, working as an assistant to the surgeon Ferdinand Sauerbruch. Though offered a professorship in Germany he returned to Switzerland in 1919. Here he opened a practice for internal medicine in Zürich, which he ran for the next fifty-seven years.

Alongside his practice, Pollag became a renowned supporter of the arts in Zürich. From around 1925 he began collecting art, in particular French artists such as Pissarro, Renoir and Matisse. Over the course of his life Pollag would collect de Vlaminck's entire graphic works.

Though it is not known how Sigmund Pollag came into contact with the London organisers, it was likely via Irmgard Burchard, who had perhaps become aware of his collection during her dealership activities in Zürich. Liebermann's *Concert at the Opera* was one of at least ten works he ultimately provided to *Twentieth Century German Art*, alongside this oil comprising works on paper by Liebermann and Max Slevogt.

Literatur

Galerie Wolfgang Ketterer: Sammlung Dr. S. Pollag Zürich, Auktionskatalog, Stuttgart, 27. November 1973.

René Neuenschwander: Gedenkblatt für einen großen Sammler. Zum Tode von Dr. Sigmund Pollag, in: Der Bund (Bern), Nr. 117, 21. Mai 1977, S. 31.

Literature

Galerie Wolfgang Ketterer: Sammlung Dr S Pollag Zürich. Auction catalogue, Stuttgart, 27 November 1973

René Neuenschwander: Gedenkblatt für einen grossen Sammler. Zum Tode von Dr. Sigmund Pollag, in Der Bund (Berne), no. 117 (21 May 1977), p. 31

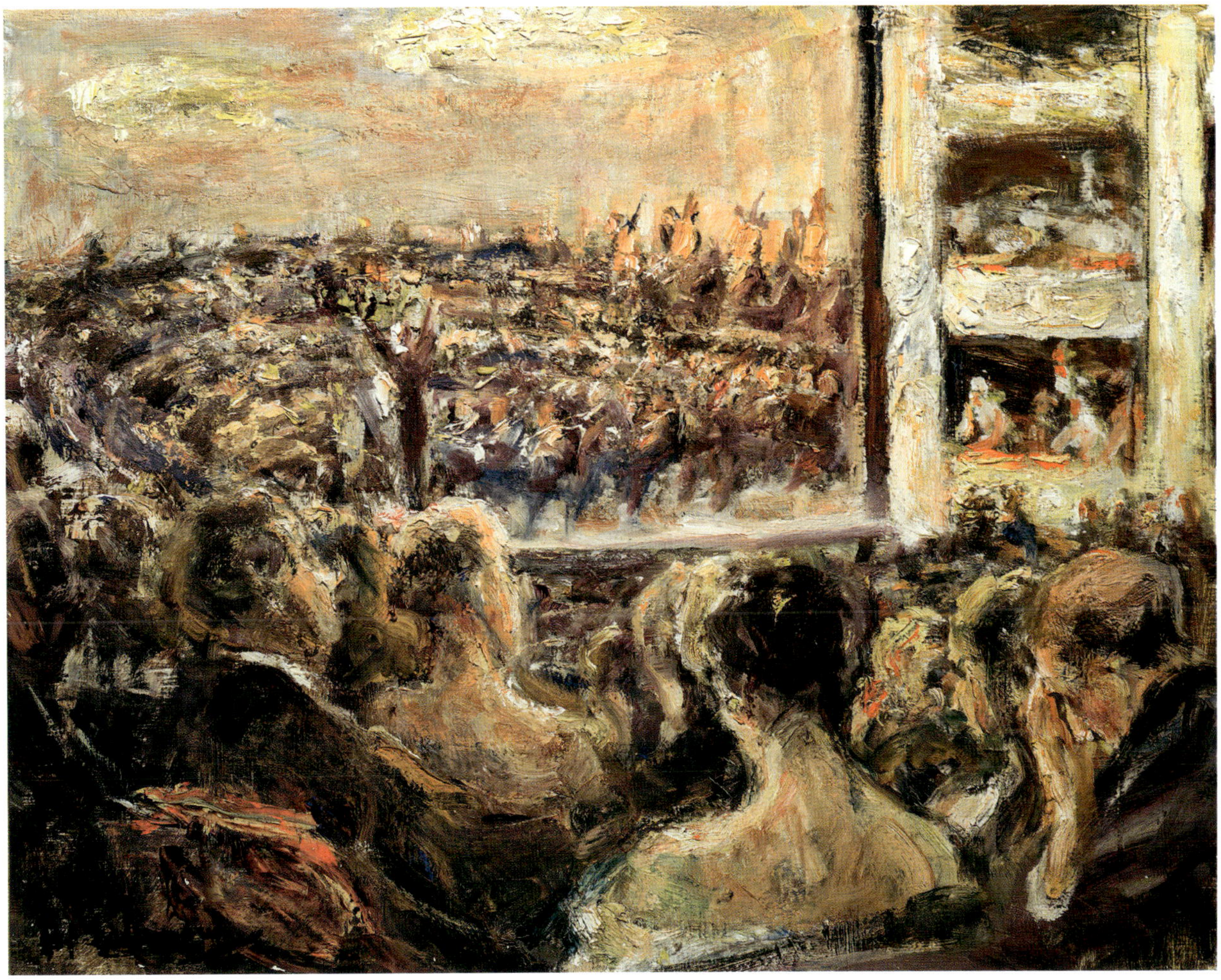

3 Max Liebermann
Konzert in der Oper | *Concert at the Opera*, 1922
Öl auf Leinwand | oil on canvas, 40 x 51 cm
Privatsammlung | private collection

Max Stern

Im Ausstellungskatalog wird dieses Gemälde als Leihgabe der «West's Gallery, London» aufgeführt. Diese Kunsthandlung wurde 1938 von dem deutsch-jüdischen Emigranten Max Stern (1904-1987) geleitet.

Zuvor hatte Stern die von seinem Vater 1913 in Düsseldorf gegründete Galerie betrieben. Als jüdischer Unternehmer war er unmittelbar nach der Machtergreifung der Nazis mit großen Schwierigkeiten konfrontiert. 1935 wurde ihm sogar die Weiterführung seiner Galerie verboten, womit das Exil unausweichlich wurde. Verzweifelt versuchte er, das Beste aus der Situation zu machen: Manche Kunstwerke verkaufte er, andere kaufte er hinzu, wie z.B. das hier gezeigte Liebermann-Gemälde. Er erwarb es im Februar 1937 vom Museum Wiesbaden, als der damalige Direktor auf Anweisung der Regierung alle Werke jüdischer Künstler verkaufen musste.

Im Herbst 1937 schloss Max Stern seine Düsseldorfer Galerie und emigrierte nach London. Die verbliebenen Kunstwerke wurden im November gleichen Jahres im Kölner Auktionshaus Lempertz versteigert. Obwohl *Kartoffelpflücker* im Auktionskatalog aufgelistet ist, wurde das Bild vor der Auktion nach London transportiert, so dass es für *Twentieth Century German Art* zur Verfügung stand. Wie viele andere Leihgaben von Kunsthändlern stand auch dieses Werk zum Verkauf.

The 1938 exhibition catalogue described this painting as a loan from 'West's Gallery, London'. This gallery was in fact run in 1938 by the German-Jewish émigré Max Stern (1904-1987).

Stern was the former owner of the Galerie Stern, an art dealership in Düsseldorf founded by his father in 1913. As Jewish business owners, the Stern family faced immediate difficulties following the National Socialist takeover; in 1935 Max Stern was banned from acting as a dealer. As exile became inevitable, Stern began a period of frantic buying and selling, in an attempt to make what he could from the gallery's remaining stock. He acquired this painting in February 1937 from the Museum in Wiesbaden, the museum's director having been ordered to sell all works by Jewish artists, including those by Max Liebermann.

With the closure of the Galerie Stern in autumn 1937, Max Stern departed Germany for Britain. The remaining stock of his gallery was sold at the Lempertz auction house in Cologne in November 1937. Though *Potato Gatherer* was included in this auction catalogue, the painting was transported to London before the sale. Like many other dealer loans to *Twentieth Century German Art* this work was marked for sale in the catalogue.

Literatur

Catherine Mackenzie: Auktion 392. Reclaiming the Galerie Stern, Montréal 2006.

Michael Dorrmann: Die Galerie Stern. Auktion 392 und das Bildnis des Jean van Eversdijk, in: Inka Bertz/Michael Dorrmann (Hg.): Raub und Restitution. Kulturgut aus jüdischem Besitz von 1933 bis heute, Göttingen, 2008, S. 98-104.

National Gallery of Canada (Ottawa), Max Stern collection and West's Galleries Limited collection.

Literature

Catherine Mackenzie: Auktion 392. Reclaiming the Galerie Stern. Montréal, 2006

Michael Dorrmann: Die Galerie Stern. Auktion 392 und das Bildnis des Jean van Eversdijk, in: Inka Bertz and Michael Dorrmann (eds.): Raub und Restitution. Kulturgut aus jüdischem Besitz von 1933 bis Heute. Göttingen, 2008, pp. 98-104

National Gallery of Canada, Ottawa, Max Stern collection and West's Galleries Limited collection

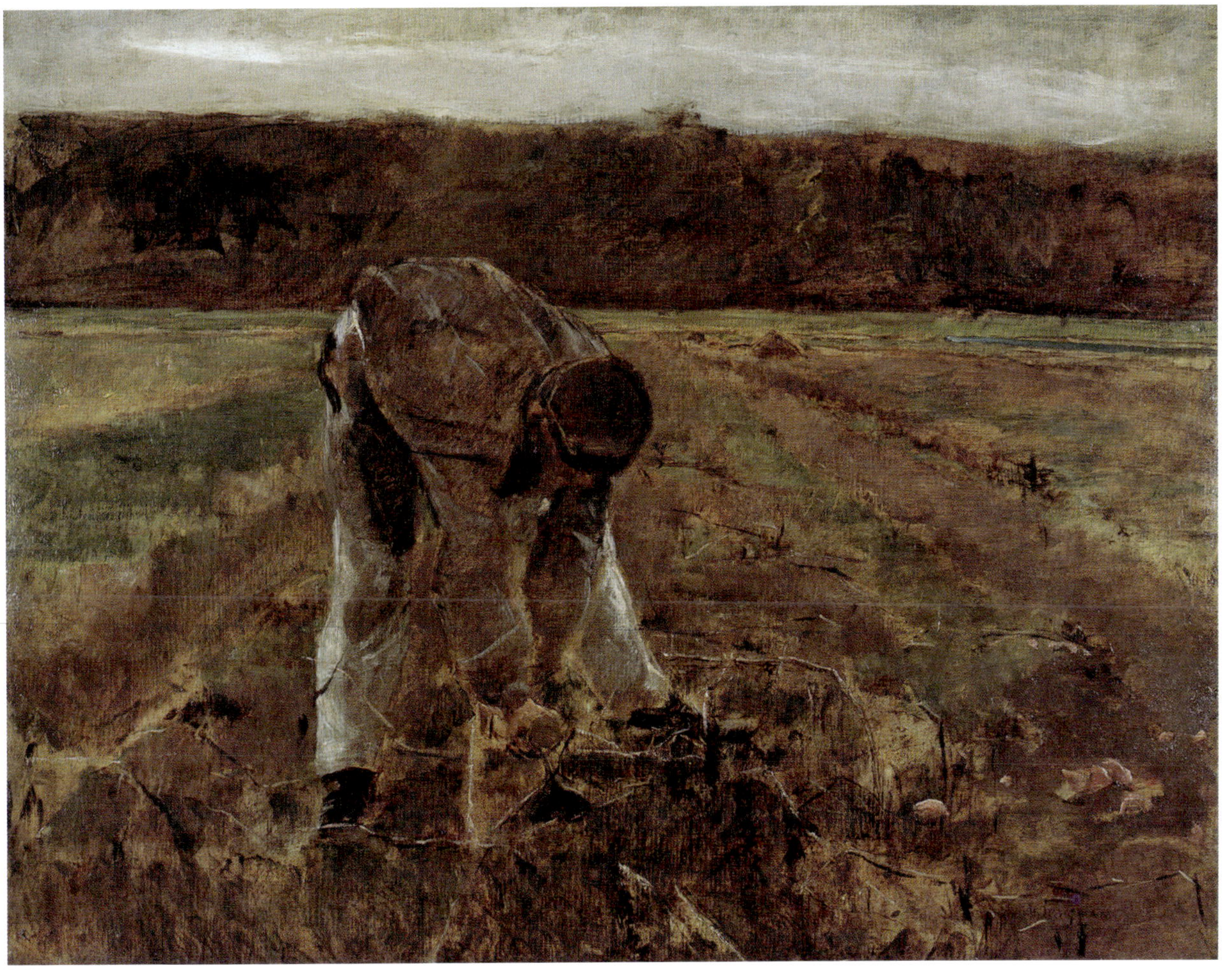

4 Max Liebermann
Kartoffelpflücker | *Potato Gatherer*, 1874
Öl auf Leinwand | oil on canvas, 90 x 116 cm
Das Kartoffelmuseum, München

Wilhelm Abegg

Die folgenden zwei Abbildungen zeigen zwei von mindestens neun Leihgaben, die Wilhelm Abbegg (1876-1951) nach London sandte. Der in Berlin geborene Verwaltungsjurist war zunächst im preußischen Staatsdienst tätig. Ab 1923 leitete er als Ministerialdirektor die Polizeiabteilung im preußischen Innenministerium. Drei Jahre später wurde er zum Staatssekretär ernannt.

Als exponierter Kritiker der Nazis verließ er Deutschland unmittelbar nach der Machtergreifung im Januar 1933. Er emigrierte nach Zürich und wurde dort in verschiedenen Widerstandsbewegungen, kulturellen Vereinigungen und Hilfsorganisationen für Flüchtlinge tätig.

Am 13. Dezember 1937 schrieb Irmgard Burchard an Paul Westheim: «Herr Dr. W. Abegg hat einige Rohlfs. Sind diese für die Ausstellung notwendig?» Westheim bejahte und bat Burchard darum, die Leihgaben zu sichern. Daraufhin beteiligte sich Abegg mit den zwei hier gezeigten Werken sowie graphischen Arbeiten von Rohlfs und Käthe Kollwitz an der Ausstellung.

Literatur

Michael Eggers: Wilhelm Abegg. Schöpfer der Deutschen Polizei und Widerstandskämpfer der ersten Stunde, in: Jahrbuch Einst und Jetzt, Bd. 56 (2011), S. 265–277.
RSMA, Brief von Irmgard Burchard an Paul Westheim, 13. Dezember 1937.

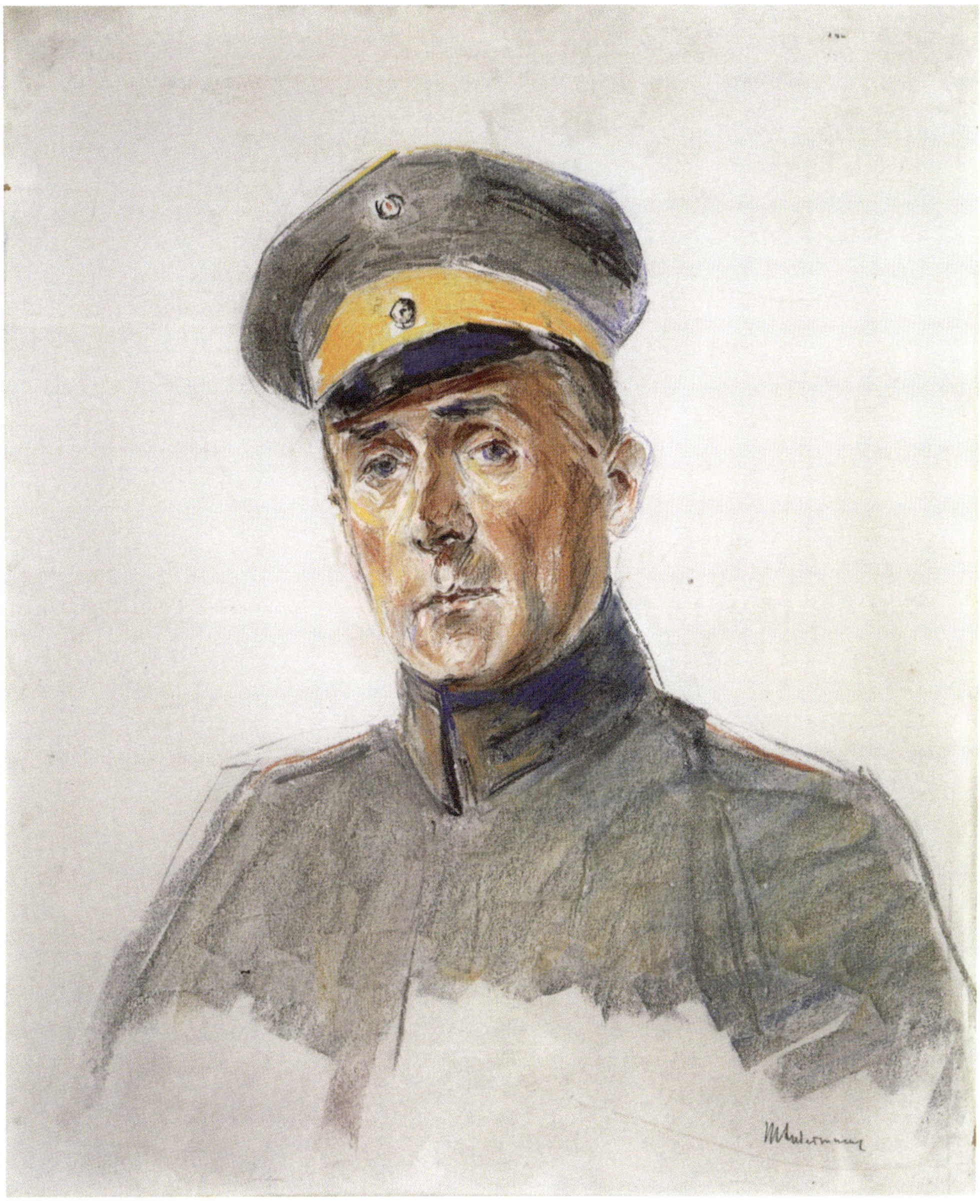

5 Max Liebermann
Harry Graf Kessler in Uniform, circa 1916
Pastell | pastel, 71 x 58.7 cm
Deutsches Literaturarchiv Marbach

Wilhelm Abegg

These are two of at least nine works provided to London by the German politician Wilhelm Abegg (1876-1951). Born in Berlin, Abegg began his career as a government lawyer. From 1923 he was Ministerial Director of the Prussian Police Department. In 1926 he was appointed State Secretary in the Prussian Interior Ministry.

Abegg was a conspicuous opponent of fascism in 1920s Berlin. He was therefore quick to leave Germany in 1933, emigrating to Zürich less than one month after Hitler's takeover. In Switzerland he became active in various German resistance movements, free cultural associations and refugee help organisations.

On 13 December 1937 Irmgard Burchard wrote to her fellow organiser Paul Westheim from her base in Zürich: "Dr W. Abegg has some works by Rohlfs ... are these needed for the exhibition?" Westheim confirmed that Burchard should secure the loans. Alongside the works illustrated here (see p. 105), Abegg provided further works on paper by Rohlfs and a selection of graphics by Käthe Kollwitz.

Literature

Michael Eggers: Wilhelm Abegg. Schöpfer der Deutschen Polizei und Widerstandskämpfer der ersten Stunde, in: Jahrbuch Einst und Jetzt, vol. 56 (2011), pp. 265-77

RSMA, letter from Irmgard Burchard to Paul Westheim, 13 December 1937

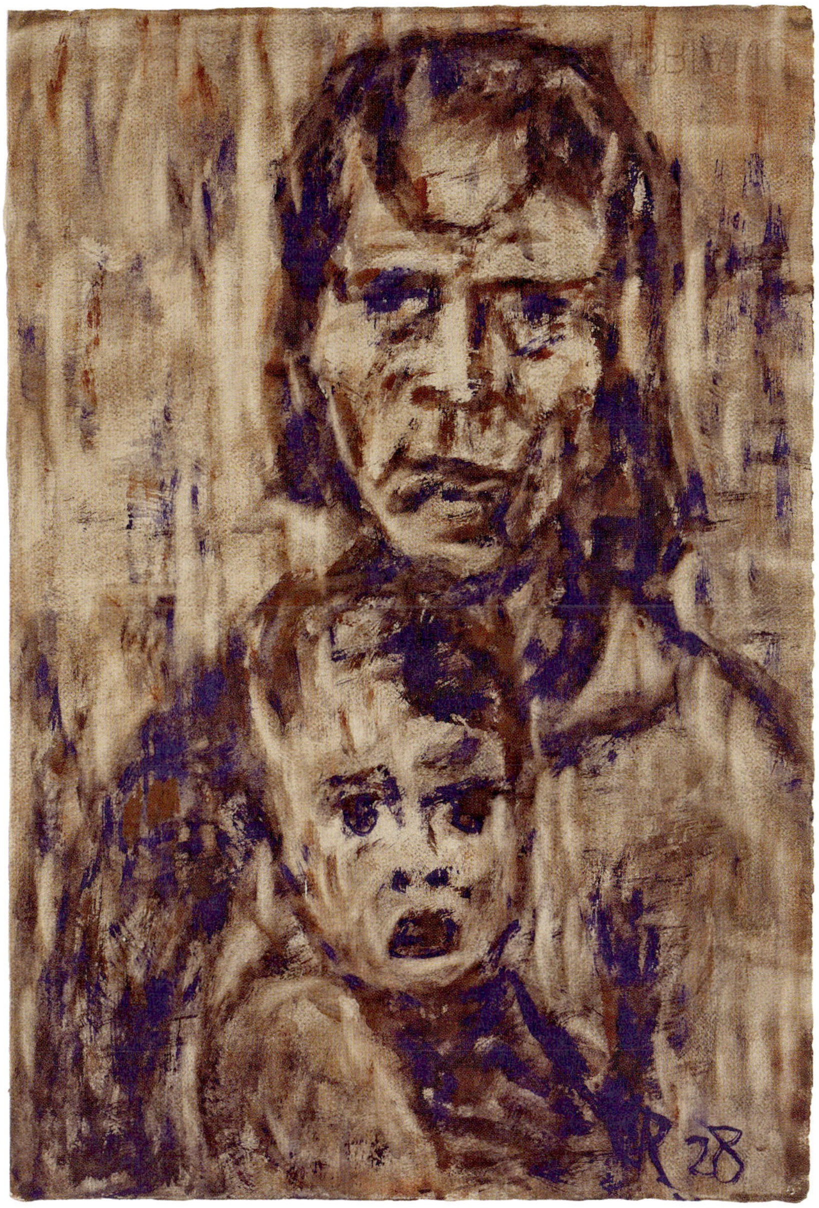

6 Christian Rohlfs
Mutter mit Kind | *Mother with Child*, 1928
Tempera auf Papier | tempera on paper, 57 x 39.5 cm
Privatsammlung | private collection

Unbekannter Leihgeber

In den 1880er und 1890er Jahren schuf Max Liebermann mindestens acht Gemälde von Kirchgängern der holländischen Stadt Laren.

Im Katalog der Ausstellung *Twentieth Century German Art* ist ein Werk «Afternoon in Laren» (Nachmittag in Laren) aufgeführt, und zwar mit den Maßen (35 × 52 cm) und dem Entstehungsdatum (1892). Als Leihgeber ist die Galerie Wolfsberg in Zürich angegeben.

Das Liebermann-Werkverzeichnis führt ein Gemälde mit dem Titel *Sonntagnachmittag in Laren* auf, das sich zwischen 1938 und 1954 im Besitz der Galerie Wolfsberg befunden hat. Dieses Gemälde ist auch in Peter Thoenes Begleitbuch zur Ausstellung *Modern German Art* abgebildet. Allerdings stimmen die Maße und das Entstehungsdatum im Werkverzeichnis (72 × 100 cm, 1894) nicht mit denjenigen im Katalog der Londoner Ausstellung überein.

Fotos der Ausstellung zeigen wiederum, dass eine andere, kleinere Fassung der Laren-Szene in London zu sehen war. Dieses Werk – *Kirchgang in Laren* (Abb. 49, S. 109) – entstand im Jahr 1882, misst 28 × 46,5 cm (dies entspricht eher den Angaben des Katalogeintrags) und trägt auf der Rückseite ein Etikett der Londoner Ausstellung. Leider ist auf dem Etikett der Name des damaligen Leihgebers nicht mehr lesbar.

Wahrscheinlich sind beide Fassungen des Laren-Motivs in London gezeigt worden. Das Gemälde aus dem Jahr 1894 war eine Leihgabe der Galerie Wolfsberg, während das Bild von 1882 aus unbekannter Quelle stammte.

Unknown lender

During the 1880s and 90s, Max Liebermann produced at least eight paintings depicting figures going to church in the Dutch town of Laren. According to the *Twentieth Century German Art* catalogue, one such Laren scene was exhibited at the New Burlington Galleries in 1938, described as "Afternoon in Laren", measuring 35 x 52 cm, dated to 1892, with the lender named as Zürich's Galerie Wolfsberg.

Turning to the Liebermann catalogue raisonné, we find that Liebermann's 1894 painting *Sunday Afternoon in Laren* was in the ownership of the Galerie Wolfsberg from 1938 until 1954. This same painting was illustrated in the book published to accompany the show, Peter Thoene's *Modern German Art*. This 1894 picture is however almost twice the size of the work listed in the London catalogue, according to the catalogue raisonné measuring some 72 x 100 cm.

Photographs of the London exhibition clearly show that a second, smaller version of this Laren scene was also exhibited in London: *Going to Church, Laren* (1882, see fig. 49, p. 84). This 1882 work measures 28 x 46.5 cm, far closer to the dimensions provided in the London catalogue. This earlier picture also bears a *Twentieth Century German Art* label on its reverse, though the details of the 1938 lender are no longer legible.

It seems therefore that two versions of this scene were on show in London: an 1894 version loaned by the Galerie Wolfsberg, and an 1882 version sent by an unknown lender.

Literatur

Matthias Eberle: Max Liebermann 1847-1935. Werkverzeichnis der Gemälde und Ölstudien, München 1995, Nrn. 1882/26 und 1894/13.

Literature

Matthias Eberle: Max Liebermann 1847-1935. Werkverzeichnis der Gemälde und Ölstudien. Munich 1995, nos. 1882/26 and 1894/13

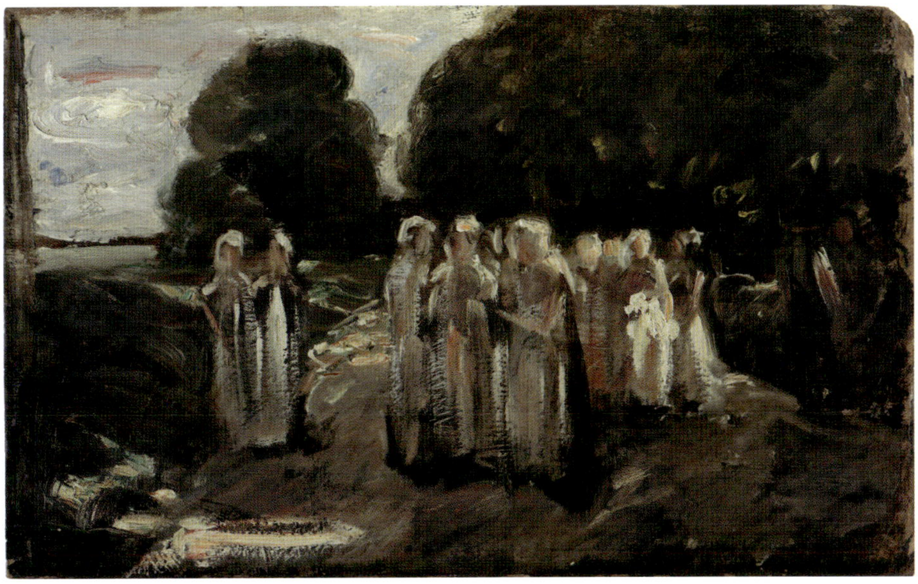

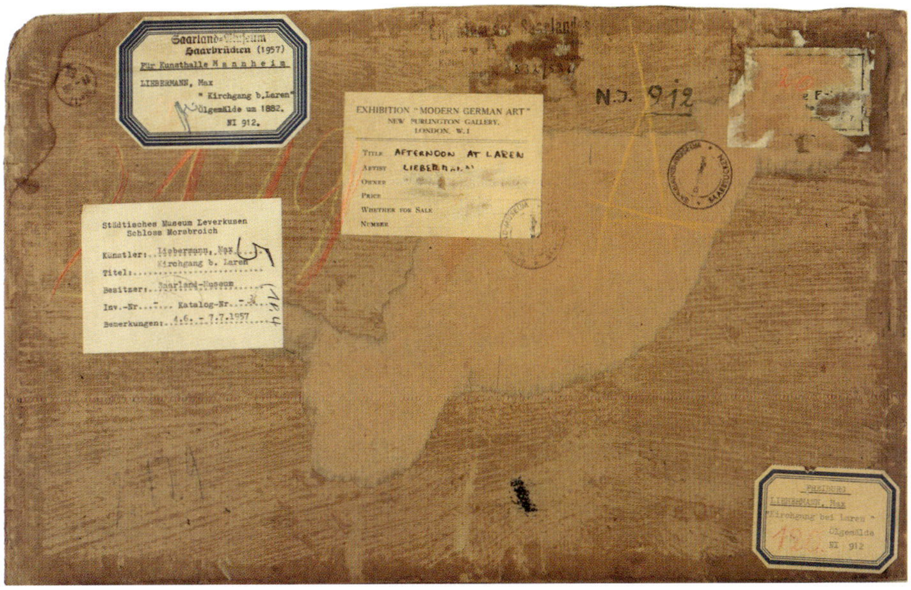

7 Max Liebermann
Kirchgang in Laren | *Going to Church, Laren,* 1882, recto | verso
Öl auf Pappe | oil on card, 28 x 46.5 cm
Saarlandmuseum Saarbrücken, Stiftung Saarländischer Kulturbesitz

Erich + Senta Göritz

Leihgeber dieses Bildes waren der deutsch-jüdische Textilfabrikant Erich Göritz (1889-1955) und seine Frau Senta (1893-1971).

Göritz zählte zu den berühmtesten Sammlern moderner Kunst im Berlin der 1920er Jahre. Eine Zeitlang gehörte ihm Manets *Un Bar aux Folies-Bergère* (1882), das er 1924 an Samuel Courtauld verkaufte. Darüber hinaus war Göritz mit Lovis Corinth befreundet und besaß Dutzende von Werken dieses Malers.

Nach der Machtergreifung der Nazis erkannten Erich und Senta Göritz rasch, wie gefährlich die Situation für Juden werden konnte. So emigrierten sie schon 1934 nach England. Einen Teil ihrer Sammlung nahmen sie ins Exil mit. Außerdem sandten sie etwa tausend Werke an das kurz davor gegründete Tel Aviv Museum of Art.

Paul Westheim kannte Göritz aus seiner Zeit in Berlin. Im November 1937 ließ seine Mitorganisatoren wissen, dass die Göritz-Sammlung jetzt in Großbritannien sei. Erich und Senta Göritz liehen mindestens sechs Ölgemälde von Corinth für die Ausstellung.

The lenders of this painting were the German-Jewish textile manufacturer Erich Göritz (1889-1955) and his wife Senta (1893-1971). Göritz was among the most prominent collectors of modernist art in Weimar-era Berlin, at one time owning Manet's *Un bar aux Folies-Bergère* (1882) which he sold to Samuel Courtauld in 1924. He was also a close friend of the painter Lovis Corinth, collecting and commissioning dozens of his works.

Erich and Senta Göritz were quick to recognise the danger for Jewish families after the National Socialist takeover. They emigrated to Britain in 1934, taking a portion of their art collection with them. A further 1000 pieces from their collection were shipped to the Tel Aviv Museum of Art.

Paul Westheim knew Göritz from his time in Berlin, in November 1937 informing his fellow organisers that the collection was now in Britain. Erich and Senta Göritz ultimately provided at least six Corinth oils to *Twentieth Century German Art*.

Literatur

Abraham Gilam: Erich Göritz and Jewish Art Patronage in Berlin During the 1920s, in: Journal of the Center for Jewish Art, The Hebrew University of Jerusalem, Bd. 11, 1985, S. 60–72.

Korrespondenz der Autorin mit Louise Millar-Göritz, London, April 2012.

Korrespondenz der Autorin mit Dr. Mario von Lüttichau, Museum Folkwang, Essen, Februar 2012.

Literature

Abraham Gilam: Erich Göritz and Jewish Art Patronage in Berlin During the 1920s, in: Journal of the Center for Jewish Art. The Hebrew University of Jerusalem, vol. 11 (1985), pp. 60-72

Correspondence between the author and Louise Millar-Göritz, London, April 2012

Correspondence between the author and Dr Mario von Lüttichau, Museum Folkwang, Essen, February 2012

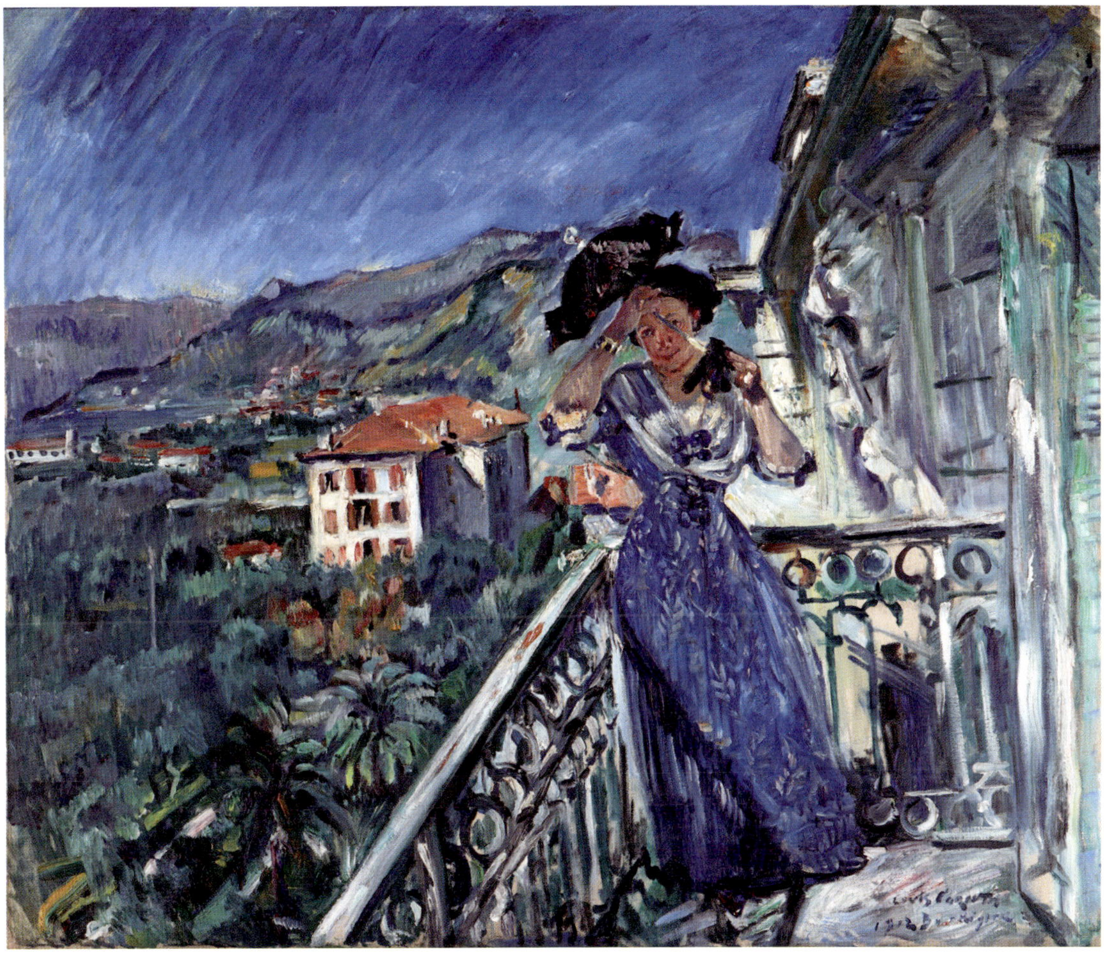

8 Lovis Corinth
In Bordighera, 1912
Öl auf Leinwand | oil on canvas, 83.5 x 105 cm
Museum Folkwang Essen

Ludwig Burchard

In der Ausstellung *Twentieth Century German Art* war Lovis Corinth mit wenigstens achtzehn Werken vertreten. Leihgeber des hier gezeigten Aquarells war der Kunsthistoriker Ludwig Burchard (1886-1960).

Nach Abschluss seines Studiums in München und Heidelberg arbeitete Burchard bis 1920 als Redakteur des renommierten Künstlerlexikon Thieme-Becker. Sein Hauptwerk, das ihn bis zu seinem Lebensende beschäftigen sollte, war jedoch das Werkverzeichnis von Peter Paul Rubens.

Da Burchards Mutter Jüdin war, musste er nach 1933 aus Deutschland emigrieren. Nach seiner Ankunft in England arbeitete er an seinem Rubens-Projekt weiter und wurde für seine umfassende Kenntnis des Künstlers berühmt, verstarb 1960 aber noch vor Fertigstellung seines Lebenswerks. Auf der Basis von Burchards Arbeit konnte jedoch das «Rubenianum› aufgebaut werden, eine auf Rubens spezialisierte kunsthistorische Einrichtung, die bis heute in Antwerpen besteht.

Lovis Corinth was well-represented in *Twentieth Century German Art*, the show containing at least 18 of his works. This watercolour self-portrait was loaned to London by the art historian Ludwig Burchard (1886-1960).

Following studies in Munich and Heidelberg, Burchard worked until 1920 as editor of the renowned 'Thieme-Becker' artists' lexicon. During this period he also began work on a catalogue raisonné of Peter Paul Rubens' works, a project which would occupy him for the rest of his life.

Burchard's mother was Jewish. He was thus forced into exile after 1933, resettling in Britain. Though he continued to work on the Rubens catalogue, and found renown as a scholar of the artist, the volume was never published and remained unfinished upon his death in 1960. His research papers formed the basis of the Rubenianum, a Rubens research centre in Antwerp which exists to this day.

Literatur
D. Sutton: Mr Ludwig Burchard. A Leading Expert on Rubens, in: The Times, 5. Oktober 1960, S. 15.
Ulrike Wendland: Biographisches Handbuch deutschsprachiger Kunsthistoriker im Exil. Leben und Werk der unter dem Nationalsozialismus verfolgten und vertriebenen Wissenschaftler, München, 1999, S. 78–83.

Literature
D. Sutton: Mr Ludwig Burchard. A Leading Expert on Rubens, in: The Times (5 October 1960), p. 15
Ulrike Wendland: Biographisches Handbuch deutschsprachiger Kunsthistoriker im Exil. Leben und Werk der unter dem Nationalsozialismus verfolgten und vertriebenen Wissenschaftler. Munich, 1999, pp. 78-83

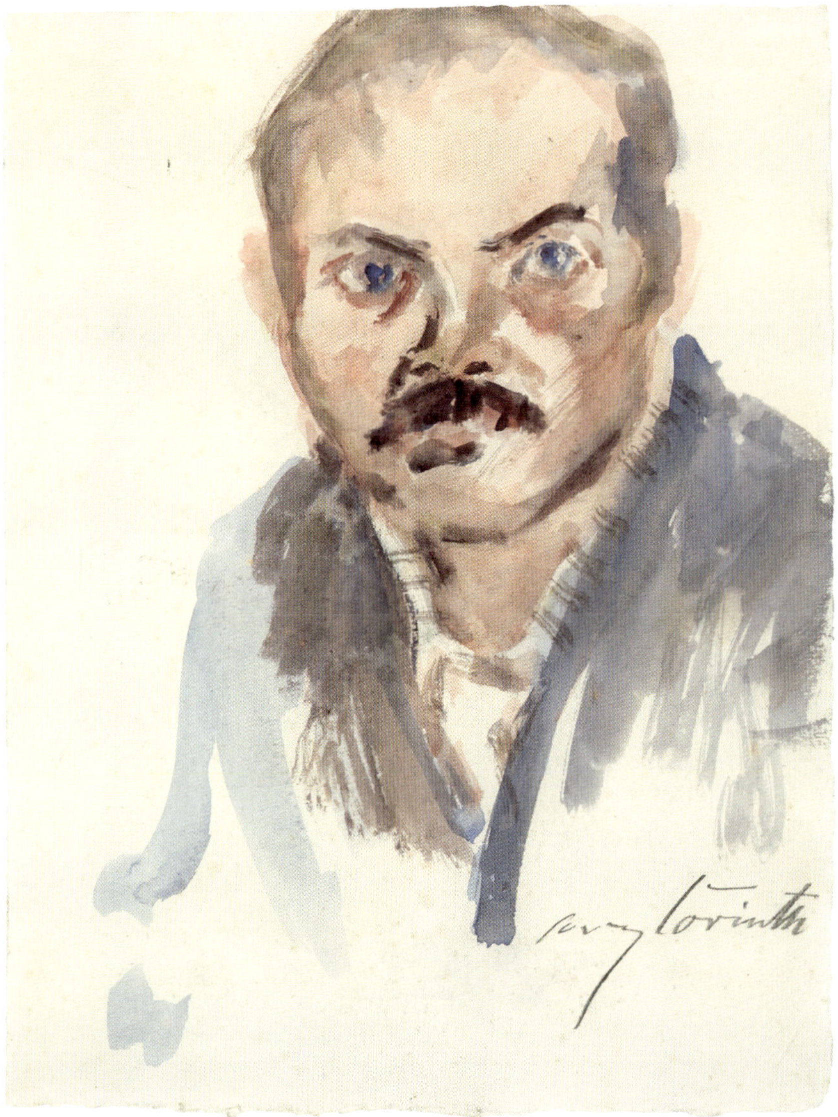

9 Lovis Corinth
Selbstbildnis | *Self Portrait*, circa 1912
Aquarell auf Papier | watercolour on paper, 28 x 21.5 cm
Daxer & Marschall Kunsthandel München

János + Melanie Plesch

Der Mediziner Dr. János Plesch (1878-1957) und seine Frau Melanie (1884-1954) beteiligten sich an der Londoner Ausstellung mit wenigstens sechs Bildern Max Slevogts.

Plesch wurde in Budapest in einer jüdischen Familie geboren. Nach seinem Medizinstudium arbeitete er ab 1902 an der Berliner Charité. 1914 heiratete er Melanie Gans aus Frankfurt; zusammen hatten sie drei Kinder.

Während der 1920er Jahre arbeitete János Plesch als Internist in Berlin. Die Familie wohnte in der Budapester Straße mit Blick auf dem Tiergarten und in der Villa Lemm am Ufer der Havel in Gatow. Unter seinen Patienten befanden sich mehrere Künstler, unter anderem auch der Maler Max Slevogt. Das Werk *Die Familie des Arztes János Plesch*, das Slevogt 1928 malte, hängt heute im Jüdischen Museum Berlin.

Familie Plesch verließ Deutschland kurz nach der Machtergreifung der Nazis und emigrierte nach England. Dr. Plesch eröffnete eine Privatpraxis in London und betrieb sie bis zu seinem Ruhestand.

Literatur

János Plesch: János. The Story of a Doctor, New York 1949.
Archiv der Familie Plesch.

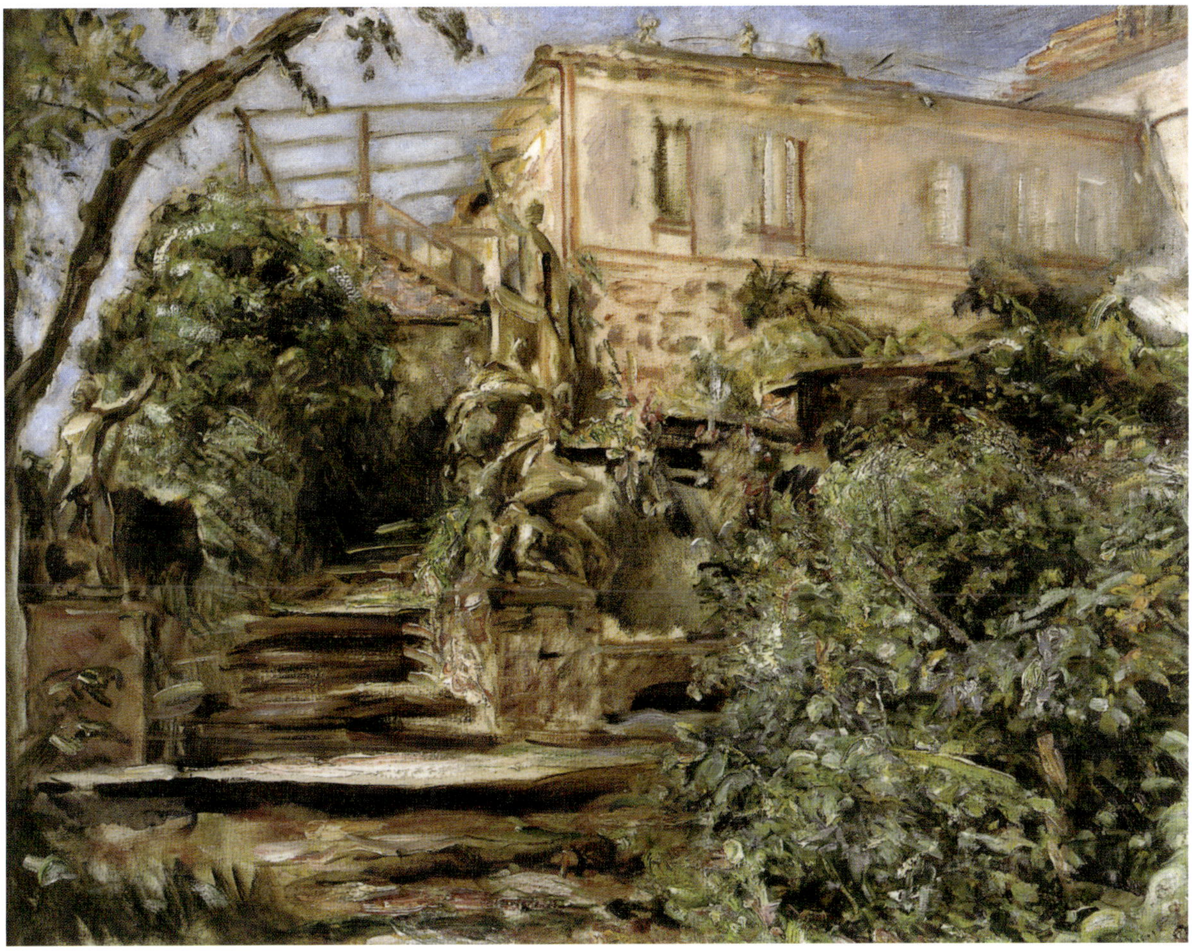

10 Max Slevogt
Der Garten in Neukastel mit der Bibliothek |
The Garden in Neukastel with the Library, 1930-31
Öl auf Leinwand | oil on canvas, 68.5 x 86.5 cm
Landesmuseum Mainz

János + Melanie Plesch

The doctor János Plesch (1878-1957) and his wife Melanie (1884-1954) provided at least six works by Max Slevogt to *Twentieth Century German Art*. Plesch was born to a Jewish family in Budapest. After training as a doctor he arrived in Berlin in 1902, to a position working at the renowned Charité hospital. In 1914 he married Melanie Gans of Frankfurt. Together the couple had three children.

Plesch became a renowned society physician in the Berlin of the 1920s. The family divided their time between a house on Budapester Straße overlooking the Tiergarten, and the Villa Lemm on the River Havel at Gatow. Plesch counted a number of artists among his patients, among them Max Slevogt. In 1928 he commissioned Slevogt to paint the family's portrait, a work which today hangs in the Jewish Museum in Berlin.

Plesch and his family departed Berlin within months of the National Socialist takeover. They resettled in London, where Plesch resumed his practice, working as a doctor in Britain until his retirement.

Literature
János Plesch: János. The Story of a Doctor. New York 1949
Plesch family archives

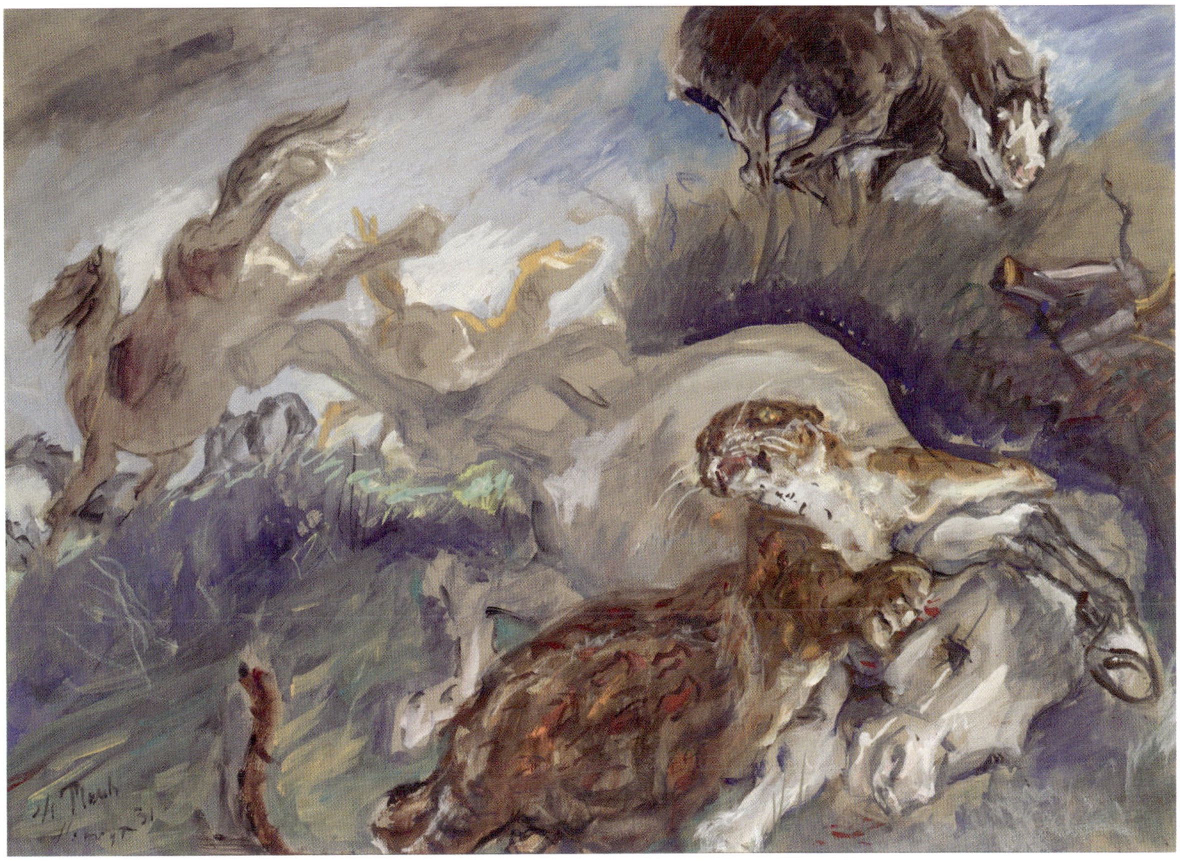

11 Max Slevogt
Der Panther | *The Panther*, 1931
Tempera, 49 x 68 cm
Privatsammlung | private collection

Paul + Elvira Bacharach

Im November 1937 aktivierte Paul Westheim sein Netzwerk, um potenzielle Leihgeber für die Ausstellung *Twentieth Century German Art* zu gewinnen. Unter seinen Kontakten in der Schweiz war der deutsch-jüdische Kunsthistoriker Curt Glaser, der ehemalige Direktor der Kunstbibliothek Berlin, der seit 1933 unweit von Ascona im Exil lebte.

Glaser wiederum kannte die Eheleute Paul und Elvira Bachrach (Lebensdaten unbekannt), die als Leihgeber in Frage kamen. Paul Bachrach hatte vor dem 1. Weltkrieg eine Pelzhandlung in Brüssel betrieben. Als deutscher Staatsbürger musste er Belgien 1914 verlassen und zog mit seiner Familie nach Worpswede. Sie kamen beim Maler Heinrich Vogeler unter, einem Freund der Familie. Während ihres dortigen Aufenthaltes kauften sie das Gemälde *Landschaft mit drei Kindern* von Paula Modersohn-Becker, die bis zu ihrem Tod 1907 dort gewohnt und gearbeitet hatte. 1919 zog Bachrach mit seiner Familie nach Ascona. Er blieb bis zum Lebensende in der Schweiz.

During November 1937, Paul Westheim reached out to his contacts in Switzerland to find potential lenders for *Twentieth Century German Art*. Among them was the German Jewish art historian Curt Glaser, former director of the Berlin Art Library, who had been living in exile near Ascona since 1933.

In early December 1937, Glaser provided Westheim with the names of Paul and Elvira Bachrach (dates of birth and death unknown) as potential lenders to London. The German-born Bachrach had worked as a fur trader in Brussels before the outbreak of the First World War forced the family back to Germany. They travelled to the village of Worpswede, where they stayed with their friend, the artist Heinrich Vogeler. Worpswede had also been the home of the artist Paula Modersohn-Becker. It was here that the Bachrachs acquired *Landscape with Three Children*. In 1919 the Bachrachs travelled on to Ascona, where they remained for the rest of their lives.

Literatur
RSMA, Brief von Curt Glaser an Paul Westheim, 1. Dezember 1938.
Korrespondenz der Autorin mit Eliana Bulteaux Bachrach (Brüssel) und Karl-Robert Schütze (Berlin).
Karl-Robert Schütze: Charlotte Bara 1901–1986, Brüssel-Worpswede-Berlin-Ascona, Berlin 2000.

Literature
RSMA, letter from Curt Glaser to Paul Westheim, 1 December 1938
Correspondence between the author and Eliana Bulteaux Bachrach, Brussels, and Karl-Robert Schütze, Berlin
Karl-Robert Schütze: Charlotte Bara 1901-1986. Brüssel-Worpswede-Berlin-Ascona. Berlin 2000

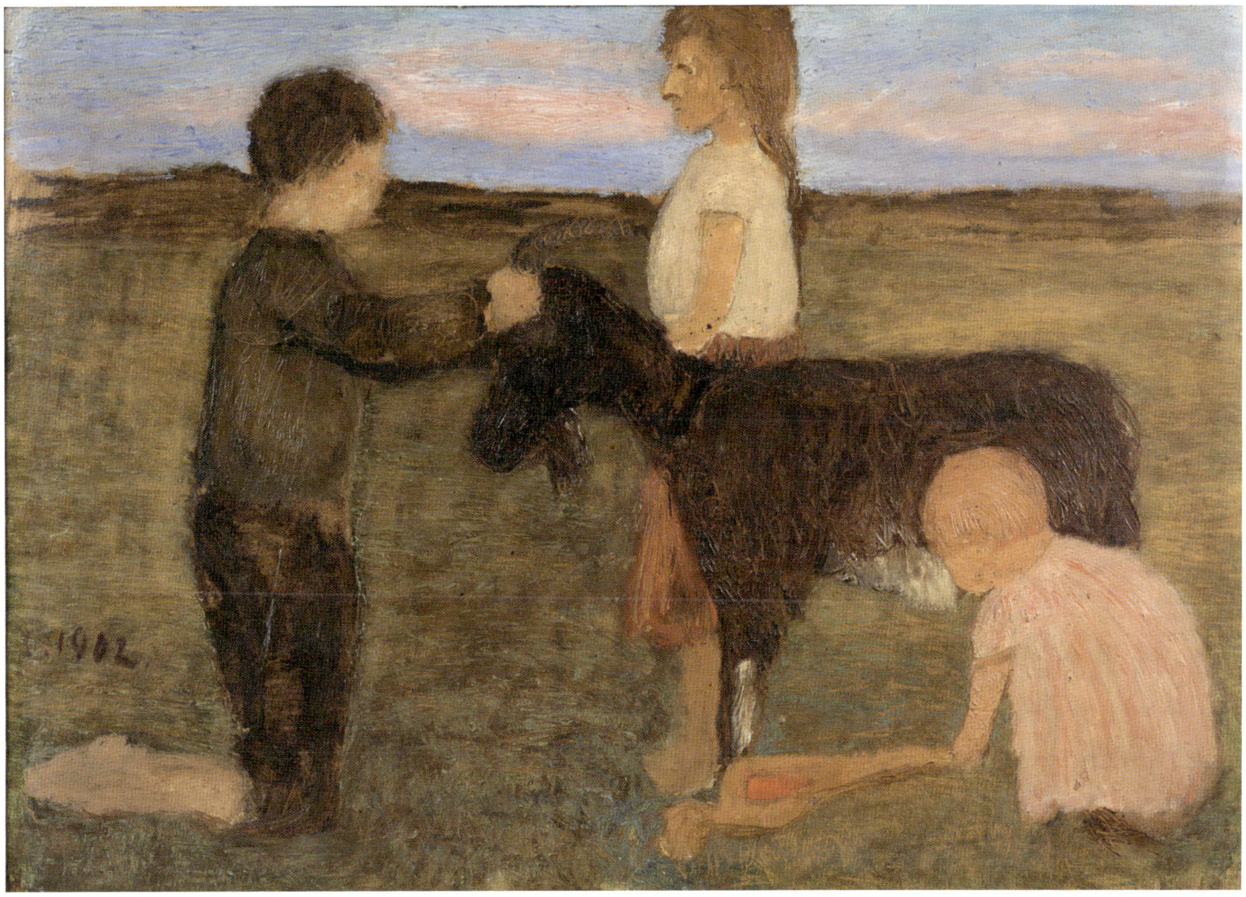

12 Paula Modersohn-Becker
Landschaft mit drei Kindern | *Landscape with Three Children*, 1902
Öl auf Pappe | oil on card, 50 x 72 cm
LENTOS Kunstmuseum Linz

Bernhard + Guste Mayer

Bernhard Mayer (1866-1946) wurde in Leufersweiler am Hunsrück als Sohn einer jüdischen Familie geboren. Wie Paul Bachrach (siehe S. 118) hatte er vor dem 1. Weltkrieg eine Pelzhandlung in Brüssel betrieben, bis er als Deutscher Belgien verlassen musste. Er übersiedelte in die Schweiz, wo er in Ascona ein neues Geschäft aufbaute.

Seine Frau Guste (1875-1958) und er sammelten Werke des Impressionismus und der klassischen Moderne. In den späten 1930er Jahren besaßen sie Bilder erstrangiger Maler wie Cézanne, Van Gogh, Renoir, Picasso, Jawlensky und Klee sowie das hier gezeigte Werk von Paula Modersohn-Becker. Wahrscheinlich machte Curt Glaser die Organisatoren von *Twentieth Century German Art* auf die Sammlung aufmerksam.

Mit Ausbruch des 2. Weltkriegs mussten Mayer und seine Familie als deutsche Staatsbürger die Schweiz verlassen. Über Kuba erreichten sie die Vereinigten Staaten. Nach dem Kriege kehrten sie in die Schweiz zurück und wohnten fortan in Zürich.

Bernhard Mayer (1866-1946) was born to Jewish family in Leufersweiler am Hunsrück, Prussia. Like his fellow London lender Paul Bachrach (see p. 118), he had built his career as a fur trader in Brussels; like Bachrach, the First World War had forced him out of Belgium, to a new life in Ascona, Switzerland.

In Ascona, Mayer and his wife Guste (1875-1958) built a remarkable art collection, which by the late 1930s included works by Cézanne, Van Gogh, Renoir, Picasso, Jawlensky, Klee – and this oil painting by Paula Modersohn Becker. As with Paul Bachrach, it was likely via Curt Glaser that Mayer's collection came to the attention of the London organisers.

With the outbreak of the Second World War in 1939, Mayer and his family – as German citizens – were unable to stay in Switzerland any longer. They travelled via Cuba to the United States. They could however return to Switzerland with the end of hostilities, settling in Zürich.

Literatur

Harald Szeemann: Die Sammlung Bernhard Mayer, Zürich 1998.

Bernhard Mayer: Interessante Zeitgenossen. Lebenserinnerungen eines jüdischen Kaufmanns und Weltbürgers, Konstanz 1998.

Literature

Harald Szeemann: Die Sammlung Bernhard Mayer. Zürich 1998

Bernhard Mayer: Interessante Zeitgenossen. Lebenserinnerungen eines jüdischen Kaufmanns und Weltbürgers. Konstanz 1998

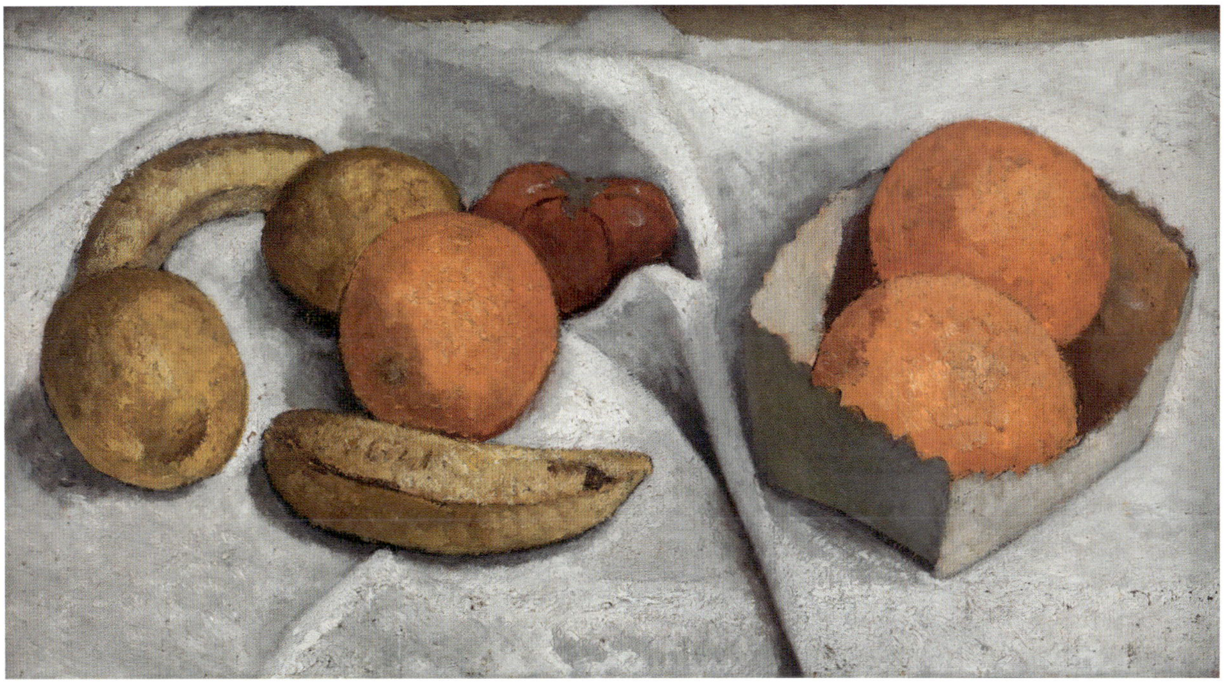

13 Paula Modersohn-Becker
Stillleben mit Orangen, Bananen, Zitrone und Tomate |
Still Life with Oranges, Bananas, Lemon and Tomato, 1906
Ölfarbe auf Pappe | oil on card, 28.2 x 52.2 cm
Staatliche Kunsthalle Karlsruhe

Willy Raeber

An *Twentieth Century German Art* beteiligten sich auch Kunsthändler – neben Londoner und Pariser Galeristen waren es mehrere aus der Schweiz, sogar solche, die mit den NS-Machthabern zusammenarbeiteten.

Das hier gezeigte Gemälde Paula Modersohn-Beckers gehörte seit 1921 zum Bestand des Stadtmuseums Dresden. Es wurde nach 1933 als ‹entartet› aus der ständigen Sammlung entfernt und 1936 vom Basler Kunsthändler Willi Raeber (1897-1976) erworben.

Seit 1933 machte Raeber Geschäfte mit hochrangigen Nazis, insbesondere mit Walter Andreas Hofer, dem persönlichen Kunstvermittler Hermann Görings. Nach erfolglosen Versuchen, das Gemälde in der Schweiz zu platzieren, schickte Raeber es nach London, wo es im Katalog von *Twentieth Century German Art* als verkäufliches Exponat eines anonymen Leihgebers erscheint. Das Bild blieb allerdings unverkauft. Nach weiteren vergeblichen Versuchen in Deutschland und den USA wurde es schließlich 1958 vom Hessischen Landesmuseum Darmstadt erworben.

Many art dealers provided works, for sale, to *Twentieth Century German Art.* Alongside dealers in London and Paris, this included Swiss dealers who worked in collaboration with the National Socialist regime.

This work by Paula Modersohn-Becker was acquired by the City Museum in Dresden in 1921. When the artist was designated 'degenerate' by the National Socialists, the painting was sold by the museum. By 1936 it had entered the stocks of the Basel dealer Willi Raeber (1897-1976).

Raeber was involved in numerous art deals with senior figures in the Third Reich after 1933. These included Walter Andreas Hofer, the personal art dealer of Hermann Göring. After attempting to sell the painting in Switzerland, Raeber sent it on to *Twentieth Century German Art* – as an anonymous loan, marked for sale in the catalogue.

The painting did not find a buyer at the New Burlington Galleries. After passing through various dealerships in America and Germany it was acquired by the Hessisches Landesmuseum Darmstadt in 1958.

Literatur

o. V.: Dr. Willi Raeber, in: Beteiligte Privatpersonen und Körperschaften am NS-Kulturgutraub, http://www.lostart.de/, besucht am 2. April 2012.

Esther Tisa Francini, Anja Heuss, Georg Kreis: Fluchtgut – Raubgut. Der Transfer von Kulturgütern in und über die Schweiz 1933–1945 und die Frage der Restitution, Zürich 2001, S. 246 und 416.

Literature

Anon.: Dr Willi Raeber, in: Beteiligte Privatpersonen und Körperschaften am NS-Kulturgutraub, available online at: http://www.lostart.de/, accessed 2 April 2012

Esther Tisa Francini, Anja Heuss and Georg Kreis: Fluchtgut – Raubgut. Der Transfer von Kulturgütern in und über die Schweiz 1933-1945 und die Frage der Restitution. Zürich 2001, pp. 246, 416

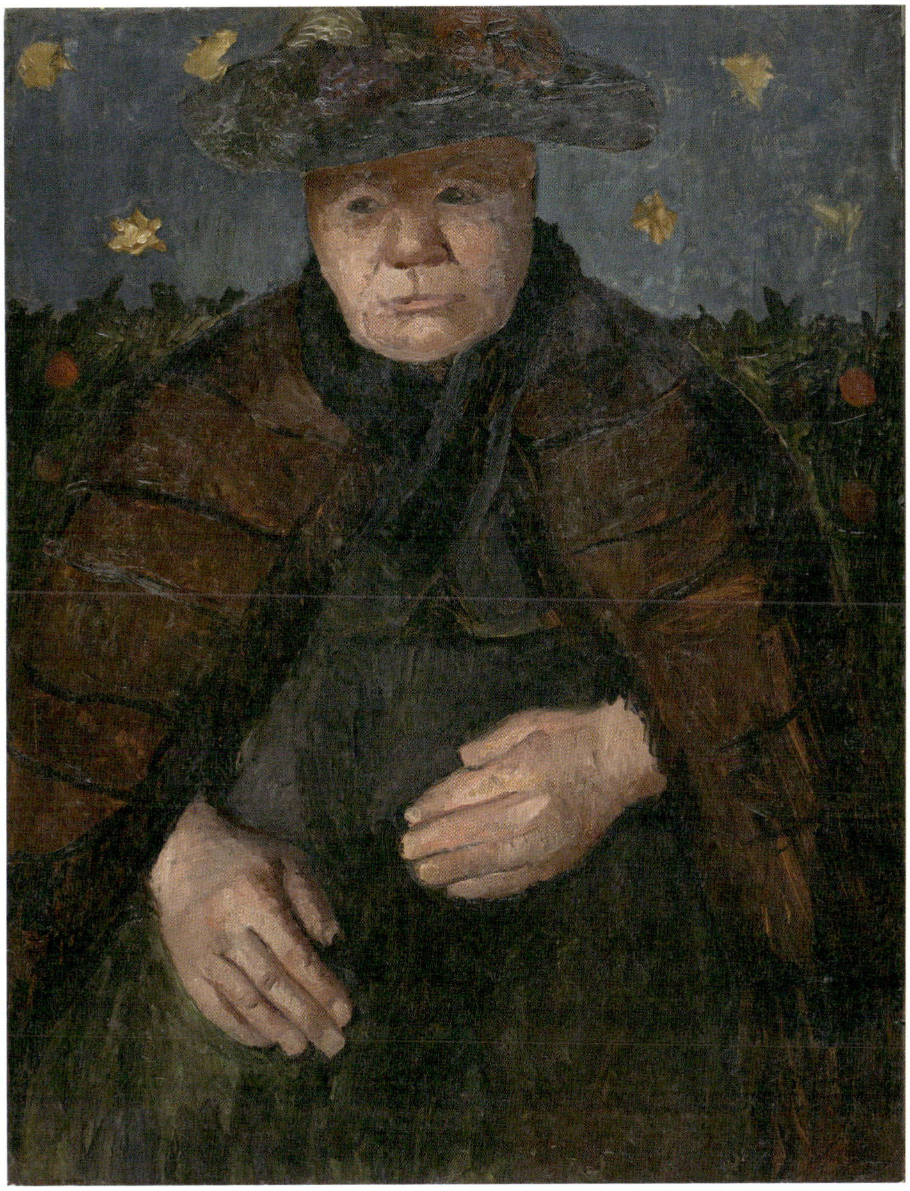

14 Paula Modersohn-Becker
Alte Armenhäuslerin | *Old Workhouse Woman*, 1906
Öl auf Karton | oil on card, 90.5 x 71 cm
Hessisches Landesmuseum Darmstadt

Hugo Simon

Dieses Werk wurde vom deutsch-jüdischen Bankier, Politiker, Sammler und Kunstförderer Hugo Simon (1880-1950) geliehen. Simon zählte zu den wichtigsten Persönlichkeiten im linken Parteienspektrum der Weimarer Republik. Als Mitglied der USPD war er 1918 Finanzminister im kurzlebigen preußischen Rat der Volksbeauftragen. 1933 flüchtete er nach Paris, wo er erneut ein Bankhaus gründete, sich politisch engagierte und die Flüchtlingshilfe unterstützte.

Da er sich frühzeitig für das Exil entschied, konnte Simon den Großteil seiner Kunstsammlung retten. Paul Westheim kannte Simon aus seiner Zeit in Berlin. Daher war vermutlich er es, der Simon zur Leihgabe von mindestens zwanzig Werken (darunter das hier gezeigte Bild Heckels) für die Ausstellung *Twentieth Century German Art* bewegte.

Nach dem Einmarsch der deutschen Truppen in Frankreich 1940 konnten Simon und seine Frau mit gefälschten tschechischen Pässe nach Brasilien flüchten. Da sie kein Visum für die Vereinigten Staaten erhielten, blieben sie bis zum Kriegsende in Südamerika. Hugo Simon starb 1950 in Brasilien.

This painting was provided to London by the German-Jewish banker and politician Hugo Simon (1880-1950). Simon was a prominent collector and supporter of the arts in Weimar-era Berlin. He was also a leading left-wing voice in the German capital – following the 1918 revolution he served as Social Democrat Finance Minister in the short-lived 'Council of the People's Deputies' government. In 1933 Simon emigrated to Paris, where he took an active role in the city's émigré community.

Thanks to his wealth and early departure from Germany, Simon was able to take a large portion of his art collection with him into exile. In 1938, it seems to have been Paul Westheim who secured him as a lender to *Twentieth Century German Art* – the two men acquainted from Berlin. This Erich Heckel painting was one of at least 20 works loaned by Simon to London.

Following the German invasion of France in 1940 Simon and his wife used faked Czech passports to escape to Brazil. Hoping to travel on to the United States, they were denied visas, and remained in South America throughout the war. Simon died in Brazil in 1950.

Literatur

Marlen Eckl: Hugo Simon. Vom Kunst liebenden Bankier in Berlin zum Seidenraupen züchtenden Autor im brasilianischen «Interior», in: Martius-Staden-Jahrbuch, Bd. 58, 2010, S. 113–137.

Edita Koch: Hugo Simon Biographie und Hugo Simon/Hubert Studenic, in: Exil. Forschung, Erkenntnisse, Ergebnisse, Bd. 3, 1983, S. 48 und 50/51.

o. V.: Wovon man nicht spricht. Eine Rundfrage über die Wertsteigerung an Werken Moderner Kunst, Hugo Simon Berlin, in: Das Kunstblatt, Bd. 15, 1931, S. 11.

RSMA, Bericht der Organisatoren der Ausstellung Twentieth Century German Art, 28. November 1937.

Literature

Marlen Eckl: Hugo Simon. Vom Kunst liebenden Bankier in Berlin zum Seidenraupen züchtenden Autor im brasilianischen "Interior"', in: Martius-Staden-Jahrbuch, vol. 58, (2010), pp. 113-37

Edita Koch: Hugo Simon Biographie, and: Hugo Simon /Hubert Studenic, in: Exil. Forschung, Erkenntnisse, Ergebnisse, vol. 3 (1983), p. 48, pp. 50-51

Anon.: Wovon man nicht spricht. Eine Rundfrage über die Wertsteigerung an Werken Moderner Kunst, Hugo Simon Berlin, in: Das Kunstblatt, vol. 15 (1931), p. 11

RSMA, report of the organisers of Twentieth Century German Art, 28 November 1937

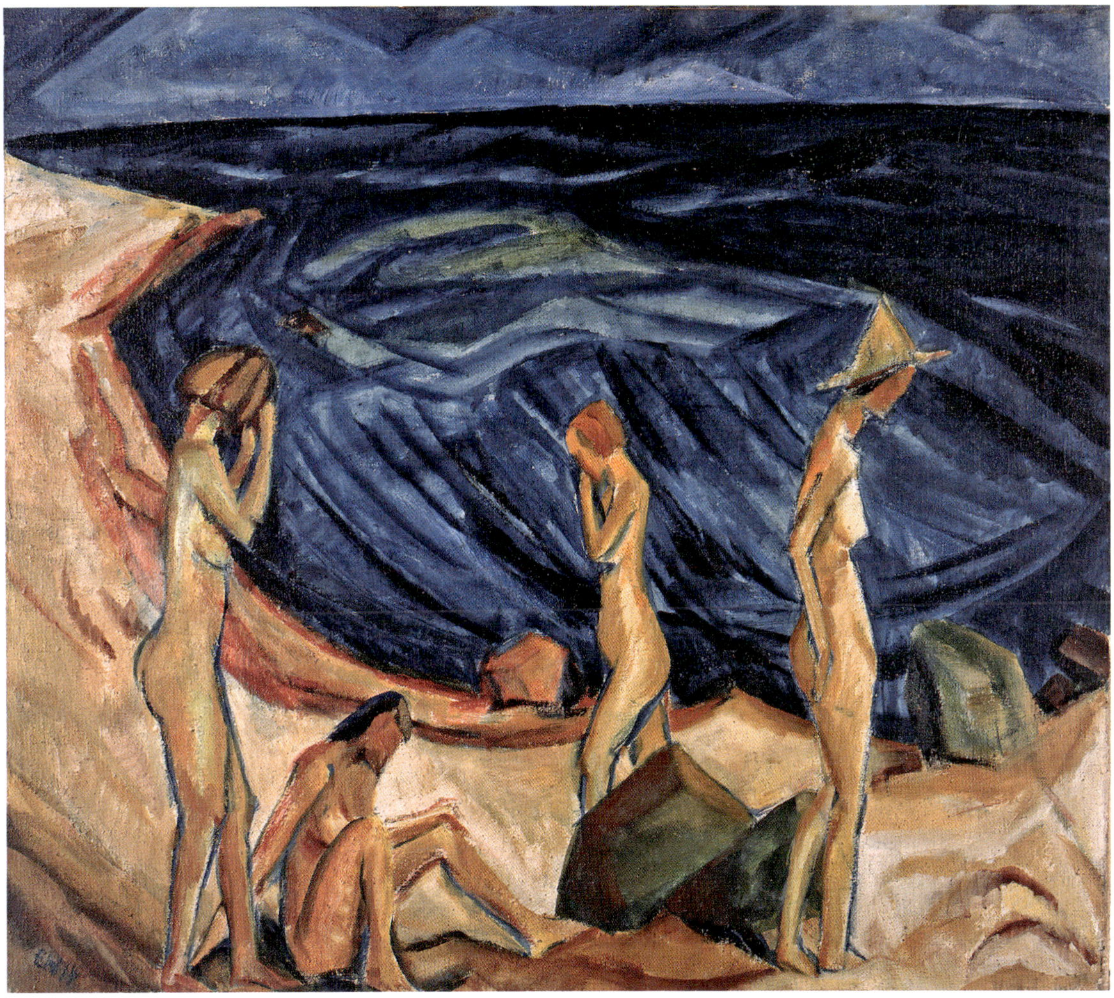

15 Erich Heckel
Badende | *Bathers*, 1914
Öl auf Leinwand | oil on canvas, 83 x 96.5 cm
Kunstmuseum Bonn

Walter + Alice Minnich

Dieses Gemälde wurde 1923 von Dr. Walter Minnich (1864-1940) erworben. Der in Deutschland geborene und in der Schweiz lebende Kunstsammler pflegte in den 1910er und 1920er Jahren eine enge Freundschaft mit Max Pechstein und erwarb in dieser Zeit mehrere Werke des Malers. Bei seinem Umzug nach Italien im Jahre 1936 vertraute Minnich die Kunstsammlung seiner Tochter Alice (1908-1989) an. Sie gab die Bilder als Dauerleihgabe an das Kunstmuseum Luzern. 1944 wandelte sie die Leihgabe in eine Schenkung um. Es war die Kunsthistorikerin Charlotte Weidler, die Verbindungsfrau Paul Westheims in Berlin, die Minnich als potentiellen Leihgeber für *Twentieth Century German Art* ins Spiel brachte. Im November 1937 hatte sie von Pechstein erfahren, dass Minnich einer der größten Sammler des Künstlers außerhalb Deutschlands sei. Obwohl das Bild *Fischerpferde* im Ausstellungskatalog nicht aufgeführt ist, bestätigt ein Etikett auf seiner Rückseite, dass es im Rahmen von *Twentieth Century German Art* ausgestellt worden ist.

This painting was acquired in 1923 by the German-born doctor, art collector and long-time resident of Switzerland, Dr Walter Minnich (1864-1940). During the 1910s and 20s Minnich had built a close friendship with the painter Max Pechstein, by the mid-1930s owning a significant collection of his works.

In 1936 Minnich left Switzerland for Italy, leaving his collection in the care of his daughter, Alice (1908-1989). She in turn passed the works on loan to the Kunstmuseum Luzern. This loan was made a permanent gift in 1944.

It was Paul Westheim's contact in Berlin, the art historian Charlotte Weidler, who identified the Minnich collection for *Twentieth Century German Art*. During November 1937 she made contact with Pechstein, who recommended Minnich as one of his most important collectors outside Germany.

Though not listed in the 1938 catalogue, a label on the reverse of *Fishermen's Horses* confirms it was exhibited in London.

Literatur

Kunstmuseum Luzern, Informationen zur Sammlung.
Isabel Greschat/Christoph Lichtin: Der Sammler Walter Minnich und das Kunstmuseum Luzern. Pechstein, Melzer, Soutine, Terechkovitch, Heidelberg 2006.
RSMA, Postkarte von Charlotte Weidler an Paul Westheim, 3. Dezember 1937.

Literature

Kunstmuseum Luzern, collection information
Isabel Greschat and Christoph Lichtin: Der Sammler Walter Minnich und das Kunstmuseum Luzern. Pechstein, Melzer, Soutine, Terechkovitch. Heidelberg, 2006
RSMA, postcard from Charlotte Weidler to Paul Westheim, 3 December 1937

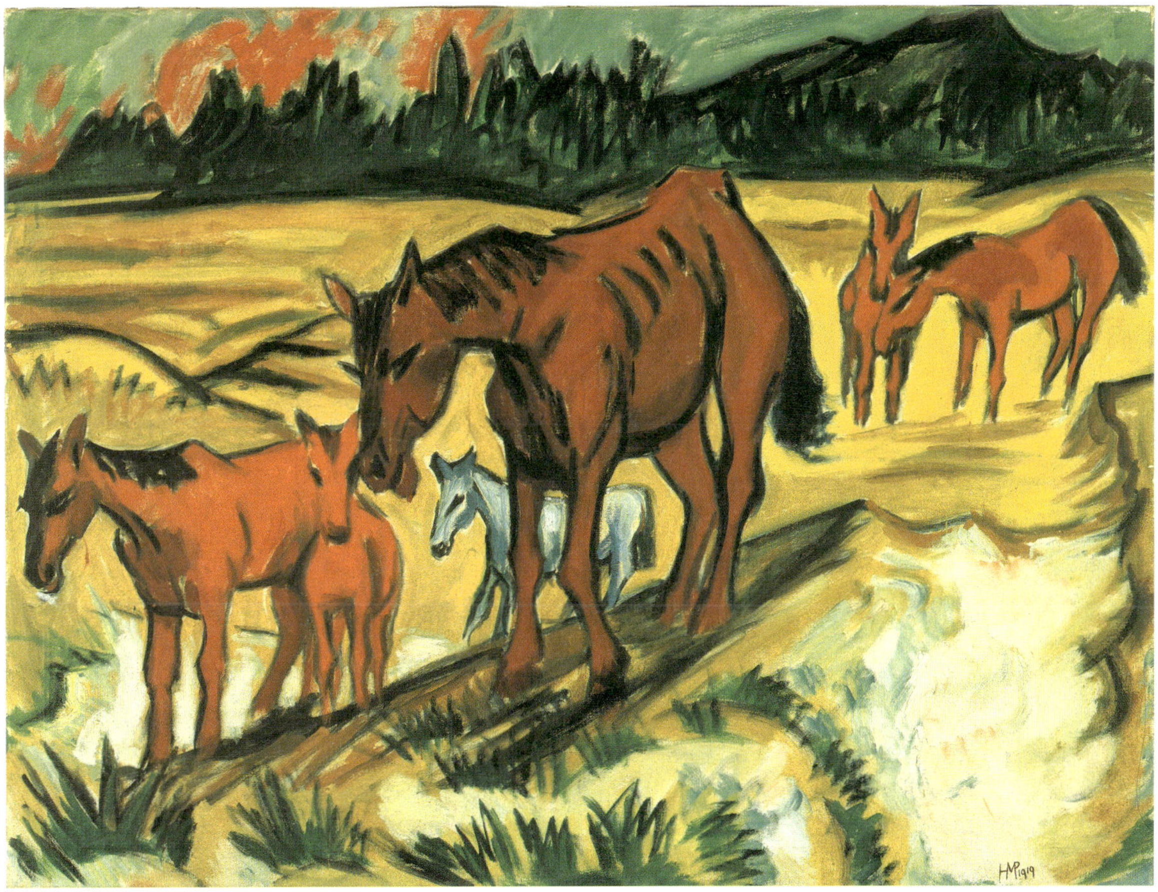

16 Max Pechstein
Fischerpferde | *Fishermen's Horses*, 1919
Öl auf Leinwand | oil on canvas, 90.5 x 120.5 cm
Kunstmuseum Luzern

Heinrich Staub

Dieses Gemälde des deutschen Malers Ernst Ludwig Kirchner war eine Leihgabe von Dr. Heinrich Staub (1866-1962), dem Chefarzt des Clavadel Sanatoriums in Davos. Kirchner, der seit 1917 in Davos lebte, war eng mit Staub befreundet. 1922 stand Hans Staub, der Sohn des Arztes, Modell für das Gemälde *Der Flötenspieler*, das heute zur Sammlung des Kirchner Museums in Davos gehört. 1927 siedelte die Familie nach Zürich über, blieb jedoch in Kontakt mit dem Maler.

Seine Diffamierung als ‹entarteter Künstler› traf Kirchner sehr. In der Folgezeit zog er sich mit seiner Frau immer mehr von der Welt zurück. Am 12. April 1938 schrieb er an Hans Staub: «Wir sind sehr, sehr einsam geworden. [...] Oft denken wir an die schönen Zeiten, da Ihre Eltern noch hier waren.» Kurz darauf besuchten Irmgard Burchard und ihr Mann Richard Paul Lohse den Künstler in Davos. Wahrscheinlich erwähnte der Maler dabei Staub als potentiellen Leihgeber für die Ausstellung *Twentieth Century German Art.*

Den Tag der Ausstellungseröffnung sollte Kirchner nicht mehr erleben. Er verfiel in eine tiefe Depression und beging am 15. Juni 1938 in Davos Selbstmord.

This work by German painter Ernst Ludwig Kirchner was loaned to London by Dr Heinrich Staub (1866-1962), who during the 1920s served as chief doctor of the Clavadel Sanatorium near Davos, Switzerland. Staub was a close friend of Kirchner's, the artist having lived in Davos since around 1918. In 1922 Staub's son Hans provided the model for Kirchner's painting *The Flute Player*, today in the collection of the Kirchner Museum in Davos. The Staub family relocated to Zürich in 1927, though they remained in contact with Kirchner.

Kirchner was deeply trouble by his defamation as 'degenerate' in Germany. He and his wife grew increasingly isolated and withdrawn in Switzerland after 1933, as he wrote to Hans Staub on 12 April 1938: "we have become very, very lonely ... we often think of the good times, when your parents were still here". Around this time, in spring 1938, Irmgard Burchard and her husband Richard Paul Lohse visited Kirchner in Davos, to gather works for London. It was perhaps on this visit that he recommended Staub as a lender.

In the final weeks before the show in London opened, Kirchner sunk into a deep depression. He committed suicide in Davos on 15 June 1938.

Literatur

Privatsammlung, Brief von Ernst Ludwig Kirchner an Hans Staub, 12. April 1938.

Richard Paul Lohse: Eine Erinnerung. Besuch bei Ernst Ludwig Kirchner 1938, in: Tages-Anzeiger (Zürich), 24. Juli 1980, Seite unbekannt.

Literature

Private collection, letter from Ernst Ludwig Kirchner to Hans Staub, 12 April 1938

Richard Paul Lohse: Eine Erinnerung. Besuch bei Ernst Ludwig Kirchner 1938, in: Tages-Anzeiger (Zurich), 24 July 1980, page unknown

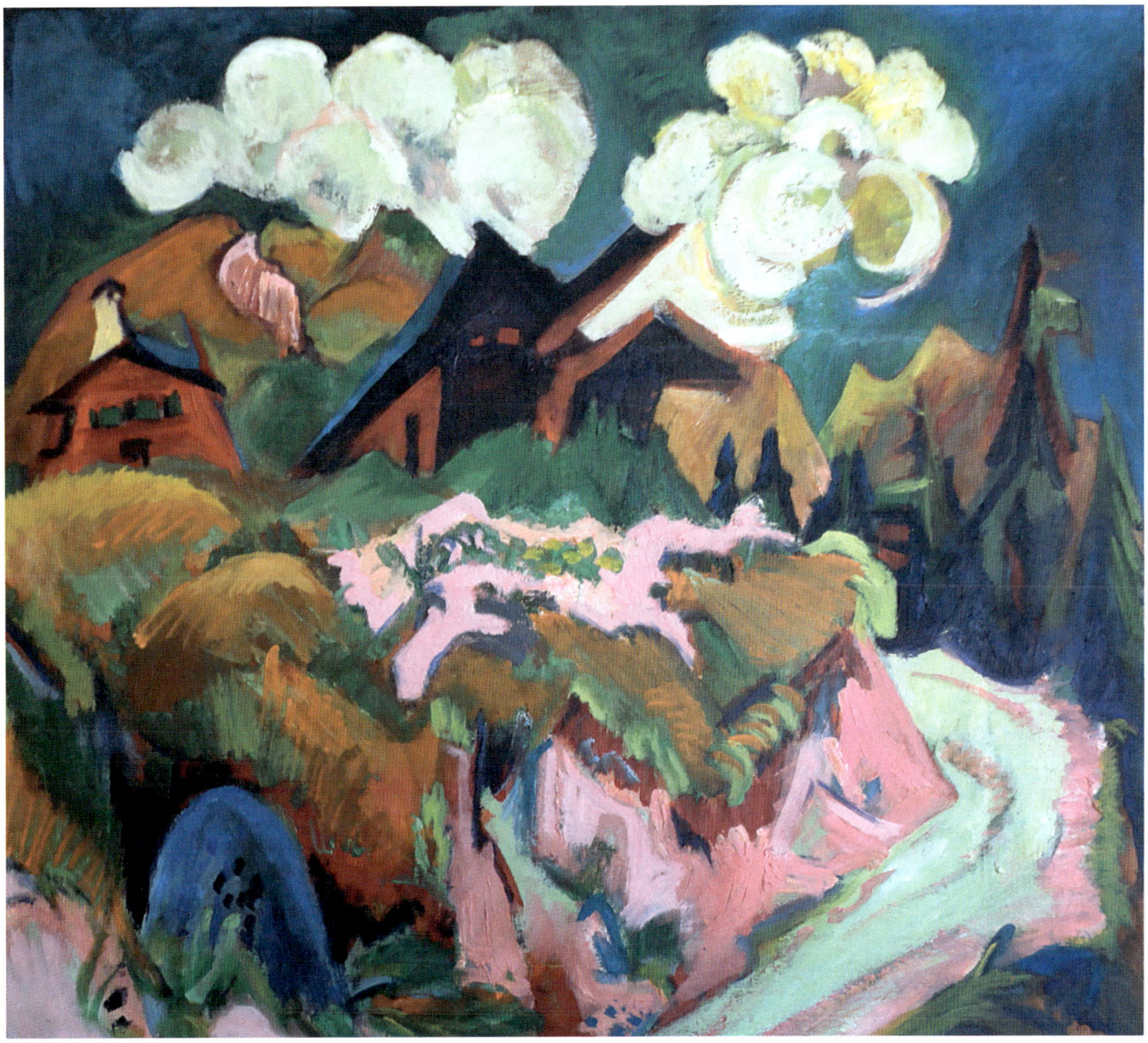

17 Ernst Ludwig Kirchner
Stafelalpweg | *Stafelalp Road*, 1918–19
Öl auf Leinwand | oil on canvas, 73.5 x 83.5 cm
Privatsammlung | private collection

Benno Elkan

Benno Elkan (1877-1960) wurde in Dortmund als Sohn einer jüdischen Familie geboren. Nach dem Studium in München und Karlsruhe und Studienaufenthalten in Paris und Rom kehrte er 1911 nach Deutschland zurück. Bald darauf wurde er als Bildhauer bekannt, vor allem für seine Denkmäler und Büsten.

Unmittelbar nach der Machtergreifung der Nazis wurde Elkan Opfer von Verfolgungsmaßnahmen. Viele seiner Werke wurden aus dem öffentlichen Raum entfernt. Deshalb flüchtete er schon 1933 nach Großbritannien und konnte viele seiner Werke mitnehmen.

Elkan beteiligte sich mit mindestens fünf Leihgaben an der Ausstellung *Twentieth Century German Art*. Er stellte drei seiner Plastiken zur Verfügung, darunter den Bronzekopf des 1937 in London verstorbenen deutsch-jüdischen Kunsthändlers Alfred Flechtheim, und zwei Gemälde von Karl Hofer und Oskar Kokoschka aus seinem Privatbesitz.

Nach dem 2. Weltkrieg wurde Elkan als Bildhauer weltweit bekannt. Nach dem Erlangen der britischen Staatsbürgerschaft wurde ihm 1957 der Order of the British Empire verliehen. Die große Menora vor der Knesset in Jerusalem zählt zu seinen bekanntesten Werken.

Benno Elkan (1877-1960) was born to a Jewish family in Dortmund. Following his studies in Munich and Karlsruhe, and travels in Paris and Rome, he returned to Germany in 1911. He soon found success as a sculptor, in particular for his public memorials and portrait busts.

Elkan faced immediate persecution following the National Socialist takeover. Many of his works were removed from public view. In 1933 he emigrated to Britain, taking a number of his pieces with him.

Elkan provided at least five works to *Twentieth Century German Art*: two paintings from his private collection (by Karl Hofer and Oskar Kokoschka), and three of his own sculptures, including this bronze of the art dealer Alfred Flechtheim. This bronze was perhaps intended as a tribute: the German Jewish Flechtheim had died in exile in London in 1937.

After the war Elkan enjoyed a successful international career. He became a British citizen and was awarded the Order of British Empire in 1957. Among his best-known works today is the Knesset Menorah, which stands outside the Israeli Parliament in Jerusalem.

Literatur

Akademie der Künste Berlin, Archiv Bildende Kunst, Beno-Elkan-Archiv.

RSMA, Brief von Irmgard Burchard an Paul Westheim, 3. April 1938.

Zentralbibliothek Zürich, Nachlass Oskar Kokoschka, Brief von Herbert Read an Oskar Kokoschka, 21. Mai 1938.

Literature

Akademie der Künste Archive, Berlin, Beno Elkan collection

RSMA, letter from Irmgard Burchard to Paul Westheim, 3 April 1938

Zentralbibliothek Zürich, Oskar Kokoschka collection, letter from Herbert Read to Oskar Kokoschka, 21 May 1938

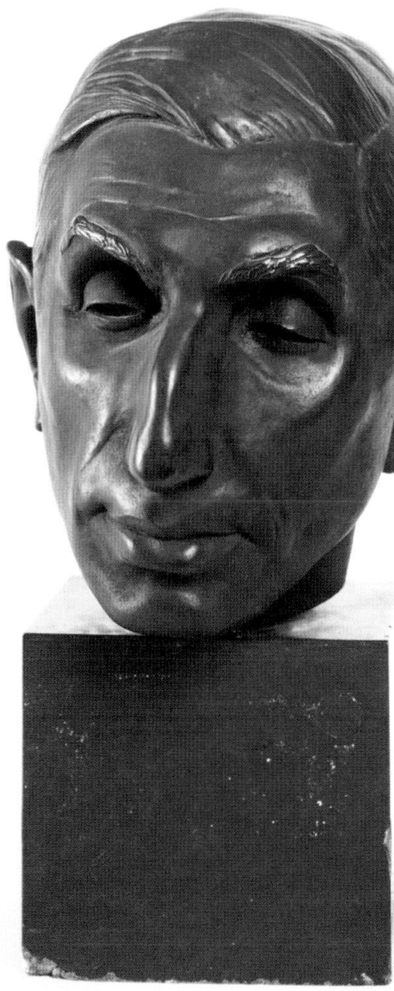

18 Benno Elkan
Alfred Flechtheim, 1912
Bronze, gegossen | bronze, cast, H 28 cm
Museum Ostwall im Dortmunder U, Dortmund

Wassiliy Kandinsky

Der in Russland geborene Maler Wassily Kandinsky (1866-1944) ist eine Zentralfigur der deutschen Moderne. 1911 war er Mitbegründer des Blauen Reiter; ab 1922 lehrte er als Meister am Bauhaus. Nach dessen Schliessung 1933 verließ er Deutschland und ließ sich in Neuilly-sur-Seine bei Paris nieder.

Irmgard Burchard nahm bereits zu Beginn ihrer Vorbereitungen für die Londoner Ausstellung Kontakt zu Kandinsky auf. Daraufhin stellte der Maler mindestens zwei Werke zur Verfügung – darunter die hier gezeigte Landschaft. Obwohl das Bild in London zum Verkauf stand, wechselte es nicht den Besitzer, sondern blieb Eigentum des Künstlers bis zu dessen Tod. Später schenkte es Nina Kandinsky, die Witwe des Malers, dem Pariser Musée National d'Art Moderne.

Nicht weniger als dreizehn Werke Kandinskys wurden in der Ausstellung *Twentieth Century German Art* gezeigt. Sie alle befinden sich heute in führenden Museen der Welt wie dem New Yorker Guggenheim Museum und der Londoner Tate Gallery.

The Russian-born painter Wassily Kandinsky (1866-1944) occupies a central place in the history of German modernist art. In 1911 he was a founding member of the expressionist Blue Rider group; from 1922 a teacher at the Bauhaus school. Following the closure of the Bauhaus Kandinsky left Germany, and settled in Neuilly-sur-Seine near Paris.

Within days of work starting on the London exhibition, Irmgard Burchard made contact with Kandinsky. This landscape was one of at least two paintings provided by the artist directly to the show. Though marked for sale in the catalogue, it was not sold in London, remaining in the artist's collection until his death. It was later gifted to the Musée National d'Art Moderne in Paris by the artist's widow, Nina.

At least 13 Kandinsky works were shown in *Twentieth Century German Art.* These are today housed in some of the world's leading museums, including the Guggenheim Museum in New York and the Tate Gallery in London.

Literatur
RSMA, Brief von Irmgard Burchard an Wassily and Nina Kandinsky, 29. November 1937.
Centre Pompidou Paris, Bibliothèque Kandinsky, Brief von Irmgard Burchard an Wassily Kandinsky, 25. März 1938.

Literature
RSMA, letter from Irmgard Burchard to Wassily and Nina Kandinsky, 29 November 1937
Centre Pompidou, Paris, Bibliothèque Kandinsky, letter from Irmgard Burchard to Wassily Kandinsky, 25 March 1938

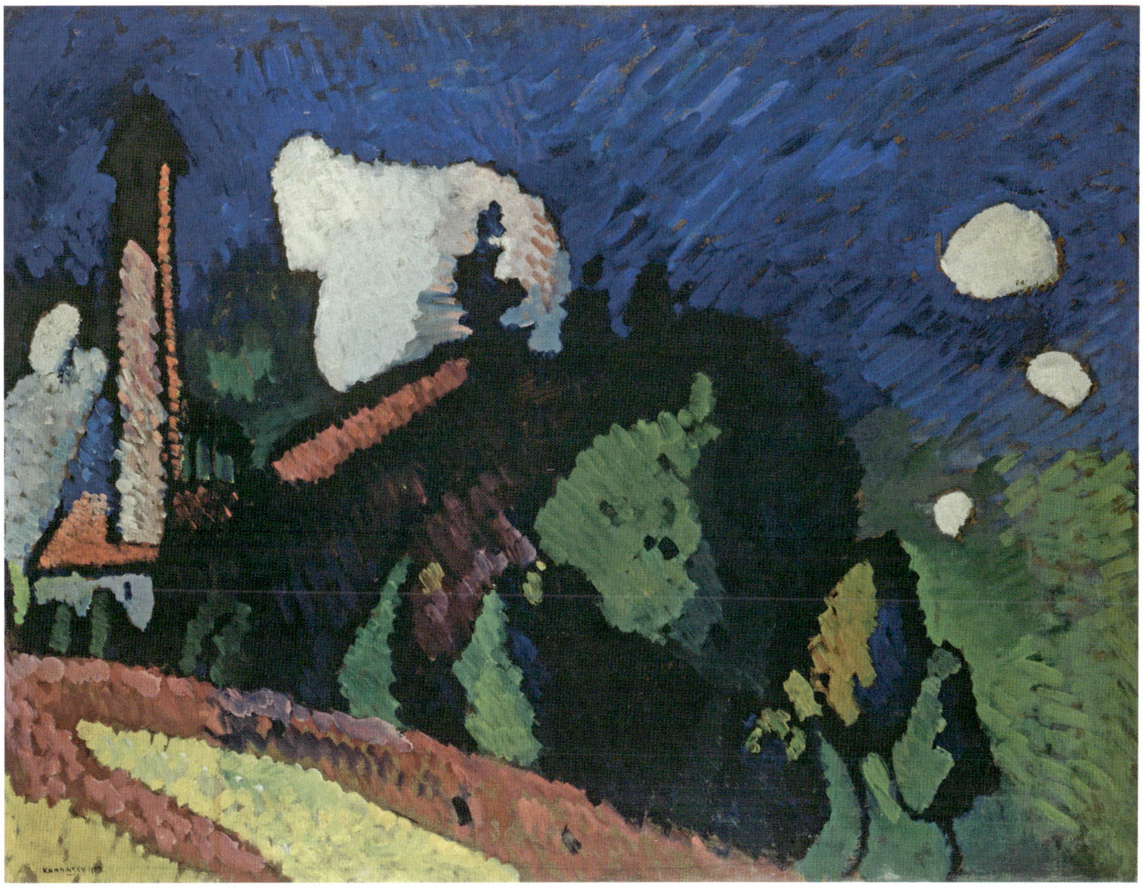

19 Wassily Kandinsky
Murnau, Landschaft mit Turm | *Murnau, Landscape with Tower*, 1908
Öl auf Pappe | oil on card, 75.5 x 99.5 cm
Centre Pompidou, National Museum of Modern Art – CCI, Paris, Geschenk Mme Nina Kandinsky, 1976

Erich Alport

Erich Alport (1903-1972) wurde als Sohn einer jüdischen Familie in Posen geboren und wuchs in Hamburg auf. 1926 studierte er zwei Semester als Gaststudent in Oxford, wo er sich mit den Schriftstellern Stephen Spender und Christopher Isherwood anfreundete.

Als Jude und Homosexueller in Deutschland doppelt ‹unerwünscht›, kehrte Alport 1933 nach Oxford zurück. Fünf Jahre später lieh er das Gemälde *Junger Mann mit buntem Halstuch* in die Ausstellung *Twentieth Century German Art*. Das Bild kann als Hommage an die Schwulenszene der 1920er Jahre gedeutet werden. Damals lebte Helmut Kolle mit dem ‹marchand amateur› Wilhelm Uhde zusammen. Nach dem Tod des Malers im Jahre 1931 verkaufte Uhde das Gemälde an Alport.

Dieser blieb bis zu seinem Tod 1972 in Oxford. In einem Nachruf beschrieb ihn die *Times* «als internationalen Liberalen und unermüdlich Reisenden [...], der in seinen musikalischen, literarischen und künstlerischen Vorlieben ebenso anspruchsvoll war wie in der Wahl seiner Freunde.»

Erich Alport (1903-1972) was born to a Jewish family in Posen, Prussia. Raised in Hamburg, in 1926 he spent two terms as a guest student at the University of Oxford, where his friends included the writers Stephen Spender and Christopher Isherwood.

Around 1933 Alport returned to Oxford: doubly 'undesirable' in Germany on grounds of his Judaism, and his homosexuality. Five years later, he provided this painting to *Twentieth Century German Art*. The work can be interpreted as a tribute to gay life in Weimar-era Germany. The artist Helmut Kolle lived for over ten years in a relationship with the art historian Wilhelm Uhde, until Kolle's death in 1931. Uhde then sold the painting to Alport before the latter's departure from Germany.

Alport remained in Oxford for the rest of his life. His 1972 obituary *The Times* described him as follows: "an international liberal, a tireless traveller ... his taste in music, literature, painting and sculpture being as fastidious as his choice of friends".

Literatur
Ingrid Mössinger/Thomas Bauer-Friedrich (Hg.): Helmut Kolle. Ein Deutscher in Paris, München u. a. 2010.
University of Oxford, Magdalen College Archives/University College Archives, Erich Alport Collections.
Richard Buckle: Erich Alport, in: The Times, 19. Februar 1972, Seite unbekannt.

Literature
Ingrid Mössinger and Thomas Bauer-Friedrich (eds.): Helmut Kolle. Ein Deutscher in Paris. Munich etc. 2010
University of Oxford, Magdalen College Archives and University College Archives, Erich Alport Collections
Richard Buckle: Erich Alport, in: The Times (19 February 1972), page unknown

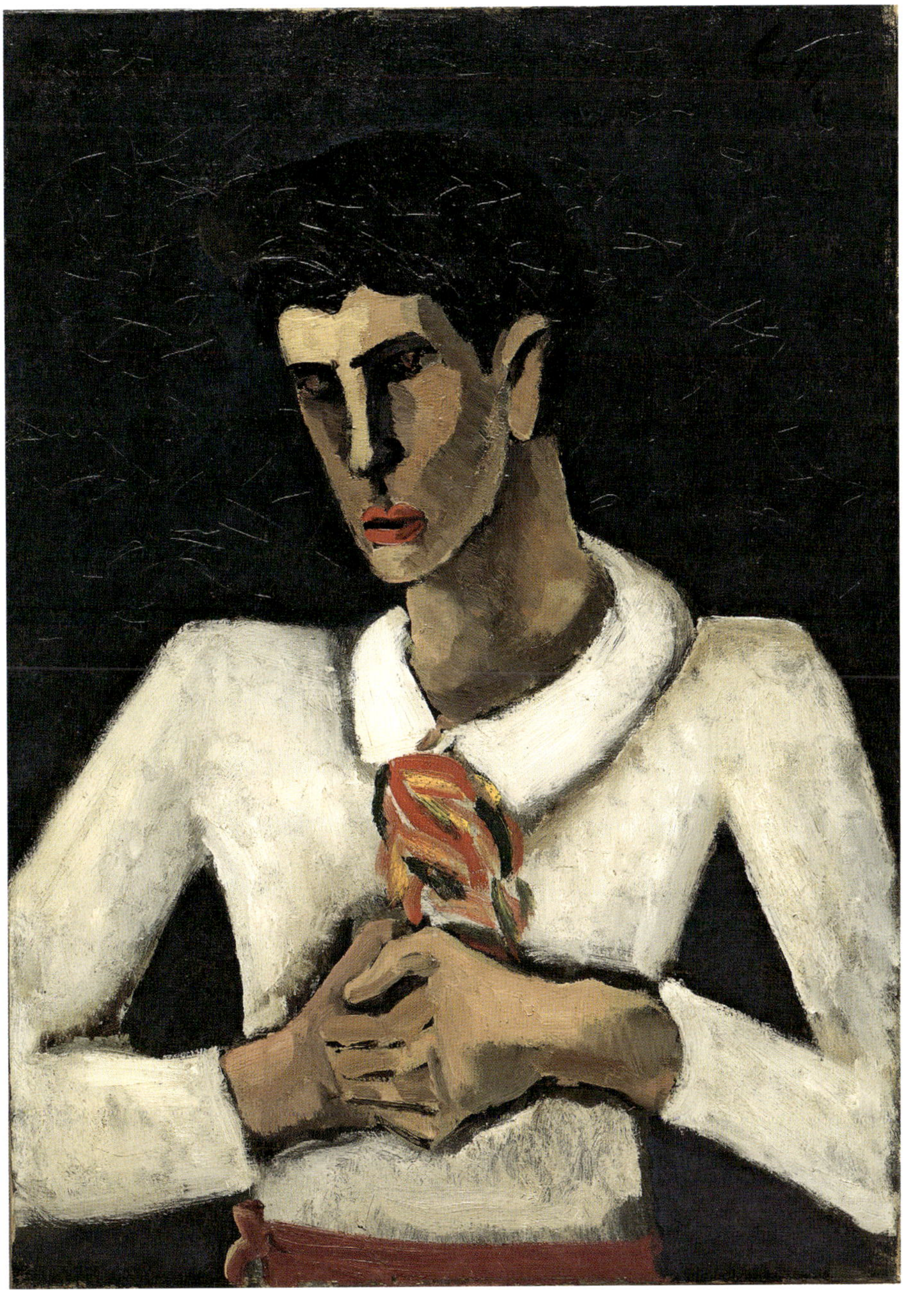

20 Helmut Kolle
Junger Mann mit buntem Halstuch
Young Man with a Coloured Scarf, ca. 1930
Öl auf Leinwand | oil on canvas, 92.4 x 65.5 cm
Kunstsammlungen Chemnitz – Museum Gunzenhauser, Stiftung Gunzenhauser

Emil Korner

Der Österreicher Oskar Kokoschka (1886-1980) zählt zu den erfolgreichsten Künstlern der klassischen Moderne in Deutschland. Nach dem Kunststudium in Wien kam er in Kontakt mit Herwarth Walden und seine ab 1910 in Berlin erscheinende Zeitschrift *Der Sturm*. Von 1919 bis 1924 hatte er eine Professur an der Kunstakademie in Dresden.

1933 zählte Kokoschka zu den ersten Künstlern, die von den Nazis als ‹entartet› diffamiert und verfolgt wurden. Deshalb ging er schon 1934 nach Prag. Im Sommer 1937 wurden mehr als 400 seiner Werke aus deutschen Museumssammlungen beschlagnahmt. 1938 floh er nach England und lebte dort bis Ende der 1940er Jahre.

An dem hier gezeigten Selbstbildnis arbeitete er ab Sommer 1937, zuerst im tschechoslowakischen Dorf Ostravice, dann in Vitkovice, wo er sich beim Industriellen und Wirtschaftwissenschaftler Prof. Dr. Emil Korner (Lebensdaten unbekannt) aufhielt. Diesem verkaufte er das Bild, als es fertig war.

Kokoschka schickte selbst kein Werk nach London, er teilte den Organisatoren der Ausstellung allerdings mit, welche Sammler sich eventuell mit Bildern an *Twentieth Century German Art* beteiligen könnten. Im Frühjahr 1938 hatte die Familie Korner die Tschechoslowakei schon verlassen. Im Katalog der Londoner Ausstellung ist das hier gezeigte Bild als «Leihgabe Prof. Dr. Korner, Zürich» notiert, was darauf hindeutet, dass die Familie zu dieser Zeit in der Schweiz lebte. Später emigrierten auch die Korners nach Großbritannien.

Literatur
Zentralbibliothek Zürich, Nachlass Oskar Kokoschka, Korrespondenz mit Irmgard Burchard und Herbert Read, 1938.
Richard Calvocoressi: Kokoschka and Scotland, Edinburgh, 1990, S. 6.
National Gallery of Scotland, Edinburgh, Informationen zur Sammlung.

The Austrian-born painter Oskar Kokoschka (1886-1980) enjoyed a successful career in early twentieth-century Germany. After studies in Vienna he established himself within the *Der Sturm* circle of Herwarth Walden. From 1919 to 1924 he served as professor at the Academy of Arts in Dresden.

Kokoschka was also one of the earliest artists to face persecution at the hands of the National Socialist regime. Included in the early exhibitions of cultural 'degeneracy' in Germany, the artist relocated to Prague in 1934. During the summer of 1937, over 400 of his works were confiscated from German museums. In 1938 he travelled on to Britain, where he remained throughout the 1940s.

Kokoschka began work on this self-portrait in the late summer of 1937, while staying in the Czechoslovakian village of Ostravice. He completed it in autumn 1937 at the home of the Czech industrialist and economist Prof. Dr. Emil Korner (dates of birth and death unknown) in nearby Vitkovice. The painting was acquired directly by Korner. Kokoschka did not send his own works directly to *Twentieth Century German Art*. He was however in correspondence with the organisers, advising them on which of his works might be available from other collections. By the spring of 1938, the Korner family had departed Czechoslovakia. In London catalogue, '*Self-Portrait of a Degenerate Artist*' was listed as a loan from 'Prof. Dr. Korner, Zürich', suggesting the family were then in Switzerland – they too would later travel on to Britain.

Literature
Zentralbibliothek Zürich, Oskar Koksochka collection, correspondence between Irmgard Burchard and Herbert Read and Oskar Kokoschka, 1938
Richard Calvocoressi: Kokoschka and Scotland. Edinburgh, 1990, p. 6
National Gallery of Scotland, Edinburgh, collection information

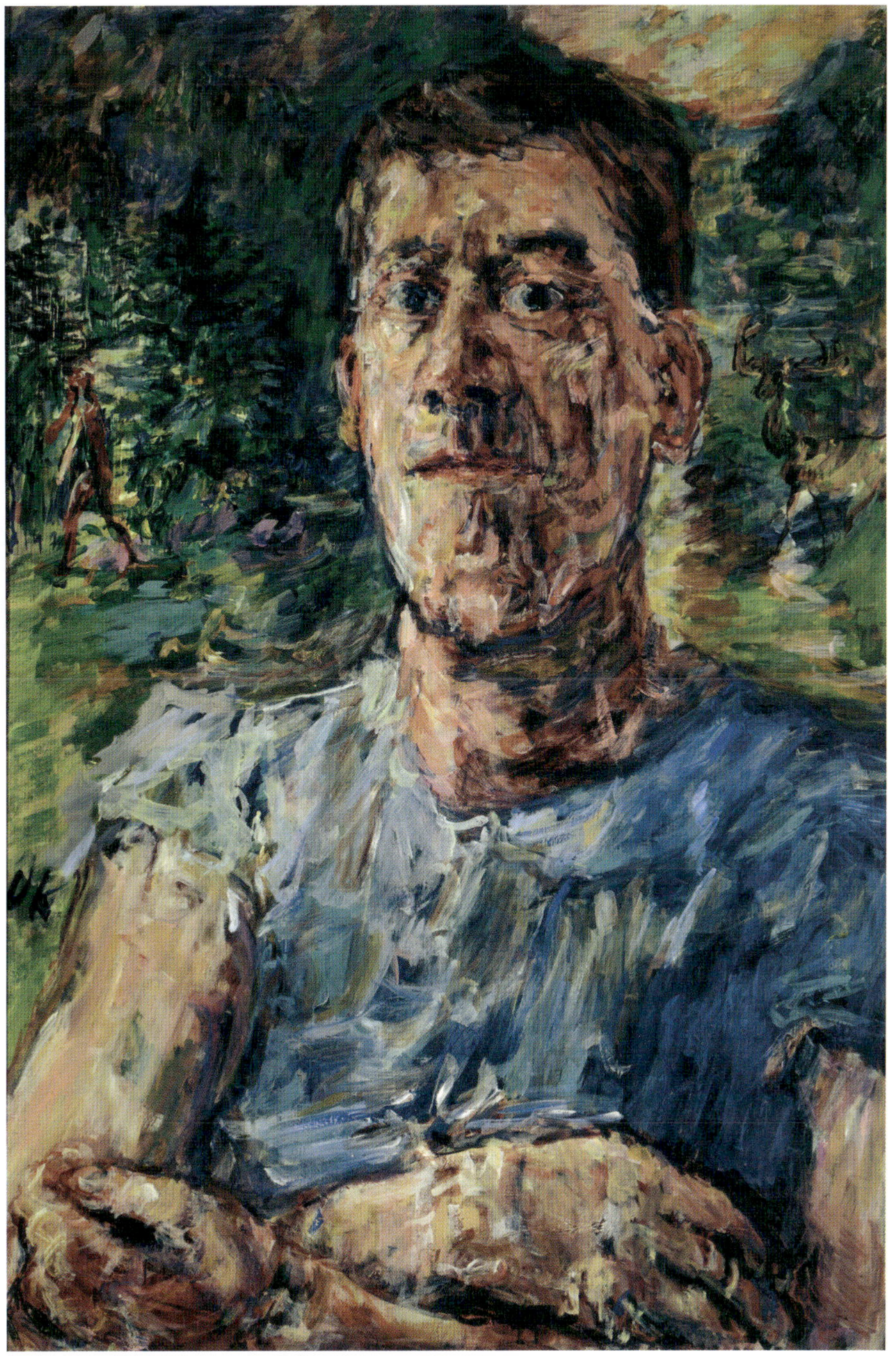

21 Oskar Kokoschka
Selbstbildnis eines «entarteten Künstlers»
Self-Portrait of a "Degenerate Artist", 1937
Öl auf Leinwand | oil on canvas, 110 x 85 cm
Private Collection on long term loan to the National Galleries of Scotland

Kunstmuseum Basel

Mehrere Museen der Schweiz beteiligten sich an *Twentieth Century German Art* mit Leihgaben. Einige schickten Bilder, die ihnen von emigrierten Künstlern anvertraut worden waren (vgl. S. 146), andere stellten Werke aus der eigenen Sammlung zur Verfügung.

Das hier gezeigte Gemälde Emil Noldes war eine Leihgabe des Kunstmuseums Basel. Im November 1937 schrieb Paul Westheim an Irmgard Burchard, sie solle sich bei «Fischer in Basel» nach potentiellen Leihgebern erkundigen. Gemeint war der deutsche Kunsthistoriker Otto Fischer, der seit 1927 das Kunstmuseum Basel leitete.

Das Bild *Blaue Iris I*, 1931 angekauft, gehört bis heute zum Sammlungsbestand des Museums. Im Katalog der Londoner Ausstellung ist es zusammen mit drei Graphiken von Rolf Nesch als Leihgaben aus Basel aufgeführt. Letzere gehörten jedoch nicht dem Museum. Sie waren Teil des Sammlungskonvoluts, das Hugo Simon (siehe S. 124) dem Museum 1938 zur Aufbewahrung anvertraut hatte.

Swiss museums were an important source of loans for the London exhibition. Many were holding works in storage for those facing exile from Germany (see also p. 146). Other museums provided loans from their permanent collections.

This Nolde oil painting was provided from the collection of the Kunstmuseum Basel. In November 1937, Paul Westheim recommended to Irmgard Burchard that she contact "Fischer in Basel" for advice on potential lenders. The German-born art historian Otto Fischer had led the Kunstmuseum Basel since 1927.

Blaue Iris I had been acquired by the museum in 1931, remaining in their collection until today. In the *Twentieth Century German Art* catalogue, the Kunstmuseum Basel is listed as lender of both this work, and three etchings by Rolf Nesch. These etchings were in fact part of the Hugo Simon collection (see p. 124), a portion of which was being held in storage at the museum during 1938.

Literatur
Kunstmuseum Basel, Archiv der Sammlung.
o. V.: Erwerbungen von Werken neuerer Kunst, Ausstellungen und Neuordnungen der öffentlichen Sammlungen im deutschen Sprachgebiet, in: Museum der Gegenwart, Bd. 1, Nr. 1, 1930, S. 47.
RSMA, Brief von Paul Westheim an Irmgard Burchard, 24. November 1937.
Hilde Flory-Fischer: Otto Fischer. Ein Kunsthistoriker des zwanzigsten Jahrhunderts, Reutlingen 1886 – Basel 1948, Reutlingen 1986.

Literature
Kunstmuseum Basel, collection archives
Anon.: Erwerbungen von Werken neuerer Kunst, Ausstellungen und Neuordnungen der öffentlichen Sammlungen im deutschen Sprachgebiet, in: Museum der Gegenwart, vol. 1, no. 1 (1930), p. 47
RSMA, letter from Paul Westheim to Irmgard Burchard, 24 November 1937
Hilde Flory-Fischer: Otto Fischer. Ein Kunsthistoriker des zwanzigsten Jahrhunderts, Reutlingen 1886 – Basel 1948. Reutlingen 1986

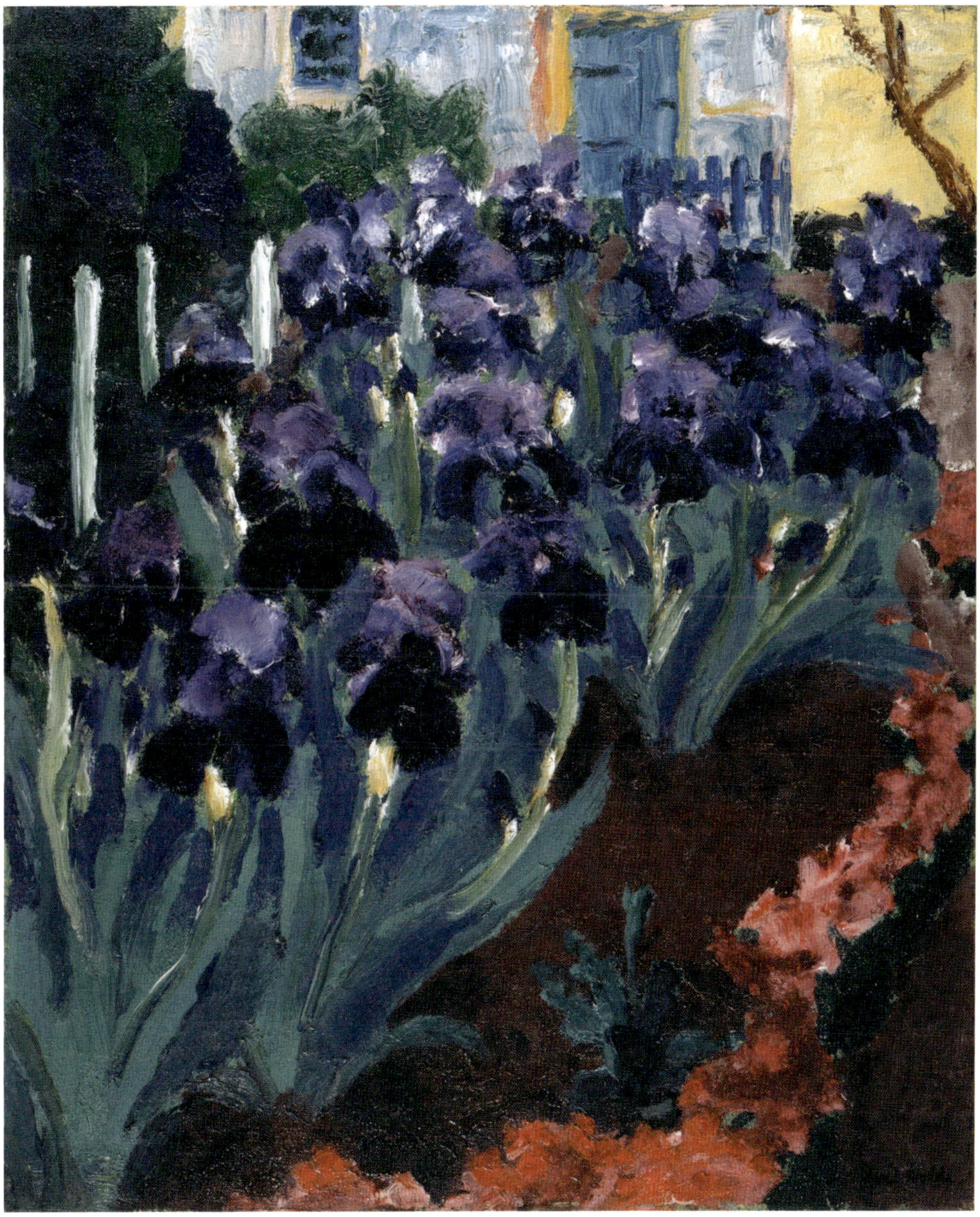

22 Emil Nolde
Blaue Iris I | *Blue Iris I*, 1915
Öl auf Leinwand | oil on canvas, 79.1 x 73.8 cm
Kunstmuseum Basel

Ernst + Emma Nelkenstock

Ernst Nelkenstock (1893-1980) wurde in Tann an der Rhön als Sohn einer jüdischen Familie geboren. Nach dem 1. Weltkrieg eröffnete er eine Anwaltskanzlei in Hanau. 1924 heiratete er Emma Berlizheimer (1900-ca. 1990), die ihm zwei Töchter schenkte. Als Mitglied der Hanauer Bürgerschaft und des Rats der Hanauer jüdischen Gemeinde war Nelkenstock eine führende Persönlichkeit der Stadt. Nelkenstock sammelte Werke des Expressionismus und besaß unter anderem dieses Gemälde von Emil Nolde.

1936 emigrierte Ernst Nelkenstock mit seiner Familie nach Großbritannien. Da es ihm untersagt war, dort als Anwalt tätig zu sein, besann er sich auf den Beruf seines Vaters und eröffnete im Norden Londons eine Metzgerei, die er bis zu seinem Ruhestand betrieb. 1938 beteiligt er sich mit dem hier gezeigten Nolde-Gemälde an der Ausstellung *Twentieth Century German Art.* Bei der Einbürgerung der Nelkenstocks im Jahr 1947 nahm die Familie den Namen «Norton» an.

Ernst Nelkenstock (1893-1980) was born to a Jewish family in Tann an der Röhn. He trained as a lawyer and, after service in World War I, established a legal practice in Hanau. In 1924 he married Emma Berlizheimer (1900-c.1990); together the couple had two daughters. Ernst Nelkenstock established himself as a prominent figure in the city of Hanau. He served on the committee of the city's Jewish Community and was also a member of the Citizen's Association. At the same time, he and his wife built a small art collection during the 1920s, including this painting by Nolde.

In 1936 the Nelkenstock family were forced out of Germany, resettling in London. Two years later, they provided this picture to *Twentieth Century German Art.* Unable to practice as a lawyer in Britain, Ernst returned to his father's trade, opening a butcher's shop in North London which he ran until his retirement. In 1947 he and his family became naturalised British citizens, changing their name to Norton.

Literatur
Korrespondenz der Autorin mit Dr. Margot S. Norton, Richmond, Juni 2012.
Korrespondenz der Autorin mit Hanna Singer, London, Mai 2012.
Archiv der Stadt Hanau.
Association of Jewish Refugees Archive, London
o. V.: Dr E. J. Norton 70, in: AJR Information, Juni 1963, S. 13.

Literature
Correspondence between the author and Dr Margot S. Norton, Richmond, June 2012
Correspondence between the author and Hanna Singer, London, May 2012
Hanau City Archive
Association of Jewish Refugees Archive, London
Anon.: Dr E. J. Norton 70, in: AJR Information (June 1963), p. 13

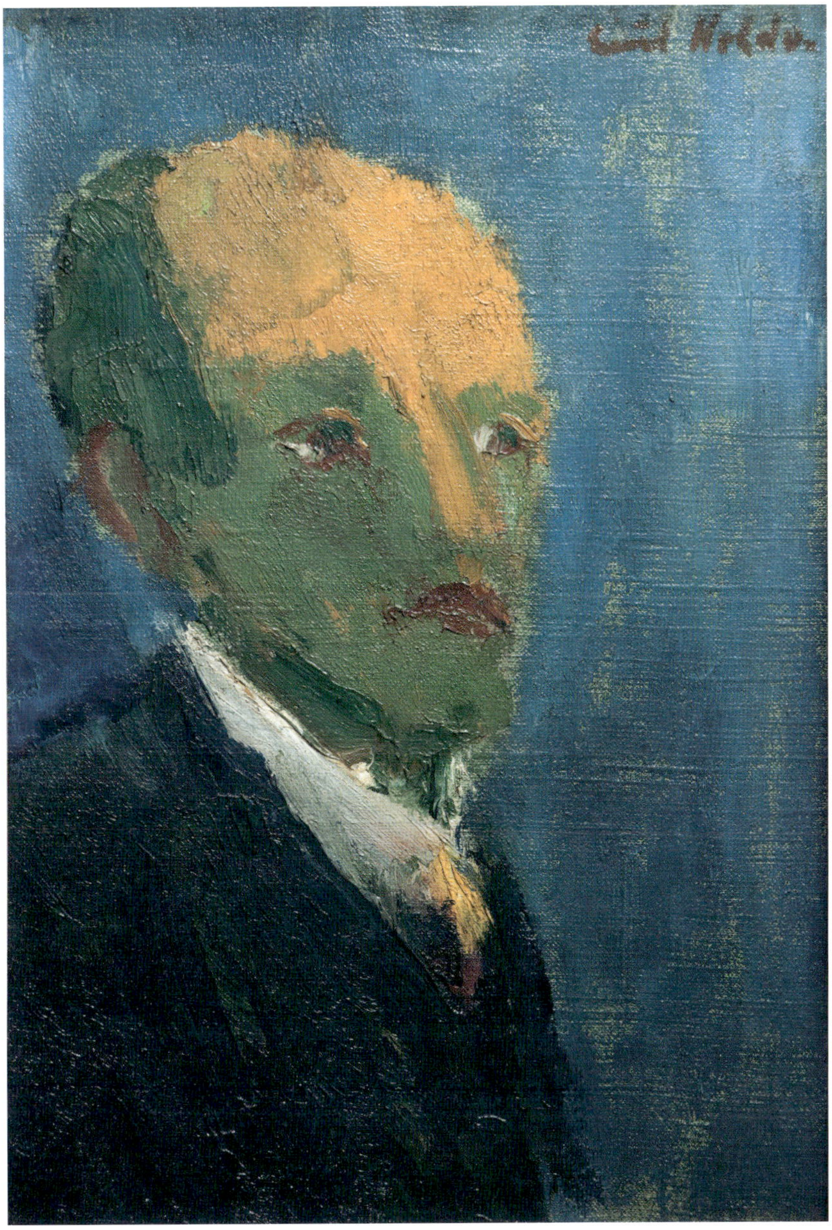

23 Emil Nolde
Junger Gelehrter | *The Young Academic*, 1918
Öl auf Leinwand | oil on canvas, 57 x 38 cm
Kunstmuseum Gelsenkirchen

Willi Baumeister

Willi Baumeister (1889-1955) wurde in Stuttgart geboren und studierte an der dortigen Kunstakademie. Nach Absolvierung des Militärdienstes reiste er 1911 nach Paris. Zwei Jahre später beteiligte er sich am *Ersten Deutschen Herbstsalon*, der von Herwarth Waldens *Sturm*-Galerie organisiert wurde. 1919 schloss er sich der Berliner Novembergruppe an.

1927 erhielt Baumeister einen Ruf als Professor an die Frankfurter Kunstgewerbeschule. Da die Nazis seinen abstrakten Stil als ‹entartet› diffamierten, wurde er 1933 entlassen. Baumeister kehrte nach Stuttgart zurück und arbeitete dort als Gebrauchsgraphiker, bis er 1938 in der Wuppertaler Lackfabrik von Dr. Kurt Herberts mit ihrem Künstlerkreis unterkam.

Schon vor der Initiierung des Londoner Projekts hatte Irmgard Burchard Kontakt mit Willi Baumeister aufgenommen und ihm angeboten, seine Werke über ihre Zürcher Galerie zu verkaufen. Dieses Angebot nahm er gerne an und schickte das Gemälde *Tennis* nach Zürich, wo es Burchard 1937 im Rahmen der Verkaufsausstellung *Art Réaliste et Abstrait* zeigte. Ein Jahr später wurde das Bild in London ausgestellt und war dort verkäuflich.

Nach dem Kriege konnte Baumeister in Deutschland erneut als Kunstmaler tätig sein. 1946 wurde er als Professor an die Kunstakademie Stuttgart berufen. Bis zu seinem Tod im Jahr 1956 war er weiterhin künstlerisch tätig und in Ausstellungen präsent.

The artist Willi Baumeister (1889-1955) was born and trained in Stuttgart. After military service he began his career as an artist, in 1911 travelling to Paris, and in 1913 taking part in the *Erste Deutsche Herbstsalon* (*First German Autumn Salon*) at Herwarth Walden's Galerie Der Sturm in Berlin. In 1919 he became a member of the Novembergruppe in Berlin.

In 1927 Baumeister was appointed Professor at the State School of Applied Arts in Frankfurt. Six years later he was dismissed from this position, his abstract style branded 'degenerate' by the National Socialist regime. He returned to his home town of Stuttgart, where he began working as a graphic designer. In 1938 he took a job at Kurt Herberts Paint and Lacquer factory in Wuppertal.

Well before planning started for the London exhibition, Irmgard Burchard made contact with Baumeister, offering to sell his works through her Zürich gallery. Baumeister agreed. The oil and sand painting *Tennis* was sent by the artist to Zürich for inclusion in a small commercial exhibition organised by Burchard during 1937 under the title *Art Réaliste et Abstrait*. The following year the painting was exhibited again at *Twentieth Century German Art*, marked for sale.

With the end of World War II, Baumeister was able to restart his career in Germany. In 1946 he was appointed Professor at the State Academy of Fine Arts in Stuttgart. He continued to work and exhibit until his death in 1955.

Literatur
Kunstmuseum Stuttgart, Archiv Baumeister, Korrespondenz zwischen Irmgard Burchard und Willi Baumeister.
Peter Beye: Willi Baumeister. Werkkatalog der Gemälde, Oslfildern-Ruit, 2002.

Literature
Kunstmuseum Stuttgart, Baumeister Archive, correspondence between Irmgard Burchard and Willi Baumeister
Peter Beye: Willi Baumeister. Werkkatalog der Gemälde. Oslfildern-Ruit, 2002

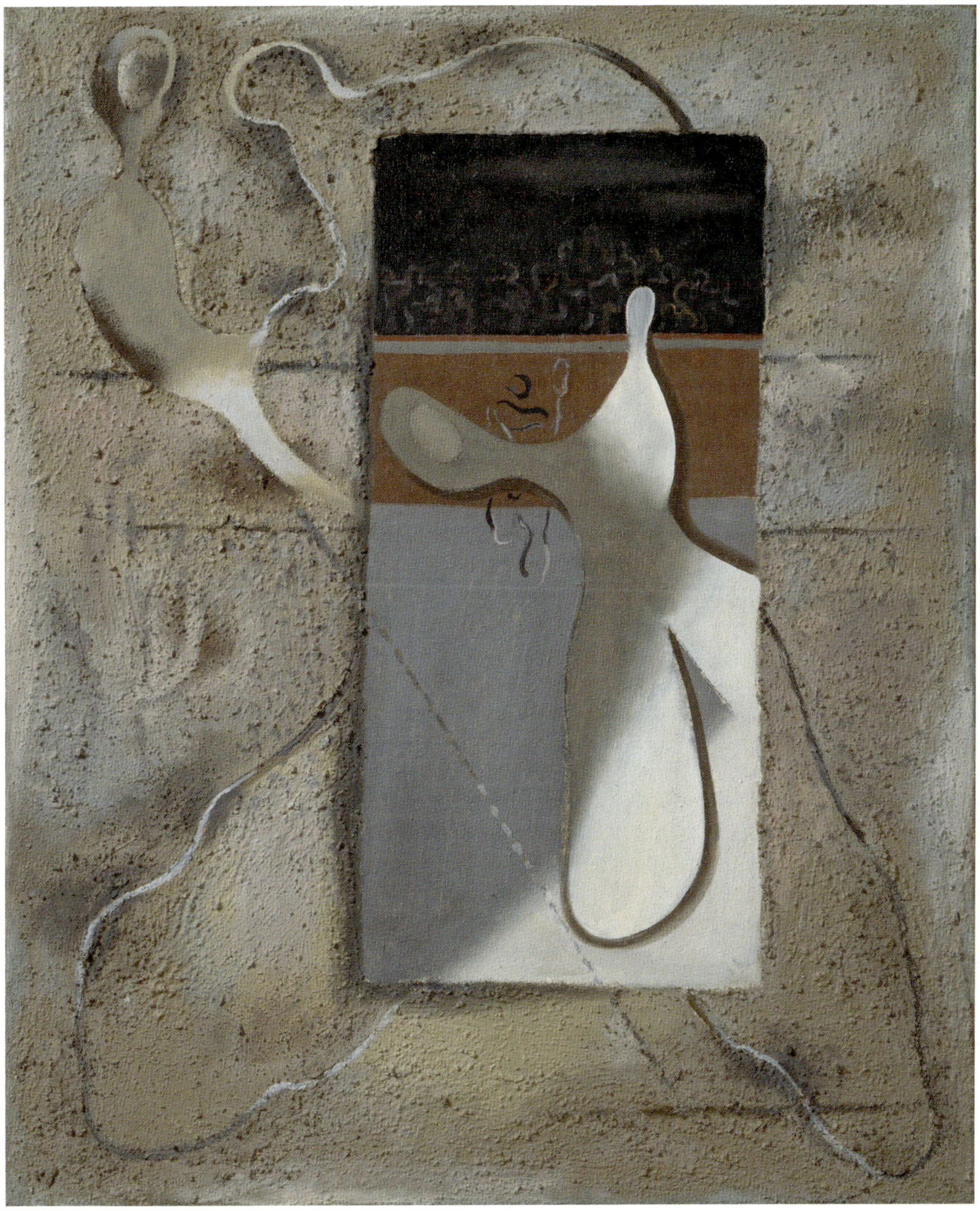

24 Willi Baumeister
Tennis, 1933
Öl und Sand auf Leinwand | oil and sand on canvas, 65 x 54 cm
Privatsammlung | private collection

Paul Klee

Paul Klee (1879-1940) zählt zu den Künstlern, die von Irmgard Burchard und ihre Zürcher Galerie vertreten wurden (siehe S. 67). Obwohl Klee in der Schweiz geboren war, arbeitete er ab 1906 hauptsächlich in Deutschland. Seit 1920 lehrte er an der Bauhaus-Schule und ab 1931 an der Düsseldorfer Kunstakademie. Zwei Jahre später gehört Klee zu den Künstlern der Moderne, die von den Nazis am heftigsten angegriffen und als ‹entartet› diffamiert wurden, so dass er im Dezember 1933 in die Schweiz zurückkehrte.

1937 zeigte Irmgard Burchard das Aquarell *Gift* in der von ihr organisierten Ausstellung *Art Réaliste et Abstrait* in Zürich.

Im Dezember desselben Jahres fragte sie Klee, ob er zur Teilnahme an der bevorstehenden Londoner Schau bereit wäre. Als der Künstler dem Vorschlag zustimmte, schickte Burchard das Aquarell mit mindestens zwei weiteren Klee-Werken nach London. Obwohl verkäuflich, fand sich für die Bilder kein Interessent, so dass sie nach der Ausstellung wieder an den Maler zurückgingen.

The painter Paul Klee (1879-1940) was another of Irmgard Burchard's Zürich dealership contacts (see p. 59). Born in Switzerland, Klee worked primarily in Germany from 1906 onwards. From 1920 he taught at the renowned Bauhaus school, from 1931 at the Düsseldorf Academy of Art. In 1933 he was branded 'degenerate' by the National Socialist regime. He returned to Switzerland in December of that year.

Klee's presence in Switzerland soon came to the attention of Irmgard Burchard. By 1936 she was acting as his dealer. The watercolour *Poison* was included in her commercial exhibition *Art Réaliste et Abstrait* in Zürich 1937.

In December 1937, Burchard asked Klee if she might send his works on to London. Klee agreed – at least three works came from him, via Burchard, to *Twentieth Century German Art*. Though marked for sale in the catalogue, none of these works found buyers in London, and were returned to the artist unsold at the end of the exhibition's run.

Literatur

Zentrum Paul Klee, Bern, Korrespondenz zwischen Irmgard Burchard und Paul Klee, 1936/37.

Paul Klee Stiftung: Paul Klee. Catalogue Raisonné, Bern 1998–2004.

Literature

Zentrum Paul Klee, Bern, correspondence between Irmgard Burchard and Paul Klee, 1936-7

Paul Klee Foundation: Paul Klee. Catalogue Raisonné. Bern 1998-2004

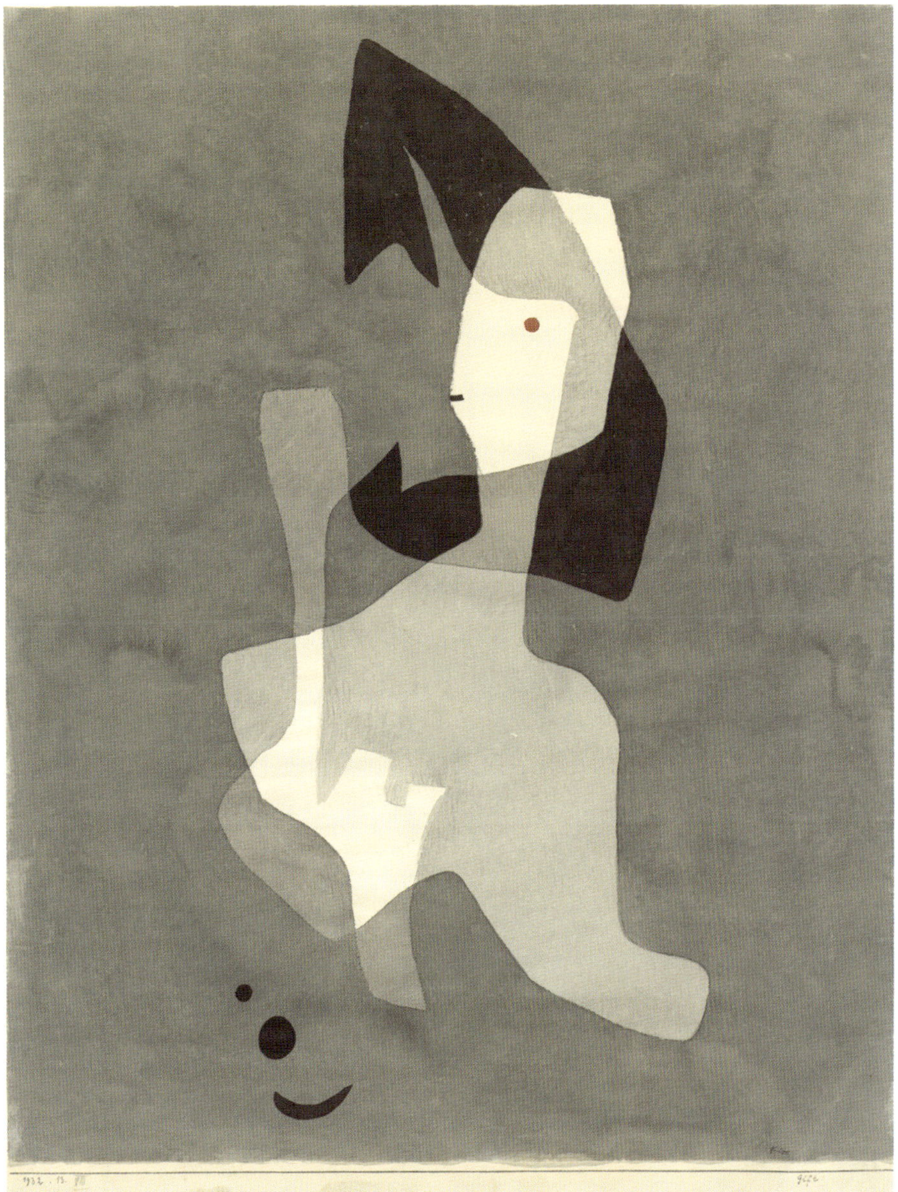

25 Paul Klee
Gift | *Poison*, 1932
Aquarell und Bleistift auf Papier über Karton |
Watercolour and pencil on paper, on card, 61.3 x 48.6 cm
Zentrum Paul Klee, Bern

Nell Walden

Nell Walden (1887-1975), die von 1912 bis 1924 mit dem Berliner Galeristen Herwarth Walden verheiratet war, zählte zu den wichtigsten Leihgebern der Ausstellung *Twentieth Century German Art.* 1913 reiste das Paar gemeinsam durch ganz Europa, um Werke für den *Ersten Deutschen Herbstsalon* zusammenzustellen, der ab September 1913 in Berlin stattfand. Diese legendäre Schau dokumentierte das gesamte Spektrum der damaligen internationalen Avantgarde-Kunst und hatte entscheidenden Einfluss auf die Kunstentwicklung in Deutschland. Parallel zu ihrer Arbeit für ihre *Sturm*-Galerie baute das Paar eine umfangreiche Kunstsammlung auf, die Walden 1919 seiner Frau übereignete.

1933 siedelte Herwarth Walden in die Sowjetunion über, während sich Nell Walden im schweizerischen Ascona niederließ und ihre Kunstsammlung in der Kunsthalle Basel deponierte.

Durch Curt Glaser erfuhr Paul Westheim im November 1937, dass sich die Sammlung Walden in der Schweiz befand. Acht Monate später wurden mindestens 39 Werke daraus in London ausgestellt. Neben den vier im folgenden reproduzierten Bildern waren darunter auch Werke folgender Künstler: Heinrich Campendonk, Franz Marc, Kurt Schwitters, August Macke, Paul Klee, Marc Chagall sowie von Nell Walden selbst.

Literatur

Antje Birthhälmer/Gerhard Finckh (Hg.): Der Sturm. Zentrum der Avantgarde, Wuppertal 2012.
Karla Bilang: Frauen im „Sturm“. Künstlerinnen der Moderne, Berlin 2013, S. 102-108.
RSMA, Brief von Curt Glaser an Paul Westheim, 1. Dezember 1937.

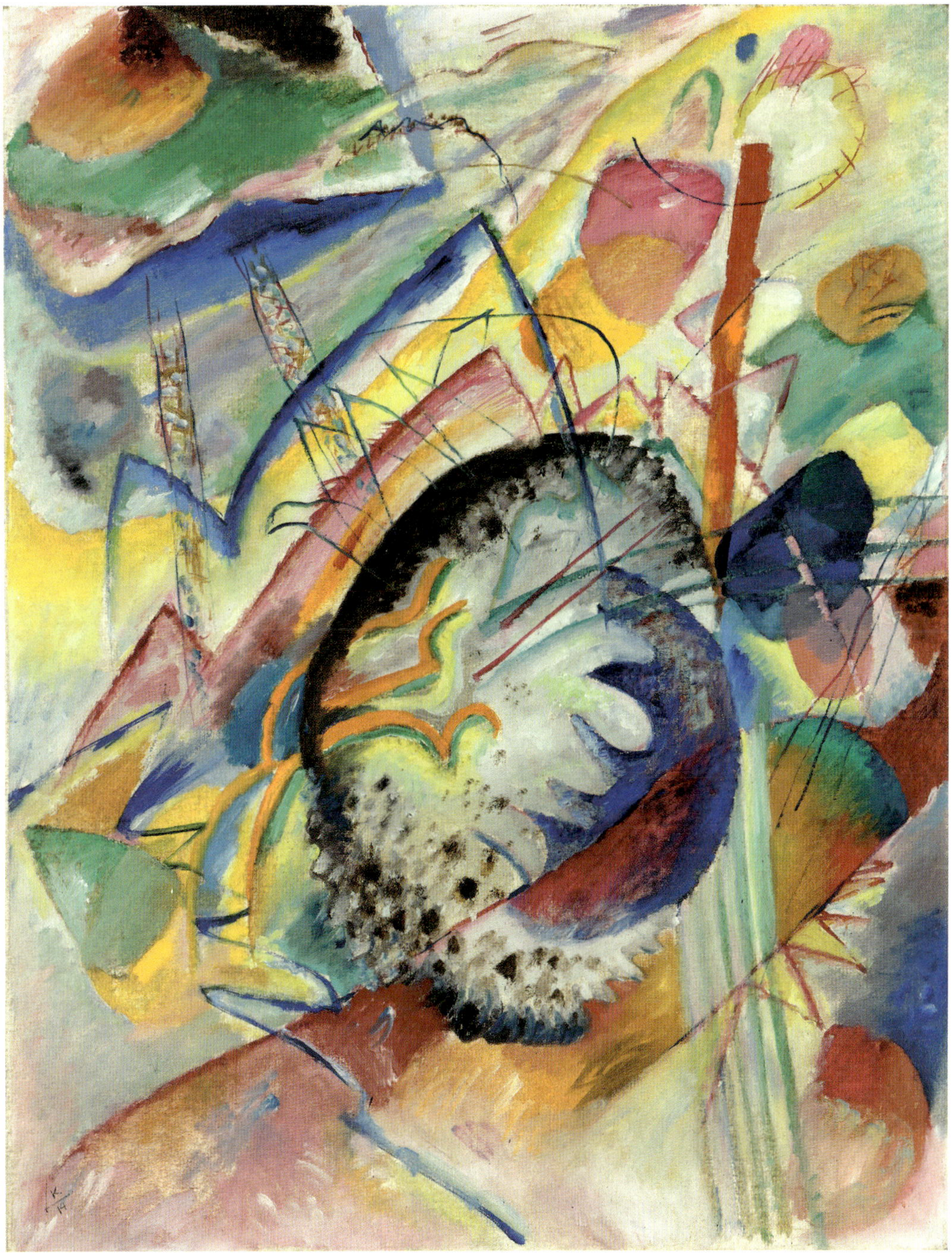

26 Wassily Kandinsky
Unbenannte Improvisation II | *Untitled Improvisation II*, 1914
Öl auf Leinwand | oil on canvas, 101 x 79.3 cm
Museum Boijmans Van Beuningen, Rotterdam

Nell Walden

Nell Walden (1887-1975) was among the most important lenders to *Twentieth Century German Art*. She was married from 1912 to 1924 to the Berlin gallerist Herwarth Walden – together they ran journal and gallery *Der Sturm* from 1912 onwards, supporting scores of modernist artists. During 1913 they travelled across Europe together, gathering works for the legendary exhibition, the *Erste Deutscher Herbstsalon* (*First German Autumn Salon*). This show was a crucial early retrospective of avant-garde art in Germany and would come to have a decisive influence of the development of modern art in the country. Nell and Herwarth Walden also built up an impressive art collection which was transferred to Nell's sole ownership in 1919.

In 1933 Herwarth Walden left Germany for Moscow. Nell meanwhile emigrated to Ascona, Switzerland. Her art collection was sent for storage at the Kunsthalle Basel.

In November 1937, Paul Westheim was informed by his contact Curt Glaser that the Walden collection was now in Switzerland. Eight months later, at least 39 of Walden's works appeared in *Twentieth Century German Art*. Alongside the four pieces illustrated here, these included works by Heinrich Campendonk, Franz Marc, Kurt Schwitters, August Macke, Paul Klee, Marc Chagall and by Nell Walden herself.

Literature

Antje Birthhälmer and Gerhard Finckh (eds.): Der Sturm. Zentrum der Avantgarde. Wuppertal 2012

Karla Bilang: Frauen im 'Sturm'. Künstlerinnen der Moderne. Berlin 2013, pp. 102-8

RSMA, letter from Curt Glaser to Paul Westheim, 1 December 1937

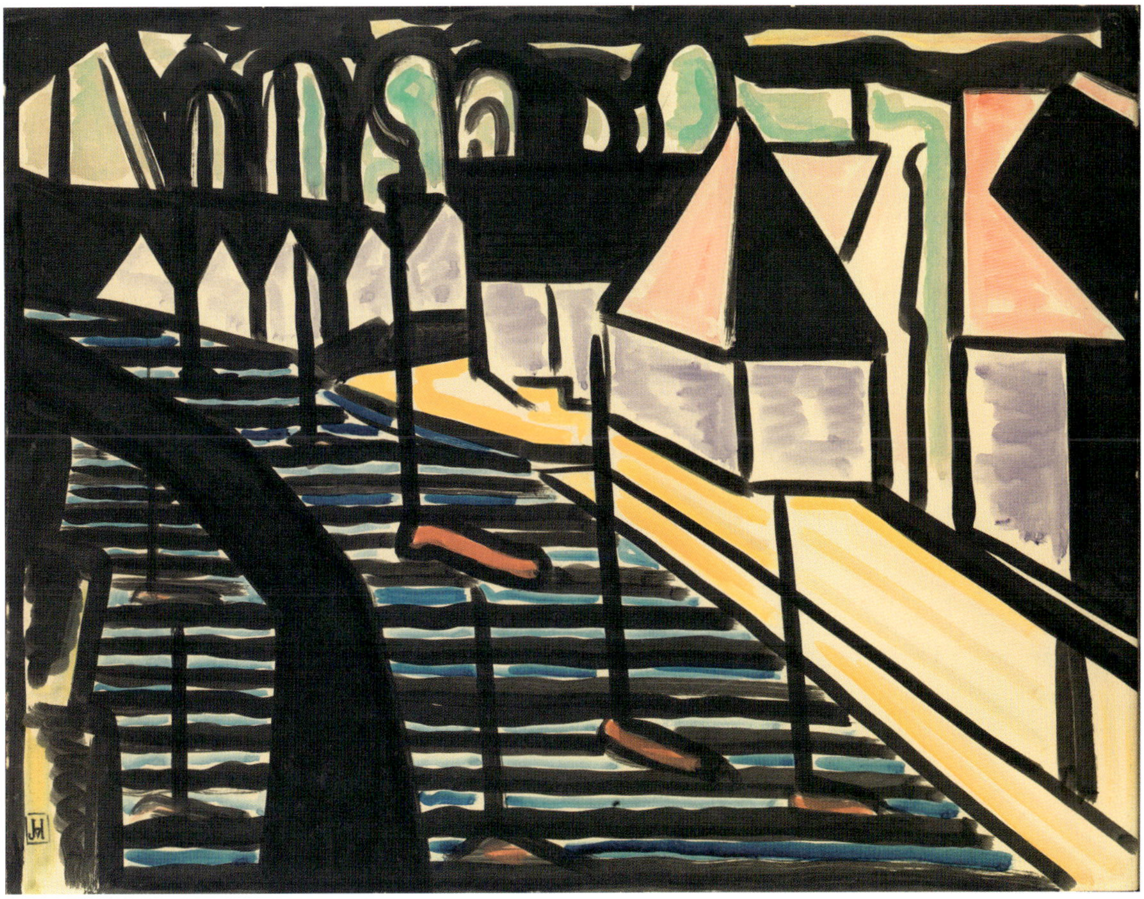

27 Jacoba van Heemskerck
Segelbild | *Sailing Picture*, circa 1915
Aquarell und Tinte auf Papier, auf Holz | watercolour and ink on paper, on wood, 48 x 63 cm
Moderna Museet, Stockholm. Donation 1958 from Nell Walden

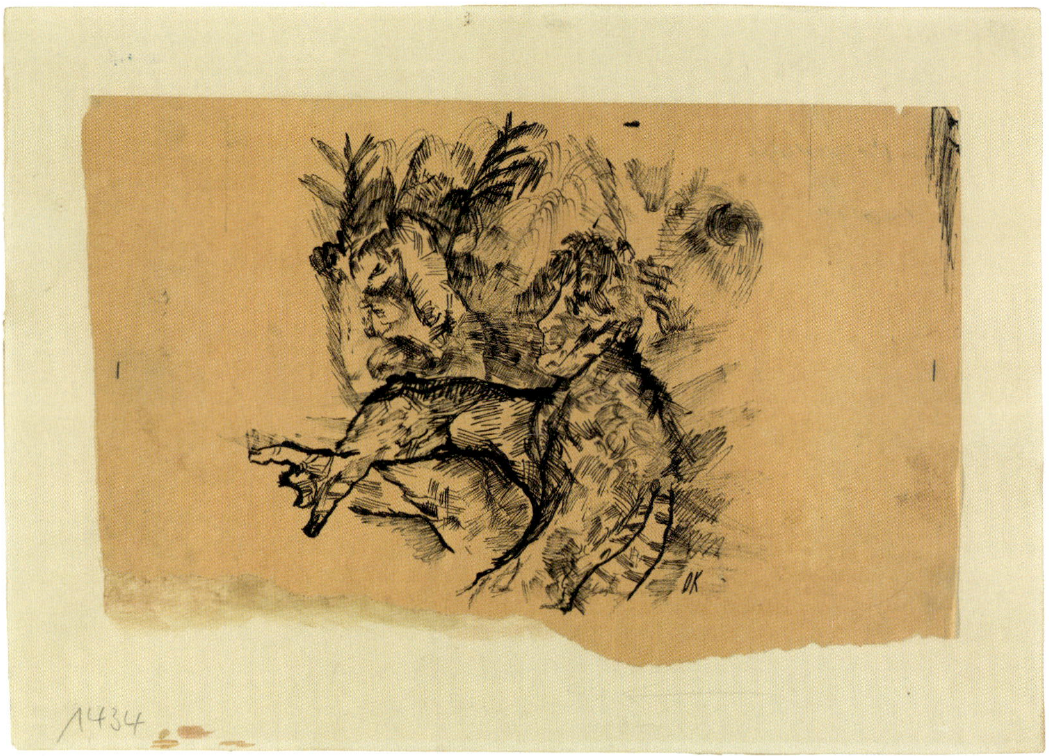

28 Oskar Kokoschka
Flucht aus dem Paradies | *Flight from Paradise*, 1910
Tuschfeder auf Papier | ink on paper, 17.5 / 20.8 x 32.5 cm
Staatliche Kunsthalle Karlsruhe

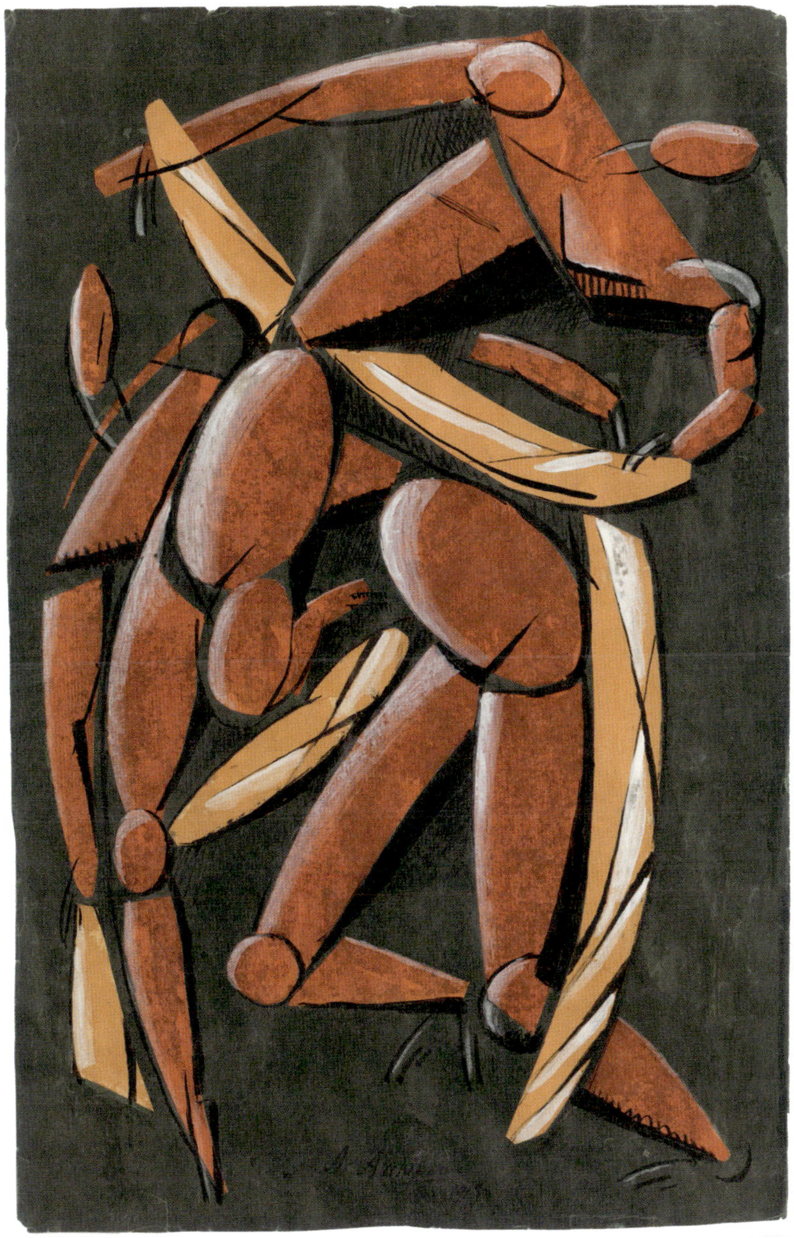

29 Alexander Archipenko
Collage, 1913
Collage mit Gouache auf Papier |
collage with gouache on paper, 47.5 x 31.5 cm
Moderna Museet Stockholm. Donation 1958 from Nell Walden

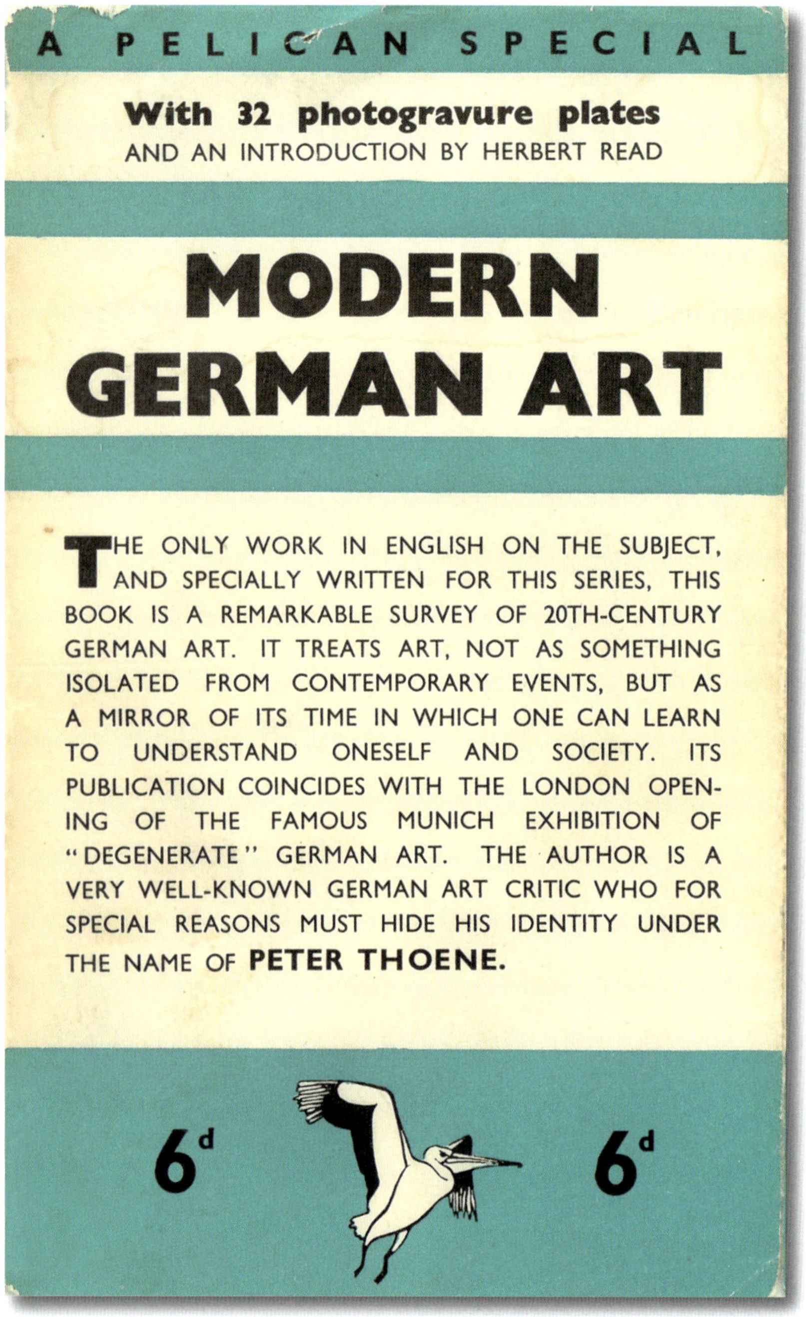

55 Peter Thoene, *Modern German Art*. London 1938, dust jacket

Modern German Art 1938: The Book

DAVID ELLIOTT

"The only work in English on the subject .... The author is a very well-known German art critic who for special reasons must hide his identity under the name of Peter Thoene".[1]

The Elusive Persona of Peter Thoene

A concise and elegantly-written essay, in a slim paperback of just 108 pages with 32 plates, comprises the corpus of *Modern German Art* (fig. 55). The first book in English on this subject, it remained the authoritative text until Peter Selz's *magnum opus* in 1957.[2] Printed on the occasion of the London exhibition *Twentieth Century German Art*, the book was handed out to visitors along with the exhibition catalogue, in exchange for their one shilling and sixpence entrance fee.

"Peter Thoene" was one of a number of aliases used by the writer later recognised as Oto Bihalji-Merin (1904-1993).[3] He was not, however, "German", but successively a citizen of the Austro-Hungarian Empire, the Kingdom of Serbs, Croats and Slovenes, the Kingdom of Yugoslavia, the German Military Occupation, Democratic Federal Yugoslavia, The Federal People's Republic of Yugoslavia, The Socialist Federal Republic of Yugoslavia and, during his last year, The State Union of Serbia and Montenegro. Against this background, it is not surprising that in the 1920s and '30s – passing through radical circles in Belgrade, Berlin, Kharkov, Paris, Moscow, Zurich and the war fronts in Spain – Bihalji-Merin recognised fluidity of identity could be an insurance policy. As a result it is difficult to track under what name, or passport, he was operating at any particular time.

Peter Thoene was born Oto Bihali to a Jewish family in the Austro-Hungarian town of Zemun (now part of Belgrade). His father David was a commercial artist. In 1915 the family moved to Budapest; in 1918, they returned to Zemun. It was at this time that Oto's surname appeared for the first time in the Serbian form "Bihalji" in official papers; he decided to adopt it, later adding a hyphenated "Merin", the surname of his wife, Lisa. Long before their 1939 marriage however, Oto had adopted the alias Peter Merin, alongside that of Peter Thoene.[4]

In 1924, Bihalji enrolled briefly in the painting school at the University of Belgrade, joined the Yugoslav Communist Party and, later in the year, moved to Berlin. While studying at the Unified State Schools for Fine and Applied Arts and attending aesthetics and philosophy courses at Berlin University, he joined the Left Student Movement and began to publish articles in newspapers and magazines. He immersed himself in every possible aspect of avant-garde culture in the German capital – his autobiography recalling for example encounters

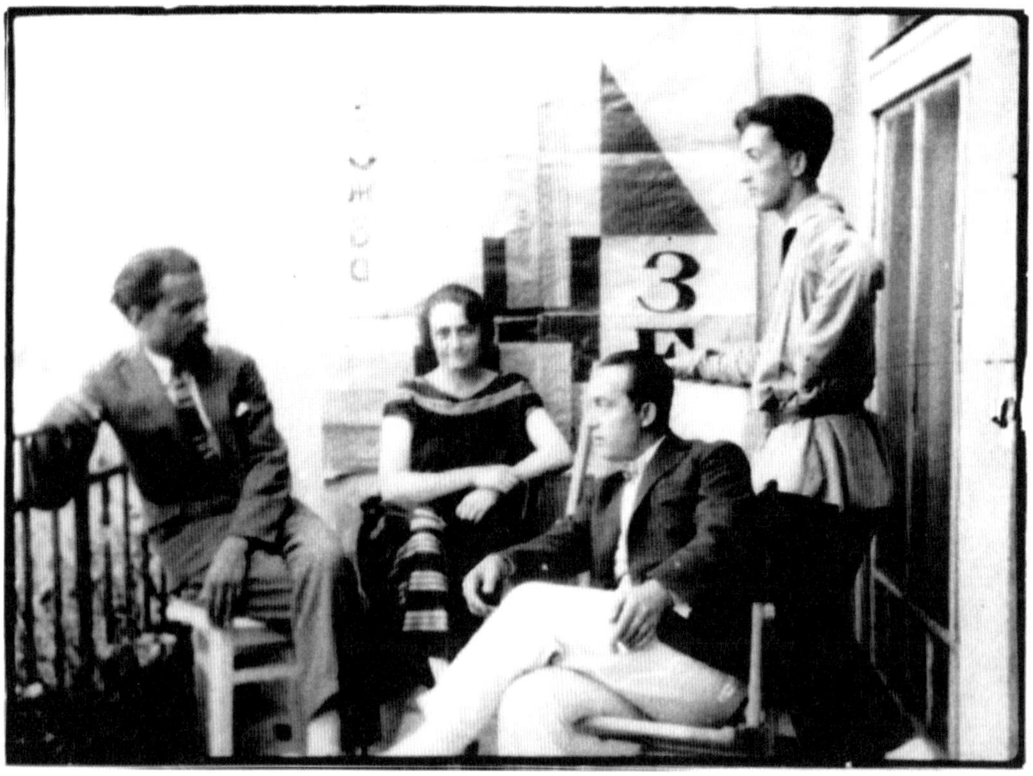

56 Left: Ljubomir Mici , founder of Zenit (left) with Anuška Nina-Naj, his wife (seated left), Pavle Bihali (seated right) and Oto Bihalji-Merin (standing), Belgrade 1925

with Herwarth Walden, publisher of the arts magazine *Der Sturm*, the Marxist-expressionist poet and novelist Johannes R. Becher, and the Hungarian Marxist aesthetician and critic, György Lukács. As a member of the 'Association of Proletarian-Revolutionary Writers', Bihalji regularly contributed to its magazine *Die Linkskurve* of which Becher was the editor.

In 1928, Bihalji returned to Yugoslavia for military service. Here he began work with his brother Pavle to set up the Nolit publishing house (fig. 56). Based on the model of Wieland Herzfelde and John Heartfield's Malik-Verlag in Berlin, Nolit was intended to continue the radical international programme of Ljubomir Micic's influential but then defunct *Zenit* (1921-26). The first editions contained contributions by authors including André Baillon, Jaroslav Hašek, Theodore Dreiser, Jack London, Otokar Keršovani and Bihalji himself. The magazine was however forcibly closed in late 1929 after just 12 issues, due to new laws forbidding leftist movements – in February 1930 Pavle was arrested for "violating state security", thrown into prison and severely tortured.[5] Oto meanwhile was released from the military on medical grounds and immediately returned to Berlin, where he persuaded Herwarth Walden to take down works by Paul Klee, Wassily Kandinsky and Marc Chagall from the *Der Sturm's* gallery in order to display *Krvava diktatura u Jugoslaviji* (*Bloody Dictatorship in Yugoslavia*), a documentation of the effects of terror and oppression.[6] After this, and the legal action it triggered in Yugoslavia, he would not be able to re-enter the country.

In Berlin, Bihalji became an activist associated with the KPD (German Communist Party), in November 1930 joining the German delegation to the Second International Congress of Revolutionary Writers in Kharkov, where he spoke on the topic of "Proletarian and Revolu-

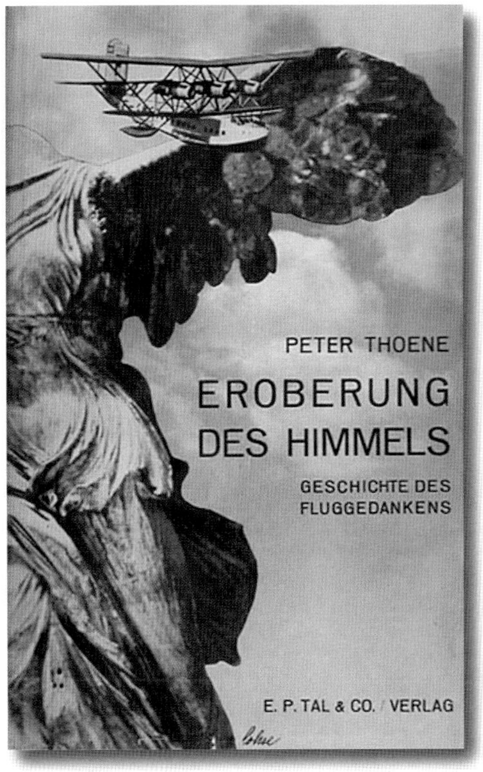

57 Richard Paul Lohse, design for the cover of Peter Thoene: *Eroberung des Himmels. Geschichte des Fluggedankens.* Wien/Leipzig 1937

tionary Literature in Germany."[7] During 1931, he wrote the first positive article to appear in the Marxist press on Bertolt Brecht, whose influence had previously been seriously criticised as 'bourgeois'. He also became the editor-in-chief of the magazine *Die Illustrierte Neue Welt* (*Illustrated New World*) and visited Spain for the first time.

Although his autobiography contains no entries for 1932, it is clear Bihalji was considering at this time the increasingly pervasive anti-intellectual impulse in culture – whether in the anti-avant-garde proletarian movement of the KPD, or in the racist, rabidly nationalistic NSDAP. In 1933, witnessing the closure of the Bauhaus school and, on 10 May, the infamous Berlin book burnings, Bihalji sought refuge in Paris. He remained there, in what he described as "exile", for almost two years.

In Paris Bihalji initially worked with fellow-communists Arthur Koestler and Manès Sperber on setting up the ultimately short-lived "Institute for the Study of Fascism". In August 1934, Maxim Gorky invited him to Moscow to attend, as a foreign observer, the All Union Congress of Soviet Writers at which Andrei Zhdanov, the Minister of Culture, promulgated the doctrine of Socialist Realism – the simplification of a chaotic and destructive system of internecine rivalry that created "order" by enforcing state power over all forms of media and art.[8]

On his return from the Congress Bihalji began to feel increasingly uncomfortable in Paris. At the beginning of 1935 he thus sought "literary asylum" in Switzerland, settling in Zürich, where he began work on a rapid succession of three books. The first, *Eroberung des Himmels: Geschichte des Fluggedankens* (*The Conquest of the Heavens: Reflections on the Changing Face of Flight*) (1937) appeared in German and French under the name of Peter

Thoene. The cover of the book's German edition (fig. 57), a photomontage combining the Nike of Samothrace with a biplane flying boat, was designed by the Swiss artist Richard Paul Lohse.[9] Lohse was the husband of gallerist Irmgard Burchard – this collaboration provides early evidence of the friendship between Bihalji and the ultimate organisers of *Twentieth Century German Art*.

Later in 1937 Bihalji published *Spanien zwischen Tod und Geburt* (*Spain Between Death and Birth*), this time under the name of Peter Merin.[10] Recording his various travels to the civil war-ravaged country during 1936, Bihalji reported his collaboration with the International Brigade volunteers, as well as his meetings with both Andreu Nin, the Catalan Minister of Justice and co-leader of the Trotskyist Workers' Party of Marxist Unification, and with Lluís Companys, the Catalan President and leader of the popular front Republican Left of Catalonia. Such political even-handedness would not have gone unnoticed, and could even have proved suicidal, had the Stalinist commissars of the International Brigades realised that the reporter was, in fact, Oto Bihalji and not Peter Merin.[11] But there is always the possibility that he was playing a double, or even treble, game: as a reporter "from the Left standpoint, but without fanaticism,"[12] as an undercover Soviet agent, or as both. In any event, he was fortunate to have lived a charmed life then, before and after.

Against this frenetic maelstrom of death, life and hope for the future, Bihalji began to prepare his book *Modern German Art*. There is no evidence that he actually visited London, either during the preparation of his book during the exhibition. But he was certainly aware of the cultural climate in Britain, of Herbert Read's position in the art world, and of masterpieces in the national art collections. It was he who provided the contact between the Zürich-based organisers, and Paul Westheim in Paris (see p. 60 of this volume); it is hard to believe that he would not have been personally acquainted with at least some of the émigrés who were living in London in 1938.

The Book and the Exhibition

Inseparable from the exhibition *Twentieth Century German Art*, the book *Modern German Art* was, as noted above, distributed at the show as part of the admission fee. The book was also available through bookshops and general stores as one of the first two "Pelican Specials" produced by the Penguin publishing house. The mission of this new imprint was to produce "books of topical importance published within as short a time as possible from receipt of the manuscript", as the dust jacket of *Modern German Art* set out. Considering his heavy publication workload, this short turnaround must have suited Bihalji. It seems the organisers provided him with little guidance however, most likely as they themselves had not reached consensus about the exhibition's composition, balance, or title – they were still collecting works for it until the last minute. Perhaps this also explains the brevity of the work descriptions in the London catalogue, and the fact that only 7 out of the 271 catalogued exhibits were illustrated in the Pelican book.

In the introduction to the exhibition catalogue, the organisers maintained that they were "not concerned with the political aspect of the situation" but wished to affirm merely "... that art as an expression of the human spirit in all its mutations, is only great in so far as it is free."[13] But even this view, no doubt carefully judged so as not to alienate those whom they hoped would support the exhibition by buying work, attracted the attention of Hitler himself (see p. 185).

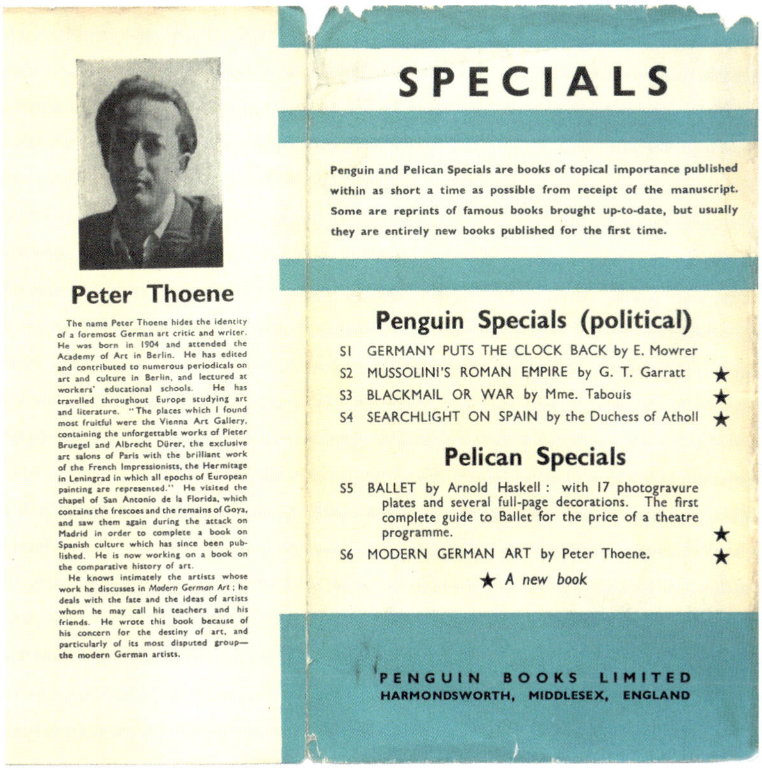

Peter Thoene

The name Peter Thoene hides the identity of a foremost German art critic and writer. He was born in 1904 and attended the Academy of Art in Berlin. He has edited and contributed to numerous periodicals on art and culture in Berlin, and lectured at workers' educational schools. He has travelled throughout Europe studying art and literature. "The places which I found most fruitful were the Vienna Art Gallery, containing the unforgettable works of Pieter Bruegel and Albrecht Dürer, the exclusive art salons of Paris with the brilliant work of the French Impressionists, the Hermitage in Leningrad in which all epochs of European painting are represented." He visited the chapel of San Antonio de la Florida, which contains the frescoes and the remains of Goya, and saw them again during the attack on Madrid in order to complete a book on Spanish culture which has since been published. He is now working on a book on the comparative history of art.

He knows intimately the artists whose work he discusses in *Modern German Art*; he deals with the fate and the ideas of artists whom he may call his teachers and his friends. He wrote this book because of his concern for the destiny of art, and particularly of its most disputed group—the modern German artists.

SPECIALS

Penguin and Pelican Specials are books of topical importance published within as short a time as possible from receipt of the manuscript. Some are reprints of famous books brought up-to-date, but usually they are entirely new books published for the first time.

Penguin Specials (political)

S1 GERMANY PUTS THE CLOCK BACK by E. Mowrer
S2 MUSSOLINI'S ROMAN EMPIRE by G. T. Garratt ★
S3 BLACKMAIL OR WAR by Mme. Tabouis ★
S4 SEARCHLIGHT ON SPAIN by the Duchess of Atholl ★

Pelican Specials

S5 BALLET by Arnold Haskell: with 17 photogravure plates and several full-page decorations. The first complete guide to Ballet for the price of a theatre programme. ★
S6 MODERN GERMAN ART by Peter Thoene. ★

★ A new book

PENGUIN BOOKS LIMITED
HARMONDSWORTH, MIDDLESEX, ENGLAND

58 Peter Thoene: *Modern German Art*. London 1938, back dust jacket

At arm's length from the exhibition, Bihalji's book provided the main conduit for expressing the political view. He explained the Nazi propaganda of *Entartete Kunst* in order to excoriate it, describing how in that exhibition "... the martyred creatures of art speak out, since the age, obedient to the voice of power, is dumb...".[14] These were innocent, but strong, works, full of worldly knowledge and emotion like those that would be shown in London that "the man at the head of the German hierarchy of power" had denigrated as "'simply the artificial stammering of people for whom God has denied the boon of genuine artistic talent and given instead the gift of prating and deception...'".[15]

With Europe at the brink of war, Bihalji recognised the potential resonance of his words. The view of modern German art history he presented, therefore, was inclusive, honest and informative, constantly making reference to the innate humanity of art, in contrast with the militant and manipulative propaganda of the Nazis.[16] Dripping with fastidious irony, and wary of writing propaganda himself, Bihaliji was careful not to mention the name of Hitler or other Nazi leaders directly, preferring to use their official titles and condemning them only through their own words.

Bihalji began his account with the Wilhelmine objections to impressionism in Germany, set as foreplay to the damaging insults and actions of the present. Describing Max Liebermann's path from realist to impressionist, the artist's own words were quoted at length, in particular his paraphrasing of Emil Zola, that "... art will be recognised as *'la nature vue à travers un tempérament'* (nature filtered through an acute sensibility)."[17] As Liebermann survives his early struggles and becomes better known, Bihalji summarises his tragedy laconically: "1905-1909: Jewish alleys, narrow streets, throngs of people ... Success began to arrive, medals, the title of Professor ... election to the Prussian Academy of Arts, President of the Berlin Secessionists. Long years of rich creativeness ... The octogenarian was fêted by a world-wide community of admirers. It thus seemed that the evening of his industrious life, rich in discoveries, love of mankind and artistic knowledge would wane peacefully and lit by fame. It turned out otherwise. In 1933 Max Liebermann left the Academy, derided, grief-stricken and wounded in spirit. He has since died."[18]

An elegiac, moral zone has been established here in which Lovis Corinth may then be accurately characterised as a proto-expressionist, his "cruelly erotic" images of women from the turn of the century contrasted with the "tempo, horror and beauty" of his later Walchensee landscapes. Yet, as throughout the book, a final, bitter layer of present circumstance is reiterated: Adolf Ziegler, president of the Reichskammer der Bildenden Künste, fanatically claims that Corinth's work "... suddenly attracted interest when, after his second stroke, he could only manage to produce morbid and incomprehensible daubs ...".[19]

Throughout the book, Bihalji maintained the same attention to detail, capturing the voices of both artists and ideologues. He weaves in the intricate rivalries of the different artistic groups and tendencies – from Die Brücke, to Der Blaue Reiter, to Bauhaus, to Die Neue Sachlichkeit – yet refusing to confine them, comparing and contrasting their works. Within a single chapter, he considered abstract artists such as Kandinsky, Schlemmer, Moholy-Nagy Willi Baumeister with their Soviet and French counterparts; he then contrasts the achievement of non-objectivity with the "super-concreteness" of socially-engaged artists who, after World War I, had been moulded by Dada: Richard Huelsenbeck, John Heartfield, Raoul Haussmann and George Grosz, extending this discussion to a consideration of the paintings of Otto Dix and Max Beckmann, the graphics of Käthe Kollwitz and the sculptures of Wilhelm Lehmbruck.[20] No British critic at this time had direct experience of such a wide range of historical and contemporary art across Europe or – with the exception of the anarchist Read – the perspective to view it humanely as a continuum of cultural activity.

The book concludes with a coda Bihalji judiciously entitles "Limitations and Possibilities." The question clearly at issue "is not Whither Art, but Whither Humanity?"[21] He continues by considering the fate of German art: "... the good name of Germany is at stake. The term 'German art' conveys the breadth and spirit of Albrecht Dürer, of Hans Holbein, of Mathias Grünewald." What relationship, he asks rhetorically, has this tradition with the virulent, racist, official art that is now being produced?[22]

Quoting Max Slevogt, Bihalji reminds us that the great painters of history "are, in fact, the great painters of humanity". As he concludes: "In what an age of darkness we must live ... when such things as these have to be stated, when art, the great protectress of the living ..., that creative force which expands the prison house of our being and allows a vision of eternity to be glimpsed beyond the brief span of our existence, has to be protected. But art, if it is to live, needs freedom. Its dreams with their abundance of solace cannot flourish in the arid atmosphere of duress."[23]

After 1938

Bihalji's cryptic autobiography records only two brief visits to London during his lifetime: on the first, in 1961, he met Herbert Read. On the second, in 1968, he travelled specifically to see the exhibition *Cybernetic Serendipity* at the ICA."[24] The most significant mention of

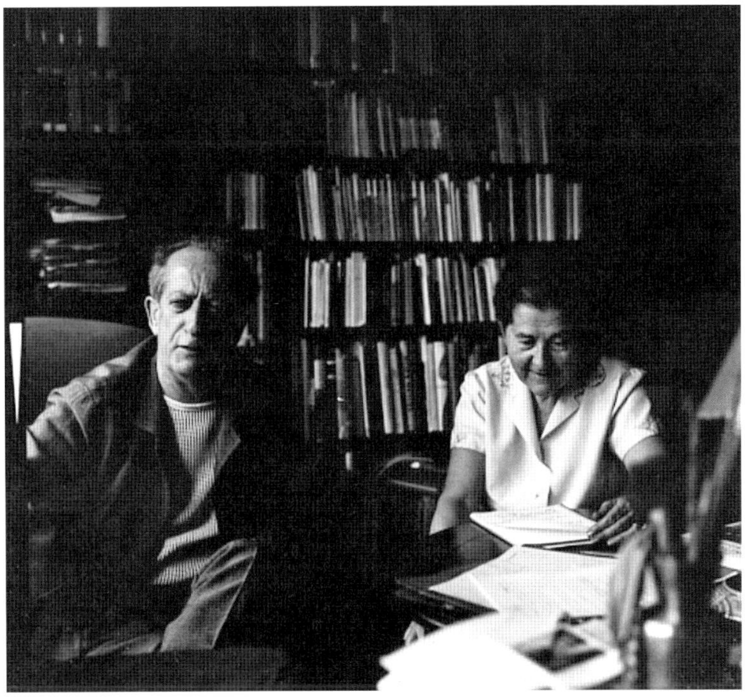

59 Oto Bihalji-Merin and his wife Lisa, 1967

his 1938 London adventure is the comment that, in 1937, it was upon his request that Picasso was made a member of the exhibition committee.[25]

Although he never said so, Bihalji's visit to Moscow in 1934, to attend the All Union Congress of Soviet Writers, may have confirmed his worst fears about the increasing totalitarianism of the Left. His book on German art does not mention the proletarian movement, or Socialist Realism, but stresses the pluralism and intrinsic anti-fascism of the avant-garde.[26] This suggests that he did not believe, or professed not to believe, in a single "party line" for culture, yet Marxist critic Anthony Blunt concluded the opposite in his review of the *Twentieth Century German Art* exhibition in the *Spectator*.[27] And it is just what Bihalji himself later championed in Yugoslavia after the war during the 1940s and '50s.

With lack of corroboration, gaps of information, manipulations and inconsistences, the facts about Oto Bihalji-Merin's life present an enigma. Was he a man of firm, humane, libertarian principles who faced and responded to tumultuous times, or was he an agent of world revolution working covertly for the USSR? According to time and circumstance, he may even have moved from being one to the other. But with the evidence available at present, these questions must remain open.

When asked in 1976 by a journalist in Belgrade if he was "an essayist, an art critic, a reporter, an author, or what is closest to him?" His answer was as follows: "The revolution of art and society, the revolt against patriarchal tyranny, the creative unrest of young people. The classical divisions of our profession are of little interest to me, much more important are the rhythms of life."[28]

This text is a shortened version of a longer essay in preparation by the author on the topic of Oto Bihalji-Merin, his life and work.

1 Peter Thoene: Modern German Art. London 1938
2 Peter Selz: German Expressionist Painting. Berkeley 1957. Alfred H. Barr's 43-page catalogue for the exhibition German Painting and Sculpture at The Museum of Modern Art, New York (1931) was Thoene's single predecessor.
3 Unless referenced otherwise, biographical details here taken from the autobiographical text Bihalji-Merin published in 1976 to mark an exhibition of his writings at Museum of Modern Art in Belgrade. Oto Bihalji-Merin: Bio-bibliografija. Belgrade 1976, hereafter "Bio-bibliografija". I am indebted to Irina Suboti, curator of the 1976 exhibition, as well as to Bojana Peji (Belgrade) and Lutz Becker (London), for their assistance.
4 Bihalji first met Lisa Merin (1900-1991), also of Zemun, in 1930. He certainly used her surname as an alias from 1936, and perhaps earlier (see fn. 10).
5 In 1941, Pavle Bihali was one of the first members of the Resistance to be murdered by the Nazi occupiers.
6 The only reference I have so far been able to locate for the *Der Sturm* exhibition is Bio-bibliografija, p. 17.
7 Bihalji became a member of the KPD once he was in Paris in 1934.
8 Zhdanov repeated here the famous line fed to him by Stalin that artists should become "Engineers of Human Souls." Bihalji noted meeting André Malraux and Louis Aragon at the Congress (both of whom he knew from Paris) as well as German writers Ernst Toller, Johannes R. Becher and Oscar Maria Graf whom he knew through *Die Linkskurve*. Bio-bibliografija, p. 19.
9 Peter Thoene: Eroberung des Himmels. Geschichte des Fluggedankens. Vienna/Leipzig 1937. Published in French as: La Conquête du Ciel. De L'antiquité à nos jours. Paris 1938. This book celebrates the history of flight and man's creative obsession with it. Although his Bio-bibliografija records an English edition of this, I have been unable to locate any record of it being published.
10 Peter Merin: Spanien zwischen Tod und Geburt. Zurich 1937. Published in English as: Spain between Death and Birth. London etc 1938, translated by Charles Fullerton who must have worked consecutively on the translation of Modern German Art.
11 Both Nin and Companys were tortured and murdered. Nin, in 1937, was flayed alive in a prison cell during the Stalinist purge. In 1940, after a show trial by the newly formed Francoist state, Companys was shot without a blindfold in front of a firing squad.
12 Quoted from the blurb on the front flap of the book jacket for Spain between Death and Birth, op. cit.
13 Anon.: Introduction, in: Anon.: Exhibition of Twentieth Century German Art. Exhibition catalogue, London 1938, p. 6
14 Peter Thoene: Modern German Art. London 1938, pp. 41-42
15 Thoene: Modern German Art, pp. 41-42. In the second quoted passage, Bihalji cites Hitler's speech of 18 July 1937 at the inauguration of the Haus der Kunst in Munich.
16 Bihalji was keenly aware of, but made no public statement about, conflicts and changes within the Soviet Union that also had consigned art as an instrument of political ideology. See note 8.
17 Thoene: Modern German Art, p. 30
18 Ibid. p. 33
19 Ibid, pp. 38-39
20 "The Abstract and the Super-Concrete". Ibid. pp. 76-103
21 Ibid. p. 104
22 Ibid, p. 107
23 Ibid, p. 108
24 Bio-bibliografija, p 28. This groundbreaking exhibition was curated by Jasia Reichardt.
25 Ibid, p. 20
26 The Bio-bibliografija (p. 17) also makes a strong point of his admiration for the work of the surrealists when he noted that he had been greatly impressed by the performance of Buñuel and Dalí's film Un Chien Andalou (1929) he had seen in 1930.
27 Anthony Blunt: Contemporary German Art, in: The Spectator (8 July 1938) p. 17. "It is the ne plus ultra of the individualist approach to art, which seems to have landed painting in a dead end, and though Hitler's method of regimenting the arts is in every way to be deplored, there is nothing intrinsically wrong in the organisation of the arts by the State. It is, in fact, the normal situation which has only not held good during the last few centuries." From the mid-1930s to at least the early 1950s, Blunt was working as a Soviet spy.
28 Bio-bibliografija, p. 7

Das Buch zur Ausstellung : *Modern German Art*, 1938

DAVID ELLIOTT

«Das einzige englischsprachige Werk zum Thema. [...] Der Autor ist ein bekannter deutscher Kunstkritiker, dessen Identität aus besonderen Gründen hinter dem Pseudonym Peter Thoene verborgen bleiben muss.»[1]

Peter Thoene, eine mysteriöse Person

Modern German Art (Abb. 55) erschien als kleinformatiges Taschenbuch, das 108 Seiten und 32 Abbildungen umfasste. Mit seinem prägnant formulierten und elegant geschriebenen Text ist es das erste Buch in englischer Sprache zur «modernen deutschen Kunst» und blieb die einzige Monographie zum Thema, bis 1957 das Hauptwerk von Peter Selzs *German Expressionist Painting* erschien.[2] Das Buch kam zur Londoner Ausstellung *Twentieth Century German Art* heraus und wurde zusammen mit dem Ausstellungskatalog und der Eintrittskarte für einen Schilling und sechs Pence abgegeben.

‹Peter Thoene› war eines von mehreren Pseudonymen, die der Autor und Kunsthistoriker Oto Bihalji-Merin (1904-1993) benutzte.[3] Trotz des gewählten Vornamens ‹Peter› war der Verfasser kein Deutscher, sondern – bedingt durch die politischen Umwälzungen des 20. Jahrhunderts – Bürger einer ganzen Reihe von Staaten: Königreich Österreich-Ungarn, Königreich der Serben, Kroatien und Slowenien, Königreich Jugoslawien, deutsches Besatzungsgebiet, Föderative Volksrepublik Jugoslawien, Sozialistische Föderative Volksrepublik Jugoslawien und, in seinem letzten Lebensjahr, Staatenbund Serbien und Montenegro. Vor diesem Hintergrund ist es nicht verwunderlich, dass Bihalji-Merin eine wechselnde Identität als Vorteil empfand; während der 1920er und 1930er Jahre verkehrte er in radikalen Kreisen in Belgrad, Berlin, Charkow, Paris, Moskau und Zürich, nahm auch am spanischen Bürgerkrieg teil, und es kam einer Lebensversicherung gleich, wenn man über mehrere Identitäten verfügte. Deshalb ist bisweilen schwer festzustellen, unter welchem Namen und mit welchem Pass er zu welcher Zeit aktiv war.

Peter Thoene entstammte einer jüdischen Familie und kam als Oto Bihali in der Stadt Zemun zur Welt (heute zu Belgrad gehörend). Sein Vater David war Gebrauchsgraphiker. 1915 zog die Familie nach Budapest, kehrte 1918 jedoch wieder nach Zemun zurück. Zu dieser Zeit erscheint der Familienname in offiziellen Dokumenten erstmals in der serbischen Form «Bihalji». Kurz darauf scheint Oto «Bihalji» beschlossen zu haben, seinen Namen von nun an immer so zu schreiben. Später fügte er mit einem Bindestrich noch «Merin» hinzu, den Nachnamen seiner Frau Lisa, die er 1939 heiratete.[4] Schon in den Jahren zuvor hat er jedoch auch die Namen «Peter Merin» «Peter Thoene» als Pseudonyme verwendet.

1924 war Bihalji kurzzeitig im Fach Malerei an der Universität Belgrad eingeschrieben. Im selben Jahr wurde er Mitglied der Kommunistischen Partei Jugoslawiens. Ende 1924 zog er nach Berlin, besuchte dort die Vereinigten Staatsschulen für freie und angewandte Kunst und hörte an der Universität Ästhetik- und Philosophie-Vorlesungen. Parallel dazu schloss er sich der linken Studentenbewegung an und begann in Zeitschriften Artikel zu veröffentlichen. Intensiv tauchte er in die Avantgarde-Szene der deutschen Hauptstadt ein; in seiner Autobiographie *Biobibliogafija* erwähnt er u.a. Kontakte zu Herwarth Walden, dem Herausgeber des *Sturm*, zu Johannes R. Becher, dem marxistisch-expressionistischen Dichter, oder zu György Lukács, dem ungarischen Marxisten, Kritiker und Theoretiker der Ästhetik. Als Mitglied des Bundes proletarisch-revolutionärer Schriftsteller schrieb Bihalji regelmäßig Beiträge für die *Linkskurve*, deren Redakteur Becher war.

1928 kehrte Bihalji nach Jugoslawien zurück, um seinen Militärdienst abzuleisten. Gemeinsam mit seinem Bruder Pavle gründete er dort den Verlag Nolit (Abb. 56), der sich am Beispiel des Berliner Malik-Verlags von Wieland Herzfelde und John Heartfield orientierte. Er sollte das radikale internationale Programm fortsetzen, das Ljubomir Micic von 1921-26 mit seiner einflussreichen Avantgarde-Zeitschrift *Zenit* verfolgt hatte. Die neue bei Nolit erscheinende Zeitschrift hieß *Nova literatura* und brachte Beiträge von Autoren wie André Baillon, Theodore Dreiser, Jaroslav Hašek, Otokar Keršovani, Jack London und Oto Bihalji selbst. Nach 12 Nummern wurde sie jedoch auf Grund neuer Zensurbestimmungen zur ‹Unterdrückung linksgerichteter Aktivitäten› verboten. Im Februar 1930 wurde Pavle wegen «Gefährdung der Staatssicherheit» festgenommen, ins Gefängnis geworfen und gefoltert.[5] Unterdessen war Oto aus medizinischen Gründen aus dem Militärdienst entlassen worden und sofort nach Berlin zurückgekehrt. Dort brachte er Herwarth Walden dazu, die in seiner *Sturm*-Galerie ausgestellten Werke Klees, Kandinskys und Chagalls abzuhängen und durch die Dokumentation *Krvava diktatura u Jugoslaviji* (Blutige Diktatur in Jugoslawien) zu ersetzen, um das Publikum über die Auswirkungen von Terror und Unterdrückung in seinem Heimatland zu informieren.[6] Diese Aktion musste naturgemäß die Aufmerksamkeit der jugoslawischen Staatssicherheit erregen, weswegen Bilhalji in der Folge nicht mehr in dorthin zurückkehren konnte.

So blieb er in Berlin und wurde dort Aktivist der KPD.[7] Als Mitglied der deutschen Delegation hielt er im November 1930 einen Vortrag über die deutsche proletarische und revolutionäre Literatur auf dem «Zweiten Internationalen Kongress für revolutionäre Literatur» in Charkow. Im darauffolgenden Jahr schrieb er den ersten von der marxistischen Presse veröffentlichten positiven Artikel über Bertolt Brecht, dessen Werk bis dahin als bürgerlich bewertet und entsprechend scharf kritisiert worden war. Außerdem wurde Bihalji Chefredakteur der Zeitschrift *Illustrierte Neue Welt* und besuchte zum ersten Mal Spanien.

Zum Jahr 1932 enthält seine Autobiografie keine Angaben. Dennoch wird Bihalji die antiintellektuellen Tendenzen wahrgenommen haben, die sich in der proletarischen KPD und der rassistischen NSDAP gleichermaßen abzeichneten. 1933 wurde er in Berlin Zeuge der Schließung des Bauhauses und der Bücherverbrennung, worauf er nach Paris flüchtete. Fast zwei Jahre lang sollte er dort nach eigenen Worten «im Exil» leben.

In der französischen Hauptstadt ging er daran, mit den Kommunisten Arthur Koestler und Manès Sperber ein Institut für das Studium des Faschismus aufzubauen, das jedoch nicht lange Bestand hatte. Im August 1934 wurde er von Maxim Gorki nach Moskau eingeladen, um als ausländischer Beobachter am Kongress des sowjetischen Schriftstellerverbandes teilzunehmen. Während dieser Tagung verkündete Kultusminister Andrei Schdanow

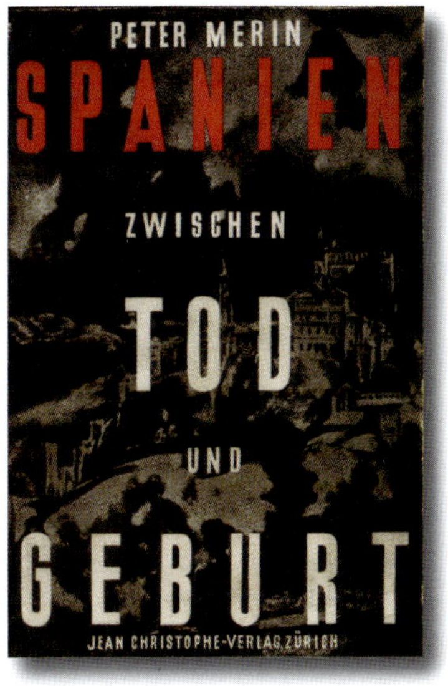

60 Peter Merin [= Oto Bihalji-Merin], *Spanien zwischen Tod und Geburt.* Zürich 1937, Schutzumschlag von Richard Paul Lohse

die Doktrin des sozialistischen Realismus. Ihr Ziel war einerseits, die chaotisch-destruktive Rivalität unter Kulturschaffenden zu beseitigen und durch staatliche Überwachung aller Medien und Kunstformen ‹Ordnung› herzustellen.[8]

Nach seiner Rückkehr aus Moskau fühlte sich Bihalji in Paris zunehmend unwohl. Anfang 1935 suchte er deshalb ‹literarisches Asyl› in der Schweiz und ließ sich in Zürich nieder, wo er in kürzester Zeit drei Bücher verfasste. Das erste, *Eroberung des Himmels – Geschichte des Fluggedankens*, erschien 1937 auf Deutsch und 1938 auf Französisch – jeweils unter dem Pseudonym ‹Peter Thoene›. Für den Umschlag der deutschen Ausgabe entwarf der Schweizer Graphiker Richard Paul Lohse eine Fotomontage mit einem Wasserflugzeug und der Nike von Samothrake (Abb. 57).[9] Lohse war der Ehemann der Galeristin Irmgard Burchard, woraus hervorgeht, dass Bihalji und die Organisatoren der Ausstellung *Twentieth Century German Art* schon früh in Verbindung standen.

Ende 1937 erschien das zweite Buch, *Spanien zwischen Tod und Geburt*, diesmal unter dem Pseudonym ‹Peter Merin›.[10] Darin schreibt Bihalji über seine verschiedenen Reisen in die spanischen Bürgerkriegsregionen, die er im Vorjahr unternommen hatte. Er berichtet von der Zusammenarbeit mit den Freiwilligen der Internationalen Brigaden und von seiner Begegnung mit zwei führenden Politikern: mit Andreu Nin, dem katalanischen Justizminister und Vorsitzenden der Arbeiterpartei der Marxistischen Einheit, sowie mit Lluís Companys, dem katalanischen Präsidenten und Anführer der Republikanischen Linken Kataloniens. Seine Sympathie für die Republik hätte ihm durchaus gefährlich werden können, wenn es den stalinistischen Politkommissaren in den Internationalen Brigaden bekannt gewesen wäre, wer sich hinter dem Pseudonym ‹Peter Merin› verbarg.[11] Möglicherweise spielte Bihalji aber auch eine doppelte, wenn nicht sogar eine dreifache Rolle: als «linksgerichteter, jedoch nicht fanatischer Reporter»,[12] und als sowjetischer Geheimagent – oder beides zugleich. Auf jeden Fall hatte er Glück – jetzt und auch später.

Mitten in diesem aufreibenden Malstrom von Tod, Leben, und Zukunftshoffnungen begann Bihalji die Arbeit am dritten Buch: *Modern German Art.* Auch wenn es keinen Beleg dafür gibt, dass er während der Entstehung des Buches oder zur der Ausstellung *Twentieth Century German Art* nach London fuhr, bleibt gleichwohl festzustellen, dass er über das kulturelle Leben Englands ausgezeichnet informiert war. Bihalji wusste um die prominente Postition von Herbert Read in der Kunstszene und kannte die Meisterwerke in den öffentlichen Kunstsammlungen. Darüber hinaus war er zwischen den Organisatoren in Zürich und Paul Westheim in Paris vermittelnd tätig (siehe S. 68). Und es ist anzunehmen, dass er wenigstens einige der in London lebenden Emigranten persönlich kannte.

Das Buch und die Ausstellung

Bihaljis Buch *Modern German Art* war, wie oben erwähnt, im Eintrittspreis zur Ausstellung enthalten und damit untrennbar mit *Twentieth Century German Art* verbunden. Gleichzeitig wurde es vom Verlag Penguin als einer der ersten Bände der Reihe «Pelican Specials» auch über den Buchhandel und in Kaufhäusern vertrieben. Laut Umschlagtext war das Ziel der Reihe, «Bücher zu aktuellen Themen unmittelbar nach Eingang des Manuskripts» zu veröffentlichen. Angesichts des umfangreichen Publikationsprogramms, das sich Bihalji aufgeladen hatte, kam ihm dieses Konzept vermutlich sehr entgegen. Von den Organisatoren der Ausstellung erhielt er anscheinend wenig inhaltliche Vorgaben, da sie selbst noch keine Einigkeit über die Auswahl der Werke, deren Präsentation und den Titel der Schau erzielt hatten – vielmehr sammelten sie noch bis zur letzten Minute Bilder. Dies dürfte auch die Kürze der Beschreibungstexte im Ausstellungskatalog erklären wie auch die Tatsache, dass nur sieben der 271 im Katalog aufgeführten Werke im Buch abgebildet sind.

In der Einleitung zum Katalog wird betont, dass es den Organisatoren von *Twentieth Century German Art* nicht um Politik gehe. Die Ausstellung solle vielmehr bekräftigen, dass «Kunst als Ausdruck des menschlichen Geistes in all seinen Formen nur in dem Maß großartig sein kann, als sie frei ist».[13] Trotz dieser vorsichtigen Formulierung, die gewählt wurde, um potentielle Käufer ausgestellter Werke nicht vom Kauf abzuschrecken, galt vielen die Londoner Ausstellung als politisches Statement – vor allem auch Hitler selbst (siehe S. 190).

Im Gegensatz zum Einführungstext des Ausstellungkatalogs war Bihaljis Text explizit politisch und verstand sich als Sprachrohr, mit dem offene Kritik an der NS-Kulturpolitik geäußert werden sollte. So prangert der Autor beispielsweise die Propaganda-Schau *Entartete Kunst* an, indem er schreibt: «[In dieser Ausstellung] bringen die gemarterten Schöpfungen der Kunst zum Ausdruck, wie ein Zeitalter dem Stumpfsinn anheimfällt, wenn es allein der Stimme der Macht gehorcht.»[14] Es seien dort unschuldige und doch starke Werke, voller Weltkenntnis und Emotion ausgestellt gewesen – vergleichbar mit denjenigen in London, Bilder, die «der Mann an der Spitze der deutschen Machthierarchie» als «bloßes Kunstgestammel» von Menschen verunglimpft habe, «denen Gott die Gnade einer wahrhaft künstlerischen Begabung versagt und dafür die Gabe des Schwätzens und Vortäuschens verliehen» habe.[15]

Europa stand damals an der Schwelle zum Krieg, und Bihalji wusste um den potentiellen Nachhall seiner Worte. Daher formulierte er seine Ausführungen über die moderne deutsche Kunst sehr sachlich und informativ, und verwies immer wieder auf die der Kunst inhärente Menschlichkeit – im Gegensatz zur aggressiven, manipulativen Propaganda der Nazis.[16] Um nicht propagandistisch zu wirken, bediente sich Bihalji der Ironie und vermied es konsequent, Hitler und andere NS-Machthaber beim Namen zu nennen. Statt dessen bezeichnete er sie ausschließlich mit ihren offiziellen Titeln und entlarvte sie allein durch ihre eigenen Worte.

An den Beginn seiner Darstellung stellte er die wilhelminischen Vorbehalte gegenüber dem Impressionismus, die er als Vorspiel für die Verunglimpfungen und Aktionen der 1930er Jahre betrachtet. In seiner Beschreibung von Max Liebermanns Weg vom Realisten zum Impressionisten zitiert er ausführlich den Künstler, besonders dessen Zola-Paraphrase, wonach «Kunst Natur sei – gesehen durch ein Temperament».[17] Bihalji fasst den Kampf Liebermanns gegen seine Widersacher, seinen späteren Erfolg und sein tragisches Ende lakonisch mit den Worten zusammen: «1905-1909: Judengassen, enge Straßen, Menschenmassen. [...] Erfolg beginnt. Ehrungen, Professorentitel. [...] Aufnahme in die Preußische Akademie der Künste, Präsident der Berliner Secession. Lange Jahre voll kreativen Schaffens. [...] Der 80-Jährige wird weltweit von einer Gemeinde von Bewunderern gefeiert. So schien es, als würde sein geschäftiges Leben, das reich war an Entdeckungen, Verehrung seiner Mitmenschen und künstlerischer Meisterschaft, friedvoll und ruhmumglänzt zu Ende gehen können. Doch es kam anders. 1933 verließ Max Liebermann die Akademie, verspottet, gramgebeugt und in seiner Seele verwundet. In der Zwischenzeit ist er verstorben.»[18]

In seinem Buch schlägt Bihalji einen wehmütigen, moralischen Ton an. Lovis Corinth charakterisiert er treffend als «Proto-Expressionist» und grenzt dessen «grausam erotischen» Frauenbilder der Jahrhundertwende von den späteren Walchensee-Landschaften mit ihrem «Tempo, dem Horror und der Schönheit» ab. Hier, wie auch an anderen Stellen des Buchs, bezieht er sich indirekt auf Exponenten der nationalsozialistischer Kulturpolitik und kritisiert ihre Äußerungen – in diesem Fall ist es Adolf Ziegler, der Präsident der Reichskammer der Bildenden Künste, der fanatisiert behauptete, Corinths Werke hätten das Publikum erst interessiert, «als der Künstler nach seinem zweiten Schlaganfall nur noch krankhafte und unverständliche Schmierereien hervorgebracht» habe.[19]

Im ganzen Buch widmet Bihalji den historischen Details eine hohe Aufmerksamkeit und lässt sowohl die Künstler wie die Ideologen zu Wort kommen. Er vertieft sich in die verwickelten Rivalitäten der verschiedenen künstlerischen Gruppen und Strömungen – Brücke, Blauer Reiter, Bauhaus, Neue Sachlichkeit –, ohne sie jedoch gegeneinander auszuspielen. Statt dessen stellt er Vergleiche unter ihren Werken an und hebt das jeweils Besondere hervor. Ein ganzes Kapitel beschäftigt sich mit der abstrakten Kunst und geht auf Kandinsky, Schlemmer, Moholy-Nagy, Baumeister sowie ihre sowjetischen und französischen Pendants ein. An anderer Stelle vergleicht Bihalji abstrakte Gemälde mit hyperrealistischen Werken sozial engagierter Künstler, wie sie nach dem Ende des 1. Weltkriegs unter dem Einfluss des Dadaismus und seiner Exponenten entstanden: Richard Huelsenbeck, John Heartfield, Raoul Haussmann und George Grosz. Anschließend weitet er die Diskussion auf Werke von Otto Dix und Max Beckmann, auf die Graphik von Käthe Kollwitz und die Skulpturen von Wilhelm Lehmbruck aus.[20] Kein britischer Autor dieser Zeit hätte über eine so weitreichende Kenntnis der euopäischen Kunst in Vergangenheit und Gegenwart verfügt. Und niemand wäre – mit Ausnahme des Anarchisten Read – in der Lage gewesen, Kunst als Kontinuum der kulturellen Aktivität des Menschen zu thematisieren.

Das Buch schließt mit einer Passage, die Bihalji zutreffend «Grenzen und Möglichkeiten» betitelt. Die Frage, die er darin aufwirft, lautet nicht «Wohin geht die Kunst?», sondern «Wohin geht die Menschheit?»[21] In diesem Kapitel denkt der Autor über das Schicksal der deutschen Kunst nach und schreibt: «Der gute Name Deutschlands steht auf dem Spiel. Der Begriff ‹deutsche Kunst› atmet den Geist Albrecht Dürers, Hans Holbeins und Mathias Grünewalds». Was hat diese Tradition, so fragt Bihalji rhetorisch, mit der aggressiven, rassistischen Staatskunst der Nazis zu tun?[22]

Max Slevogt zitierend, erinnert er daran, dass die großen Maler der Geschichte «tatsächlich die großen Maler der Menschlichkeit» waren. Und Bihalji folgert: «In welch dunklen

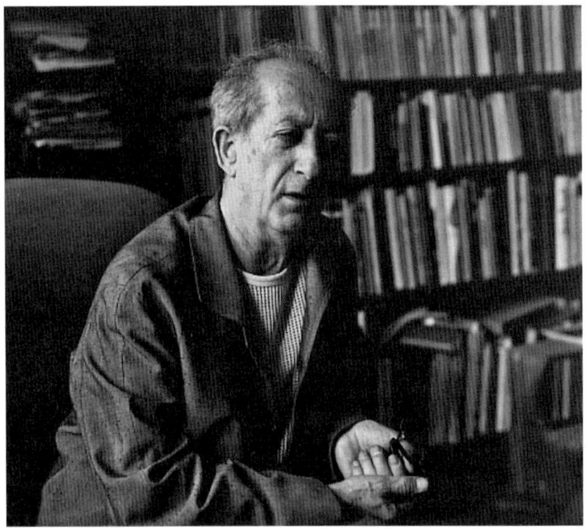

61 Oto Bihalji-Merin im Jahr 1967

Zeiten leben wir [...], wenn solche Dinge gesagt werden müssen, wenn die Kunst, jene großartige Beschützerin der Lebenden [...], jene kreative Kraft, die das Gefängnis unseres Daseins sprengt und uns einen Blick auf die Ewigkeit jenseits der kurzen Spanne unserer Existenz gewährt, selbst beschützt werden muss? Um zu leben, braucht die Kunst doch Freiheit. Ihre trostreichen Traumvisionen können in der öden Atmosphäre des Zwangs nicht gedeihen.»[23]

Nach 1938

Bihaljis kryptische Autobiographie berichtet nur von zwei kurzen Aufenthalten in London. 1961 traf er dort Herbert Read. Die zweite Reise unternahm er 1968, um die Ausstellung *Cybernetic Serendipity* im Institute of Contemporary Art zu besuchen.[24] Die wichtigste Information zu seiner Beteiligung an *Twentieth Century German Art* ist die Bemerkung, dass Picasso 1937 auf sein Betreiben hin in das Patronat aufgenommen worden sei.[25]

Auch wenn es Bihalji nie öffentlich aussprach, dürfte er beim Kongress des sowjetischen Schriftstellerverbands in Moskau 1934 seine schlimmsten Befürchtungen bezüglich eines linken Totalitarismus bestätigt gefunden haben. Auffällig ist jedenfalls, dass er in *Modern German Art* weder die Arbeiterbewegung noch den Sozialistischen Realismus hervorhebt, sondern den Pluralismus und das spezifisch antifaschistische Wesen der Avantgarde .[26] Daraus könnte man schließen, dass er eine «einheitliche Parteilinie» im Bezug auf Kultur ablehnte – oder abzulehnen vorgab. Der marxistische Kunstkritiker Anthony Blunt vertrat in seiner Rezension der Ausstellung *Twentieth Century German Art* in *The Spectator* dazu die Gegenposition. Er sah das Problem nicht in einer staatlichen Steuerung der Kunst, sondern im schrankenlosen Individualismus, der die Kunst in eine Sackgasse geführt habe.[27] Auf diese Position schwenkte auch Bihalji ein, als er nach dem 2. Weltkrieg nach Jugoslawien zurückkehrte.

Wegen fehlender Quellen und Informationen, Manipulationen und Widersprüchen ist das Leben Oto Bihalji-Merins bis heute rätselhaft. War er ein unerschütterlicher Verfechter humanistischer und liberaler Prinzipien, der sich stürmischen Zeiten anpassen musste, oder bloß ein Agent der weltweiten Revolution, der verdeckt für die Sowjetunion arbeitete? War er vielleicht sogar je nach Zeit und Umständen mal das eine, mal das andere? Auf der Basis der heute zur Verfügung stehender Informationen müssen diese Fragen offen bleiben.

1976 wurde er in Belgrad von einem Journalisten gefragt, ob er sich als Essayist, Kritiker, Reporter, Autor oder was sonst begreife. Bihalji antwortete darauf: «Die Revolution der Kunst und der Gesellschaft, die Revolte gegen patriarchalische Tyrannei, die kreative Unruhe junger Menschen. Die klassischen Aufteilungen unseres Berufs interessieren mich wenig. Viel wichtiger ist für mich der Rhythmus des Lebens.»[28]

Beim vorliegenden Text handelt es sich um die gekürzte Version einer ausführlichen in Vorbereitung befindlichen Darstellung zu Oto Bihalji-Merins Leben und Werk.

1 Peter Thoene: Modern German Art. London 1938.

2 Peter Selz: German Expressionist Painting, Berkeley 1957. Der von Alfred H. Barr verfasste, 43-seitige Katalog der 1931 im New Yorker Museum of Modern Art gezeigten Ausstellung German Painting and Sculputure ist die erste Publikation, die sich vor Thoenes Buch der deutschen moderner Kunst gewidmet hat.

3 Soweit nicht anders vermerkt entstammen die Angaben des vorliegenden Textes der Autobiographie, die Bihalji-Merin 1976 zu einer Ausstellung seiner Schriften im Museum für Moderne Kunst Belgrad verfasst hat (Oto Bihalji-Merin: Bio-bibliografija, Belgrad 1976, im folgenden «Bio-bibliografija»). Der Autor dankt Irina Suboti, Kuratorin der Ausstellung von 1976, sowie Bojana Peji (Belgrad) und Lutz Becker (London) für ihre Hilfe.

4 Bihalji lernte die ebenfalls aus Zemun stammende Lisa Merin (1900-1991) im Jahre 1930 kennen. Nachgewiesen ist die Verwendung von Lisas Nachnamens als Pseudonym ab 1936. Eventuell geschah dies allerdings schon früher (siehe Fußnote 10).

5 1941 gehörte Pavle Bihali zu den ersten Widerstandskämpfern, die von den NS-Besatzern ermordet wurden.

6 Zur Ausstellung in der *Sturm*-Gallerie siehe Bio-bibliografija, S. 17.

7 Allerdings trat er erst 1934 in Paris der KPD bei.

8 Schdanow vertrat somit Stalins Ansicht, wonach Künstler zu «Ingenieuren der Seele» werden sollten. Beim Kongress traf Bihalji u.a. André Malraux und Louis Aragon, die er in Paris kennengelernt hatte, sowie Ernst Toller, Johannes R. Becher und Oscar Maria Graf, die er aus seiner Zeit als Mitarbeiter der *Linkskurve* kannte. Siehe Bio-bibliografija, S. 19.

9 Peter Thoene: Eroberung des Himmels. Geschichte des Fluggedankens, Wien/Leipzig 1937. Dieses Buch zur Geschichte der Fliegerei und zur kreativen Obsession des Menschen für das Fliegen wurde in französischer Sprache unter dem Titel *La Conquête du ciel – De L'Antiquité à nos jours* (Paris 1938) veröffentlicht. Obwohl in Bio-bibliografija eine englische Ausgabe erwähnt ist, war diese bislang nicht nachzuweisen.

10 Peter Merin: Spanien zwischen Tod und Geburt, Zürich 1937. Die englische Fassung (*Spain between Death and Birth*, London u. a. 1938) wurde von Charles Fullerton übersetzt, der kurz danach auch *Modern German Art* übertragen haben muss.

11 Sowohl Nin als auch Companys wurden später gefoltert und ermordet. Im Zuge der stalinistischen «Großen Säuberung» wurde Nin 1937 bei lebendigem Leib enthäutet. Companys wurde 1940 nach einem Schauprozess durch das neu etablierte Franco-Regime ohne Augenbinde erschossen.

12 Auszug aus dem Klappentext des Schutzumschlags von *Spanien zwischen Tod und Geburt.*

13 o. V.: Exhibition of Twentieth Century German Art. Exhibition catalogue, London 1938, S. 6.

14 Peter Thoene: Modern German Art, London 1938, S. 41 f.

15 Ebd., S. 41/42. Im zweiten Zitat übernahm Bihalji einen Auszug aus Hitlers Rede zur Einweihung des Münchner Hauses der Kunst am 18. Juli 1937.

16 Bihalji wusste von den Konflikten und Veränderungen in der Sowjetunion sowie von den Bestrebungen, dort Kunst ebenfalls propagandistisch zu instrumentalisieren. Doch äußerte er sich dazu nie öffentlich. Siehe Fußnote 8.

17 Thoene, S. 30. Thoene zitierte den originalen Wortlaut des Satzes: «L'art, cest la nature vue à travers un tempérament.»

18 Ebd., S. 33.

19 Ebd., S. 38/39.

20 Ebd., S. 76-103.

21 Ebd., S. 104.

22 Ebd., S. 107.

23 Ebd., S. 108.

24 Bio-bibliografija, S. 28. Diese bahnbrechende Ausstellung wurde von Jasia Reichardt kuratiert.

25 Ebd., S. 20.

26 In Bio-bibliografija (S. 17) spricht Bihalji von seiner Verehrung für die Werke der Surrealisten und erwähnt, wie beeindruckend er 1930 *Un Chien andalou* fand, den Film von Luis Buñuel und Salvador Dalí.

27 Anthony Blunt: Contemporary German Art, in: The Spectator, 8. Juli 1938, S. 17: «Anscheinend wurde die Kunst durch den individualistischen *ne plus ultra* Ansatz in eine Sackgasse geführt. Obwohl Hitlers Reglementierung der Kunst in jeder Hinsicht beklagenswert ist, so ist doch nichts eigentlich Falsches daran, dass der Staat die Kunst organisiert. Tatsächlich ist dies sogar die normale Situation, die lediglich während der letzten Jahrhunderte verändert wurde.» Seit Mitte der 1930er bis mindestens zum Beginn der 1950er Jahre war Blunt sowjetischer Spion.

28 Bio-bibliografija, S. 7.

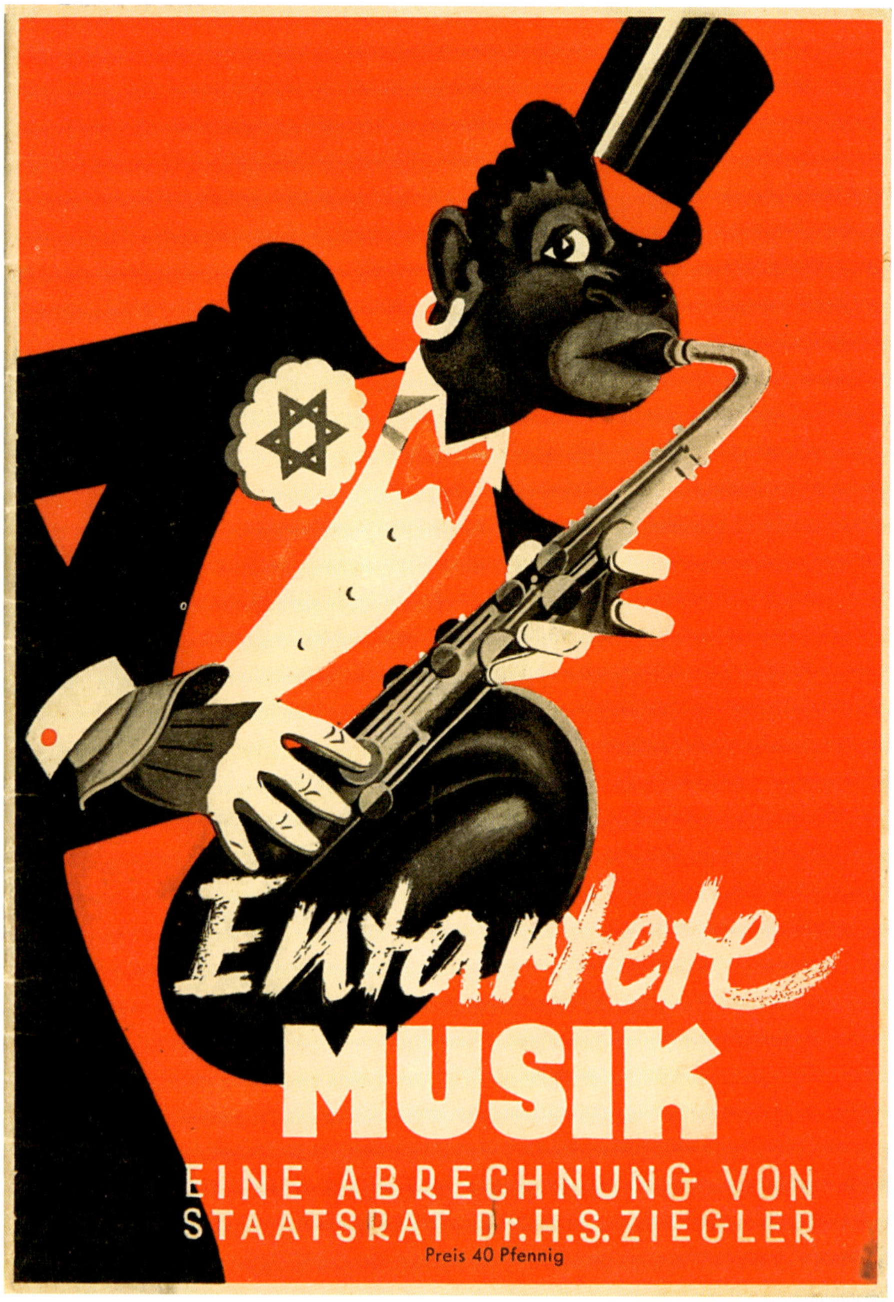

62 Titel der Broschüre «Entartete Musik» Düsseldorf 1938

Ehrenrettung für diffamierte Komponisten: Das Londoner *Festival of German Music*

ALBRECHT DÜMLING

Ein Jahr nach der Münchner Ausstellung *Entartete Kunst* wurde im Mai und Juni 1938 bei den Düsseldorfer Reichsmusiktagen eine ähnliche Propaganda-Schau unter dem Titel *Entartete Musik* gezeigt (Abb. 62 u. 68). Der Weimarer Staatsrat Hans Severus Ziegler, ein persönlicher Freund Adolf Hitlers, hatte sie initiiert. Er wandte sich gegen ‹fremdrassige› Einflüsse im Musikleben der Weimarer Republik und stellte dabei die Atonalität Arnold Schönbergs und den als ‹Negermusik› diffamierten Jazz in den Vordergrund. Zur allgemeinen Verwunderung waren auch die nichtjüdischen Komponisten Paul Hindemith und Igor Strawinsky einbezogen worden. Sogar Peter Raabe, der Präsident der Reichsmusikkammer, protestierte scharft gegen die Ausstellung. Um weiteren Ärger zu vermeiden, ordnete Joseph Goebbels knappe Presseberichte sowie die vorzeitige Schließung der Veranstaltung an.

Vergleichsweise zurückhaltend äußerte sich die britische Presse. Die Londoner *Times* schrieb am 26. Mai: «Die Ausstellung soll die traurige Notlage der deutschen Musik in der Zeit des ‹jüdischen Einflusses› von 1920 bis 1933 illustrieren und zeigen, wie dieser Auflösungsprozess jetzt gestoppt wird.»[1] Mehr kritische Distanz zeigte der *Manchester Guardian*, als er die in Düsseldorf aufgestellten Tonkabinen beschrieb, bei denen man bewusst auf Schallisolierung verzichtet hatte, um das Nebeneinander gleichzeitig vorgeführter Klangbeispiele «entarteter Musik» zum chaotischen Missklang werden zu lassen.[2]

Überlagert wurde die Wahrnehmung der Propagandaschau *Entartete Musik* durch Hitlers Einmarsch in Österreich, der in Großbritannien und international großes Aufsehen erregte. Für manche Briten war sofort klar, welche gravierenden Auswirkungen dieses Ereignis auf das kulturelle Leben in Wien haben würde. Benjamin Britten notierte am 13. März 1938 in sein Tagebuch: «Scheußliche Nachrichten aus Wien – man stelle sich Wien unter Nazi-Kontrolle vor: kein Mahler mehr, keine Leichtigkeit, keine Kultur, nichts als ihre dreckige, unanständige Herzlichkeit, ihre abscheuliche Arroganz und unaussprechliche Dummheit.»[3] Der junge Komponist war wie viele englische Musikfreunde entsetzt über die Art, wie das ‹Dritte Reich› anerkannte Künstler wie Paul Hindemith, Arnold Schönberg, Franz Schreker und Kurt Weill behandelte.

Als Ergänzung zur Ausstellung *Twentieth Century German Art* fand deshalb in den New Burlington Galleries ein *Festival of German Music* statt, das der in Deutschland diffamierten Musik ein Forum bieten sollte (Abb. 63). Es wurden insgesamt drei Konzerte gegeben: Das erste am 20. Juli mit Kammermusik von Paul Hindemith, Anton Webern, Alban Berg, Arnold

Schönberg, Ernst Krenek und Hanns Eisler, das zweite, am 28. Juli, mit einer halbszenischen Teil-Aufführung der *Dreigroschenoper*, und das letzte, am 4. August, mit Liedern von Johann Sebastian Bach, Wolfgang A. Mozart, Franz Schubert, Hugo Wolf, Gustav Mahler und Ernst Krenek. Die drei Konzerte fanden in den Ausstellungsräumen der New Burlington Galleries statt und standen unter der Schirmherrschaft eines Komitees mit Edward J. Dent, Präsident der Internationalen Gesellschaft für Neue Musik, an der Spitze; weitere prominente Mitglieder waren die Komponisten Ralph Vaughan Williams, Sir Arnold Bax, William Walton und Stanley Marchant, dazu der Musikwissenschaftler Sir Donald Tovey und George Dyson, Präsident des Londoner Royal College of Music. Mit dem Festival reagierten diese Fachleute auf die Verunglimpfung ihrer deutschen Kollegen. Während die NS-Ideologen Werke jüdischer Komponisten als ‹undeutsch› ansahen, präsentierten die Londoner Konzerte Werke von Bach, Mozart und Schubert wie von Mahler, Schönberg, Webern, Hindemith, Krenek und Weill als «deutsche Musik» – ohne jede rassische oder stilistische Einschränkung.

Kammermusik des 20. Jahrhunderts

Die erste der im Wochenabstand stattfindenden Veranstaltungen war am 20. Juli der deutschen Kammermusik des 20. Jahrhunderts gewidmet. Die hier ausgewählten Komponisten Schönberg, Webern, Eisler, Hindemith, Krenek und Berg, welche die Düsseldorfer Ausstellung als ‹entartet› geschmäht hatte (Abb. 67), waren in England keineswegs unbekannt. Schönberg hatte schon 1914 in der Londoner Queen's Hall seine *Orchesterstücke op. 16* dirigiert, Webern war ab 1929 mehrfach Gast bei Konzerten der BBC gewesen. In der BBC war im Vorjahr Eislers Liedzyklus *Zeitungsausschnitte* zu hören gewesen. Musik von Hindemith und Krenek wurde regelmäßig in London aufgeführt. Alban Berg hatte die britische Hauptstadt nie persönlich besucht; jedoch fand 1934 hier die konzertante Aufführung seiner *Wozzeck*-Oper große Beachtung.

Schönbergs *Drei Klavierstücke op. 11* von 1908 gehörten zu den frühesten atonalen Kompositionen überhaupt. Anders als Berg, Webern, Eisler und Krenek hatte Paul Hindemith, den die Düsseldorfer Ausstellung in einem Atemzug mit Schönberg als «Theoretiker der Atonalität» bezeichnete, die Tonalität nie ganz preisgegeben. Beim Konzert im Rahmen der Londoner Ausstellung vom 20. Juli war er sogar mit einer Uraufführung vertreten. Dies ging auf den Schönberg-Schüler und BBC-Programmberater Edward Clark zurück, der sich in England immer wieder für die europäische Avantgarde eingesetzt hatte. Auf seine Initiative hin war Hindemiths Oratorium *Das Unaufhörliche* im März 1933 bei einem BBC-Konzert aufgeführt und der Komponist im Januar 1934 zu Rundfunkaufnahmen eingeladen worden. Aufsehen erregte Hindemith, als er im Januar 1936 in London vom Tod des englischen Königs erfuhr und innerhalb kürzester Zeit eine Trauermusik komponierte und spielte. Aufführungen seiner Musik waren im ‹Dritten Reich› verboten, obwohl Hindemith weiterhin eine Professur an der Berliner Hochschule für Musik bekleidete. Noch immer versuchte er – unterstützt von Wilhelm Furtwängler und anderen Prominenten – die Uraufführung seiner Oper *Mathis der Maler* in Deutschland durchzusetzen, allerdings vergeblich. Diese fand schließlich im Mai 1938 in Zürich statt – in Anwesenheit des Komponisten.

Von Zürich aus reiste Hindemith (Abb. 69) in den schweizerischen Ferienort Chandolin, wo er am 23. Juni eine neue Oboen-Sonate fertigstellte. Leon Goossens, der herausragende Oboist des London Philharmonic Orchestra, sollte sie in London erstmals spielen. Ende Juni erhielt Hindemith ein Telegramm von Edward Clark, der ihm von dem geplanten Konzert

New Burlington Galleries, W.1.

F E S T I V A L O F G E R M A N M U S I C

Thursday, 21st July, at 9 p.m.

XXTH CENTURY GERMAN CHAMBER MUSIC

Harriet Cohen C.B.E.
Leon Goossens

NEW OBOE SONATA (First performance) — Hindemi

Antonia Brosa

FOUR PIECES FOR VIOLIN & PIANOFORTE (First Performance) — Webern

Frederick Grinke
Dorothy Manley

ADAGIO FROM "KAMMERKONZERT" FOR VIOLIN AND PIANOFORTE (First Performance) — Berg

Eileen Ralph

THREE PIANO PIECES (Op.II) — Schoenburg

Sophie Wyss
Benjamim Britten

"DURCH DIE NACHT" SONG CYCLE (Poems by Karl Kraus) — Krenek

Parry Jones
Alan Rawsthorne

"NEWSPAPER CUTTINGS" (Excerpts from the Daily Press) — Eisler

THURSDAY, 28TH JULY, at 9 p.m.

S O N G S & S A T I R E S

WEDEKIND, KASTNER, BRECHT, EISLER

"DREIGROSCHENOPER"

Brecht-Weill

(English Version by C.Dennis Freeman)

Hedli Anderson
Lisa Desterre
The Opera Group

(Director: Ernst Schoen)

THURSDAY, 4TH AUGUST, at 9 p.m.

RECITAL

by

E L I Z A B E T H S C H U M A N N

Songs by Bach, Mozart, Schubert, Hugo Wohlf, Mahler and Krenek.

At the Piano: Professor Leo Rosenek

63 Festival of German Music, Konzertübersicht. Der erste Abend fand bereits am 20. Juli statt, vielleicht um Hindemith für eine Teilnahme zu gewinnen, der am 21. Juli die Uraufführung seines Balletts *Nobilissima Visione* in Londeon leitete.

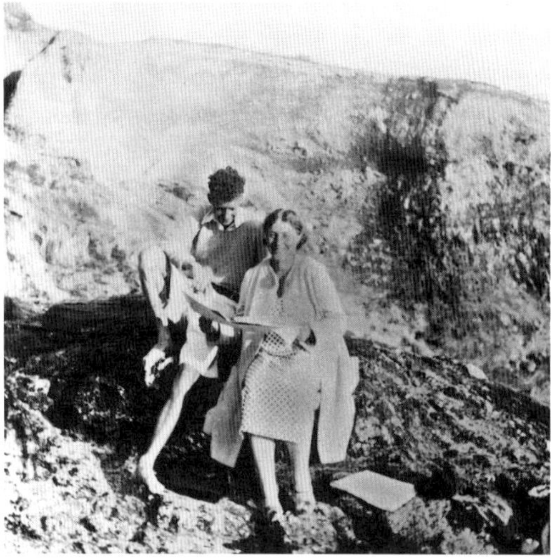

64 Benjamin Britten mit Sophie Wyss, Crantock UK, 1936

im Rahmen von *Twentieth Century German Art* berichtete. Der Komponist bezweifelte jedoch, dass dies ein guter Rahmen für eine Uraufführung sei. Vermutlich hatte er schon in Zürich von den Debatten um die Londoner Ausstellung gehört. Am 5. Juli schrieb er seinem Verleger Willy Strecker: «Die Ausstellung ‹German Art of the 20th Century› scheint nicht so ganz hasenrein zu sein – was ich gleich vermutete und ihn [Clark] darum vertraulich um Auskunft bat, ob man das Konzert dort spielen könne. Zwar sei der Musikausschuss Tovey, Dent, V. Williams über alle Verdächte erhaben, aber es gäbe andere Personen.»[4] Hindemith entschied schließlich, der Uraufführung zwar zuzustimmen, persönlich aber nicht anwesend zu sein. Hindemith wohnte damals aber noch in Berlin und wollte jede offene Kritik am Hitler-Staat vermeiden. Schon 1934 hatte Willy Strecker die BBC gebeten, den Komponisten bei seinem London-Besuch nicht zur Situation in Deutschland zu befragen.[5]

Am 14. Juli reiste Paul Hindemith mit seiner Frau Gertrud nach London, wo er am 21. Juli die Uraufführung seines Balletts *Nobilissima Visione* im Theatre Royal Drury Lane leiten wollte. Zuvor ließ er sich von Leon Goossens und Harriet Cohen seine neue Oboensonate vorspielen, die – ein Tag vor dem Ballett – beim Konzert in den New Burlington Galleries erstmals aufgeführt werden sollte. Der Pianistin zufolge war auch Stefan Zweig zugegen und assistierte ihr durch Umblättern der Noten, die die Interpreten erst eine Woche zuvor erhalten hatten.[6] Obwohl bei der Festival-Ankündigung die Hindemith-Uraufführung besonders hervorgehoben wurde (Abb. 63),[7] nahm der Komponist wie geplant nicht daran teil. Seinem Tagebuch zufolge war er an diesem Tag an der Generalprobe seines Balletts.

Dagegen erschienen zu dem Galerie-Konzert Hindemiths Kollegen William Walton, John Ireland und Arthur Bliss sowie der 24-jährige Benjamin Britten, der bei Kreneks Zyklus *Durch die Nacht* die Sängerin Sophie Wyss am Klavier begleitete (Abb. 64). Wie Britten wenig später dem jungen Sohn des Dirigenten Hermann Scherchen schrieb, war er mit Aufführung und Resonanz insgesamt zufrieden. Die Presse sprach von einem interessanten Programm und kompetenter Wiedergabe, erwähnte aber nur fünf Komponisten; offenbar war Eislers Liedzyklus kurzfristig entfallen. Während der *Times*-Kritiker sich auch Schönberg und Webern respektvoll widmete, meinte sein *Telegraph*-Kollege: «Wenn Schönberg und Hindemith beide den Zeitgeist ihrer Epoche ausdrücken wollen, muss einer von ihnen Unrecht haben.»[8] Im

65 Porträt Kurt Weill, ca. 1937

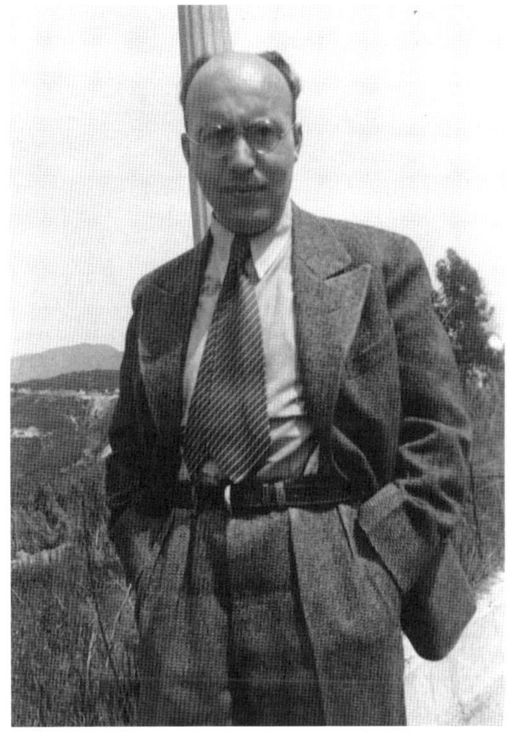

Daily Herald las man: «Umgeben von Bildern, die Hitler verboten hat, hörte ein großes Publikum gestern Abend von ihm verbotene Musik. Schönbergs unverständliche *Drei Klavierstücke* und Weberns vier fragmentarische Piepser für Klavier und Violine schienen kaum wesentlich genug für eine feierliche Exkommunikation Sie waren *in-Fuehreriatingly*[9] langweilig.»[10]

Dagegen wurde Hindemiths Sonate als anmutig und spritzig gelobt. Eine Kritikerin, der das Gehörte insgesamt besser gefiel als das Gesehene, schrieb: «Beim Blick auf die Bilder wurde mir ganz klar, in welcher Kunst die Deutschen herausragen.»[11]

Eine halbszenische *Dreigroschenoper*

Das zweite Konzert brachte Songs aus der *Dreigroschenoper* von Brecht und Weill zur Aufführung, die in der Düsseldorfer Propagandaschau besonders schrill aus den Tonkabinen dröhnten und als Musterbeispiele der *Entartete Musik* diffamiert wurden. Dieses in Deutschland so erfolgreiche Werk stieß in England nur auf wenig Verständnis. Kurt Weill (Abb. 65) war im März 1933 von Berlin zunächst nach Paris geflohen. Von dort übersiedelte er im Januar 1935 nach London, wo er eine von Edward Clark dirigierte Rundfunkaufführung der *Dreigroschenoper* hörte. Weill hielt sie für ein Missverständnis. Trotz miserabler Presseberichte erstellte der beteiligte Produzent Dennis Freeman eine englische Übersetzung, die am 28. Juli 1938 in Auszügen halbszenisch aufgeführt wurde. Ernst Schoen leitete dabei The Opera Group. Er war ein Jugendfreund Walter Benjamins, hatte bei Ferruccio Busoni und Edgard Varèse studiert und als Programmleiter am Frankfurter Sender auch mit Brecht und Eisler zusammengearbeitet. 1933 wurde er entlassen und floh nach KZ-Haft nach England, wo er sich zunächst als Notenkopist durchschlug. 1936 kam Schoen ebenso wie das von ihm gemeinsam mit Georg Knepler geleitete kleine Opernensemble bei der BBC unter.

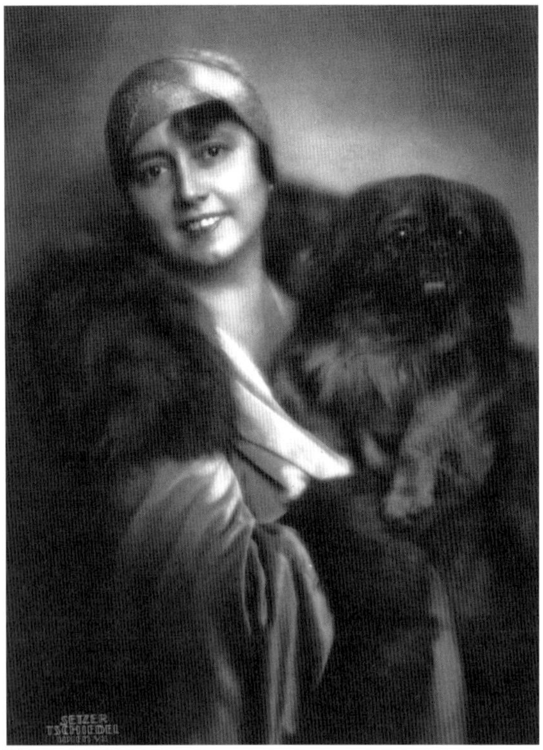

66 Elisabeth Schumann, 1932

Star der Brecht-Weill-Aufführung beim *Festival of German Music* war Hedli Anderson. Sie war als Opernsängerin ausgebildet, pflegte einen von Yvette Guilbert beeinflussten Gesangsstil und wirkte bei diversen Londoner Kabarett-Programmen mit. Den jungen Benjamin Britten beeindruckte sie so sehr, dass er für sie mehrere Kabarett-Songs schuf. Zu ihrer Beteiligung beim Programm vom 28. Juli liegen leider keine Presseberichte vor.

Es sollten noch fast zwei Jahrzehnte vergehen, bis 1956 endlich eine erste erfolgreiche Aufführung der *Dreigroschenoper* in London stattfand.

Liederabend mit Elisabeth Schumann

Unmittelbar nach einem Auftritt des weltbekannten afro-amerikanischen Sängers und Schauspielers Paul Robeson am 3. August in den New Burlington Galleries[12] bildete am 4. August ein Liederabend mit der ebenso berühmten Sopranistin Elisabeth Schumann (Abb. 66) den Abschluss des Festivals. Diese Sängerin hatte schon 1914 an der New Yorker Metropolitan Opera gastiert, bevor sie 1919 eine feste Position an der Wiener Staatsoper erhielt. Am Tage des ‹Anschlusses› verließ sie Wien, nicht zuletzt wegen ihres jüdischen Lebensgefährten Hans Krüger, dem sie die Ausreise ermöglichte. Vorübergehend übersiedelten beide nach England, wo sie heirateten. Elisabeth Schumann war für ihre Rollen in Opern von Mozart, Wagner und Strauss ein gefeierter Star, ebenso wie für ihre Lied-Interpretationen. Bei ihrem Londoner Auftritt sang sie Lieder von Bach bis Krenek. Mit der Krenek-Oper *Jonny spielt auf*, die in der Düsseldorfer Ausstellung als Musterbeispiel für ‹Entartung› galt, war sie besonders verbunden: An der Wiener Staatsoper hatte sie 1928 die Partie der Yvonne gesungen. Den Kritiker des *Daily Herald* interessierten allerdings mehr die älteren Lieder. Unter der Überschrift «Die Nazis verlieren eine weitere Sängerin» schrieb er: «Die deutsche Sängerin Elisabeth Schumann hat mit den Nazis gebrochen. Sie folgt Lotte Lehmann, der ebenso berühmten österreichischen Sopranistin, nach Amerika. Gestern Abend sang sie zugunsten der verjagten deutschen Künstler, die Hitler als entartet bezeichnete. [...] Indem sie dies tat, verließ sie die Nazi-Umklammerung. Dabei ist Elisabeth Schumann, ebenso wie Lotte Lehmann, rein arisch. Sie sang Lieder von Bach, Mozart, Brahms und Hugo Wolf, Lieder welche die Atmosphäre der Romantik atmeten, für die Deutschland einmal berühmt war.»[13]

Noch im gleichen Jahr zogen die Sängerin und ihr Pianist Leo Rosenek in die USA, wo beide in Philadelphia am Curtis Institute of Music unterrichteten.

In Musikzeitschriften wie *Monthly Musical Record*, *Musical Opinion* und *The Chesterian* sucht man vergebens nach zusammenfassenden Berichten über das *Festival of German Music*. Lag es daran, dass es in einer Galerie und nicht in einem Konzertsaal stattfand oder weil die führenden Kritiker im Urlaub waren? Oder war das Interesse so gering, weil bereits im Juni Werke von Krenek, Hindemith und Webern beim Londoner Festival der Internationalen Gesellschaft für Neue Musik erklungen waren?

Auch wenn die Wirkung der drei Konzerte auf das englische Publikum offenbar begrenzt blieb, den beteiligten Komponisten öffneten sie die Augen für das ganze Ausmaß der nationalsozialistischen Kulturbarbarei. Paul Hindemith räumte noch im August 1938 seine Berliner Wohnung und verließ Deutschland. Als Benjamin Britten, die große Hoffnung der britischen Musik, im September von der BBC das Angebot erhielt, im nächsten Jahr beim Festival für zeitgenössische Musik in Baden-Baden eines seiner Werke aufführen zu lassen, reagierte er mit scharfer Ablehnung: «Zugegebenermaßen hat Musik nichts mit Politik zu tun», erklärte er. «Aber wenn die Politik ihre schmierigen Finger in die Musik steckt, ist das eine andere Sache.»[14]

1 o. V.: «Degenerate Music». Anti-Jewish Exhibition in Germany; in: The Times, 26. Mai 1938, S. 18.
2 o.V.: Atonal Music Condemned. Campaign at Nazi Exhibition, in: The Manchester Guardian (8. Juni 1938), S. 10.
3 Donald Mitchell and Philip Reed (Hg.): Benjamin Britten. Letters from a Life, volume 1: 1923-39. Selected Letters and Diaries. London 2011, S. 552.
4 Luitgard Schader (Hg.): Paul Hindemith Bläserkammermusik III. Bd. V, 3 (PHA 503). Mainz 2013, S. XVI f.
5 BBC Written Archives, Caversham, Hindemith file. Freundlicher Hinweis von Erik Levi, London.
6 Harriet Cohen: A Bundle of Time. The Memoirs of Harriet Cohen. London 1969, S. 275 f.
7 o.V.: Festival of German Modern Music. Hindemith's Oboe Sonata; in: The Times, 18. Juli 1938, S. 10.
8 J. A. W.: Modern German Music. New Hindemith Sonata; in: Daily Telegraph and Morning Post, 21. Juli 1938, S. 10.
9 Wortspiel «infuriatingly» (aufreizend) mit «unführerhaft».
10 S. F.: Listening to the Banned; in: Daily Herald, 21. Juli 1938, S. 3.
11 Mariegold: What Every Woman Wants to Know; in: The Sketch, 27. Juli 1938 , S. 21.
12 vgl. o.V., Manchester Guardian, 3. August 1938, S. 18 ‹Today's Arrangements›.
13 A. E.: Nazis lose another singer; in: Daily Herald, 5. Aug. 1938, S. 9.
14 Benjamin Britten, a.a.O., S. 581 f.

Restoring the Honour of Defamed Composers. The London *Festival of German Music*

ALBRECHT DÜMLING

During the May and June of 1938, one year after the exhibition of *Entartete Kunst* (*Degenerate art*) held in Munich, a similar propaganda show was staged in Düsseldorf: *Entartete Musik* (*Degenerate Music*), organised as part of the Reich Music Festival in the city (fig. 62 and 68). The exhibition was initiated by Weimar State Councillor Hans Severus Ziegler. A friend of Adolf Hitler's, Ziegler had strongly opposed 'foreign racial' influences on the 1920s German music scene, in particular the atonal music of Arnold Schönberg and the 'Negro-Music' of jazz. To widespread astonishment however, the Düsseldorf show also included a number of non-Jewish German composers, among them Paul Hindemith and Igor Strawinsky. Even high-ranking Nazis protested violently against the Düsseldorf exhibition – among them Peter Raabe, the President of the Reich Chamber of Music. To prevent further backlash against the *Degenerate Music* exhibition, Joseph Goebbels ordered limited press reporting in Germany, later organising the show's early closure.

The response of the British press was more restrained. *The Times*, for example, wrote on 26 May: "The object of the exhibition is to illustrate the sorry plight of German music during the period of 'Jewish influence' from 1920 to 1933 and to show how this process of disintegration is now being checked."[1] The *Manchester Guardian* displayed more critical distance in its report on the Düsseldorf exhibition, claiming that the organisers had deliberately dispensed with acoustic insulation in the sound booths at the exhibition, to make the pieces of 'degenerate music' played simultaneously next to each other sound like a cacophony.[2]

Against the backdrop of the significant attention paid to Hitler's annexation of Austria, the exhibition of *Degenerate Music* went largely uncommented abroad. There was however clearly an awareness of the impact of Nazism on musical culture. As Benjamin Britten for example noted in his diary on 13 March 1938: "Bloody news from Vienna – to think of Vienna, under Nazi control – No more Mahler, no lightness, no culture, nothing but their filthy, lewd, heartiness, their despicable conceit and unutterable stupidity."[3] Like many English music lovers, the young composer was horrified by the Third Reich's treatment of recognised artists such as Paul Hindemith, Arnold Schönberg, Franz Schreker and Kurt Weill.

It was in this context that a festival of German music was organised to coincide with the exhibition of *Twentieth Century German Art* (fig. 63), the festival designed as a platform for the defamed musicians. Three concerts were held in the rooms of the New Burlington Gal-

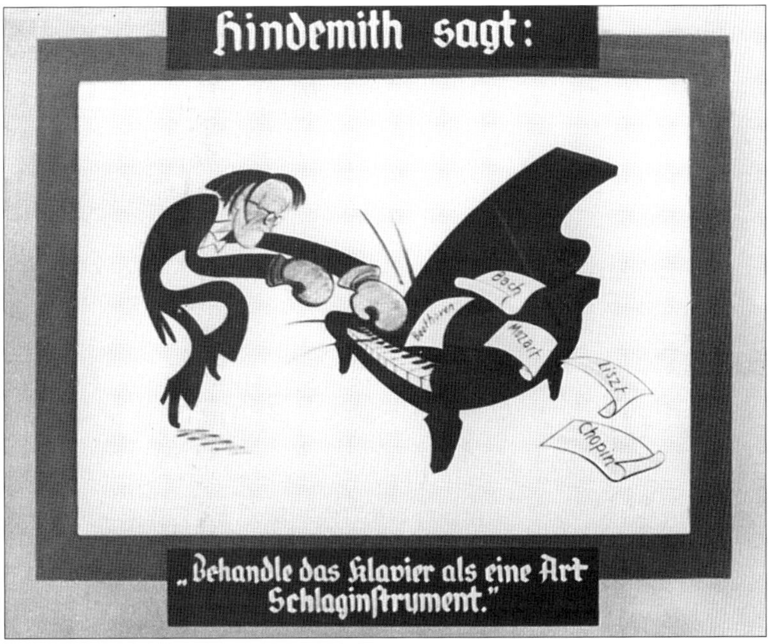

67 Poster regarding Paul Hindemith from the Degenerate Music exhibition, 1938, citing the composer: "Treat the piano as a sort of percussion instrument".

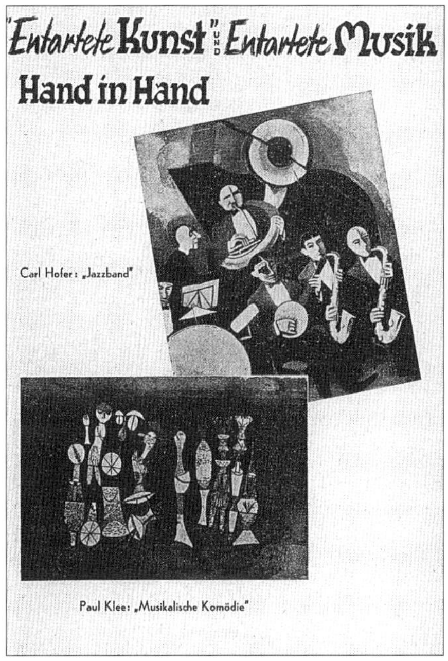

68 "Degenerate art and degenerate music hand in hand", poster of the Düsseldorf exhibition.

leries during the exhibition's run: on 20 July, with chamber music by Paul Hindemith, Anton Webern, Alban Berg, Arnold Schönberg, Ernst Krenek and Hanns Eisler; on 28 July with an abridged, semi-staged performance of *The Threepenny Opera*; and on 4 August with songs by Johann Sebastian Bach, Wolfgang A. Mozart, Franz Schubert, Hugo Wolf, Gustav Mahler and Ernst Krenek. The concerts were supported by a committee of patrons headed by Edward J. Dent, President of the International Society for Contemporary Music; other prominent committee members included the composers Ralph Vaughan Williams, Sir Arnold Bax, William Walton and Stanley Marchant, the musicologist Sir Donald Tovey and George Dyson, President of the London Royal College of Music. While the Nazi regime sought to present Jewish composers as 'un-German', the London concerts presented German music without racial or stylistic constraints, including pieces by Bach, Mozart and Schubert alongside those by Mahler, Schönberg, Webern, Hindemith, Krenek and Weill.

20th Century Chamber Music

The first of these weekly musical events, on 20 July 1938, was devoted to contemporary German chamber music. The composers selected – Arnold Schönberg, Anton Webern, Hanns Eisler, Paul Hindemith, Ernst Krenek and Alban Berg, all of whom had been branded 'degenerate' in Düsseldorf (fig. 67) – were by no means unknown in England. Schönberg had already conducted his *Orchestra Pieces Op. 16* at Queen's Hall in London in 1914. Webern had appeared in several BBC concerts from 1929 onwards; Eisler's song cycle *Zeitungsausschnitte* had been played at the BBC the previous year. Music by Hindemith and Krenek was regularly performed in London, and while Alban Berg had never visited the British capital, a 1934 performance of his opera *Wozzeck* had been well-received in the city.

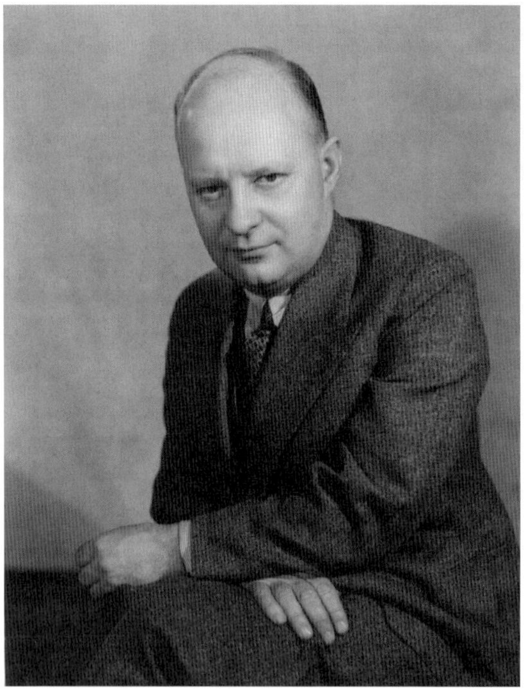

69 Paul Hindemith, New York, 1937.

Schönberg's *Three Piano Pieces Op. 11* of 1908 was one of the earliest ever atonal compositions. Paul Hindemith however (fig. 69), though denounced as a "theorist of atonality" in Düsseldorf, had never fully relinquished tonality. One of his compositions was premiered at the 21 July concert. This occurred on the initiative of Edward Clark, a former pupil of Schönberg who had repeatedly championed Central European avant-garde musicians. As a BBC programme adviser, Clark had arranged for Hindemith's oratorio *Das Unaufhörliche* to be broadcast in March 1933, and for the composer to be invited to radio recordings in the following January. Hindemith had also caused a sensation in London when, upon learning of the death of King George V in 1936, he had swiftly composed and performed a funerary piece. Though the composer continued to hold a professorship at the Music Academy in Berlin, performances of his works were banned in Germany. Hindemith did campaign for the premier of his opera *Mathis der Maler* to be staged in Germany, with the backing of Wilhelm Furtwängler and other prominent figures. This campaign proved unsuccessful however, the piece eventually receiving its premier in Zürich in May 1938, in the presence of the composer.

After this performance in Zurich, Hindemith travelled on to the Swiss resort of Chandolin, where he completed a new oboe sonata on 23 June. The premier was planned take place in London, performed by Leon Goossens, star oboist from the London Philharmonic Orchestra. At the end of June 1938, Hindemith received a telegram from Edward Clark, asking him if the new sonata might be performed during the concert planned for the New Burlington Galleries. The composer was however sceptical, perhaps having heard about the controversial exhibition during his time in Zurich. On 5 July he wrote to his publisher Willy Strecker: "The 'German Art of the 20th Century' exhibition does not seem to be all that respectable – which I immediately suspected and asked [Clark] quietly for information on whether the concert

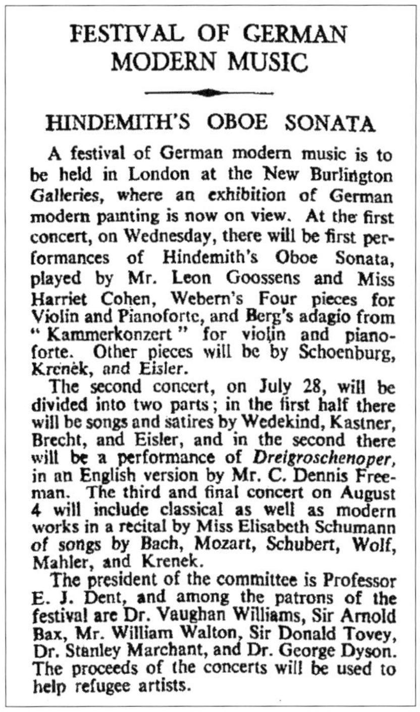

FESTIVAL OF GERMAN MODERN MUSIC

HINDEMITH'S OBOE SONATA

A festival of German modern music is to be held in London at the New Burlington Galleries, where an exhibition of German modern painting is now on view. At the first concert, on Wednesday, there will be first performances of Hindemith's Oboe Sonata, played by Mr. Leon Goossens and Miss Harriet Cohen, Webern's Four pieces for Violin and Pianoforte, and Berg's adagio from "Kammerkonzert" for violin and pianoforte. Other pieces will be by Schoenburg, Krenèk, and Eisler.

The second concert, on July 28, will be divided into two parts; in the first half there will be songs and satires by Wedekind, Kastner, Brecht, and Eisler, and in the second there will be a performance of *Dreigroschenoper*, in an English version by Mr. C. Dennis Freeman. The third and final concert on August 4 will include classical as well as modern works in a recital by Miss Elisabeth Schumann of songs by Bach, Mozart, Schubert, Wolf, Mahler, and Krenek.

The president of the committee is Professor E. J. Dent, and among the patrons of the festival are Dr. Vaughan Williams, Sir Arnold Bax, Mr. William Walton, Sir Donald Tovey, Dr. Stanley Marchant, and Dr. George Dyson. The proceeds of the concerts will be used to help refugee artists.

70 Article on Paul Hindemith's Oboe Sonata during the Festival of German Modern Music, *The Times*, 18 July 1938, p. 10.

could be played there. He answered that the members of the organisation committee (Tovey, Dent and V. Williams) were above any suspicion, but other persons are also involved."[4] As a result, Hindemith decided not to attend the concert personally. The composer was still living in Berlin and wanted to avoid any open criticism of the Hitler regime. During the composer's visit to London in 1934, Strecker had already asked the BBC not to ask him about the situation in Germany.[5]

On 14 July 1938 Hindemith travelled to London with his wife Gertrud to conduct the premiere of his ballet *Nobilissima Visione* at Theatre Royal Drury Lane on 21 July. In the days beforehand, he asked Leon Goossens and the pianist Harriet Cohen to play him the newly composed oboe sonata which should be performed for the first time in the New Burlington Galleries – the day before the prmeiere of his ballet. According to Cohen, Stefan Zweig had also been present, helping Cohen by turning the pages of the handwritten score, which the musicians had only received one week earlier.[6] Despite the prominent place afforded to Hindemith's new Oboe Sonate in the London festival programme (fig. 63)[7], the composer stuck by his decision not attend the performance, according to his diary choosing visit a rehearsal of his ballet instead.

By contrast, Hindemith's peers William Walton, John Ireland and Arthur Bliss all attended the concert at the New Burlington Galleries, as did the 24-year-old Benjamin Britten (fig. 8), who provided the piano accompaniment for singer Sophie Wyss's performance of the Krenek cycle *Durch die Nacht*. A few days after the concert, Britten wrote to the son of director Hermann Scherchen that he was pleased with the performance and its echo in the press. The contemporary press did indeed praise the festival for its interesting, well-executed programme; though they only referred to five composers – suggesting that Eisler's song cycle was cancelled after the programme went to press. While *The Times* praised both Schönberg and Webern, *The Telegraph* wrote: "If Schönberg and Hindemith both claim to express the spirit of the age, one of them must be wrong."[8] *The Daily Herald* was even more cutting: "Surrounded by pictures banned by Hitler a big audience last night listened to music banned by Hitler. Schoenberg's uncommunicative *Three Piano Pieces* and Webern's four fragmentary squeaks for piano and violin seemed hardly important enough for solemn excommunication. They were *in-Fuehreriatingly* dull."[9]

Hindemith's sonata, on the other hand, was lauded as charming and sprightly. As one critic wrote, clearly more impressed by the music than the paintings on display: "Gazing at the pictures during the intervals, I thought how obvious it was in what art the Germans excelled."[10]

A semi-staged version of *The Threepenny Opera*

The second concert in the New Burlington Galleries festival featured songs from Brecht and Weill's *The Threepenny Opera*. These songs had boomed with particular shrillness from the listening booths at the Düsseldorf propaganda exhibition, branded there as a prime example of 'degenerate music'. Despite its great success in Germany, *The Threeepenny Opera* had proven something of a flop in England. Kurt Weill (fig. 65), who had fled from Berlin to Paris in March 1933, arrived in London in January 1935, where he in fact heard an early radio performance of the opera, conducted by Edward Clark. Weill recognised this as a misunderstanding of his work. Yet despite miserable reviews, the performance did prompt producer Dennis Freeman to translate the piece into English. Extracts from this English translation were performed at the New Burlington Galleries on 28 July 1938, performed by The Opera Group under the direction of Ernst Schoen. A childhood friend of the philosopher Walter Benjamin, Schoen had studied under Ferruccio Busoni and Edgard Varèse, and even worked with Brecht and Eisler as programme director at the radio station in Frankfurt. He was dismissed in 1933 and, after being detained in a concentration camp, fled to England, where he initially scraped a living transcribing musical scores. In 1936 he found a job at the BBC, together with the opera ensemble he led with Georg Knepler.

The star of the Brecht/Weill performance at the Festival of German Music was Hedli Anderson, an opera singer influenced by Yvette Guilbert who featured on various London cabaret programmes. She made such a strong impression on Benjamin Britten that the young composer wrote several cabaret songs for her. Unfortunately, there are no known press reports on her performance during the event on 28 July.

It would be almost two decades before *The Threepenny Opera* finally encountered success in London in 1956.

"Lieder" Recital by Elisabeth Schumann

The day after a performance by the world-famous African-American singer and actor Paul Robeson at the New Burlington Galleries on 3 August,[11] a song recital by the equally famous soprano Elisabeth Schumann (fig. 66) rounded off the *Festival of German Music*. Schumann had appeared at the New York Metropolitan Opera as a guest performer in 1914 before being offered a permanent position at the Vienna State Opera in 1919. On the day of the German annexation of Austria in March 1938, Schumann and her Jewish partner Hans Krüger left Vienna. They settled first in England, where they were married.

Elisabeth Schumann was renowned for her roles in operas by Mozart, Wagner and Strauss, and for her performances of German "Lieder". At the New Burlington Galleries she performed songs by a wide array of composers, from Johann Sebastian Bach to Ernst Krenek. Schumann was particularly associated with the part of Yvonne in Krenek's opera *Jonny spielt auf*, which she had sung at the Vienna State Opera in 1928; this piece had also been cited as a prime example of 'degenerate' music at the Düsseldorf exhibition. The music critic in the British *Daily Herald* however was more interested in the older songs performed by Schumann. Under the heading "Nazis lose another singer", he wrote: "Elisabeth Schumann, the German singer, has broken with Nazism. She is following Lotte Lehmann, the equally famous Austrian soprano, in going to America. Last night she sang for the benefit of expelled German artists branded as degenerate by Hitler at the New Burlington Galleries, where an exhibition of Twentieth Century German Art is being held. [...] In doing so, she put herself outside the Nazi pale. Yet Elisabeth Schumann, like Lotte Lehmann, is a pure Aryan. She sang songs of Bach, Mozart, Brahms and Hugo Wolf, songs that breathed the atmosphere of romanticism for which Germany once was famous."[12]

Later in 1938, Schumann and her pianist Leo Rosenek emigrated onwards to the United States, where they found teaching positions at the Curtis Institute of Music in Philadelphia.

Dedicated music periodicals such as *Monthly Musical Record*, *Musical Opinion* and *The Chesterian* carried no reports on the *Festival of German Music*. Is this because the festival was held in a gallery rather than a concert hall, or because the leading critics were on holiday? Or was the lack of interest due to the fact that pieces by Krenek, Hindemith and Webern had already been played in London in June 1938 at the Festival of the International Society for Contemporary Music?

While these three concerts may only have had a limited impact in England, they nonetheless opened the eyes of the participants to the full extent of Nazi cultural barbarism. In August 1938 Paul Hindemith emptied his Berlin apartment, and left Germany. In September the BBC asked Benjamin Britten if he might perform a Hindemith piece at the following year's Festival of Contemporary Music in Baden-Baden. Britten sharply refused, as he explained: "Admittedly music has nothing to do with politics, but when politics pokes its slimy fingers into music that's a different matter."[13]

1 Anon.: «Degenerate Music». Anti-Jewish Exhibition in Germany; in: The Times, 26 May 1938, p. 18
2 Anon.: Atonal Music Condemned. Campaign at Nazi Exhibition, in: The Manchester Guardian, 8 June 1938, p. 10
3 Donald Mitchell/Philip Reed (eds.): Benjamin Britten. Letters from a Life, Vol. 1, 1923-1939, Selected Letters and Diaries, London 2011, p. 552
4 Luitgard Schader (ed.): Paul Hindemith Bläserkammermusik III, Vol. V, 3 (PHA 503), Mainz 2013, p. XVI f.
5 BBC Written Archives, Caversham, Hindemith file (friendly advice from Erik Levi, London)
6 Harriet Cohen: A Bundle of Time. The Memoirs of Harriet Cohen, London 1969, p. 275 f.
7 Anon.: Festival of German Modern Music. Hindemith's Oboe Sonata, in: The Times, 18 July 1938, p. 10
8 J.A.W.: Modern German Music. New Hindemith Sonata, in: Daily Telegraph and Morning Post, 21 July 1938, p. 10
9 S.F.: Listening to the Banned, in: Daily Herald, 21 July 1938, p. 3
10 Mariegold: What Every Woman Wants to Know, in: The Sketch, 27 July 1938, p. 21
11 Anon.: Manchester Guardian, 3. August 1938, p. 18 'Today's Arrangements'
12 A.E.: Nazis lose another singer, in: Daily Herald, 5 August 1938, p. 9
13 Mitchell/Reed, p. 581 f.

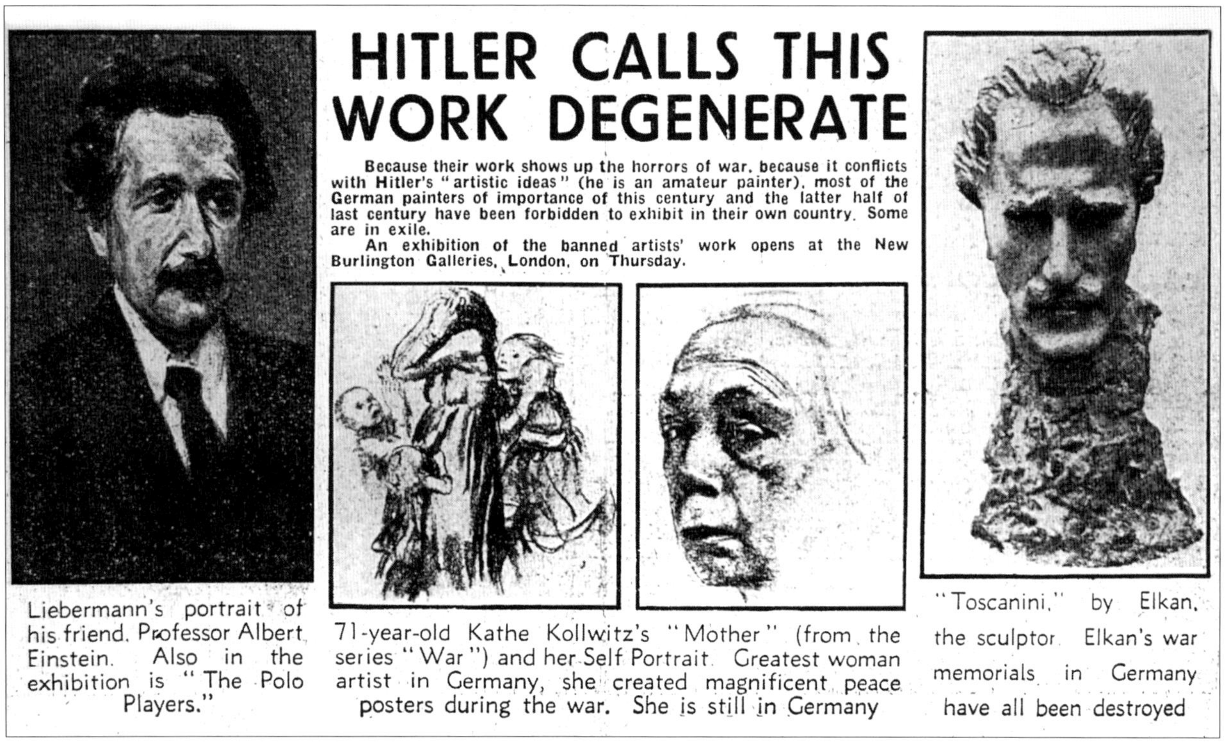

HITLER CALLS THIS WORK DEGENERATE

Because their work shows up the horrors of war, because it conflicts with Hitler's "artistic ideas" (he is an amateur painter), most of the German painters of importance of this century and the latter half of last century have been forbidden to exhibit in their own country. Some are in exile.

An exhibition of the banned artists' work opens at the New Burlington Galleries, London, on Thursday.

Liebermann's portrait of his friend, Professor Albert Einstein. Also in the exhibition is "The Polo Players."

71-year-old Kathe Kollwitz's "Mother" (from the series "War") and her Self Portrait. Greatest woman artist in Germany, she created magnificent peace posters during the war. She is still in Germany

"Toscanini," by Elkan, the sculptor. Elkan's war memorials in Germany have all been destroyed

71 Anon.: "Hitler Calls This Work Degenerate", newspaper and date unknown (before 7 July 1938).

The Public Response to *Twentieth Century German Art*

LUCY WASENSTEINER

The public reaction to *Twentieth Century German Art* was in many respects hard to predict. Never before had so much German modernist art been shown in Britain; never before had art been used so explicitly to counter the policies of a foreign regime. Would the show be of interest to the London public? And would it hit its mark as a statement against Nazi policy?

'Entrance Jam at Art Show'

Twentieth Century German Art opened its doors on Thursday 7 July 1938. The painter Augustus John (fig. 72) was invited to give the opening speech – astonishing those present with his brief address, "I have the great pleasure and privilege to declare this exhibition open". This sense of caution was echoed in a second introductory speech, made by the British diplomat Sir Ronald Storrs (fig. 73). Though Storrs spoke at greater length, he too was keen to emphasise that the exhibition was "non-political", that it "was not be approached politically at all".[1]

These claims for political neutrality were however roundly ignored by British journalists. In the preceding weeks, numerous titles had begun reporting on the forthcoming exhibition, with headlines referring to "Banned 'Degenerates'" and the "Reply to Munich", among others.[2] In the week of the opening, other titles took the exhibition as a chance to criticize Nazi cultural policy more broadly (fig. 77).[3] Indeed, the attempts made by organisers to neutralize the show's political message were explicitly identified as concealment, as the *Daily Express* concluded on 6 July, "how can the show ... be anything but political? Its very existence is an implied criticism of a political regime".[4]

Perhaps as a result of this advance reporting, from the moment of its opening *Twentieth Century German Art* attracted huge crowds to the New Burlington Galleries (fig. 74 and 80). According to the *Star* newspaper (fig. 75), over one thousand people were in attendance at the opening event on 7 July 1938, causing a "jam" which forced visitors to wait in the street.[5] This was confirmed by the German critic Alfred Kerr (fig. 78), himself in attendance, writing for the German exile periodical the *Pariser Tageszeitung* on 13 July: "Anyone who saw the crush at the opening of this show of banned Germans ... must tip their hat in the manner of Charlie Chaplin to the promotional talents of the organiser Irmgard Burchard. The street was blocked. An elderly British lady begged me to take her in on my ticket, to which I agreed.»[6]

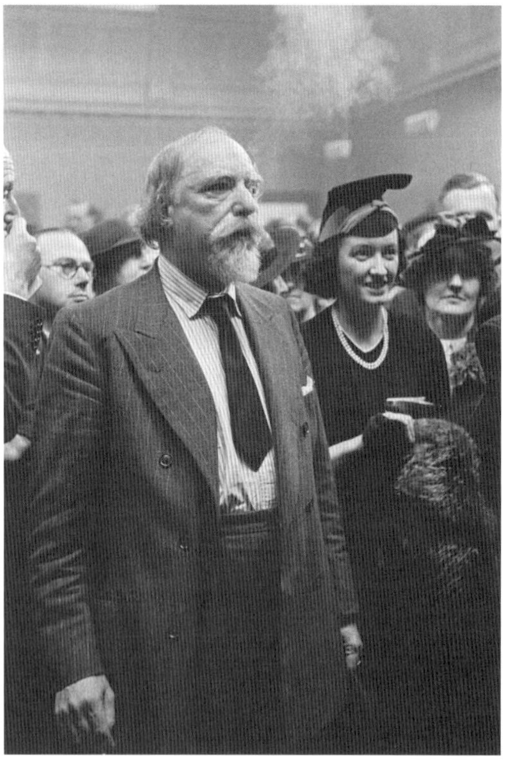

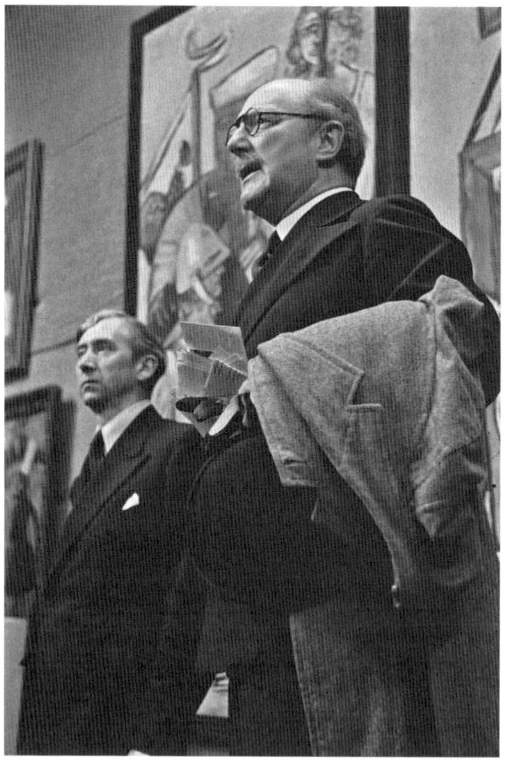

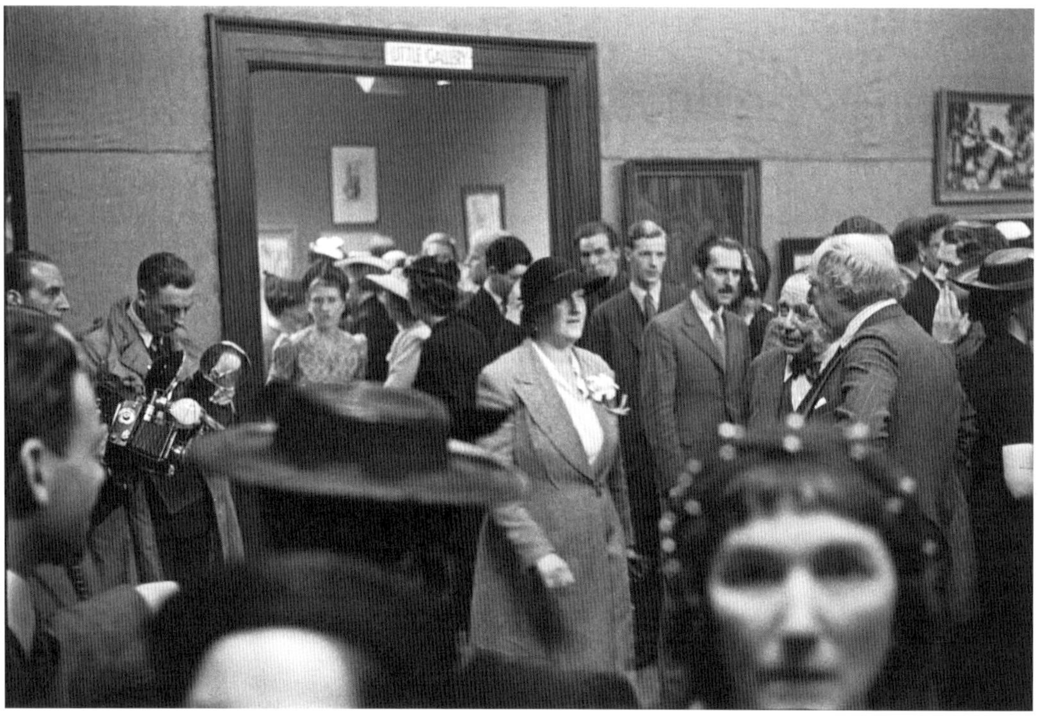

72 Augustus John at the opening of *Twentieth Century German Art*, 7 July 1938.
73 Ronald Storrs speaking at the opening, with Herbert Read (left).
74 Crowds at the opening of *Twentieth Century German Art*.

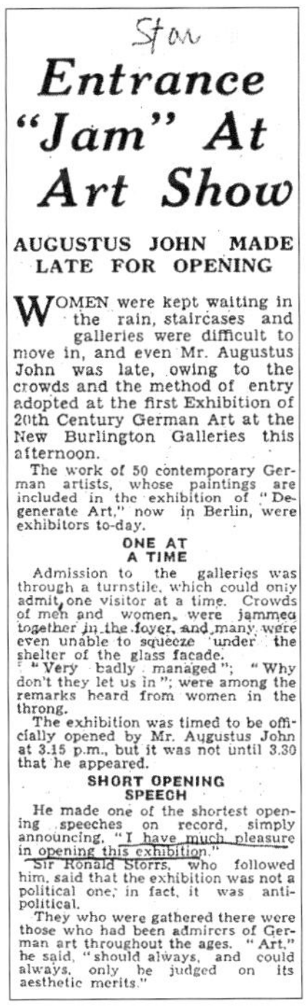

Star

Entrance "Jam" At Art Show

AUGUSTUS JOHN MADE LATE FOR OPENING

WOMEN were kept waiting in the rain, staircases and galleries were difficult to move in, and even Mr. Augustus John was late, owing to the crowds and the method of entry adopted at the first Exhibition of 20th Century German Art at the New Burlington Galleries this afternoon.

The work of 50 contemporary German artists, whose paintings are included in the exhibition of "Degenerate Art," now in Berlin, were exhibitors to-day.

ONE AT A TIME

Admission to the galleries was through a turnstile, which could only admit one visitor at a time. Crowds of men and women were jammed together in the foyer, and many were even unable to squeeze under the shelter of the glass facade.

"Very badly managed"; "Why don't they let us in"; were among the remarks heard from women in the throng.

The exhibition was timed to be officially opened by Mr. Augustus John at 3.15 p.m., but it was not until 3.30 that he appeared.

SHORT OPENING SPEECH

He made one of the shortest opening speeches on record, simply announcing, "I have much pleasure in opening this exhibition."

Sir Ronald Storrs, who followed him, said that the exhibition was not a political one; in fact, it was anti-political.

They who were gathered there were those who had been admirers of German art throughout the ages. "Art," he said, "should always, and could always, only be judged on its aesthetic merits."

75 Anon. "Entrance 'Jam' at Art Show: Augustus John Made Late for Opening", *The Star*, 7 July 1938, p. 1

76 Anon.: "'Entartete Kunst' – diesmal in London", *Völkischer Beobachter* (Vienna), 11 July 1938, p. 10

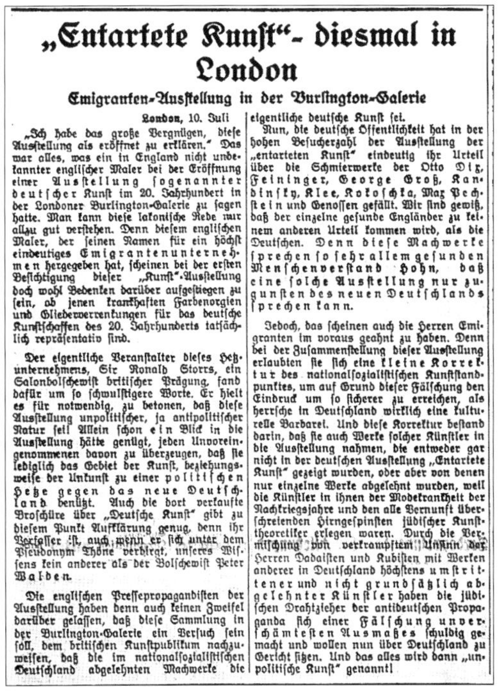

„Entartete Kunst"- diesmal in London

Emigranten-Ausstellung in der Burlington-Galerie

London, 10. Juli

„Ich habe das große Vergnügen, diese Ausstellung als eröffnet zu erklären." Das war alles, was ein in England nicht unbekannter englischer Maler bei der Eröffnung einer Ausstellung sogenannter deutscher Kunst im 20. Jahrhundert in der Londoner Burlington-Galerie zu sagen hatte. Man kann diese lakonische Rede nur allzu gut verstehen. Denn diesem englischen Maler, der seinen Namen für ein höchst eindeutiges Emigrantenunternehmen hergegeben hat, scheinen bei der ersten Besichtigung dieser „Kunst"-Ausstellung doch wohl Bedenken darüber aufgestiegen zu sein, ob jenen krankhaften Farbenorgien und Gliederverrenkungen für das deutsche Kunstschaffen des 20. Jahrhunderts tatsächlich repräsentativ sind.

Der eigentliche Veranstalter dieses Hetzunternehmens, Sir Ronald Storrs, ein Salonbolschewist britischer Prägung, fand dafür um so schwulstigere Worte. Er hielt es für notwendig, zu betonen, daß diese Ausstellung unpolitischer, ja antipolitischer Natur sei! Allein schon ein Blick in die Ausstellung hätte genügt, jeden Unvoreingenommenen davon zu überzeugen, daß sie lediglich das Gebiet der Kunst, beziehungsweise der Unkunst zu einer politischen Hetze gegen das neue Deutschland benützt. Auch die dort verkaufte Broschüre über „Deutsche Kunst" gibt zu diesem Punkt Aufklärung genug, denn ihr Verfasser ist, auch wenn er sich unter dem Pseudonym Thöne verbirgt, unseres Wissens kein anderer als der Bolschewist Peter Walden.

Die englischen Pressepropagandisten der Ausstellung haben denn auch keinen Zweifel darüber gelassen, daß diese Sammlung in der Burlington-Galerie ein Versuch sein soll, dem britischen Kunstpublikum nachzuweisen, daß die im nationalsozialistischen Deutschland abgelehnten Machwerke die eigentliche deutsche Kunst sei.

Nun, die deutsche Öffentlichkeit hat in der hohen Besucherzahl der Ausstellung der „entarteten Kunst" eindeutig ihr Urteil über die Schmierwerke der Otto Dix, Feininger, George Groß, Kandinsky, Klee, Kokoschka, Max Pechstein und Genossen gefällt. Wir sind gewiß, daß der einzelne gesunde Engländer zu keinem anderen Urteil kommen wird, als die Deutschen. Denn diese Machwerke sprechen so sehr allem gesunden Menschenverstand Hohn, daß eine solche Ausstellung nur zugunsten des neuen Deutschlands sprechen kann.

Jedoch, das scheinen auch die Herren Emigranten im voraus geahnt zu haben. Denn bei der Zusammenstellung dieser Ausstellung erlaubten sie sich eine kleine Korrektur des nationalsozialistischen Kunststandpunktes, um auf Grund dieser Fälschung den Eindruck um so sicherer zu erreichen, als herrsche in Deutschland wirklich eine kulturelle Barbarei. Und diese Korrektur bestand darin, daß sie auch Werke solcher Künstler in die Ausstellung nahmen, die entweder gar nicht in der deutschen Ausstellung „Entartete Kunst" gezeigt wurden, oder aber von denen nur einzelne Werke abgelehnt wurden, weil die Künstler in ihnen der Modekrankheit der Nachkriegsjahre und den alle Vernunft überschreienden Hirngespinsten jüdischer Kunsttheoretiker erlegen waren. Durch die Vermischung von verkrampftem Unsinn der Herren Dadaisten und Kubisten mit Werken anderer in Deutschland höchstens umstrittener und nicht grundsätzlich abgelehnter Künstler haben die jüdischen Drahtzieher der antideutschen Propaganda sich einer Fälschung unverschämtesten Ausmaßes schuldig gemacht und wollen nun über Deutschland zu Gericht sitzen. Und das alles wird dann „unpolitische Kunst" genannt!

This popularity only increased during the show's run. Scheduled to close on 2 August, it was extended three times over the following weeks, eventually closing on Saturday 27 August. As reported in *Daily Telegraph* and *Morning Post* on 12 August, "The exhibition of *Twentieth Century German Art* ... has already been seen by about 12,000 people ... a remarkable figure for a heat wave in the holiday season".[7]

Germany Responds

It did not take long for the National Socialist regime in Germany to respond to the London exhibition. Three days after the *Twentieth Century German Art* opening, the second annual *Große Deutsche Kunstausstellung* opened to great fanfare in Munich. The opening address on Sunday 10 July was provided by Hitler himself. In this speech, Hitler made reference to the London exhibition, as quoted on the front page of the Berlin *Völkischer Beobachter* the following day: "... there are now only a few immeasurably foolish individuals ... who now and again still repeat overseas the stupid drivel of the time before 1933. So we have in a country – that has already allowed itself the frivolity of a special court, which claimed to have proven the innocence of Van der Lubbe ... – today we see it once again delighting the world with an exhibition, which is supposed to show the opposition between the cultural achievements of the great 'November' names in the line of Dada, Cubism etc., and the poverty of today's German art."[8]

Between September and December 1933, the Dutch communist Marinus van der Lubbe had been tried by a National Socialist court, charged with starting the Reichstag Fire. He was found guilty and executed in 1934. Over one week in September 1933 a group of prominent anti-Nazis had organised a counter-trial in London. To the Führer's German audience, these references to the British capital would have been immediately clear.

Hitler's speech was reproduced in full across the National Socialist press, sparking a flurry of reporting on the topic of the London show. Under headlines including "Degenerate Art in London" and "The Art Swindle in London", *Twentieth Century German Art* was widely recognised as a statement against the new Germany (fig. 76, 79).[9] Though these German journalists clearly had few concrete details regarding the identity of the organisers, there was no doubt who was ultimately behind the project. As the Berlin edition of the *Völkischer Beobachter* reported on 1 August: "Once again Judaism and Moscow are united ... to encourage insurrection. As always, the Jewish-bolshevist puppet masters of this inflammatory propaganda have tried to camouflage their intentions, in doing so biasing both the no-doubt politically clueless English, and the misguided un-political artistic idealists, in favour of their actions."[10]

The British Response to German Modernism

Twentieth Century German Art seems to have hit its mark as political propaganda. How then did it fare finding new and responsive audiences for the art being forced out of Germany?

The response of London's art journals was certainly far from enthusiastic. Many were repulsed by the "bad form" and "wild smears" of the German modernists, in particular in comparison to their French contemporaries.[11] Such opinions were echoed in certain general interest titles. As critic Raymond Mortimer memorably concluded in his 16 July review for the *New Statesmen and Nation*, "People who go to see the exhibition are only too likely to say: 'If Hitler doesn't like these pictures, it's the best thing I've heard about Hitler' ... for the general impression made by the show on the ordinary public must be one of extraordinary ugliness".[12]

Yet these kinds of responses were by no means universal. Writing in the *Spectator* on 8 July for example, critic Anthony Blunt argued against a comparison with French modernism, claiming that Germany possessed "a school of painting as original as that of Paris, of equal vitality, and with quite independent characteristics".[13] A similar approach was taken by art historian Nicolette Gray in her review published in the *Catholic Herald* on 15 July.[14] The problem lay not in the quality of the German works, she argued, but in the standards of judgement applied, as she wrote: "our traditional ... power of appreciation has been almost wiped out by the violent and persistent Gallicism of English art criticism since the eighteen nineties ... the result is an obvious unmitigated loss."

Gray proceeded with glowing praise of a number of the artists represented in London – Kokoschka "magnificent"; Modersohn-Becker and Dix "artists of real importance" – characterising the entire exhibition as one of "extraordinary richness and variety".

Across dozens of shorter reviews, the exhibition was similarly praised. In the *Manchester Guardian* the show was "brutal, violent ... but not undisciplined", while in the *Belfast News-Letter* the works of Max Beckmann were singled out for "the skill with which the figures have been drawn ... the vividness of the colour ... the strength and vigour of the brushwork". *The Western Morning News* highlighted Franz Marc's work as "outstanding"[15] while the *Daily Herald* simply implored its readers: "Go and see the Goya-esque lithographs by Käthe Kollwitz ... the tense wood-sculptures of Barlach; the astonishing landscapes of Kokoschka; the profoundly moving sculpture of Lehmbruck; the engaging fantasies of Paul Klee; oh, and everything."[16]

An unqualified success?

It seems only to have been in financial terms that the London exhibition seriously failed to meet expectations. Though there were some early sales, of works on paper by Kollwitz, Klee and Nolde,[17] the most significant sale from the show seems to have been Liebermann's portrait of Albert Einstein (see cat. no. 1), acquired by London's Royal Society following an appeal for public donations.[18] As Irmgard Burchard summarized on 5 September, around one week after the show's closure: "In spite of the very great moral success that the exhibition has had ... and the wide interested it arouse [sic] ... we have not been able to sell as many works as we hoped."[19]

Despite this lack of sales, the exhibition was clearly a "great moral success", recognised as a statement against Nazi cultural policies both in the Third Reich, and in Britain. And, despite some critical voices, the *Twentieth Century German Art* brought huge audiences to the New Burlington Galleries: audiences who were at least curious, and at most impressed, by the German modernism on show.

1 Anon.: Our London Correspondent. Mr John Opens the German Art Exhibition; in: Manchester Guardian, 8 July 1938, p. 10

2 Anon.: Banned "Degenerates"; in: The Scotsman, 8 June 1938, p. 10; F. Watson: Banned German Art. London Exhibition of Movements Condemned in Germany; in: Yorkshire Post, 4 July 1938, page unknown; and Anon.: "Degenerate Art" Show. A Reply to Munich; in: Manchester Guardian, 6 July 1938, p. 7

3 W. P. Hamsher: Where Painters Must Do What They're Told; in: News Chronicle, 6 July 1938, page unknown. See also Anon.: Hitler Tells Artists "Work Like This"; in: Evening Standard, 11 July 1938, p. 4

4 Anon.: Banned but Cautious; in: Daily Express, 6 July 1938, p. 6

5 Anon.: Entrance "Jam" at Art Show. Augustus John Made Late for Opening; in: The Star, 7 July 1938, p. 1

6 Alfred Kerr: Kulturchronik; in: Pariser Tageszeitung, 13 July 1938, p. 3

7 Anon.: German Art Exhibition to Continue. 12,000 Visitors in a Month, Nazis Protest; in: Daily Telegraph and Morning Post, 12 August 1938, p. 8

8 Anon.: Der Führer Sprach bei der Eröffnung der zweiten Großen Deutschen Kunstausstellung; in: Völkischer Beobachter (Berlin), 11 July 1938, p. 1

9 See for example Anon.: Entartete Kunst – diesmal in London; in: Völkischer Beobachter (Vienna), 11 July 1938, p. 10; Robert Scholz: Der Kunstschwindel von London; in: Völkischer Beobachter (Vienna), 3 August 1938, p. 9; Werner Rittich: Saison-Ausverkauf in bolschewistischer Kunst; in: Der Angriff, 3 August 1938, p. 4.

10 Scholz, ibid.

11 See for example Anon.: Modern German Art – Till Now; in: Studio, July 1938, pp. 160-4; Anon.: Some Topics of the Moment. Twentieth Century German Art; in: Connoisseur, vol. 102 no. 443, July 1938, p. 101; and Anon.: German Art. Exhibition of XXth-Century German Art at the New Burlington Galleries; in: Apollo, vol. 28, July 1938, pp. 94-5

12 Raymond Mortimer: Miscellany. German Artists; in: New Statesman and Nation, no. 286, 16 July 1938, pp. 112-3

13 Anthony Blunt: Art. Contemporary German Art; in: Spectator, vol. 161, 8 July 1938, p. 61

14 Nicolete Gray: German XXth Century Art. London Sees the Pictures Hitler Condemns as Decadent; in: Catholic Herald, 15 July 1938, p. 2

15 Anon.: London Letter. Modern German Art; in: Western Morning News and Daily Gazette, 15 July 1938, p. 6

16 Anon.: One Picture in Four Parts; in: Daily Herald, 7 July 1938, p. 3

17 Anon.: German Art Exhibition; in: The Times, 25 July 1938, p. 7, 'up to the present 30 works have been sold, including six by Käthe Kollwitz and five by Paul Klee'

18 Correspondence between the author and Keith Moore, Royal Society, London, February 2012

19 RSMA, letter from Irmgard Burchard to Fred Uhlman, 5 September 1938 [in English]

Die Resonanz auf *Twentieth Century German Art*

LUCY WASENSTEINER

Die Reaktion des Publikums und der Presse auf die Ausstellung *Twentieth Century German Art* war kaum vorhersehbar, und zwar aus verschiedenen Gründen. Nie zuvor wurden so viele Werke der deutschen Moderne auf einmal in Großbritannien gezeigt; nie zuvor wurde Kunst so explizit dafür eingesetzt, die Regierung eines anderen Landes zu kritisieren. Würde sich das Londoner Publikum für die Schau überhaupt interessieren? Und würde die Ausstellung tatsächlich als ein Statement gegen die Politik der Nazis verstanden werden?

«Warteschlange bei Kunstausstellung»

Die Vernissage von *Twentieth Century German Art* fand am 7. Juli 1938 statt. Der Maler Augustus John war für die Eröffnungsrede vorgesehen (Abb. 72); er überraschte die Anwesenden allerdings damit, dass er sich auf eine bloße Eröffnungsformel beschränkte: «Es ist mir eine große Freude, diese Ausstellung als eröffnet zu erklären.» Der britische Diplomat Sir Ronald Storrs (Abb. 73) sprach etwas länger. Aber auch er zeigte sich in seinen Formulierungen zurückhaltend. Dabei war ihm wichtig, den «nicht-politischen» Charakter der Ausstellung hervorzuheben, und zu betonen, dass sie nicht die «geringsten politischen Absichten» verfolge.[1]

Die britische Presse ließ sich durchs Storrs Beteuerungen allerdings nicht vom unpolitischen Charakter der Schau überzeugen. In den vorangegangenen Wochen hatten bereits zahlreiche Zeitungen über die bevorstehende Ausstellung berichtet, und zwar unter Überschriften wie «Verbotene ‹entartete› Künstler» oder «Antwort an München».[2] Auch unmittelbar vor der Eröffnung nutzten verschiedene Blätter die Gelegenheit, die Nationalsozialistische Kulturpolitik im allgemein zu kritisieren (Abb. 77).[3] Der Versuch der Organisatoren, die politische Dimension der Veranstaltung herunterzuspielen, wurde als bloße Verschleierung bewertet. Oder, wie der *Daily Express* am 6. Juli schrieb: «Wie kann diese Schau [...] unpolitisch sein? Schon die Tatsache, dass sie stattfindet, ist eine implizite Kritik an einer bestimmten Regierung.»[4]

Die Presseartikel im Vorfeld trugen dazu bei, dass die Ausstellung vom ersten Moment an wahre Besuchermassen anzog (Abb. 74, 80). Wie der *Star* berichtete (Abb. 75), kamen zu Eröffnung mehr als tausend Menschen; der Andrang so groß, dass Besucher bis auf die Straße Schlange standen.[5] Der Kunstkritiker Alfred Kerr (Abb. 78), selbst unter den Wartenden, bestätigte diese Berichte, und schrieb am 13. Juli in der *Pariser Tageszeitung*: «Wer den Andrang zur Eröffnung dieser deutschen Verbanntenschau sah, [...] der muss vor der

Where Painters Must Do What They're Told

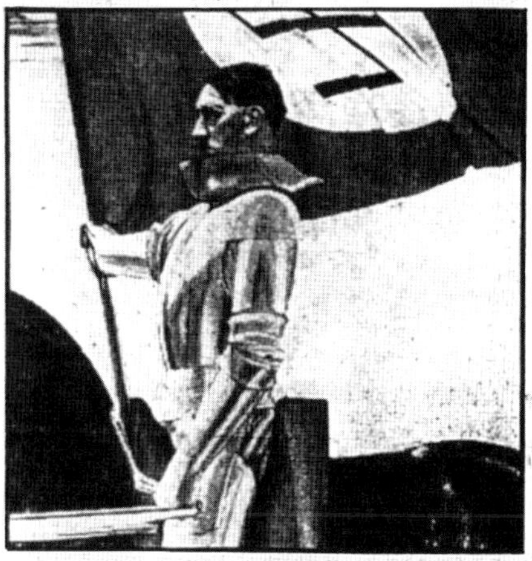

The Nazis Call This Art

THE Exhibition of Twentieth Century German Art, which opens in London today, is more than a display of paintings and sculpture. It is a guide to the mind and spirit of Nazism. For of its artists, the Third Reich ranks none worthy of wall space.

A thoroughgoing museum purge has by now taught the Nazi pretty effectively what is not art—in the eyes of the Propaganda Ministry. Hence the first significance of the collection at the New Burlington Galleries, as revealing the type of treatment which merits the official German epithet "degenerate."

This exhibition in London, enriched by fruits of the Anschluss purge, will be the fourth by these "degenerate" artists I have seen within twelve months. The original drew enormous crowds at Munich, and was then transplanted to Berlin. Yet it was not the same, for a regime sensitive to the point of touchiness in these matters listened to what the foreign critics said, and discreetly removed various exhibits.

As arranged in Munich, the exhibition was a herded display of the uncatalogued condemned. Suspicion was at once aroused by the choice of red as the colour for the curtains draping the entrance. I was prepared to believe that this was fortuitous,' but it was certainly by design that every wall in every room was so crowded with exhibits that the visitor not yet half-way round found himself ready to cry "Hold, enough!" and confess the horrors of art run off the (Nazi) rails.

★

Confusion was increased by canvas screens, cunningly dividing rooms, so that pictures depending on distance for their effect could be viewed only at close range, where the best of them became but meaningless daubs.

Beside each picture was a tab giving the price the German workers, "out of hard-paid taxes, were forced to pay for it." It would have been a fairer commentary, I thought, if the coincident inflationary price of bread had been mentioned, too.

Munich was fortunate, however, in that its "degenerates" were on parade almost opposite the new House of German Art, thus permitting quick comparison with pictures which had passed the party sieve, and received from the appropriate department the rubber stamp of approval without which nothing breathes freely in the Germany of today.

I studied particularly the war pictures of each parallel display:

The "degenerate" that stands out in memory was an unlabelled painting by Otto Dix who also will be represented in London. It showed four maimed and blinded war-victims, walking on peg legs past a shoemaker's shop. One has shell-shock ague and to depict this the artist adopted the rather elementary device of painting several trembling outlines of hand, arm and face. An Iron Cross, on one breast, was perhaps a trifle bigger than the perspective demanded.

★

These four might have posed, before the battle began, and they fell wounded, for any of a dozen bright-eyed hero-pictures in the House of German Art: that Labour Service man, shouldering a spade shining as none ever could in the trenches; this soldier, full of fearless nobility; this Black Guard, a tower of Nazi strength. But when these brave uniforms have come to dust, then no more will they be fit subject for an artist. For to portray the end of the fight would be to reverse the effect of colours-flying, forward-marching propaganda.

Art, says the handbook to the House of German Art, must have as the one essential a purifying, uplifting influence in form and content. It must again become the expression of the ennobling powers of the nation.

Art, in short, must serve the sentimental-heroic, and be ever docile to the propaganda mentality of the Third Reich.

Take as an example the big canvas showing the warship Admiral Scheer bombarding Almeria: a geometrical composition, cliffs running parallel to the ship's bows, whose blue-grey colouring matches that of the sea, with a vivid contrast of yellow stabbing smoke and flame from the guns. And high at each masthead the swastika ensign, undisturbed by the noise and racket of bombardment, painted flat against the sky, to inform the youngest among us of the nationality of the attacking ship.

A pity London cannot also see this Home of Orthodox Art.

It is a pet concern of the Fuehrer's. With half a dozen museums in keeping with Munich's tradition, all within a stone's throw, it was hither he led Mussolini, and even on the very day of his departure for the last Nazi Party Congress at Nuremberg he stepped across from his flat in the Prince Regent Street for another quick look round.

★

On such hurried visits as these it must seem to Hitler—there are so many busts and portraits of himself on show—that the place is stuffed with mirrors.

Chief item in this pantheistic cult of Hitlerism is a painting of the leader of the German people attired in crusading armour, mounted on a charger, and in his hand a flowing swastika pennon. Thus religion among the orthodox artists.

W. P. Hamsher

News Chronicle 6. 7.

77 W. P. Hamsher, "Where Painters Must Do What They're Told", in: *News Chronicle*, 6. Juli 1938, Seite unbekannt.

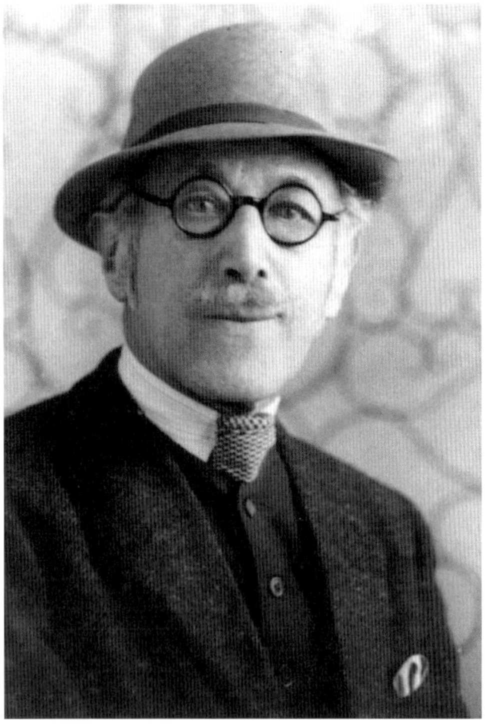

78 Alfred Kerr, 1936

Werbungskraft der Einrichterin Irmgard Burchard einen Augenblick das Hütchen wie Charlie Chaplin lüften. Der Straßendamm war gesperrt. Eine bejahrte Britin flehte zu mir, sie auf meiner Karte mitzunehmen, was gelang.»[6]

Der Erfolg setzte sich in den folgenden Wochen unvermindert fort. Die Ausstellung wurde dreimal verlängert und schloss nicht wie geplant am 2., sondern erst am 27. August. Schon am 12. August stand im *Daily Telegraph* and *Morning Post*, «Etwa 12.000 Menschen [...] haben die Ausstellung *Twentieth Century German Art* bis jetzt gesehen [...] eine beeindruckende Zahl trotz Hitzewelle und Ferienzeit.»[7]

Die Reaktion aus Deutschland

Die Antwort der NS-Regierung ließ nicht lange auf sich warten. Am 10. Juli, d.h. drei Tage nach der Vernissage von *Twentieth Century German Art*, wurde in München die zweite *Große Deutsche Kunstausstellung* eröffnet. Hitler selbst hielt die Eröffnungsrede und nahm dabei Bezug auf die Londoner Ausstellung. Die Berliner Ausgabe des *Völkischen Beobachters* zitierte ihn am folgenden Tag mit den Worten: «Es gibt nur noch vereinzelte, schon unermesslich törichte Menschen, [...] die im Ausland das stupide Gerede der Zeit vor dem Jahre 1933 auch heute noch ab und zu wiederholen. So hat man in einem Staat, der sich schon einmal den Spaß eines besonderen Gerichtshofes erlaubte, der im Gegensatz zum Deutschen Reichsgericht in einem ebenso kindlichen wie verletzenden Verfahren die Unschuld van der Lubbes erweisen sollte, in diesen Tagen wieder einmal die Welt mit einer Ausstellung beglückt, die bestimmt sein soll, den Gegensatz aufzuzeigen zwischen den kulturträchtigen Leistungen bekannter Novembergrößen vom Stamme der Dada, der Kubi usw. und der Armut der heutigen deutschen Kunst.»[8]

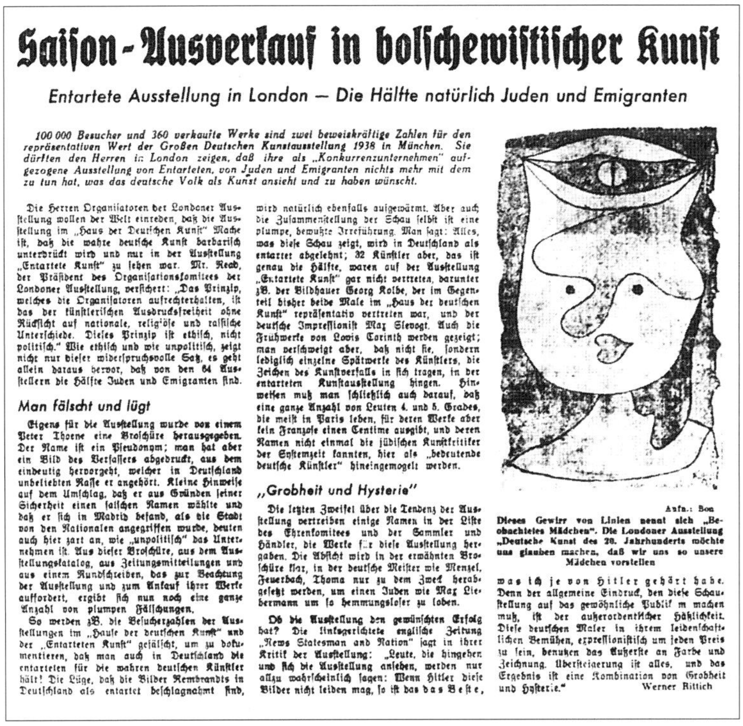

Saison-Ausverkauf in bolschewistischer Kunst

Entartete Ausstellung in London — Die Hälfte natürlich Juden und Emigranten

100 000 Besucher und 360 verkaufte Werke sind zwei beweiskräftige Zahlen für den repräsentativen Wert der Großen Deutschen Kunstausstellung 1938 in München. Sie dürften den Herren in London zeigen, daß ihre als „Konkurrenzunternehmen" aufgezogene Ausstellung von Entarteten, von Juden und Emigranten nichts mehr mit dem zu tun hat, was das deutsche Volk als Kunst ansieht und zu haben wünscht.

Die Herren Organisatoren der Londoner Ausstellung wollen der Welt einreden, daß die Ausstellung im „Haus der Deutschen Kunst" Mache ist, daß die wahre deutsche Kunst barbarisch unterdrückt wird und nur in der Ausstellung „Entartete Kunst" zu sehen war. Mr. Read, der Präsident des Organisationskomitees der Londoner Ausstellung, versichert: „Das Prinzip, welches die Organisatoren aufrechterhalten, ist das der künstlerischen Ausdrucksfreiheit ohne Rücksicht auf nationale, religiöse und rassische Unterschiede. Dieses Prinzip ist ethisch, nicht politisch." Wie ethisch und wie unpolitisch, zeigt nicht nur dieser widerspruchsvolle Satz, es geht allein daraus hervor, daß von den 64 Ausstellern die Hälfte Juden und Emigranten sind.

Man fälscht und lügt

Eigens für die Ausstellung wurde von einem Peter Thoene eine Broschüre herausgegeben. Der Name ist ein Pseudonym; man hat aber ein Bild des Verfassers abgedruckt, aus dem eindeutig hervorgeht, welcher in Deutschland unbeliebten Rasse er angehört. Kleine Hinweise auf dem Umschlag, daß er aus Gründen seiner Sicherheit einen falschen Namen wählte und daß er sich in Madrid befand, als die Stadt von den Nationalen angegriffen wurde, deuten auch hier zart an, wie „unpolitisch" das Unternehmen ist. Aus dieser Broschüre, aus dem Ausstellungskatalog, aus Zeitungsmitteilungen und aus einem Rundschreiben, das zur Beachtung der Ausstellung und zum Ankauf ihrer Werke auffordert, ergibt sich nun noch eine ganze Anzahl von plumpen Fälschungen.

So werden zB. die Besucherzahlen der Ausstellungen im „Hause der deutschen Kunst" und der „Entarteten Kunst" gefälscht, um zu dokumentieren, daß man auch in Deutschland die entarteten für die wahren deutschen Künstler hält! Die Lüge, daß die Bilder Rembrandts in Deutschland als entartet beschlagnahmt sind, wird natürlich ebenfalls aufgewärmt. Aber auch die Zusammenstellung der Schau selbst ist eine plumpe, bewußte Irreführung. Man sagt: Alles, was diese Schau zeigt, wird in Deutschland als entartet abgelehnt; 32 Künstler aber, das ist genau die Hälfte, waren auf der Ausstellung „Entartete Kunst" gar nicht vertreten, darunter zB. der Bildhauer Georg Kolbe, der im Gegenteil bisher beide Male im „Haus der deutschen Kunst" repräsentativ vertreten war, und der deutsche Impressionist Max Slevogt. Auch die Frühwerke von Lovis Corinth werden gezeigt; man verschweigt aber, daß nicht sie, sondern lediglich einzelne Spätwerke des Künstlers, die Zeichen des Kunstverfalls in sich tragen, in der entarteten Kunstausstellung hingen. Hinweisen muß man schließlich auch darauf, daß eine ganze Anzahl von Leuten 4. und 5. Grades, die meist in Paris leben, für deren Werke aber kein Franzose einen Centime ausgibt, und deren Namen nicht einmal die jüdischen Kunstkritiker der Systemzeit kannten, hier als „bedeutende deutsche Künstler" hineingemogelt werden.

„Grobheit und Hysterie"

Die letzten Zweifel über die Tendenz der Ausstellung vertreiben einige Namen in der Liste des Ehrenkomitees und der Sammler und Händler, die Werke für diese Ausstellung hergaben. Die Absicht wird in der erwähnten Broschüre klar, in der deutsche Meister wie Menzel, Feuerbach, Thoma nur zu dem Zweck herabgesetzt werden, um einen Juden wie Max Liebermann um so hemmungsloser zu loben.

Ob die Ausstellung den gewünschten Erfolg hat? Die linksgerichtete englische Zeitung „News Statesman and Nation" sagt in ihrer Kritik der Ausstellung: „Leute, die hingehen und sich die Ausstellung ansehen, werden nur allzu wahrscheinlich sagen: Wenn Hitler diese Bilder nicht leiden mag, so ist das das Beste, was ich je von Hitler gehört habe. Denn der allgemeine Eindruck, den diese Schaustellung auf das gewöhnliche Publikum machen muß, ist der außerordentlicher Häßlichkeit. Diese deutschen Maler in ihrem leidenschaftlichen Bemühen, expressionistisch um jeden Preis zu sein, benutzen das Äußerste an Farbe und Zeichnung. Übersteigerung ist alles, und das Ergebnis ist eine Kombination von Grobheit und Hysterie."

Werner Rittich

Aufn.: Bon

Dieses Gewirr von Linien nennt sich „Beobachtetes Mädchen". Die Londoner Ausstellung „Deutsche Kunst des 20. Jahrhunderts möchte uns glauben machen, daß wir uns so unsere Mädchen vorstellen

79 Werner Rittich: "Saison-Ausverkauf in bolschewistischer Kunst", *Der Angriff*, 3. August 1938, S. 4.

Der niederländische Kommunist Marinus van der Lubbe hatte zwischen September und Dezember 1933 als Hauptangeklagter beim Reichtagsbrandprozess vor Gericht gestanden, war schuldig gesprochen und im Januar 1934 hingerichtet worden. Im September 1933 hatten prominente Nazigegner dazu einen Gegenprozess in London organisiert. Was Hitler mit seiner Anspielung sagen wollte, war dem Eröffnungspublikum natürlich sofort klar.

Hitlers Rede wurde von der gesamten NS-Presse in extenso wiedergegeben, gefolgt von einer Flut von Artikel mit Überschriften wie «Der Kunstschwindel in London» oder «Entartete Kunst – diesmal in London», in denen die Ausstellung eindeutig als Angriff auf das neue Deutschland bewertet wurde.[9] Auch wenn die deutschen Journalisten keine detaillierten Informationen zur Identität der Organisatoren besaßen, ließen sie keinen Zweifel daran, wen sie für die eigentlichen Drahtzieher hielten. So war beispielsweise am 1. August in der Berliner Ausgabe des *Völkischen Beobachters* zu lesen: «Hinter dieser Hetzausstellung gegen Deutschland [stehen] wieder einmal Juda und Moskau vereint als Agenten einer planmäßig betriebenen Völkerentfremdung und -verhetzung [...] Wie immer haben die jüdisch-bolschewistischen Drahtzieher dieser Hetzpropaganda ihre Absichten zu tarnen versucht, indem sie auch einige sicher politisch ahnungslose Engländer und irregeführte unpolitische Kunstidealisten dieser Aktion vorgespannt haben.»[10]

Britische Reaktionen auf die deutschen Moderne

Damit schien die Ausstellung *Twentieth Century German Art* ihr politisches Ziel erreicht zu haben. Hat sie aber auch dazu beigetragen, das Verständnis des britischen Publikums für die aus Deutschland vertriebene Kunst zu verbessern?

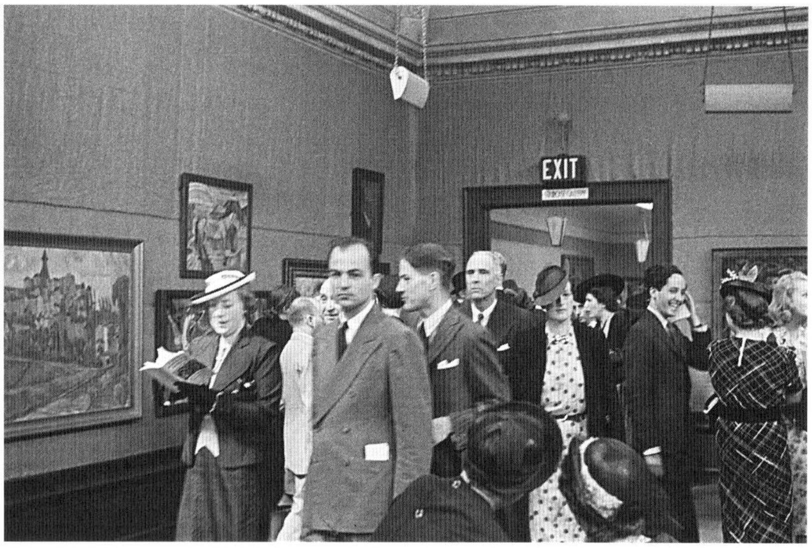

80 Besucherandrang bei der Vernissage der Ausstellung *Twentieth Century German Art*, 7. Juli 1938

Die Reaktion der Londoner Kunstzeitschriften war von Begeisterung weit entfernt. Viele fühlten sich abgestoßen von der «schlechten Form» und den «wilden Flecken» in den Werken der deutschen Künstler, besonders im Vergleich mit der Kunst ihrer französischen Zeitgenossen.[11] Ähnliche Töne wurden auch in der übrigen Presse angeschlagen. Der Kritiker Raymond Mortimer beispielsweise schrieb in *New Statesmen and Nation*: «Viele Besucher der Ausstellung werden womöglich denken: ‹Wenn Hitler diese Bilder nicht mag, ist es das Beste, was ich bisher über ihn gehört habe› [...] Denn der Gesamteindruck, den die Ausstellung beim normalen Besucher hinterlässt, ist der äußerster Hässlichkeit.»[12]

Allerdings entsprachen diese Stimmen keineswegs dem allgemeinen Tenor. Antony Blunt zum Beispiel wies den Vergleich mit der französischen Moderne zurück, indem er in *The Spectator* schrieb: «Die deutsche Schule ist genauso originell und lebendig wie die französische und besitzt eigene Qualitäten.»[13] Die Kunsthistorikerin Nicolette Gray vertrat eine ähnliche Meinung und unterstrich, dass die angelegten Maßstäbe, nicht die Qualität der deutschen Kunst das Problem seien. Am 15. Juli schrieb sie im *Catholic Herald*: «Unser traditionell gutes Urteilsvermögen in Sachen Kunst wurde seit den 1890er Jahren durch die gewaltige, anhaltende Vorliebe unserer Kritiker für die französische Kunst wie ausgelöscht. [...] Dadurch entstand ein gravierendes Manko.»[14] Anschließend pries Gray eine Reihe von Künstlern und bezeichnete Kokoschka als «großartig» sowie Dix und Modersohn-Becker als «wirklich wichtige Künstler». Die Ausstellung sei insgesamt «äußerst vielfältig und reichhaltig».

Dutzende von kleineren Blättern reagierten ebenfalls positiv auf die Londoner Ausstellung, so der *Manchester Guardian*, dem die Ausstellung «brutal und heftig [...] aber nicht undiszipliniert» erschien. Der *Belfast News-Letter* lobte die Werke Max Beckmanns für «die Präzision der Zeichnung, [...] die lebendige Palette, [...] den kräftigen und energischen Pinselstrich». Die *Western Morning News* bezeichnete Frank Marcs Werk als «hervorragend», während der *Daily Herald* an seine Leser den Appell richtete: «Gehen Sie und bewundern Sie die Goya-ähnlichen Lithographien von Käthe Kollwitz, [...] die spannungsgeladenen Holzplastiken Barlachs, die überraschenden Landschaften Kokoschkas, die beeindruckenden Skulpturen Lehmbrucks, die bezaubernden Phantasien Paul Klees. Ach, bewundern Sie alles».[15]

Ein uneingeschränkter Erfolg?

Nur wirtschaftlich erfüllte die Ausstellung die Erwartungen der Organisatoren nicht. Zwar wurden in den ersten Tagen ein paar Arbeiten auf Papier von Kollwitz, Klee und Nolde verkauft,[16] für die Hauptwerke fanden sich jedoch anscheinend keine Käufer – mit Ausnahme von Liebermanns Einstein-Porträt (siehe Kat.-Nr. 1), das dank öffentlicher Spenden durch die Royal Society erworben werden konnte.[17] Etwa eine Woche nach dem Ende der Ausstellung zog Irmgard Burchard folgendes Fazit: «Trotz des großartigen moralischen Erfolgs [...] und der Begeisterung des Publikums, [...] konnten wir nicht so viele Werke verkaufen, wie wir uns es gewünscht hatten.»[18]

Twentieth Century German Art war in der Tat ein «großartiger moralischer Erfolg», trotz der geringen Verkäufe. Sie wurde sowohl in Großbritannien als auch in Deutschland als klares Statement gegen die nationalsozialistische Kulturpolitik verstanden. Und trotz einiger kritischer Stimmen zog die Ausstellung Tausende von Besuchern in die New Burlington Galleries, ein Publikum, das zumindest neugierig war auf die moderne deutsche Kunst und sich von ihr auch größtenteils beeindruckt zeigte.

1 o. V.: Our London Correspondent. Mr John Opens the German Art Exhibition, in: Manchester Guardian, 8. Juli 1938, S. 10.

2 o. V.: Banned «Degenerates», in: The Scotsman, 8. Juni 1938, S. 10; F. Watson: Banned German Art. London Exhibition of Movements Condemned in Germany, in: Yorkshire Post, 4. Juli 1938, Seite unbekannt; o. V.: «Degenerate Art» Show. A Reply to Munich, in: Manchester Guardian, 6. Juli 1938, S. 7.

3 W. P. Hamsher: Where Painters Must Do What They're Told, in: News Chronicle, 6. Juli 1938, Seite unbekannt; o. V.: Hitler Tells Artists «Work Like This», in: Evening Standard, 11. Juli 1938, S. 4.

4 o. V.: Banned but Cautious, in: Daily Express, 6. Juli 1938, S. 6.

5 o. V.: Entrance «Jam» at Art Show. Augustus John Made Late for Opening, in: The Star, 7. Juli 1938, S. 1.

6 Alfred Kerr: Kulturchronik, in: Pariser Tageszeitung, 13. Juli 1938, S. 3.

7 o. V.: German Art Exhibition to Continue. 12.000 Visitors in a Month, Nazis Protest, in: Daily Telegraph and Morning Post, 12. August 1938, S. 8.

8 o. V.: Der Führer sprach bei der Eröffnung der zweiten Großen Deutschen Kunstausstellung, in: Völkischer Beobachter (Berlin), 11. Juli 1938, S. 1

9 Siehe zum Beispiel: o. V.: Entartete Kunst – diesmal in London, in: Völkischer Beobachter (Wien), 11. Juli 1938, S. 10; Robert Scholz: Der Kunstschwindel von London, in: Völkischer Beobachter (Wien), 3. August 1938, S. 9; Werner Rittich: Saison-Ausverkauf in bolschewistischer Kunst, in: Der Angriff, 3. August 1938, S. 4.

10 Scholz, ibid.

11 Siehe zum Beispiel: o. V.: Modern German Art – Till Now, in: Studio, Juli 1938, S. 160-164; o. V.: Some Topics of the Moment. Twentieth Century German Art, in: Connoisseur, Bd. 102, Nr. 443, Juli 1938, S. 101; o. V.: German Art. Exhibition of XXth-Century German Art at the New Burlington Galleries, in: Apollo, Bd. 28, Juli 1938, S. 94-95.

12 Raymond Mortimer: Miscellany. German Artists, in: New Statesman and Nation, Nr. 286, 16. Juli 1938, S. 112-113

13 Anthony Blunt: Art. Contemporary German Art, in: The Spectator, Bd. 161, 8. Juli 1938, S. 61.

14 Nicolete Gray: German XXth Century Art. London Sees the Pictures Hitler Condemns as Decadent, in: Catholic Herald, 15. Juli 1938, S. 2.

15 o. V.: One Picture in Four Parts, in: Daily Herald, 7. Juli 1938, S. 3.

16 o. V.: German Art Exhibition, in: The Times, 25. Juli 1938, S. 7: «Bis dato wurden dreißig Werke verkauft, darunter sechs von Käthe Kollwitz und fünf von Paul Klee.»

17 Korrespondenz zwischen der Autorin und Keith Moore, Royal Society, London, Februar 2012.

18 RSMA, Brief von Irmgard Burchard an Fred Uhlman, 5. September 1938.

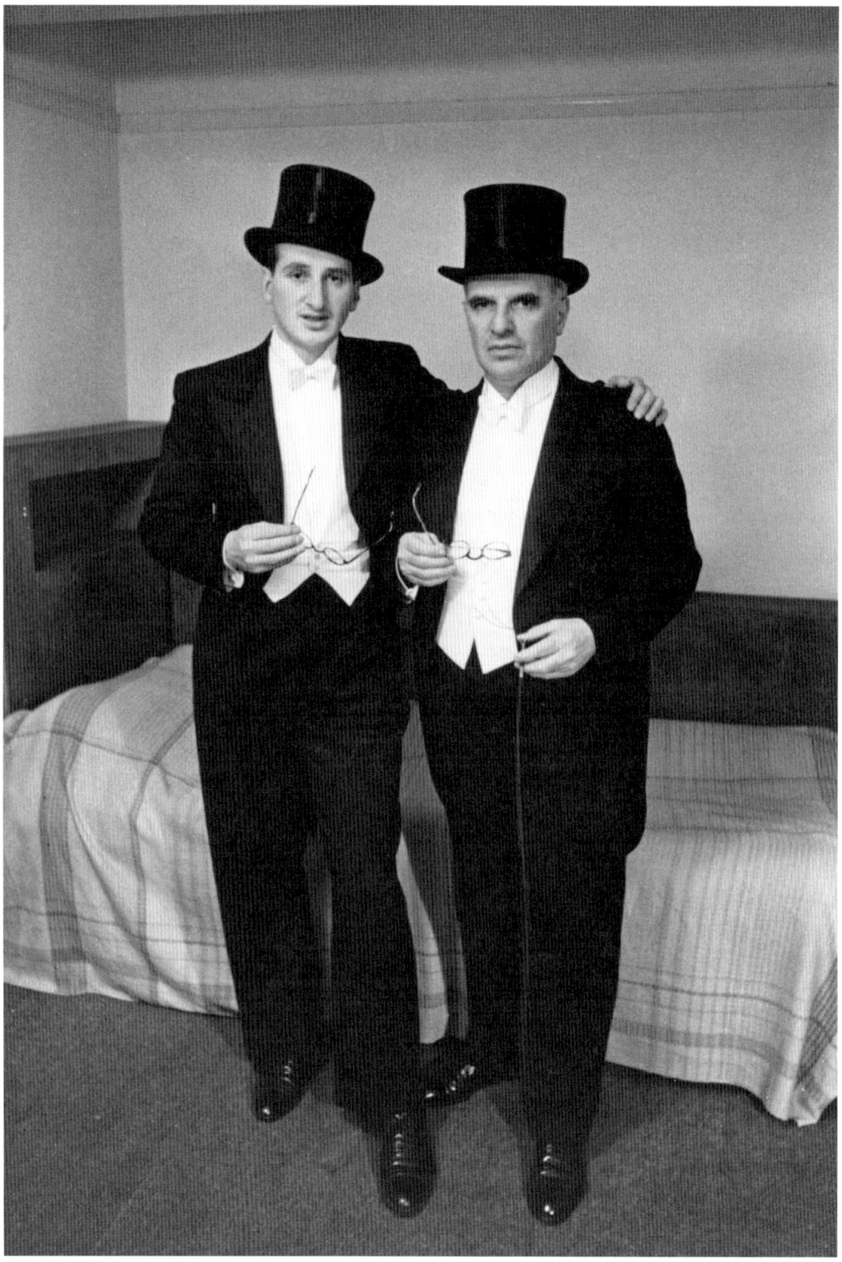

81 Otto (left) and Erich Salomon, London 1935.

Otto Salomon / Peter Hunter: immigrant photographer in London

VERONICA HEKKING

Only one set of photographs survives from the opening of *Twentieth Century German Art*. These were taken by a photographer working in London in 1938, later known as Peter Hunter, born in Berlin as Otto Erich Salomon (1913-2006).

Salomon had grown up in an assimilated, Jewish Berlin family. His father was the renowned press photographer Dr Erich Salomon. At an early age the young Otto helped his father in the dark room. Like his father, Otto began his career by studying law, starting university in 1931. This was the year Erich Salomon published the photobook *Berühmte Zeitgenossen in unbewachten Augenblicken* (*Famous Contemporaries in Unguarded Moments*), which established him as one of Germany's best-known photographers.[1]

Otto Salomon's parents were visiting family in The Hague when Hitler took power in January 1933. They decided to stay. After witnessing the Nazi boycott of Jewish businesses, which took effect from 1 April 1933, Otto was prompted to follow in their footsteps. Contrary to his parents, Otto developed an interest in Zionism during this period. Considering emigration to Palestine, during 1934 he travelled to Lithuania, to train as an agricultural labourer at a Hechalutz farm near Memel. These plans were never realised however, and in May 1935 he moved to London, to work as a trainee with Associated Press.

After a few months Otto Salomon decided to start a career as a photographer, equipped with an old Leica camera which had belonged his father (fig. 81). As his assistant from the Amsterdam period later noted, 'for many immigrants, who were not allowed more than 10 Marks out of Germany, such a camera was their starting capital ... you could make your living with it'.[2] Otto was soon acting as his father's agent in London, for example organising an Erich Salomon exhibition at the Ilford Galleries in the autumn of 1937.

Otto had inherited his father's talent to move with grace and charm in the upper circles of society – he soon had access to the political and diplomatic circles of 1930s London. In 1937, at the yearly dinner of the Foreign Press Association, he captured the elegant British Foreign secretary, Anthony Eden; one year later, at yet another dinner, the Prime Minister Neville Chamberlain. Other renowned and influential subjects were the American newspaper magnate William Randolph Hearst, society photographer Cecil Beaton, the author George Bernard Shaw, Lord Mayor Frank Bowater and Sir Winston Churchill. His subjects included the famous tenor Richard Tauber, in the company of Marlene Dietrich and her friend, the

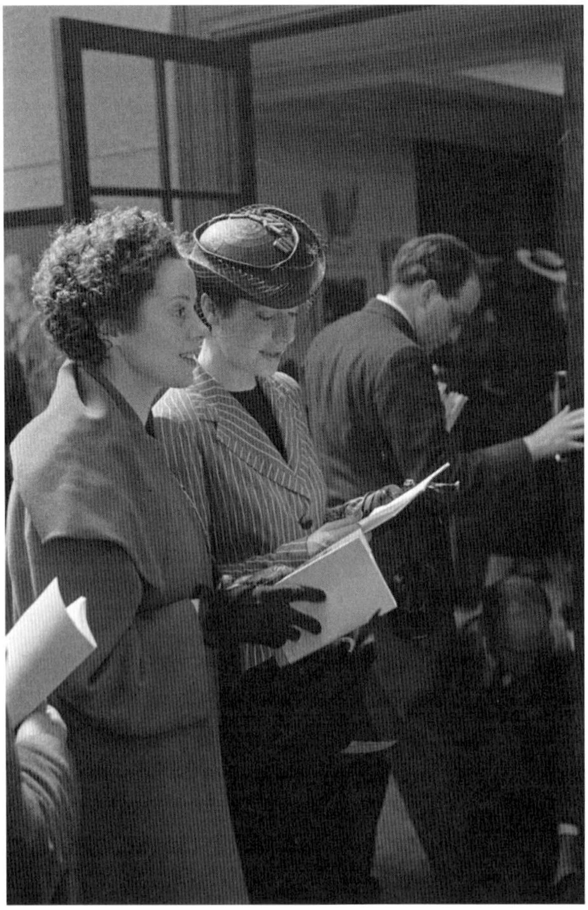

82 Elsa Lanchester at the opening of *Twentieth Century German Art*, 7 July 1938

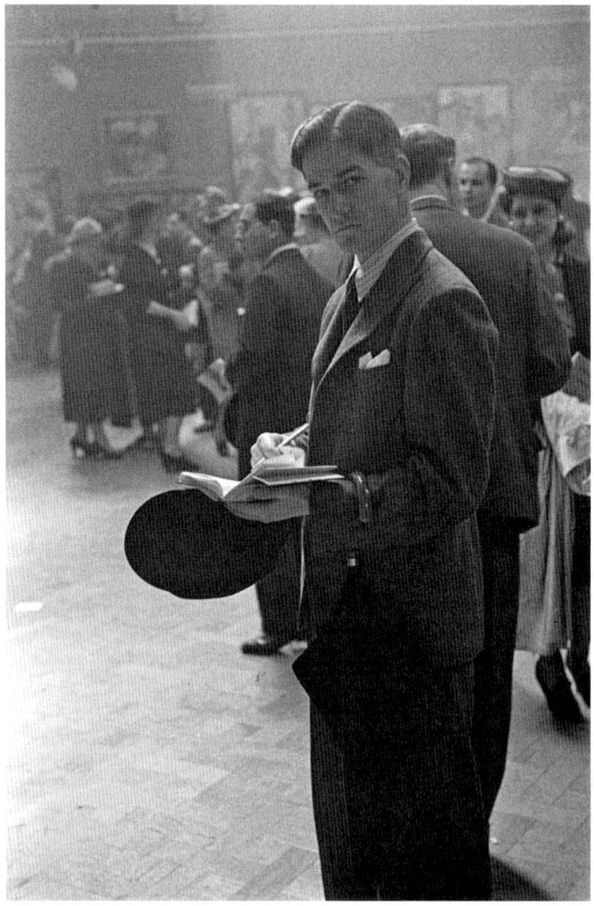

83 David F. Ritchie at the opening of *Twentieth Century German Art*, 7 July 1938.

film star Douglas Fairbanks. Many of these figures – for example Marlene Dietrich – had been photographed earlier in their careers by Erich Salomon.

Though his photographs displayed some similarities with those of his father, Otto developed his own interests and style. In December 1936 he seized the chance to see the other side of London, visiting the Dockland Settlements, a charity organisation in the city's East End. Again he showed his unconventional spirit, depicting the kitchen staff during a reception at a Kensington mansion. A growing interest in the social and political problems of the time can be seen in his various photo-reportages, of the National Birth Control Association (1937) and of Woburn House, the centre of the German-Jewish Aid Committee (25 October 1938). On 9 December 1938 he was also present at an event in support of Zionism, which featured as speakers Lord Rothschild and Chaim Weizmann, leader of the British Zionist Federation.

It was this growing political awareness, coupled with an interest in the arts, which brought Otto Salomon to the opening of *Twentieth Century German Art* on 7 July 1938. During the well-attended opening he took 25 photographs, mainly focussing on the visitors, among them Herbert Read, chairman of the show's organising committee (fig. 73). Salomon's eye also fell upon the actress Elsa Lanchester (fig. 82), and on an elegant young man looking

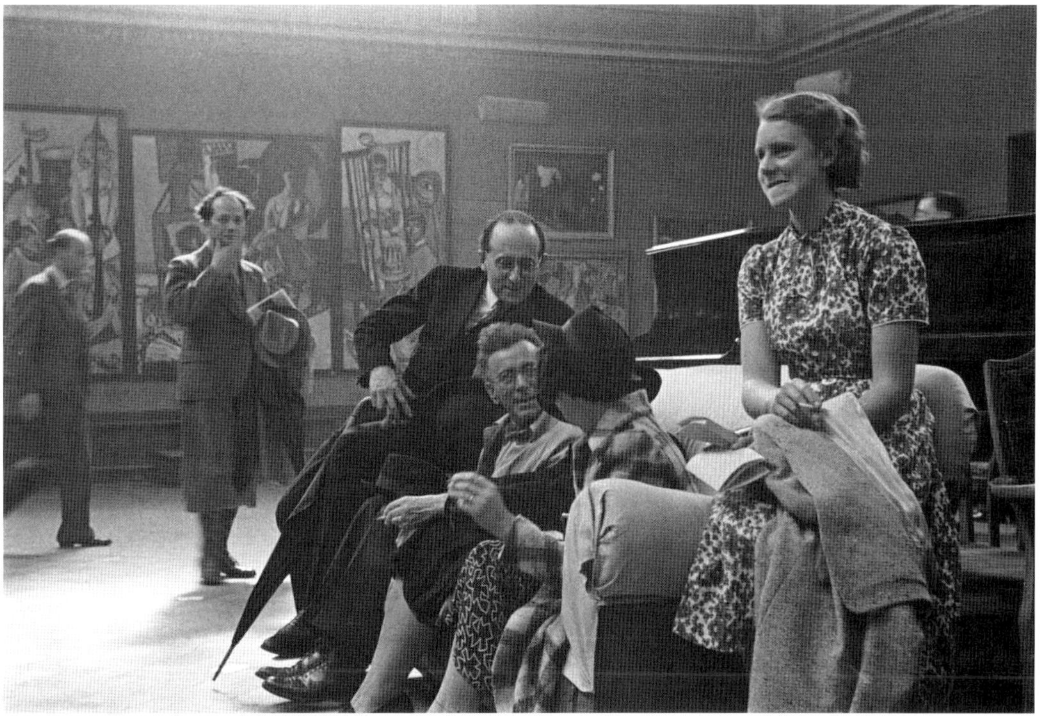

84 Group at the opening of *Twentieth Century German Art*, 7 July 1938

up into the camera: the photo editor of *Life* magazine, David F. Ritchie (fig. 83). Several photographs depicted the painter Augustus John, who made the first opening speech (fig. 72), in lively conversation or listening attentively. The paintings themselves appear only in the background – most notably Max Beckmann's triptych *Temptation* (fig. 84). Salomon's primary concern was the people, their attitudes and their gestures; a quick look, an informal moment, carefully observed before his Leica did its work. In the weeks following the opening, a further set of interior photographs was made by the art historian Ewan Philips, his collection of over 70 shots documenting the artworks on show (see p. 8, 11-14). As one of the founding members of the Artist's Refugee Committee, Philips too was closely involved with the troubles faced by artists who had been forced to flee their country.

After five years working in Britain, in April 1940 Salomon had to apply for the renewal of his work permit. When it looked as if this might be denied, the editor at *Life* David F. Ritchie came to his rescue, writing a letter of recommendation to the British authorities. Nonetheless, like many other German émigrés, Salomon was arrested two months later as an 'enemy alien' and shipped to an internment camp in Australia. After two months he was able to return to Britain where he joined the army, changing his name to Peter Hunter after a pseudonym of his father's.

1 See also Flip Bool and Veronica Hekking (eds.): Erich Salomon, Emigrant in Holland – Peter Hunter, Emigrant in London: Fotos 1933-1940. Amsterdam 1996

2 Paul Hellmann: Peter Hunter. Fotograaf in de schaduw van Erich Salomon; in: NRC-Handelsblad, 11 June 1993

Otto Salomon alias Peter Hunter: Ein emigirierter Photograph in London

VERONICA HEKKING

Zur Vernissage der Ausstellung *Twentieth Century German Art* hat sich nur eine einzge Serie von Fotos erhalten. Sie wurden von einem Fotografen aufgenommen, der in London arbeitete und später unter dem Namen ‹Peter Hunter› bekannt wurde. Er stammte jedoch aus Berlin und war dort als Otto Erich Salomon geboren worden.

Otto Salomon (1913-2006) wuchs in einer assimilierten jüdischen Familie auf. Sein Vater war der berühmte Pressefotograf Dr. Erich Salomon. Schon als Kind half Otto seinem Vater in der Dunkelkammer. Und genauso wie dieser studierte er zunächst Rechtswissenschaften. Als er 1931 mit dem Studium begann, veröffentlichte sein Vater den Bildband *Berühmte Zeitgenossen in unbewachten Augenblicken*, durch den er zu einem der bekanntesten Pressefotografen in Deutschland aufstieg.[1]

Otto Salomons Eltern besuchten gerade Verwandte in Den Haag, als Hitler Ende Januar an die Macht kam. Sie beschlossen, nicht nach Deutschland zurückzukehren. Nach dem Boykott der jüdischen Geschäfte am 1. April schien es Otto geraten, seinen Eltern ins Exil zu folgen. Im Gegensatz zu ihnen fing er in dieser Zeit an, sich für den Zionismus zu interessieren und eine Auswanderung nach Palästina in Erwägung zu ziehen. In diesem Zusammenhang reiste er 1934 nach Litauen und absolvierte dort eine Ausbildung als Landarbeiter auf einem Gut der zionistischen Organisation «Hechaluz» in der Nähe von Memel. Seine Pläne zerschlugen sich jedoch; stattdessen emigrierte er im Mai 1935 nach London, wo er zunächst als Lehrling bei Associated Press arbeitete.

Ausgerüstet mit einer alten Leica seines Vaters entschied sich Otto Salomon nach ein paar Montaten, Fotograf zu werden (Abb. 81). Erich Salomons Assistent aus dessen Amsterdamer Zeit hat dazu später einmal bemerkt: «Viele Emigranten durften nur zehn Mark aus Deutschland mitnehmen. Unter diesen Bedingungen konnte eine solche Kamera eine Existenzgrundlage darstellen.»[2] Bald fungierte Otto als Londoner Agent seines Vaters und organisierte im Herbst 1937 beispielsweise eine Ausstellung von dessen Bilder in den Ilford Galleries.

Otto hatte das Talent seines Vaters geerbt, sich mit Charme und Geschick auf gesellschaftlichem Parkett zu bewegen, so dass er rasch Zugang zu den politischen und diplomatischen Kreisen Londons fand. Beim jährlichen Empfang der Foreign Press Association 1937 machte er Aufnahmen von Anthony Eden, dem eleganten britischen Außenminister. Im darauf folgenden Jahr konnte er während eines anderen Empfangs Premierminister Neville Chamberlain fotografieren. Als weitere Prominente seien der amerikanische Pressemagnat William

Randolph Hearst, der Gesellschaftsfotograf Cecil Beaton, der Autor George Bernard Shaw, der Londoner Bürgermeister Sir Frank Bowater und Sir Winston Churchill erwähnt. Oder er fotografierte den berühmten Tenor Richard Tauber in Begleitung von Marlene Dietrich und Douglas Fairbanks. Einige dieser Persönlichkeiten – unter anderem Marlene Dietrich – waren früher auch schon von Erich Salomon fotografiert worden.

Trotz gewisser Ähnlichkeiten mit den Bildern seines Vaters entwickelte Otto Salomon eigene Interessen und einen eigenen Stil. Im Dezember 1936 ergriff er beispielsweise die Gelegenheit, die andere Seite Londons kennenzulernen, als er die «Dockland Settlements», eine Wohltätigkeitsorganisation in den Arbeitervierteln, besuchte. Seine unkonventionelle Art wurde auch deutlich, als er während eines Empfangs im Schloss Kensington das Küchenpersonal fotografierte. Von wachsendem sozialpolitischen Interesse zeugen seine Bildreportagen über das Nationale Zentrum für Geburtenkontrolle (1937) und über das Woburn House, dem Sitz des Deutsch-jüdischen Hilfskomitees (25. Oktober 1938). Am 9. Dezember 1938 besuchte er eine Veranstaltung zur Unterstützung des Zionismus, auf der Lord Rothschild und Chaim Weizmann, der Chef der British Zionist Federation, Ansprachen hielten.

Sein wachsendes politisches Bewusstsein, verbunden mit seinem Interesse an der Kunst dürften Otto Salomon auch bewogen haben, am 7. Juli 1938 zur Eröffnung der Ausstellung *Twentieth Century German Art* zu gehen. An der gutbesuchten Veranstaltung machte er 25 Aufnahmen, wovon die meisten das Publikum zeigen. Außerdem fotografierte er Herbert Read, den Präsidenten des Organisationskomitees (Abb. 73). Daneben fiel sein Auge auf die Schauspielerin Elsa Lanchester (Abb. 82) und auf einen eleganten jungen Mann: David F. Ritchie, den Bildredakteur des *Life*-Magazins (Abb. 83). Den Maler Augustus John, der die Eröffnungsworte gesprochen hatte (Abb. 72), hielt er mehrfach in lebhaftem Gespräch mit Gästen fest. Auf den Fotos der Ausstellung sind die Gemälde – unter anderem das Triptychon *Versuchung* von Max Beckmann (Abb. 84) – nur im Hintergrund zu sehen, da es Salomon hauptsächlich um die Menschen, um ihre Haltung und Gestik ging. Er hatte einen schnelles Auge für den unverstellten Moment – und schon trat die Leica in Aktion.

In den Wochen nach der Eröffnung hat der Kunsthistoriker Ewan Philips mehr als siebzig Fotos der Ausstellungsräume und gezeigten Kunstwerke aufgenommen (siehe S. 8, 11-14). Als Gründungsmitglied des Artist's Refugee Committee war Philips bestens über die Probleme informiert, mit denen die aus Deutschland vertriebenen Künstler konfrontiert waren.

Nach fünf Jahren in Großbritannien musste Otto Salomon im April 1940 um eine Verlängerung seiner Arbeitsgenehmigung nachsuchen. Als sich abzeichnete, dass sie ihm verweigert werden würde, versuchte David F. Ritchie ihm zu helfen und schrieb einen Empfehlungsbrief an die britischen Behörden – vergebens. Zwei Monate später wurde Salomon wie zahlreiche andere deutsche Emigranten als ‹feindlicher Ausländer› interniert und in ein Lager nach Australien gebracht. Zwei Monate später konnte er nach Großbritannien zurückkehren, trat in die Armee ein und nannte sich fortan ‹Peter Hunter›, nach einem früheren Pseudonym seines Vaters.

1 Siehe auch Flip Bool/Veronica Hekking (Hg.): Erich Salomon, Emigrant in Holland – Peter Hunter, Emigrant in London: Fotos 1933-1940, Amsterdam 1996.

2 Paul Hellmann: Peter Hunter. Fotograaf in de schaduw van Erich Salomon, in: NRC-Handelsblad, 11. Juni 1993.

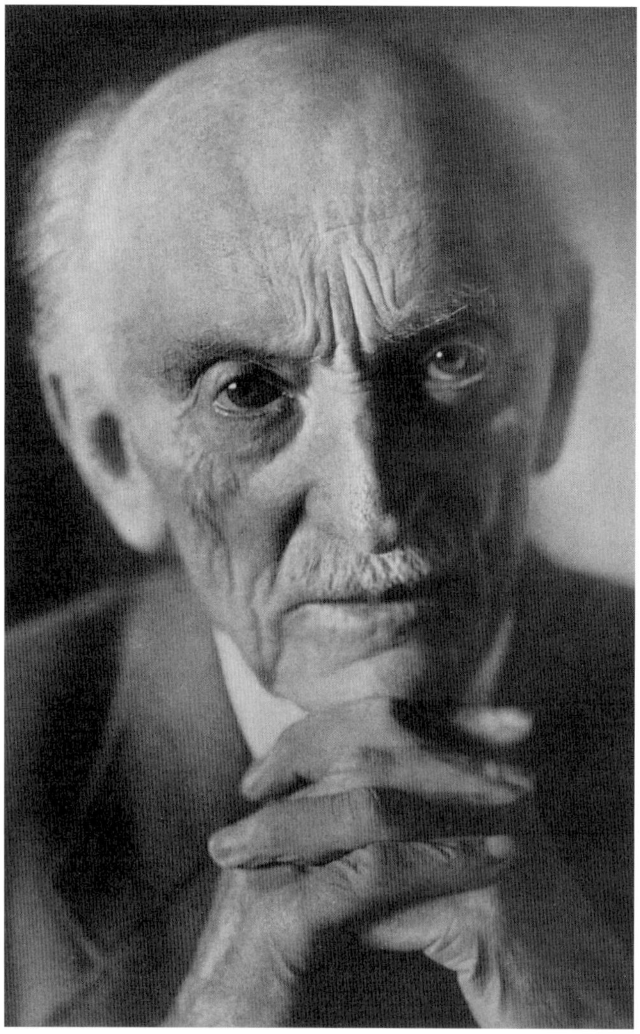

85 Emil Nolde, um 1938.

Ein Künstler reagiert: Emil Nolde und die Ausstellung *Twentieth Century German Art*

AYA SOIKA

Zahlreiche biografische Übersichten zum Leben Emil Noldes verweisen auf seine Teilnahme an der Londoner Ausstellung im Jahr 1938. In solchen Chronologien wird die Schau in einen zeitlichen und inhaltlichen Zusammenhang mit Noldes Diffamierung im Zuge der *Entartete Kunst*-Kampagne von 1937 gestellt. Die Assoziation Noldes mit der inzwischen legendären Ausstellung in den Burlington Galleries, einer «Gegenveranstaltung zur Propaganda-Schau *Entartete Kunst*»[1], fügt sich nahtlos ein in das tradierte Narrativ von Nolde als einem Künstler, der in erster Linie Leidtragender der nationalsozialistischen Kunstpolitik war und mit dessen Situation als ‹Entartetem› sich die Londoner Organisatoren im Sommer 1938 solidarisch erklärten. Doch diese Lesart lässt die Haltung Noldes außer Acht: Bereits im Vorfeld stellte der Künstler klar, dass seine Arbeiten gegen seinen Willen gezeigt würden, und verurteilte die Absicht der Londoner Ausstellung. Dies tat er mit Hilfe seines Freunds Hans Fehr. Der Schweizer Rechtsprofessor war im Frühjahr 1938 um Nolde-Leihgaben für die Schau gebeten worden und machte Nolde überhaupt erst auf die Vorbereitungen aufmerksam. In Noldes Namen wandte er sich am 16. Mai 1938 an das Auswärtige Amt in Berlin (Abb. 86) und teilte Staatssekretär Ernst von Weizsäcker mit: «Nolde und ich sind der Meinung, daß diese Ausstellung (unter jüdischer Führung) zu einer Art Demonstrations-Ausstellung ausgebaut wird. Davon will Nolde nichts wissen und sich nicht beteiligen. Sollten sich trotzdem, etwa aus Privatbesitz, Bilder meines Freundes dort finden, so geschieht dies *gegen seinen Willen*. Ich wäre Ihnen sehr dankbar, wenn Sie dies an kompetenter Stelle mitteilen oder mir sagen würden, wohin ich ev. eine solche Mitteilung richten soll. Denn ich möchte, daß man im Reiche weiß, wie solidarisch sich Nolde mit dem deutschen Staat fühlt. Sie verstehen gut, wie wichtig diese Haltung ev. für meinen Freund werden kann.»[2]

Ernst von Weizäcker bestätigte Fehr, daß seine «Äußerungen betreffend die Haltung des Herrn Nolde an die dafür zuständige Stelle gelange.»[3] Dies leitete Fehr beruhigt an Nolde weiter: «Du siehst, lieber Freund, soweit wäre alles in Ordnung. Der Staat weiß nun, daß mit Deinem Willen keine Bilder ausgestellt werden dürfen. Das ist wichtig.»[4] Damit hatte Nolde im Vorfeld das in seiner Macht Stehende getan, um sich aktenkundig von den Organisatoren zu distanzieren und dem nationalsozialistischen Staat gegenüber vorsorglich seine Loyalität zu bekunden.[5] Auf die Möglichkeit, dass Leihgaben ihm nicht bekannter Besitzer in der Ausstellung gezeigt wurden, hatte er dagegen keinen Einfluss. So kam es, dass Nolde unfreiwillig als einer von insgesamt 64 Künstlern mit mindestens zwei Gemälden, sieben Aquarellen und

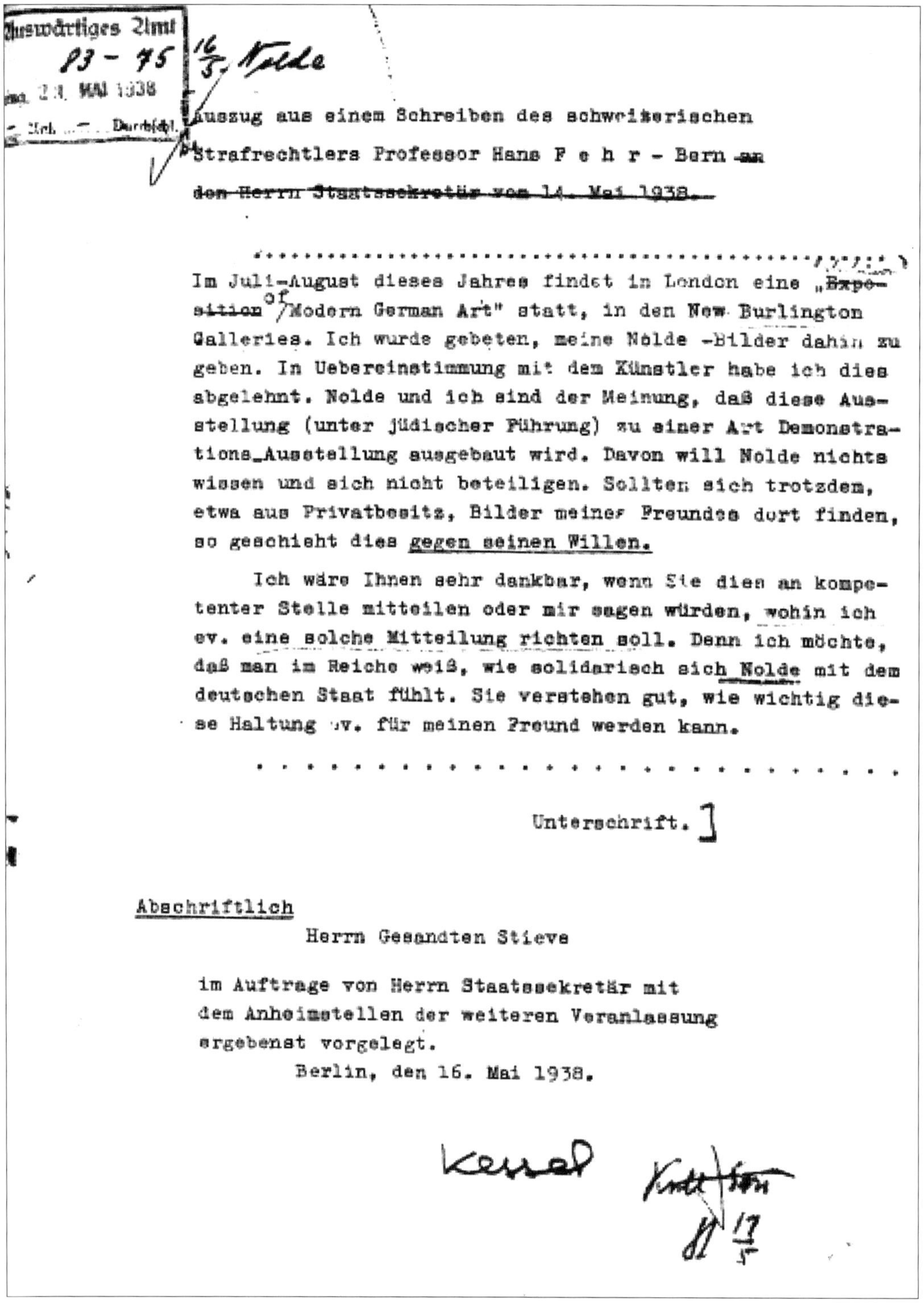

Auswärtiges Amt
83 – 75
24. MAI 1938

16/5. Nolde

Auszug aus einem Schreiben des schweizerischen Strafrechtlers Professor Hans F e h r – Bern ~~an den Herrn Staatssekretär vom 14. Mai 1938.~~

. . . .

Im Juli-August dieses Jahres findet in London eine „~~Exposition~~ of Modern German Art" statt, in den New Burlington Galleries. Ich wurde gebeten, meine Nolde -Bilder dahin zu geben. In Uebereinstimmung mit dem Künstler habe ich dies abgelehnt. Nolde und ich sind der Meinung, daß diese Ausstellung (unter jüdischer Führung) zu einer Art Demonstrations_Ausstellung ausgebaut wird. Davon will Nolde nichts wissen und sich nicht beteiligen. Sollten sich trotzdem, etwa aus Privatbesitz, Bilder meines Freundes dort finden, so geschieht dies gegen seinen Willen.

Ich wäre Ihnen sehr dankbar, wenn Sie dies an kompetenter Stelle mitteilen oder mir sagen würden, wohin ich ev. eine solche Mitteilung richten soll. Denn ich möchte, daß man im Reiche weiß, wie solidarisch sich Nolde mit dem deutschen Staat fühlt. Sie verstehen gut, wie wichtig diese Haltung ev. für meinen Freund werden kann.

. . . .

Unterschrift.

Abschriftlich

Herrn Gesandten Stieve

im Auftrage von Herrn Staatssekretär mit dem Anheimstellen der weiteren Veranlassung ergebenst vorgelegt.

Berlin, den 16. Mai 1938.

86 Auszug aus dem Schreiben von Hans Fehr an das Auswärtige Amt, Berlin, Abschrift vom 16.5.1938.

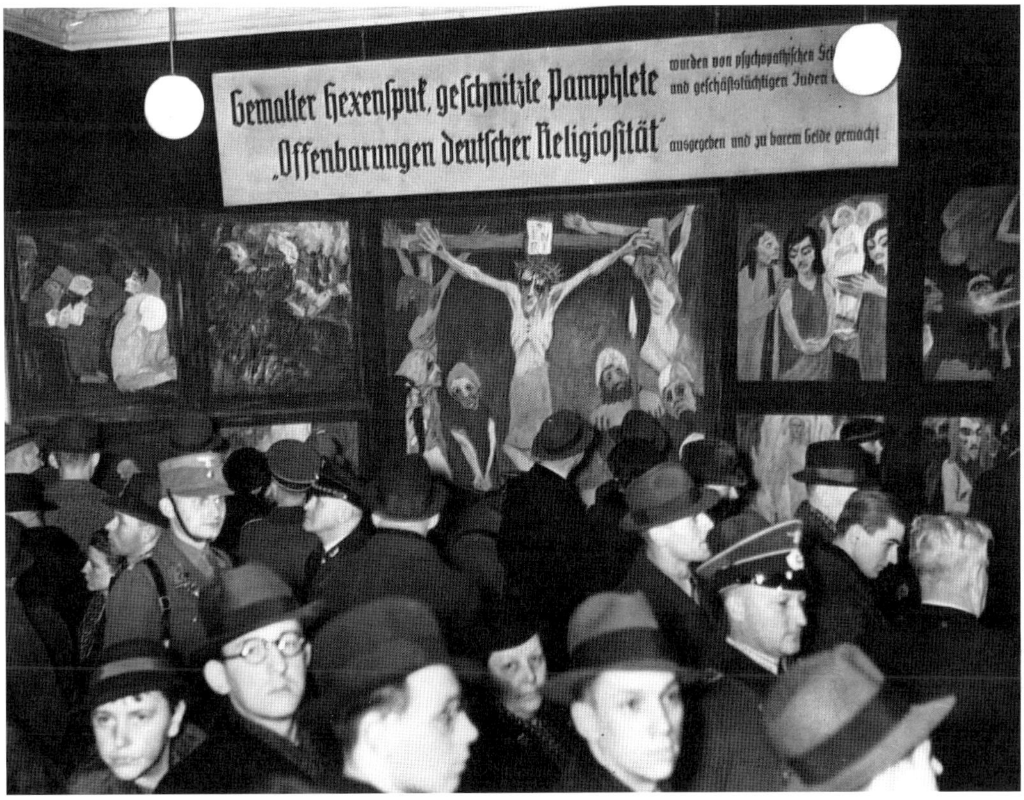

87 Emil Noldes *Das Leben Christi* auf der Ausstellung *Entartete Kunst* in Berlin, Februar 1938.

jeweils einer Zeichnung und Lithographie vertreten war (Abb. 89). Im Vergleich zu Max Beckmann, dessen Triptychon *Versuchung* vielfach publiziert wurde, oder zu Franz Marc, dessen *Blaue Pferde* als Farbabbildung den Katalog zierte, spielten Noldes Werke allerdings eine weniger zentrale Rolle.[6] Dies war in der Münchner *Entartete Kunst*-Ausstellung von Juli 1937 anders gewesen, hier war Nolde mit 33 Gemälden nicht nur der am prominentesten vertretene Künstler, sondern mit seinem neunteiligen Hauptwerk *Das Leben Christi* auch das Aushängeschild der Schau (Abb. 87). Für Nolde war dies eine «Entehrung», die ihn tief verletzte und dazu führte, dass er sich aktiv um die Rückgabe seines Gemälde-Zyklus einsetzte, der ihm persönlich gehörte und anders als die meisten übrigen Exponate nicht aus Museumsbesitz stammte.

Warum also positionierte sich Nolde, ein Opfer der Kampagne *Entartete Kunst*, als Gegner des Londoner Ausstellungsprojekts? Hätte er nicht allen Grund gehabt, die Initiative der Organisatoren als Geste der Solidarität dankbar anzuerkennen?

Die Schau *Twentieth Century German Art* fand zu einer Zeit statt, in der Nolde mit Nachdruck seine Loyalität zum Regime zu bekräftigen versuchte, indem er sich sowohl von anderen ‹Entarteten› als auch von einer angeblich jüdisch dominierten Kunstszene abgrenzte. Ohne es zu ahnen, erwiesen ihm die Londoner Organisatoren nun einen Bärendienst, der Noldes Bemühungen um demonstrative Linientreue (er war seit Herbst 1934 Mitglied der NSDAP in Nordschleswig) zu unterlaufen drohte – zumal die Nolde-Leihgaben größtenteils von jüdischen Eigentümern stammten, die aus Deutschland nach Großbritannien oder in die Schweiz geflohen waren: Zwei Blumenaquarelle hatte der nach London emigrierte Berliner Sammler Leo Finkelstein zur Verfügung gestellt; aus der Sammlung des ebenfalls nach London geflohenen Hanauer Juristen Dr. Ernst J. Nelkenstock (später Norton) wurde ein Ölporträt gezeigt (Kat.-Nr. 23); von dem in Zürich ansässigen Sammler Dr. Goldberg kam ein weiteres Aquarell, und die ausgestellte Lithographie gehörte dem von den Nazis als Halbjuden eingestuften Frankfurter Kunsthändler und Antiquar Mario Uzielli, der Anfang 1936 in die Schweiz emigriert war. Im Katalog waren diese Leihgeber namentlich genannt, direkt hinter dem Titel des jeweiligen Nolde-Werks. Diese öffentliche Nachbarschaft von Nolde und jüdischen Sammlern lief den Anstrengungen des Künstlers unmittelbar zuwider, sich als Pionier im Kampf gegen die jüdischen Akteure der Berliner Kunstszene zu stilisieren, wie er es in seinen schriftlichen Loyalitätsbekundungen gegenüber verschiedenen Parteifunktionären mehrfach getan hatte. Damit wollte er belegen, dass er weder ‹entartet› noch ‹undeutsch› war. Sein Schreiben an Kultusminister Bernhard Rust vom August 1937 enthielt eine systematische Argumentation in sieben Punkten, deren erster lautete: «Als fast einzigster deutscher Künstler habe ich um die Jahre 1910 einen Kampf gegen das damalige, unsaubere Kunsthändlertum, gegen Überfremdung der deutschen Kunst und gegen die Liebermannsche und Cassirersche Macht geführt. – und verloren.»[7] Am 2. Juli 1938, also nur fünf Tage vor Eröffnung der Londoner Schau, schrieb Nolde einen Brief an Propagandaminister Joseph Goebbels, indem er erneut betonte, er habe «vor Beginn der Nationalsozialistischen Bewegung als fast einzigster deutscher Künstler in offenem Kampf gegen die Überfremdung der deutschen Kunst, gegen das unsaubere Kunsthändlertum und gegen die Machenschaften der Liebermann- und Cassirerzeit gekämpft ... ein Kampf gegen eine große Übermacht, der mir jahrzehntelange materielle Not und Nachteile brachte.»[8] Noldes Argumentation in beiden Briefen lief nun Gefahr, unglaubwürdig zu erscheinen.

Denn auch die NS-Führungsriege erfuhr von der Schau in London. Den ersten öffentlichen Angriff startete Adolf Hitler persönlich, und zwar in seiner Eröffnungsrede zur *Großen Deutschen Kunstausstellung* am 10. Juli 1938. Sowohl in dieser Rede als auch in den folgenden NS-Presseberichten (siehe S. 185, 190 f.) wurde die enge Beziehung zwischen moderner Kunst und jüdischen Händlern, Sammlern und Emigranten angeprangert. Am 5. August 1938 schrieb Ernst Gosebruch, der ehemalige Direktor des Essener Museums Folkwang, in einem Brief an Nolde: «Meine Tochter wird in London die moderne deutsche Kunstausstellung sehen, deren Veranstalter ja [Max] Sauerland[t]s Freund, H[erbert] Read, ist. Aus der Berichten geht aber schon hervor, daß man dort in der Hauptsache Bilder sehen wird, wie sie bei Flechtheim und Consorten gezeigt wurden.»[9] Auch Gosebruch übernahm das Klischee eines durch den jüdischen Kunsthandel geprägten modernen Kanons, eventuell ohne zu wissen, dass Flechtheim bereits am 9. März 1937 im Londoner Exil verstorben war.

Eine Auswertung der englischen Presseberichterstattung durch die deutschen Behörden scheint allerdings erst mit Verzögerung erfolgt zu sein. Nach Ende der Ausstellung am 27. August 1938 sollte genauer ermittelt werden, welchen Anteil die jeweiligen Künstler daran hatten, so sie – wie Nolde – als Mitglieder der Reichskammer geführt wurden. Nolde erhielt am 3. Dezember 1938 vom Präsidenten der Reichskammer der bildenden Künste folgende Nachfrage: «Es ist mir bekanntgeworden, dass Sie sich im Juli d. J. an der Ausstellung der New Burlington Galleries in London beteiligt haben. Ich bitte Sie um Mitteilung, von welcher Stelle die Einladungen zu dieser Ausstellung ergangen sind und welche Stelle Ihnen die Ausfuhrgenehmigung für Ihre Werke erteilte.»[10]

Nolde erhielt dieses Schreiben frühestens am 4. Dezember. Am 6. Dezember 1938 entwarf er einen Brief an die «Führung und Partei» der NSDAP, in dem er mit antisemitischen Loyalitätsbekundungen reagierte. Um den Eindruck einer Verbindung zu einem jüdischen Kunstnetzwerk aus dem Weg zu räumen, stellte Nolde dem Propagandaministerium und dem Reichspressechef gegenüber klar: «Es wird gesagt, dass meine Kunst von Juden gefördert und gekauft worden ist. Auch das ist falsch. Einzelne versprengte Bilder sind in späteren Jahren durch den Kunsthandel zu Juden gekommen, im Allgemeinen jedoch bekämpfen sie mich. Die Reinheit und das ursprüngliche Deutsche in meiner Kunst haben sie bespöttelt und nie gewollt. Meine wesentlichsten Bilder sind alle im deutschen Besitz, von Deutschen gekauft, die durchaus nicht fremdländisch angekränkelt, sondern bewusst Deutsche sind.»[11]

Außerdem betonte Nolde, dass er auch in der Vergangenheit kein Nutznießer des jüdischen Kunstsystems gewesen sei: «Als 15 oder 20 Jahre später [nach seinem Liebermann-Streit 1910/11] die Grossjuden Cassirer und Flechtheim dem Drängen der Künstlerjugend folgend, mich zu grossen Kollektivaustellungen aufforderten, lehnte ich es jeweils ab, – innerstem Widerspruch folgend.»[12]

Im Zuge der antisemitischen Radikalisierung hielten es Nolde und seine Frau Ada für nötig, die offiziellen Stellen über seine Haltung aufzuklären. Ausschlaggebend hierfür war aber nicht nur die Anfrage der Reichskammer, sondern vor allem auch die Berichterstattung in der Presse, die nagelegte, dass auch Nolde Teil der jüdischen Kunstverschwörung sei, ja, die aufgrund der gewählten Formulierungen suggerierte, Nolde sei selbst Jude.

Bereits am 25. November 1938 hatte Ada Nolde eine Beschwerde an den Redakteur des *Flensburger Generalanzeigers* geschickt. In dem Artikel «Der Feind im eigenen Land – Juden als Kulturbolschewisten» fiel Noldes Name «im Zusammenhang mit den Namen: Alfred Kerr, Paul Cassirer u. a. und zwar als ob er dazugehört hätte».[13] Auch Nolde bezog sich in der erwähnten Stellungnahme anderthalb Wochen später auf diesen Beitrag, in dem er mit dem nach London emigrierten Schriftsteller Alfred Kerr, dem verstorbenen Kunsthändler Paul Cassirer und dessen nach Oxford emigrierten Cousin, dem Verleger Bruno Cassirer, sowie dem der modernen Kunst gegenüber aufgeschlossenem Unternehmer Ludwig Katzenellenbogen assoziiert wurde. Die genannten Personen bezeichnete er als «die ärgsten Feinde meines Lebens» und beklagte, dass das «Verkennen und Nichtwissen des Tatsächlichen alles verdreht.»[14]

Seine Erklärung vom 6. Dezember schickte er mit ausgewählten Passagen seiner Autobiografie *Jahre der Kämpfe* (1934, Abb. 88) an Ernst Schröder in Flensburg, der sie dem Adjutanten des Reichspressechefs Otto Dietrich übergab. Auch an das Propagandaministerium ging eine Version. Noldes Stellungnahme trug schon einige Tage später erste Früchte. Am 8. Dezember 1938 gab das Propagandaministerium die folgende Presseanweisung aus: «Der Maler Emil *Nolde* ist kein *Jude* … [er ist] sogar Pg. [Parteigenosse].»[15]

In seinem Weihnachtsbrief schrieb Nolde an Fehr, dass seine an die Ämter gerichtete Bitte, «meinen ehrlichen deutschen Namen nicht mit den benannten jüdischen Grössen durch die Presse schleifen zu wollen», Erfolg gehabt habe.[16] Ihm war sowohl vom Reichspressechef sowie vom Propagandaministerium mitgeteilt worden, «daß eine solche Verquickung künftig nicht mehr geschehen werde.»[17] Um die in Gang gesetzte Rehabilitierung Noldes auf möglichst vielen Ebenen fortzuführen und dem Ministerium dessen Loyalität gegenüber der Partei überzeugend zu beweisen, kontaktierte der mit dem Künstler befreundete Staatsrecht-

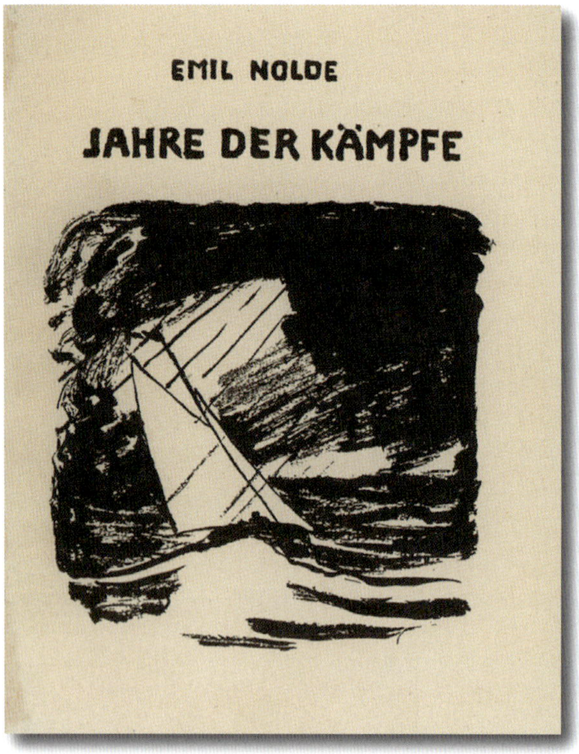

88 Emil Nolde: *Jahre der Kämpfe*. Berlin 1934, Schutzumschlag

ler Carl Schmitt den Leiter der Hauptgeschäftsstelle der Organisation Volksbund für das Deutschtum im Ausland in Berlin. Dieser schickte Carl Schmitt am 16. Dezember die gewünschte Bestätigung: «Die Partei schätzt Herrn Nolde als Parteigenossen und als Landsmann.»[18]

So endete für Nolde das Jahr 1938 befriedigend, denn seine Stellungnahmen brachten den gewünschten Erfolg. Sein beschlagnahmter Gemälde-Zyklus *Das Leben Christi* wurde ihm zurückerstattet, und Anfang des Jahres 1939 erhielt er sogar die Nachricht, dass sein Name mit der Ausstellung *Entartete Kunst* nicht mehr in Verbindung gebracht werden dürfe. Tatsächlich wurden auf den folgenden Stationen der Schau keine Nolde-Gemälde mehr gezeigt. Ada Nolde berichtete am 9. Februar 1939, im Propagandaministerium soll ein «Umschwung zu unsern Gunsten geschehen sein».[19] Um diesen ‹Umschwung› hatten sich die Eheleute Nolde und ihr gut vernetzter Bekanntenkreis seit Juli 1937 intensiv bemüht. Dass Nolde in London mit Werken aus jüdischem Besitz Seite an Seite mit emigrierten Künstlern ausgestellt worden war, hatte diese Bemühungen zu untergraben gedroht und sein Bedürfnis verstärkt, sich durch Betonung seines Antisemitismus von den Zielen der Schau abzugrenzen. Er fürchtete eine Vereinnahmung durch die dortigen Organisatoren, zumal sie seine Kunst in einem Kontext präsentierten, der seinem nationalistisch geprägten Selbstverständnis nicht entsprach. Sowohl das Schreiben Fehrs im Vorfeld als auch Noldes Stellungnahme vom 6. Dezember 1938 müssen als Ausdruck seiner Haltung verstanden werden, die noch 1938/39 das nationalsozialistische Regime befürwortete und dessen antijüdische Politik akzeptierte. Die *Exhibition of Twentieth Century German Art* und ihre Darstellung in der deutschen Öffentlichkeit war damit nicht vereinbar.

Mit Dank an Dr. Christian Ring und die Ada und Emil Nolde Stiftung Seebüll/Neukirchen, in der Folge abgekürzt als ANS, für den Zugang zu den Quellen infolge eines Forschungsprojekts zur Aufarbeitung Emil Noldes im Nationalsozialismus. In enger inhaltlicher Verbindung zu diesem Beitrag steht mein Text zu Emil Nolde und der Wanderausstellung *Entartete Kunst* (Erscheinungstermin 2018).

1 Vgl. z. B. die Biografie zusammengestellt von Julia Bremer, in: Felix Krämer (Hg.): Emil Nolde. Retrospektive. Ausst.-Kat. Staedel Museum Frankfurt a. M., München 2014, S. 281-285, hier S. 285

2 Auszug aus dem Schreiben von Hans Fehr, maschinenschriftliche Abschrift vom 16.5.1938, Inland II A/B, ‹Deutsche Emigranten im Ausland›, Bd. 18 [R 99592 / Stempel: Auswärtiges Amt / 83-75 16/5 Nolde / eing. 23. Mai 1938 / Abt. – Deutschl.]. Das Schriftstück wurde bereits 2001 zitiert in: Alexander Stephan: Hetz- und Greuelpropaganda. Die Überwachung der deutschen Exilschriftsteller in Grossbritannien durch das Auswartige Amt, in: James M. Ritchie (Hg.): German-speaking Exiles in Great Britain, Leiden/Boston 2001, Bd. 3, S. 23-40, hier S. 32

3 Hans Fehr an Emil Nolde, 20.5.1938, mit Abschrift des Schreiben vom Staatssekretär des Auswärtigen Amts Weizäcker, ANS

4 Ebd.

5 Nolde war eigentlich bekannt, dass Herbert Read bereits vor 1933 eine Ausstellung deutscher Kunst in London plante. Damals hatte Max Sauerlandt ihn gebeten, Read den ersten Band seiner Memoiren zu senden. Read bedankte sich auch bei Nolde persönlich und Sauerlandt berichtete Nolde im August 1932, Read «hat das Buch gelesen und ist ganz begeistert.» Bei einem geplanten Vortrag Sauerlandts über moderne deutsche Kunst in Edinburgh und Glasgow im Winter 1932 plante er, Nolde «als Zentralfigur» darzustellen (Max Sauerlandt an Ada und Emil Nolde, 6.8.1932, ANS)

6 Allerdings war Nolde unter den zwanzig namentlich genannten Künstlern auf der Einladung zur Eröffnung genannt. Max Pechstein, der auch vertreten war, wurde auf der Einladung hingegen nicht erwähnt. Vgl. Ausst.-Kat. 1988/89 (Stationen der Moderne), Abb. 10/3, S. 316.

7 Emil Nolde an den Reichsminister für Wissenschaft, Bernhard Rust, 5.8.1937, Abschrift ANS. Zum Beweis verwies Nolde auf seine Autobiografie *Jahre der Kämpfe*, die eine ausführliche Schilderung des Liebermann-Konflikts enthielt.

8 Emil Nolde an Joseph Goebbels, 2.7.1938, Bundesarchiv Berlin, R 55 21014.

9 Ernst Gosebruch an Emil Nolde, 5.8.1938, Abschrift in ANS.

10 Der Präsident der Reichskammer, gez. v. Kittlitz, an Emil Nolde, 3.12.1938, ANS.

11 Typoskript Noldes mit Korrekturen in der Handschrift Noldes, Entwurf eines Briefes an den Reichspressechef, 6.12.1938, S. 2-3, ANS.

12 Ibid.

13 Ada Nolde an Otto Entmayr, 25.11.1938, ANS. Die Tageszeitung, auf die Ada sich beruft, ist im Stadtarchiv Flensburg unter diesem Titel für das Jahr nicht bekannt. In den *Flensburger Nachrichten* war am 23.11. 1938, Nr. 274, ein ähnlicher Artikel mit dem Titel «Judas Verbrechen am deutschen Volk» abgedruckt – mit Erwähnung einiger der auch von Ada Genannten in der Sektion «Kunst und Wissenschaft», allerdings ohne Nennung Noldes. Mit Dank an Marvin Nissen, Stadtarchiv Flensburg, für die freundliche Auskunft und Übermittlung.

14 Ibid.

15 Hans Bohrmann und Gabriele Toepser-Ziegert (Hg.): NS-Presseanweisungen der Vorkriegszeit. Edition und Dokumentation, Bd. 6, München 1999, S. 1173, Eintrag zum 8.12.1938.

16 Emil Nolde an Hans Fehr, o. D. «Weihnachten 1938» [ca. 24.12.1938], ANS.

17 Ibid.

18 Dr. von Türke an Carl Schmitt, 16.12.1938, beigelegt als Abschrift in einem Brief vom 04.02.1939 von Duska Schmitt an Ada Nolde, ANS.

19 Ada Nolde an Duska Schmitt, 9.2.1939, Landesarchiv Düsseldorf, Nachlass Carl Schmitt [RW 265-10422/1]. Trotz dieser Entwicklungen wurde Nolde 1941 aus der Reichskammer der bildenden Künste ausgeschlossen.

An Artist Reacts: Emil Nolde and the *Twentieth Century German Art* Exhibition

AYA SOIKA

Biographical studies of the painter Emil Nolde often refer to his participation in the 1938 London exhibition *Twentieth Century German Art*. In most cases, the London show is mentioned in the context of Nolde's defamation as a 'degenerate artist' during 1937. Associating Nolde with the legendary show in the New Burlington Galleries, presented as "a counter-event to the *Degenerate Art* propaganda exhibition",[1] fits seamlessly into the traditional image of the artist as a victim of Nazi cultural policies, who stood in solidarity with the organisers of the London show. Yet this narrative ignores the fact that Nolde condemned *Twentieth Century German Art* before the exhibition had even opened, declaring – through his friend, the Swiss Law Professor Hans Fehr – that his works were being shown against his will. It was Fehr who had first informed Nolde of the London project, having been asked in the spring of 1938 to lend works to the exhibition. Writing on the artist's behalf, on 16 May 1938 Fehr made contact with the German Foreign Office, as he set out to State Secretary Ernst von Weizsäcker (fig. 86): "[...] Nolde and I are of the opinion that this show (under Jewish management) is being expanded into a kind of demonstration exhibition. Nolde doesn't want to know anything about it, and does not want to participate. But if any works by my friend are shown there, for example from private collections, this will be against his will. I would be very grateful if you could convey this to the relevant office or tell me where I should direct such a communication. Because I want those in the Reich to know the solidarity Nolde feels with the German state. You understand how important this stance may become for my friend."[2]

In his answer, von Weizsäcker reassured Fehr that the "remarks concerning Mr Nolde's position will reach the competent authority."[3] Relieved, Fehr forwarded the news to Nolde: "You see, dear friend, thus far everything is in order. The state knows that no works have been exhibited with your permission. This is important."[4] Nolde had done what he could both to officially distance himself from the organizers of Twentieth Century German Art, and to carefully avow his loyalty to the National Socialist state.[5] The possibility of unknown collectors lending works was, however, beyond his control. In the end Nolde was indeed among the 64 artists shown in London, represented against his will by at least two oil paintings, one drawing, one lithograph and seven watercolours (fig. 89). Compared to artists such as Max Beckmann, whose triptych *Temptation* was reproduced across the contemporary press, or Franz Marc, whose *Blue Horses* adorned the catalogue cover, Nolde's works played a less central role. At the exhibition Degenerate Art staged in Munich the previous year, the story

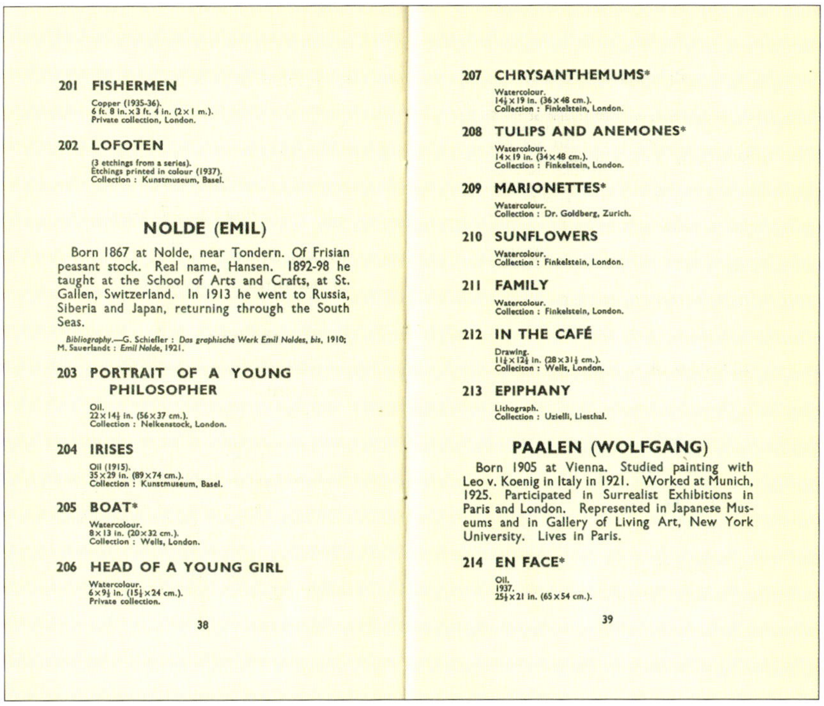

201 **FISHERMEN**
Copper (1935-36).
6 ft. 8 in.×3 ft. 4 in. (2×1 m.).
Private collection, London.

202 **LOFOTEN**
(3 etchings from a series).
Etchings printed in colour (1937).
Collection : Kunstmuseum, Basel.

NOLDE (EMIL)

Born 1867 at Nolde, near Tondern. Of Frisian peasant stock. Real name, Hansen. 1892-98 he taught at the School of Arts and Crafts, at St. Gallen, Switzerland. In 1913 he went to Russia, Siberia and Japan, returning through the South Seas.

Bibliography.—G. Schiefler : *Das graphische Werk Emil Noldes, bis*, 1910; M. Sauerlandt : *Emil Nolde*, 1921.

203 **PORTRAIT OF A YOUNG PHILOSOPHER**
Oil.
22×14½ in. (56×37 cm.).
Collection : Nelkenstock, London.

204 **IRISES**
Oil (1915).
35×29 in. (89×74 cm.).
Collection : Kunstmuseum, Basel.

205 **BOAT***
Watercolour.
8×13 in. (20×32 cm.).
Collection : Wells, London.

206 **HEAD OF A YOUNG GIRL**
Watercolour.
6×9½ in. (15½×24 cm.).
Private collection.

38

207 **CHRYSANTHEMUMS***
Watercolour.
14½×19 in. (36×48 cm.).
Collection : Finkelstein, London.

208 **TULIPS AND ANEMONES***
Watercolour.
14×19 in. (34×48 cm.).
Collection : Finkelstein, London.

209 **MARIONETTES***
Watercolour.
Collection : Dr. Goldberg, Zurich.

210 **SUNFLOWERS**
Watercolour.
Collection : Finkelstein, London.

211 **FAMILY**
Watercolour.
Collection : Finkelstein, London.

212 **IN THE CAFÉ**
Drawing.
11½×12½ in. (28×31½ cm.).
Colleciton : Wells, London.

213 **EPIPHANY**
Lithograph.
Collection : Uzielli, Liesthal.

PAALEN (WOLFGANG)

Born 1905 at Vienna. Studied painting with Leo v. Koenig in Italy in 1921. Worked at Munich, 1925. Participated in Surrealist Exhibitions in Paris and London. Represented in Japanese Museums and in Gallery of Living Art, New York University. Lives in Paris.

214 **EN FACE***
Oil.
1937.
25½×21 in. (65×54 cm.).

39

89 Page from the *Twentieth Century German Art* exhibition catalogue, with a list of the works by Emil Nolde and their lenders.

had been quite different: with 33 oil paintings Nolde was not only among the best-represented artists; his nine-panel *The Life of Christ* (fig. 87) was among the highest-profile pieces in the show. Nolde saw his presence in Munich as a "dishonour" which wounded him deeply, leading him to actively seek the return of *The Life of Christ*. Unlike many other exhibits in Munich this work had not belonged to the museum from which it was confiscated, and still belonged to the artist in 1937.

Why then did Nolde, a victim of the 'degenerate art' campaign, position himself as an opponent of the London exhibition project? Did he not in fact have every reason to thank the organisers for their support?

Twentieth Century German Art took place during a period in which Nolde was working hard to emphasise his loyalty to the new government, to set himself apart from both the other 'degenerate' artists, and the allegedly Jewish-dominated art scene. Thus the organisers of *Twentieth Century German Art* unknowingly worked against him, as he sought to strengthen this position (indeed, the artist had been a member of the Nazi Party in Nordschleswig since autumn 1934). To make matters worse, most of the Nolde loans to London came from German-Jewish collectors, who had been forced into exile in Britain or Switzerland: two watercolours came from the Berlin collector Leo Finkelstein, in exile in London; one oil portrait from the lawyer Ernst Nelkenstock (later Norton), formerly of Hanau, then also living in London (Kat.-Nr. 23); one further aquarelle from the Zürich collector Dr. Goldberg; and a lithograph from the Frankfurt art dealer Mario Uzielli, who had been categorised as a 'half Jew' by the Nazi authorities and who had been living in exile in Switzerland since 1936. Each of these lenders were named in the London catalogue, directly next to their works. This public association of Nolde with Jewish collectors strongly contradicted the artist's own position, specifically the repeated declarations he had made to various Nazi officials, styling himself as a pioneer in the struggle against Jewish actors on the Berlin art scene and offering this as proof that he was neither 'degenerate' nor 'un-German'. A letter send to the Minister of Science, Education and Culture Bernhard Rust for example in August 1937 presented a systematic argumentation in seven points, the first of which read: "In around 1910, I was almost the only German artist to wage a battle against the unclean art trade of the time, against the infiltration of German art by foreigners, against the powers of Liebermann and Cassirer – a battle which I lost."[7] On 2 July 1938, just five days before the opening of the London show, Nolde sent a similar letter to Propaganda Minister Joseph Goebbels, stressing once again that he was "almost the only German artist to have fought openly, before the beginning of the National Socialist movement, against the foreign infiltration of German art, against an unclean art trade and the machinations of the Liebermann and Cassirer period [...], a struggle against a much stronger power that caused me decades of material hardship and disadvantage".[8] With his inclusion in London, the truth of these repeated statements was now thrown into question.

Indeed, the National Socialist rulers did become aware of *Twentieth Century German Art*. Adolf Hitler himself publicly attacked the London show in his speech opening the *Große Deutsche Kunstausstellung* on 10 July 1938. Both this speech, and the following reports in the Nazi-controlled press (see pp. 185, 190 f.), denounced the close relationship between modern art and Jewish dealers, collectors and émigrés. On 5 August 1938, Ernst Gosebruch, the former director of the Folkwang Museum in Essen, wrote to Nolde: "My daughter will see the exhibition of modern German art that H[erbert] Read, a friend of [Max] Sauerland[t], organised in London. But several reports already suggest that most of the works on display there are of the same kind as those favoured by Flechtheim and the like."[9] Gosebruch too employed the cliché of a modern canon determined by Jewish dealers, possibly unaware that Flechtheim had already died in exile in London on 9 March 1937.

It seems to have taken the German authorities some time to fully analyse the British press response to *Twentieth Century German Art*. Following the closure of the London exhibition on 27 August 1938 it was attempted to discover exactly how far the exhibited artists – included Nolde – had participated in the show. On 3 December 1938 Nolde received a letter from the President of the Reich Chamber of Fine Arts with the following request: "I have been informed that you took part in the exhibition at the New Burlington Galleries in London in July of this year. Please let me know from which office the invitations to this exhibition were issued, and by what authority you were granted the export licence for your works."[10]

Nolde would have received this letter on 4 December 1938 at the earliest. On 6 December 1938 he prepared a response, to the "leadership and party" of the NSDAP, reacting once again with an anti-Semitic statement of loyalty. As he set out, attempting to dispel any suspicion of his association with a Jewish art network: "It is said that my work was promoted and bought by Jews. That too is false. In recent years one or two paintings have found their way via the art trade into Jewish hands, but in general Jews fight against against me. They have mocked the purity and the genuine German character of my work, and never wanted it. My most important paintings are all in German possession, purchased by Germans, who are not afflicted with the sickness of foreign influence, who are consciously German."[11]

Nolde also emphasised that he had never been a beneficiary of this Jewish art system: "Fifteen or twenty years [after my conflict with Liebermann in 1910/11], when young artists urged the Grand Jews Cassirer and Flechtheim to invite me to participate in their large group exhibitions, I always declined – in accordance with my deep-felt opposition."[12]

As anti-Semitism became more radical in Germany, Emil Nolde and his wife Ada felt it was important to clarify the artist's position to the authorities. Not only due to the inquiries from the Reich Chamber of Fine Arts, but also as a result of press reports suggesting the artist was part of a Jewish art conspiracy – some even hinting that Nolde was actually a Jew.

On 25 November 1938 Ada Nolde sent a letter to the editor of the *Flensburger Generalanzeiger*. Her complaint: that in an article titled "The enemy in our own country – Jews as cultural Bolsheviks", Emil Nolde was mentioned "in connection with the names Alfred Kerr, Paul Cassirer etc. as if he was one of them."[13] Nolde himself also referred to this article, in his 6 December letter referred to above. He too objected to his association with the writer Alfred Kerr, in exile in London, the deceased art dealer Paul Cassirer, his cousin Bruno, in exile in Oxford, and the pro-modernist businessman Ludwig Katzenellenbogen. According to Nolde, these individuals were "the worst enemies of my life", the artist lamenting how "misjudgement and ignorance of the facts distorts everything."[14]

Together with selected passages from his autobiography *Years of Struggle* (1934; fig. 88), Nolde sent his statement of 6 December to Ernst Schröder in Flensburg, who passed it on to an aide of Otto Dietrich, Press Chief of the Third Reich. A copy was also sent to the Ministry of Propaganda. The first sign of success came just two days later, when the Propaganda Ministry issued the following statement: "The painter Emil *Nolde* is not *Jewish* [...] he is even a member of the Nazi party."[15]

Writing around Christmas 1938, Nolde informed his friend Fehr that the authorities had taken his wishes into account, that they would no longer "drag [his] honest German name through the press with those noted Jews."[16] Both the Reich Press Chief and the Ministry of Propaganda had affirmed that "such a conflation would not happen again."[17] To promote Nolde's rehabilitation on as many levels as possible, and to further demonstrate the artist's loyalty to the Nazi party, his friend Carl Schmitt, a constitutional lawyer, also contacted an official at the headquarters of the Volksbund für das Deutschtum im Ausland (People's Association for Germans Abroad) in Berlin. The desired response was dated 16 December: "The party values Mr Nolde as a member and as a fellow countryman."[18]

The year 1938 thus came to a satisfactory close for Emil Nolde. His letters had achieved the desired results. His polyptych *The Life of Christ* was returned to him, and in early 1939 he even received the news that his name would no longer be associated with the Degenerate Art exhibition – no works by Nolde were displayed at the show's subsequent venues. Moreover, Ada Nolde reported on 9 February 1939 that a "change in our favour had taken place" at the Ministry of Propaganda.[19] Ada and Emil Nolde, and their well-connected circle, had worked hard to effect this 'change' in the months since July 1937. Nolde's appearance in London alongside Jewish lenders and émigré artists had to some extent undermined these efforts, increasing the need for him to emphasis his anti-Semitism and thus his distance from the show's intentions. Nolde feared that his works would be misinterpreted in London, presented in a context at odds with his nationalistic convictions. The letters prepared by Fehr and Nolde must be recognised as an expression of the artist's position in 1938/39, in support of the National Socialist regime and in acceptance of their anti-Semitic policies. This position was entirely incompatible with the exhibition of *Twentieth Century German Art* and its presentation to the German public.

Judas Verbrechen am deutschen Volk

Der Hintermann entschied

Werner Sombart hat einmal, vor etwa zwanzig Jahren, den Ausspruch getan, daß der Anteil der Juden am Aufbau unserer Volkswirtschaft kleiner erscheinen müsse, als er in Wirklichkeit sei. Zum Beweise führte er ein Beispiel aus Wien an, wo nach dem amtlichen Handelsschema von 1845 nur 63 Juden als „tolerierte jüdische Handelsleute" vorhanden gewesen seien, in deren Händen sich aber der gesamte Textil-Engroshandel befunden hätte. Wie die Verhältnisse sich damals in einem ganz kleinen Sektor gestalteten, so beherrschten sie nach Jahrzehnten das ganze Deutschland. Das Judentum nützte seine Chancen rücksichtslos aus. Blinde Regierungen duldeten die Entwicklung wohlwollend. Das unaufgeklärte Volk hat sich widerspruchslos zum Opfer machen lassen.

Lange Jahre wußte man nichts von einer jüdischen Herrschaft. Der Jude eroberte sich anonym Schlüsselstellung um Schlüsselstellung. Gute deutsche Namen mußten für Geschäfte und Regierungs-Verhandlungen herhalten, hinter denen sich jüdische Drahtzieher verborgen hielten. Dabei gliederten sich die Juden nicht so ein, daß sie sich mit dem auserwählten Betätigungsfeld verwurzelten. Sie schwebten gewissermaßen in der Luft und angelten nach der Berührung mit den Spitzenzweigen. Worauf es ihnen ankam, war die Macht.

Die Macht war für sie das „Jerusalem". Sie waren aber klug genug, lange Zeit

im Schatten der Anonymität

sich dieser Macht zu bedienen. Gar viele Wege gab es. Sie scheuten sich nicht, ihre Töchter und ihr Geld an maßgebende verschuldete Kreise zu verheiraten. Sie deckten sich mittels Aktien und Börsenpapieren, um die Wirtschaft zu beherrschen und zu beeinflussen.

Erst nach der Revolte des Jahres 1918 glaubten sie die Zeit gekommen, auch „ihre Leit" in die vordersten Stellungen zu schieben und sichtbar zu machen.

Es war aber wirklich nur die zweite Garnitur, die das deutsche Judentum in die Schützengrabenstellungen — Gefahr war ja nicht mehr zu befürchten — schickte. Diese Herrschaften waren photographenreif. Sie lüfteten vielleicht den Schleier. Viel gefährlicher waren aber die jüdischen „Generalstabschefs", die hinter ihnen standen. Es gab keine wichtige Stellung, die nicht — gleichgültig von wem sie besetzt war — eine Filiale ihrer Tätigkeit war.

Man braucht bloß auf das Gebiet der Politik überzugreifen, um einer Reihe von Menschen zu begegnen, die vor oder hinter den Kulissen in der Kriegs- und Nachkriegszeit bestimmend auf die Gestaltung der Dinge eingewirkt haben. Da ist Walter Rathenau, da sind die marxistischen Abgeordneten Hugo Haase, Oskar Cohn, Kurt Eisner und die vielen anderen Vaterlandsverräter, denen nicht die Ehre angetan sein soll, daß man ihre Namen hier noch eigens nennt. Da sind die vielen Hilfsgenossen, die auf dem Gebiet der Presse und im Kulturleben die jüdische Auffassung den unpolitischen Schichten des deutschen Volkes aufzwangen. Nur wenige Namen genügen, um „tonangebende Richtungen" zu kennzeichnen: George Bernhard, Theodor Wolff und Maximilian Harden.

Das Wirtschaftsleben

war noch in ganz anderem Ausmaße in den Händen der Juden. Es gab schließlich keinen Konzern und keinen maßgebenden Geschäftszweig mehr, in dem nicht der Jude dominierte und seine „Befehle" nach unten weitergeben konnte.

Die Geldwirtschaft lag vollständig in den Händen von Juden und Nichtariern.

Von der Deutschen Bank und Diskonto-Gesellschaft waren die Juden Steinthal und Salomonsohn die Vorsitzenden des Aufsichtsrates. Die anderen großen Banken hatten soviel Juden in ihren Aufsichtsräten und Direktionen, daß der Betrieb nach jüdischen Methoden gewährleistet war. Die Industrie, die in der Hauptsache durch die jüdischen Banken kontrolliert wurde, hatte Vorstände nach dem Herzen der jüdischen Kontrolleure.

Kunst und Wissenschaft

waren ebenfalls — das, was sie zu bieten hatten, fand nicht den Beifall des Volkes und war nur eine Angelegenheit von Snobs und jüdisch infizierten Konventikeln — eine Stätte, von der aus man bewußt Kulturbolschewismus predigte und eine vollständige Umwertung der sittlichen Werte propagierte. Vom jüdischen Kapital (Katzenellenbogen) wurde der bolschewistische (volljüdische) Intendant Piscator zum Starten gebracht und zum Durchhalten veranlaßt. Was ansonsten an jüdischen Elementen die Kunst „befruchten" wollte, sei wirklich verschwiegen.

Den Beitrag, den die akademische Welt dazu lieferte, daß die Juden an allen Schlüsselstellungen sich festsetzen konnten, kann man erst in seiner ganzen Größe dem deutschen Volke zeigen, wenn die abschließenden Zahlen feststehen. Es ist ja inzwischen bekanntgeworden, wie sehr der ärztliche, der chemische, der juristische, der volkswirtschaftliche Beruf von Juden übersetzt war und wie sich der Jude auch in den akademischen Lehrberuf selbst „hineinzuwanzen" verstanden hat. Vom Film ist erst gar nicht zu reden.

Mehr noch als der offizielle, im Rampenlicht des Tages stehende Jude, ist aber derjenige Jude, der als „Hintermann", „Ratgeber", „graue Eminenz"

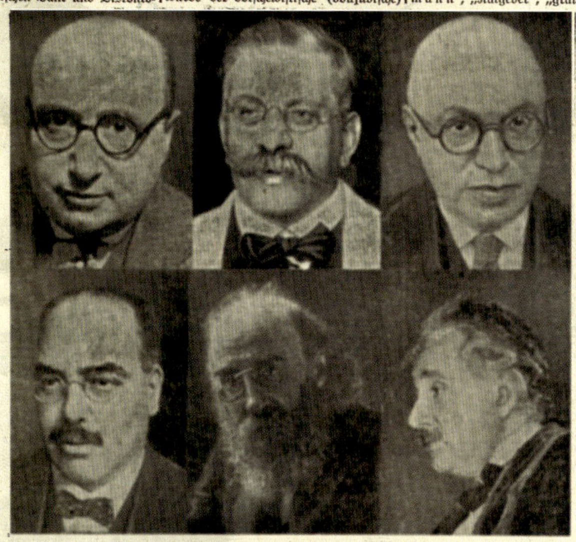

Judas Schuldkonto in Deutschland

Oben von links: Der Theaterjude Zickel, der wie seine Rassegenossen Piscator und Rotter das Theater zu einem Tummelplatz für die unverschämtesten Triebe gegen alles machte, was Ehre, Sitte und Würde darstellt. — Der Sexual-„Professor" Magnus Hirschfeld, einer jener jüdischen Pornographenliteraten, die systematisch die kulturelle Aushöhlung des deutschen Kulturlebens anstrebten und der unter Mißachtung aller Moralbegriffe die Vernichtung von Ehe und Familie betrieb. — Der jüdische Rechtsverdreher Werthauer, der u. a. die These aufstellte, der Staat habe für Verbrecher überhaupt kein Recht zur Strafe. — **Unten von links:** Der Jude Hilferding, der als Chefredakteur der „Freiheit" (USPD.) im Jahre 1919 die bedingungslose Unterzeichnung des Versailler Schanddiktats forderte und später als Finanzminister seinen landesverräterischen Instinkten zugunsten seiner Rasse freien Lauf ließ. — Der Jude Kurt Eisner, der im November 1919 in München glatten Landesverrat trieb, indem er auf die Lostrennung Bayerns vom Reich hinarbeitete und gefälschte Dokumente veröffentlichte, um Deutschlands Schuld am Weltkrieg zu beweisen. — Der Jude Albert Einstein, der unter der Maske des Wissenschaftlers sich als übler Schreier für den Bolschewismus betätigte und heute zu den gemeinsten Hetzern gegen Deutschland gehört. (Weltbild, K.)

90 Anon. "The Crime of Judas against the German people", *Flensburger Nachrichten*, 23 November 1938, No. 274.

Many thanks to Dr. Christian Ring and the Ada and Emil Nolde Foundation in Seebüll/Neukirchen (hereinafter ANS) for access to the sources within the scope of a research project examining the artist's position under Nazi rule. The present essay is closely linked to the author's article on Emil Nolde and the touring version of the Munich *Degenerate Art* exhibition to be published in 2018.

1 Cf. e.g. the biography compiled by Julia Bremer, in: Felix Krämer (ed.): Emil Nolde. Retrospektive, Staedel Museum Frankfurt/Main (exib. cat.), Munich 2014, p. 281-285; here: p. 285.

2 Excerpt from a typewritten copy of the letter dated 16 May 1938, Inland II A/B, 'Deutsche Emigranten im Ausland', Vol. 18 [R 99592 / stamp: Federal Foreign Office / 83-75 16/5 Nolde / rec'd. 23 May 1938 / Dept. – Germany]. Document previously cited in 2001 in: Alexander Stephan, Hetz- und Greuelpropaganda. Die Überwachung der deutschen Exilschriftsteller in Großbritannien durch das Auswärtige Amt, in: James M. Ritchie (ed.): German-speaking Exiles in Great Britain, Leiden/Boston 2001, Vol. 3, p. 23-40, here: p. 32.

3 ANS, letter from Hans Fehr to Emil Nolde, 20 May 1938, with a copy of the letter from Weizsäcker, State Secretary in the Foreign Office.

4 Ibid.

5 Nolde knew that Herbert Read had already planned an exhibition of German art in London before 1933. At that time Max Sauerlandt had asked him to send Read the first volume of his memoirs. Read also thanked Nolde personally and Sauerlandt reported to Nolde in August 1932 that Read was very enthusiastic about the book. During a planned lecture in Edinburgh and Glasgow in the winter of 1932, Sauerlandt intended to make Nolde "a central figure" of modern German art (ANS, letter from Max Sauerlandt to Ada and Emil Nolde, 6 August 1932).

6 Nolde was, however, among the twenty artists listed on the invitation to the private viewing, whereas Max Pechstein, whose works were also shown, was not. Cf. Stationen der Moderne (exhib. cat. 1988/89), fig. 10/3, p. 316.

7 ANS, copy of the letter from Emil Nolde to Bernhard Rust, 5 August 1937. To prove his statement, Nolde referred to his autobiography Jahre der Kämpfe ("Years of Battles"), which included a detailed account of his conflict with Max Liebermann.

8 Bundesarchiv Berlin, letter from Emil Nolde to Joseph Goebbels, 2 July 1938, R 55 21014.

9 ANS, copy of the letter from Ernst Gosebruch to Emil Nolde, 5 August 1938.

10 ANS, letter from the President of the Reich Chamber of Fine Arts, signed by a certain Kittlitz, to Emil Nolde, 3 December 1938.

11 Typescript draft of a letter from Nolde to the Press Chief of the Reich (with corrections in the artist's handwriting), 6 December 1938, pp. 2/3.

12 Ibid.

13 ANS, letter from Ada Nolde to Otto Entmayr, 25 November 1938. The daily newspaper to which Ada refers is not known in the Flensburg City Archive under this title for the year given. A similar article entitled "Judas Verbrechen am deutschen Volk" was published in *Flensburger Nachrichten* on November 23, 1938, No. 274. Some of those mentioned by Mrs Nolde are also named under "Art and Science", but there is no mention of Emil Nolde. Many thanks to Marvin Nissen, Flensburg City Archive, for his kind assistance.

14 Ibid.

15 Hans Bohrmann, Gabriele Toepser-Ziegert (eds.): NS-Presseanweisungen der Vorkriegszeit. Edition und Dokumentation, Vol. 6, Munich 1999, p. 1173, entry for 8 December 1938.

16 ANS, letter from Emil Nolde to Hans Fehr, n. d., "Weihnachten 1938" [c. 24 December 1938].

17 Ibid.

18 ANS, letter from Dr von Türke to Carl Schmitt, 16 December 1938, enclosed as a copy in a letter from Duska Schmitt to Ada Nolde, 4 February 1939.

19 Landesarchiv Düsseldorf, Estate of Carl Schmitt [RW 265-10422/1], letter from Ada Nolde to Duska Schmitt, 9 February 1939. Notwithstanding these positive developments, Nolde was expelled from the Reich Chamber of Fine Arts in 1941.

This collection has been assembled through the Organizing Committee of the Exhibition of Twentieth Century German Art, held in London, July and August, 1938.

President, Augustus John
Chairman, Herbert Read
Honorary Organizer, Irmgard Burchard
Honorary Secretary, Patrick Blackwood
The Rt. Hon. The Earl of Listowel
Brian Howard — Dunstan Curtis
Roland Penrose — John Harrison

BAUMEISTER, WILLI
2. Tennis Player. Watercolor — Not for Sale

BECKMANN, MAX
3. The Skaters — Not For Sale
4. Working Figures — £ 450.

CORINTH, LOVIS
5. Self Portrait — £ 325.

ERNST, MAX
7. La Colombe Blanche — £ 42.
8. Acolade — 52.

FEININGER, LYONEL
12. Longeuil, Village in Normandy — £ 100.

GROSZ, GEORGE
13. Street in Paris. Watercolor — £ 55.
14. Restaurant. Watercolor — 55.
15. The Agitator. Watercolor — 55.

HECKEL, EHRICH
16. Portrait — Not For Sale
17. Horses in Field — £ 35.

HOFER, CARL
18. Liebespaar — £ 275.
19. Two Children with Sunflowers — 100.

KIRCHNER, ERNST LUDWIG
20. Farm House in Fehman — £ 240.
21. Laburnum Tree — £ 100.

KLEE, PAUL
22. Garden after the Storm — £ 145.
23. Arab Song — 145.
24. New Harmony — 175.
25. In the Country of Precious Stones. Watercolor — £ 50.

KOKOSCHKA, OSKAR
28. Mother and Child — £ 230.

KRAUSKOPF, BRUNO
29. Still Life — £ 67.

LANGE, OTTO
30. Bridge at Arles. Watercolor — £ 25.
31. Dresden. Watercolor — 25.

LEHMBRUCK, WILHELM
32. Woman. Drawing — £ 75.
33. Man. Drawing — 60.
34. The Kiss. Drawing — 30.
35. Figures. Lithograph — 30.

LIEBERMANN, MAX
36. Self Portrait — Not For Sale
37. Horses on the Sea Shore — Not For Sale

MARC, FRANZ
38. Long Yellow Horse — Not for Sale
39a Blue Horses — £ 1,200.
39b Blue Horses
40. Cosmic Cow — Not For Sale
41. St. Christopher — £ 550.
42. Yellow Cow — 475.

MODERSOHN-BECKER, PAULA
44. Seated Peasant Woman — £ 200.

MULLER, OTTO
46. Bathing in the Brook — £ 70.
47. Self Portrait — 45.

NOLDE EMIL
48. Peasant Girl — £ 100.
49. Still Life — 75.
50. Chrysanthemums. Watercolor — £ 50.
51. Tulips and Anemones. Watercolor — 50.
52. Sunflowers. Watercolor — 50.

PECHSTEIN, MAX
53. Appletrees — £ 125.
54. Still Life — 125.
55. Sea Shore — 125.

ROHLFS, CHRISTIAN
56. Street — £ 240.
57. Flowers. Watercolor — £ 125.
58. Houses. Watercolor — 65.

SCHLEMMER, OSKAR
60. Figures — £ 50.
61. Study of Torso — 50.
62. Woman — 50.

SCHMIDT-ROTTLUFF, KARL
63. Oriental Forest — £ 50.
64. Village Street — 65.
65. Man Sharpening Scythe. Watercolor — £ 40.

SLEVOGT, MAX
66. Self Portrait — Not For Sale
67. Landscape — £ 100.
68. Still Life — 100.

BLOCH, MARTIN
69. Hammersmith Bridge — £ 75.

FEIBUSCH, HANS
71. Two Heads — £ 50.

TRIER, WALTER
74. Old Toy Shop — £ 30.

UHLMAN, FRED
75. Gypsies — £ 20.
76. Streets in Paris — 20.

PRICE LIST

EXHIBITION OF
20th
century
(BANNED)
GERMAN ART

CIRCULATED BY BLANCHE A. BYERLEY
NEW YORK

91 *Exhibition of 20th century (Banned) German Art,* catalogue with typed "Price List."

The United States tour of *20th Century (Banned) German Art*

KEITH HOLZ

Uncertainties engulf the end of the *Twentieth Century German Art* exhibition. This is especially true of the dispersion of the collected and exhibited artworks. As historian Marc Masurovsky recently observed: "There has never been a proper accounting of these 'banned' works, those that were returned unsold to the sources which lent them, those works which were then shipped to the United States or other destinations".[1] While this essay does bring us closer to an account of the artworks' dispersal, its focus is instead upon organisation and reception of the later tour of the exhibition which travelled through at least nine US cities between June 1939 and April 1940.

Extended three times, the London exhibition closed on 27 August 1938.[2] In early September, the show's honorary organiser, Irmgard Burchard, shared plans for a selection of the exhibited artworks to travel to the City Art Gallery of Leeds and to the Palais des Beaux Arts, Brussels.[3] The only verified British or continental version of the exhibition however was held between 14 March to 1 April at the McLellan Galleries in Glasgow, Scotland.[4]

To spark interest in the United States, as early as May 1938, Herbert Read had approached the dealer J. B. Neumann in New York.[5] Though Burchard was back in Zürich by mid-September 1938, before leaving London she and her team had initiated preparations sufficient for her co-workers – perhaps Noel Norton's colleague at the London Gallery Patrick Blackwood, or Herbert Read himself – to continue planning for about seventy-five artworks to tour U.S. museums.[6] Included on the U.S. checklist (provided to each venue), around thirty works previously listed in the London catalogue.[7]

Also before quitting London, Burchard posted several standard-form letters soliciting U.S. art museum directors to take the exhibition. To "The Director, St. Louis Art Institute" she wrote: "The exhibition has been a great success ... We are very anxious that America shall have an opportunity to see these pictures ... The Exhibition has been organised to supply artists called 'degenerate' with stipendiums, and to sell their pictures. It is under the patronage of the Tate and the National Galleries. We should be very grateful for any help or advice you can give us."[8]

The purpose underscored by Burchard, to "supply artists called 'degenerate' with stipendiums, and to sell their pictures", loosely concurs with the purpose stated in the New Burlington Galleries exhibition catalogue: "Profits will be devoted to the relief of refugee artists." Yet, the shift in language is telling: "refugee artists" (for London) and "artists called 'degenerate'" (for the United States). Although true that very few of the exhibited artists were refugees, by August 1938 refugees were a hot political issue in the U.S. and Burchard may have consciously sought to remove this label from the exhibitors. She may however simply have been describing the status of the represented artists more accurately. Surprising too is her overstated claim that the exhibition stood under the patronage of the Tate and National Galleries.

By May 1939 at least seventy-six works – including the thirty exhibited in London – had been shipped to the United States. On June 1, the exhibition opened at the Milwaukee Art Institute in Wisconsin under the title *Exhibition of 20th Century (Banned) German Art*. But how did this exhibition circulate around the United States? And where would it actually travel before closing in spring 1940? Enter one Blanche A. Byerley of Westport, Connecticut.[9]

Byerley, was the organiser of the U.S. exhibition tour. She operated the "Blanche A. Byerley Lecture Bureau" from an office in New York and from her home in Westport. She also enjoyed some affiliation with the Ferargil Gallery (63 East 57th Street) founded and operated by Fredric Newlin Price.[10] A letter from Jere Abbott, then-director of the Smith College Museum of Art in Northampton, Massachusetts, to Alfred Barr at the Museum of Modern Art in New York suggests both men were on a first name basis with her.[11] Her interests lay with modern European art as well as organising exhibitions of contemporary African-American women artists. During the war, she also raised monies for the Russian War Relief.[12] For the German exhibition she proved herself a highly attentive administrator. A long correspondence trail documents her successes securing at least nine museums to host the exhibition, scheduling (and rescheduling) the venues that ran for just less than one month each, forwarding 500 copies of the checklist ("catalogue") to each venue, conducting communications about insurance and shipping, and gathering press clippings from each museum. She also distributed advance press materials: photographs of artworks exhibited in London, a press release derived from the London catalogue text, and articles from British newspapers such as *The Yorkshire Post* and *The Sunday Times*.[13]

The exhibition's U.S. premier at the Milwaukee Art Institute ran from June 1 to 25, 1939. Days before the opening, an anonymous essay appeared in the local newspaper (fig. 96). After asking readers to recall earlier opinions about the "disgraceful" *Blue Horses* of Franz Marc, the "wickedness" of Expressionism and the time when Die Brücke was nearly a synonym for "Lost Souls", it relegated those dismissive opinions to an earlier period: examples of intolerance that time had "softened." Viewers were now encouraged to value the "vitality" of modern German pictures, such as those by Marc, Feininger and Klee. It was also noted that the Art Institute already owned a Hofer. As for Grosz: "we accept George Grosz as the most brilliant satirist since Daumier. We were delighted to learn that he is on the way to American citizenship and we smile at the humanizing effect America is having on his sting."[14] Striking is how this essay anticipates a conservative and potentially intolerant audience's efforts to engage with this art, while smiling upon the assimilation of one of the artists now living in the United States.

Four weeks later, on 26 June, Milwaukee director Alfred G. Pelikan wrote to Meyric Rogers, director of the Saint Louis City Art Museum, the next station on Byerley's U.S. programme. Pelikan enclosed a letter "typical [of] ones addressed to me and to the Board of Trustees" – from the Senior Canon of All Saints Cathedral, Milwaukee. Karl Hofer's painting Liebespaar [Pair of Lovers] was the subject of the churchman's concern (fig. 92). As the canon wrote,

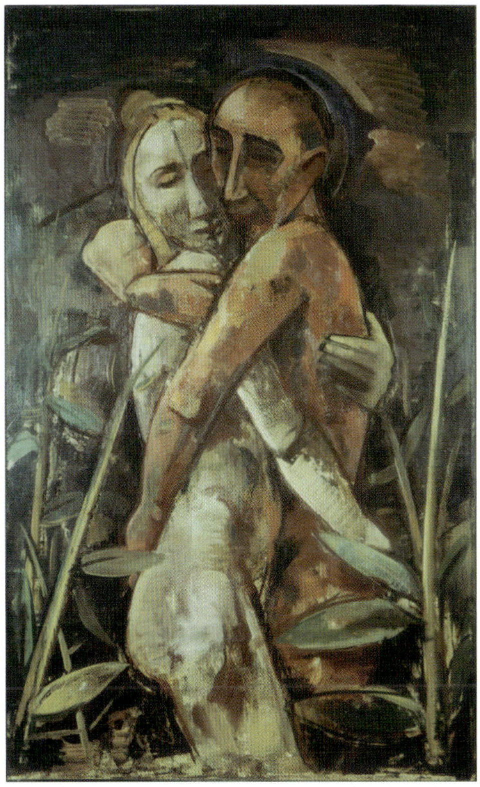

92 Karl Hofer, *Liebespaar, Pair of Lovers*, a.k.a. *Love: Human Couple*. 1922. Oil on canvas, 128.8 x 80.4 cm. Private Collection.

the picture was "decidedly crude and vulgar to such an extent that it was nothing less than lewd and pornographic. If police were to arrest a person with a photograph of this picture, he would certainly be charged with possessing an indecent picture. Several other subjects were far from edifying."[15] Glossed over by Pelikan, but recently analyzed by art historian Gregor Langfeld, one Elizabeth Oehlenschlaeger similarly weighed in during the exhibition with forceful anti-modernist criticism that concurred with the racist and populist arguments and politics of the National Socialists in Germany.[16] To Rogers, awaiting the exhibition's arrival in St. Louis, Pelikan also warned: "... a small but determined and active group of 'Sanity in Art' followers took advantage of the opportunity to attack modern art in general and the *Twentieth Century German Art* in particular. Through the press some of these people openly advocated the belief that in matters of art Hitler must be right".[17]

The Society for Sanity in Art was a network of anti-modernist art world figures, founded in 1936, which purported to represent popular opinion and taste. They had members in many U.S. cities, including Chicago, Boston, New York and San Francisco. It was led in nearby Chicago by arts patron and heiress Josephine Hancock Logan (1862-1943). In the decade prior to her death in November 1943, Logan had disseminated her anti-modernist views widely, views that did not elude the attention of Paul Westheim in Paris. Writing in the exile press, he addressed how Logan and the Sanity in Art groups opposed modern art that was not "rationally beautiful" or that they considered sickly and degenerate. He also described Logan's efforts to cleanse the art museums of Chicago, inviting obvious comparison with the anti-modernist campaigns of National Socialists in Germany.[18]

In the days after the outrage caused by Hofer's *Lovers* in Milwaukee, Byerley herself wrote to director Rogers in St. Louis. Appended to information about transport and frames she also offered some rather singular guidance: "... I am leaving it to the discretion of the museums [sic] directors to omit any work when hanging the group, which they may consider it inadvisable to show."[19] This offer stands out as an unusual concession from any exhibition organiser, to self-censor in order to align the exhibition with perceived local tastes or opinion. But the St. Louis museum did not remove the Hofer and appears to have hung all exhibits during the September 1 – 25 exhibition. The local press also reckoned with the exhibition in two newspaper articles. On the eve of Germany's invasion of Poland, the banning of these artists "in Germany by the Nazi government" was at the forefront of all these commentators' engagement with the show.[20]

The exhibition's third venue was the Smith College Museum of Art in Northampton, Massachusetts. Few details have emerged about this exhibition, other than its comparatively short run (October 6 to 25). The museum's director, Jere Abbott, had studied with Alfred Barr at Harvard, later serving with him as the first associate director of the New York Museum of Modern Art. Two weeks before the exhibition opened at Smith College, Abbott opined to Barr: "I am now, because of what I have subsequently heard, getting a little cold feet about the exhibition, not by any political consideration but because I hear that the works in it are really not representative of the men. If this is the case, the show would do more harm than good because it would give people the opportunity to say, quite rightly, that the pictures were not worth hanging in museums."[21]

Writing to a Cincinnati collector on 5 October 1939, the eve of the Smith opening, Barr picked up on Abbott's criticism of how the exhibition fell short: "this is confidential ... there is a large exhibition of German art, rather badly chosen, touring museums. It seems to be doing a lot of harm so far as the reputation of German painting is concerned and is even causing people who are not in sympathy with modern art to say, with a certain relief, that Hitler is right."[22]

As with certain critics in London[23] and Milwaukee, Barr privately acknowledged that unsympathetic popular opinion toward modern art in the democracies might rally support for Hitler – no minor concern in the weeks following the outbreak of war. Yet Barr offered a rationale for his position, stating that these particular paintings were "badly chosen." "Badly chosen" appears to refer to the artistic quality of the artworks (compared to ones Barr had access to in New York). But one might also wonder whether poor physical condition of artworks might have stoked their negative assessment. Consider the December 27, 1939 condition report prepared by the Portland Art Museum, the sixth stage of the U.S. tour. Notations were made for about half of the works as having damage to the canvas, the paper, or the frames (fig. 98).[24] Their value was also implicitly questioned at the seventh venue, the San Francisco Museum of Art, where director Grace L. McCann Morley challenged the exhibition's $300 fee, writing: "with so many watercolors and drawings I find the fee a bit stiff."[25]

These touring versions of the London exhibition are sometimes confused with, and overshadowed in the scholarly literature by, other American exhibitions of modern German art during 1939 and 1940. These include *Modern German Art* at the Museum of Fine Arts in Springfield, Massachusetts. This January 1939 exhibition was comprised chiefly of loans from Curt Valentin at the Buchholz Gallery in New York.[26] Karl Buchholz was authorised to continue operating his Berlin gallery as one of four dealers officially appointed by the National Socialist German government to liquidate confiscated degenerate art abroad. This allowed him to acquire high quality, recently confiscated, modernist artwork from German museums at low prices and export, sell and promote them in the United States, which he did through Valentin.[27] In November 1939, an even larger exhibition – *Contemporary German Art* – was held at the Institute of Contemporary Art, Boston. In this extensively studied exhibition, organised by James Plaut and Mary Udall, again with the support of Curt Valentin, prime examples of German expressionism were exhibited together with their German museum provenances. Also included were many works from major U.S. museums.[28] One Boston Globe review once again echoed concerns that the public might sympathise with National Socialist policy, as the journalist wrote: "There are probably many people – art lovers – in Boston, who will side with Hitler in this particular purge ... So it is that the war of opinions has come to Boston – the judgment seat of the United States in art matters – with the emphasis slightly on the side of traditions which Hitler seems to respect."[29] A third exhibition staged with Valentin's involvement took place at the Buchholz Gallery in New York in April 1940, under the title *Landmarks in Contemporary German Art*.

From Smith College in Northampton, the *Exhibition of 20th Century (Banned) German Art* meanwhile travelled to its fourth venue, the William Rockhill Nelson Gallery in Kansas City, Missouri (for the month of November 1939). It was then shipped back to the Northeast, for its firth stage at the Albright Art Gallery in Buffalo where it ran from 1 to 22 December 1939.

The Albright Art Gallery, directed by Gordon B. Washburn, provided the exhibition with a thoughtful essay in its newsletter Gallery Notes. It emphasised the cultural politics of the exhibition in relation to Germany's National Socialist art and racial policies. It also issued an invitation card, with a diagonal text printed in German fraktur "Degenerate Non-Aryan" as if stamped over the exhibition's title (fig. 93).[32] Under the headline "Hitler-Banned Art

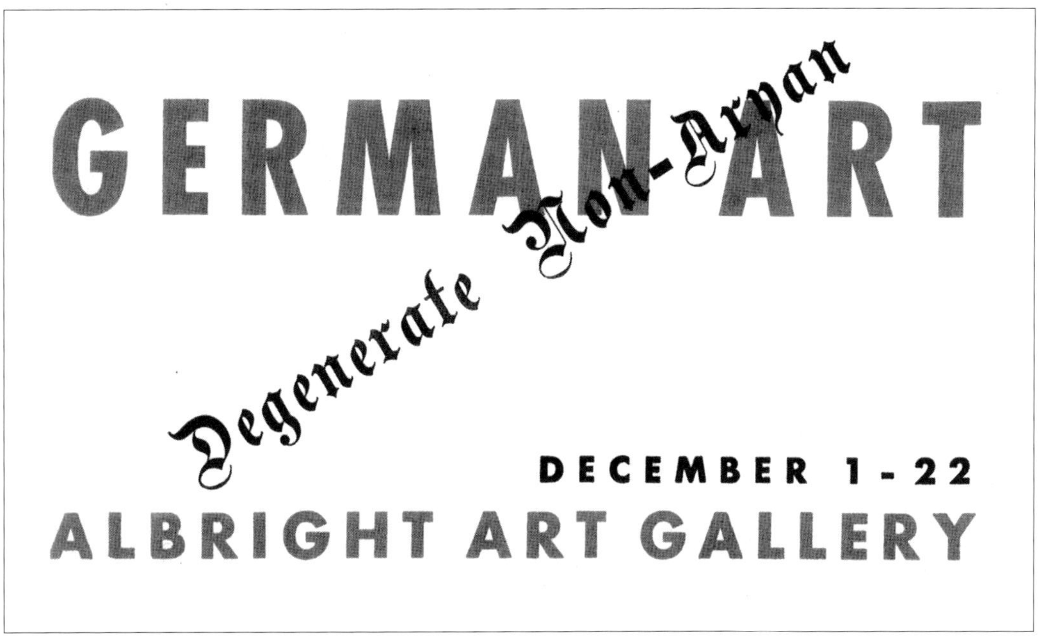

93 Albright Art Gallery, Buffalo, invitation card, recto only, 1939. *Exhibition of 20th Century Germany Art.*

Buffalo N. Y. Evening News
Saturday, December 9, 1939

sketching stroll through Buffalo. It would spoil the fun (for art can be fun, too, they say) to disclose the exact

even a slight bit about the history of the city. Next week, Mrs. Durston leaves downtown Buffalo for an East Side trip.

HITLER-BANNED ART DISCLOSED IN SADLY-DEPLETED CONDITION

By NORA LEE ROHR

THE exhibition of German "degenerate" art now current at the Albright Gallery in no way bears out the rather drastic expectations which go with the title and the publicity that has heralded the show since its arrival in the States last June. It has already been seen in Milwaukee, St. Louis and Kansas City. From here it will go on to Portland, Ore., San Francisco and finally to New York.

The collection, as shown here, is not nearly as effective as was the original one in Munich in 1937 and viewed at the time by your critic. The show then was vastly larger comprising several hundreds of paintings and pieces of sculpture and hung closely together for dramatic effect. Even since the organization of the present group at the New Burlington Galleries in London, under the sponsorship of Augustus John, H. G. Wells, Clive Bell, the Bishop of Birmingham and other notables, the contents have dwindled and changed for one reason or other, until today all we see is a none-too-representative remnant of Hitler's once-condemned art.

For this reason also the term non-Aryan today may seem somewhat startling, for, like the "bolshevist art" applied at the time, non-Aryan had the general connotation of a subtitle, including anything not strictly national. Today the Third Reich has enlisted art in its campaign to provide party propaganda through a new race-conscious art which combines a vague Aryan mythology with a summons to "be natural, be God-like, be beautiful."

Not Art in Revolt

As the Art Gallery Bulletin explains, "this art is not an attack on the Hitler regime by a rebellious group of discontented artists. On the contrary the new regime has attacked the established national art. "As a result of World War I, Germanic culture was isolated from the French impressionist and post-impressionist movements and branched out in a new direction — expressionist movement. Much of this school reflected the bitter cynicism and hopeless morbidity of the post-war period. No sooner had this new growth begun to establish itself than it was swept aside, condemned on political grounds and suppressed.

The artists of widest international fame in this exhib't are of course George Grosz and Oscar Kokoshka. Grosz is now in New York where he has taught at the National Academy for a number of years. His style of painting has gone from drastic to mild without losing any of its vigor. Of Oscar Kokoshka the same is not true, he has continued his startling expressionism to this day.

Ironically enough, Lionel Feininger is included because of his former association with the Bauhaus Group, today he is well recognized here as an American painter.

One of the leaders in pre-war modern German art was Franz Marc, who died in action during the World War. He was the organizer of the famous group of "Blaue Reiter" in Munich in 1910, together with Kandinski and Klee. Out of the six of Marc's canvases only the "Blue Horses" are really representative of his best work. "Three Red Horses" (1909) an even better example of that period, has just been acquired by the Cincinnati Art Museum, together with other once condemned art from the Folkwang Museum in Essen.

An Understanding

Among the typically German artists, less well known abroad, Max Liebermann and Lovis Corinth are well worth noting. They were among the earliest artists to swing German painting from impressionism to expressionism and the successive movements that followed. Others, more independent, were Otto Schlemmer, Max Pechstein, Max Slevogt and Emil Nolde. Wilhelm Lehmbruck, the sculptor, is represented with fine drawings and a lithograph. It is Lehmbruck's "Kneeling Woman," in the permanent collection of the Gallery, which served as one of the prize pieces of "banned" sculpture in Hitler's selection.

It is essential to remember, in viewing this exhibit, that the Hitler ban was directed less against the artist himself than against the content and spirit of paintings of that neurotic and decadent period which followed immediately upon the war. It is also to be understood that the Art Gallery presents this exhibit as an esthetic document of an era, without any indication of approval and with no political interest at all.

Drawings Are Shown

Thirteen contemporary drawings, presented to the Gallery by Mr. A. Conger Goodyear last month, have now been placed on exhibit in the Room for Contemporary Art together with additional drawings loaned from his private collection. The whole makes a striking and representative show.

Among the drawings now in the Gallery collection are a number of studies in the nude which are interesting to compare. As always we find the artists, in their drawings, less conventional, more forthright than in their more formal finished painting or sculpture. These somewhat casual, yet serious studies, toward the solving of specific problems give the artist a more human aspect than usual, and their personalities are more easily recognized.

Salvador Dali, in his "Woman Leaning Against the Ledge of a House," is indiscribably subtle, serene and less puzzling than in his work of late. There is the "Torso of a Woman" by Aristide Maillol, only faintly indicated with a soft pencil, yet these few lines seem so much more expressive than the rather stiff and orthodox nude by Eugene Speicher. George Kolbe's seated nude is plastic and solidily modeled while Jules Pascin expresses himself in persuasive color as usual. Muirhead Bone, best known as British etcher, is exceedingly powerful in his drawing of "Armistice Night," and Maurice Sterne's "Ball Boy" fairly sways with rhythm.

The additional drawings loaned by Mr. Goodyear all seem to be of exceptional quality. Augustus John, the British portraitist, shows himself particularly versatile in lithe sketches, so unlike his powerful, somewhat stolid type of portraiture. "Woman Gathering Sticks," has the tenseness of a Daumier and the drawing of two boys is full of charm.

There is a delightful "Inspector" by Rockwell Kent, a terrifying "Old Woman" by Pable Picasso (1902), a poignant satire, "Our Masters," by Louis Forain, a classical "Horse" by Edgar Degas, a meticulously beautiful still life by Diego Rivera and a vivid color composition by Paul Gauguin.

Two of the best in this group are indubitably Georges Seurat's ethereal "La NOU-Nou" in his pointilist style, and Charles Despiau's "Nude," a very sculptural rendering in sanguine of a figure seen in drastic foreshortening.

Among the Exhibits

This month the Rochester Memorial Art Gallery is fortunate in having the National Ceramic Exhibition, the eighth in a comprehensive series assembled by the Syracuse Museum of Fine Arts. The exhibition this year consists of 88 items in a rich variety of techniques, materials and designs. Today the American Potter and Ceramic Sculptor are almost technically perfect artists.

• • •

The Tatler Club in Niagara Falls has put on an exhibition of the work of local artists. Of real interest are the sculptural pieces by Ceramists Wenonan Davidson and Mary Metcalf Langs. Among the painters are Anna Knauff, Polly King, Harlan Dickinson and Eugene Dyzckowski, native of the Falls.

• • •

Paintings by Ethlyn P. Cobb, member of the Patteran Society are now on view at the Jane Keeler Theater, in the lobby recently redecorated by Mrs. Urquhart Wilcox.

Patron's Need Cited

John Rothenstein M. A., Ph.D., director and keeper of the Tate Gallery, Millbanks, London, spoke on 19th Century English Painting at the Garret Club Thursday. He stressed the importance of the patron in art, for lack of commissions, he said, have caused in great part the artists drifting off into the field of abstraction.

Besides Augustus John, he spoke of W. R. Sickert, Ethel Walker, Duncan Grant, Windham Lewis, Paul and John Nash, Stanley Spencer and Christopher Wood. The latter and Augustus John are represented at the Albright: Windham Lewis has just completed a portrait of Chancellor Samuel P. Capen of the University, which he executed while residing in this city.

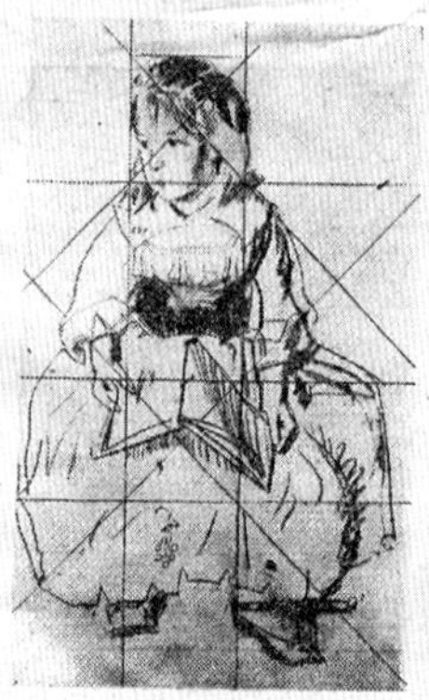

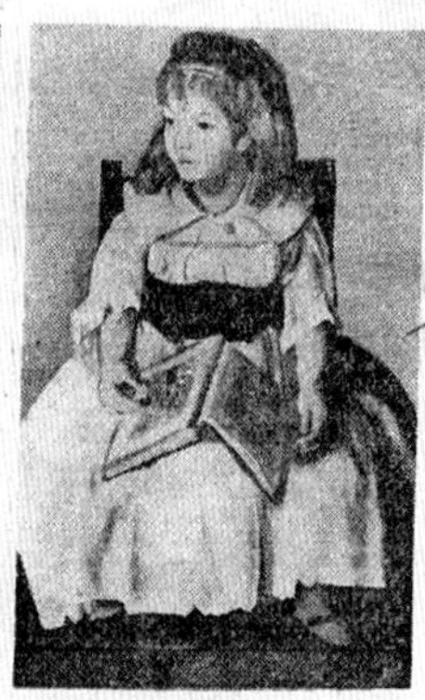

Among the 13 contemporary drawings recently presented to the Albright by A. Conger Goodyear is the George Bellows item illustrated above. It is the preliminary sketch for Jean, the central figure of the Bellows painting, "Eleanor, Jean and Anne," which has become familiar to Buffalo art lovers as part of the Albright permanent collection. It will be noted how carefully the sketch was proportioned and how closely the figure in the painting (shown at the right as a detail) follows the Bellows plan.

94 Nora Lee Rohr, "Hitler Banned Art Disclosed in Sadly-Depleted Condition", *Buffalo Evening News*, 9 December 1939.

95 Lyonel Feininger, *Longeuil, Normandie*, 1909. Oil on canvas, 80.6 x 101 cm. Art Institute of Chicago

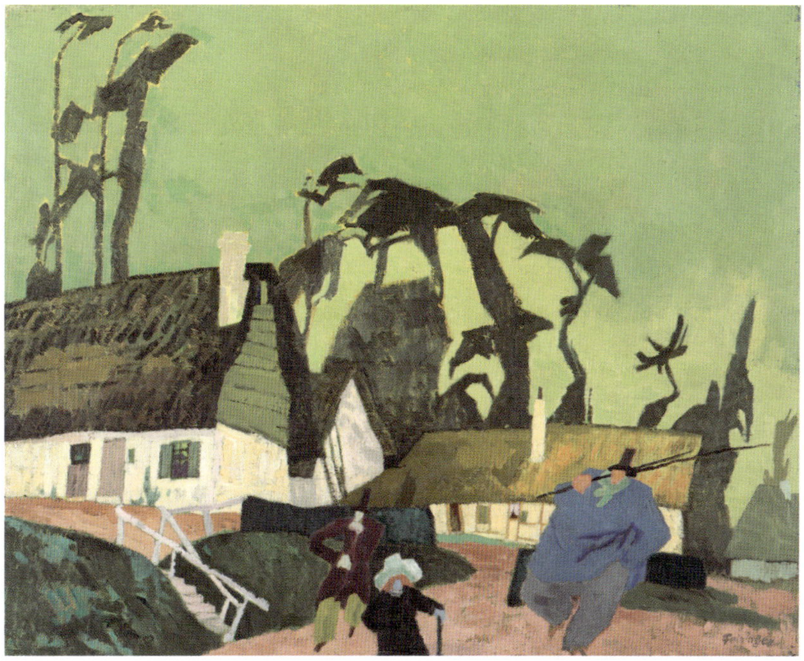

Disclosed in Sadly-Depleted Condition" an art critic for the *Buffalo Evening News* compared the show to Degenerate Art in Munich and London's New Burlington Galleries exhibition (fig. 94). She reported how the exhibition had "dwindled" now offering "a none-too-representative remnant of Hitler's once-condemned art." After reviewing exhibition highlights and relating the art to its political contexts in interwar Germany, she closed by parroting the museum's press release: "It is also to be understood that the Art Gallery presents this exhibit as an esthetic document of an era, without any indication of approval and with no political interest at all.[33]

As noted above, the sixth venue was the West coast's Portland Art Museum, in Oregon (3-25 January 1940). After Portland the exhibition travelled 770 miles south to the San Francisco Museum of Art where it ran from February 1 to 25, 1940. After an eighth showing at the Dayton Art Institute, Ohio (3-24 March 1940), the final (verified) stage of the exhibition took place from 1 to 25 April 1940 at the Josyln Memorial Museum in Omaha, Nebraska. Byerley had sought additional, yet-to-be confirmed venues; like many questions raised by this overview, these await further research.

Evaluating Impact

Measured by Burchard's stated aim for this travelling exhibition – to sell pictures and raise funds for "stipendiums" for artists – the U.S. tour undoubtedly failed. Although a few artworks sold from the exhibition – among them paintings by Feininger, Hofer (fig. 95 and 99), and by Franz Marc[34] – no evidence of aid distributed to defamed artists in need has surfaced. Although persons in England were consulted on incoming offers for artworks less than the asking price, it does not appear that any of the exhibition's European lenders ever saw any proceeds from sales.

Yet, other less emphatically stated results were achieved by the exhibition. Firstly, it motivated U.S. audiences outside of the metropolitan New York area to wrestle with the suppression, oppression, and expulsion of artists and banning of artworks in National Socialist Germany. It also aligned this art with democracy and freedom as valued by Americans facing the prospect of war with Nazi Germany. By doing so, it also provided U.S. museum directors with an instrument to measure the extent to which regional American audiences shared views on art approximating those of the Nazis. Tellingly, even when the exhibition encountered focused populist criticism, prompting Byerley to offer the option of excluding works "inadvisable to show," American museums did not remove potentially offending artworks.

Finally, the exhibition played a role related to a key issue isolated in recent scholarship, namely the canonisation of Expressionism (and to a lesser extent Bauhaus-related modernism) as the most important visual art of the pre-Nazi era.[35] In doing so, it helped initiate the often oversimplified and heavily instrumentalised binary distinction between the "banned," modernist (Expressionist and Bauhaus-related) art of Germany and the art of the National Socialist government.

1 Marc Masurovsky: Franz Marc's "The Large Blue Horses"; in: Plundered Art, 5 January 2012, available online: http://plundered-art.blogspot.de/; accessed 27 December 2017. I thank Lucy Wasensteiner for this reference and for the excerpts related to the U.S. tour she sent me from her forthcoming book that promises to rectify some of these mysteries (Lucy Wasensteiner: The Twentieth Century German Art Exhibition. Answering Degenerate Art in 1930s London. New York, forthcoming).

2 Anon.: German Art Exhibition to Continue; The Times, August 22, 1938, p. 8

3 RSMA, letter from Irmgard Burchard to Fred Uhlmann, 5 September 1938. According to a 3 June 1992 letter from Les Expositions du Palais des Beaux-Arts, Bruxelles (D. Favart) to Paul Klee-Stiftung Kunst*museum Bern (S. Frey) the Twentieth Century German Art* exhibition never took place at the Palais des Beaux-Arts. With thanks to Stefan Frey for sharing this letter from the Collection Paul Klee-Stiftung Kunstmuseum Bern.

4 See Anon.: Modern German Art. Exhibition in Glasgow, Banned Pictures; in: Scotsman, 15 March 1939, p. 17. According to this article, this show was organised under the auspices of the Saltire Society, by 'Mrs Alison Bonfield and Mrs John Doogan'.

5 Archives of American Art, J. B. Neumann Papers, letter from Herbert Read to J. B. Neumann, 24 May 1938

6 RSMA, letter from Irmgard Burchard to Fred Uhlmann 5 September 1938

7 An exact count is not possible as the U.S. catalogue varies titles, and lists no dimensions or collections.

8 Saint Louis Art Museum Archives, Director's Correspondence, letter from Irmgard Burchard to "The Director, St. Louis Art Institute", 11 August 1938

9 Blanche A. Byerley Pousland (b. ca. 1882? - d. May 12, 1960), Obituary and Death Notice Archive, Connecticut, available at: www.genlookups.com, accessed 23 November 2017.

10 Dayton Art Institute Archives, Folder: Banned German Art, Letter from Byerley to Siegfried R. Weng, Director, Dayton Art Institute, 16 September 1939

11 Letter from Abbott to Barr, 23 August 1939, cited in Vivian Endicott Barnett: Banned German Art. Reception and Institutional Support of Modern German Art in the United States, 1933-1945; in: Stephanie Barron (ed.): Exiles and Emigrés. The Flight of European Artists from Hitler. New York 1997, pp. 273-284, pp. 279 and 284, fn. 26.

12 Masurovsky, as in note 1

13 Eric Newton: 'Degenerate' Art. Expressionism in Germany; in: Sunday Times, 10 July 1938; Francis Watson: Banned German Art. London Exhibition of Movements Condemned in Germany; in: Yorkshire Post, 4 July 1938. See also: Albright Knox Art Gallery Archives, Buffalo, letter from Byerley to John Hagerty, The Buffalo Fine Arts Academy, 9 November 1939

14 Anon.: Modern Art of Germany here June 1; in: The Milwaukee Journal, 28 May 1939. I thank Lucy Wasensteiner for sharing this reference.

15 The Saint Louis Art Museum Archives, Director's Office Exhibition Correspondence, letter from Senior Canon, All Saints Cathedral Milwaukee, Wisconsin to Alfred G. Pelikan, 26 June 1939

16 Gregor Langfeld: Deutsche Kunst in New York. Vermittler – Kunstsammler – Ausstellungsmacher 1904-1957. Berlin 2011, pp. 140-141

17 The Saint Louis Art Museum Archives, Director's Office Exhibition Correspondence, letter from Alfred G.

Pelikan to Meyric Rogers, Director, City Art Museum, St. Louis, Missouri, 30 August 1939

18 Paul Westheim: Sanity in Art; in: Die Neue Weltbühne, XXXIV, no. 50 (15 December 1938), pp. 1589-1590. I have discussed this episode at greater length in Keith Holz: 'Brushwork thick and easy' or a 'beauty-parlor mask for murder'? Reckoning with the Great German Art Exhibitions in the Western democracies; in: RIHA Journal, 0055 (28 September 2012), available at: www.riha-journal.org/articles/2012/2012-jul-sep/holz-reckoning; accessed 6 February 2018.

19 The Saint Louis Art Museum Archives, Director's Office Exhibition Correspondence, letter from Byerley to Meyric Rogers, 5 July 1939

20 The Saint Louis Art Museum Archives, Publicity Scrapbooks: Harry R. Burke: Protest Theme of German Art. Vivid Works Now on Display Show Cause of Exile Orders; in: Globe-Democrat, 27 August 1939, page unknown; Anon.: Works of Art Banned by Nazis Draw Attention. Some Smile at Modernistic Paintings in Display at City Museum; in: Star-Times, 25 August 1939, page unknown; Anon.: Banned German Art; in: Star-Times, 26 August 1939, page unknown.

21 Letter from Abbott to Barr, 23 August 1939, cited in Barnett, 1997, pp. 279 and 284, fn. 26. Without making the connection to the concurrent exhibition at Smith College, Barnett notes a similar point discussed at a meeting of the trustees of the Institute of Modern Art in Boston on October 19, 1939. Director's Office Archives, Institute of Contemporary Art, Boston.

22 Letter from Barr to Paul E. Geier, 5 October 1939, cited in Barnett, 1997, pp. 279 and 284, fn. 27

23 For example the review of Raymond Mortimer, cited in this volume p. 186.

24 Albright Knox Art Gallery Archives, Buffalo, condition report Exhibition of 20th Century Germany Art, Portland Art Museum, 27December 1939

25 SFMOMA Archives, Call no. ARCHEXH001, Box 12, Folder 3, copy letter from Grace L. McCann Morley, Director to Blanche A. Byerley, 24 March 1939

26 For an excellent analysis of this Springfield exhibition and the November 1939 ICA Boston exhibition, see: Langfeld 2011, pp. 142-150, 209

27 Among the ballooning literature on the complex ethical, financial, and political questions dogging Valentin's dealing, especially valuable are: Jennifer McComas: Canonizing Hitler's 'Degenerate Art' in Three American Exhibitions, 1939 1942; in: Ruth Iskin (ed.): Re-envisioning the Contemporary Art Canon. Perspectives in a Global World. London 2017, pp. 205-208, and Anja Tiedemann: Die 'Entartete' Moderne und Ihr Amerikanischer Markt. Berlin 2013. Tiedemann, pp. 133-145 shows that the Buchholz Gallery was the widest channel of 'degenerate' artworks entering the United States between early 1939 and June 1940 when naval warfare interrupted transatlantic shipping.

28 Reinhold Heller: The Expressionist Challenge. James Plaut and the Institute of Contemporary Art; in: Reinhold Heller: Dissent: The Issue of Modern Art in Boston, Boston 1985, pp. 16-51; Barnett, 1997, pp. 280-281; Pamela Kort: The Myths of Expressionism in America; in: Renée Price (ed.): New Worlds. German and Austrian Art, 1890–1940. New York etc. 2001, pp. 275-276; Judith Bookbinder: Boston Modern. Figurative Expressionism as Alternative Modernism. Durham, NH 2005, pp. 52-56; Langfeld 2011, pp. 144-150; and McComas 2017, pp. 207-208.

29 A. I. Philpott: Contemporary German Art at the Institute of Modern Art; in: Boston Globe, 2 November 1939, p. 12; cited in Heller 1985, p. 32

30 McComas 2017, pp. 209-212

31 Gallery Notes, Vol. VII, No. 3, December, 1939

32 Albright-Knox Art Gallery Archives, Exhibition of 20th Century Germany Art. Unfortunately only the recto of this folded announcement remains in the museum's archive.

33 Albright-Knox Art Gallery Archives, Clipping File: Nora Lee Rohr: Hitler Banned Art Disclosed in Sadly-Depleted Condition; in: Buffalo Evening News, 9 December 1939, page unknown

34 Copy of November 22, 1939 letter from Byerley to Gordon Washburn, Buffalo Academy of Fine Arts, informing him that "Two Children with Sunflowers", by Carl Hofer, has been acquired in Kansas City ... It will not, therefore, be included in the collection when it is expressed to you..." Exhibition of 20th Century Germany Art, Albright Knox Art Gallery Archives.

35 In a January 12, 1940 letter from Byerley to Dr. Grace L. McCann Morley, Director, San Francisco Museum of Art, Byerley advised: "Should you wish to make an offer off the list price, and will let me know by night letter, I will endeavor to get a reply from England by cable." SFMOMA Archives, Call no: ARCHEXH 001, Box 12, Folder 3. But who in England was consulted remains unknown.

36 Langfeld 2011; and McComas 2017

Ausstellungstournee *20th Century (Banned) German Art* durch die USA

KEITH HOLZ

Über das Ende der Ausstellung *Twentieth Century German Art* herrscht bis heute Unklarheit, und zwar vor allem hinsichtlich des Verbleibs der zusammengetragenen und ausgestellten Werke. Zu diesem Thema bemerkte kürzlich der Historiker Marc Masurovsky: «Eine genaue Auflistung der ‹verbotenen› Kunstwerke hat es nie gegeben, so dass man weder weiß, welche unverkauft an die Leihgeber zurückgingen, noch welche nach Amerika oder sonst wohin geschickt wurden.»[1] Der vorliegende Essay nimmt die Spuren auf, wohin sich die Werke verstreut haben, auch wenn das Hauptaugenmerk dabei auf der Organisation und Rezeption einer Wanderausstellung liegt, die zwischen Juni 1939 und April 1940 in mindestens neun amerikanischen Städten gezeigt wurde.

Nach dreimaliger Verlängerung wurde die Londoner Ausstellung am 27. August 1938 endgültig geschlossen.[2] Anfang September sprach Irmgard Burchard von Plänen, eine Auswahl der Werke in der City Art Gallery Leeds sowie im Brüsseler Palais des Beaux-Arts zu zeigen.[3] In Großbritannien und auf dem Kontinent ist allerdings nur eine einzige Folgestation nachzuweisen, und zwar in Glasgow, wo vom 14. März bis 1. April 1939 ein Teil der Werke in den McLellan Galleries präsentiert wurde.[4]

Schon im Mai 1938 war Herbert Read auf den Kunsthändler J. B. Neumann in New York zugegangen, um in den USA Interesse für das Projekt zu wecken.[5] Bevor Burchard Mitte September nach Zürich zurückkehrte, hatte sie mit den übrigen Mitgliedern des Organisationsteams (entweder mit Read oder Patrick Blackwood, einem Mitarbeiter von Noel Nortons London Gallery) die nötigen Vorbereitungen getroffen, dass eine Tournee von rund 75 Werken durch amerikanische Museen ins Auge gefasst werden konnte.[6] An die in Frage kommenden amerikanischen Einrichtungen wurde eine Liste von Exponaten geschickt, unter ihnen ca. 30 Werke, die auch im Katalog der Londoner Ausstellung aufgeführt sind.[7]

Außerdem hatte Burchard noch aus London einen Rundbrief an amerikanische Museen geschickt, um ihnen die Übernahme der Ausstellung *Twentieth Century German Art* anzubieten. Dem Direktor des Saint Louis Art Museum schrieb sie beispielweise: «Die Ausstellung [in London] ist ein großer Erfolg. [...] Wir würden Amerika gern die Möglichkeit bieten, diese Bilder zu sehen. [...] Unsere Ausstellung ist mit dem Ziel organisiert worden, Stipendien für sogenannte ‹entartete› Künstler zu beschaffen und ihre Bilder zu verkaufen. Sie steht unter der Schirmherrschaft der Tate Gallery und der National Gallery. Über jede Form von Rat und Hilfe würden wir uns sehr freuen.»[8]

Die hervorgehobene Absicht, sogenannte ‹entartete› Künstler mit Stipendien zu unterstützen und ihre Werke zu verkaufen, entspricht zwar ungefähr der Ankündigung im Londoner Katalog: «Der Erlös wird geflüchteten Künstlern zugute kommen.» Doch hat sich der Akzent etwas verschoben: Aus den «geflüchteten Künstlern» im Londoner Katalog sind im Schreiben an die amerikanischen Museen ‹entartete› Künstler geworden. Auch wenn einige der in London ausgestellten Künstler wirklich Flüchtlinge waren, hat Burchard dieses Wort in ihrem Anschreiben vermutlich bewusst gestrichen – denn im August 1938 war die Frage der ‹Flüchtlinge› in den Vereinigten Staaten ein heiß diskutiertes Thema. Womöglich hat sie den Status der Künstler aber auch nur genauer bezeichnen wollen. Eine Übertreibung ist in jedem Fall die Behauptung, die Londoner Ausstellung stehe unter der Schirmherrschaft der Tate Gallery und der National Gallery.

Bis Mai 1939 wurden mindestens 76 Kunstwerke – darunter 30 aus der Londoner Ausstellung – in die USA verschickt, und am 1. Juni eröffnete das Milwaukee Art Institute (Wisconsin) die Schau unter dem Titel *Exhibition of 20th Century (Banned) German Art.*

Doch wie entstand daraus eine Tournee durch die gesamten Vereinigten Staaten? Und in welchen Museen wurde die Schau anschließend gezeigt, ehe sie vermutlich im Frühjahr 1940 endete? In diesem Kontext ist eine gewisse Blanche A. Byerley aus Westport (Connecticut) von Bedeutung.[9] Sie betrieb in New York und Westport, wo sie zu Hause war, das «Blanche A. Byerley Lecture Bureau», und wurde zur Organisatorin der Ausstellungstournee. Byerley unterhielt gute Beziehungen zur New Yorker Ferargil Gallery, die von Fredric Newlin Price in der 63 East 57th Street gegründet worden war.[10] Außerdem stand sie auf Du und Du mit Jere Abbott, dem Direktor des Smith College Museum of Art in Northampton (Massachusetts) sowie mit Alfred Barr, dem Gründungsdirektor des Museum of Modern Art in New York.[11] Ihre Interessen reichten von der europäischen Moderne bis zur zeitgenössischen Kunst afroamerikanischer Frauen, über die sie Ausstellungen organisiert hatte. Später, während des Krieges, koordinierte sie auch Spendenaktionen zugunsten des Russian War Relief. Für die Ausstellung deutscher Kunst wurde sie zu einer außerordentlich engagierten und umsichtigen Organisatorin, wie zahlreiche Briefe belegen. Es gelang ihr, mindestens neun Museen zur Übernahme der Schau zu bewegen. Sie entwarf Zeitpläne für die Veranstaltungen, die jeweils einen knappen Monat dauerten, versorgte jeden Veranstaltungsort mit 500 Exemplaren der Exponatliste d.h. des Katalogs, führte die Korrespondenz mit Versicherungen und Transportfirmen. Außerdem übernahm sie die Öffentlichkeitsarbeit, verschickte Pressemappen mit Textauszügen aus dem Londoner Katalog und Fotos der dort ausgestellten Werke sowie mit Artikeln aus britischen Zeitungen, zum Beispiel aus der *Yorkshire Post* und der *Sunday Times.*[13] Schließlich erstellte sie einen Pressespiegel zu jeder Ausstellungsstation.

Den Auftakt der Tournee bildete, wie bereits erwähnt, die Ausstellung im Milwaukee Art Institute (1.-25. Juni 1939). In einem einführenden Artikel, der kurz vor Eröffnung in der lokalen Presse erschien (Abb. 96), erinnerte ein unbekannter Journalist an die Zeit, als die blauen Pferde Franz Marcs noch als «schändlich», der Expressionismus als «widerlich» und die Maler der Brücke als Inbegriff «toter Seelen» galten. Nach der abschließenden Bemerkung, solche Wertungen seien Beispiele überholter Intoleranz, ermutigte der Autor seine Leser, die Vitalität deutscher moderner Künstler wie Marc, Klee und Feininger zu erkennen. Außerdem bemerkte er, das Milwaukee Art Institute habe bereits ein Werk Hofers erworben. Und zu Grosz heißt es: «Wir sehen in George Grosz den brillantesten Satiriker seit Honoré

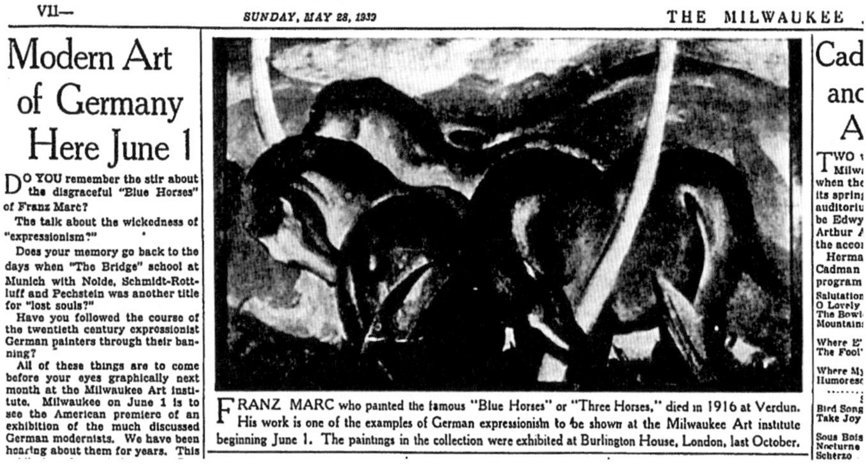

VII— SUNDAY, MAY 28, 1939 THE MILWAUKEE

Modern Art of Germany Here June 1

DO YOU remember the stir about the disgraceful "Blue Horses" of Franz Marc?

The talk about the wickedness of "expressionism?"

Does your memory go back to the days when "The Bridge" school at Munich with Nolde, Schmidt-Rottluff and Pechstein was another title for "lost souls?"

Have you followed the course of the twentieth century expressionist German painters through their banning?

All of these things are to come before your eyes graphically next month at the Milwaukee Art institute. Milwaukee on June 1 is to see the American premiere of an exhibition of the much discussed German modernists. We have been hearing about them for years. This

FRANZ MARC who painted the famous "Blue Horses" or "Three Horses," died in 1916 at Verdun. His work is one of the examples of German expressionism to be shown at the Milwaukee Art institute beginning June 1. The paintings in the collection were exhibited at Burlington House, London, last October.

96 o. V., «Modern Art of Germany Here June 1», *The Milwaukee Journal*, 28. Mai 1939

Daumier und freuen uns, zu erfahren, dass er bald die amerikanische Staatsbürgerschaft erhalten wird. Und schon jetzt lachen wir bei der Vorstellung, welch humanisierenden Effekt Amerika auf seinen Stachel haben wird.»[14]

Auffällig ist, wie der Essay die Mühen eines konservativen und womöglich intoleranten Publikums antizipiert, sich auf diese Kunst einzulassen, wobei der Autor sich zugleich darüber amüsiert, dass einer der betreffenden Künstler sich als neuer US-Bürger an diese Maßstäbe werde anpassen müssen.

Vier Wochen später, am 26. Juni, schrieb Alfred G. Pelikan, der Direktor des Milwaukee Art Institute, einen Brief an Meyric Rogers, den Direktor des Saint Louis City Art Museum, welches die nächste Station der Tournee sein sollte. Seinem Brief legte Pelikan ein Schreiben bei, das er als Reaktion auf die Ausstellung deutscher Kunst vom Kirchenvorstand der Kathedrale von Milwaukee erhalten hatte und das «typisch für viele ähnliche Briefe» sei. Gegenstand des Schreibens war Karl Hofers Bild *Liebespaar*, das die Aufmerksamkeit des Kirchenmannes erregt hatte (Abb. 92). Er beschrieb es als «dermaßen roh und vulgär, dass es nur als unanständig und pornografisch» gelten könne. Sollte jemand von der Polizei angehalten werden und ein Foto dieses Gemäldes bei sich tragen, so würde er mit Sicherheit dafür angeklagt werden. Auch andere Bilder der Ausstellung seien alles anderes als erbaulich.[15] Pelikan mochte es vielleicht beschönigen, doch standen – wie Gregor Langfeld kürzlich analyisert hat – die massiv anti-modernen Zuschriften, zu der auch der Brief einer gewissen Elizabeth Oehlenschlaeger zählte, den populistischen und rassistischen Ansichten der deutschen NS-Politik in nichts nach.[16] Während Meyric Rogers die Ankunft der Bilder in St. Louis erwartete, schrieb ihm Pelikan erneut einen warnenden Brief: «Eine kleine, jedoch sehr aktive Gruppe von Anhängern der ‹Society Sanity in Art› (Gesellschaft für gesunde Kunst) hat während der Ausstellung die moderne Kunst im allgemeinen und *Twentieth Century German Art* im besonderen angegriffen. In Zeitungsartikeln haben diese Leute offen ihre Überzeugung zum Ausdruck gebracht, dass Hitler in Fragen der Kunst durchaus im Recht sei.»[17]

Die Society for Sanity in Art war 1936 als eine Vereinigung von Persönlichkeiten aus der Kunstwelt gegründet worden, die behaupteten, Meinung und Geschmack des Volkes zu

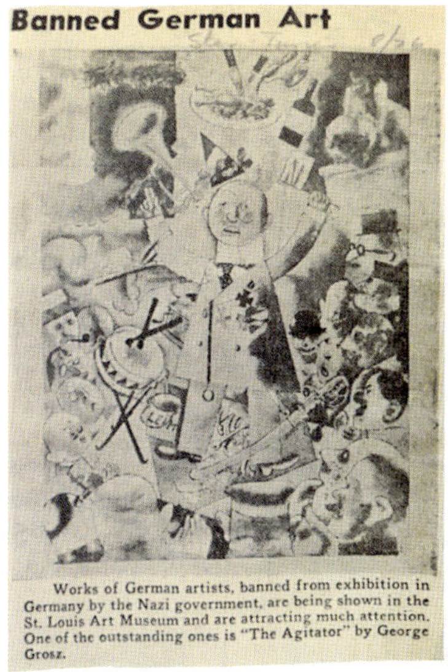
Banned German Art

Works of German artists, banned from exhibition in Germany by the Nazi government, are being shown in the St. Louis Art Museum and are attracting much attention. One of the outstanding ones is "The Agitator" by George Grosz.

97 o.V., «Banned German Art» (mit einer Abbildung von George Grosz, *Der Agitator*, in: *Star-Times*, 26. August 1939.

repräsentieren. Die Gesellschaft hatte Anhänger in vielen Städten, unter anderem in Chicago, Boston, New York und San Francisco. Vorsitzende war die reiche Erbin und Kunstmäzenin Josephine Hancock Logan (1862-1943), die in der Nähe von Chicago wohnte. Seit Anfang der 1930er Jahre hatten sich Logans antimoderne Ansichten so stark verbreitet, dass sogar Paul Westheim in Paris auf sie aufmerksam wurde. Daraufhin verfasste er mehrere Artikel für die deutsche Exilpresse in Frankreich und beschrieb, wie Logan und die Society for Sanity in Art alles bekämpften, was ihnen in der modernen Kunst, «nicht rationell schön» erschien und als ‹krank› bzw. ‹entartet› abgelehnt werden musste. Westheim berichtete auch über Logans Bestrebungen zur ‹Säuberung› der Kunstmuseen von Chicago und unterstrich dabei die Parallelen mit den antimodernen Kampagnen der Nazis.[18]

Nachdem es in Milwaukee wegen Hofers *Liebespaar* zu empörten Reaktionen gekommen war, schrieb Blanche A. Byerley einen Brief an Direktor Rogers in St. Louis. Zwar ging es dabei vornehmlich um Informationen zum Transport und zur Rahmung der auszustellenden Werke, doch gab sie zugleich einen ziemlich einmaligen Rat: «Ich überlasse es», schrieb sie, «der Einschätzung des Museumsdirektors, das eine oder andere der geschickten Kunstwerke nicht zu zeigen, falls dies erforderlich sein sollte.»[19] Aus dem Munde einer Ausstellungsorganisatorin war dies ein recht ungewöhnliches Zugeständnis und konnte als eine Lizenz zur Selbstzensur verstanden werden, um auf diesem Weg die Schau dem angenommenen Publikumsgeschmack anzunähern. Dennoch wurde zwischen dem 1. und 25. September 1939 Hofers Bild samt allen anderen Werken in Saint Louis gezeigt. Die lokale Presse setze sich mit der Ausstellung in zwei Artikeln auseinander, wobei für die Kommentatoren – kurz vor Deutschlands Überfall auf Polen – im Vordergrund stand, dass die Künstler vom Nazi-Regime verboten worden waren.[20]

Die dritte Station der Tournee war das Smith College Museum of Art in Northampton, Massachusetts. Über diese Veranstaltung ist wenig bekannt, nur dass sie vom 6. bis 25. Oktober dauerte und damit relativ kurz war. Der Museumsdirektor Jere Abbott hatte zusammen mit Alfred Barr in Harvard studiert und anschließend zunächst als stellvertretender Direktor des New Yorker Museum of Modern Art gearbeitet. Zwei Wochen vor der Vernissage schrieb

Abbott seinem ehemaligen Kommilitonen: «Aufgrund der Informationen, die ich im Nachhinein erhalten habe, bekomme ich langsam kalte Füße. Nicht aus irgendwelchen politischen Gründen, sondern weil ich höre, dass die Werke nicht repräsentativ für die jeweiligen Künstler seien. In diesem Fall würde die Ausstellung eher schaden als Positives bewirken, denn es gäbe den Leuten Gelegenheit zu sagen, alles gut und schön, doch museumswürdige Bilder sind das nicht.[21]

In einem Brief vom 5. Oktober 1939, dem Tag vor der Ausstellungseröffnung in Northampton, schrieb Barr einem Kunstsammler in Cincinnati und übernahm darin Abbotts Kritik: «Unter uns gesagt, gibt es da eine große Wanderausstellung deutscher Kunst mit ziemlich schlecht ausgewählten Werken. Sie wird in verschiedenen Museen gezeigt, doch es sieht so aus, als würde sie dem Ansehen der deutschen Kunst eher schaden, denn Leute, die keine Freunde der Moderne sind, können dadurch mit einer gewissen Erleichterung behaupten, Hitler habe Recht.»[22]

Wie manche Kritiker zuvor in London[23] und Milwaukee äußerte also auch Barr im privaten Kreis die Sorge, dass eine Ablehnung der modernen Kunst in den demokratischen Ländern eine Parteinahme für Hitler auslösen könne, eine Sorge, die in den ersten Wochen nach Kriegsausbruch keinesfalls irrelevant war. Barr begründete seine Position mit der ‹schlechten Auswahl› der Bilder. Vermutlich meinte er damit eine minderwertige künstlerische Qualität der Werke – zumindest im Vergleich mit denjenigen, zu denen er in New York Zugang hatte. Auch der schlechte konservatorische Zustand der Exponate mag seine Meinung negativ beeinflusst haben. Das Empfangsprotokoll des Portland Art Museum, der sechsten Station der Tournee, hielt am 27. Dezember 1939 bei fast der Hälfte der Leihgaben Beschädigungen der Leinwand, des Papiers oder des Rahmens fest (Abb. 98).[24] Ihr Wert wurde dann bei der siebten Station, dem San Francisco Museum of Art, implizit in Frage gestellt, als die Direktorin Grace L. McCann Morley die Höhe der Leihgebühr von 300 Dollar kritisierte: «Bei so vielen Aquarellen und Zeichnungen», bemängelte sie, «erscheint mir die Gebühr ganz schön happig.»[25]

Die auf Basis der Londoner Schau realisierte Wanderausstellung wird manchmal mit anderen Ausstellungen moderner deutscher Kunst verwechselt, die in den Jahren 1939 und 1940 zu sehen waren. Dies gilt vor allem für die Ausstellung *Modern German Art* vom Januar 1939 im Museum of Fine Arts in Springfield (Massachusetts). Sie bestand jedoch hauptsächlich aus Leihgaben, die Curt Valentin von der New Yorker Buchholz Gallery vermittelt hatte. Buchholz war einer von vier deutschen Kunsthändlern, die von der NS-Regierung offiziell damit beauftragt waren, beschlagnahmte Werke ‹entarteter Kunst› ins Ausland zu verkaufen. Über seine Berliner Galerie konnte er günstig qualitativ hochwertiges Material aus konfisziertem deutschem Museumsbestand erwerben, in die USA exportieren und dort über seinen Mitarbeiter Curt Valentin verkaufen.[27]

Im November 1939 wurde im Institute of Contemporary Art Boston eine weitere Ausstellung *Contemporary German Art* veranstaltet, die sogar noch größer war. Diese später eingehend erforschte Schau wurde – erneut mit Unterstützung Curt Valentins – von James Plaut und Mary Udall organisiert und enthielt einige herausragende Werke des deutschen Expressionismus aus ehemaligem deutschem Museumsbesitz, was kenntlich gemacht war. Weitere Werke stammten aus führenden amerikanischen Museen.[28] Auch der *Boston Globe* wiederholte in seiner Besprechung die Sorge, die Öffentlichkeit könne wegen einer solchen Ausstellung mit der NS-Kulturpolitik sympathisieren. So schrieb der Kritiker unter anderem:

PORTLAND ART MUSEUM

WEST PARK AND MADISON   PORTLAND, OREGON

ROBERT TYLER DAVIS, DIRECTOR

Received from ALBRIGHT ART GALLERY, Decmber 27, 1939,

7 boxes containing the loan EXHIBITION OF 20th CENTURY GERMAN ART:

BAUMEISTER, WILLI
1. Tennis Player. Watercolor

BECKMANN, MAX
2. The Skaters. Oil
3. Working Figures. Oil (frame chipped in different places)

CORINTH, LOVIS
4. Self Portrait. Oil

ERNST, MAX
5. La Colombe Blanche. Oil (frame slightly marred)
6. Acolade. Oil

FEININGER, LYONEL
7. Longeuil, Village in Normandy. Oil (gilt frame chipped in lower right hand corner)

GROSZ, GEORGE
8. Street in Paris. Watercolor
9. The Agitator. Watercolor
10. Restaurant. Watercolor

HECKEL, EHRICH
11. Portrait. Oil
12. Horses in Field. Oil (canvas slightly cracked in places)

HOFER, CARL
13. Liebespaar. Oil

KIRCHNER, ERNST LUDWIG
14. Farmhouse in Fehman. Oil (canvas cracked all over surface, due to age)
15. Laburnun Tree. Oil (canvas cracked in several places, due to age)

KLEE, PAUL
16. Arab Song. Oil (frame cracked on lower right side and marred all over due to age and much handling)
17. New Harmony. Oil (framed marred due to much handling)
18. Garden after the Storm. Oil (canvas chipped in lower part of picture due to age)
19. In the Country of Precious Stones. Watercolor

KOKOSCHKA, OSKAR
20. Mother and Child. Oil (canvas cracked all over surface due to age and bad paint)

98 Erste Seite des Empfangsprotokolls mit Zustandsbeschreibung der Leihgaben, Portland Art Museum, 27. Dezember 1939

«Es wird in Boston unter Kunstliebhabern wahrscheinlich viele geben, die Hitlers Säuberungsaktion begrüßen. [...] Boston, die amerikanische Hauptstadt der Künste, ist somit zum Schlachtfeld eines Meinungskrieges geworden, wobei die Tendenz eben jenen Traditionen zuneigt, die Hitler zu respektieren scheint.»[29] Eine dritte Ausstellung unter Mitwirkung Curt Valentins wurde im April 1940 unter dem Titel *Landmarks in Contemporary German Art* in der New Yorker Buchholz Gallery gezeigt.[30]

Unterdessen war die *Exhibition of 20th Century (Banned) German Art* vom Smith College Museum of Art, Northampton, an ihre vierte Station weitergewandert: die William Rockhill Nelson Gallery in Kansas City (Missouri), wo sie im November 1939 gastierte. Für ihre fünfte Station wurde sie dann in den Nordosten der USA gebracht und war vom 1. bis 22. Dezember in der Albright Art Gallery in Buffalo zu sehen.

Dieses Museum wurde von Gordon B. Washburn geleitet und veröffentlichte in der hauseigenen Zeitschrift *Gallery Notes* einen interessanten Artikel zur Ausstellung.[31] Darin wurde die politische Dimension der Veranstaltung im Hinblick auf die Kultur- und Rassenpolitik der Nationalsozialisten unterstrichen. Außerdem wurde eine Einladungskarte gedruckt, auf welcher der Ausstellungstitel diagonal mit den Worten «Degenerate Non-Aryan» überdruckt war, und zwar in Fraktur (Abb. 93).[32] Die *Buffalo Evening News* berichtete über die Schau unter dem Titel «Von Hitler verbotene Kunst in traurig abgespeckter Form eröffnet» (Abb. 94). Dabei zog die Journalistin Nora Lee Rohr einen Vergleich mit der *Entarteten Kunst* in München und der Ausstellung in den Londoner New Burlington Galleries. Die Schau sei arg «zusammengeschrumpft», bemerkte sie und stehe «nicht mehr wirklich repräsentativ für die damals von Hitler angeprangerte Kunst». Nachdem Kritikerin die Hauptwerke der Ausstellung besprochen und die Bilder in Beziehung zum politischen Kontext der 1920er und 1930er Jahre in Deutschland gesetzt hatte, schloss sie mit einem Satz aus der Pressemitteilung des Museums: «Es muss betont werden, dass die Art Gallery die Ausstellung als künstlerisches Dokument einer Epoche versteht, ohne dass damit irgendeine Zustimmung oder politische Absicht zu signalisieren.»[33]

Wie oben erwähnt, fand die sechste Station der Ausstellung im Portland Art Museum, Oregon, statt (3. bis 25. Januar 1940). Danach wanderte sie 1200 Kilometer die Atlantikküste nach Süden und war vom 1. bis 25. Februar 1940 im San Francisco Museum of Art zu sehen. Nach einer achten Station (3. bis 24. März 1940) im Dayton Art Institute (Ohio) erreichte die Tournee im Josyln Memorial Museum in Omaha (Nebraska) ihren Abschluss (1. bis 25. April 1940). Obwohl Blanche A. Byerley noch weitere Orte geplant hatte, sind nach heutigem Stand der Forschung keine Folgestationen nachgewiesen. Wie viele andere aus dieser Übersicht resultierende Fragen wird auch diese erst durch weitere Forschungen geklärt werden können.

Bedeutung aus heutiger Sicht

Gemessen an Irmgard Burchards erklärten Zielen – Verkauf von Kunstwerken und finanzielle Unterstützung der Künstler –, war die Wanderausstellung durch die USA zweifellos ein Fehlschlag.

Obwohl einige wenige Bilder verkauft wurden – unter anderem Gemälde von Feininger, Hofer (Abb. 95 und 99) und Marc –,[34] ist bislang kein Beleg dafür aufgetaucht, dass mit dem Geld notleidende verfolgte Künstler unterstützt worden wären. Zwar wurden verschiedentlich Besitzer von Bildern in England wegen Kaufangeboten und Bitten um Preisnachlässe

99 Karl Hofer, *Kinder mit Sonnenblumen*, 1929. Öl auf Leinwand, 100 x 74 cm. Privatbesitz

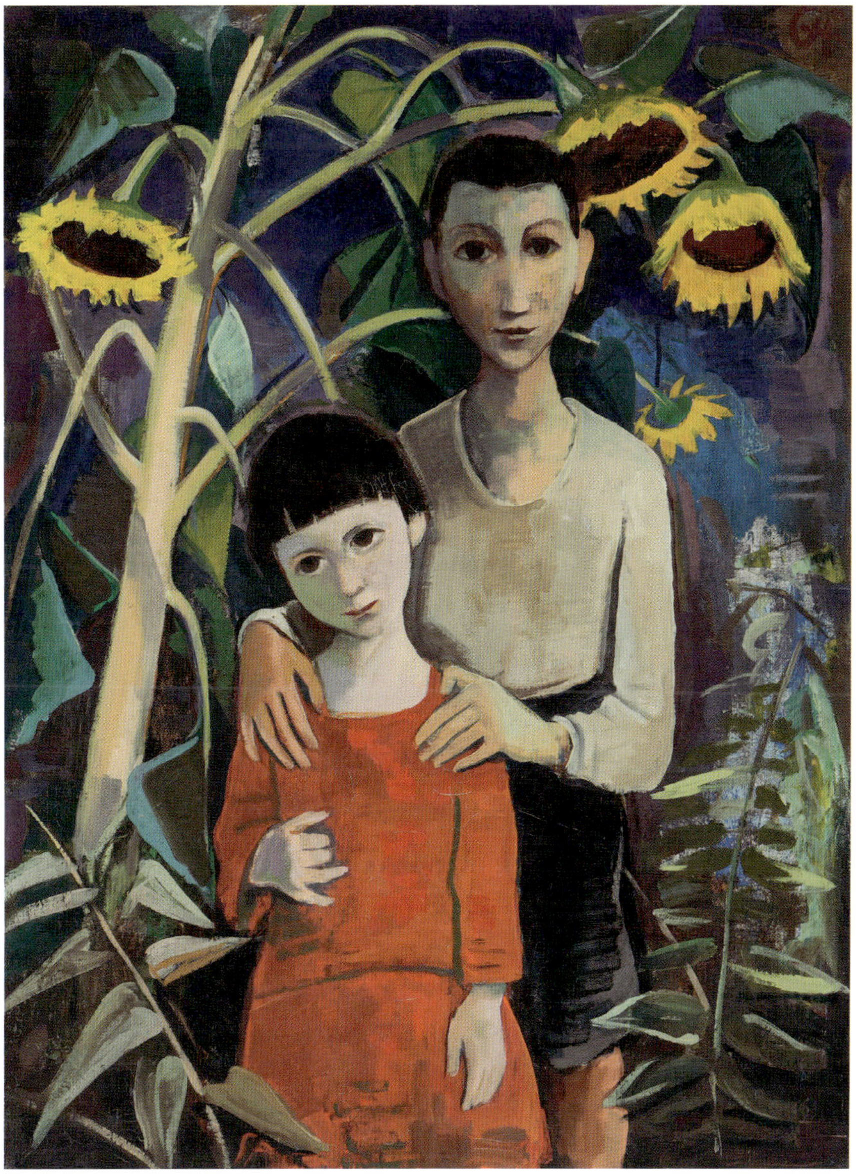

kontaktiert,[35] doch ist bis heute nicht bekannt, ob auch nur ein einziger der europäische Leihgeber Verkaufserlöse erhalten hat.

Gleichwohl konnte die Ausstellung in weniger vordringlichen Belangen positive Ergebnisse für sich verbuchen. Zum einen regte sie die amerikanischen Kunstinteressierten außerhalb der Metropole New York dazu an, sich mit den Verbot, Verfolgungen und Vertreibungen von Künstlern und ihren Werken in NS-Deutschland auseinanderzusetzen. Zum anderen wurde im Vorfeld des Kriegseintritts der USA eine Verbindung zwischen der verfolgten Kunst und den in Amerika hochgehaltenen Werten ‹Demokratie› und ‹Freiheit› etabliert. Und drittens konnten die Direktoren der Museen anhand der Reaktionen auf die Ausstellung feststellen, in welchem Maß das regionale amerikanische Publikum der Kunstauffassung der Nazis nahestand. Auch wenn die Schau an all ihren Stationen im Kreuzfeuer der Kritik stand, so wurde Byerleys Angebot, umstrittene Werke gegebenenfalls wegzulassen, von keinem Museum in Anspruch genommen.

Abschließend bleibt zu bemerken, dass die Ausstellung für einen Schlüsselbereich der jüngeren Forschung von Bedeutung ist, und zwar hinsichtlich der Kanonisierung des Expressionismus und (in geringerem Maße) des Bauhauses als den beiden wichtigsten Kunstströmungen der Moderne vor 1933.[36] Damit trug *20th Century (banned) German Art* allerdings auch zur Etablierung eines simplifizierenden und leicht instrumentaliserbaren Gegensatzpaares bei: der verfolgten deutschen Moderne (Expressionismus und Bauhaus) einerseits und der Kunst der NS-Regierung andererseits.

1 Marc Masurovsky: Franz Marc's «The Large Blue Horses», in: Plundered Art, 5. Januar 2012, http://plundered-art.blogspot.de/, aufgerufen am 27. Dezember 2017. Der Autor bedankt sich bei Lucy Wasensteiner für diese Link sowie die Informationen zur Ausstellungstournee in den USA. Diese werden in ihrem bald erscheinenden Buch zu nachzulesen sein und manche der obenerwähnten Aspekte beleuchten (Lucy Wasensteiner: The Twentieth Century German Art Exhibition. Answering Degenerate Art in 1930s London. New York, im Druck)

2 o. V.: German Art Exhibition to Continue; in: The Times, 22. August 1938, S. 8.

3 RSMA, Brief von Irmgard Burchard an Fred Uhlmann, 5. September 1938. Aus einem Brief vom 3. Juni 1992, den Dominique Favart (Palais des Beaux-Arts Brüssel) an Stefan Frey (Paul Klee-Stiftung/Kunstmuseum Bern) schrieb, geht hervor, dass *Twentieth Century German Art* nie in Brüssel gezeigt wurde. Der Autor dankt Stefan Frey für diese Information.

4 Siehe o. V.: Modern German Art. Exhibition in Glasgow, Banned Pictures, in: Scotsman, 15. März 1939, S. 17. Aus diesem Zeitungsartikel geht hervor, dass diese Ausstellung unter der Schirmherrschaft der Satire Society durch «Mrs Alison Bonfield and Mrs John Doogan» organisiert wurde.

5 Archives of American Art, J. B. Neumann Papers, Brief von Herbert Read an J. B. Neumann, 24. Mai 1938.

6 RSMA, Brief von Irmgard Burchard an Fred Uhlmann, 5. September 1938.

7 Eine genaue Zahlenangabe ist nicht möglich, da im amerikanischen Katalog andere Titel und weder Maße noch Leihgeber notiert sind.

8 Saint Louis Art Museum Archives, Korrespondenz des Direktors, Brief von Irmgard Burchard an den Direktor der «St. Louis Art Institute», 11. August 1938.

9 Blanche A. Byerley Pousland (ca. 1882-12. Mai 1960), Obituary and Death Notice Archive, Connecticut, www.genlookups.com, aufgerufen am 23. November 2017.

10 Dayton Art Institute Archives, Banned German Art, Brief von Byerley an Siegfried R. Weng, Direktor des Dayton Art Institute, 16. September 1939.

11 Brief von Jere Abbott an Alfred Barr, 23. August 1939, zitiert in Vivian Endicott Barnett: Banned German Art. Reception and Institutional Support of Modern German Art in the United States, 1933–1945, in: Stephanie Barron (Hg.): Exiles and Emigrés. The Flight of European Artists from Hitler, New York 1997, S. 273-284.

12 Masurovsky, siehe Fußnote 1.

13 Eric Newton: ‹Degenerate› Art. Expressionism in Germany, in: Sunday Times, 10. Juli 1938; Francis Watson: Banned German Art. London Exhibition of Movements Condemned in Germany, in: Yorkshire Post, 4. Juli 1938; Albright Knox Art Gallery Archives Buffalo, Brief von Blanche A Byerley an John Hagerty (Buffalo Fine Arts Academy), 9. November 1939.

14 o. V.: Modern Art of Germany here June 1, in: The Milwaukee Journal, 28. Mai 1939. Der Autor dankt Lucy Wasensteiner für die Information.

15 The Saint Louis Art Museum Archives, Korrespondenz des Direktors, Brief von Dompropst der Kathedrale von Milwaukee an Alfred G. Pelikan, 26. Juni 1939.

16 Gregor Langfeld: Deutsche Kunst in New York. Vermittler – Kunstsammler – Ausstellungsmacher 1904-1957, Berlin 2011, S. 140-141.

17 The Saint Louis Art Museum Archives, Korrespondenz des Direktors, Brief von Alfred G. Pelikan (Milwaukee Art Institute) an Meyric Rogers (City Art Museum, St. Louis), 30. August 1939.

18 Paul Westheim: Sanity in Art, in: Die Neue Weltbühne, 34. Jg, Nr. 50 (15. Dezember 1938), S. 1589-1590. Siehe dazu Keith Holz: «Brushwork thick and easy» or a «beauty-parlor mask for murder»? Reckoning with the Great German Art Exhibitions in the Western democracies, in: RIHA Journal, 0055 (28. September 2012), www.riha-journal.org/articles/2012/2012-jul-sep/holz-reckoning, aufgerufen am 6. Februar 2018.

19 The Saint Louis Art Museum Archives, Korrespondenz des Direktors, Brief von Blanche Byerley an Meyric Rogers, 5. Juli 1939.

20 The Saint Louis Art Museum Archives, Pressespiegel, Harry R. Burke: Protest Theme of German Art. Vivid Works Now on Display Show Cause of Exile Orders, in: Globe-Democrat, 27. August 1939, Seite unbekannt; o. V.: Works of Art Banned by Nazis Draw Attention. Some Smile at Modernistic Paintings in Display at City Museum, in: Star-Times, 25. August 1939, Seite unbekannt; o. V.: Banned German Art, in: Star-Times, 26. August 1939, Seite unbekannt.

21 Brief von Jere Abbott an Alfred Barr, 23. August 1939, zitiert in Barnett 1997, S. 279/284, fn. 26. Obgleich sie keine Verbindung zur Ausstellung im Smith College herstellt, unterstreicht Barnett, dass eine ähnliche Auffassung bei einem Treffen des Kuratoriums des Bostoner Institute of Modern Art am 19. Oktober 1939 geäußert wurde (Institute of Contemporary Art, Boston, Offizielles Archiv des Direktors).

22 Brief von Alfred Barr an Paul E. Geier, 5. Oktober 1939, zitiert in Barnett 1997, S. 279/284, fn. 27.

23 Siehe z.B. das Zitat von Raymond Mortimer auf S. 192.

24 Albright Knox Art Gallery Archives Buffalo, Empfangsprotokolls für die Werke der Ausstellung *20th Century Germany Art*, Portland Art Museum, 27. Dezember 1939.

25 SFMOMA Archives, Signatur: ARCHEXH001, Box 12, Folder 3, Kopie des Briefes von Grace L. McCann Morley an Blanche A. Byerley, 24. März 1939.

26 Eine ausgezeichnete Analyse der Ausstellungen in Springfield und Boston findet sich in Langfeld 2011, S. 142-150 sowie 209.

27 Unter den vielen Abhandlungen über die ethischen, finanziellen und politischen Aspekte der Aktivitäten von Curt Valentin sind folgende Werke hervorzuheben: Jennifer McComas: Canonizing Hitler's «Degenerate Art» in Three American Exhibitions, 1939-1942, in: Ruth Iskin (Hg.): Re-envisioning the Contemporary Art Canon. Perspectives in a Global World, London 2017, S. 205-208; Anja Tiedemann: Die «Entartete» Moderne und ihr amerikanischer Markt, Berlin 2013, S. 133-145. Im letzteren Werk wird dargestellt, wie die New Yorker Buchholz Gallery ab Anfang 1939 zum Hauptumschlagplatz für ‹entartete› Kunst in den USA wurde, bis der transatlantische Handelsverkehr ab Juni 1940 durch den Seekrieg nicht mehr möglich war.

28 Reinhold Heller: The Expressionist Challenge. James Plaut and the Institute of Contemporary Art, in: Reinhold Heller: Dissent: The Issue of Modern Art in Boston, Boston 1985, S. 16-51; Barnett 1997, S. 280-281; Pamela Kort: The Myths of Expressionism in America, in: Renée Price (Hg.): New Worlds. German and Austrian Art, 1890-1940, New York u.a. 2001, S. 275-276; Judith Bookbinder: Boston Modern. Figurative Expressionism as Alternative Modernism, Durham 2005, S. 52-56; Langfeld 2011, S. 144-150; McComas 2017, S. 207-208.

29 A. I. Philpott: Contemporary German Art at the Institute of Modern Art, in: Boston Globe, 2. November 1939, S. 12; zitiert in Heller 1985, S. 32.

30 McComas 2017, S. 209–212.

31 Gallery Notes, Bd. VII, Nr. 3, Dezember 1939.

32 Albright-Knox Art Gallery Archives, Exhibition of 20th Century Germany Art. Leider ist nur die Vorderseite der Karte erhalten.

33 Albright-Knox Art Gallery Archives, Presseausschnitte: Nora Lee Rohr: Hitler Banned Art Disclosed in Sadly-Depleted Condition, in: Buffalo Evening News, 9. Dezember 1939, Seite unbekannt.

34 Am 22. November 1939 schrieb Blanche A. Byerley an Gordon B. Washburn, den Direktor der Albright Art Gallery: «Das Gemälde *Zwei Kinder mit Sonnenblumen* von Carl Hofer wurde in Kansas City verkauft. [...] Deshalb wird es nicht unter den Werken sein, die Ihnen zugesandt werden sollen.» (Albright-Knox Art Gallery Archives, Exhibition of 20th Century Germany Art).

35 Am 12. Januar 1940 schrieb Blanche A. Byerley an Dr. Grace L. McCann Morley, die Direktorin des San Francisco Museum of Art: «Sollten Sie mir ein Angebot machen, das unter dem im Katalog gedruckten Preis liegt, würde ich dieses unverzüglich nach England mit der Bitte um Antwort telegrafieren.» (SFMOMA-Archives, Signatur: ARCHEXH 001, Box 12, Folder 3). Die Kontaktperson in England ist allerdings nicht bekannt.

36 Langfeld 2011 sowie McComas 2017.

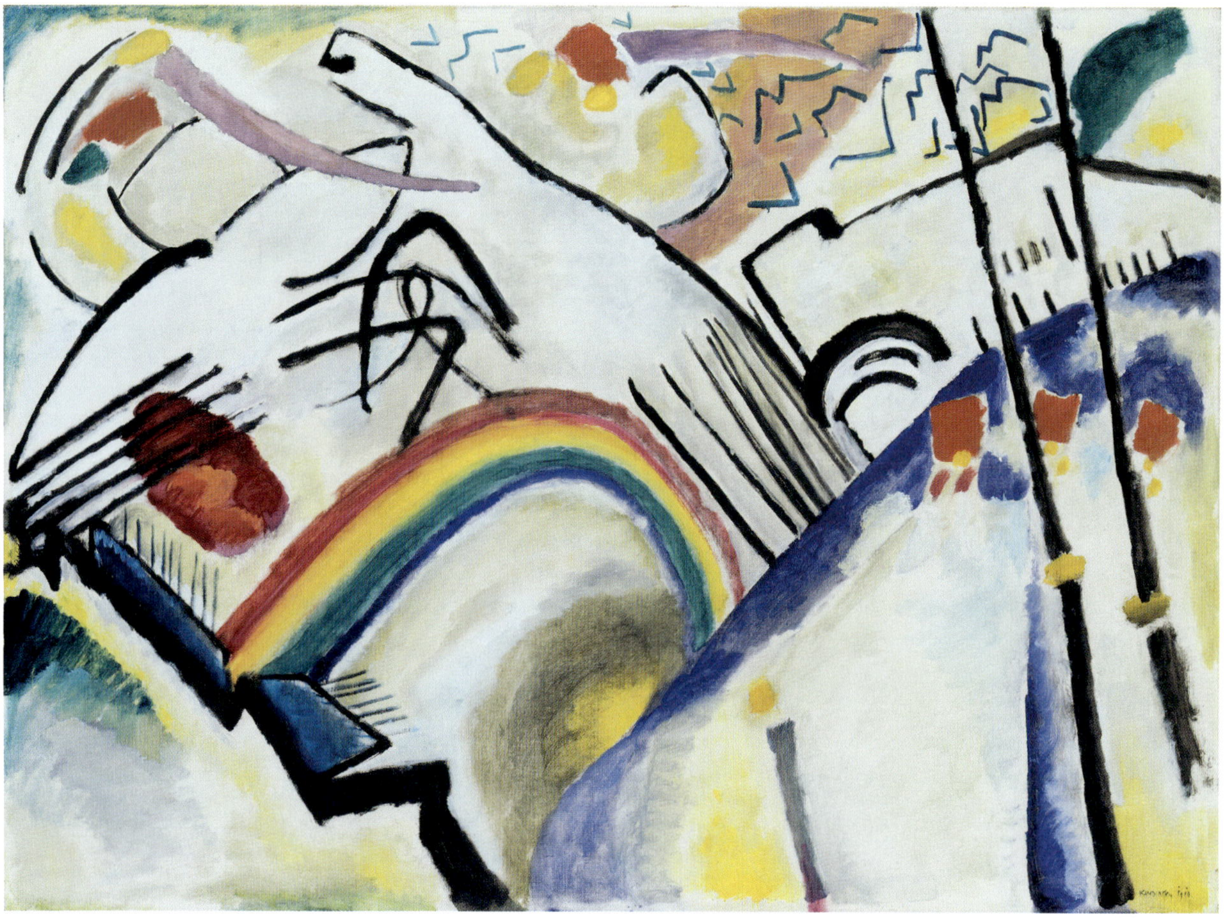

100 Wassily Kandinsky, *Cossacks*, 1910-11. Oil on canvas, 94.6 x 130.2 cm. Tate Gallery London

Modern German Art in Britain after 1938: Recolletions of a Curator[1]

RICHARD CALVOCORESSI

"An American woman living in London has bought a pre-war painting from me and presented it to the Tate Gallery in London! It is the first truly modern painting in the famous museum in London."[2] Wassily Kandinsky, writing in January 1939 to his old friend and supporter in the US, Galka Scheyer, was referring to *Cossacks* (1910-11, fig. 100), which had recently been donated to the Tate by Hazel McKinley, Peggy Guggenheim's sister. Although ex-catalogue, *Cossacks* was included in the *Twentieth Century German Art* exhibition at the New Burlington Galleries in Mayfair, together with other works by Kandinsky on loan from Guggenheim Jeune, Peggy Guggenheim's gallery in nearby Cork Street. It remains the only Kandinsky from the early Blaue Reiter period in a British public collection.

Despite the open-minded reaction of the British public to *Twentieth Century German Art* (see pp. 181-184 of this volume), the story of British attitudes to modern German art after 1938 is generally one of ignorance, prejudice and missed opportunities, redeemed ultimately by the actions of a handful of convinced individuals in prominent positions in the public as well as the private sector.

If we start by looking at national collections, it was to be another eight years before the Tate actually purchased a work by a modern German artist. During the Second World War, two oils by Oskar Kokoschka and a gouache by Paul Klee were acquired by the gallery but all three were gifts. In 1946, however, John Rothenstein – a director not known for his love of continental modernism – bought three top-quality 1920s watercolours by Paul Klee from the artist's widow, Lily. Rothenstein was encouraged by the success of the Tate's exhibition *Paul Klee 1879-1940*, shown at the National Gallery from December 1945 to February 1946 while the bomb-damaged Tate was undergoing repairs. A smaller version of this exhibition was afterwards toured to six cities in England and Scotland by the Arts Council.

The idea for the Klee show came from the art historian and collector Douglas Cooper. He selected the 137 works together with Lily Klee (who lent three quarters of the exhibition) and Rolf Bürgi, Klee's financial adviser in Switzerland and owner of an important collection of his work. On a diplomatic level they were supported by Noel 'Peter' Norton (fig. 35) and her husband Clifford. Eight years after their involvement in the planning of *Twentieth Century German Art*, the Nortons were now in Bern, where Clifford was a minister at the British Embassy. This was also the city where both Lily Klee and Bürgi lived, and where Cooper was working as a 'monuments man', tracking down Nazi-looted art that had been sold to Swiss collectors.

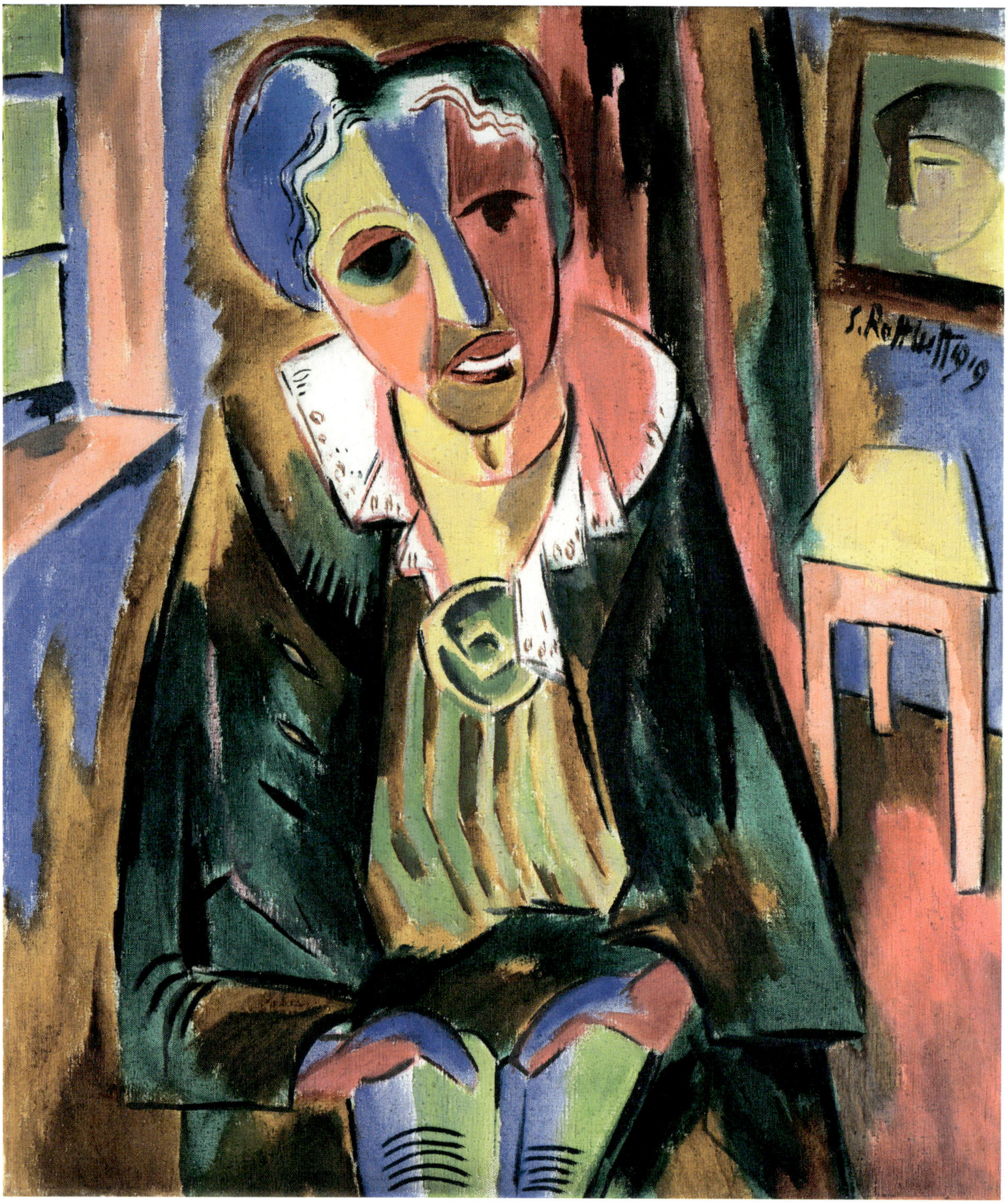

101 Karl Schmidt-Rottluf, *Portrait of Dr Rosa Schapire*, 1919. Oil on canvas, 100.6 x 87.3 cm. Tate Gallery London

It is worth pausing for a moment to reflect on the appetite for new German art in London in the 1930s. For a brief period Peter Norton was a neighbour of Douglas Cooper's in Cork Street. As a director of the Mayor Gallery (until 1938), a few doors down from Norton's London Gallery, Cooper gave Max Ernst and Klee their first one-man shows in Britain, in 1933 and 1934 respectively; in 1933 he also held a Kandinsky exhibition. The Mayor Gallery was committed to showing German art from the outset owing partly to its relationship with the renowned dealer Alfred Flechtheim, who was in the process of moving his stock from Germany now that the Nazis were in power. At the Mayor Gallery's opening show in 1933, which included work by Ernst, Klee and Willi Baumeister, Cooper's co-director Freddy Mayor told the press: "... the Germans will be the great novelty, as none of their works has been seen in England before".[3] But business was slow and only a few British collectors took the opportunity to buy: in the case of a George Grosz exhibition at the gallery in 1934 not a single work was sold.

The situation after 1945 was if anything worse. Had Klee not been marketed as a Swiss artist – his German nationality and service in the German army in the First World War conveniently overlooked – it is debatable whether the Tate trustees would have agreed to buy his work. But antipathy towards Germany for having dragged Britain into two world wars does not fully explain the negative reaction to modern German art, many of whose practitioners were, after all, Jewish or anti-Nazi (or both). The main reason, I suspect, has to do with taste. The teaching of art history and the collecting of modern art in Britain were heavily influenced by the doctrine of formalism – the insistence on the superiority of 'significant form' over representational or narrative content – preached by the influential critic Roger Fry and his Bloomsbury circle, leading them to promote French art, and virtually ignore German. Reviewing Herbert Read's book *Art Now* in 1934, Fry accused German art, with its "Teutonic" tendency to Expressionism, of "artistic bad manners" in contrast to French or Italian art.[4] Read was one of the few in Britain at the time publicly to champion German art.

The Klee acquisition aside, Rothenstein's subsequent record at the Tate as far as German art is concerned was dismal. It was only after her death in 1954 that Rosa Schapire's offer of an outstanding group of paintings and a sculpture by her friend, the Brücke artist Karl Schmidt-Rottluff, was accepted as a gift (a gift which included, for example, Schmidt-Rottluff's portrait *Dr Rosa Schapire* of 1919, fig. 101). The British Museum's department of prints and drawings behaved even less creditably, turning down Schapire's offer of her almost complete collection of Schmidt-Rottluff's graphics. However, it went some way towards making up for this a generation later when its curators Antony Griffiths and Frances Carey embarked on a sustained programme of collecting, culminating in their ground-breaking 1984 exhibition, *The Print in Germany 1880-1933: The Age of Expressionism*, which included no less than 170 recent acquisitions.

Rosa Schapire, a respected art historian with socialist and feminist beliefs who championed Die Brücke, left most of her prints to museums in Germany but donated a few to the Victoria and Albert Museum and to Leicester Art Gallery. Thanks to an enlightened director, Trevor Thomas, Leicester had succeeded in putting together a small but impressive collection of German Expressionism during the war, in itself a remarkable achievement. This included Franz Marc's *Red Woman* (1914) and Lyonel Feininger's *Behind the Church* (1916), both oils bought from the family of Tekla Hess, widow of the wealthy Erfurt shoe manufacturer Alfred Hess. Like Dr Schapire, Mrs Hess had emigrated to Britain in 1939, bringing a fraction of her once extensive collection of modern German art with her.[5]

Rothenstein's successor as director of the Tate Gallery was Norman Reid. Reid was not unsympathetic to German art, buying the occasional work by, for example, Emil Nolde, Ernst Barlach and Max Beckmann, as well as – more controversially – Grosz's savage satire on the link between bought sex and death, *Suicide* (1916). But it was not until Alan Bowness became director in 1980 that the Tate started to treat German art, both modern and contemporary, with the seriousness it deserved. If I had to single out one acquisition from this period it would be Beckmann's mysterious, dream-like *Carnival* (1920, fig. 102), a masterpiece of the artist's Neue Sachlichkeit phase, which the Tate bought in 1981. *Carnival* had been shown at the Hayward Gallery in 1978-79 in the Arts Council of Great Britain's large exhibition *Neue Sachlichkeit and German Realism of the Twenties*, curated by the distinguished Austrian art historian Wieland Schmied – the first substantial exhibition of this period in German art outside Germany. The government-funded Arts Council had a respectable record when it came to touring shows around the country of classic German masters such as Feininger and Klee. Simultaneously the German government-funded Goethe Institutes in London and Glasgow, under the lead of enlightened directors such as Günter Coenen and Hilmann von Halem respectively, worked quietly but effectively to promote an informed understanding of German culture and history through a stimulating programme of exhibitions, performances, recitals, films and talks.

In his relatively brief tenure at the Tate (1980-88) Bowness also acquired important works by Ernst Ludwig Kirchner, Kurt Schwitters (a large and striking assemblage, *Picture of Spatial Growths* of 1920/1939), Ernst, Kokoschka and Wols. As Bowness's curator responsible for German art, I found him refreshingly responsive to my proposals for purchasing the work of living artists such as Joseph Beuys, Georg Baselitz, Anselm Kiefer (the three 1973 *Parsifal* pictures) and A R Penck, and by Austrians such as Arnulf Rainer, Hermann Nitsch and Günter Brus. I felt that what was happening in cities such as Cologne, Berlin and Vienna was at least as interesting as the widely trumpeted art scene in New York. The Tate failed, however, to acquire a painting by Otto Dix, having been outbid at auction in London in 1986 when the artist's *Der Salon I*, a sardonic brothel scene of 1921, sold for a record price to the Galerie der Stadt (now Kunstmuseum) in Stuttgart, the pre-eminent institutional collector of Dix's work.

The only public collection in Britain to possess an oil by Dix is the Scottish National Gallery of Modern Art (SNGMA) in Edinburgh, founded in 1960. In 1980 it acquired Dix's *Nude Girl on a Fur* 1932, a portrait of a well-worn prostitute that recalls earlier German masters such as Cranach in the pose of the figure and Baldung in Dix's meticulous attention to the texture of hair, fur and sagging flesh. The Scots, it seems, were appreciative of modern German art earlier than the English. It is significant, for instance, that a version of the *Twentieth Century German Art* exhibition travelled to Glasgow in 1939, where it was thoughtfully reviewed.[6] Throughout the 1930s a series of shows devoted to northern European and German artists had taken place at the Royal Scottish Academy in Edinburgh: Edvard Munch (1931, his first in Britain), Klee (1934), German sculpture (1936), Max Ernst (1937). Later, in the 1960s, the SNGMA under Douglas Hall acquired a fine early Brücke painting by Kirchner (15 years before he was bought by the Tate, fig. 103), and expressionist paintings by Nolde and Alexei Jawlensky. In 1970 the Richard Demarco Gallery brought Beuys, Gerhard Richter, Blinky Palermo and other contemporary Düsseldorf artists to the Edinburgh Festival. For Beuys, it was the first of many visits to Scotland.

The 1980s marked a turning point in Scotland as in England. The SNGMA acquired a 1913 oil by Feininger, Beckmann's print cycle *Hell* (1919); and, after I took over the running of the gallery from Hall in 1987, a beautiful chalk drawing by Oskar Kokoschka of his lover and muse Alma Mahler, as well as two striking carved wooden figures separated in date by almost half a century: Barlach's *The Terrible Year 1937* (1936. fig. 104) and Baselitz's *Untitled* (1982-84) – his first sculpture to enter a museum collection anywhere. Even rarer, *The Terrible Year 1937* is the only wood carving by Barlach in a public collection in Britain. Although he carved it in 1936, the artist did not title his sculpture of a mourning woman, inspired by northern Gothic art, until the following year, in response to the notorious *Entartete Kunst* action and exhibition in Germany. To mark their fiftieth anniversary in 1987, I curated a display juxtaposing the Barlach with Kokoschka's *Portrait of a 'Degenerate Artist'* (1937), which was then on loan to the gallery from a private collection (and still is). It had been one of at least seven oils by Kokoschka shown in *Twentieth Century German Art* in London in 1938.

If the climate was generally more receptive to German art, much of the credit is due to the commitment shown by a very small number of commercial galleries. Chief among these was Marlborough Fine Art, founded in London after the war by two émigrés from Vienna, Frank Lloyd and Harry Fischer (who later broke away to open his own gallery, Fischer Fine Art). From the late 1950s Marlborough staged a series of pioneering exhibitions on aspects of 20th-century German art, and in 1964 mounted the first ever Egon Schiele exhibition in Britain. It also held regular exhibitions of Kokoschka's work, eventually representing his estate. Another estate it managed was that of Schwitters. Its important 1981 exhibition re-evaluating Schwitters's late work included the assemblage, *Picture of Spatial Growths* (1920/1939), which Bowness later purchased for the Tate.

Marlborough and Fischer Fine Art's dedication to classic modern German and Austrian art was later echoed with almost missionary zeal in relation to contemporary German art by the Anthony d'Offay gallery in London. Joseph Beuys's installation at the gallery in 1980, *Stripes from the House of the Shaman*, was followed by further revelatory shows devoted to Beuys, Baselitz, Richter, Sigmar Polke and Kiefer, culminating in 1991 in d'Offay's sale to the Tate of Beuys's final, multi-part sculptural environment, *The End of the Twentieth Century.* By this time Nicholas Serota had succeeded Alan Bowness as director, following 12 years at the Whitechapel Art Gallery. Here he organised shows of Kiefer, Baselitz, Rainer and, most memorably, Beckmann's triptychs, including *Temptation* (Bayerische Staatsgemäldesammlungen, Munich) which had last been seen in London at the New Burlington Galleries in 1938. Before the Whitechapel, Serota had been director of the Museum of Modern Art in Oxford where, in 1974, he invited Beuys to show for the first time his large and expanding group of drawings, *The Secret Block for a Secret Person in Ireland*, which gives a crucial insight into the artist's sculptural thinking.

Serota belongs to a younger generation of art historians born at the end of the war or just afterwards who did not share the reservations about modern German art – or aggressively figurative, sexually explicit or socially critical art, which much German art tends to be – that had bothered their predecessors, with notable exceptions such as Bowness. Like-minded peers in positions of influence included David Elliott, Norman Rosenthal and Neil MacGregor. While still a student at Durham University in 1970 Elliott organised the multidisciplinary exhibition *Germany in Ferment: Art and Society in Germany 1900-1933*, which travelled afterwards via Sheffield to Leicester Art Gallery, where Elliott became an assistant. He later succeeded Serota in Oxford. At London's Institute of Contemporary Arts in 1974 Rosenthal, together with the Berlin-based 'Ausstellungsmacher' Christos M. Joachimedes, curated an exhibition of radical contemporary German art, *Art into Society: Society into Art*, featuring Beuys, Hans Haacke and others. In 1981 Rosenthal collaborated with Serota and Joachimides on the seminal exhibition *A New Spirit in Painting* at the Royal Academy, where he was by now exhibitions secretary. It introduced the work of Baselitz, Markus Lüpertz, Kiefer, Polke and others to the British public for the first time. Four years later Rosenthal organised, again with Joachimedes (and Wieland Schmied), a massive survey of 20th-century German art in the same venue.

From 1981-87 Neil MacGregor was editor of *The Burlington Magazine*. In an early editorial he drew attention to the historical neglect of 20th-century German art in Britain's museums and galleries – a neglect that Bowness and others were in the process of remedying.[7] MacGregor's first – in retrospect, symbolic – act on assuming the directorship of the National Gallery in 1987 was to buy a landscape by Caspar David Friedrich, the artist's first in a public collection in Britain. What MacGregor wrote then about the British indifference to German Romantic painting applies equally to the negative perception a century later of German Expressionism (whose liberating spirit owed much to the ideals of Romanticism) – doubts that he and others of his generation have gone a long way to dispel.

Most German painters of the last century found ready patrons at home, so few chose or needed to export their works during their lifetime. This century's wars ensured that no British connoisseur would buy Menzel or Runge in the way that Keynes or Courtauld bought Cézanne and the Impressionists. To these practical obstacles were added theoretical ones. Critics concerned primarily to investigate art as a formal progression from Cézanne through Cubism to full Abstraction were unlikely to linger on the spiritual narrative of an artist like Friedrich, whose formal repertoire owes a great deal to earlier art and whose contribution to the European tradition is as much in his content as in his handling of it.[8]

1 The author was a curator at the Tate Gallery (1979-1987), director of the Scottish National Gallery of Modern Art (1987-2007) and director of the Henry Moore Foundation (2007-2015). He now works for the Gagosian Gallery, London

2 Ronald Alley: Catalogue of The Tate Gallery's Collection of Modern Art, other than works by British Artists. London 1981, p.381

3 Richard Calvocoressi: Klee's Reception in Scotland and England 1930-1945; in: Stefan Frey and Josef Helfenstein (eds.) Paul Klee Rediscovered. Works from the Bürgi Collection. London 2000, p. 235.

4 Roger Fry: Art Now. An Introduction to the Theory of Modern Painting and Sculpture; in: The Burlington Magazine, 64 (1934), pp. 242 and 245

5 The Hess family were also among the lenders to *Twentieth Century German Art*. See the forthcoming volume by Lucy Wasensteiner; The Twentieth Century German Art Exhibition. Answering Degenerate Art in 1930s London. New York, forthcoming

6 Anon.: Modern German Art Exhibition in Glasgow. Banned Pictures; in: The Scotsman, 15 March 1939, p. 17. I am grateful to Lucy Wasensteiner for drawing my attention to this review

7 Editorial: The Tate Gallery's foreign collection. A new catalogue; in: The Burlington Magazine, 124 (1982), p.539

8 Neil MacGregor: Foreword; in: John Leighton and Colin J. Bailey: Caspar David Friedrich. Winter Landscape. London 1990, p. 5

Deutsche Kunst der Moderne in Grossbritannien nach 1938 – Erinnerungen eines Kurators[1]

RICHARD CALVOCORESSI

«Eine in London lebende Amerikanerin hat ein Bild von mir aus der Zeit vor dem Kriege gekauft und es der Tate Gallery geschenkt. Es ist das erste wirklich moderne Werk in diesem berühmten Londoner Museum»,[2] schreibt Wassily Kandinsky im Januar 1939 an seine langjährige amerikanische Freundin Galka Scheyer und bezieht sich dabei auf das Gemälde Fragment zu *Komposition IV* (auch bekannt als *Cossacks*) (1910/11, Abb. 100). Hazel McKinley, die Schwester von Peggy Guggenheim, hatte es kurz zuvor der Tate Gallery übereignet. Auch wenn das Bild im Katalog von *Twentieth Century German Art* nicht erwähnt ist, war es in der Ausstellung der New Burlington Galleries dennoch zu sehen. Gleiches gilt für weitere Werke Kandinskys, die von Guggenheim Jeune kamen, der Galerie, die Peggy Gugenheim an der Cork Street betrieb. Bis heute ist *Cossacks* das einzige Kandinsky-Gemälde aus der Zeit des Blauen Reiter, das sich in einer öffentlichen britischen Sammlung befindet.

Trotz der aufgeschlossenen Reaktion des britischen Publikums auf *Twentieth Century German Art* (siehe S. 186-190), war die Haltung der Briten gegenüber der deutschen modernen Kunst nach 1938 vor allem durch Ignoranz, Vorurteile und verpasste Gelegenheiten gekennzeichnet. Nur sehr wenige einflussreiche Privatpersonen und Vertreter öffentlicher Stellen bildeten dazu ein Gegengewicht. Betrachtet man die britischen Museumssammlungen, so sollte es nach Ende der Londoner Ausstellung noch acht Jahre dauern, bis die Tate Gallery das erste Werk eines modernen deutschen Künstlers ankaufte. Zwar waren während des 2. Weltkrieges zwei Ölgemälde von Oskar Kokoschka und eine Gouache von Paul Klee in die Sammlung gelangt, jedoch nicht durch Kauf, sondern als Schenkung. Erst 1946 erwarb John Rothenstein, der Direktor der Tate, bei Klees Witwe drei bedeutende Aquarelle des Künstlers aus den 1920er Jahren. Er hegte zwar keine Vorliebe für die europäische Moderne, sah sich zu diesem Kauf jedoch durch den Erfolg der Ausstellung *Paul Klee 1879-1940* veranlasst, die vom Dezember 1945 bis Februar 1946 in der damals noch von deutschen Bomben beschädigten Tate Gallery stattgefunden hatte. Eine kleinere Version der Ausstellung tourte im Anschluss durch sechs Städte Englands und Schottlands, organisiert vom Arts Council of Great Britain.

Initiant der Klee-Ausstellung war der Kunstsammler und -historiker Douglas Cooper. Zusammen mit Lily Klee, die drei Viertel der Exponate zur Verfügung stellte, und Rolf Bürgi, dem Sammler und Finanzberater des Künstlers, wählte Cooper insgesamt 137 Werke aus. Noel ‹Peter› Norton (Abb. 35) und ihr Ehemann Clifford, die acht Jahre zuvor an der Vor-

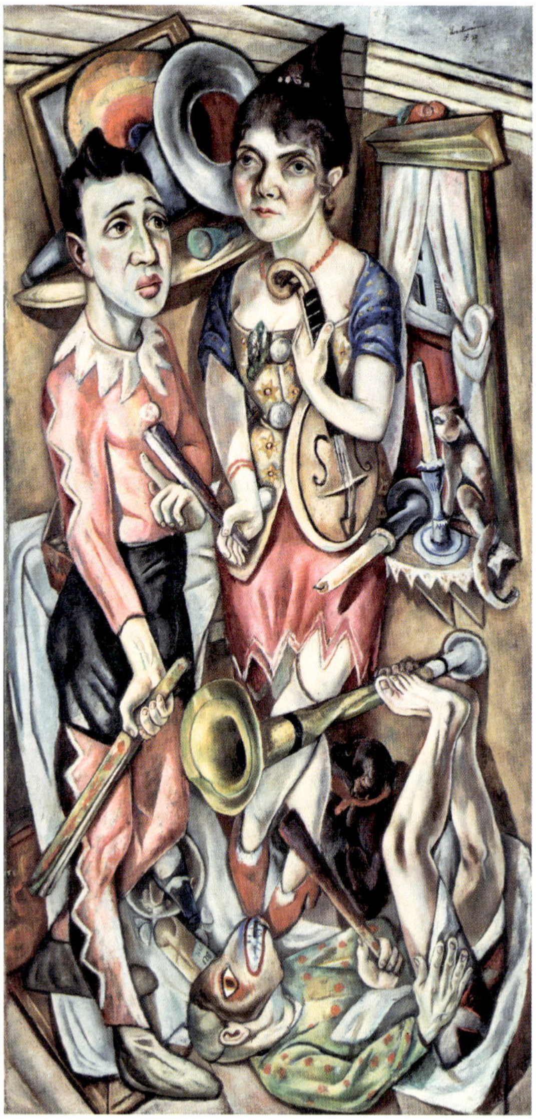

102 Max Beckmann, *Karneval*, 1920. Oil on canvas, 186.4 x 91.8 cm. Tate Gallery London

bereitung der Ausstellung *Twentieth Century German Art* beteiligt gewesen waren, konnten das Projekt auf diplomatischer Ebene unterstützen. Mittlerweile lebten sie in Bern, wo Clifford Norton an der britische Botschaft tätig war. In Bern wohnten auch Lily Klee und Rolf Bürgi, während Douglas Cooper als ‹Monuments Man› hier Kunstwerke aufzuspüren versuchte, die von den Nazis geraubt und von Schweizer Sammlern gekauften worden waren.

Es empfiehlt sich, an diesem Punkt kurz auf das Interesse zurückzublicken, das in London während der 1930er Jahre für deutsche Kunst bestanden hat. Für eine kurze Zeit waren Noel Norton und Douglas Cooper Nachbarn an der Cork Street. Bis 1938 führte Cooper dort die Mayor Gallery, nur wenige Meter von Noel Nortons London Gallery entfernt, und er war es, der Max Ernst und Paul Klee zu einer ersten Einzelausstellung in Großbritannien verhalf (1933 und 1934). Zudem veranstaltete er 1933 eine Kandinsky-Ausstellung. Dieses Engagement für die deutsche Kunst verdankte sich unter anderem der Verbindung zum bekannten Kunsthändler Alfred Flechtheim, der nach der Machtergreifung der Nazis dabei war, seine Galeriebestände ins Ausland zu bringen. Anlässlich der Eröffnungsausstellung in der Mayor Gallery, bei der Werke von Max Ernst, Paul Klee and Willi Baumeister gezeigt wurden, sagte Freddy Mayor, der stellvertretende Direktor der Galerie, vor Journalisten: «Die deutschen Künstler sind *die* große Neuigkeit, da ihre Werke noch nie in England ausgestellt worden sind.»[3] Allerdings entwickelten sich die Geschäfte schleppend, und nur wenige Sammler ergriffen damals die Gelegenheit zum Kauf. So wurde bei der George Grosz-Ausstellung der Mayor Gallery im Jahr 1934 kein einziges Werk verkauft.

Nach 1945 verschlechterte sich die Lage sogar noch. Wenn Klee nicht als Schweizer gehandelt worden wäre – seine deutsche Staatsbürgerschaft und sein Militärdienst im 1. Weltkrieges wurden geflissentlich übergangen –, hätte der Vorstand der Tate dem Erwerb der oben genannten Werkgruppe möglicherweise gar nicht zugestimmt. Die Antipathie gegen Deutschland, das Großbritannien in zwei Weltkriege hineingezogen hatte, erklärt die Ablehnung der deutschen modernen Kunst allerdings nicht ganz – schließlich waren viele ihrer Exponenten Nazigegner, Juden oder beides. Meines Erachtens hatte die ablehnende Haltung eher mit dem britischen Kunstgeschmack zu tun. Sowohl die Kunstgeschichtsschreibung als auch die Sammler waren stark von der Idee des Formalismus beeinflusst, der die «bedeutungsvolle», d.h. das Wesen zur Anschauung bringende Form höher bewertete als die äußere Erscheinung des Motivs oder dessen narrativen Inhalt. Zu den Wortführern des Formalismus gehörte der einflussreiche Kunstkritiker Roger Fry und andere Mitglieder der Bloombury Group, die wegen ihrer Kunstauffassung die französische Kunst bevorzugten und die deutsche tendenziell ignorierten. In einer 1934 veröffentlichten Rezension zu Herbert Reads *Art Now* warf Fry der deutsche Kunst eine «teutonische» Tendenz zum Expressionismus und «schlechte künstlerische Manieren» vor, wodurch sie sich von der französischen und italienischen Kunst grundsätzlich unterscheide.[4] Read gehörte damals zu den wenigen Briten, die sich öffentlich für die deutsche Moderne einsetzten.

Abgesehen vom Erwerb der Klee-Werke zeigte Rothenstein gegenüber der deutschen Kunst weiterhin Zurückhaltung. Er lehnte sogar ein herausragendes Ensemble von Werken Karl Schmidt-Rottluffs ab, das Rosa Schapire dem Museum schenken wollte. Erst nach dem Tode der Gönnerin und Freundin des Brücke-Malers im Jahre 1954 nahm das Museum das Geschenk an, darunter eine Plastik und mehrere Gemälde wie das Porträt von Dr. Rosa Schapire aus dem Jahre 1919 (Abb. 101). Noch weniger verständlich war das Verhalten des British Museum, dessen Graphikabteilung die von Frau Schapire angebotene, fast vollständige Sammlung von Graphiken Schmidt-Rottluffs ebenfalls ablehnte. Es bedurfte eines Generationswechsels, ehe sich Anzeichen für eine Wende zeigten. Anthony Griffiths und Frances Carey initiierten als neue Kuratoren des Museums ein Programm zum Ankauf von Werken deutscher Kunst, dessen außergewöhnliche Dimensionen 1984 deutlich wurden, als ihre wegweisende Ausstellung *The Print in Germany 1880-1933: The Age of Expressionism* etwa 170 Neuerwerbungen zeigte.

Rosa Schapire hatte als Feministin, Sozialistin und anerkannte Kunsthistorikerin die Brücke tatkräftig unterstützt. Obwohl sie den Großteil ihrer Graphiksammlung schließlich an deutsche Museen gab, schenkte sie auch der Leicester Art Gallery und dem Victoria and Albert Museum einzelne Blätter. Dank des Engagements von Trevor Thomas, dem Direktor der Leicester Art Gallery, hatte dieses Museum bereits während des Krieges – was an sich schon bemerkenswert ist – eine kleine hochwertige Sammlung deutscher expressionistischer

Werke aufgebaut. Darunter befanden sich *Rote Frau* von Franz Marc (1914) und *Hinter der Kirche* von Lyonel Feininger (1916), zwei Ölgemälde, die Angehörige von Tekla Hess, der Witwe des wohlhabenden Erfurter Schuhfabrikanten Alfred Hess, an das Museum verkauft hatten. Ebenso wie Rosa Schapire war Tekla Hess 1939 nach Großbritannien emigriert, wobei sie allerdings nur einen Bruchteil ihrer einst beträchtlichen Sammlung moderner deutscher Kunst mitnehmen konnte.[5]

Rothensteins Nachfolger als Direktor der Tate Gallery, Norman Reid, war der deutschen Kunst gegenüber durchaus aufgeschlossen. Er kaufte einige Werke von Emil Nolde, Ernst Barlach und Max Beckmann und sogar *Selbstmord* (1916) von George Grosz – ein Bild, das wegen seiner satirischen Darstellung von Tod und käuflichem Sex umstritten war. Allerdings wurde bei der Tate die moderne und zeitgenössische deutsche Kunst erst dann gebührend ernst genommen, als Alan Bowness 1980 zum neuen Direktor des Museums berufen wurde.

Sollte ich eine besondere Erwerbung aus dieser Zeit hervorheben, würde ich *Karneval* (1920, Abb. 102) von Max Beckmann nennen. Dieses rätselhafte und traumartige Meisterwerk wurde 1981 von der Tate erworben. Es war 1978/79 in der Hayward Gallery im Rahmen der Ausstellung *Neue Sachlichkeit and German Realism of the Twenties* gezeigt worden, der ersten substantiellen Ausstellung zu dieser Epoche außerhalb Deutschlands, die vom angesehenen österreichischen Kunsthistoriker Wieland Schmied kuratiert und vom Arts Council of Great Britain organisiert wurde. Der staatliche Arts Council hatte zuvor bereits die oben erwähnte Klee-Tournee sowie weitere Ausstellungen anderer deutscher Künstler u.a. Lyonel Feininger veranstaltet. Zu dieser Zeit entwickelte die deutsche Regierung über die Standorte des Goethe-Instituts in London und Glasgow ein Programm mit Ausstellungen, Konferenzen, Filmen, Konzerten und anderen kulturellen Veranstaltungen, dessen Ziel es war, das Verständnis für deutsche Kultur und Geschichte beim britischen Publikum zu fördern. Verantwortlich für die Umsetzung dieses Programms waren die beiden fortschrittlichen Direktoren Günter Coenen und Hilmann von Halem, die dabei geräuschlos, aber sehr effizient agierten.

Während seiner relativ kurzen Amtszeit als Direktor der Tate (1980-1988) kaufte Alan Bowness wichtige Werke von Ernst Ludwig Kirchner, Max Ernst, Oskar Kokoschka, Alfred Otto Wolfgang Schulze, alias Wols, und Kurt Schwitters (die beeindruckende, großformatige Collage *Bild mit Raumgewächsen*, 1920/1939). In meiner Position als Kurator für deutsche Kunst fand ich Bowness stets offen, wenn ich ihm den Erwerb von Werken deutscher Künstler wie Joseph Beuys, Georg Baselitz, A. R. Penck und Anselm Kiefer (*Parsifal I, II* und *III*, 1973) oder österreichischer Künstler wie Arnulf Rainer, Hermann Nitsch und Günter Brus vorschlug. Meines Erachtens war die Kunstszene in Köln, Berlin oder Wien zu dieser Zeit mindestens genauso interessant wie die in New York. Beim Versuch, ein Gemälde von Otto Dix zu erwerben, wurde die Tate allerdings überboten. Als das Gemälde *Der Salon I* (1921), eine sardonische Bordelldarstellung, 1986 auf einer Auktion angeboten wurde, zahlte die Galerie der Stadt Stuttgart (jetzt Kunstmuseum) eine Rekordsumme und ist heute die führende öffentliche Sammlung für das Werk des Malers.

Die einzige britische Institution, die heute ein Werk von Otto Dix besitzt, ist die 1960 in Edinburgh gegründete Scottish National Gallery of Modern Art (SNGMA). 1980 erwarb sie das Gemälde *Mädchen auf Fell* (1932), das Portrait einer verlebten Prostituierten, deren Haltung auf Werke von Lucas Cranach anspielt, während die sorgfältige Wiedergabe der Haare, des Fells und des Hängebauchs an Bilder von Baldung Grien erinnert. Anscheinend entwickelten die Schotten früher als die Engländer eine Wertschätzung für die deutsche Moderne. Es

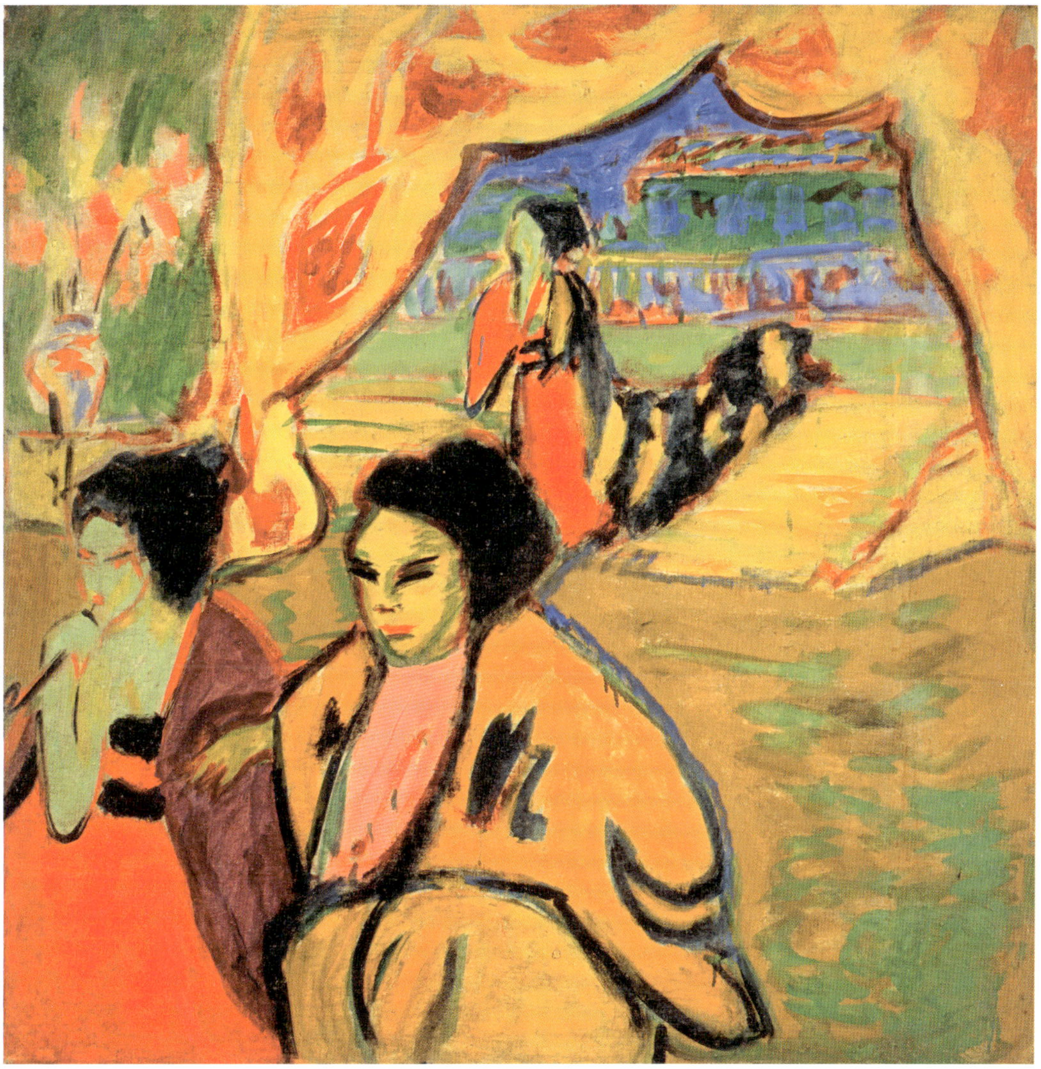

103 Ernst Ludwig Kirchner, *Japanisches Theater*, 1909. Öl auf Leinwand, 113.7 x 113.7 cm. Scottish National Gallery of Modern Art Edinburgh

ist bezeichnend, dass eine abgewandelte Version von *Twentieth Century German Art* 1939 in Glasgow gezeigt und in der schottischen Presse sehr ausführlich besprochen wurde.[8] Darüber hinaus fanden in den 1930er Jahren in der Royal Scottish Academy in Edinburgh mehrere Ausstellungen deutscher und nordeuropäischer Kunst statt. So wurden Werke von Edvard Munch (1931, eine Premiere in Großbritannien), Paul Klee (1934) und Max Ernst (1937) sowie von verschiedenen deutschen Bildhauern (1936) gezeigt. Später, in den 1960er Jahren, erwarb die SNGMA unter der Leitung von Douglas Hall expressionistische Gemälde Emil Noldes und Alexei Jawlenskys sowie ein großartiges frühes Gemälde aus Kirchners Brücke-Phase, das fünfzehn Jahre zuvor von der Tate angekauft worden war (Abb. 103). 1970 schließlich brachte die Richard Demarco Gallery im Rahmen des Edinburgh Festivals Joseph Beuys, Gerhard Richter, Blinky Palermo und andere zeitgenössische Düsseldorfer Künstler nach Schottland. Für Beuys war es der erste Besuch, viele weitere sollten folgten.

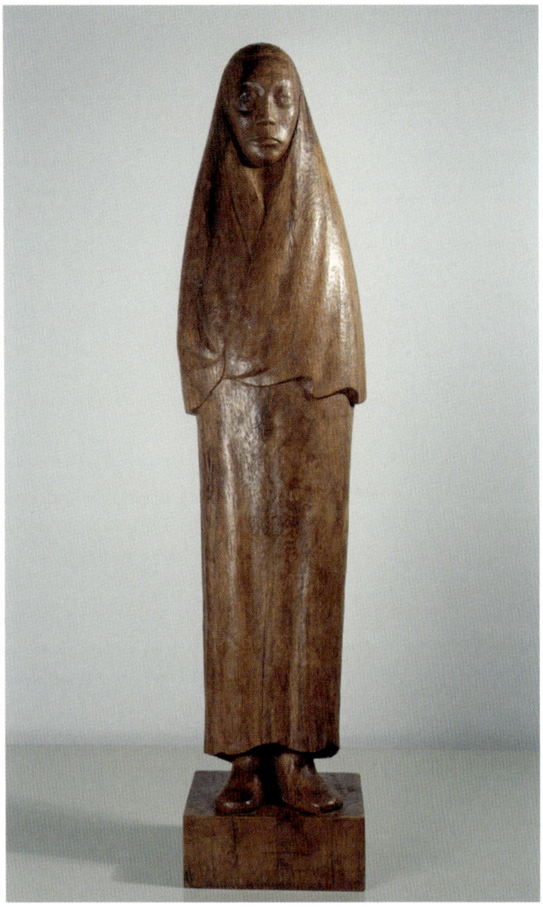

104 Ernst Barlach *Das schlimme Jahr 1937*. Holz (Eiche), Höhe 142 cm. Scottish National Gallery of Modern Art Edinburgh

Das Jahr 1980 markiert einen Wendepunkt, sowohl in Schottland als auch in England. Die SNGMA erwarb in diesem Jahr ein Feininger-Gemälde von 1913 sowie den Lithographie-Zyklus *Die Hölle* (1919) von Max Beckmann; nach meiner Berufung zum Direktor des Museums im Jahr 1987 folgten drei weitere Werke deutscher Maler. Das erste war ein schönes Kreideporträt Oskar Kokoschkas, das seine Muse und Geliebte Alma Mahler zeigt. Bei den zwei anderen Werken handelte es sich um bemerkenswerte Holzskulpturen: *Das schlimme Jahr 1937* (1936, Abb. 104) von Ernst Barlach sowie ein fast fünfzig Jahre später entstandenes Werk von Georg Baselitz *Ohne Titel* (1982/84) – es war die erste Holzskulptur des Künstlers in einer öffentlichen Sammlung. Noch bedeutender ist Barlachs *Das schlimme Jahr 1937*, bei dem es sich um die einzige Holzskulptur des Künstlers in einem britischen Museum handelt. Obwohl Barlach sie 1936 in Anlehnung an Werke der Gotik schuf, erhielt sie ihren Titel erst im darauffolgenden Jahr in Anspielung auf die berüchtigte Ausstellung *Entartete Kunst* in München. Anlässlich des fünfzigsten Jahrestags dieser von der NS-Regierung initiierten Aktion stellte ich im Jahre 1987 in den Sammlungsräumen des SNGMA die Plastik Barlachs neben Kokoschkas *Portrait eines entarteten Künstlers* (1937), das sich damals als private Leihgabe im Museum befand (und noch immer befindet). Mit mindestens sechs weiteren Werken des Malers war es 1938 in London in der Ausstellung *Twentieth Century German Art* vertreten gewesen.

Dass sich die Rezeption der deutschen Kunst in Großbritannien im Laufe der Zeit verbessert hat, ist größtenteils dem Engagement einiger privater Galerien zu verdanken. Besonders hervorzuheben ist dabei Marlborough Fine Art, ein Unternehmen, das nach dem Krieg von zwei emigrierten Österreichern in London gegründet wurde: Frank Lloyd und Harry Fischer. Letzterer machte sich später selbständig und gründete die Galerie Fischer Fine Art. Ab Ende der 1950er Jahre wurden bei Marlborough zahlreiche bahnbrechende Ausstellungen deutscher Kunst des 20. Jahrhunderts organisiert. 1964 fand dort auch die erste britische Egon-Schiele-Ausstellung statt. Darüber hinaus wurden hier die künstlerischen Nachlässe von Kokoschka und Schwitters betreut und ausgestellt. Die wichtige Schwitters-Ausstellung 1981 trug zu einer entscheidenden Neubewertung seines Spätwerks bei und präsentierte unter anderem die Collage *Bild mit Raumgewächsen* (1920/1939), die später von Bowness für die Tate erworben wurde.

Das Engagement der Galerien Marlborough und Fischer für die klassische Moderne aus Deutschland und Österreich fand später in der Londoner Galerie Anthony d'Offay ein Pendant, die sich mit geradezu missionarischem Eifer für die zeitgenössische deutsche Kunst einsetzte. 1980 wurde dort die Installation *Streifen aus dem Haus des Schamanen* von Joseph Beuys gezeigt. Anschließend organisierte die Galerie weitere Ausstellungen mit Werken von Beuys, Baselitz, Richter, Polke und Kiefer. Dieses Engagement erlebte 1991 einen Höhepunkt, als die Galerie ein monumentales Spätwerk von Beuys, *Das Ende des 20. Jahrhunderts*, an die Tate verkaufen konnte. Zu dieser Zeit wurde das Museum nicht mehr von Alan Bowness, sondern von Nicholas Serota geleitet. Dieser war zuvor Direktor der Whitechapel Art Gallery gewesen. Während seiner zwölfjährigen Amtszeit hatte er dort Ausstellungen mit Werken von Kiefer, Baselitz, Rainer und Beckmann organisiert. Unvergessen ist die Schau, bei welcher mehrere Triptychen Beckmanns zu sehen waren. Darunter befand sich auch die *Versuchung* (Bayerische Staatsgemäldesammlungen München), die 1938 Teil der Ausstellung in den New Burlington Galleries gewesen war. Vor seiner Zeit in Whitechapel leitete Serota Direktor das Museum of Modern Art in Oxford, wohin er Beuys 1974 einlud, ertsmals seine große, umfangreiche Gruppe von Zeichnungen mit dem Titel *The Secret Block for a Secret Person in Ireland* zu zeigen, die wesentliche Einblicke in das skulpturale Denken von Beuys ermöglichten.

Serota gehört zu einer jüngeren Generation von Kunsthistorikern. Gegen Ende des 2. Weltkriegs oder unmittelbar danach geboren, teilten er und seine Kollegen nicht die Vorbehalte ihrer Vorgänger, die der aggressiven Gegenständlichkeit, der expliziten Sexualisierung und der offenen Sozialikritik der deutschen Moderne ablehnend gegenüberstanden (mit wenigen Ausnahmen wie beispielsweise Bowness). Zu den ähnlich denkenden Kollegen in einflussreichen Positionen gehörten David Elliott, Norman Rosenthal und Neil MacGregor. Schon als Student organisierte Elliott die interdisziplinäre Ausstellung *Germany in Ferment: Art and Society in Germany 1900-1933*, die in Durham, Sheffield und Leicester gezeigt wurde. Anschließend war er Assistent in der Leicester Art Gallery, bis er als Nachfolger Serotas nach Oxford berufen wurde. Norman Rosenthal kuratierte 1974 zusammen mit dem Berliner Ausstellungsmacher Christos M. Joachimedes im Londoner Institute of Contemporary Arts eine Ausstellung radikaler zeitgenössischer deutscher Kunst mit dem Titel *Art into Society: Society into Art*. Hier wurden Werke von Joseph Beuys, Hans Haacke und anderen Künstlern gezeigt. Sieben Jahre später, nachdem er zum Ausstellungsbeauftragten der Royal Academy berufen worden war, organisierte Rosenthal in Zusammenarbeit mit Serota und Joachimedes die wegweisende Ausstellung *A New Spirit in Painting*. Sie war insofern eine Premiere, als sie erstmals Werke von Baselitz, Lüpertz, Kiefer, Polke und anderen deutschen Künstlern in Großbritannien präsentierte. 1985 schließlich veranstaltete Norman Rosenthal erneut mit Christos M. Joachimedes im gleichen Haus (unterstützt von Wieland Schmied) eine große Retrospektive der deutschen Kunst des 20. Jahrhunderts.

Neil MacGregor war von 1981 bis 1987 Herausgeber des *Burlington Magazine*. In einem seiner ersten Editorials machte er auf die Vernachlässigung der deutschen Kunst des 20. Jahrhunderts in den britischen Museen und Galerien aufmerksam[7] – ein Defizit, das Bowness und andere Museumsdirektoren zu dieser Zeit gerade zu beheben anfingen. 1987 wurde MacGregor zum Direktor der National Gallery berufen. Eine der ersten (im Nachhinein geradezu programmatischen) Amtshandlungen als neuer Direktor stellte der Erwerb eines Landschaftsbildes von Caspar David Friedrich dar. Es war das erste Werk des Künstlers, das in eine öffentliche britische Sammlung aufgenommen wurde. Was MacGregor damals über die Gleichgültigkeit der Briten gegenüber der deutschen Romantik schieb, gilt in gleicher Weise für die negative Rezeption des hundert Jahre später folgenden Expressionismus, da die Betonung des Geistigen bei den Expressionisten in vieler Hinsicht auf Ideen der Romantiker zurückgeht. MacGregor und die Kunsthistoriker seiner Generation waren unermüdlich darin, dieser Gleichgültigkeit entgegenzuwirken.

Die meisten deutschen Maler des letzten Jahrhunderts fanden Sammler und Mäzene im eigenen Land. Somit mussten nur wenige ihre Werke zu Lebzeiten exportieren. Darüber hinaus sorgten zwei Weltkriege dafür, dass kein britischer Kunstsammler Werke von Menzel oder Runge mit der Begeisterung gesammelt hat, wie Keynes oder Courtauld es bei Gemälden von Cézanne und den Impressionisten taten. Zu diesen praktischen Hindernissen kam noch eine Schwierigkeit theoretischer Natur hinzu: Kritiker, welche die Kunst hauptsächlich als eine formale Entwicklung von Cézanne über den Kubismus bis zur Abstraktion begriffen, konnten sich kaum für die spirituellen Dimensionen eines Malers wie Friedrich interessieren, dessen Formrepertoire viel der alten Kunst verdankt und dessen Beitrag zur europäischen Tradition ebenso sehr in seinen Motiven wie im Umgang mit ihnen besteht.[8]

1 Der Autor dieses Essays war Kurator der Tate Gallery (1979-1987), Direktor der Scottish National Gallery of Modern Art (1987-2007) und Direktor der Henry Moore Foundation (2007-2015). Heute arbeitet er in der Londoner Gagosian Gallery.

2 Ronald Alley: Catalogue of The Tate Gallery's Collection of Modern Art, other than works by British Artists, London 1981, S. 381.

3 Richard Calvocoressi: Klee's Reception in Scotland and England 1930-1945, in: Stefan Frey/Josef Helfenstein (Hg.): Paul Klee Rediscovered. Works from the Bürgi Collection, London 2000, S. 235.

4 Roger Fry: Art Now. An Introduction to the Theory of Modern Painting and Sculpture, in: The Burlington Magazine, Nr. 64 (1934), S. 242 und 245.

5 Die Familie Hess war unter den Leihgebern der Ausstellung *Twentieth Century German Art*. Siehe dazu Lucy Wasensteiner: The Twentieth Century German Art Exhibition. Answering Degenerate Art in 1930s London, New York (in Vorbereitung).

6 o. V.: Modern German Art Exhibition in Glasgow. Banned Pictures, in: The Scotsman, 15. März 1939, S. 17. Der Autor dankt Lucy Wasensteiner, dass sie ihn auf diesen Artikel aufmerksam gemacht hat.

7 Neil MacGregor: Editorial: The Tate Gallery's foreign collection. A new catalogue, in: The Burlington Magazine, Nr. 124 (1982), S. 539.

8 Neil MacGregor: Foreword, in: John Leighton and Colin J. Bailey: Caspar David Friedrich. Winter Landscape, London 1990, S. 5.

Transcript of the 1938 exhibition catalogue
Der Katalog von 1938: Die Exponate

Auf den folgenden Seiten sind die Exponate der Londoner Ausstellung aufgelistet, wie sie im damaligen Katalog verzeichnet sind. Bei verschiedenen Künstlern war den Werken eine Kurzbiographie vorangestellt; diese Texte werden hier nicht wiedergegeben. Die Angaben zu den Werken entsprechen denjenigen des Katalogs. Der Asterisk* nach dem Titel zeigt an, dass das betreffende Werk verkäuflich war. Wie sich einer Notiz auf der Katalogrückseite entnehmen lässt, waren von den ausstellenden Künstlern noch weitere Werke in der Galerie vorrätig und konnten auf Anfrage besichtigt werden. Die ausgestellten Werke und ihre Leihgeber sind identifiziert bei Lucy Wasensteiner, *The Twentieth Century Art Exhibition. Answering Degenerate Art in 1930s London*. New York (im Erscheinen).

The following pages reproduce the list of works which appeared in the 1938 London exhibition catalogue. Certain artists were listed with short biographies; these biographies are not reproduced here. Work details and subheading reflect those used in the original catalogue. The asterisk* beside the work indicated that it was for sale in London. A notice affixed to the back of each catalogue stated that further works by all exhibiting artists were in stock at the galleries and available for viewing upon request. The forthcoming book by Lucy Wasensteiner (*The Twentieth Century Art Exhibition. Answering Degenerate Art in 1930s London*) identifies the exhibited artworks and their lenders in 1938.

BARLACH (ERNST)

1 VISION*
Sculpture in wood (1912).
45 ¾ x 38 ½ in. (119 x 98 cm)
Exhibited at: Religiöse Kunstausstellung, Düsseldorf. Reproduced in: Ernst Barlach, "Ein Selbsterzähltes Leben", Paul Cassirer, Berlin, 1928.
Collection: Hugo Simon, Paris.

2 HUNGER*
Sculpture in wood (1914).
26 ¾ x 27 ¼ in. (68 x 69 cm)
Exhibited at: Private collection, Berlin.
Reproduced in: Ernst Barlach, "Ein Selbsterzähltes Leben", Paul Cassirer, Berlin, 1928.
Lent by: Galerie Fischer, Lucerne.

3 MARTYRDOM OF MANKIND*
Sculpture in wood (1919).
76 ½ x 57 in. (195 x 145 cm)
Exhibited at: Private collection, Berlin.
Reproduced in: Ernst Barlach, "Ein Selbsterzähltes Leben", Paul Cassirer, Berlin, 1928.
Lent by: Galerie Fischer, Lucerne.

4 MOTHER AND CHILD*
Sculpture in wood (1920).
37 ¾ x 20 ½ in. (96 x 52,5 cm)
Reproduced in: Ernst Barlach, "Ein Selbsterzähltes Leben", Paul Cassirer, Berlin, 1928.
Lent by: Galerie Fischer, Lucerne.

5 CUTTING MELON
Bronze (1933). 13 ½ in. (34 cm)
Collection: Hugo Moser, Heemstede.

6 DEATH
Drawing. 37 x 14 in. (43 x 36 cm)
Private collection.

7 PROMETHEUS
Drawing. Collection: Dr. Goldberg, Zurich.

8 A WOMAN*
Drawing (1923). 19 ½ x 14
(50 x 36 cm) Collection: Wells, London.

9 THE FUGITIVES
Lithograph. Collection: Dr. Goldberg, Zurich.

BAUMEISTER (WILLI)

10 TENNIS*
Oil (1933). 21 x 26 in. (54 x 66 cm)
Private Collection, Basle.

11 KNEELING GROUP
Oil (1933). 26 x 31 ½ in. (66 x 79 cm)
Exhibited at: Leicester Gallery, London.
Collection: Sir Michael Sadler, K.C.S.I., C.B., Oxford.

12 FOOTBALL PLAYERS, NO. 1*
Drawing. Private collection.

13 FOOTBALL PLAYERS, NO. 2*
Drawing. Private collection.

BECKMANN (MAX)

14 GENOA
Oil (1927). 38 x 77 in. (95 x 193 cm) Exhibited at: Paris, Galerie la Renaissance, 1931. Reproduced in: Heinrich Simon, Max Beckmann.
Private collection.

15 THE SKATERS*
Oil (1932). 52 x 40 in. (131 x 100 cm) Exhibited at: Kunsthaus Winterthur, 1938. Private collection.

16 WOODCUTTERS
Oil (1933). 19 x 47 ½ in. (48 x 118 cm) Exhibited at: Galerie la Renaissance, Paris, 1931. Private collection.

17 THE KING*
Oil (1937). 53 x 40 in. (133 x 100 cm) Exhibited at: Kunsthaus Winterthur, 1938. Collection: Irmgard Burchard, Zurich.

18 TRIPTYCH: TEMPTATION
Oil (1937). Reproduced in: (centrepiece) Peter Thoene, Modern German Art, Pelican Books, 1938.
Collection: Stefan Lackner, Paris.

19 QUAPPI*
Oil (1937). 43 ½ x 26 in.
(110 x 66 cm)
Exhibited at: Kunsthaus Winterthur, 1938; Aktuarius Zurich, 1938. Reproduced in: Peter Thoene, Modern German Art, Pelican Books, 1938.

20 TAMERLAN
Lithograph.
Collection: Stefan Lackner, Paris.

CAMPENDONCK (HEINRICH)

21 JUMPING BEAST*
Oil (1913). 33 ½ x 25 ½ in.
(85 x 65 cm)
Private collection.

22 THE HORSEMAN
Oil (1921). 55 x 43 in.
(140 x 110 cm)
Collection: Sacher-Stehlin, Pratteln.

CORINTH (LOVIS)

23 BORDIGHERA
Oil (1912). 33 x 39 in. (82,5 x 98 cm) Exhibited at: Kronprinzen-Palais, Berlin; Landesmuseum, Karlsruhe; Kunsthalle Basel.
Collection: Erich Goeritz, London.

24 FLOWERS
Oil (1914). 42 x 56 in. (110 x 143 cm) Exhibited at: Kunsthalle Basel 1936. Kronprinzen-Palais, Berlin; Landesmuseum, Karlsruhe.
Collection: Erich Goeritz, London.

25 NUDE WITH BATH-TOWEL
Oil (1917). 25 x 20 ½ in. (63 x 52 cm) Collection: Mrs. F. R., London.

26 WALCHENSEE
Oil (1921). 47 x 37 in. (95 x 120 cm) Exhibited at: Kunsthause, Zurich, 1934. Reproduced: Peter Thoene, Modern German Art, Pelican Books, 1938. Collection: Mrs. F. R., London.

27 FRIENDS OF ART
Oil (1921). Exhibited: Kronprinzen-Palais, Berlin; Kunsthalle, Hamburg; Landesmuseum Karlsruhe; Kunsthalle, Basel. Collection: Erich Goeritz, London.

28 SELF PORTRAIT AT WALCHENSEE*
Oil (1922). 22 x 18 ½ in. (56 x 47 cm) Collection: Irmgard Burchard, Zurich.

29 AMAZONE
Lithograph. Collection: Richard Baer, Zug.

30 STREET IN KOENIGSBERG
Lithograph. Collection: Richard Baer, Zug.

31 NUDE
Etching. Collection: Richard Baer, Zug.

32 CHARLOTTE BEHRENDT
Drawing. Collection: Mrs. F. R., London.

33 SELF-PORTRAIT
Watercolour. 23 ½ x 17 cm.
Collection: Dr. L. Burchard, London.

34 SELF PORTRAIT WITH WIFE
Etching. Collection: Richard Baer, Zug.

35 PORTRAIT
Etching. Collection: Richard Baer, Zug.

36 WALCHENSEE
Etching. Collection: Richard Baer, Zug.

37 MONUMENT
Drawing. Collection: Mrs. F. R., London.

DEMETER (WOLF)

38 HELMUTH VON GERLACH*
Bronze (1935). 17 in. (43 cm).
Exhibited at: Galerie Renou et Colle, Paris. Collection: Hugo Simon, Paris.

DIX (OTTO)

39 PORTRAIT UZARSKY*
Oil (1923).50 x 29 in. (126 x 73 cm) Reproduced in: "Junge Kunst", Volume of Otto Dix. Collection: Dr. D. Hagmann, Zurich.

40 HOHENTWIEL*
Oil (1933). 28 x 35 ½ in. (70 x 80 cm) Exhibited at: Galerie Wolfsberg, Zurich, 1938. Collection: Galerie Wolfsberg, Zurich.

EGGELING (VIKING)

41 CHORD*
Drawing (1919). 23 ½ in. (60 cm) Exhibited at: Museums of Basel, Hannover, Bremen, Cologne; Grosse Berliner Kunstausstellung, 1923; Exposition Internationale de Moscow, 1924; New York, 1926. Collection: Hans Richter, Zurich.

ELKAN (BENNO)

42 HEAD OF PRINCE EDWARD*
Study in Plasticine (1937). 8 in. (20 cm)

43 HEAD OF TOSCANINI*
Study in Plaster (1938). 23 ½ in.
(160 cm)

44 HEAD OF ALFRED FLECHTHEIM*
Bronze (1912). 12 ½ in. (32 cm)
Exhibited at: Kronprinzen-Palais, Nationalgalerie, Berlin; Städtische Kunsthalle, Düsseldorf.

ERNST (MAX)

45 SUNSET
Oil (1926). 67 x 55 in. (170 x 140 cm)
Collection: Sacher-Stehlin, Pratteln.

46 CELESTIAL ARMY
Oil (1927). 32 x 25 in. (81,5 x 63,5 cm)
Collection. Sacher-Stehlin, Pratteln.

47 OISEAUX SPECTRAUX
Oil. 21 x 26 ½ in. (53 x 67 cm)
Collection: Sir Michael Sadler, K.C.S.I., C.B., Oxford.

48 SURREALIST FIGURE
Oil. 32 x 25 in. (81,5 x 32,5 cm)
Collection: Sir Michael Sadler, K.C.S.I., C.B., Oxford.

FEININGER (LYONEL)

49 HIGH HOUSES*
Oil (1916). 39 x 31 in. (98 x 79 cm)
Private collection.

50 PORTRAIT*
Oil (1916). 15 x 18 ½ in. (39 x 47 cm)
Collection: Erich Mendelssohn, London.

51 MARKET PLACE
Watercolour (1910). 18 x 20 in. (45,5 x 50,5 cm)
Collection: Wells, London.

52 STREET*
Drawing (1915). 22 x 17 in. (56 x 43 cm) Private collection.

FREUNDLICH (OTTO)

53 UNIVERSAL SYNTHESIS*
Oil (1934). 42 ½ x 28 ¼ in. (108 x 72 cm) Exhibited at: Kunsthalle, Basel, 1937; Musée Municipale, Amsterdam, 1938.

GROSZ (GEORGE)

54 HEAD OF A MAN AND FIGURES
Etching. Collection: Richard Bear, Zug.

55 AUTUM LEAVES*
Watercolour (1931). 24 x 17 in. (61 x 43 cm) Private collection.

56 STREET IN PARIS*
Watercolour. 18 x 24 in. (44 x 62 cm)
Collection: Finkelstein, London.

57 RESTAURANT*
Watercolour. 17 ½ x 27 in. (46 x 69 cm)
Collection: Finkelstein, London.

HAUSMANN (RAOUL)

58 DADA CONSTRUCTION*
(1919). 10 x 8 in. (25 x 20 cm)

59 OPTOFONETIK CONSTRUCTION 2*
(1922). 12 ½ x 9 in. (32 x 23 cm)

60 OPTOFONETIK CONSTRUCTION 3*
(1922). 12 ½ x 9 in. (32 x 23 cm)

HECKEL (ERICH)

61 BATHING SCENE*
Oil (1914). 19 x 21 ½ in. (48 x 55 cm)
Collection: Hugo Simon, Paris.

62 GHENT*
Oil. 38 x 47 ½ in. (97 x 120 cm)
Collection: Hugo Simon, Paris.

63 HIGH MOUNTAINS
Watercolour. 24 x 19 in. (60 x 47 cm)
Collection: Kunsthalle, Bern.

64 BASQUE
Watercolour. 23 x 17 ¼ in. (58 x 44 cm)
Collection: Kunsthalle, Bern.

65 PORTRAIT OF M. H.*
Etching. Private Collection.

66 CLOWNS
Etching. Collection: Wells, London.

HOFER (CARL)

67 LOVE*
Oil (1922). 48 ¾ x 31 in. (124 x 79 cm)
Private collection, London.

68 GIRL WRITING
Oil (1930). 27 x 32 in. (69 ½ x 82 cm)
Collection: Marcel Fleischmann, Zurich.

69 TWO CHILDREN WITH SUNFLOWERS*
Oil (1932). 29 x 39 in. (74 x 100 cm)
Exhibited at: Berlin Academy, 1932.
Collection: Finkelstein, London.

70 FRIENDS
Lithograph. Collection: Richard Baer, Zug.

71 NUDE
Etching. Collection: Richard Baer, Zug.

72 HEADS OF WOMEN*
Lithograph. Collection: Dr. Goldberg, Zurich.

73 EGYPTIAN DANCER*
Lithograph. Collection: Dr. Goldberg, Zurich.

KANDINSKY (WASSILIJ)

74 LANDSCAPE, 1909*
Oil (1909). 30 x 39 in. (75 x 100 cm)
Reproduced in: Monographie Kandinsky, Edition Cahiers d'art.

75 CRINOLINE
Oil (1910). 37 x 58 in. (94 x 148 cm)
Collection: Beffie, Brussels.

76 COMPOSITION NO. 2*
Oil (1912). 51 x 38 in. (129 x 97 cm)
Reproduced in Modern Painting by W. H. Wright.

77 SUR FOND BLANC*
Oil (1923). 38 x 41 in. (98 x 105 cm)
Exhibited: Kunsthalle, Bern. Reproduced: The Exhibition Catalogue, Bern.

78 PLAISANTERIE SÉRIEUSE*
Oil (1930). 20 x 29 in. (51 x 71 cm)
Lent by Guggenheim Jeune Gallery, London.

79 LIBREMENT ACCENTUE*
Oil (1930). 20 x 28 in. (51 x 71 cm)
Lent by Guggenheim Jeune Gallery, London.

80 BAGATELLE
Watercolour. 17 ¾ x 17 ¾ in.
(45 x 45 cm)
Collection: Beffie, Brussels.

81 COMPOSITION
Watercolour. 15 ½ x 30 ¾ in. (38,5 x 34 cm)
Collection: Beffie, Brussels.

82 STUDY IN PALE PINK
Watercolour. 15 ½ x 13 ½ in.
(47,5 x 33 cm). Private collection.

83 STUDY*
Watercolour. 15 x 12 in.
(47,5 x 53,5 cm) Private collection.

KIRCHNER (ERNST LUDWIG)

84 RED HOUSES*
Oil (1913). 47 x 35 in (120 x 89 cm)
Collection: Hugo Simon, Paris.

85 SERTIG VALLEY
Oil (1926). 43 x 59 in. (109 x 150 cm)
Exhibited: Kunsthalle, Bern.
Lent by Kunsthalle, Bern.

86 MAN WITH CAT
Oil (1930). 16 x 13 in. (41 x 33 cm)
Exhibited: Kunsthalle, Bern, 1933. Reproduced: The Catalogue of Exhibition, Bern. Lent by Kunsthalle, Bern.

86a STAFFELALP
Oil. 34 x 29 in. (85 x 72,5 cm)
Collection: Dr. Staub, Zurich.

87 DANCER
Pastel (1914). 26 x 18 ½ in.
(67 x 96 cm) Collection: Hugo Simon, Paris.

KLEE (PAUL)

88 HOUSE IN THE NIGHT*
Oil (1908). 9 x 12 ½ in. (25 x 31 cm)
Private collection.

89 GARDEN AFTER THE STORM*
Oil (1932). 29 x 41 in. (75 x 105 cm)
Lent by Galerie Simon, Paris.

90 ARAB SONG*
Oil (1932). 24 ½ x 35 ½ in. (91 x 64 cm) Lent by Galerie Simon, Paris.

91 WATCHED GIRL*
Oil (1933). 8 x 12 ½ in. (20 x 32 cm)
Exhibited: Art realiste et abstrait, Zurich. Reproduced: Peter Thoene, Modern German Art, Pelican Books, 1938.
Collection: Irmgard Burchard, Zurich.

92 HARMONIE NOUVELLE*
Oil (1936). 40 x 26 in. (93 x 66 cm)
Lent by Galerie Simon, Paris.

93 ABSTRACT PICTURE WITH YELLOW BALL
Oil. 13 ½ x 9 ½ in. (61 x 85 cm)
Collection: Fleischmann, Zurich.

94 FERTILITY*
Watercolour (1933). 10 ¼ x 7 ¾ in.
(24 x 19,5 cm) Private Collection.

95 CITY OF GRAVES
Coloured Drawing (1914). 5 ¾ x 6 ½ in. (14 x 16 cm) Collection: Beffie, Brussels.

96 COFFEE-GARDEN
Drawing. Collection: Beffie, Brussels.

97 POISON*
Watercolour (1934). Private collection.

98 IN THE COUNTRY OF PRECIOUS STONES*
Watercolour (1929).
Lent by Galerie Simon, Paris.

99 SWAMP
Watercolour (1929). 18 x 12 in.
(27 x 21 cm) Collection: Sir Michael Sadler, K.C.S.I., C.B., Oxford.

100 STARS OVER EVIL HOUSES*
Watercolour (1916). 11 ½ x 10 in.
(30,5 x 23,5 cm) Private collection.

101 LITTLE COMMUNITY*
Watercolour (1916). 11 ½ x 10 in.
(30,5 x 23,5 cm) Private collection.

102 MEMORY OF A NIGHT*
Watercolour (1916). 11 ½ x 10 in.
(30,5 x 23,5 cm) Private collection.

KOKOSCHKA (OSKAR)

103 FRANZ LISZT*
Plaque (1910). Private collection.

104 HERWARTH WALDEN*
Oil (1911). 27 x 39 in.
(68½ x 112 cm) Private collection.

105 SELF PORTRAIT
Oil (1912). 27 ½ x 42 in.
(70 x 107 cm) Exhibited: Kunsthaus Zurich, 1927; Cassirer, Berlin, 1927; Fischer, Lucerne, 1931.
Lent by Galerie Fischer, Lucerne.

106 MADRID*
Oil (1925). 39 x 26 in. (99 x 66 cm)
Exhibited: Cassirer, Berlin, "Kokoschka Exhibition". Lent by Galerie Fischer, Lucerne.

107 VIEW OF MARSEILLES*
Oil (1927). 39 x 28 ¾ in.
(100 x 73 cm) Collection: Hugo Simon, Paris.

108 LANDSCAPE WITH ANIMALS
Oil (1927). 45 x 32 in (114 x 81 cm)
Exhibited: Kronprinzen-Palais, Berlin. Collection: Marcel Fleischmann, Zurich.

109 ALGERIENNE AU TONNEAU
Oil. 38 ½ x 31 ½ in. (97 x 79 cm)
Collection: Marcel Fleischmann, Zurich.

110 SELF PORTRAIT OF A DEGENERATE ARTIST
Oil (1937). 43 x 33 ½ in.
(85 x 110 cm)
Collection: Prof. Dr. Korner, Zurich.

111 WOMAN'S DESIRE*
Four drawings (1910).
Private collection.

112 BIRTH OF CHRIST*
Drawing (1910).
Private collection.

113 A LILY TO BE KISSED*
Drawing. Private collection.

114 PASSED*
Drawing. Private collection.

115 SNAKE DANCE*
Drawing. Private collection.

116 FLIGHT FROM PARADISE*
Drawing. Private collection.

117 JEWESS*
Watercolour. Private collection.

118 BATTLE*
Watercolour. Private collection.

119 SELF-PORTRAIT*
Pen drawing.
Lent by Guggenheim Jeune Gallery, London.

120 SELF-PORTRAIT*
Pen drawing.
Lent by Guggenheim Jeune Gallery, London.

121 RESCUE*
Pen drawing.
Lent by Guggenheim Jeune Gallery, London.

KOLBE (GEORG)

122 HEAD OF PAUL CASSIRER
Bronze (1927). 8 in. (20 cm)
Exhibited: Kronprinzen-Palais, Berlin.
Collection: Hugo Simon, Paris.

KOLLE (HELMUT)

123 CYCLIST*
Oil (1929). 40 x 26 in (100 x 65 cm)
Exhibited: Exposition Kolle, Georges Bernheim, Paris, 1929. Exposition Retrospective, Paris, 1932. Collection: Uhde, Paris.

124 YOUNG MAN IN WHITE SWEATER
Oil (1930). 25 x 35 ½ in.
(63 x 88 cm) Reproduced: W. Uhde: Der Maler Helmut Kolle.
Collection: E. A. Alport, London.

KOLLWITZ (KAETHE)

125 PLOUGHING
Lithograph. Collection: Dr. Abegg, Zurich.

126 HELP FOR RUSSIA
Lithograph. Collection: Dr. Abegg, Zurich.

127 PRISONER
Lithograph. Collection: Dr. Abegg, Zurich.

128 TO BATTLE
Lithograph. Collection: Dr. Abegg, Zurich.

129 PARENTS*
Lithograph. Collection: Dr. Goldberg, Zurich.

130 SELF-PORTRAIT*
Lithograph. Collection: Dr. Goldberg, Zurich.

131 FALLEN SOLDIER*
Lithograph. Collection: Dr. Goldberg, Zurich.

132 WOMAN WORKER*
Lithograph. Collection: Dr. Goldberg, Zurich.

LEHMBRUCK (WILHELM)

133 TORSO*
Sculpture in Cement (1910). 32 in. (81 cm) Reproduced: Paul Westheim Lehmbruck. Coll.: Hugo Simon, Paris.

134 BUST*
Terracotta (1910). 16 in. (40 cm)
Collection: Hugo Simon, Paris.

135 TORSO*
Sculpture in Cement (1910-1911). 27 ½ in. (70 cm). Reproduced: Paul Westheim: Lehmbruck.
Collection: Hugo Simon, Paris.

136 BUST*
Terracotta (1911). 17 in. (42 cm)
Reproduced: Paul Westheim: Lehmbruck. Collection: Hugo Simon, Paris.

137 HEAD OF FRITZ VON UNRUH
Terracotta. 16 ½ in. (42 cm). Last work before his death).
Private collection.

138 HEAD OF A GIRL
Plaster. 16 in. (40 cm) Collection: The Rt. Hon. The Earl of Sandwich.

139 WOMAN AND FAUN*
Coloured etching. Collection: Wells, London.

140 THREE FIGURES*
Etching. Collection: Wells, London.

141 FIGURE*
Etching. Collection: Wells, London.

142 STUDY OF A HEAD*
Charcoal. 20 ¾ x 16 ¼ in. (52,5 x 41 cm) Collection: Uzielli, Liesthal.

LIEBERMANN (MAX)

143 THE POTATO GATHERER*
Oil (1876). 35 x 46 in. (89 x 116 cm)
Reproduced: Karl Schiefler Max Liebermann, Munich, 1922. Peter Thoene Modern German Art, Pelican Books, 1938. Lent by West's Gallery, London.

144 AFTERNOON IN LAAREN*
Oil (1892). 10 ½ x 21 in. (35 x 52 cm)
Exhibited: Galerie Henneberg, Zurich; Galerie Wolfsberg, Zurich. Reproduced in: Peter Thoene Modern German Art, Pelican Books, 1938.
Collection: Galerie Wolfsberg, Zurich.

145 THE PARROT MAN
Oil (1902). 39 x 23 in. (98 x 60 cm)
Exhibited: Kunsthalle, Bern, 1937.
Collection: G. Weill, Zurich.

146 STUDIO*
Oil (1902). 31 x 27 in. (82 x 68 ½ cm)
Exhibited: Collection Rothermund, Dresden.Reproduced and mentioned: Georg Pauli, Max Liebermann, Stuttgart, 1911; Erich Hanke, Max Liebermann, Berlin, 1914; Max Friedlaender, Max Liebermann, coloured reproduction by A. Seemann, Dresden. Private collection.

147 POLO PLAYERS
Oil (1902). 22 x 33 in. (55 x 82 cm) Exhibited: Kronprinzen-Palais, Berlin, Landesmuseum, Karlsruhe; Kunsthalle, Basel; National galerie, Berlin; Tate Gallery, London. Collection: K. Goeritz, Aerdenhout, Holland.

148 PORTRAIT OF PROF. EINSTEIN*
Oil (1922). 38 ½ x 28 in. (98 x 71 cm) Private Collection, London.

149 SELF-PORTRAIT
Oil (1922). 39 x 28 in. (99 x 71 cm) Exhibited: Grosse Kunstausstellung, Dresden, 1925. Kunsthuette Chemnitz. Collection: Karl Goeritz, Aerdenhout, Holland.

150 CONCERT AT THE OPERA
Oil (1930). 16 x 19 ½ in. (40 x 50 cm) Exhibited: Kunsthalle, Basel, 1937. Collection: Dr. Pollag, Zuich.

151 RIDER BY THE SEA
Oil. 27 x 35 in. (69 x 87 cm) Collection: Sir Kenneth Clark, K.C.B., London.

152 DUTCH PEASANT GIRL
Pastel (1895).25 x 38 in. (63 x 95 cm) Private collection.

153 ALMSHOUSE
Etching. Collection: Dr. Pollag, Zurich.

154 THE JEWRY IN AMSTERDAM (1)
Etching. Collection: Dr. Pollag, Zurich.

155 THE JEWRY IN AMSTERDAM (2)
Etching. Collection: Dr. Pollag, Zurich.

156 REARING HORSES
Lithograph. Collection: Dr. Pollag, Zurich.

157 CORSO ON MONTE PINCIO
Etching. Collection: Dr. Pollag, Zurich.

158 SELF-PORTRAIT
Lithograph. Collection: Dr. Pollag, Zurich.

159 THE HORSE-RACE
Lithograph. Collection: Dr. Pollag, Zurich.

160 WANNSEE, BERLIN
Coloured Etching. Collection: Dr. Pollag, Zurich.

MACKE (AUGUST)

161 THE YELLOW COAT*
Watercolour (1913).11 ½ x 17 ½ in. (30 x 45 cm) Private collection.

162 MEN ON A BRIDGE*
Watercolour. 8 x 6 in. (20 x 15 cm) Collection: Wells, London.

MARC (FRANZ)

163 ANIMALS*
Oil on glass (1912). 42 x 21 in. (108 x 54 cm) Exhibited: Kunstmuseum, Bern, 1938. Private collection.

164 YELLOW COW*
Oil (1912). 71 x 55 in. (140 x 190 cm) Exhibited: Kunstmuseum, Bern, 1938. Private collection.

165 THE POOR COUNTRY OF TYROL
Oil (1913). 51 x 78 in. (130 x 200 cm) Collection: Beffie, Brussels.

166 DIE WELTENKUH*
Oil (1913). 27 x 55 in. (70 x 140 cm) Private collection.

167 LONG YELLOW HORSE
Oil (1913). 24 x 32 in. (60 x 80 cm) Collection: Beffie, Brussels.

168 THE BLUE HORSES*
Oil. 41 x 71 in. (104 x 180 cm) Reproduced: Kunstsalon Wolfsberg, Zurich. Private collection.

169 RESTING HORSES
Watercolour. 15 ½ x 18 ½ in. (39 x 46 cm) Collection: Beffie, Brussels.

170 MOUNTAIN GOAT*
Watercolour. 15 x 18 in. (38 x 45 cm) Collection: Dr. Goldberg, Zurich.

171 HORSE
Watercolour (1912). 14 ½ x 17 in. (36 x 42 cm) Collection: Sir Michael Sadler, K.C.S.I., C.B., Oxford.

172 WOODCUT
Woodcut. Collection: Beffie, Brussels.

173 TIGER
Woodcut. Collection: Beffie, Brussels.

174 SHEPHERDESS
Woodcut (1913-1914). Private collection.

175 TIGER
Woodcut (1913-1914). Private collection.

176 RECONCILIATION
Woodcut (1913-1914). Private collection.

177 LION FIGHT
Woodcut (1913-1914). Private collection.

178 ANIMALS
Woodcut. Collection: Wells, London.

MARCKS (GERHARD)

179 REBECCA
Bronze. 37 in. (78 cm) Collection: K. Goeritz, Aerdenhout, Holland.

MATTARÉ (EWALD)

180 RESTING COW
Bronze (1932). 19 in. (48 cm) Collection: Hugo Simon, Paris.

MEIDNER (LUDWIG)

181 PORTRAIT
Etching. Collection: Dr. Goldberg, Zurich.

MEYER-AMDEN (OTTO)

182 ENTERING THE CLASSROOM
Two oil sketches (1912-1928).
Exhibited: Kunsthaus, Zurich, 1933; Kunsthalle, Basel, 1934; Kunsthalle, Bern, 1934.
Collection: Paul Meyer, Laupen.

183 BOY
Oil. 7 x 5 in. (16,5 x 12,5 cm)
Collection: Paul Meyer, Laupen.

184 CHOIR PRACTICE
Three sketches.
1. Oil. 26 x 33 in. (65 x 82,5 cm)
2. Pastel. 22 x 25 in. (55 x 62,5 cm)
3. Oil on paper. 30 x 14 in. (75 x 35 cm) Exhibited: Kunsthaus, Zurich, 1933; Kunsthalle Basel, 1934; Kunsthalle, Bern, 1934.
Collection: Paul Meyer, Laupen.

185 TWO SYMBOLS
Drawings (1912-1928).
Exhibited: Kunsthaus, Zurich, 1933; Kunsthalle, Basel, 1934; Kunsthalle, Bern, 1934. Collection: Paul Meyer, Laupen.

186 CONFIRMATION
Three coloured drawings (1912-1928).Exhibited: Kunsthaus, Zurich, 1933; Kunsthalle, Basel, 1934; Kunsthalle, Bern, 1934.

187 ADORATION OF THE SHEPHERDS
Drawing (1912-1928).
Collection: Paul Meyer, Laupen.

188 COMPOSITION
Pencil and Wash Drawing. 23 x 15 ½ in. (57,5 x 38,5 cm) Collection: Kunsthalle, Bern.

189 STREET SCENE
Water colour (1928-1932).
Collection: Paul Meyer, Laupen.

MODERSOHN BECKER (PAULA)

190 CHILDREN WITH GOAT*
Oil (1902). 18 ½ x 27 in. (47 x 68 cm)
Private collection.

191 PEASANT WOMAN*
Oil (1904). 28 x 20 ½ in. (71 x 52 cm)
Private collection.

192 WORKHOUSE WOMAN*
Oil. Private collection.

193 STILL LIFE
Oil. 10 ½ x 20 in. (27 x 51 cm)
Collection: Bernhard Mayer, Ascona.

194 RED HAIRED CHILD
Oil. 19 ½ x 31 ½ in. (50 x 80 cm.)
Collection: Nadolny, Basel.

195 CHILDREN PLAYING*
Oil. 23 ½ x 17 in. (60 x 45 cm)
Private collection.

196 ON THE HEATH
Oil (1901). 14 x 20 in. (36 x 51 cm)
Exhibited: Kunsthalle, Basel, 1936.
Collection: Münzhandlung, Basel.

MUELLER (OTTO)

197 BATHING IN THE BROOK*
Oil. 30 ½ x 42 in. (78 x 108 cm)
Private collection.

198 SELF-PORTRAIT*
Oil. 27 ½ x 19 in. (70 x 48 cm)
Collection: Hugo Simon, Paris.

199 SUMMER
Watercolour (1918). 14 ¼ x 12 ½ in. (36 x 31 cm) Private collection.

NESCH (ROLF)

200 WOMAN RECLINING
Zinc and copper construction (1934). 8 ft. 4 in. x 3 ft. 4 in. (2,50 x 1 m.). Private collection, London.

201 FISHERMEN
Copper (1935-36). 6 ft. 8 in. x 3 ft. 4 in. (2 x 1 m.). Private collection, London.

202 LOFOTEN
(3 etchings from a series). Etchings printed in colour (1937). Collection: Kunstmuseum, Basel.

NOLDE (EMIL)

203 PORTRAIT OF A YOUNG PHILOSOPHER
Oil. 22 x 14 ½ in. (56 x 37 cm)
Collection: Nelkenstock, London.

204 IRISES
Oil (1915). 35 x 29 in. (89 x 74 cm)
Collection: Kunstmuseum, Basel.

205 BOAT*
Watercolour. 8 x 13 in. (20 x 32 cm)
Collection: Wells, London.

206 HEAD OF A YOUNG GIRL
Watercolour. 6 x 9 ½ in. (15 ½ x 24 cm) Private collection.

207 CHRYSANTHEMUMS*
Watercolour. 14 ½ x 19 in. (36 x 48 cm) Collection: Finkelstein, London.

208 TULIPS AND ANEMONES*
Watercolour. 14 x 19 in. (34 x 48 cm) Collection: Finkelstein, London.

209 MARIONETTES*
Watercolour. Collection: Dr. Goldberg, Zurich.

210 SUNFLOWERS
Watercolour. Collection: Finkelstein, London.

211 FAMILY
Watercolour. Collection: Finkelstein, London.

212 IN THE CAFÉ
Drawing. 11 ¼ x 12 ½ in. (28 x 31 ½ cm)
Collection: Wells, London.

213 EPIPHANY
Lithograph. Collection: Uzielli, Liesthal.

PAALEN (WOLFGANG)

214 EN FACE*
Oil (1937). 25 ½ x 21 in. (65 x 54 cm)

PECHSTEIN (MAX)

215 ITALIAN LANDSCAPE
Oil (1913). 13 ½ x 17 ½ in. (34 x 44 cm) Collection: Hugo Simon, Paris.

216 HEAD OF A GIRL
Oil (1919). Exhibited at Kunsthütte, Chemnitz. Collection: Karl Goeritz, Aerdenhout, Holland.

217 SUNRISE*
Oil (1932). 27 x 31 in. (69 x 79 cm) Collection: Finkelstein, London.

218 THE BATHER
Drawing (1912). 22 ½ x 17 ½ in. (56 x 44 cm) Collection: Sir Michael Sadler, K.C.S.I., C.B., Oxford.

219 HARBOUR
Drawing. Collection: Finkelstein, London.

ROHLFS (CHRISTIAN)

220 THE PRODIGAL SON*
Oil (1917). 31 ½ x 23 ½ in. (80 x 60 cm) Private collection.

221 WOMAN WITH VASE
Oil (1924). 31 x 23 in. (78 x 59 cm) Collection: Dr. Wilhelm Abegg, Zurich.

222 NEGRO
Water colour. 27 x 21 ½ in. (69 x 54 cm) Collection: Dr. Wilhelm Abegg, Zurich.

223 RED FLOWERS*
Watercolour (1915). 19 x 25 in. (48 x 73 cm) Private collection.

224 WHITE TULIPS*
Watercolour (1916). 26 x 20 in. (66 x 51 cm) Private collection.

225 MOTHER AND CHILD
Watercolour (1928). 22 x 15 in. (54 x 37,5 cm). Collection: Dr. Wilhelm Abegg, Zurich.

225a CHINESE HEAD
Watercolour. 27 x 19 in. (67,5 x 47 cm) Private collection.

226 LANDSCAPE
Watercolour. 14 x 22 in. (36 x 56 cm) Collection: Uzielli, Liesthal.

227 DEATH WITH CROWN AND SCEPTRE
Woodcut. Collection: Dr. Abegg, Zurich

SCHLEMMER (OSKAR)

228 SCENE AT A TABLE*
Oil. 25 ½ x 19 ½ in. (65 x 50 cm) Collection: John Harrison, London.

229 GROUP IN LIGHT GRAY*
Oil. 25 x 18 in. (64 x 46 cm) Collection: John Harrison, London.

230 TWO FRIENDS*
Oil. 25 x 17 in. (64 x 43 cm) Exhibited: Art Realiste et Abstrait, Zurich. Collection: Irmgard Burchard, Zurich.

SCHMIDT-ROTTLUFF (KARL)

231 FISHERMEN'S HOUSES
Oil. 24 ½ x 31 ½ in. (62 x 82 cm) Exhibited: Kunsthuette, Chemnitz. Collection: Karl Goeritz, Aerdenhout, Holland.

232 TREES*
Watercolour (1920). 16 x 21 in. (37 x 52 cm) Private collection.

233 MAN SHARPENING SCYTHE
Watercolour. 26 ¼ x 19 in. (67 x 48 cm) Collection: Finkelstein, London.

234 BRIDGE
Watercolour (1930). 19 ¼ x 26 ¾ in. (47 x 67 cm) Collection: Meyer-Wedell, London.

SCHOLZ (WERNER)

235 WOMAN*
Coloured Lithograph. 18 x 25 in. (47 x 63 cm) Private collection.

SCHWITTERS (KURT)

236 THE GOLDEN EAR
Construction (1935). 26 ½ x 21 ¾ in. (67,5 x 55,6 cm) Private collection, London.

237 COLLAGE
9 ½ x 7 ½ in. (24 x 18,5 cm) Private collection.

SLEVOGT (MAX)

238 ARGENTINA*
Oil (1926). 61 x 41 in. (152 x 102 cm) Collection. Professor Dr. Plesch, London.

239 PORTRAIT OF THE ACTRESS, SADA JAKHO
Oil (1925-26). 53 x 44 in. (133 x 110 cm) Exhibited at the Berlin Academy.Collection: Professor Dr. Plesch, London.

240 LILIES
Oil (1925). Collection: Professor Dr. Plesch, London.

241 NEUKASTELL
Oil (1930). Collection: Professor Dr. Plesch, London.

242 SELF-PORTRAIT
Oil (1931). 12 x 9 in. (31 x 23 cm) Collection: Prof. Dr. Plesch, London.

243 THE PANTHER
Tempera (1931). 19 ½ x 26 in. (49 x 68 cm) Collection: Professor Dr. Plesch, London.

244 D'ANDRADE
Etching. Collection: Dr. Pollag, Zurich.

245 SELF-PORTRAIT*
Etching. Collection: Richard Bear, Zug.

VORDEMBERGE (FRIEDEL)

246 COMPOSITION 56
32 x 24 in. (80 x 60 cm) Private collection.

WALDEN (NELL)

247 FLOWER*
Tempera (1926). 15 ½ x 12 ½ in. (39,5 x 31,5 cm) Private collection.

248 GARDEN OF THE HESPERIDES*
Tempera (1926). 13 ¼ x 10 ½ in. (33,5 x 27,5 cm) Private collection.

249 MELANCHOLY*
Tempera (1926). 13 ¼ x 17 ¼ in. (33.5 x 43,5 cm)

WOLLHEIM (GERT)

250 CHESTNUT FLOWERS
Oil. 36 x 32 in. Private collection.

Artists now working in England

AUERBACH (ERNA)

251 THE SWIMMING POOL*
Oil (1931). 18 x 27 in. (45 x 68 cm)

BLOCH (MARTIN)

252 RAILWAY BRIDGE NEAR BERLIN*
Oil (1933). 29 x 37 in. (73 x 92 cm)

EHRLICH (GEORG)

253 HEAD OF A YOUTH*
1936. 12 ½ in. high (31 cm.)
Exhibited at the Austrian Exhibition Jeu de Paumes, Paris, 1937.

FREIBUSCH (HANS)

254 DEATH OF NARCISSUS*
Oil (1938). 20 x 35 in. (50 x 86 cm)

HAMANN (PAUL)

255 FIGURE IN BRONZE (1930).
19 in. (47 cm) Collection: The Hon. Harold Nicolson, M.P., London.

HECKROTH (HEIN)

256 THE DANCER*
Oil (1937). Collection: John Harrison, London.

HESS (TIZA)

257 SISTERS*
Wood (1936). 27 in. (57,5 cm)
Collection: Wells, London.

HOEFNER (WALTER)

258 BOAT*
Watercolour (1937). 24 x 19 in. (60 x 45,5 cm)

KORMIS (FRITZ J.)

259 TWO HEADS* Stone.

KOENIGSBERGER (PAUL)

260 PROFESSOR SIGMUND FREUD
Bronze (1930). 18 in. (45 cm)

KRAEMER (FRITZ)

261 STILL LIFE*
Oil. 13 x 23 in. (32,5 x 57,5 cm.)

MARKS (MARGARETHE)

262 LANDSCAPE*
Watercolour. 13 x 19 in. (32,5 x 45,5 cm)

SOKOL (MAX)

263 RECLINING NUDE*
Bronze.

TRIER (WALTER)

264 CARNIVAL
Tempera (1935). 7 ½ x 9 ½ in. (19 x 24 cm)

UHLMAN (FRED)

265 FRENCH CEMETERY*
Oil (1938). 25 ½ x 32 in.

The following works were included after the Catalogue had gone to press.

GRAUMANN (ERWIN)

266 COQUILLAGE*
Oil (1932).
16 x 26 ½ in. (40 x 67 cm)
Exhibited at: Exposition Cubisme-Surréalisme, Copenhagen, 1935; "Surindépendants", Paris, 1937.

HARTUNG (HANS)

267 COMPOSITION*
Oil (1935-6).
Collection: Mrs. Basil Gray.

JENE (EDGAR)

268 AQUARELLE*
23 x 18 ½ in. (58,5 x 47 cm)
Watercolour (1937).

269 LES BARQUES*
23 x 18 ½ in. (58,5 x 47 cm)
Watercolour (1936). 48 x 60 cm.

The Authors
Die Autorinnen und Autoren

Richard Calvocoressi is an art historian and curator. He was educated at Oxford University and at the Courtauld Institute, University of London. He was curator at the Tate Gallery in London from 1979 to 1987, and director of the Scottish National Gallery of Modern Art from 1987 to 2007. He directed the Henry Moore Foundation from 2007 to 2015, and is now director and senior curator at Gagosian London. Calvocoressi has published widely, on artists including Georg Baselitz, Lucian Freud, Anselm Kiefer, Paul Klee, Oskar Kokoschka, Lee Miller and Joan Miró. In 2008 he was appointed CBE for services to the arts in Scotland.

Albrecht Dümling is a music historian and critic based in Berlin. He wrote his doctoral thesis in 1978 under Carl Dahlhaus on the topic of Arnold Schönberg and Stefan George. He then worked until 1998 as music critic for the Berlin *Tagesspiegel* newspaper. Today he works for the *Neue Musikzeitung* and for various other media outlets. His exhibition *Degenerate Music: A Reconstruction* toured to over 60 cities worldwide. He has led the "musica reanimata" society since 1990, organising concerts and publications for the musicians and composers persecuted by the National Socialist regime. For this work he was awarded KAIROS Prize for European culture in 2007.

David Elliott is a British art historian, curator, writer and professor. He was previously director of the Museum of Modern Art, Oxford, of the Moderna Museet in Stockholm, and of Tokyo's Mori Art Museum. During 2007 he was the first director of Istanbul Modern. He is currently Vice Director and Senior Curator at the Redtory Museum of Contemporary Art (RMCA) and Arts District in Guangzhou, China. A specialist in Soviet and Russian avantgarde, as well as in modern and contemporary Asian art, he has published widely in these fields as well as on many other aspects of contemporary art.

Richard Calvocoressi ist Kunsthistoriker und Kurator. Er studierte in Oxford und am Courtauld Institute of Art in London. Anschließend war er Kurator an der Tate Gallery (1979-1987), Direktor der Scottish National Gallery of Modern Art (1987-2007) und Direktor der Henry Moore Foundation (2007-2015). Heute ist er Direktor und Hauptkurator der Londoner Gagosian Gallery. Zahlreiche Publikationen zu Künstlern wie Georg Baselitz, Lucian Freud, Anselm Kiefer, Paul Klee, Oskar Kokoschka, Lee Miller und Joan Miró. Für seinen Verdienst im Bereich der Künste in Schottland wurde er 2008 zum Commander of the Order of the British Empire ernannt.

Albrecht Dümling lebt als Musikwissenschaftler und -kritiker in Berlin. 1978 promovierte er über Schönberg und Stefan George, danach war er bis 1998 Musikkritiker des Berliner *Tagesspiegel*. Heute ist er Mitarbeiter der *Neuen Musikzeitung* und verschiedener Rundfunkanstalten. Die von ihm kuratierte Ausstellung *Entartete Musik. Eine kommentierte Rekonstruktion* reiste weltweit in über 60 Städte. Seit 1990 leitet Dümling den Förderverein «musica reanimata», der sich mit Gesprächskonzerten und Buchveröffentlichungen für NS-verfolgte Komponisten und ihre Werke einsetzt. Für diese Aktivitäten wurde er 2007 mit dem Europäischen Kulturpreis KAIROS ausgezeichnet.

David Elliott ist ein britischer Autor, Historiker, Kurator und Professor. Er leitete folgende Museen: Museum of Modern Art (Oxford), Moderna Museet (Stockholm) und Mori Art Museum (Tokio). 2007 war er der erste Direktor von Istanbul Modern. Heute ist er stellvertretender Direktor und Hauptkurator des Redtory Museum of Contemporary Art and Arts District in Guangzhou (China). Als Spezialist der russischen und sowjetischen Avantgarde sowie der modernen und zeitgenössischen asiatischen Kunst veröffentlichte er zahlreiche Bücher über diese und andere Aspekte der zeitgenössischen Kunst.

Martin Faass is the director of the Liebermann-Villa am Wannsee. He studied art history and German in Marburg and Berlin. His doctoral thesis considered Lyonel Feininger and Cubism. Since 1996 he has curated numerous exhibitions, among others at the Hamburger Kunsthalle, the Museum Kurhaus Kleve, the Kunsthaus Apolda and the Museum of Applied Arts in Hamburg, where he worked from 2001 to 2005. In 2006 he was appointed director of the Liebermann-Villa am Wannsee. He is editor of the publication series of the Max Liebermann Society and is since 2013 on the committee of the Berlin State Museums Association.

Veronika Hekking studied social and cultural history at the Erasmus Universiteit in Rotterdam. She previously worked as editor at *GKf Bulletin*, and as editor and author at *Hollands Licht* (1995-1998) and *GKf 50, Fotografie 1945-1995*. She has worked as chief editor at *Kunstenaarswijzer* (1999-2003) and *Optrek in Transvaal. Over de rol van publieke kunst in de Stedelijke ontwikkeling. Interventies en onderzoek* (2010). She has (co-)authored publications on diverse subjects in art and photographic history, including *De Dam 7 mei 1945. Foto's en Documenten* (1992), *De Illegale Camera* (1995), *Het ondergewone: 55 kunstenaars uit Den Haag* (2005), and *Dutch Eyes. A Critical History of Photography in the Netherlands* (2007).

Meike Hoffmann holds a doctorate in art history and is an expert in 19th and 20th century art. She is academic project coordinator at the Degenerate Art Research Centre / Mosse Art Research Initiative at the Freie Universität, Berlin. She is also a lecturer in provenance research and National Socialist cultural policy at the Freie Universität. Since 2012 she has undertaken research into the recently-discovered Gurlitt collection, has acted as an expert adviser for the Public Prosecutor's Office in Augsburg, and serves as member of the "Schwabinger Kunstfund Taskforce". She has published widely in her field of research, most recently a biography of the art dealer Hildebrand Gurlitt: *Hitlers Kunsthändler. Hildebrand Gurlitt (1895-1956): Die Biographie* (2016).

Keith Holz is Professor of Art History at Western Illinois University. He was awarded his doctorate by Northwestern University. He has held fellowships from the Getty, Fulbright, IREX, the German Academic Exchange Service (DAAD) and from the German Historical Institute in Moscow. His publications have examined representations of modern German art and its audiences in the democracies. He is currently writing *Placing Kokoschka, Kokoschka and Place*. Previous books include: *Modern German Art for Thirties Paris, Prague, and London* (2004). His recent articles address German exile artists groups as networks (2012), the Großen Deutsche Kunstausstellungen (2012), Kokoschka's private life in Czechoslovakia (2014), Neue Sachlichkeit painting beyond German borders (2016), and the study of German-Bohemia artists (forthcoming).

Martin Faass ist Direktor der Liebermann-Villa am Wannsee. Er studierte Kunstgeschichte und Germanistik in Marburg und Berlin und dissertierte über *Lyonel Feininger und der Kubismus*. Er kuratierte seit 1996 zahlreiche Ausstellungen, u.a. für die Hamburger Kunsthalle, das Museum Kurhaus Kleve, das Kunsthaus Apolda und das Museum für Kunst und Gewerbe Hamburg und war von 2001-05 Mitarbeiter des Museums für Kunst und Gewerbe Hamburg. 2006 übernahm er die Leitung der Liebermann-Villa am Wannsee. Er gibt die Schriftenreihe der Max-Liebermann-Gesellschaft Berlin e.V. heraus und ist seit 2013 im Vorstand des Landesverbandes der Museen zu Berlin.

Veronika Hekking studierte Sozial- und Kulturgeschichte an der Erasmus Universität in Rotterdam. Sie war Redakteurin bei *GKf Bulletin* sowie Redakteurin und Verfasserin bei *Hollands Licht* (1995-1998) und *GKf 50, Fotografie 1945-1995*. Sie war Chefredakteurin bei Kunstenaarswijzer (1999-2003) und *Optrek in Transvaal. Over de rol van publieke kunst in de Stedelijke ontwikkeling. Interventies en onderzoek* (2010). Darüber hinaus schrieb sie Beträge für verschiedene Bücher zur Kunstgeschichte und Fotografie, unter anderem *De Dam 7 mei 1945. Foto's en Documenten* (1992), *De Illegale Camera* (1995), *Het ondergewone: 55 kunstenaars uit Den Haag* (2005), und *Dutch Eyes. A Critical History of Photography in the Netherlands* (2007).

Meike Hoffmann ist promovierte Kunsthistorikerin und Expertin für Kunst des 19. und 20. Jahrhunderts. Sie ist wissenschaftliche Projektkoordinatorin für die Forschungsstelle «Entartete Kunst» / Mosse Art Research Initiative der Freien Universität Berlin und arbeitet zudem als Dozentin für Provenienzforschung und NS-Kunstpolitik an der Freien Universität. Seit 2012 Recherche zu den Werken der «Entarteten Kunst» im Gurlitt-Bestand, zunächst als Gutachterin für die Staatsanwaltschaft Augsburg, danach als Mitglied der Taskforce «Schwabinger Kunstfund» und der Folgeprojekte in Berlin und Bern. Zahlreiche Publikationen zu ihrem Forschungsbereich, zuletzt *Hitlers Kunsthändler. Hildebrand Gurlitt (1895-1956) Die Biographie* (2016).

Keith Holz promovierte an der Northwestern University und ist Professor für Kunstgeschichte an der Western Illinois University. Er war Stipendiat verschiedener Institute (Getty, Fulbright, IREX, DAAD, Deutsches Historisches Institut Moskau). Er schrieb mehrere Bücher über die deutsche Moderne und ihre Rezeption in den demokratischen Ländern (z. B. *Modern German Art for Thirties Paris, Prague, and London*, 2004). Zurzeit arbeitet er an dem Buch *Placing Kokoschka, Kokoschka and Place*. In den letzten Jahren hat er Beiträge zu folgenden Themen veröffentlicht: Die emigrierten deutschen Künstler und ihre Netzwerke (2012), Die Großen Deutschen Kunstausstellungen (2012), Kokoschkas Privatleben in der Tschechoslowakei (2014), Die Neue Sachlichkeit außerhalb Deutschlands (2016) und eine Studie zu deutsch-böhmischen Künstlern (in Vorbereitung)

Matthew C. Potter is an Associate Professor and Reader in Art and Design History at Northumbria University, Newcastle, UK. His research explores the role played by visual culture in the construction of national identities and international exchange, mainly between 1850 and 1950. Matthew's publications include *The Inspirational Genius of Germany: British Art and Germanism, 1850-1939* (2012), the edited collection *The Concept of the 'Master' in Art Education in Britain and Ireland, 1770 to the Present* (2013) and *British art for Australia: The acquisition of artworks from the United Kingdom by Australian national galleries, 1860-1953* (forthcoming).

Aya Soika studied art history in Berlin and Cambridge. She was awarded her doctorate in 2001 by the University of Cambridge, with a thesis considering the Brücke artists' group. She has taught art history at Bard College Berlin since 2005, with a focus on German modernist art. In 2011 she published the two-volume catalogue raisonné of the oil paintings of Max Pechstein. In 2012 she published the biography: *Max Pechstein. The Rise and Fall of Expressionism* (together with Bernhard Fulda). In 2014 she published a study considering the artists of the Brücke group during the First World War: *Weltenbruch. Die Künstler der Brücke im Ersten Weltkrieg. 1914 bis 1918*, followed in 2016 by a study considering Max and Lotte Pechstein's travels in the South Pacific: *Der Traum vom Paradies. Max und Lotte Pechsteins Reise in die Südsee*. She also curated the accompanying exhibition. Since 2012 she has researched Emil Nolde and National Socialism.

Barbara Warnock is the Education and Outreach Manager of The Wiener Library and the co-curator of the London stage of the *London 1938* exhibition project. She obtained her doctorate in History from Birkbeck College, University of London in 2016. Her thesis, entitled *The First Bailout: The Financial Reconstruction of Austria 1922-1926*, explored the political, social, economic and financial crisis in Austria in the early 1920s, and international responses to this. She also holds an MA in European History from Birkbeck, and previously worked as a history teacher for many years.

Lucy Wasensteiner studied law at the universities of Bristol and Oxford, coming to art history through the topic of provenance research. She was awarded her PhD from the Courtauld Institute of Art in London, her thesis considering modern art in German-speaking Europe from 1871, National Socialist cultural policy and its international implications, with particular focus on the exhibition *Twentieth Century German Art*. She has worked as researcher and writer for the Tate Gallery and as Associate Lecturer at the Courtauld Institute. She has worked at the Liebermann-Villa am Wannsee since 2015 and is curator of the *London 1938* exhibition project.

Matthew C. Potter ist Associate Professor and Reader an der Fakultät für Kunst und Design der Northumbria University in Newcastle. Seine Forschungsarbeiten galten vor allem der Rolle der visuellen Kultur bei der Entwicklung der Nationalidentität und des internationalen Austauschs zwischen 1850 und 1950. Zu seinen Veröffentlichungen zählen unter anderem: *The Inspirational Genius of Germany: British Art and Germanism, 1850-1939* (2012), *The Concept of the ‹Master› in Art Education in Britain and Ireland, 1770 to the Present* (2013) und *British art for Australia: The acquisition of artworks from the United Kingdom by Australian national galleries, 1860-1953* (in Vorbereitung).

Aya Soika studierte Kunstgeschichte in Berlin und Cambridge. Sie promovierte 2001 an der University of Cambridge mit einer Arbeit über die Künstlergemeinschaft Brücke. Seit 2005 lehrt sie Kunstgeschichte am Bard College Berlin, mit Forschungsschwerpunkt im Bereich der deutschen Moderne. 2011 publizierte sie das zweibändige Werkverzeichnis der Ölgemälde Max Pechsteins. 2012 folgte die Pechstein-Biographie *Max Pechstein: The Rise and Fall of Expresisonism* (gemeinsam mit Bernhard Fulda). 2014 veröffentlichte sie die Studie *Weltenbruch. Die Künstler der Brücke im Ersten Weltkrieg. 1914 bis 1918*, 2016 das Buch *Der Traum vom Paradies. Max und Lotte Pechsteins Reise in die Südsee* und konzipierte die gleichnamigen Ausstellungen. Seit 2012 beschäftigte sie sich mit der Rolle Emil Noldes im Nationalsozialismus.

Barbara Warnock leitet die pädagogische Abteilung der Wiener Library und ist Co-Kuratorin der Londoner Station von *London 1938*. 2016 promovierte sie am Birkbeck College der Londoner Universität in Geschichte. Ihre Dissertation mit dem Titel *The First Bailout: The Financial Reconstruction of Austria 1922-1926* war dem Wiederaufbau Österreichs nach der politischen, sozialen, wirtschaftlichen und finanziellen Krise der frühen 1920er Jahre und dessen internationalem Kontext gewidmet. Zuvor hatte sie am Birkbeck College ihren Mastertitel in europäischer Geschichte erlangt und mehrere Jahre als Geschichtslehrerin gearbeitet.

Lucy Wasensteiner studierte Jura an den Universitäten Bristol und Oxford, bevor sie durch die Thematik der Provenienzforschung zur Kunstgeschichte kam. Sie promovierte am Courtauld Institute of Art in London mit einer Arbeit über moderne Kunst im deutschsprachigen Raum ab 1871, nationalsozialistische Kulturpolitik und ihre internationale Wirkung mit besonderem Forschungsschwerpunkt auf der Ausstellung *Twentieth Century German Art*. In den letzten Jahren war sie als Forscherin und Autorin für die Tate Gallery tätig sowie als Associate Lecturer am Courtauld Institute. Seit 2015 ist sie Mitarbeiterin an der Liebermann-Villa am Wannsee und kuratiert die Ausstellung *London 1938*.

Bildnachweis | Picture Credits

Die Bildvorlagen stammen aus den Archiven der im Folgenden genannten Museen, Galerien und Fotoateliers. Trotz intensiver Bemühungen ist es nicht in allen Fällen gelungen, Urheberschaft und Herkunft der Abbildungen zu klären. Berechtigte Ansprüche werden bei entsprechendem Nachweis im Rahmen üblicher Tarife abgegolten.

The images in this volume were sourced from the following museums, galleries and photographic studios. Despite our best efforts, it has not been possible in all cases to determine the origins of the images. We welcome claims by the owners of these images for any royalties legitimately owed.

Katalog | Catalogue

1 Royal Society, London; **2** Foto | Photo: Andreas Weiss Privatbesitz | Private collection; **3** Courtesy Arnoldi-Livie, München; **4** Stiftung Otto Eckart, Foto | Photo: Alexander Bernhard; **5** Archiv Nimbus. Kunst und Bücher AG, Wädenswil; **6** Courtesy Ketterer Kunst; **7** Foto | Photo: Raphael Maass © Saarlandmuseum Saarbrücken, Stiftung Saarländischer Kulturbesitz; **8** Museum Folkwang Essen – ARTOTHEK; **9** Daxer & Marschall Kunsthandel, München; **10** GDKE, Landesmuseum Mainz. Foto | Photo Axel Brachat; **11** Privatbesitz | Private collection, Fotol Photo: Andy Johnson; **12** LENTOS Kunstmuseum Linz, Foto | Photo: Reinhard Haider; 13 Staatliche Kunsthalle Karlsruhe – bpk, Foto | Photo Wolfgang Pankoke; **14** Hessisches Landesmuseum Darmstadt, Foto | Photo: Wolfgang Fuhrmannek; **15** Kunstmuseum Bonn, Foto | Photo: Reni Hansen, © Pro Litteris, Zürich; **16** Kunstmuseum Luzern, © Pro Litteris, Zürich; **17** Privatbesitz | Private Collection; **18** Museum Ostwall im Dortmunder U, Dortmund; **19** CNAC-MNAM – bpk, Fotol Photo Bertrand Prévost; **20** Kunstsammlungen Chemnitz – Museum Gunzenhauser; **21** Private Collection on long term loan to the National Galleries of Scotland Edinburgh, Foto | Photo: Antonia Reeve, © Fondation Oskar Kokoschka, Pro Litteris, Zürich; **22** Kunstmuseum Basel, Foto | Photo Martin P. Bühler, © Nolde Stiftung Seebüll; **23** Kunstmuseum Gelsenkirchen © Nolde Stiftung Seebüll; **24** Privatbesitz | Private Collection © Willi Baumeister Pro Litteris, Zürich; **25** Zentrum Paul Klee, Bern; **26** Museum Boijmans Van Beuningen, Rotterdam; Foto | Photo: Studio Tromp, Rotterdam; **27** Moderna Museet, Stockholm; **28** Staatliche Kunsthalle Karlsruhe – bpk, Foto | Photo Annette Fischer, Heike Kohler, © Fondation Oskar Kokoschka, Pro Litteris, Zürich; **29** Moderna Museet, Stockholm, © Alexander Archipenko, Pro Litteris, Zürich.

Illustrationen | Illustrations

1-4 Tate Archive, Ewan Phillips collection, Foto | Photo: Ewan Phillips, © Tate, London 2018; **5-6** Courtesy of The Wiener Library, London; **7** Privatbesitz | Private collection; **8-11** Internetressource; **12** Ullstein-Bild, Axel Springer Syndication GmbH, Berlin; **13** aus: Gestalt und Seele. Das Werk des Malers Leo von König. Leipzig 1936, ill. 53; **14-15** Courtesy of The Wiener Library, London; **16** Ullstein-Bild, Axel Springer Syndication GmbH, Berlin; **17** Wiener Library Archives, London, The Bernard Simon Collection; **18** Courtesy of Bexhill Museum; **19** Wiener Library Archives, London; **20** Privatbesitz | Private collection; **21** Wiener Library Archives, London, The Bernard Simon Collection; **22** Ullstein-Bild, Axel Springer Syndication GmbH, Berlin; **23** Wiener Library Archives, London; **24** Staatliche Kunsthalle Karlsruhe – bpk, Foto | Photo Annette Fischer | Heike Kohler; **25** Museum Georg Schäfer, Schweinfurt; **26** Privatbesitz | Private collection; **27** aus: Museum I, Tafel 16; **28** SMPK Berlin Nationalgalerie; **29** National Galleries of Scotland Edinburgh; **30** San Francisco Museum of Modern Art, Gift of Charlotte Mack; **31** Royal Collection Trust | Her Majesty Queen Elizabeth II; **32** Museum Bautzen; **33** Victoria and Albert Museum, London; **34** Courtesy of The Wiener Library, London; **35** Courtesy Rosie Alison; **36** Tate Archive, Ewan Phillips collection, Foto | Photo: Ewan Phillips, © Tate, London 2018; **37** Foto | Photo: Franz Pfemfert. Courtesy Yonna Yapou-Kromholz; **38** Stiftung Archiv Akademie der Künste, Berlin **39** Ullstein-Bild, Axel Springer Syndication GmbH, Berlin; **40** National Portrait Gallery, London, © Howard Coster; **41** London Metropolitan Archives, City of London; **42** Courtesy of The Wiener Library, London; **43** Max-Liebermann-Gesellschaft Berlin; **44** Privatbesitz | Private collection; **45** Tate Gallery, London; **46** Max-Liebermann-Gesellschaft Berlin; **47** Privatbesitz | Private collection; **48** Kunstmuseum St. Gallen;

49 Tate Archive, Ewan Phillips collection, Foto I Photo: Ewan Phillips, © Tate, London 2018; **50** Privatbesitz I Private collection; **51** Courtesy Ketterer Kunst; **52** Westfälisches Landesmuseum, Münster; **53-54** Tate Archive, Ewan Phillips collection, Foto I Photo: Ewan Phillips, © Tate, London 2018; **55** Privatbesitz I Private collection; **56** Natio- nal Museum, Belgrade, Courtesy Irina Subotic, Ljubomir Micic Estate; **57** Privatbesitz I Private collection © Richard Paul Lohse, Pro Litteris, Zürich; **58** Privatbesitz I Private collection; **59** Foto I Photo: Klaus Eschen. © SLUB I Dt. Fotothek I Klaus Eschen; **60** Privatbesitz I Private collection © Richard Paul Lohse, Pro Litteris, Zürich; **61** Foto I Photo: Klaus Eschen. © SLUB I Dt. Fotothek I Klaus Eschen; **62** Archiv Albrecht Dümling; **63** Privatbesitz I Private collection; **64** Courtesy of the Britten-Pears Foundation; **65** Courtesy of the Weill-Lenya Research Centre, Kurt Weill Foundation for Music, New York; **66** Courtesy Joy Puritz; **67** Fondation Hindemith, Blonay (CH); **68** Archiv Albrecht Dümling; **69** Fondation Hindemith, Blonay (CH); **70** Privatbesitz I Private collection; **71** Privatbesitz I Private collection; **72-74** Foto I Photo: Peter Hunter. © Peter Hunter I Nederlands Fotomuseum; **75-77** Privatbesitz I Private collection; **78** Stiftung Archiv Akademie der Künste Berlin; **79** Privatbesitz I Private collection; **80** Foto I Photo: Peter Hunter. © Peter Hunter I Nederlands Fotomuseum; **81** © Anja Elisabeth Witte I Berlinische Galerie; **82-84** Foto I Photo: Peter Hunter. © Peter Hunter I Nederlands Fotomuseum; **85** SLUB I Deutsche Fotothek; **86** Privatbesitz I Private collection; **87** © ullstein bild – Südddeutsche Zeitung, Photo; **88** Archiv Nimbus. Kunst und Bücher AG, Wädenswil; **89** Courtesy of The Wiener Library, London; **90** Stadtarchiv Flensburg, mit Dank an Marvin Nissen; **91** Image courtesy of the Albright-Knox Art Gallery Digital Assets Collection and Archives; **92** VAN HAM Kunstauktion, Foto I Photo: Saša Fuis. © Karl Hofer, Pro Litteris, Zürich; **93-94** Image courtesy of the Albright-Knox Art Gallery Digital Assets Collection and Archives; **95** The Art Institute of Chicago – bpk I © Art Resource NY I Lyonel Feininger, Pro Litteris, Zürich; **96** Privatbesitz I Private collection; **97** Saint Louis Art Museum Archives; **98** Image courtesy of the Albright-Knox Art Gallery Digital Assets Collection and Archives; **99** Privatbesitz I Private collection. © Karl Hofer, Pro Litteris, Zürich; **100** Tate Gallery, London; **101** Tate Galleries, London, © Karl Schmidt-Rottluff – Pro Litteris, Zürich; **102** Tate Gallery, London – bpk, Foto I Photo Hermann Buresch I © Max Beckmann, Pro Litteris, Zürich; **103-104** National Galleries Scotland Edinburgh, Foto I Photo: Antonia Reeve.

Dank | Acknowledgments

Das Projekt *London 1938* wäre nicht möglich gewesen ohne die großzügige Unterstützung der Leihgeber:
The *London 1938* project would not have been possible without the generous support of the lenders:

Kunstmuseum Basel; Zentrum Paul Klee, Bern; Kunstmuseum Bonn; Kunstsammlungen Chemnitz, Museum Gunzenhauser; Hessisches Landesmuseum Darmstadt; Museum Ostwall, Dortmund; National Gallery of Scotland, Edinburgh; Museum Folkwang, Essen; Kunstmuseum Gelsenkirchen; Staatliche Kunsthalle Karlsruhe; LENTOS Kunstmuseum, Linz; The Royal Society, London; Kunstmuseum Luzern; GDKE – Landesmuseum Mainz; Deutsches Literaturarchiv Marbach; Daxer & Marschall Kunsthandel, München; Das Kartoffelmuseum, München; Centre Pompidou, National Museum of Modern Art, Paris; Museum Boijmans Van Beuningen, Rotterdam; Saarlandmuseum Saarbrücken, Stiftung Saarländischer Kulturbesitz; Moderna Museet, Stockholm

und jener Leihgeber, die namentlich nicht genannt werden wollen.
together with those lenders, who do not wish to be named.

Wir danken der Wiener Library Holocaust Archive, London, für die großartige Zusammenarbeit.
We would like to thank the Wiener Library, London, for their cooperation and support.

Für Rat und Unterstützung bedanken wir uns bei:
For advice and support we would like to thank:

Susanne Brogi; Dr Nicholas Clark; Dorothea Dörries-Koubenec; Hildegard Findeklee; Sandra Köhler; Grit Jehmlich; Keith Moore; Cornelia Muessig, Galerie Arnoldi-Livie; Thomas Pauling; Carolien Provaas; Marga Quiring; Dina Schlote; Frank Steffen; Barbara Stursberg; Chris Sutherns, Ruth Ur; Dorothee Veltrup; Oliver Max Wenske; Dr. Heinz-Jürgen Winkler.

Inhalt | Contents

Dieses Buch erscheint anlässlich der Ausstellungen | This book accompanies the exhibitions:

London 1938. Defending 'degenerate' German Art
The Wiener Library for the Study of the Holocaust & Genocide, London
13.06.2018 – 14.09.2018

London 1938: Mit Kandinsky, Liebermann und Nolde gegen Hitler
Liebermann-Villa am Wannsee, Berlin
07.10.2018 – 14.01.2019

Herausgegeben von | Edited by
Lucy Wasensteiner | Martin Faass

Mit Beiträgen von | With contributions by
Richard Calvocoressi, Albrecht Dümling, David Elliott, Martin Faass, Veronika Hekking, Meike Hoffmann, Keith Holz, Matthew C. Potter, Aya Soika, Barbara Warnock, Lucy Wasensteiner

Übersetzungen | Translations
Übersetzungsdienst Marcel Saché,
Bernhard Echte, Lucy Wasensteiner

Koordination | Organisation
Julia Knapp

Lektorat | Editing
Bernhard Echte

Gestaltung | Layout
NIMBUS. Kunst und Bücher AG, Wädenswil

Erste Auflage 2018

Villa zum Abendstern, Bürglistrasse 37,
CH 8820 Wädenswil am Zürichsee, Schweiz
www.nimbusbooks.ch

Druck: Gulde Druck GmbH, Tübingen
Bindung: Josef Spinner GmbH, Ottersweier

ISBN 978-3-03850-049-0
Printed in Germany

Die Realisierung der beiden Ausstellungen wurde ermöglicht durch die großzügige Unterstützung von:
The realisation of the two exhibitions was made possible thanks to the generous support of:

KULTURSTIFTUNG DES BUNDES
EvS ERNST VON SIEMENS KUNSTSTIFTUNG
BRITISH COUNCIL UK/DE 2018
Sotheby's EST. 1744

Die Publikation des vorliegenden Bandes wurde ermöglicht durch die großzügige Unterstützung von:
The publication of this catalogue was made possible thanks to the generous support of:

IMAF INTERNATIONAL MUSIC & ART FOUNDATION